Praxis® Core

FOR DUMMIES®

A Wiley Brand

P9-CSE-300

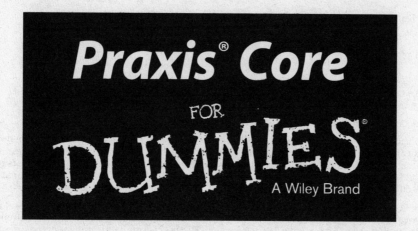

Praxis® Core

FOR

DUMMIES®

A Wiley Brand

by Carla Kirkland and Chan Cleveland

FOR

DUMMIES®

A Wiley Brand

Praxis® Core For Dummies®

Published by: John Wiley & Sons, Inc.
111 River Street
Hoboken, NJ 07030-5774
www.wiley.com

Copyright © 2014 by John Wiley & Sons, Inc., Hoboken, New Jersey

Media and software compilation copyright © 2014 by John Wiley & Sons, Inc. All rights reserved.

Published simultaneously in Canada

No part of this publication may be reproduced, stored in a retrieval system or transmitted in any form or by any means, electronic, mechanical, photocopying, recording, scanning or otherwise, except as permitted under Sections 107 or 108 of the 1976 United States Copyright Act, without the prior written permission of the Publisher. Requests to the Publisher for permission should be addressed to the Permissions Department, John Wiley & Sons, Inc., 111 River Street, Hoboken, NJ 07030, (201) 748-6011, fax (201) 748-6008, or online at http://www.wiley.com/go/permissions.

Trademarks: Wiley, For Dummies, the Dummies Man logo, Dummies.com, Making Everything Easier, and related trade dress are trademarks or registered trademarks of John Wiley & Sons, Inc., and may not be used without written permission. Praxis is a registered trademark of Educational Testing Service (ETS). This product is not endorsed or approved by ETS. All other trademarks are the property of their respective owners. John Wiley & Sons, Inc., is not associated with any product or vendor mentioned in this book.

LIMIT OF LIABILITY/DISCLAIMER OF WARRANTY: WHILE THE PUBLISHER AND AUTHOR HAVE USED THEIR BEST EFFORTS IN PREPARING THIS BOOK, THEY MAKE NO REPRESENTATIONS OR WARRANTIES WITH RESPECT TO THE ACCURACY OR COMPLETENESS OF THE CONTENTS OF THIS BOOK AND SPECIFICALLY DISCLAIM ANY IMPLIED WARRANTIES OF MERCHANTABILITY OR FITNESS FOR A PARTICULAR PURPOSE. NO WARRANTY MAY BE CREATED OR EXTENDED BY SALES REPRESENTATIVES OR WRITTEN SALES MATERIALS. THE ADVICE AND STRATEGIES CONTAINED HEREIN MAY NOT BE SUITABLE FOR YOUR SITUATION. YOU SHOULD CONSULT WITH A PROFESSIONAL WHERE APPROPRIATE. NEITHER THE PUBLISHER NOR THE AUTHOR SHALL BE LIABLE FOR DAMAGES ARISING HEREFROM.

For general information on our other products and services, please contact our Customer Care Department within the U.S. at 877-762-2974, outside the U.S. at 317-572-3993, or fax 317-572-4002. For technical support, please visit www.wiley.com/techsupport.

Wiley publishes in a variety of print and electronic formats and by print-on-demand. Some material included with standard print versions of this book may not be included in e-books or in print-on-demand. If this book refers to media such as a CD or DVD that is not included in the version you purchased, you may download this material at http://booksupport.wiley.com. For more information about Wiley products, visit www.wiley.com.

Library of Congress Control Number: 2014933459

ISBN 978-1-118-53280-5 (pbk); ISBN 978-1-118-61257-6 (ebk); ISBN 978-1-118-61266-8 (ebk)

Manufactured in the United States of America

10 9 8 7 6 5 4 3 2 1

Contents at a Glance

Table of Contents

Introduction

If you want to be a teacher, you generally have to take the Praxis Core Academic Skills for Educators at least once. "What?! What do you mean by 'at least once'?" Yes, it's true that you may have to take the Praxis twice in your quest to shape the minds of future generations. Many colleges and universities require that students who want to enroll in an education major take the exam. And if that isn't bad enough, most states and some U.S. territories require that you pass the Praxis in order to be licensed to teach. But don't panic. You've come to the right place for help in acing the exam.

The goal of this book is to help you brush up on what you need to know to pass the Praxis with flying colors. We don't cover every topic that will be tested in detail; instead we offer an overview of those topics. The overview allows you to review a topic and say to yourself either, "Yep, got it! I can move onto the next topic." or "I don't get it. I'd better focus on my statistics knowledge." (If you decide you need more review on a topic, check out the many *For Dummies* books that relate to the chapters in this book.)

You can also use the two practice tests in this book and the additional three practice tests online to test yourself in a lifelike testing situation. You may want to take one test before you read any chapters to see where your strengths and weaknesses are; then you'll know where to focus your attention. After you've studied your weak areas and reviewed the topics you're better at, you can take another practice test to see how much you've improved and where you still may need more work.

So we have you covered when it comes to studying for and passing the Praxis. Take a couple of tests, review the chapters, and get the confidence you need to score well on the test when it really counts.

About This Book

Praxis Core For Dummies breaks down the exam's main objectives into understandable sections. This book is organized into parts that align with the test's subsections so you can find the answers to your most challenging areas quickly. If you're struggling with math, you can find all those topics grouped together. If writing makes you want to pull your hair out, you can get a comprehensive overview in Part IV.

In addition to reviewing Praxis topics, we offer strategies that you can practice and keep in mind so you don't fall for the booby traps that others seem to. We outline the different types of questions so you know where to expect the hurdles you'll see on the Praxis Core Academic Skills for Educators exam. (Okay, this is the last time we will spell out the official title of the test. From now on it will be referred to as the Praxis or the Praxis Core.)

A test-prep book wouldn't be a test-prep book without a couple of practice tests. This book offers two tests in the book, those same two tests online, and then another three tests online to help you become familiar with the content and question types you'll encounter when you take the exam. They say practice makes perfect. With these practice tests, you can put that theory to the "test."

Foolish Assumptions

In writing this book, we've made some assumptions about you. The biggest assumption we've made applies to all readers: You have decided to teach, which is one of the most rewarding professions known to man. Beyond that, you fall into one of the following categories:

- ✔ You are a first-time test-taker who wants to pass the test on your first try.

- ✔ You are a retester who has taken the test and failed based on your state cut score requirement. You can still successfully reach the passing score goal. You're actually in a better situation than the first-time test-taker because you possess a detailed report that outlines your strengths and weaknesses. That way you can truly attack the sections that challenge you the most.

- ✔ You are a traditional teacher candidate in college who is currently enrolled or trying to enroll as an education major in an undergraduate program, and you need to pass this test to start taking your specialized courses.

- ✔ You are an alternative route teacher candidate who possesses a four-year degree and you need to pass this test as one of your first steps toward certification.

Regardless of your category, we have written this book to fit your specific needs.

Icons Used in This Book

Icons are the drawings in the margins of this book, and we use several icons to call out special kinds of information.

Examples are sample test questions that appear at the ends of sections and that highlight particular ideas that you should be familiar with. We provide an answer and explanation immediately after the question. (And there's more — at the end of a chapter, you usually find a handful of numbered sample questions, which we don't mark with the icon because they're in their own practice-questions section.)

The Remember icon points out something you should keep in mind while you're taking the exam.

A Tip is a suggestion that usually points out a trick for remembering information for the test.

The Warning icon flags traps and tricks that the creators of the Praxis often employ to trip you up when it comes to choosing the correct answer. Pay special heed to these paragraphs.

Beyond the Book

In addition to the material in the print or e-book you're reading right now, this product also comes with some access-anywhere goodies on the web. Check out these features:

- **Cheat Sheet:** (www.dummies.com/cheatsheet/praxiscore): When you're down to the last few days before the test, not only do you have to remember everything you've studied for the test, but you have to remember what to take with you to the testing site. Check out the online Cheat Sheet for a handy list of what to take with you. You'll also find some general tips for succeeding on the Praxis. Review this a week or so before you're scheduled to take the test so you can make sure you're as prepared as you can be.

- **Dummies.com articles** (www.dummies.com/extras/praxiscore): Each part in this book is supplemented by a relevant online article that provides additional tips and techniques related to the subject of that part. Read helpful articles that reveal even more test-taking tips and hints for each subtest of the exam.

- **Online practice and study aids:** In addition to the two complete practice exams contained in this book, your book purchase also comes with a free one-year subscription to additional practice questions that appear online — enough to fill three more exams. You can access the content whenever you want. Create your own question sets and view personalized reports that show what you need to study most.

To gain access to the online practice, all you have to do is register. Just follow these simple steps:

1. **Find your PIN access code.**

   Print book users: If you purchased a hard copy of this book, turn to the front of this book to find your access code.

   E-book users: If you purchased this book as an e-book, you can get your access code by registering your e-book at www.dummies.com/go/getaccess. Go to this website, find your book and click it, and answer the security question to verify your purchase. Then you'll receive an e-mail with your access code.

2. **Go to** www.prep.dummies.com/proed/go/accesscode.

3. **Enter your access code.**

4. **Follow the instructions to create an account and establish your personal login information.**

That's all there is to it! You can come back to the online program again and again — simply log in with the username and password you chose during your initial login. No need to use the access code a second time. If you have trouble with the access code or can't find it, please contact Wiley Product Technical Support at 877-762-2974 or http://support.wiley.com. Your registration is good for one year from the day you activate your access code. After that time frame has passed, you can renew your registration for a fee. The website gives you all the important details about how to do so.

Where to Go from Here

Use this book as a reference. You don't need to read this book from front to back. Feel free to skip around to the sections that you find most useful. If you can't decide, begin with Chapter 1 — it includes an overview of the Praxis, and you'll probably need to read it at some point. If you know that geometry (Chapter 6) is your Achilles heel or that reading comprehension questions (Chapter 9) make your eyes cross, go straight to the corresponding chapter. We give you an index, too, at the back of the book to help you find specific information. Or, if you like, you can take one of the tests to see how well you do and determine what you need to brush up on.

Part I

Getting Started with the Praxis Core

getting started with the

Praxis Core

 web extras

Visit www.dummies.com for free access to great Dummies content online.

In this part . . .

✔ Get the details about who takes the Praxis, what's on the test, and how your score is calculated.

✔ Figure out how to schedule your study time in advance of test day, find out what to expect on test day, and get some pointers if you're retaking the test.

✔ Try out some practice Praxis questions to discover the areas in which you're strong and the areas where you need more review. Then develop a plan to strengthen the areas in which you're weak.

Chapter 1

Previewing the Praxis

In This Chapter

▶ Knowing why you're taking the Praxis

▶ Finding out what's on the Praxis

▶ Seeing how the Praxis is scored

*F*or decades teacher candidates have been taking assessments in order to meet certification requirements. Praxis Core Academic Skills for Educators is the latest version of these tests that measure core skills in the areas of reading, writing, and mathematics for potential teacher candidates. This chapter gives you an overview of what you need to know about the exam.

Why Take the Praxis?

If you want to become a teacher, you may face the Praxis at some point on the road to certification. You may take it to get into a teaching program at college, or you may take it to get your teaching license before starting a second career. If you're lucky, you may only take it once, but our bet is that you'll take it twice before you're fully qualified to work in a classroom.

Colleges and universities use the Praxis Core testing series to determine whether teaching program candidates meet the minimum requirements to enter into the field of teaching. Most colleges and universities won't allow admission into their teacher preparation programs until candidates complete this basic skills exam. Undergraduate students generally take the Praxis early in their college career. Some students may be able to skip taking certain parts of the Praxis if they have a high score on college entrance exams like the ACT.

Most states also use the Praxis as a certification test to show that you've mastered the skills needed to be a highly competent teacher. In many cases, teaching licenses are directly tied to this test. Age doesn't get you out of this standardized test.

Almost every state in the country uses some form of the Praxis. Contact your state department of education for specific licensure details.

Breaking Down the Praxis

The newly developed Praxis Core evaluates the core academic abilities of prospective educators in the areas of reading, writing, and math. Previously, this test was called the Praxis I Pre Professional Skills Test, but ETS (Educational Testing Services, the folks who create the exam) decided to make a change to reflect the requirement to get potential teachers up to the level needed to meet the Common Core State Standards. According to ETS, the test is broken down into the following three parts:

- **The reading test:** This test poses multiple-choice questions based on reading passages and statements.

- **The writing test:** This test is divided into two sections. The multiple-choice section tests grammar usage, sentence correction, revision in context, and research skills. The test also requires you to write two essays based on information presented; one is an argumentative essay, and the other is an explanation of a topic.

- **The mathematics test:** This test measures multiple mathematics topics up to the advanced high-school level. The format of the test has numeric entry questions and multiple-choice questions that may require you to select one or more choices. They do give you access to an on-screen calculator.

The following sections give you more details about the subtests and the question types so you don't encounter any (or too many) surprises when you sit down to take the test.

Knowing what topics are covered

Just like most other standardized tests you've taken, the Praxis includes long reading passages, complicated math problems, and detailed essay topics. You'll have a set number of questions about certain topics to answer in a given amount of time. Check out Table 1-1 for the breakdown.

Table 1-1	Breakdown of the Praxis	
Test Subject	*Number of Questions*	*Time*
Reading	56 multiple-choice questions	85 minutes
Writing	40 multiple-choice questions and 2 essays	100 minutes
Mathematics	56 multiple-choice questions	85 minutes

Each subject is broken down further into specific concepts:

- **Reading:**

  - **Key ideas and details:** This section requires you to closely read text, make logical inferences, connect specific details, address author differences, and determine uncertain matters. You'll see 17 to 22 questions about these concepts.

  - **Craft, structure, and language skills:** This section requires you to interpret words and phrases, recognize the tone of word choices, analyze text structure, assess points of view, apply language knowledge to determine fact or opinion, determine word meanings, and understand a range of words and word nuances. You'll see 14 to 19 questions about these concepts.

  - **Integration of knowledge and ideas:** This section requires you to analyze diverse media content, evaluate arguments in texts, and analyze how two or more texts address similar themes. You'll see 17 to 22 questions about these concepts.

- **Writing:**

  - **Text types, purposes, and production:** This section requires you to produce one argumentative and one informative/explanatory essay. This section also requires you to edit and revise text passages. You'll see 6 to 12 multiple-choice questions about these concepts.

- **Language and research skills:** This section requires you to demonstrate command of English grammar, usage, capitalization, and punctuation. This section also requires you to apply and recognize research skills. You'll see 28 to 34 multiple-choice questions about these concepts.

✔ **Mathematics:**

- **Number and quantity:** This section focuses on the understanding of order among number integers, representation of a number in more than one way, place value, whole number properties, equivalent computational procedures, ratio, proportion, and percentages. You'll see 17 questions about these concepts.

- **Algebra and functions:** This section assesses the ability to handle equations and inequalities, recognize various ways to solve a problem, determine the relationship between verbal and symbolic expressions, and interpret graphs. In this section, you also encounter function questions that test the knowledge of basic function definitions and the relationship between the domain and range of any given functions. You'll see 17 questions about these concepts.

- **Geometry:** This part assesses the understanding and application of the characteristics and properties of geometric shapes, the Pythagorean theorem, transformation, and use of symmetry to analyze mathematical situations. (Knowledge of basic U.S. and metric systems of measurement is assumed.) You'll see 11 questions about these concepts.

- **Statistics and probability:** This part assesses the ability to read and interpret visual display of quantitative information, understand the correspondence between data and graph, make inferences from a given data display, determine mean, median, and mode, and assign a probability to an outcome. You'll see 11 questions about these concepts.

The good news about the math subtest is that an on-screen four-function calculator is available for your use, which reduces the chance that you'll select a wrong answer choice based on a simple arithmetic error.

Seeing what types of questions you'll face

The Praxis Core gives you multiple types of questions. Taking all of our practice tests will give you a consistent idea of what you will see on the actual test. Before you get to the practice tests, check out this list of question types you'll encounter in the different subtests:

✔ **The reading test** has four categories of text paragraph sections.

- Reading Category 1 questions deal with paired passages of about 150 to 200 words combined with four to seven questions, such as "Unlike the author of Passage 2, the author of Passage 1 mentions . . ." or "Which of the following statements best describes the relationship between the two passages?"

- Reading Category 2 questions deal with lengthy paragraphs of about 175 to 200 words combined with four to seven questions that may ask, "Which of the following best describes the organization of the passage?" or "The author would be *most* likely to agree with which of the following statements?"

- Reading Category 3 questions deal with abbreviated passages of 75 to 100 words with two or three questions such as "The passage is primarily concerned with . . ." or "Which of the following is an unstated assumption made by the author of the passage?"

- Reading Category 4 questions deal with short statements followed by a single question.

✔ **The writing test** has four categories of multiple-choice questions and two essays.

- The multiple-choice writing questions are straightforward questions covering sentence correction, revision in context, usage, and research skills. You have to find only one correct answer for each of these questions.

- The argumentative and informative/explanatory essay sections test your skills to write a detailed essay in a very short period of time. See Chapter 11 for more on the essay questions.

✔ **The mathematics test** has several question categories:

- One of the categories deals with numeric entry. These types of questions require you to input an integer or decimal into a single box or a fraction into two separate boxes.

- The other categories contain multiple-choice questions followed by five answers, with either one or two of those choices being correct. Be aware that the test may not tell you the number of choices to select, but the directions will tell you to check all that apply.

Understanding How the Test Is Scored

The Praxis Core exam is divided into three tests: reading, writing, and mathematics. Take careful note of the difference between our use of "exam" and "test." Each test is scored separately, and every state that requires passing scores for the exam requires that exam-takers pass each of the three tests that compose the exam. Your score on a given test is based on a raw score and adjusted to a scale that ranges from 100 to 200 points.

Your raw score is the number of questions you answer correctly. You don't lose any points for answering a question incorrectly. If you were to answer every single question incorrectly, your raw score would be 0, which is exactly what it would be if you didn't answer any questions at all. That's why you have nothing to lose by guessing if you don't know the answer to a question.

Your score for each test involves taking your raw score, or the number of questions you answer correctly, and comparing it to the number of questions on the test. This comparison determines your final score, the number that exists in the range from 100 to 200. Your final score determines whether you pass the test. (*Note:* When you take the practice tests in the book or online, there is no way to convert your raw score to a final score.) You pass the test in most states by answering at least 60 percent of the questions correctly. This gives you a benchmark to measure yourself against as you go through the practice tests.

When you receive your test results, you'll see a raw score for each test, and you'll also get a raw score for each content category into which the test is divided. Your total raw score is converted to a scaled score that adapts for the level of rigor of that particular testing edition.

If you fail the Praxis the first time you take it (or if you've already failed it), you can look at your scores for each content category to see where you did well and where you struggled. Use those scores to direct your studies in anticipation of taking the test again.

Each state that requires passing the exam has its own minimum scores for each of the tests that make up the exam. What constitutes a passing score in one state may not be a passing score in another state. Contact your state local department of education for the actual cut scores.

Chapter 2

Getting Ready for Test Day

You've known for months, if not years, that you need to take the Praxis exam to be certified to teach in your state. And just like any other major undertaking in life, you need to prepare for the test. You wouldn't run a marathon without doing some training, would you? You shouldn't just show up to take the Praxis either.

Before you take the Praxis, you should put a strategy in place. Ideally you'll give yourself a couple of months to get ready for the test. In that time you'll study and review concepts the test covers, take practice tests to familiarize yourself with the format and timing of the test, and brush up in areas where you're weak so you can ace the test.

In this chapter, we offer suggestions about how to prepare for the test, whether you're taking it for the first time or taking it again.

Registering for the Test

Before you register to take the Praxis, check with the local department of education to make sure you're taking the right test. Don't ask ETS or your mom or anyone else who isn't in a position to admit you to a teaching program; they may give you wrong information, which can lead to wasted time and money.

You can find out how to register to take the Praxis Core by going to www.ets.org. The Praxis Core is offered during testing windows at more than 300 Prometric testing sites across the country. Contact your local Prometric testing site for specific questions regarding its testing windows. Test-takers must register at least three days prior to their intended test date, and you must pay the testing fee online. At the time of this writing, individual tests (reading, writing, or mathematics) cost $85; the price to take all three tests at once is $135; and the cost to register for two tests is $125.

After you register, read all the admission ticket info to make sure all the content is correct. Contact ETS if you have any disabilities that require accommodations.

Consider taking one test per day instead of multiple tests per day. You know your limits and abilities. Some people take all three tests on the same day, and they bomb all three. If you aren't super confident that you can pass multiple tests in one sitting, you may want to schedule them for different days. This approach will also help you map out your study plan more strategically (see the next section). You can study for one test at a time instead of all three.

Using Your Time Wisely

When preparing for the Praxis, you need to think of time in two different ways. First, you need to plan your study time. Expect to spend many hours over the next several weeks reviewing the material that could be on the test. Then you need to know how much time is allotted for the test itself. Knowing these details will help you pace yourself as you answer questions during the test when it really counts. We cover both aspects of using your time wisely in the following sections.

Budgeting your study time leading up to test day

When you budget your study time ahead of your test date, you increase your chances of passing the first time. Do you really want to face the Praxis more than once to enroll in a teacher education program? We didn't think so.

If you can't put in adequate study time before taking the test, seriously consider rescheduling. The Praxis Core is given several times each year at the local testing center. Rather than taking the test with no preparation, contact the testing center or go online to reschedule to take the test at a later date.

Creating a schedule and penciling in the practice tests

The best way to prepare to take the Praxis is to set up a study schedule and then stick to it. Block off an amount of time each day to prepare for the test and note what topics you plan to study or review. You may need to ask your sister to baby-sit the kids, or you may need to turn down drinks with friends for a few weeks, but it will be worth it. This test will affect your life for a short amount of time. After you receive a passing score, you can commit to the bowling league. Use all of your extra time to focus on the Praxis.

Create an adjustable timetable that you can revise to best meet your needs as test time gets closer. The latest that you should begin studying is four to six weeks before the test.

During your study sessions, familiarize yourself with the question types for each section. Not all the questions are straightforward, multiple-choice questions. Some of them ask you to choose *all* the right answers. Other questions require you to calculate an answer and write it in a box. Knowing the variations in question types gives you a better chance of answering them correctly. As you get familiar with the question types, also pay attention to the test's directions. Understanding the directions ahead of time can save you valuable time on test day and can reduce test anxiety.

This book includes two full-length tests in Part V and three more online. You may want to take a test now and save the others to take in the days leading up to the exam.

When you take the practice tests, take them under timed conditions in a quiet setting where you won't be disturbed. Taking the practice tests in a test-like environment gives you a better sense of how you'll perform on the Praxis when it counts. After you take a practice test, be sure to review the answer explanations. These help you see what you did right or where you went wrong; they're another learning opportunity beyond the review material.

You can also take partial timed exams at different times in your long-term study schedule and focus on your weakest objective areas. Different subjects call for different study habits. If the subject is math, then work problems — don't just read over the info like you would writing and reading.

Joining forces with others

Sometimes people gain more knowledge when they study with others. Others may have a different way to solve an algebra problem or a better way to get to the heart of a reading passage, and their explanations may help you learn what you need for the test. So consider creating or joining a study group. Most teacher assistants need the same tests, and they may have different strengths in the same areas and can help each other.

If you can't find a group to study with, look for a Praxis prep course. The instructors of these courses know the ins and outs of what's on the test, and during the class, they review material that you're likely to encounter. Yes, you'll have to pay for the course, but the advantage is that the instructor should know the material in depth and be able to answer your questions or explain the material in a way that suits your learning style. The Kirkland Group has been conducting Praxis workshops for several years. For more details, go to www.kirklandgroup.org.

Take the test within a week after the prep class ends. This will increase your chances of remembering the information until you take the test. Don't wait six months after completing the course before you take the test, or you may end up back in the same boat.

Employing some other study techniques

Even when you're not officially studying, try to sneak in some learning or review. Pull out your old textbooks for grammar, reading, and math, and skim through them during lunch or while you're on the treadmill. The info in your old textbooks may jog your memory about something you learned a while back. The only way to study math is to practice on the problems in the books. You need to know certain grammar rules that may only be explained in a traditional grammar book. If you think the verb "to be" is one of Shakespeare's famous lines, then you need to go back and read the grammar books.

Gather up crossword puzzle books, Sudoku challenges, and other mind games, and work them while you're relaxing in front of the TV. If you're a whiz at English, work numbers games. If numbers are your thing, try your hand at crossword puzzles. Your goal is to strengthen the areas where you're weak, and puzzles or games are a fun way to accomplish that.

You are what you eat. You can't run a marathon by eating candy bars and drinking soft drinks every day for breakfast. There are some foods that assist you during the learning process. They naturally increase the memory and release chemicals that are helpful to the brain. These foods include eggs, fish, whole grains, leafy greens, fruits, and — thank goodness — coffee.

Budgeting your time while taking the test

On test day, it's all about pacing yourself. We like to look at the test from the perspective of how many questions you have to answer per minute:

- The math and reading sections give you 85 minutes to answer 56 questions. This gives you a little over a minute and a half to answer each question.
- The writing section gives you 40 minutes to answer 40 multiple-choice questions. That comes out to one question per minute.
- The essay section gives you 60 minutes to write two essays.

You may look at those numbers and think, "There's no way I can answer questions that quickly!" But fear not. Here are some tips that will help you shave seconds off the amount of time it takes you to answer many of the questions:

- ✔ **Watch the clock on the computer screen.** Monitor the time on the computer screen like it's your million-dollar countdown. Remember that you'll have at least one minute per question, and you need to use every minute wisely.

- ✔ **Don't make time your sole focus.** Don't get so caught up on timing that you aren't paying attention to what the questions are asking. Strike a balance between monitoring the time and concentrating on the task at hand.

- ✔ **Watch for the traps.** The people who write the assessment questions always add "trap" answers into the mix. These incorrect answers look like they're correct, but they're not. For example, you may see an answer to a word problem that's achieved by multiplying when you should be dividing. It's a trap. Watch out for it.

- ✔ **Use the process of elimination.** If you don't know the answer immediately after reading the answer choices, try to eliminate as many answers as possible. Then guess at the answer. Your chances of guessing correctly increase as you eliminate more answer choices.

- ✔ **Read all possible answers.** Sift through each answer choice and ensure that you aren't overlooking a better answer. Don't select Choice (A) before looking at the alternative answer choices.

When Test Day Has Arrived

If you've followed the advice up to this point, you'll begin test day well prepared for the task at hand. By this time, you should be in shape and ready to concentrate on the test.

Print testing-center map directions to make sure you know where you're going. Drive to the testing center the day before to find out exactly where the testing center is located. Try to make the drive at the same time that you'll make the drive on test day; that way you'll know what traffic may be like and can plan accordingly for backups.

Arrive at the testing center at least 30 minutes early. Arriving late could cause you to forfeit registration. And make sure you bring a picture ID. Without your ID, you won't be admitted to the test center, and you'll lose your registration fee.

Don't take the test while you are fatigued. Sleep deprivation can lead to failing test scores. Make sure you get a good night's sleep the night before you're scheduled to take the test.

After you arrive at the testing center, you'll need to follow a few rules and sit through a bit of training. We cover those details in the sections that follow.

Knowing what to bring and what to leave at home

You must bring two items to the testing center:

- ✔ **Your admission ticket:** You receive your admission ticket when you register online.

- ✔ **Picture identification:** The picture ID must include your name, signature, and photo. Acceptable IDs include a valid government-issued driver's license, a passport, a state-issued ID, a national ID, or a military ID. See www.ets.org for more details.

If you don't have these items, you won't be allowed to take the exam.

Thousands of people take the Praxis every year. To make sure everyone has a fair chance at passing, ETS has set up guidelines for what isn't allowed in the test center. Following is a list of items to leave at home:

- **Cellphones, smartphones, laptops, tablets, MP3 players, or any other electronic devices:** You can't even bring these into the building, so lock them in your car or leave them at home. ETS takes the confidentiality of the test *seriously*.

- **Dictionaries, books, or other reading materials:** Yes, that includes this book. Study *Praxis Core For Dummies* either in the car or at home.

- **Scratch paper:** The testing center will provide scratch paper that you can use for math computations, notes, and outlines.

- **Personal items:** You may be asked to empty your pockets before entering the test room. You'll be given a place to store your belongings while you take the test, but don't plan on leaving anything valuable in there.

Be sure you wear the right clothing. Sometimes buildings are colder than expected. Dress in layers so that you can make adjustments for the temperature.

Getting familiar with computer testing

You will take the Praxis Core on a computer. This allows you to take the test any day of the week and almost on demand at the local Prometric testing center. It also allows for faster scoring of your test, meaning you'll get your results faster than you would if the test were administered on paper.

Before you take the test, ETS gives you 30 minutes of practice time during which you can figure out how the computer test works. Pay attention during this online computerized testing tutorial session. Tips like how to use the computer, answer questions, and review previous pages can be helpful. Take advantage of this time because you're on your own once the test starts.

Make sure to figure out how to mark questions. Occasionally you'll come to an item that you aren't sure about. If you have extra time left at the end of the test, you can go back and check your answers.

If You Are Retaking the Test

The reality is that sometimes you study for, prepare for, and focus on the Praxis Core only to receive the bad news that you didn't achieve a passing score. Don't panic. According to ETS, you can take the test once per calendar month, but no more than six times within a 12-month period.

If you do need to retake the test, spend some time analyzing the areas where you fell short and then create a plan to improve your score the next time. Examine your previous test scores. The numbers can tell you how close you were to passing and how much work you have to do to bring up your score.

Don't make the same mistakes the second time around. A wise saying defines insanity as doing the same thing over and over again and expecting different results. Don't repeat your previous mistakes on subsequent tests. If you didn't pass because you just don't understand decimals or grammatical rules, spend extra time studying those areas.

Some people miss passing the test by 15 points or more. If that's the case, don't rush to retake the test. Enroll in a review course in order to increase your chances of passing the test on your next try. You may spend a little money on the class, but you'll save money in the long run because you won't have to take the test repeatedly. Sometimes individuals who work together, take the same college course, or go to the same church can form a study group. Or you can look for a personal tutor.

When test day rolls around again, try to minimize negative circumstances, and know that uncontrollable ones aren't likely to reoccur. You may have argued with your spouse on the morning you took the first test. Maybe the baby contracted diarrhea the night before, or perhaps the chicken salad you ate didn't agree with your stomach. These factors may have contributed to your failure to pass the test. Take it again and the conditions will probably be better.

Chapter 3

Practicing the Praxis: Trying Out Some Practice Questions

In This Chapter

▶ Trying your hand at some sample Praxis questions

▶ Checking out the right and wrong answers

▶ Determining the areas where you need to study

If you're just beginning to prepare to take the Praxis, this chapter is a good place to start. It gives you a sense of the types of math, reading, and writing questions you'll encounter when you face the real exam.

In this chapter, we give you an opportunity to see where your strengths and weaknesses lie. You can determine whether you need to spend the next few weeks studying statistics and probability questions, grammar rules, or reading comprehension strategies. Or maybe you'll decide that you just need to fine-tune one or two specific areas of knowledge, and that's fine too.

Focus first on the areas you need to study most. Later you can review the areas you're more familiar with.

Going through the Preassessment Questions

In just a minute here, we'll be tossing some practice questions at you. Actually, because there are complete practice tests later in the book, maybe you should think of these upcoming questions as "practice for the practice." The questions in this chapter can help you determine your strengths and weaknesses, and then align your study appropriately.

When you answer the questions in the upcoming sections, we don't recommend setting a timer or anything like that yet. You should learn how to do something right before you start to worry about doing it fast, and there'll be plenty of time to time yourself later.

Because time won't be an issue, you also don't need to worry about skipping hard questions and coming back to them later. Try your best to answer each one, even if it's just a guess (there's no penalty for guessing on the Praxis, so on the actual test, there'll be no reason to leave a question blank).

Finally, we recommend that you resist the urge to flip to the answers after each question to see whether you got it right. That can wait until you've completed all the practice questions. Seeing that you've gotten a few questions wrong early on can dishearten you, and seeing that you've gotten a bunch right in a row can make you paranoid about jinxing yourself. Either way, there's no advantage to checking your answers on a question-by-question basis: Take your time, and complete all the questions to the best of your ability. You can worry about how many you got right when you're finished, and you can worry about how fast you are later in the book.

(**Note:** We don't provide essay questions in this chapter for you to practice on because we want you to get an overview of your skills. If you want to spend some time on essay writing, flip to Part IV.)

When you're ready to try your hand at a full-length practice test, head to Part V, where you'll find two full-length Praxis exams (with essay questions included).

Reading practice questions

Directions: Each passage in this test is followed by a question based on its content. After reading each passage, choose the best answer to each question from among the five choices given. Answer all questions following a passage on the basis of what is stated or implied in that passage. You are not expected to have any previous knowledge of the topics treated in the passages.

Line   Although "an elephant is an elephant" to the untrained eye, African elephants and Asian elephants are actually two distinct species, and it's not so hard to tell the difference. In African ele-
(05)   phants, the head is higher than the back, whereas the Asian elephant's back is higher than its head. Among African elephants, both males and females are almost always born with tusks, while female Asian elephants are usually tuskless. If you can
(10)   get close enough to examine the trunk, you'll notice that African elephants have two finger-like protrusions at the tip of the trunk, as opposed to an Asian elephant's one.

1. According to the passage, an elephant with no tusks is

   (A) definitely a female elephant.

   (B) definitely an Asian elephant.

   (C) probably a male Asian elephant.

   (D) probably a female Asian elephant.

   (E) more likely to be a male Asian elephant than a female African elephant.

   Nowadays, most people are aware that Christopher Columbus was not only a pretty terrible guy, but that he also didn't really discover America. Even leaving out the obvious objection that vast populations of indigenous peoples were (05) already living here, there's also indisputable evidence that the Vikings reached North America and established settlements centuries before Columbus (it was a quicker and an easier trip for them, however, as all they had to do was sail (10) along the ice of the Arctic Circle as though it were a coastline). What far fewer people know is that it seems likely that seafaring Pacific Islanders reached the west coast of South America in the early second millennium, possibly even before (15) the Vikings touched down in the Northeast. Archaeological evidence indicates the sudden appearance of yams (originally native to South America) in Polynesia and of chickens (originally native to Asia) in Chile at about the same time. (20)

2. The primary purpose of the passage is to

   (A) explain how chickens appeared in South America.

   (B) discern whether the Vikings or Pacific Islanders reached the Americas first.

   (C) argue that Columbus Day should no longer be celebrated as a holiday.

   (D) examine the question of whose journey to the Americas was most difficult.

   (E) provide information about journeys to the Americas before that of Columbus.

Though many might understandably assume that it was a long and complex process, the transformation of the Republican Party from a single-issue organization dedicated to ending slavery into the "party of big business" was both predictable and more-or-less instantaneous. Knowing that freed slaves would have no choice but to travel north and take factory jobs, which would result in more competition for employment and therefore lower wages, northern industrialists joined forces with idealistic abolitionists. When slavery ended, the abolitionists considered their duty done and got out of politics, and the captains of industry were left in charge of the party.

3. The passage characterizes the shift in priorities of the 19th-century Republican Party as

(A) very nearly inevitable.

(B) the surprising result of a long struggle.

(C) the fault of naïve abolitionists.

(D) a logical reaction to unforeseen circumstances.

(E) an attempt to reduce competition for employment.

It is arguably Shakespeare's finest comedy, but modern productions of *As You Like It* find themselves awkwardly having to negotiate a plot point that doesn't sit right with contemporary audiences: In this day and age, we roll our eyes at the idea that the intelligent, resourceful, and independent heroine Rosalind would fall madly in love with Orlando simply because she sees him win a wrestling match.

4. The author of the passage uses the word *negotiate* most nearly to mean

(A) imperceptibly alter

(B) make the best of

(C) draw attention away from

(D) apologize for

(E) rush through safely

Perhaps no issue in popular music divides both critics and fans more bitterly than the seemingly endless debate over what music, and which bands, do or do not count as "punk rock." People can't even seem to agree on whether punk is a genre of rock or was a historical movement within rock, specific to a particular place and time. Were 1990s rock groups like Nirvana and Blink-182 punk bands, or were they only bands that were influenced by punk as it was "authentically" played in the 1970s by bands like the Ramones and the Clash? Did punk "end" at a certain point in music history, and if so, then when, and what case is to be made for saying it ended then as opposed to at an earlier or later date? After all, if a word refers only to a style of music, then music of that style can be played by anyone at any time — but if the word refers to a contextualized historical movement, then calling contemporary bands "punk" would be as absurd as calling contemporary feminists "bluestockings" or calling contemporary Midwesterners "settlers."

5. The organization of the passage can best be described by which of the following?

(A) A compromise between two sides in a controversy is suggested.

(B) A popular misconception is corrected.

(C) A tricky question is analyzed for a general audience.

(D) A comparison is made between seemingly dissimilar things.

(E) A problematic term is suggested to be meaningless.

Line   I don't feel old, but when I examine all the
data, it seems to point to the fact that I just
might be. Perhaps the most crucial piece of evidence is that I haven't dressed up for Halloween
(05) in nearly four years. This wasn't a decision I
made; it was just a string of bad luck. One year, I
happened to be moving on Halloween. The next
year, I was helping a friend move. Last year, there
was a hurricane — surely that's not my fault,
(10) right? I can make all the excuses I want, but deep
down inside I know that if I were ten years
younger I would have found a way to dress up on
Halloween no matter what. Maybe that's what
getting old is: a loss of energy disguised as a
(15) series of coincidences.

6. In the passage, the author's tone can best
    be described as one of

    (A) nostalgic self-justification.

    (B) annoyed defensiveness.

    (C) paranoid hypothesizing.

    (D) blissful ignorance.

    (E) melancholy philosophizing.

Line   Despite the hand-wringing that intellectuals
love to do about the blockbuster sales of "silly"
books like *The DaVinci Code,* one might justifi-
ably make the claim that we are currently living
in a golden age of literature — not because more   (05)
"good" books are being written, but merely
because far more books of any kind are being
read, and by more people, than at any point in
history so far. Most studies indicate that about
as many "serious" books by "good" authors are   (10)
being written now as at any other time and that
they are being read by about as many people. It's
just that they are no longer the most famous books.
But the reason behind this is actually cause for
celebration: Classes of people that would have   (15)
been either illiterate or at the very least uninter-
ested in reading in former times are now buying
and reading books. Even the success of the much-
maligned *Twilight* series should be putting smiles
on the faces of those who look at it the right way: (20)
Young people are reading books of their own free
will, outside of school. Granted, they're not reading Shakespeare, but it wasn't so long ago that
they wouldn't have been reading at all.

7. The phenomenon characterized by the
    author as "cause for celebration" is

    (A) the fact that fewer people are making
        silly distinctions about what does or
        doesn't count as a "serious" book.

    (B) the fact that reading is popular enough
        among the masses for bad books to be
        outselling good ones.

    (C) the fact that young people are reading
        without being forced to.

    (D) the fact that maligned books like *The
        DaVinci Code* and the *Twilight* series
        are actually not as bad as many people
        claim.

    (E) the fact that people who are uninter-
        ested in reading are reading books
        anyway, because there is suddenly
        social pressure on them to do so.

Writing practice questions

Directions: Each question consists of a sentence that contains four underlined portions. Read each sentence and decide whether any of the underlined parts contains a grammatical construction, a word use, or an instance of incorrect or omitted punctuation or capitalization that would be inappropriate in carefully written English. If so, select the underlined portion that must be revised to produce a correct sentence. If there are no errors in the sentence as written, select "No error." No sentence has more than one error.

1. Don't <u>be offended</u> when the cat headbutts
   _A
   <u>you, you</u> should <u>be flattered because it's</u> a
   _B   _C
   sign <u>of affection</u>. <u>No error</u>.
        _D   _E

2. When I <u>saw you</u> covered in <u>feathers, I just</u>
   _A   _B
   <u>naturally</u> assumed <u>that you were</u> the
   _C
   person <u>to which</u> I mailed all those ducks.
          _D
   <u>No error</u>.
   _E

3. <u>You're computer</u> seems to have a <u>virus but</u>,
   _A   _B
   <u>as far</u> as I can <u>tell, it should be possible</u> for
   _A   _C
   us to remove it without any <u>of the data being</u>
                               _D
   lost. <u>No error</u>.
         _E

4. <u>It's</u> remarkable <u>that, even though</u> you are
   _A   _B
   not <u>any taller than he, you</u> are still <u>heavily</u>
       _C
   <u>favored to win the scheduled</u> one-on-one
   _D
   basketball game. <u>No error</u>.
                    _E

Directions: Read each of the following sentences. The answer choices present five ways of writing the sentence. The first of these repeats the original, but the other four are all different. If you think the original sentence is better than any of the suggested changes, you should select the first answer choice; otherwise, you should select one of the other choices.

This is a test of correctness and effectiveness of expression. In choosing answers, follow the requirements of standard written English; i.e., pay attention to acceptable usage in grammar, diction (choice of words), sentence construction, and punctuation. Choose the answer that expresses most effectively what is presented in the original sentence; this answer should be clear and exact without awkwardness, ambiguity, or redundancy.

5. Coulrophobia is the fear of clowns, and a phenomenon more widespread than many realize.

    (A) Coulrophobia is the fear of clowns, and a phenomenon more widespread than many realize.

    (B) Coulrophobia, it is the fear of clowns, a phenomenon more widespread then many realize.

    (C) Coulrophobia, the fear of clowns, is a phenomenon more widespread than many realize.

    (D) Coulrophobia, which is the fear of clowns, being a phenomenon more widespread then many realize.

    (E) Coulrophobia is the fear of clowns, it is a phenomenon more widespread than many realize.

6. The octopus is a surprisingly smart animal, they can solve mazes amazing skillfully.

    (A) The octopus is a surprisingly smart animal, they can solve mazes amazing skillfully.

    (B) The octopus is a surprisingly smart animal, that can solve mazes amazing and skillful.

    (C) The octopus is a surprisingly smart animal, it can solve mazes amazingly skillful.

    (D) The octopus is a surprisingly smart animal; which can solve mazes amazingly skillfully.

    (E) The octopus is a surprisingly smart animal: It can solve mazes amazingly skillfully.

7. Although it was believed for years that they weren't, biologists have recently proven that pandas are in fact true bears.

    (A) Although it was believed for years that they weren't, biologists have recently proven that pandas are in fact true bears.

    (B) Although it was believed for years that they weren't, but biologists have recently proven that Pandas are in fact true bears.

    (C) Although it was believed for years that they weren't, biologists have recently proven that Pandas are in fact true Bears.

    (D) It was believed for years that they weren't, however, biologists have recently proven that Pandas are in fact true bears.

    (E) It was believed for years that they weren't, biologists have recently proven that pandas are in fact true bears.

8. Whomever parked the car, that is in the driveway, could of done a better job.

    (A) Whomever parked the car, that is in the driveway, could of done a better job.

    (B) Whoever parked the car that is in the driveway could have done a better job.

    (C) Whoever parked the car that is in the driveway, could of done a better job.

    (D) Whomever parked the car which is in the driveway could have done a better job.

    (E) Whomever parked the car, which is in the driveway, could have done a better job.

Mathematics practice questions

Directions: Questions 1–20 are followed by five suggested answers. Select the one that best answers the question.

The following graph shows the number of bicycles sold by Brad's Bicycle Company for the years 2006–2011. Use the graph to answer Questions 1–4.

Brad's Bicycle Company Annual Sales

© John Wiley & Sons, Inc.

1. Which year showed the greatest number of bicycles sold by Brad's Bicycle Company?

    (A) 2006

    (B) 2007

    (C) 2008

    (D) 2009

    (E) 2010

2. Between which two years did the number of bicycles sold change the most?

    (A) 2006–2007

    (B) 2007–2008

    (C) 2008–2009

    (D) 2009–2010

    (E) 2010–2011

3. What is the average number of bicycles sold for the 6-year period?

    (A) 1,125,000

    (B) 11,250

    (C) 19,000

    (D) 187,500

    (E) 18,750

4. What is the median number of bicycles sold for the 6-year period?

    (A) 210,000

    (B) 220,000

    (C) 215,000

    (D) 430,000

    (E) 225,000

Following are the results from Mrs. Lowe's science test. Use the stem-and-leaf plot to answer Questions 5–7.

Science Test Results	
Stem	Leaf
5	0 0 5 5 5 9
6	0 9
7	0
8	5 5 5 5
9	0 0 0 9

© John Wiley & Sons, Inc.

5. In which interval did most students score?

    (A) 50–59

    (B) 60–69

    (C) 70–79

    (D) 80–89

    (E) 90–99

6. What is the median score on the math test?

    (A) 60

    (B) 65

    (C) 70

    (D) 85

    (E) 90

7. What is the mode of the data set?

    (A) 85

    (B) 55

    (C) 90

    (D) 95

    (E) 50

Use the Venn diagram that follows to answer Questions 8–9.

Favorite Food of 50 Students

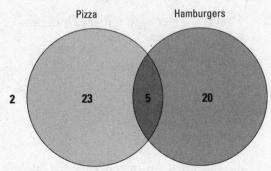

Pizza   Hamburgers

2   23   5   20

© John Wiley & Sons, Inc.

8. Pizza is the favorite food of what percentage of students in the Venn diagram?

   (A) 46 percent

   (B) 40 percent

   (C) 10 percent

   (D) 23 percent

   (E) 4 percent

9. What percentage of students do not like pizza or hamburgers?

   (A) 46 percent

   (B) 40 percent

   (C) 10 percent

   (D) 23 percent

   (E) 4 percent

10. The Hornet football team won eight football games and lost four games. Find the ratio of wins to total games in simplest form.

   (A) 8:4

   (B) 2:1

   (C) 8:12

   (D) 2:3

   (E) 4:12

11. A grocery store sells 5 pounds of apples for $3.50. How much would you pay for 2 pounds of apples?

   (A) $0.70

   (B) $0.75

   (C) $1.40

   (D) $1.50

   (E) $1.43

12. Which problem situation could be solved with the following equation?

   $$15d + 50 = m$$

   (A) Cassie earns $15 each day she works plus a flat rate of $50 per month. What is m, the total amount she earns in a month when she works d number of days?

   (B) Cassie earns $15 for every purchase she sells at her job. What is m, the total amount she earns in 100 months?

   (C) Cassie earns $50 each day she works plus a flat rate of $15 per month. What is m, the total amount she earns in a month when she works d number of days?

   (D) Cassie earns d amount of dollars for every 15 items she sells. She makes $50 per day at her job. What is m, the total dollar amount Cassie earns in a year?

   (E) Cassie earns d amount of dollars for every 50 items she sells. She makes $15 per day at her job. What is m, the total dollar amount Cassie earns in a year?

13. There are 10 yellow counters and 15 red counters in a bag. What is the probability of picking a yellow counter from the bag?

   (A) 5/8

   (B) 1/2

   (C) 2/5

   (D) 2/3

   (E) 3/8

14. A spinner with the numbers 1 through 15 is spun. Find P (prime numbers).

(A) 2/5

(B) 5/15

(C) 6/15

(D) 3/5

(E) 7/15

15. The approximate mass of a dust particle is 0.000000000753 kilograms. Write in scientific notation.

(A) 7.53×10^9

(B) 7.53×10^{-10}

(C) 7.53×10^{10}

(D) 7.53×10^{-9}

(E) 7.53×10^7

16. In the following rectangle ABCD, $\overline{AC}$ is 6 inches long. If the rectangle's perimeter is 34 inches, how many inches long is $\overline{AB}$?

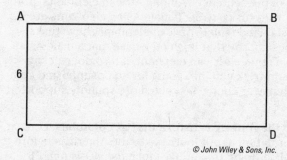

© John Wiley & Sons, Inc.

(A) 28

(B) 13

(C) 22

(D) 11

(E) 17

17. What is the length in centimeters of the hypotenuse of a right triangle with legs of 5 centimeters and 12 centimeters?

(A) 13

(B) 17

(C) 7

(D) 4.12

(E) 5

18. The length of each leg of an isosceles triangle is 17 centimeters, and the perimeter is 62 centimeters. What is the length of the base?

(A) 45

(B) 17

(C) 28

(D) 14

(E) 20

19. Simplify $(-3a^5)^2$.

(A) $-9a^{10}$

(B) $-9a^7$

(C) $9a^{-7}$

(D) $9a^{10}$

(E) $-3a^7$

20. Which number is NOT expressed in scientific notation?

(A) 6×10^5

(B) 0.25×10^9

(C) 1.5×10^1

(D) 5.2×10^5

(E) 4.2×10^3

Looking at the Preassessment Answers

Now it's time to see how you did on the three sets of practice questions. When you score your answers, keep track of which questions you answered incorrectly. Then go back and determine which category the question fits into (algebra, subject-verb agreement, and so on). This will allow you to determine what areas you need to spend more time studying.

Reading answers and explanations

Use this answer key to score the practice reading questions in this chapter. The answer explanations give you some insight as to why the correct answer is better than the other choices.

1. **D. probably a female Asian elephant.** The passage explicitly states that "female Asian elephants are usually tuskless." While the passage implies that it's possible for a male or female of either elephant species to be born without tusks, it remains the case that only female Asian elephants are tuskless *most of the time.*

   Choice (A) is wrong because there's no reason to think that a tuskless elephant is *definitely* female. The passage states that female Asian elephants are usually tuskless, but it also mentions that female African elephants usually have tusks, and that it's possible, though rare, for a male of either species to be tuskless. (As a general rule, on reading-comprehension tests like the Praxis, you should never go for a "definitely" when a "probably" will do.)

   Choice (B) is wrong because the passage states that "among African elephants, both males and females are *almost* always born with tusks." The "almost" implies that it's possible, though rare, for an African elephant of either gender to be tuskless.

   Choice (C) is wrong because, although male Asian elephants are not *explicitly stated* to be either tusked or tuskless, the construction of the sentence "Among African elephants, both males and females are almost always born with tusks, while female Asian elephants are usually tuskless" *clearly implies* that male Asian elephants usually have tusks.

   Choice (E) is wrong because the structure of the sentence "Among African elephants, both males and females are almost always born with tusks, while female Asian elephants are usually tuskless" implies that both male Asian and female African elephants have tusks most of the time. Although the passage does *not* say that it *isn't* the case that a male Asian elephant is more likely to be tuskless than a female African elephant, it *also* doesn't say that it *is* the case. This answer choice tries to trick you into going for an unsupported complex answer even though another, simpler answer choice is much more soundly supported by the passage. Don't be fooled!

2. **E. provide information about journeys to the Americas before that of Columbus.** Look at it this way: *Does* the passage "provide information about journeys to the Americas before that of Columbus?" Yes, indisputably. And is it doing this pretty much *the whole time?* It sure is. So there's no real way that Choice (E) can be wrong. There's no reason to go for an overly specific answer choice when another answer choice contains a broad statement that isn't wrong.

   Choice (A) is wrong because, although the passage *does* provide an explanation of how chickens ended up in South America, this is *not* the *primary purpose* of the passage — it's a detail brought up in the course of exploring a larger idea. If something isn't brought up until the end, it's probably not the primary purpose of the passage. (Did you notice how the passage *closed* with the chicken detail and then that detail was mentioned in the *first* of the wrong choices so it would be fresh in your mind? Watch out for that trick!)

   Choice (B) is wrong because, although the passage does seem to be unsure about whether Vikings or Pacific Islanders reached the Americas first ("*possibly* even before. . . ."), it doesn't seem to be primarily concerned with which of them "won." The passage only seeks to establish that both the Vikings and the Pacific Islanders got here before Columbus.

   Choice (C) is wrong because, although it may be logical to assume that the author isn't a big fan of Columbus Day, based on the fact that he calls Columbus a "terrible guy" and points out that he didn't really discover America, the passage never gets into the issue of whether Columbus Day should still be celebrated. If arguing this were really the *primary purpose* of the passage, then the author would have made his opinion clear.

   Choice (D) is wrong because although the passage mentions that the Vikings' journey was easier than Columbus's, it does so in a parenthetical, and this is the only comparison in the entire passage involving the difficulty of the respective journeys. A concern brought up only once isn't likely to be the *primary purpose* of a passage.

3. **A. very nearly inevitable.** The first sentence of the passage ends by calling the transformation of the Republican Party from an abolitionist organization to a pro-business party "predictable and more-or-less instantaneous." The rest of the passage offers an explanation for this appraisal, framing the course of events as the only thing that could realistically have happened — in other words, *very nearly inevitable*.

   Choice (B) is wrong because the opening sentence establishes that the transformation of the Republican Party was *not* "a long and complex process" (a near-paraphrase of "the surprising result of a long struggle"), despite the fact that "many might understandably assume" it was. As an argumentative passage will often do, this passage opens by explaining what is *not* the case before going on to explain what *is* the case.

   Choice (C) is wrong because, while the passage explains that the abolitionists who founded the Republican Party "considered their duty done and got out of politics" after the end of slavery, it doesn't call them naïve and blame them for the party's subsequent course. This answer choice is too strongly worded — something that should make you suspicious on the actual exam.

   Choice (D) is wrong because while the passage does characterize the shift in priorities of the Republican Party as "logical" in the sense that it happened due to a series of identifiable and predictable steps, it does *not* bring up any "unforeseen circumstances." On the contrary, the passage explains that northern businessmen *did* foresee the desirable financial effect that abolition of slavery would have on their businesses, and that they joined the party specifically for that reason.

   Choice (E) is wrong because the passage clearly states that the businessmen who joined the Republican Party *wanted* there to be "more competition for employment," so they were hardly trying to *reduce* such competition.

4. **B. make the best of.** The close-in-context adverb *awkwardly* is a clue to the fact that a troupe playing *As You Like It* would expect the wrestling-inspired love scene to seem cheesy or even sexist to a modern audience and would therefore have to try and find a way to present the plot device as inoffensively as possible — in other words, to "make the best of" it.

   Choice (A) is wrong because there is no indication in the passage that modern troupes are in the habit of actually *changing* the scene in question. They have to "play it down," but the passage doesn't say that they *rewrite* Shakespeare.

   Choice (C) is wrong because, while "draw attention away from" is possibly the best of the wrong answers, it's not as good as "make the best of." Why not? Drawing attention away from the plot point in question *would be a form of* making the best of it — so if Choice (C) is right, then *so is* Choice B, but only *one* answer choice can be right. Conversely, Choice (B) can be right on its own, because Choice (C) goes too far. There's no real way to "draw attention away from" a scene in a play. You can, however, make decisions about different ways of staging it — so "make the best of" works, but "draw attention away from" goes too far.

   Choice (D) is wrong because the passage never implies that modern troupes "apologize for" the wrestling plot point in *As You Like It*. It is implied that they have to stage it cautiously and creatively, but "apologize for" is too extreme.

   Choice (E) is wrong because, while "rush through safely" can be a good synonymous phrase for *negotiate* in other contexts — one might speak of *negotiating* hurdles or river rapids, for example — it doesn't fit here.

5. **C. A tricky question is analyzed for a general audience.** At the very least, the passage definitely implies that the question of which bands count as "punk" bands is *tricky* — it does hardly anything aside from explain why the question is difficult to answer. And the passage does definitely appear to have been written for a general audience. Because these things are all that Choice C asserts to be true of the passage, there's really no way it can be wrong.

   Choice (A) is wrong because the passage never implies that there are precisely *two sides* to the debate about punk rock. On the contrary, the passage gives the impression that there are as many opinions as there are people involved in the discussion! Additionally, the passage never really "suggests a compromise." It summarizes what others have said, but the author never offers an argument of his own.

Choice (B) is wrong because the passage never says anything along the lines of "many people think that such-and-such is true, but it's not, and here is what's true instead." It summarizes points that many music critics and fans have made, but it never says anything about who is wrong or who is right.

Choice (D) is wrong because the passage never makes any comparisons.

Choice (E) is wrong because, while the passage certainly characterizes "punk" as "a problematic term," it never goes so far as to suggest that it is *meaningless*. The idea of the passage seems to be that the term does mean *something*, but that people can't agree on what.

6. **E. melancholy philosophizing.** The author is certainly *philosophizing* — in other words, he is tossing out analyses and characterizations of a particular concept (aging). And it seems inarguable that he is *melancholy* — that is, mournful and blue. Because those two things are all that Choice (E) asserts, and they're both true, there's no way that Choice (E) can be wrong.

Choice (A) is wrong because the passage is not really *nostalgic* — the author is talking more about a present that he isn't enjoying than about a past that he did enjoy. And he certainly isn't being *self-justifying*. If anything, he is beating up on himself, which is exactly the opposite.

Choice (B) is wrong because the author seems more sad than *annoyed*. He doesn't like what he's talking about, but it's making him depressed, not angry. And he isn't being *defensive* about anything. He's admitting his faults rather than making excuses for them.

Choice (C) is wrong because while the author is *hypothesizing* — in other words, coming up with possible explanations for a phenomenon — nothing in the passage suggests that he's *paranoid*. The author is feeling blue about getting older, not freaking out because he thinks people are out to get him.

Choice (D) is wrong because the author seems much more sad than he does *blissful*. And as for *ignorance*, it seems as though he is only too aware of his problems, not oblivious to them.

7. **B. the fact that reading is popular enough among the masses for bad books to be outselling good ones.** In context, the author says that the "cause for celebration" is the "reason behind" the fact that "serious" books "are no longer the most famous books." He then explains that this is because certain "classes of people" (that is, the masses) who once would not have read at all are now reading frequently. The result is that bad books outsell good ones, but the way the author sees it, this is better than back when most people didn't read at all.

Choice (A) is wrong because, although the author puts words like "good" and "serious" in quotes to acknowledge the fact that such distinctions about literature are subjective, there is no indication that the author *doesn't think there is actually such a thing* as the distinction between good and bad books. He is being politic and self-effacing about it, but the author does, in fact, appear to believe that some books really are better than others.

Choice (C) is wrong because although the author definitely does say that more young people are reading without being forced to and that this is a good thing, this particular fact is not the specific "cause for celebration" that the question asks about. The author uses the phrase "cause for celebration" earlier in the passage, about something else.

Choice (D) is wrong because, though he's trying to be as nice as possible about it, the author does, in fact, appear to think that *Twilight* and *The DaVinci Code* are not exactly the greatest books in the world. After all, the assertion that some books (like popular bestsellers) are not as good as others (like serious literature) is necessary for the author to make his point. If he didn't think this was the case, then he wouldn't have written the passage.

Choice (E) is wrong because the passage doesn't argue that the masses are only reading because of social pressure. Nothing about societal pressure is mentioned or alluded to in the passage.

Writing answers and explanations

Use this answer key to score the practice writing questions in this chapter. The answer explanations give you some insight as to why the correct answer is better than the other choices.

1. **B. you, you.** This section of the sentence contains a comma splice.

   Choice (A) is wrong because this imperative clause is properly constructed. Choice (C) is wrong because no comma before the *because* clause is necessary, and the correct spelling of *it's* is used.

   Choice (D) is wrong because the correct preposition is used, and *affection* is spelled correctly. Choice (E) is wrong because there is in fact an error in the sentence.

2. **D. to which.** The speaker is talking about a human being, and the pronoun is the object of a preposition, so it should be *whom* instead of *which*.

   Choice (A) is wrong because the normal past tense is correct here. Choice (B) is wrong because the comma correctly joins an initial subordinate *when* clause and a subsequent independent clause.

   Choice (C) is wrong because *that* is the appropriate relative pronoun for an essential clause. Choice (E) is wrong because there is in fact an error in the sentence.

3. **A. You're computer.** The possessive pronoun is spelled *your,* and that's the one you need here (*you're* means "you are").

   Choice (B) is wrong because a comma after a conjunction is correct in the rare instances where an appositive clause immediately follows the conjunction. Choice (C) is wrong because the comma here correctly marks the end of the appositive clause and the beginning of the final independent clause.

   Choice (D) is wrong because *data* is plural. Choice (E) is wrong because there is in fact an error in this sentence.

4. **E. No error.** There is no error in this sentence.

   Choice (A) is wrong because this is the correct spelling of *it's* in this context (the one that means "it is"). Choice (B) is wrong because a comma is necessary here, as an appositive clause interrupts the subordinate *that* clause.

   Choice (C) is wrong because, although many people would say "taller than *him*," it is actually correct to say "taller than *he*" because *than* is not a preposition. Choice (D) is wrong because the infinitive form of the verb ("to win") is correct in this context.

5. **C. Coulrophobia, the fear of clowns, is a phenomenon more widespread than many realize.** This sentence correctly presents a single independent clause that is interrupted by an appositive clause set off with a pair of commas.

   Choice (A) is wrong because a comma before the conjunction is incorrect here, as an independent clause does not follow it. Choice (B) is wrong because the comma and *it* after the subject of the sentence is unnecessary, and the spelling should be *than* instead of *then*.

   Choice (D) is wrong because the sentence has no main verb, and the spelling should be *than* instead of *then*. Choice (E) is wrong because this sentence contains a comma splice.

6. **E. The octopus is a surprisingly smart animal: It can solve mazes amazingly skillfully.** Both independent clauses are correctly constructed, and a colon is an acceptable way (though not the only way) of joining them.

   Choice (A) is wrong because the sentence contains a comma splice, the subject and pronoun do not agree in terms of number, and we need the adverb *amazingly* rather than the adjective *amazing*. Choice (B) is wrong because a comma is not needed before the *that* clause and because the adjectives *amazing* and *skillful* appear to modify the noun *mazes*, when we want them to be adverbs (*amazingly* and *skillfully*) modifying the verb *solve*.

Choice (C) is wrong because the sentence contains a comma splice, and because we want the adverb *skillfully* rather than the adjective *skillful*. Choice (D) is wrong because the semicolon does not join two independent clauses (a *which* clause is not an independent clause).

7. **A. Although it was believed for years that they weren't, biologists have recently proven that pandas are in fact true bears.** The sentence correctly presents an independent clause preceded by a subordinate *although* clause and a comma, and it doesn't incorrectly capitalize the names of animals.

Choice (B) is wrong because it is incorrect to include both *although* and *but* (you need one or the other, but not both), and because *Pandas* should not be capitalized. Choice (C) is wrong because *Pandas* and *Bears* should not be capitalized.

Choice (D) is wrong because *however* should be used to interrupt a single independent clause, not join two of them, and because *Pandas* should not be capitalized. Choice (E) is wrong because this sentence contains a comma splice.

8. **B. Whoever parked the car that is in the driveway could have done a better job.** The subjective case *whoever* is correctly used for the subject of the sentence, the essential *that* clause is not set off with any commas, and the correct *could have* is used in place of the incorrect *could of*.

Choice (A) is wrong because *whoever*, rather than *whomever*, should be used for the subject of the sentence, a *that* clause should not be set off with commas, and *could have* is correct, not *could of*. Choice (C) is wrong because no comma is needed, and because *could have* is correct, not *could of*.

Choice (D) is wrong because *whoever*, rather than *whomever*, should be used for the subject of the sentence, and because a *which* clause would need to be set off with commas. Choice (E) is wrong because *whoever*, rather than *whomever*, should be used for the subject of the sentence.

Math answers and explanations

Use this answer key to score the practice mathematics questions in this chapter.

1. **E. 2010.** The year 2010 yielded the highest bicycle sales of $230,000.

2. **B. 2007–2008.** Bicycle sales changed the most between the years 2007–2008. The change was $70,000.

3. **D. 187,500.** The average sales are found by adding the total sales for all years and dividing the total by the number of years: $100,000 + 140,000 + 210,000 + 225,000 + 230,000 + 220,000 = 1,125,000 \div 6 = 187,500$.

4. **C. 215,000.** Put the sales in order from least to greatest:

    ~~100,000~~, ~~140,000~~, 210,000, 220,000, ~~225,000~~, ~~230,000~~

Cross out the numbers alternating between one on the left and one on the right until you reach the numbers in the middle of the data set. There are two numbers in the center; take the average of them and you have the median:

   $(210,000 + 220,000) \div 2 = 215,000$

5. **A. 50–59.** The stem of 5 indicates that six people scored between 50–59 with the scores of 50, 50, 55, 55, 55, 59.

6. **C. 70.** Extract the data from the stem-and-leaf plot and highlight the middle number:

    50, 50, 55, 55, 55, 59, 60, 69, **70**, 85, 85, 85, 85, 90, 90, 90, 99

7. **A. 85.** The score that occurs the most often is 85, so 85 is the mode.

8. **A. 46 percent.** Fifty people were surveyed regarding their favorite foods. $\frac{23}{50}$ or 46 percent liked pizza; $\frac{20}{50}$ or 40 percent liked hamburgers; $\frac{5}{50}$ or 10 percent liked pizza and hamburgers; $\frac{2}{50}$ or 4 percent did not like either.

9. **E. 4 percent.** Fifty people were surveyed regarding their favorite foods. $\frac{23}{50}$ or 46 percent liked pizza; $\frac{20}{50}$ or 40 percent liked hamburgers; $\frac{5}{50}$ or 10 percent liked pizza and hamburgers; $\frac{2}{50}$ or 4 percent did not like either.

10. **D. 2:3.** The ratio of wins to total games played is 8:12. Set up the ratio of wins to total games played and reduce your answer using 4.

$$\frac{\text{wins}}{\text{total games}} = \frac{8}{12} \div \frac{4}{4} = \frac{2}{3}$$

11. **C. $1.40.** Set up a proportion to compare the cost of apples for 5 pounds to the cost of apples for 2 pounds. Cross multiply to find that 2 pounds of apples cost $1.40.

$$\frac{3.50}{5} = \frac{x}{2}$$
$$3.50(2) = 5x$$
$$7.00 = 5x$$
$$\frac{7.00}{5} = \frac{5x}{5}$$
$$1.40 = x$$

12. **A. Cassie earns $15 each day she works plus a flat rate of $50 per month. What is *m*, the total amount she earns in a month when she works *d* number of days?** The amount for *m* is the total Cassie earns each day she works at a rate of $15 per day, plus a flat rate of $50.

13. **C. 2/5.** There are 25 counters in the bag; 10 out of 25 are yellow, or 2/5 when simplified.

14. **A. 2/5.** There are six prime numbers between 1 and 15: 2, 3, 5, 7, 11, and 13. This is 6/15, which is 2/5 when simplified.

15. **B. 7.53×10^{-10}.** 0.000000000753 when written in scientific notation is 7.53×10^{-10}. A number written in scientific notation has two parts: The first part is the digits or a number between 1 and 10 (the decimal point must be placed after the 7 in 7.53). The second part is $\times$ 10 raised to a power. The power indicates how many spaces you moved the decimal point to get to the 7 in 7.53, which was 10 times. When the decimal point is moved right, the power is negative.

16. **D. 11.** The perimeter, in this case 34, is the sum of all the sides. You were given the width of 6 in the problem. Using $P = 2l + 2w$, you can find the missing side.

$$P = 2l + 2w$$
$$34 = 2l + 2(6)$$
$$34 = 2l + 12$$
$$22 = 2l$$
$$l = 11$$

17. **A. 13.** Using the Pythagorean theorem formula $a^2 + b^2 = c^2$, substitute the value of the legs for a and b and solve for c.

$$a^2 + b^2 = c^2$$
$$5^2 + 12^2 = c^2$$
$$25 + 144 = c^2$$
$$169 = c^2$$
$$\sqrt{169} = c$$
$$13 = c$$

18. **C. 28.** An isosceles triangle has two sides of equal length. Given that the perimeter or distance around the triangle is 62, we can solve for the base.

$$\text{length of side } 1 + \text{length of side } 2 + \text{base} = 62$$
$$17 + 17 + \text{base} = 62$$
$$34 + \text{base} = 62$$
$$\text{base} = 62 - 34$$
$$\text{base} = 28$$

19. **D. $9a^{10}$.** The exponent of 2 on the outside of the parenthesis indicates that you are to raise everything inside the parenthesis to the second power.

$$(-3)^2 = 9$$
and
$$(a^5)^2 = a^{10}$$
so
$$9a^{10}$$

20. **C. 0.25×10^9.** A number written in scientific notation has two parts: The first part is the digit or a number between 1 and 10 (the decimal point must be placed after the first digit). The second part is $\times 10$ raised to a power. The first part of the number in Choice (C) is not a number between 1 and 10.

Assessing Your Results

Now that you've answered and reviewed a representative sample of Praxis questions, you can evaluate how you did and figure out which subjects you need to spend more time reviewing. Even if you missed a couple of questions, don't worry. That was the point of answering the assessment questions. You're still at an early stage in your process of preparation for the Praxis, and there's a lot of book left to go.

Every time you take a practice test, you can benefit by assessing your results and focusing your studying and skills improvement accordingly.

Identifying categories where you struggled

The areas where you struggled the most are the areas you need to focus on the most. To figure out where you struggled, focus on each section of the practice test and outline the areas in which you need the most improvement. Briefly describe everything you missed, and look for patterns. Under each test subject (math, reading, writing), write the names of more specific categories, and then write even more specific categories under those. (Use the table of contents for help identifying specific categories within each test.) You may need to have a subcategory titled "Other."

For example, the first level of subheadings for math consists of the four major categories of Praxis Core math questions — number and quantity (basic math), algebra and functions, geometry, and statistics and probability. Each of those categories has its own categories (look at the chapters for each of the broad categories to break them down further). Continue to drill down into the topics until you identify the specific area you need to review. What matters is that you organize your weakest areas in a way that you can keep up with them and work on them.

After you've identified the categories that gave you trouble, look at the answer choices you picked incorrectly. Compare them to the correct answer choice. Review your mistakes and be sure you understand why any incorrect answers were incorrect. If something is unclear, ask a professor to help you understand where you went wrong (see the next section for more on this).

Taking notes on the areas where you succeeded can also help you. Improving your knowledge and skills concerning those areas can give you an edge for getting difficult questions correct.

Understanding where you went wrong specifically

Along with making an outline of the types of questions you missed, look for reasons for not getting the ones you missed. Did you lack knowledge that you need to review? Did you simply make an error? Did you confuse one idea with another? Did you not use a strategy you could have used that would have made the difference? Make a list of these reasons and keep them in mind as you work on gaining the necessary knowledge and practice as well as the test-taking skills that will help you.

The Praxis Core exam requires critical thinking beyond mere knowledge, but knowledge is extremely important, and so is strategy. The chapters in Parts II, III, and IV review the knowledge you need to know for each topic on the Praxis, and the Parts conclude with a strategy chapter to help you increase your chances of answering a question right when you're not 100 percent sure of the answer.

However, don't focus only on how many questions you missed and what types of questions they were. You can improve your future scores by asking yourself right now: *What did the wrong answers you picked have in common?* After all, if you failed to pick the right answer to a given question, that means you were fooled by one of the wrong answers. Go back over the explanations to the questions you missed, examine the differences between the right answers and the wrong answers that fooled you, and try to develop a sense of *what type of wrong answers you have a tendency to be fooled by.* Then you'll know what to watch out for!

When it comes to math questions, you'll likely have to go back and look at how you worked the problem to identify where you went wrong.

When it comes to the reading and writing questions, think about these questions: Do you tend to jump after the wrong answer with the biggest words in it? Or are you fooled by something that's probably true in real life, but that the passage never actually mentions? Did they get you with the wrong answer that mentions a detail from the end of the passage because they know it's fresh in your mind? Do you have a weakness for the wrong answer that uses the greatest number of exact words from the passage?

Maybe your weakness is emotional — you may tend to go for the most optimistic answer or for the most pessimistic one. You may have an unconscious bias toward picking the longest one or the shortest one. You may even be falling back on the tried-and-true, junior-high-school method of "when in doubt, pick C" without even realizing it (old habits die hard)!

There's an old saying among test-prep tutors: "I can tell you how to get a question right, but only you can tell yourself why you got one wrong." Okay, fine, it's not an old saying — we just made it up. But it *should* be an old saying, because it makes a good point.

Part II
Mastering Math Concepts

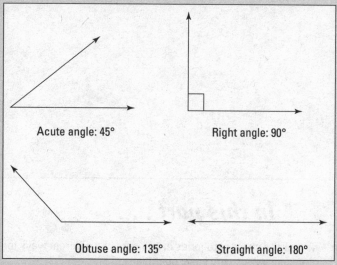

Acute angle: 45°

Right angle: 90°

Obtuse angle: 135°

Straight angle: 180°

© John Wiley & Sons, Inc.

Get a handle on the relationships between angles and transverse lines with the free article at
www.dummies.com/extras/praxiscore.

In this part . . .

- ✔ Review the major categories of numbers, the different ways to represent values, and basic operations.

- ✔ Brush up on how to use variables to represent quantities, perform operations with variable expressions, and solve equations and inequalities.

- ✔ Strengthen your understanding of geometric concepts, principles, and formulas.

- ✔ Gain mastery of the major forms of data representation and analysis.

- ✔ Understand the best test-taking strategies for math.

Chapter 4

Count on It: Number and Quantity

• •

In This Chapter

▶ Brushing up on integers

▶ Rewriting fractions and mixed numbers

▶ Determining decimal and percent forms of numbers

▶ Looking at number lines and the order of operations

▶ Figuring out quantities

• •

A good review of math begins with the basics of numbers and the major operations you do with them. The Praxis Core exam involves the basic operations, as well as more complicated ones, using different types of numbers. About 30 percent of the 56 math questions on the exam fall into the "number and quantity" category (that's about 17 questions if you haven't warmed up your math muscles yet). Plus, you have to understand these basics in order to perform more-complicated math problems.

If you were reviewing how to ride a bike, you might want to start with a discussion of pedals and tires and how to make them move. Doing math is like riding a bike, and this chapter starts at the beginning of your ride down the road to complete preparation for Praxis Core math.

You will have an on-screen calculator to use when you take the Praxis Core exam.

Working with Integers: Whole Numbers and Their Opposites

Think about the first numbers you ever learned. The first numbers you named belong to the most basic category of numbers — *whole numbers.* They begin with 0 and go on forever: 1, 2, 3, and so on. Each whole number is separated from the next by a quantity of 1. Partial numbers — that is, fractions such as $\frac{2}{5}$ and decimals such as 0.4 — are *not* whole numbers.

All whole numbers other than 0 are *positive*, which means that they're greater than 0. A number with no sign before it is understood to be positive. All numbers less than 0 are *negative* and are represented with a minus sign (–). Every negative number is the opposite of a positive number, and vice versa. For example, the opposite of 8 is –8, and the opposite of –12 is 12.

The *integers* are all the whole numbers and their opposites. In other words, all the whole numbers and all the negatives of whole numbers make up the entire set of integers. The only integer that doesn't have an opposite is 0. Poor thing.

Doing basic operations with integers

The basic operations you can perform with integers are addition, subtraction, multiplication, and division. You can perform the same operations with all numbers, but this part of the review focuses on integers because they're the best numbers to use in the early part of your math review. After all, they're basic numbers, and this discussion is about basic operations. They make a good fit, basically.

To add or subtract integers, it may help to understand *absolute value,* which is an integer's positive distance from 0. The absolute value of any integer is its value without a negative sign. So, the absolute value of any positive integer is the number, and the absolute value of any negative integer is its opposite, or the integer that remains when you drop the negative sign. The| |symbols represent absolute value. Here are a couple examples:

The absolute value of a positive number: $|7| = 7$

The absolute value of a negative number: $|-7| = 7$

Recall a few facts about working with integers:

✔ Subtracting an integer is the same as adding its opposite, and adding a number is the same as subtracting its opposite.

✔ If an even number of negative integers are multiplied or divided, the product is positive. If an odd number of integers are multiplied or divided, the product is negative.

✔ To add two integers with the same sign, add their absolute values and give the sum the sign that both numbers have.

✔ To add two integers with opposite signs, subtract the smaller absolute value from the greater absolute value and give the difference the sign of the number with the greater absolute value.

Find the product of the following: $-2 \cdot 4 \cdot -1 \cdot -3 \cdot -2$

(A) −48

(B) 24

(C) 48

(D) 25

(E) −24

The correct answer is Choice (C). The product of the absolute values of the integers is 48. Because the number of negative integers in the problem is four (−2, −1, −3, and −2), an even number, the product is positive.

$$(-2)(4)(-1)(-3)(-2) =$$
$$(-8)(-1)(-3)(-2) =$$
$$(8)(-3)(-2) =$$
$$(-24)(-2) = 48$$

Therefore, the answer is 48. Choice (A) is not correct because 48 is a positive number. You could accidentally forget to multiply one of the integers and get Choice (B) for an answer or add −1 instead of multiplying it to get Choice (D). This is a major area for errors. Try not to lose focus even for a split second when multiplying with negative numbers. Accidents cause false conclusions.

No matter how well you understand a mathematical concept or process, the threat of careless errors exists. To help avoid them on the Praxis Core exam, make sure you work every step, talk the problem out in your head as you work it, and, if you have time, go back over all the problems you worked after you reach the end of the math section. Danger lurks in the shadows, so be careful out there!

Finding factors of whole numbers

A *factor* of a whole number is a whole number that can be divided into it a whole number of times. For example, 4 is a factor of 20 because 4 can be multiplied by the whole number 5 (which is also a factor of 20) to get 20. The number 4 is not a factor of 21, 19, or any other number that is not evenly divisible by 4. And if you can break down a number's factor even further into its own factors, those smaller factors are also factors of the original number you started with. For example, because 2 is a factor of 4, 2 is also a factor of 20.

Every whole number has itself and 1 for factors. If those are the only two factors of a number, it's a *prime number*. For example, 3, 17, 31, and 79 are prime numbers.

To determine the factors of a number, first determine one factor and what it has to be multiplied by to get the number. Then find factors of those numbers the same way. Continue the process until no numbers can be broken down further. At this point, you've found the *prime factorization* of the number — a representation of the number as a product of all its prime factors. From there, all the number's factors, other than 1, can be found by multiplying every possible combination of the prime factors.

Find all the factors of 30.

(A) 30 and 1

(B) 2, 3, and 5

(C) 1, 2, 3, 5, 6, 10, 15, and 30

(D) 2, 3, 5, 6, 10, and 15

(E) 2 and 15

The correct answer is Choice (C). All the numbers listed are either prime factors of 30, products of combinations of those prime factors, or 1. However, Choice (C) is the only choice that includes all of them.

$$30 = 3 \cdot 10$$
$$= 3 \cdot 5 \cdot 2$$

The number 1 is a factor of 30 because 30 is a whole number, and every whole number is a factor of itself. The prime factors of 30 are 5, 2, and 3. By multiplying combinations of those numbers, the other factors can be determined.

$5 \times 2 = 10; 10 \times 3 = 30$

$5 \times 3 = 15; 15 \times 2 = 30$

$2 \times 3 = 6; 6 \times 5 = 30$

Employing some helpful divisibility rules

Knowing the divisibility rules concerning single-digit numbers and 10 can be helpful for finding factors of numbers. Check out Table 4-1.

Table 4-1	Divisibility Rules	
A whole number is divisible by . . .	*. . . if . . .*	*Examples*
0	No number is divisible by 0.	Sorry. Nothing to see here.
1	No ifs, ands, or buts apply here: All whole numbers are divisible by 1.	Every whole number is an example of this rule.
2	The last digit is an even number (0, 2, 4, 6, 8).	12; 728; 4; 962
3	The sum of the digits of the number is divisible by 3.	27 (2 + 7 = 9) 138 (1 + 3 + 8 = 12) 10,011 (1 + 0 + 0 + 1 + 1 = 3)
4	The last two digits form a number that's divisible by 4.	124 (24); 736 (36); 13,112 (12)
5	The last digit is 0 or 5.	25; 360; 4; 195
6	The number is divisible by both 2 and 3.	12; 54; 270; 906
7	You can double the last digit and subtract it from the rest of the number to get either 0 or a number with an absolute value that's divisible by 7.	14; 63; 175; 707
8	The last 3 digits form a number that's divisible by 8. (This rule, of course, is useful only with numbers with more than three digits.)	2,800; 16,384; 596,656
9	The sum of the digits is divisible by 9.	18; 72; 108; 918
10	The last digit of the number is 0.	100; 810; 21,370

Finding multiples of integers

A *multiple* of a number can be obtained by multiplying the number by an integer. For example, multiples of 5 include 5, 10, 15, 20, 25, and so forth. The phrases *a multiple of* and *divisible by* have basically the same meaning, but *divisible by* generally refers specifically to whole numbers, while *multiple* is used to label whole numbers as well as other types of numbers. If an integer is evenly divisible by another integer, it's automatically a multiple of it.

Each of the following is a multiple of 3 EXCEPT

(A) 96

(B) 123

(C) 3,000

(D) 761

(E) 903

The correct answer is Choice (D). By using the divisibility rule for 3 (see Table 4-1), you can determine that 96, 123, 3,000, and 903 are divisible by 3. The digits of each number add up to a number that's divisible by 3. That means each one is a multiple of 3 because you can multiply 3 by another integer to obtain each number. However, the digits of 761 add up to 14, which is not divisible by 3. You can also use long division to determine whether each number is a multiple of 3 by seeing whether 3 goes into it an even number of times, but that takes longer. Keep in mind that time is a factor on the Praxis Core exam.

Determining the greatest common factor and least common multiple

Two whole numbers can have factors in common. Such factors are called *common factors*. The greatest of those factors is the *greatest common factor* of the two numbers. To find the greatest common factor of two numbers, find all the factors of both numbers, determine which factors the numbers have in common, and then determine which of those common factors is the greatest (largest).

For example, to determine the greatest common factor of 20 and 45, you must first determine the factors of both numbers. You can use the prime factorization technique to find them.

20 : 1, 2, 4, 5, 10, 20

45 : 1, 3, 5, 9, 15, 45

What factors do 20 and 45 have in common? The common factors are 1 and 5. Because 5 is the greatest of the common factors, 5 is the greatest common factor.

The *least common multiple* of two numbers is like the greatest common factor, except that it's the lowest number instead of the highest one, and it's a multiple instead of a factor. To find the least common multiple of two numbers, write out several multiples of each and then determine the lowest multiple that they have in common.

For example, to find the least common multiple of 3 and 5, first write multiples of both numbers until you see one that they have in common.

3 : 3, 6, 9, 12, 15, 18, 21

5 : 5, 10, 15

For 5, you can stop at 15 because 15 is also a multiple of 3. Because 15 is the lowest of the multiples that 3 and 5 have in common, 15 is the least common multiple of 3 and 15.

You can't just multiply the factors together to get the least common multiple. Multiplying the factors will give you a multiple, but it may not be the smallest one. For example, if you want the least common multiple of 4 and 6, you can't multiply them because that gives you 24, when the least common multiple is actually 12.

Exponents and square roots

Have you ever taken a shortcut? If so, you're not alone, and you can relate to the idea of using exponents to represent multiplication. The people who invented the language we use to represent numbers decided to use shortcuts in representing multiplication involving a factor more than once. Imagine reading and writing stuff like this all the time:

$7 \times 7 =$

Fortunately, an easier way was created. In the preceding example, 7 is multiplied 21 times. That 21 can be used as an exponent:

$$7 \times 7 = 7^{21}$$

An *exponent* represents how many times a number is a factor. A number with an exponent is said to be set to that *power*. 7^{21} is "7 to the 21st power," for example. On the Praxis Core exam, you're almost guaranteed to see exponents. You may also see two very common exponents. When a number has 2 for an exponent, the number is *squared*, which means the number is multiplied by itself. When a number has an exponent of 3, the number is *cubed*, or multiplied by itself two times.

5^2 is "5 squared" $(5 \cdot 5)$, or 25.

10^3 is "10 cubed" $(10 \cdot 10 \cdot 10)$, which equals 1,000.

Math questions on the Praxis Core exam can involve numbers with exponents as parts of larger operations, but they can also ask you flat out what the value of a number with an exponent is.

Which of the following numbers is the cube of 4?

(A) 16

(B) $\frac{1}{4}$

(C) 43

(D) 64

(E) 256

The correct answer is Choice (D). 4 cubed is 4^3, which represents $4 \cdot 4 \cdot 4$. The value of $4 \cdot 4 \cdot 4$ is 64.

Often in math, if you can ride one way down a road, you can turn around and ride the other way. As you can find the value of the square of a number, you can find what has to be squared to get a number. What you have to square to get a number is the number's *square root*. For example, the square root of 81 is 9 because 9 squared $(9 \cdot 9)$ is 81. The symbol for square root is $\sqrt{}$. The number you are taking the square root of goes inside the symbol. $\sqrt{9}$ represents "the square root of 9." The positive number that is squared to get 9 is 3, so the square root of 9 is 3. Thus, $\sqrt{9} = 3$ because $3^2 = 9$.

What is the value of $\sqrt{36}$?

(A) 36

(B) 6

(C) 1,296

(D) 72

(E) 18

The correct answer is Choice (B). The positive number that is squared to get 36 is 6; $6^2 = 36$. Choice (A) is incorrect because 36 is simply the number in the square root symbol. Choice (C) is false because 1,296 is 36 squared. Choice (D) is the product of 36 and 2. Choice (E) is the value of $6 \cdot 3$ and also the value of $\frac{1}{2} \cdot 36$, but it's not the square root of 36.

Computing with Fractions and Mixed Numbers

Not all numbers are whole. Fractions represent partial numbers and are represented through the use of integers. The integer on top is the *numerator,* and the integer on the bottom is the *denominator.* In the fraction $\frac{3}{4}$, 3 is the numerator and 4 is the denominator. What the fraction represents is "3 out of 4." If 3 of the people in a rock group have music degrees, and the band has 4 members, $\frac{3}{4}$ of the members of the band have music degrees. A fraction also represents a *ratio,* which is a comparison of two quantities. The fraction $\frac{3}{4}$, for example, represents the ratio "3 to 4."

If you eat a whole pie and $\frac{2}{3}$ of another one, the number of pies you eat can be represented by a *mixed number,* $1\frac{2}{3}$. A mixed number is an integer followed by a fraction. Every mixed number represents a fraction with an absolute value that is greater than 1.

A fraction also represents division. The numerator is divided by the denominator. Every integer is understood to be over 1. For example, $8 = \frac{8}{1}$.

Simplifying fractions

Different fractions can have equal values. The fractions $\frac{1}{2}$ and $\frac{100}{200}$ represent the same amount, for example. They both represent half. If 20 out of 50 people vote for a political candidate, 2 out of every 5 people vote for the candidate. The difference is that a group of 50 people involves multiple sets of 5 people, while a group of 5 people does not. It only involves 1. The fraction $\frac{2}{5}$ is *simplified,* which means it cannot be written with two integers with smaller absolute values. It is written in the simplest form possible.

To simplify a fraction, you find the greatest common factor of the numerator and the denominator, and then write the number of times the greatest common factor goes into each. The greatest common factor of 20 and 50 is 10. To simplify $\frac{20}{50}$, write the number of times 10 goes into 20 and write it over the number of times 10 goes into 50.

$$\frac{20}{50} = \frac{2}{5}$$

Using any common factor will lead you in the right direction. If you don't use the greatest common factor, however, you'll have to repeat the process of finding common factors and simplifying the numbers until they can't be simplified anymore.

Which of the following represents $\frac{18}{24}$ in simplest form?

(A) $\frac{3}{4}$

(B) $\frac{9}{12}$

(C) $\frac{36}{48}$

(D) –6

(E) $\frac{3}{24}$

The correct answer is Choice (A). The greatest common factor of 18 and 24 is 6, which goes into 18 three times and 24 four times. The simplest form of the fraction is therefore $\frac{3}{4}$.

Choice (B) is another form of the fraction, but not the simplest form. If you arrive at such an answer, you must continue to look for common factors. Choice (C) results from multiplying the numerator and denominator by 2, and Choice (D) is the result of subtracting 24 from 18. Choice (E) is the result of dividing only the numerator by the greatest common factor.

Knowing how to simplify fractions is important because answers that are the results of operations with fractions must always be in simplest form unless otherwise indicated.

Converting between fractions and mixed numbers

Mixed numbers can be written as fractions. Knowing how to write mixed numbers as fractions is important when you perform operations with mixed numbers, and writing fractions as mixed numbers is necessary if your answer choices on the Praxis Core exam are mixed numbers.

To write a mixed number as a fraction, multiply the denominator of the fraction by the absolute value of the integer. Then add the numerator to that product. Write the result over the denominator of the fraction.

$$4\frac{3}{7} = \frac{(7 \cdot 4) + 3}{7}$$
$$= \frac{28 + 3}{7}$$
$$= \frac{31}{7}$$

Put a negative sign before the fraction if the mixed number is negative.

To go the opposite way down that road and convert a fraction to a mixed number, write the highest integral (the adjectival form of *integer*) number of times the denominator fits completely into the numerator. Then write what remains as the numerator of a fraction beside the integer. The denominator of the fraction will be the denominator of the fraction you are converting. The number 7 goes into 31 completely 4 times because $7 \cdot 4 = 28$, which is 3 short of 31.

$$\frac{31}{7} = 4\frac{3}{7}$$

Performing basic operations with fractions and mixed numbers

Knowing how to convert between fractions and mixed numbers is useful in performing basic operations with them. We highly recommend converting mixed numbers to fractions when performing addition, subtraction, multiplication, or division. Working with fractions is much easier than working with mixed numbers.

Adding and subtracting fractions

To add fractions with the same denominator, add the numerators and write the sum over the denominator both fractions have, which is called the *common denominator*. If you add two apples and three apples, you get five apples. Similarly, if you add two sevenths and three sevenths, you get five sevenths.

$$\frac{2}{7} + \frac{3}{7} = \frac{5}{7}$$

Now, what do you do if you want to add two fractions that don't have the same denominator? You turn them into two fractions that do have the same denominator, by force. The way to do that is to write at least one of the fractions in a different but equal form. Usually, you need to convert both fractions into new forms. To convert fractions into new forms, you can multiply the numerator and the denominator by the same number, which should be the number you have to multiply by to get the denominator you want.

$$\frac{1}{5} + \frac{3}{7} = \frac{1(7)}{5(7)} + \frac{3(5)}{7(5)}$$
$$= \frac{7}{35} + \frac{15}{35}$$
$$= \frac{22}{35}$$

 Any common multiple of the denominators of fractions will work as a common denominator, but the best common denominator to use is the least common multiple. If you use another common denominator, you'll have to simplify the sum of the fractions. A guaranteed way to find a common multiple of two numbers is to multiply them by each other. However, this does not always result in the least common multiple. It only guarantees a common multiple, not necessarily the smallest one.

You follow the same procedure to subtract fractions, except you, well, subtract. That's the only difference.

$$\frac{5}{8} - \frac{1}{6} = \frac{5(3)}{8(3)} - \frac{1(4)}{6(4)}$$
$$= \frac{15}{24} - \frac{4}{24}$$
$$= \frac{11}{24}$$

Multiplying fractions

To multiply fractions, multiply the numerators and then multiply the denominators. Write the product of the numerators over the product of the denominators.

$$\left(\frac{3}{10}\right)\left(-\frac{5}{8}\right) = -\frac{15}{80}$$
$$= -\frac{3}{16}$$

 Unless otherwise suggested, all fractions that are final answers must be in simplest form.

Dividing fractions

Dividing by a fraction is the same as multiplying by its *reciprocal*, which is what you get when you switch the numerator and denominator of a fraction.

$$\frac{6}{7} \div \frac{2}{3} = \frac{6}{7} \cdot \frac{3}{2}$$
$$= \frac{18}{14}$$
$$= \frac{9}{7}$$

The fraction $\frac{9}{7}$ is an example of an *improper fraction,* which is a fraction in which the numerator is greater than the denominator. Improper fractions make acceptable answers as long as they're simplified and the correct one is among the choices you are given.

Working with mixed numbers

To perform the basic operations with mixed numbers, convert them to improper fractions and then perform the operations as you would with any fractions, as shown in the following examples:

$$5\frac{4}{7} + 3\frac{6}{7} = \frac{39}{7} + \frac{27}{7}$$
$$= \frac{66}{7}$$

$$\left(-3\frac{4}{5}\right)\left(-2\frac{1}{6}\right) = \left(-\frac{19}{5}\right)\left(-\frac{13}{6}\right)$$
$$= \frac{247}{30}$$

If every section of each box is the same size, what is the sum of the fractions of the boxes that are shaded?

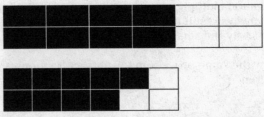

© John Wiley & Sons, Inc.

(A) $\frac{12}{17}$

(B) $\frac{17}{12}$

(C) $\frac{7}{12}$

(D) $\frac{9}{24}$

(E) $\frac{3}{8}$

The correct answer is Choice (B). The fraction of the first box that is shaded is $\frac{8}{12}$, and the fraction of the second box that is shaded is $\frac{9}{12}$. The sum of those two fractions is $\frac{17}{12}$. Choice (A) is the reciprocal of the answer, Choice (C) is the result of adding the unshaded fractions of the boxes, and Choice (D) is the sum of the numerators of both fractions over the denominators of both fractions. Choice (E) is the simplified form of Choice (D).

Working with Decimals and Percents

Now the review comes to one of the most famous types of fractions — the percent. A *percent* is a representation of a number of hundredths, and it's represented by the symbol %. The % sign and the word "hundredths" have the same meaning. Their meanings are 100% the same. A percent greater than 100% represents a quantity greater than 1.

Percents are related to decimals. *Decimals* represent whole and partial numbers. Both 0.17 and 64 are decimals. In 64, the ".0" is implied. Decimals can be written as percents, and percents can be written as decimals. Both can be written as fractions. Techniques can be used for converting numbers from any one of those forms to either of the other two. (Note that the word *decimal* refers to both the punctuation mark and numbers that use the punctuation mark but not a %.)

Converting between decimals and percents

A percent is nothing more than another way to express a fraction. For example, 100% means 100 hundredths, or $\frac{100}{100}$, which is 1. To convert a percent to a fraction, drop the percent sign and put the number over 100. Don't forget to simplify.

$$5\% = \frac{5}{100}$$
$$= \frac{1}{20}$$

A fraction represents division. The numerator is divided by the denominator.

A decimal has an integer followed by a decimal point and at least one digit after the decimal point. Because the second place after the decimal point is the hundredths place, dividing a decimal number by 100 is the same as moving its decimal point two places to the left.

Moving a decimal point two places to the left results in a number that is $\frac{1}{100}$ of the original number.

$$275.34\% = 275.34 \div 100 = 2.7534$$

That's why changing a percent to a decimal number involves just dropping the percent sign and moving the decimal two places to the left. For example, 73% (which is 73.0 percent) is equal to 0.73.

To go in the other direction, do the reverse. Converting a decimal into a percent involves moving the decimal two places to the right and adding a percent sign. That's because multiplying by 100 and dividing by 100 undo each other. It's like taking a step forward and taking a step back.

$$0.589 = 0.589 \times 100 = 58.9\%$$

Every time you move a decimal point one place to the left, you divide by 10. Every time you move a decimal one place to the right, you multiply by 10.

In order to change a fraction to a decimal, divide the numerator by the denominator with your calculator.

$$\frac{3}{8} = 0.375$$

To convert a fraction to a percent, divide the numerator by the denominator to write the fraction in decimal form. Then convert the decimal form to a percent by multiplying by 100.

$$\frac{3}{8} = 0.375$$
$$= 0.375 \times 100$$
$$= 37.5\%$$

Which of the following percents is equal to the fraction $\frac{3}{5}$?

(A) 60%

(B) 30%

(C) 35%

(D) 65%

(E) $\frac{3}{5}\%$

The correct answer is Choice (A). By dividing 3 by 5, you get 0.6. If you move the decimal two places to the right and add a percent sign, you get 60%. Choices (B), (C), and (D) involve mis-calculations, and Choice (E) results from the false method of simply adding a percent symbol.

Performing basic operations with decimals

Doing the basic operations with decimals isn't very different from doing the same operations with integers. The only major difference is that decimal placement has to be taken into account. Beyond that, everything is pretty much the same.

Adding and subtracting decimals

To add or subtract decimal numbers, line up the decimals points (even the one in the answer) and then add the numbers as if they were integers. Digits with nothing under them can be dropped, though some may have digits carried over them that need to be added. Also, after the last non-zero digit after a decimal point, you can add as many 0's as you want, though it's not a requirement. Doing so doesn't change the value of the number.

$$
\begin{array}{r}
3,542.1478 \\
+85.4120 \\
\hline
3,627.5598
\end{array}
$$

Multiplying decimals

You multiply decimals exactly the same way you multiply integers, except the total number of digits after the decimal point in the answer equals the number of places after the decimal points in the numbers you're multiplying. So, if you have a total of three places after the decimal points in the numbers you're multiplying, you need to have three numbers after the decimal point in your answer.

Don't line up the decimal points if they don't happen to already be lined up when you align the numbers to the right, unless you want to confuse yourself.

$$
\begin{array}{r}
89.7 \\
\times 3.48 \\
\hline
7176 \\
35880 \\
269100 \\
\hline
312.156
\end{array}
$$

Dividing decimals

To divide with decimals, you can use long division the way you would with integers. However, you move the decimal in the number being divided as many places to the right as you need to in order to get an integer. To make up for the change, you move the decimal in the number it is divided into the same number of places to the right. Then, you bring the decimal in the number in the division box to the top of the box, right above the decimal inside the box.

$82.64 \overline{)305.768}$ is the same as $8264 \overline{)30576.8}$. If you put the decimal in the answer directly above the decimal in 30576.8, you can divide as you would without the decimal. Just remember where the decimal belongs in the answer, which is 3.7.

Understanding the Number Line

The *number line* is a tool that's used to illustrate orders of numbers. The numbers represented on it can vary. On all versions of the number line, numbers decrease to the left and increase to the right. Although only a few numbers are shown in any given instance, the numbers represented by suggestion are all the real numbers. The arrows indicate that the numbers go on infinitely in both directions.

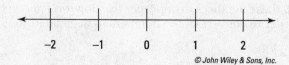

© John Wiley & Sons, Inc.

Interpreting numeration and place values

The numbers represented by points on the number line are *coordinates*. The points are named not only by their coordinates, but also sometimes by letters that appear above the points. The coordinate of Point C could be 4, for example. The point can also be called 4.

Questions on the Praxis Core exam may go beyond identifying points by the numbers under them. Questions can involve distances, and those questions are rooted in placements of coordinates.

Point C is not labeled, but it is halfway between Points A and D. What is the distance from Point C to Point D?

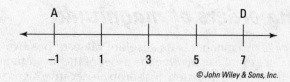

© John Wiley & Sons, Inc.

(A) 4

(B) 3

(C) 5

(D) 2

(E) 7

The correct answer is Choice (A). Since the coordinate of point A is –1 and the coordinate of point D is 7, the distance between them is 8. Half of that distance is 4, and 3 is 4 units from both –1 and 7. Choice (B) is the coordinate of Point C. Choice (C) is the coordinate of the point that is halfway between Points C and D. Choice (D) is the distance from one labeled coordinate to the next, and Choice (E) is merely the coordinate of Point D.

The number that's halfway between two numbers is the average of the two numbers. Recall that the average of a group of numbers is the sum of the numbers divided by the number of numbers in the group.

Knowing the basics of order

The number line can be helpful for putting numbers in order. A question about order on the Praxis Core exam can involve differing types of numbers. For example, an order question can involve a mixture of integers, fractions, mixed numbers, and decimal numbers. The best way to put such an assortment of numbers in order is to rewrite all of them as one type of number, such as all fractions or decimals. Then you can use the number line as a mental and visual aid to put the numbers in order.

Suppose you need to put the numbers 2.78, $\frac{5}{2}$, 2, and $\frac{8}{3}$ in order from least to greatest. You can put all these numbers in improper fraction form and get a common denominator, but it may be easier to convert all the numbers to decimal form.

$$2.78 = 2.78$$

$$\frac{5}{2} = 2.5$$

$$2 = 2.0$$

$$\frac{8}{3} = 2.666...$$

Because the order of the decimal forms is 2.0, 2.5, 2.666. . . , 2.78, the order of the numbers as given is 2, $\frac{5}{2}$, $\frac{8}{3}$, 2.78. Placing the decimal form numbers on the number line, or at least thinking about where they are on the number line, can help put the task into focus.

The number line can also be useful for addition and subtraction problems that involve negative numbers. Left is the negative direction, and right is the positive direction.

Finding orders of magnitude

The *magnitude* of a number is its absolute value, or positive distance from 0. A question on the Praxis Core exam can involve the order of the magnitudes of numbers. To find the answer to this type of question, just drop all negative signs that may be involved and put the remaining numbers in order.

Determine which answer choice has the following numbers in order of magnitude from least to greatest: $9, -2, 5.7, -\frac{15}{2}$.

(A) $-2, -\frac{15}{2}, 5.7, 9$

(B) $9, 5.7, -\frac{15}{2}, -2$

(C) $9, -\frac{15}{2}, 5.7, -2$

(D) $-2, 5.7, -\frac{15}{2}, 9$

(E) $-\frac{15}{2}, 9, 5.7, -2$

The correct answer is Choice (D). Without the negative signs, the order of the numbers from least to greatest is $-2, 5.7, -\frac{15}{2}, 9$, so that is the order of magnitude from least to greatest.

Choice (A) is the order of the numbers from least to greatest without magnitude taken into account, Choice (B) is the actual order of the numbers from greatest to least, and Choice (C) is the order of magnitude of the numbers from greatest to least. Choice (E) has no excuses for itself.

Finding numbers in sequences

A *sequence* is a list of numbers in a certain type of order. Have you ever heard a person talk about doing something in sequence? It means doing the parts of the task in order. Sequences are important because many types of orders of numbers exist. For example, a sequence can be a list of prime numbers in which order increases. One of the most common classifications is the *arithmetic sequence,* in which the same quantity is added to each number to get the next. In the following arithmetic sequence, 4 is added to each number to determine the next number.

3, 7, 11, 15, 19, 23, 27. . .

Another is the *geometric sequence,* for which each number is multiplied by the same quantity to get the next.

2, 6, 18, 54, 162, 486. . .

On the Praxis Core exam, you may be asked to determine a number that should appear in a certain position in a sequence. To make the determination, first decide what is done to each number in order to create the value of the one that follows. Then, make the calculation for each number up to the position in question.

What is the ninth term of the following sequence? 3, 6, 12, 24, 48. . .

(A) 96

(B) 2,304

(C) 768

(D) 72

(E) 1536

The correct answer is Choice (C). The sequence is geometric, so each term must be multiplied by 2 to result in the next. The fifth term is 48, so it must be multiplied by $2 \cdot 2 \cdot 2 \cdot 2$ for the multiplication to result in the ninth term of the sequence, which is 768. Choice (A) is the sixth term, Choice (B) is the square of 48, and Choice (D) is the sum of 48 and 24. Choice (E) is the tenth term of the sequence.

Following Orders: The Order of Operations

After you have the basic mathematical principles down, you're ready to tackle the order of operations.

When multiple computations are involved in finding a value represented by multiple numbers and operations signs, the rules concerning the order in which the operations are to be worked must be applied. Doing them in the wrong order can cause answers to be false, which is not the ideal situation. To avoid such examination misfortune, you must follow the *order of operations,* or the correct procedure for working multiple computations.

Think about how you would determine the value of the following expression:

$$3 + 2^3 + 5(4 - 7)$$

What would you do? Hold that thought. We have an idea.

Remembering "GEMDAS"

The acronym "GEMDAS" is formed by the initials of the order of operations, in order:

- **G:** *Grouping* symbols (such as parentheses, brackets, and fraction bars)
- **E:** *Exponents*
- **MD:** *Multiplication* and *Division* in order from left to right
- **AS:** *Addition* and *Subtraction* in order from left to right

Notice that multiplication and division are represented together, as are addition and subtraction. That indicates that you must do those operations in the order in which they appear. For example, you don't want to add all the way from left to right and then go back and do all the subtraction from left to right.

Okay, we believe an unresolved issue is still waiting for an answer. How do you find the value of $3 + 2^3 + 5(4 - 7)$? Well, the first step is to find the value within the grouping symbols, the parentheses. Then the exponent needs to be used. Next comes the indicated multiplication, and then the addition.

$$
\begin{aligned}
3 + 2^3 + 5(4 - 7) &= 3 + 2^3 + 5(-3) \\
&= 3 + 8 + 5(-3) \\
&= 3 + 8 - 15 \\
&= 11 - 15 \\
&= -4
\end{aligned}
$$

Using the order of operations within itself

What should you do if the issue of operations order arises within a step of the order of operations? Don't worry. The order of operations is a principle of its word. It applies even within steps of itself. If multiple operations are needed within parentheses, for example, apply the order of operations inside the parentheses.

$$[(8-3)^2 + 2 \cdot 5] - 7 + 4 \cdot 6 =$$

(A) 22

(B) 152

(C) 192

(D) 52

(E) –52

The correct answer is Choice (D). The value within the parentheses must be determined first, and then it must be squared because exponents come next in the order of operations. The product of 2 and 5 should be added to the value. At this point, the value within the brackets can be determined. Then, you need to find the product of 4 and 6 and add it to the result of subtracting 7 from the value within the brackets. Here's how the math looks when you work it out:

$$
\begin{aligned}
[(8-3)^2 + 2 \cdot 5] - 7 + 4 \cdot 6 &= [5^2 + 2 \cdot 5] - 7 + 4 \cdot 6 \\
&= [25 + 2 \cdot 5] - 7 + 4 \cdot 6 \\
&= [25 + 10] - 7 + 4 \cdot 6 \\
&= 35 - 7 + 4 \cdot 6 \\
&= 35 - 7 + 24 \\
&= 28 + 24 \\
&= 52
\end{aligned}
$$

Reasoning with Quantities

The Praxis Core exam tends to involve questions about quantities and how they are related. Various categories of quantities exist, and two major systems are used for measuring them.

Using the two major systems of measurement

The two mainstream systems of measurement in the United States are the English system and the metric system. Table 4-2 shows the basic units of measurement for each system.

Table 4-2	Systems of Measurement	
Form of Measurement	**English System**	**Metric System**
Distance	Inch, foot, yard, mile	Meter
Volume	Cup, pint, quart, gallon	Liter
Weight	Ounce, pound, ton	Gram

The metric system has fewer units because each category of measurement uses the same base unit. However, you can add prefixes to the unit that give you more-specific information about the size of the measurement. For example, 1,000 grams is the same as 1 kilogram. All the prefix meanings in the metric system are multiples of 10 or multiples of $\frac{1}{10}$. Check them out in Table 4-3.

Table 4-3	Metric System Prefixes
Metric Prefix	*Meaning*
Milli-	$\frac{1}{1,000}$
Centi-	$\frac{1}{100}$
Deci-	$\frac{1}{10}$
Main unit (meter, liter, gram)	1
Deca-	10
Hecto-	100
Kilo-	1,000

The English system doesn't have consistent base units for categories of measurement. The English units for each type of measurement are based on each other, but not in ways that mere suffixes are sufficient for changing terminology with varying levels. Here's how the different units of measurement relate within each form:

✔ **Distance:** 12 inches make up a foot, 3 feet make a yard, and 5,280 feet compose a mile.

✔ **Volume:** 2 cups form a pint, 2 pints make a quart, and 4 quarts make up a gallon.

✔ **Weight:** 16 ounces make a pound, and a ton is 2,000 pounds.

Converting units of measurement

Problems on the Praxis Core exam may involve converting one unit of measurement to another. For example, you may need to determine that 5 feet is the same as 60 inches or figure out how many deciliters are in 3 hectoliters.

To make such conversions, use the more basic unit to multiply if the answer involves the bigger unit and divide if the answer involves the smaller unit. For example, say you want to know how many inches of twine are in 4 yards. You have to convert yards to feet to inches:

1. **Convert yards to feet.**

   4 yards = 4(3 feet) = 12 feet

2. **Convert feet to inches.**

   (12 feet)(12 inches) = 144 inches

Therefore, 4 yards is equal to 144 inches.

To convert from greater to lesser units, divide instead of multiply. The same applies to metric units, but the conversions are easier because you can simply multiply by multiples of 10 or $\frac{1}{10}$.

How many kilograms are in 7 centigrams?

(A) 0.00007

(B) 7,000

(C) 700

(D) 70

(E) 7

The answer is Choice (A). Moving from kilograms to centigrams, the number gets smaller, so multiply 7 by $\frac{1}{10}$ for every space the prefixes are apart on the table. Choice (B) falsely involves the result of multiplying 7 by 10^5 instead of by $\frac{1}{10}$ as a factor that many times.

Choices (C) and (D) involve too few factors and multiplying in the wrong direction. Choice (E) falsely implies that a kilogram is the same as a centigram.

Basic word problems

Conversions with units can be involved in answering word problems, but often they also require performing other operations. You need to memorize the meanings of the units and prefixes for the Praxis Core exam because they won't be provided. You also need to understand how words used in each system for each type of measurement are connected to each other.

If a cook pours 5 quarts of water out of a 3-gallon container and then another cook takes his place and adds 2 pints of water, how many cups of water are in the container?

(A) 8

(B) 16

(C) 72

(D) 32

(E) 64

The correct answer is Choice (D). The best way to determine the answer is to convert all the measurements to numbers of cups and then calculate the number of cups remaining. You could also convert the measures to numbers of pints and convert to cups on the last step. 5 quarts is equal to 5(4) cups; 3 gallons is the same as 3(16) cups; and 2 pints is a measure equal to 2(2) cups. 48 – 20 + 4 = 32, so the answer is 32. Choice (A) is the number of quarts that result, and Choice (B) is the equivalent measure in pints. Choice (C) is the number of quarts that would result if all of the mentioned quantities were added, and Choice (E) could be the correct answer if there were 4 cups in a pint instead of 2.

Practice Questions about Number and Quantity

These practice questions are similar to the questions about number and quantity that you'll encounter on the Praxis.

1. Which of the following is a counterexample to the following statement?

   All prime numbers are odd.

   (A) 4

   (B) 2

   (C) 7.5

   (D) 1

   (E) 0

2. $[(9 - 4)^3 - 25 \cdot 2] - [7 + 4(2 - 3)] =$

   (A) −3

   (B) 172

   (C) 64

   (D) 72

   (E) 103

3. Which of the following numbers is the lowest?

   (A) $3\frac{1}{3}$

   (B) 3.25

   (C) $3\frac{1}{2}$

   (D) $\frac{23}{7}$

   (E) 3.271

4. The following table represents the percentages regarding the favorite movie categories of students at a college attended by 1,000 students. How many students have a favorite movie category that is either drama, comedy, or horror?

Movie Category	Percent of Students
Comedy	26%
Musical	11%
Drama	22%
Documentary	6%
Horror	19%
Science Fiction	12%
Other	4%

   (A) 220

   (B) 67

   (C) 670

   (D) 6,700

   (E) 26

5. Each of the following numbers is a common factor of 150 and 300 EXCEPT

   (A) 5

   (B) 25

   (C) 50

   (D) 75

   (E) 300

Answers and Explanations

Use this answer key to score the practice number and quantity questions in this chapter.

1. **B. 2.** The number 2 is both an even number and a prime number. It's a prime number because it has exactly two factors — itself and 1. As a matter of fact, 2 is the only even prime number. Choice (A) has three factors, 1, 2, and 4. Choice (C) isn't odd or even because 7.5 is not an integer, and it's not prime because it isn't a positive integer. Choice (D) isn't prime because 1 has only one factor. Choice (E) is incorrect because 0 is divisible by all numbers.

2. **D. 72.** Follow the order of operations to solve this correctly (remember GEMDAS).

$$
\begin{aligned}
\left[(9-4)^3 - 25 \cdot 2\right] - \left[7 + 4(2-3)\right] &= \left[5^3 - 25 \cdot 2\right] - \left[7 + 4(2-3)\right] \\
&= \left[125 - 50\right] - \left[7 + 4(2-3)\right] \\
&= 75 - \left[7 + 4(-1)\right] \\
&= 75 - \left[7 + (-4)\right] \\
&= 75 - 3 \\
&= 72
\end{aligned}
$$

   All other answer choices can be reached through following an incorrect order of operations.

3. **B. 3.25.** The best way to determine the answer is to write all the numbers in the same type of form. For example, you can write all the numbers as decimal numbers: 3.33, 3.25, 3.50 and 3.271, respectively. Then you can put them in order and see that 3.25 is the lowest number, making Choice (B) correct.

4. **C. 670.** The sum of the drama, comedy, and horror percentages is 67 percent, and 67 percent of 1,000 is 670. To get 67 percent of 1,000, you can write 67 percent in decimal form by dropping the percent sign and moving the decimal two places to the left. That gives you 0.67, which you can multiply by 1,000 to get 670. Choice (A) is the number of students whose favorite type of movie is drama. Choice (B) is 6.7 percent of 1,000, and Choice (D) is 670 percent of 1,000. Choice (E) is merely the numerical part of the term 26 percent, the percent of students whose favorite genre is comedy.

5. **E. 300.** If you find the prime factorizations of 150 and 300 and use those prime factors to find all the other factors, you can see that Choices (A), (B), (C), and (D) are common factors of 150 and 300. However, 300 is a factor of 300 but not 150, though it is a multiple of 150.

Chapter 5

Introducing Letters: Algebra and Functions

In This Chapter

▶ Coming to terms with variables

▶ Solving equations and inequalities

▶ Facing the facts of factoring

▶ Making quick work of word problems

▶ Looking at patterns and conditional statements

*N*ow's the time to revisit your days as an algebra student. When you start treating letters as numbers, you're entering algebra territory. That's what this chapter is about. The Praxis Core exam tests basic algebra knowledge, generally the material that's covered in pre-algebra and perhaps some Algebra I courses, depending on where you went to school and when. Algebra questions make up 30 percent of the math section of the Praxis Core. Also, many of the geometry questions on the test involve algebra, so this chapter goes a long way toward preparing you for the math test of the exam.

Variables: When Letters Represent Numbers

You are very familiar with letters, and algebra just involves using letters in some different ways. Algebra is the area of math that focuses on the basics of working with *variables,* which are letters that represent numbers. That's all it is. A large portion of algebra involves determining the numbers represented by variables, which requires knowledge of some basic rules.

The most common letter used to represent numbers is x. Other letters that are commonly used are y, n, a, and b. Most of the letters in our alphabet, and many of the letters in the Greek alphabet, are used as variables at times. But thankfully, you don't have to know Greek to take the Praxis Core exam.

Here's an example of using a variable:

$$x + 3 = 7$$

This equation means that when 3 is added to some number (x), the result is 7. In this case, the number that the variable x represents is 4. When 3 is added to 4, the result is 7, so x equals 4. Later in this chapter, you review how to determine what a given variable represents. In this section, we cover the basics of variables.

Laying out the terms: Variable terms and expressions

What makes algebra interesting is when variables and numbers meet. When a number comes right before a variable, it means that the number is multiplied by the variable. For example, $3y$ means "3 times y." A number can also be multiplied by more than one variable at a time. $10xyz$ means "10 times x times y times z." A number that precedes a variable or variables to indicate that it is multiplied by them is a *coefficient*. In $10xyz$, 10 is the coefficient. If no coefficient is given, the coefficient is understood to be 1. In other words, x is the same as $1x$, and xyz is the same as $1xyz$.

A variable or group of variables next to a coefficient, or with an understood coefficient of 1, is called a *term*. A number followed by no variables is also a term. In a term, variables can have exponents, which indicate how many times a variable is multiplied (see Chapter 4 for a review of exponents). All of the following are examples of terms:

x

$-17n^2$

5

$156abc$

xy

A single term or a group of terms separated by + or – forms an *expression*. There is no maximum number of terms an expression can have, but the minimum number is one. Yes, a term is an expression, but not all expressions are terms. $48x^3y^5$ is a term, so it is an expression. $48x^3y^5 + 15x^2y^2 - xy + 87x - 9$ has five terms, but it is one expression.

Let's get together: Combining like terms

After you've come to terms with terms (see the preceding section), it's time to see how to make them join forces and become one term, when they can. *Like terms* are terms that have either exactly the same variable or variables with only one exponent for each variable, or no variables.

If two terms are like terms and both have x, y, and z, every x has the same exponent, every y has the same exponent, and every z has the same exponent. Numbers without variables, such as 3 and 5, are also like terms. $17x$ and $12x$ are like terms, and so are $15a^3b^{15}c^8$ and $4a^3b^{15}c^8$.

Like terms can be combined. In other words, one can be added to or subtracted from the other to form one term. To combine like terms, combine their coefficients to get a new coefficient and follow that with the common variables and their exponents.

$$17x + 12x = (17 + 12)x = 29x$$

$$15a^3b^{15}c^8 - 4a^3b^{15}c^8 = (15 - 4)a^3b^{15}c^8 = 11a^3b^{15}c^8$$

$$5 + 7 = 12$$

If you have 2 apples and you add 3 apples, you have 5 apples. The same principle works with variables. If you have 2 of x and add 3 of x, you have 5 of x.

$$2 \text{ apples} + 3 \text{ apples} = 5 \text{ apples}$$

$$2x + 3x = 5x$$

Multiplying and dividing with terms and expressions

Just as you can add and subtract terms and expressions (see the preceding section), you can multiply and divide them. Remember that variables represent numbers, which means operations with variables involve the same principles that apply to operations without variables. So, when in doubt, just think about how numbers work.

Multiplying expressions

In multiplying algebraic expressions, the number of times a number or variable is a factor is part of what determines what the product is. To multiply different variables, simply put them next to each other.

$$x \cdot y = xy$$
$$a \cdot b = ab$$

To multiply a number times a variable or variables, put them all next to each other.

$$3 \cdot a \cdot b = 3ab$$

The next question is what you should do when the same variable is a factor more than once. Do you write the variable next to itself? Nope. The product has to be written with exponents because a letter times a letter does not equal another letter. The letters have to remain the same, but their exponents do not. The final answer should have exponents representing how many times a variable is a factor.

$$(x)(x)(x) = x^3$$
$$j \cdot j = j^2$$
$$p \cdot p \cdot p \cdot p = p^4$$

Using 1 as an exponent isn't necessary. A variable without an exponent shown is understood to have an exponent of 1.

Now put these principles together in your mind, and you're ready to multiply algebraic terms that have coefficients.

$$(4ab)(2ab) = 4 \cdot 2 \cdot a \cdot a \cdot b \cdot b$$
$$= 8a^2b^2$$

Now, what do you do when the terms you are multiplying already have exponents? For each variable, you just add its exponents.

$$(5p^2q^4r^3)(3p^3q^2r^2) = (5 \cdot 3) \, p^2p^3q^4q^2r^3r^2$$
$$= 15p^{2+3}q^{4+2}r^{3+2}$$
$$= 15p^5q^6r^5$$

With these skills, you can multiply any algebraic terms. On the Praxis Core, you may be asked to multiply two-term expressions. For example, you may need to multiply $(x + 2)(x + 3)$. To find the product of two two-term expressions, the best method to use is FOIL, which is the best-known algebra acronym. It stands for "first, outer, inner, last." The words apply to the terms in the problem. In this case, the first terms are x and x, the outer terms are x and 3, the inner terms are 2 and x, and the last (as in last in each expression) terms are 2 and 3. To use FOIL, multiply the first, outer, inner, and last terms, and then add them together (according to the rules for combining terms) in the same order.

$$(x+2)(x+3)=(x\cdot x)+(x\cdot 3)+(2\cdot x)+(2\cdot 3)$$
$$=x^2+3x+2x+6$$
$$=x^2+5x+6$$

Subtracting a number is the same as adding its opposite. A minus sign in a FOIL problem must be treated as a negative sign.

Find the following product: $(3j + 4)(2j - 5)$

(A) $5j^2 - 7j - 20$

(B) $6j^2 - 7j - 20$

(C) $6j^2 + 7j + 20$

(D) $13j^3 - 1$

The correct answer is Choice (B). By using FOIL, you can determine that the product of the two expressions is $(3j)(2j) + (3j)(-5) + (4)(2j) + (4)(-5)$, which is $6j^2 - 15j + 8j - 20$. By combining those terms, you get $6j^2 - 7j - 20$.

Dividing expressions

Dividing algebraic terms isn't as common as multiplying them, but it does happen, so you should know how to perform this operation.

In a fraction, the numerator is divided by the denominator.

$$\frac{8x^3y^4z^2}{2x^2y^2z^2} = \frac{8\cdot x\cdot x\cdot x\cdot y\cdot y\cdot y\cdot y\cdot z\cdot z}{2\cdot x\cdot x\cdot y\cdot y\cdot z\cdot z}$$

Recall that factors that appear in a term that is a numerator and a term that is the denominator of the same fraction can be cancelled once in both numerator and denominator for every appearance in both. In other words, anything that is a factor of a fraction's numerator and denominator can be cancelled from both, but it can be cancelled only one time for each instance.

$$\frac{8x^3y^4z^2}{2x^2y^2z^2} = \frac{8\cdot \cancel{x}\cdot \cancel{x}\cdot x\cdot \cancel{y}\cdot \cancel{y}\cdot y\cdot y\cdot \cancel{z}\cdot \cancel{z}}{2\cdot \cancel{x}\cdot \cancel{x}\cdot \cancel{y}\cdot \cancel{y}\cdot \cancel{z}\cdot \cancel{z}}$$

What's left in the preceding ratio? $\frac{8}{2}=4$, so 4 is left in the numerator. With 3 x's on top and 2 on the bottom, 1 is left on top because $3 - 2 = 1$. By the same reasoning, 2 y's are left in the numerator. The z's cancel each other out. Therefore, you're left with $4xy^2$.

Because of this principle, you can easily find the difference of a variable's numerator and denominator exponents. Just subtract the smaller exponent from the bigger exponent and make the difference the variable's resulting exponent. Put the variable with that exponent in the place where the bigger exponent was before you subtracted. If a variable in a problem has the same exponent in the numerator and denominator, you can cancel the variable completely. The result of exponent subtraction would be the variable with an exponent of 0, and any value with an exponent of 0 equals 1.

$$\frac{12a^3b^4c^7d^5}{9a^5b^2c^2d^5} = \frac{4b^{4-2}c^{7-2}}{3a^{5-3}}$$
$$= \frac{4b^2c^5}{3a^2}$$

Similarly, when you divide one product of multi-term expressions by another, you can cancel expressions that are factors of both the dividend and the divisor.

$$\frac{(y+2)(y-3)}{(y-1)(y+2)} = \frac{\cancel{(y+2)}(y-3)}{(y-1)\cancel{(y+2)}}$$

Now you're left with one expression on top and one on the bottom. The quotient is $\frac{y-3}{y-1}$.

On the Praxis Core exam, you may be asked to divide with expressions that have three or more terms. The upcoming section "Factoring in Algebra" shows you how to work such problems.

When variable values are given

The values of expressions can be determined when the values of the variables in them are known. To find the value of an expression is to *evaluate* the expression. When you evaluate an expression, you replace each variable with its given value. Then you can solve for the value of the expression. Here's how:

1. **Replace each variable with its given value.**

2. **Follow the order of operations.**

   Recall GEMDAS from Chapter 4.

3. **Simplify the resulting expression by following the order of operations as many times as necessary.**

4. **Mark the final number as your answer.**

Evaluate the following expression for $p = 2$, $q = 5$, and $r = 1$.

$5p - q + 2r$

(A) –2

(B) 16

(C) 7

(D) –1

The correct answer is Choice (C). To evaluate the expression, simply replace each variable with its value.

$$
\begin{aligned}
5p - q + 2r &= 5(2) - 5 + 2(1) \\
&= 10 - 5 + 2 \\
&= 5 + 2 \\
&= 7
\end{aligned}
$$

A number immediately next to a variable indicates that the number is multiplied by the variable.

Working with Equations

An equation is a mathematical statement in which one expression is set equal to another. For example, $8n + 1 = 17$ is an equation. Very commonly in algebra, the value of a variable in an equation can be determined when the value is not given. To determine the value of a variable in an equation is to *solve* the equation.

The two sides of an equation have the same value. If $8n + 1 = 17$, then $8n + 1$ has the same value as 17. The value of n can be determined from the equation.

Solving for x and other variables

Solving equations is an enormous part of algebra. Understanding how to do it puts you in an excellent position for conquering Praxis Core algebra completely.

To solve an equation, you need to get the variable by itself on one side of the equal sign (=). If you are solving for x, the goal is to work with the equation until you have $x =$ something, like $x = 4$ or $x = -12$. Notice that in both cases, x is by itself on one side of the equal sign and a value is on the other side. Once you reach that point correctly, you have solved the equation. The point of solving an equation is to determine what the variable equals.

To get a variable by itself on one side of the equal sign, you need to perform whatever operations are necessary. Then, if necessary, combine like terms so the variable is in only one term in the equation. The next step is to undo everything that is being done to the variable by doing the opposite. Addition and subtraction are opposite operations, and multiplication and division are opposite operations. You can use opposite operations to undo each other.

Because the two sides of an equation are equal, anything done to one side of the equation must be done to the other side so the two sides will remain equal. If you have a set of weights with 50 pounds on one side and 50 pounds on the other side and you want to add a certain amount of weight to one side, you must add the same amount of weight to the other side to keep the weights of the two sides equal. The values on either side of an equation work the same way. If you add 10 to one side of an equation but not the other, the two sides will no longer be equal. An equation is wrong if its sides aren't equal.

Here's how you get a variable by itself to determine its value (also known as solving for x):

1. **Isolate the variable.**

   Get all the x's on one side of the equal sign and the numbers without variables on the other side.

2. **Combine like terms.**

   Add or subtract all the x's on one side; add or subtract whatever is on the other side of the equal sign.

3. **Divide both sides of the equation by whatever number (coefficient) is in front of the x (or other variable).**

You can see how these steps work by solving for y in this equation: $3y - 12 = y + 6$.

1. **Isolate the variable.**

   Move the y to the left side of the equation by subtracting y from both sides. Move the 12 to the right side by adding it to both sides of the equation. This gives you $3y - y = 6 + 12$.

2. **Combine like terms.**

   Do the operations to get $2y = 18$.

3. **Divide both sides of the equation by whatever number (coefficient) is in front of the x.**

   When you divide 18 by 2, you get 9. Therefore, $y = 9$. Problem solved!

Undoing addition and subtraction

Consider the equation $y + 4 = 9$. The variable y is not by itself on one side of the equal sign because 4 is being added to y. Getting rid of the addition of 4 will cause y to be by itself on one side of the equation. By subtracting 4, the addition of 4 will be undone. If you add 4 to a number and then subtract 4 from the result, you're back at the original number. If you have 5 sandwiches and someone gives you 4 sandwiches, and then you give away those 4 sandwiches, you'll be back to having 5 sandwiches. Algebra works the same way.

$y + 4 = 9$	*Original equation*
$y + 4 - 4 = 9 - 4$	*Subtract 4 from both sides to get y by itself on one side.*
$y = 5$	*Determine the value of each side.*

The equation has been solved. The value of y is 5 because $y = 5$. If you replace y with 5 in the original equation, you will see that the value of y is 5 because $5 + 4 = 9$. All solutions to equations can be checked that way.

Keep in mind that anything done to one side of an equation must also be done to the other side.

Just as subtraction can be used to undo addition, addition can be used to undo subtraction.

$$j - 8 = 12$$
$$j - 8 + 8 = 12 + 8$$
$$j = 20$$

In the solution, j is by itself on one side of the equal sign, so the value of j is on the other side of the equal sign. The value of j is 20, so 20 is the solution to the equation. It is true that $20 - 8 = 12$, so j is 20.

Undoing multiplication and division

Like addition and subtraction (see the preceding section), multiplication and division are opposite operations. When a variable is multiplied by a number, the multiplication can be undone if the term is divided by the same number. Recall that a fraction represents a numerator divided by a denominator. The easiest way to divide a term by a number is to create a denominator with that number. However, you must do this to both sides.

$$5m = 30$$
$$\frac{5m}{5} = \frac{30}{5}$$
$$m = 6$$

Now m is by itself on one side of the equation. The solution is 6 because that is what m equals.

Because multiplication and division are opposite operations, multiplication can undo division. Think about how to solve the following equation.

$$\frac{p}{4} = 10$$

The variable, _p,_ is not by itself on one side of the equal sign because it's being divided by 4. Because you don't have any addition or subtraction to worry about, you can go ahead and multiply by 4 to undo the division by 4. Multiplying by 4 gets _p_ by itself on one side of the equal sign. The equation is then solved because you're left with the statement of what _p_ equals.

$$\frac{p}{4}(4) = 10(4)$$
$$p = 40$$

The solution is 40 because $p = 40$.

Whatever you do to a side must be done to the entire side, not just some small part of it. A common mistake is to do something like multiply a term on one side by a number and then multiply just one term among several on the other side by the same number. So not only do you have to do the same thing to each side, but you must do that operation to the complete value of each side to make both sides equal.

Multistep equations

In many algebraic equations, you have to undo more than one operation. The best way to solve such equations is to use whatever addition or subtraction is necessary first and then use multiplication or division.

You can't multiply or divide just one term by a number when other terms are on the same side. Anything you do to both sides of an equation has to be done to the entire side, not just parts of it.

The following equation requires undoing both multiplication and subtraction. Undo the subtraction first so you can then divide both entire sides by the same number.

$$5x - 3 = 12$$
$$5x - 3 + 3 = 12 + 3$$
$$5x = 15$$
$$\frac{5x}{5} = \frac{15}{5}$$
$$x = 3$$

The solution is 3 because 3 is what _x_ equals.

Proportions

A _proportion_ is an equation in which one ratio (usually in the form of a fraction) is set equal to another. This is an example of a proportion:

$$\frac{9}{3} = \frac{12}{4}$$

On the Praxis Core exam, you may need to solve one or more proportions in which one term is unknown (represented by a variable). You can save a lot of time by setting the products of the numerator of one ratio and the denominator of the other equal to each other and then cross multiplying. To cross multiply, you multiply the numerator of the left fraction by the denominator of the right fraction, and then you do the same with the right numerator and left denominator. Finally, divide both sides by the coefficient to get the variable by itself and solve the equation.

$$\frac{20}{x} = \frac{15}{3}$$
$$20(3) = 15(x)$$
$$60 = 15x$$
$$\frac{60}{15} = \frac{15x}{15}$$
$$4 = x$$
$$x = 4$$

Solve the following proportion: $\frac{10}{5} = \frac{6a}{21}$

(A) 7

(B) 42

(C) 2

(D) $\frac{1}{2}$

The correct answer is Choice (A). By cross multiplying, you get the equation $210 = 30a$, the solution to which is 7. The other choices are misleading because both ratios equal 2, each denominator is equal to $\frac{1}{2}$ its fraction's numerator, and 42 is the value of the numerator of the second fraction. The Praxis Core uses such tricks, so be ready to see through them. Use your academic street smarts at all times.

Systems of equations

Equations with two variables can be solved if they are accompanied by a second equation with at least one of the variables. When presented with such sets of equations, or *systems of equations,* the trick is to use the information to get an equation with one variable. Two major methods exist for accomplishing this: the substitution method and the elimination method.

Solving by substitution

The *substitution* method involves finding the value of one variable in terms of the other in one equation. Then you can substitute that expression for the variable in the second equation. The result is an equation with one variable, and you can solve an equation with one variable by using the earlier discussed techniques.

$$4x + 2y = 22$$
$$x + y = 8$$

The concept is that x has the same value in both equations and so does y. To solve the system of equations using the substitution method, you state either what y equals in terms of x or what x equals in terms of y. You can use either equation to make the determination, but the second equation is easier to work with in this case because neither variable has a pesky coefficient.

$$x + y = 8$$
$$x + y - y = 8 - y$$
$$x = 8 - y$$

Because x has exactly the same value as $8 - y$, you can substitute $8 - y$ for x in the other equation. Then you have an equation with just one variable.

$$4x + 2y = 22$$
$$4(8 - y) + 2y = 22$$
$$32 - 4y + 2y = 22$$
$$32 - 2y = 22$$
$$-2y = -10$$
$$y = 5$$

You can solve the equation to determine that $y = 5$. Then, you can substitute 5 for y in either equation and solve for x, which is 3.

When using the substitution method to solve a system of equations, make sure you don't substitute a variable expression for the other variable in the equation you used to determine the expression. You must use the other equation; otherwise, the result will be an equation with no variable. An equation with no variable can't be solved.

Solving by elimination

Another method used for solving systems of equations is *elimination*. It's based on the fact that adding the same value to or subtracting the same value from both sides of a true equation results in another true equation. In this case, the added or subtracted value is what is represented by both sides of one of the given equations. Check out this example:

$$3x + 4y = 34$$
$$-3x + 5y = 29$$

Because both sides of the second equation (and the first, for that matter) have the same value, the second equation can be added to the first equation. The result is a third equation that is also true. That's an ideal thing to do here because adding $3x$ and $-3x$ gets rid of x, leaving you an equation with only one variable, y. The coefficients of x have the same absolute value, so elimination can work immediately. You may sometimes have to subtract.

$$3x + 4y = 34$$
$$\underline{-3x + 5y = 29}$$
$$9y = 63$$
$$y = 7$$

Knowing that $y = 7$, you can put 7 in for y in either equation to determine that $x = 2$.

With both elimination and substitution, putting a variable value in place of the variable does not cause trouble. Just don't substitute an algebraic expression for a variable in the equation that gave you the expression. That's where chaos awaits.

To use elimination when neither variable has coefficients with the same absolute value, you can multiply both sides of an equation by the same number and get a new equation. In some cases, you must do that to both equations. Consider the following equations:

$$3j + 5p = 29$$
$$2j + 4p = 22$$

Neither variable has coefficients with the same absolute value, but you can multiply both sides of the top equation by 2 and both sides of the bottom equation by 3 to give j the same coefficient. Then you can subtract one equation from the other and get an equation with one variable.

$$2(3j + 5p) = 2(29)$$
$$3(2j + 4p) = 3(22)$$
$$6j + 10p = 58$$
$$6j + 12p = 66$$
$$-2p = -8$$
$$p = 4$$

Now that you know $p = 4$, you can substitute 4 in for p in either equation and solve for j, which has a value of 3.

Substitution is the ideal method to use when at least one of the variable terms has a coefficient of 1 (understood). Elimination is the generally preferred method to use when both variables have coefficients other than 1 in all cases.

Solving Inequalities

All men and women are created equal, but not all expressions are. An *inequality* is a mathematical statement in which one side is (or may be) greater than or less than the other side. Some inequalities also suggest that the sides may be equal.

The signs used in inequalities are

- ✔ <, which means "less than"
- ✔ >, which means "greater than"
- ✔ ≤, which means "less than or equal to"
- ✔ ≥, which means "greater than or equal to"

The underlining of < and > to create ≤ and ≥ means "or equal to." Those signs indicate that the sides may be equal.

The following table shows examples of inequalities and what they mean.

$2x + 14 < 24$	"$2x + 14$ is **less than** 24."
$y + 6 > 11$	"$y + 6$ is **greater than** 11."
$9w - 20 \leq 34$	"$9w - 20$ is **less than or equal to** 34."
$8b \geq 48$	"$8b$ is **greater than or equal to** 48."

An inequality sign always points to the side that is (or may be) the one that is less. You can also think of it as a mouth that's trying to eat the greater side.

Like equations, inequalities can be solved when they involve only one variable of unknown value. For the most part, you solve inequalities the same way you do equations, but a couple of the rules change. We cover those in the next section.

Following two more rules when solving inequalities

To solve an inequality, you use exactly the same rules you use to solve equations. However, unlike an equal sign, an inequality sign can change directions. Because of this, you must follow two extra rules when you solve inequalities. The sign in an inequality must change direction when either of the following happens:

✔ Both sides are multiplied or divided by a negative number.

✔ The sides are switched.

Consider the following:

$3 < 7$

You have a true inequality. However, what happens when you multiply both sides by a negative number?

$$3(-1) < 7(-1)$$
$$-3 < -7$$

The resulting inequality is false; –3 is not less than –7. However, if the sign were to change direction, the resulting inequality would be true.

$$-3 > -7$$

The example illustrates that when both sides of an inequality are multiplied or divided by a negative number, the sign must change direction.

Now consider what happens when the two sides of an inequality are switched.

$$3 < 7$$
$$7 < 3$$

It's true that 3 is less than 7, but 7 is not less than 3. Because the sides were switched, the direction of the sign has to change.

$$3 < 7$$
$$7 > 3$$

So 3 is less than 7, and 7 is greater than 3.

Here's how you would solve this inequality: $47 \geq -10x - 3$.

1. **Isolate the term with the variable.**

   Add 3 to both sides to undo subtracting 3 from $10x$.

   $$47 + 3 \geq -10x - 3 + 3$$

2. **Combine like terms and simplify each side.**

   $$50 \geq -10x.$$

3. **Divide both sides of the equation by whatever number (coefficient) is in front of the x.**

   Divide both sides by –10 to undo multiplying x by –10.

   $$\frac{50}{-10} > \frac{-10x}{-10}$$

4. **Simplify each side, and switch the direction of the sign because the sides were divided by a negative number.**

$-5 \leq x$

5. **Switch the sides to make x the subject of the sentence, as a formality. Also change the direction of the sign because the sides were switched.**

$x \geq -5$

The solution to the inequality is $x \geq -5$, which represents –5 and all numbers greater than –5. Any number that is –5 or greater will make the original inequality true.

Graphing inequalities

Inequalities with one variable can be graphed on the number line.

To graph an inequality on the number line, place a circle on the line at the point representing the solution. If the number used in the solution is included by the inequality, darken in the circle. This happens when $\leq$ or $\geq$ is used. When < or > is used, the number used in the solution only marks the boundary of what makes the inequality true, and it's not included in the set of numbers that make the inequality true. In those situations, make the circle hollow, not darkened. Next, darken in the part of the number line that includes the solution.

For example, if $g \geq 3$, a $\geq$ sign is used, so g can be 3. Therefore, darken in the circle on the number line to show that 3 is included. Then, darken the part of the number line that includes everything greater than 3. If $g < 4$, g cannot be 4. 4 would only be the boundary for what g can be, so you would not darken in the circle on the number line.

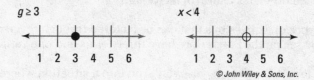

© John Wiley & Sons, Inc.

Factoring in Algebra

In Chapter 4, we review factoring numbers. Factoring algebraic terms involves the same general concepts, but variables can be involved. On the Praxis Core exam, you may be asked to factor expressions with varying numbers of terms.

Factoring terms out of bigger terms

To factor an expression with more than one term, first see whether you can combine like terms. After that, take the greatest common factor of all the terms and put it on the outside of a set of parentheses. Then write what the factor has to be multiplied by to get each term in the expression. Don't forget to take signs into account.

$$6x^4y^2 + 15x^3y^2 - 3xy = 3xy(2x^3y + 5x^2y - 1)$$

An exam question may also ask you about factors of a single term.

Which of the following is a factor of $90a^2b^5c^3$?

(A) $90a^2b^6c^3$

(B) $80abc$

(C) $9a^3b$

(D) $10ac^2$

(E) $180a$

The correct answer is Choice (D). $10ac^2$ is the only term listed that can be factored out of $90a^2b^5c^3$. To determine this, write out the factorization of $90a^2b^5c^3$:

$$90a^2b^5c^3 = 3 \cdot 3 \cdot 2 \cdot 5 \cdot a \cdot a \cdot b \cdot b \cdot b \cdot b \cdot b \cdot c \cdot c \cdot c$$

$10ac^2$ is the only factor among the five answer choices because $5 \cdot 2 \cdot a \cdot c \cdot c$ can be taken out of the factorization.

Choice (A) is incorrect because b^6 cannot be factored out of $90a^2b^5c^3$ since b^6 has an exponent greater than the exponent in b^5. Choice (B) is incorrect because 80 is not a factor of 90. Choice (C) is incorrect because a^3 is not a factor of a^2 since the exponent of a^3 is greater. Choice (E) is incorrect because 180 is not a factor of 90. It is a multiple of it.

Using reverse FOIL

While FOIL (first, outer, inner, last) can be used for multiplying two-term expressions, *reverse FOIL* can take you in the opposite direction from one expression to two-term expressions times each other. It's a form of factoring.

Many types of expressions that can be factored through reverse FOIL exist, but the ones you'll typically see on the Praxis Core have three terms and one variable: for example, $w^2 + 2w - 15$.

On the Praxis Core exam, you won't run into a situation where you'll need to use reverse FOIL to factor an expression in which the largest exponent is greater than 2. If you need to factor a three- or four-term expression in which a variable has an exponent of 2, checking to see whether the expression can be factored through reverse FOIL is worthwhile.

To use reverse FOIL, create two sets of parentheses in which the first terms contain the variable that is squared in the expression you're factoring, if the expression has only one variable. If more than one variable is in the expression, you'll need to try combinations of first terms until you find the one that works. Then think of the numbers that can be multiplied to get the final term of the factored expression. One of the combinations will form the last terms (the "L" in FOIL) in the parentheses. If the coefficient of the variable squared is understood to be 1 and the factored expression has one middle term, you have it made. All you have to do is pick the combination that adds up to the middle term coefficient. Otherwise, use trial and error. What matters is that the product of the two term expressions in the parentheses is the factored expression. You can always test that.

Here's how the earlier expression would be factored using reverse FOIL:

$$w^2 + 2w - 15 = (w + 5)(w - 3)$$

In some cases, the coefficient of the term with the variable squared will not be 1. With those, the coefficients of the first terms of the factors have to be considered, as in this example:

$$3q^2 + 14q + 8 = (3q + 2)(q + 4)$$

Always multiply what you determine to be the factors after performing reverse FOIL to make sure they are the real factors.

Decoding Algebra Word Problems

Algebra can be used to represent and figure out situations that are described with words. Variables can be used to represent quantities that are not yet known, and every equation and inequality makes a statement. Using a variable in a mathematical statement can sum up what has been described with words, and mathematical statements with one variable can usually be solved.

Translating English into mathematical language

Whenever you're given a description of a scenario that involves a number you don't know, you need to represent that number with a variable. That's always the first step. If another number isn't known, it may be possible to represent it by using the same variable by doing something to the variable, such as adding something to it or multiplying it by something. Think about the following description:

7 more than twice a number

The first step in representing the description mathematically is to use a variable to represent the unknown number. Just pick a letter, such as x. Write down how the number is represented so you can keep up with it.

x: the number

Now think about what is being done to the number. The description involves twice the number, which can be represented by $2x$. "7 more than" indicates that 7 is added to the amount, so the result is $2x + 7$. "7 more than twice a number" and "$2x + 7$" have the same meaning. However, "$2x + 7$" is much easier to use in algebraic equations.

Algebraic word problems

Algebraic word problems can look complicated, but they simply involve representing a quantity with a variable (see the preceding section), writing a statement about it, solving for the variable, and using the variable's value to answer the question. Sometimes you have to figure out the values of other numbers after the value of the variable has been determined. Here's an example of an algebraic word problem:

3 times a number is decreased by 5. The result is 25. What is the number?

To solve the problem, first use a variable to represent the number.

n: the number

Next, write a mathematical statement about the number by translating the word problem into mathematical language. "Decreased by" means "minus (−)," and "the result is" means "equals (=)." So, the word problem can be directly translated into mathematical language with this equation:

$3n - 5 = 25$

From there, you can simply solve the equation. The value of n, the number, is 10.

In some word problems, more than one quantity is described but only one variable needs to be used. These problems work like the one that was just demonstrated, but you need to represent more than one quantity. Let a variable represent one unknown quantity, and let a more detailed expression involving the same variable represent another quantity.

Two consecutive even integers have a sum of 34. What are the integers?

Use a variable to represent one of the integers and use a longer expression to represent the other integer. Because consecutive even integers are always 2 apart, one is 2 greater than the other.

y: the first integer

$y + 2$: the second integer

Now just directly translate the word problem into mathematical language. A sum is the result of adding, so add the expressions and show that the result is 34.

$$y + y + 2 = 34$$

You can combine like terms to get the equation $2y + 2 = 34$ and then solve the equation. In this case, $y = 16$, so the first integer is 16 and the second integer is 2 more than that, which is 18. The two integers are 16 and 18. You can check the answer by adding 16 and 18. Their sum is 34.

When solving algebraic word problems, make sure you know exactly what the question is. Don't make the mistake of assuming the question. The preceding word problem could have asked for just the first integer, just the second integer, or both integers. You need to take careful note of what the question is asking because it won't always be what you may otherwise assume.

Figuring Out Functions

Functions are generally presented in the form of equations on the Praxis Core. A function may look scary with the $f(x)$ notation at the beginning of the equation, but you have nothing to worry about. If you can solve basic equations, you can solve functions. The following sections give you more details about exactly what a function is and how to solve them.

Identifying functions

In order to understand functions, you need to understand some other basic terminology. To start with, know that a set of ordered pairs is a *relation*. For example, {(3, 5), (7, 10), (8, –1)} is a relation. It is a set of three ordered pairs. Relations can be represented in other ways. A table is a means of representing ordered pairs by listing x-coordinates next to the y-coordinates with which they are paired. Check out the following table:

x	y
–7	–2
–1	4
2	3
5	0

The table represents the ordered pairs (–7, –2), (–1, 4), (2, 3), and (5, 0).

Relations can also be represented by points on the coordinate plane and by graphs of equations (see Chapter 6 for more on these concepts). The graph of an equation represents an infinite number of ordered pairs.

The set of x values in a relation is the *domain,* and the set of y values is the *range* of a relation. Variables other than x and y can be represented by a relation. However, universally, the domain of a relation is the set of the ordered pairs' first variable values, and the range is the set of second variable values.

Now that you are familiar with the terms *relation, domain,* and *range,* you're ready to see the bigger picture of functions. A *function* is a relation in which each number in the domain is paired with only one number in the range. Generally, since the first variable of the ordered pairs in a function tends to be x, a function involves x but no repeat of an x value. In other words, each domain value is paired with just one range value, so a value of x never repeats, unless the same range value repeats with it, which is rare. However, a range value can repeat in a function without the same domain value repeating with it.

The requirement for a function is that no number in the domain is paired with more than one number in the range, not that no number in the range is paired with more than one number in the domain. The relation {(1, 2), (1, 3), (1, 4)} is not a function because 1 is paired with three different range values, but the relation {(1, 5), (2, 5), (3, 5)} is a function. The fact that 5 is paired with three different domain values does not matter. 5 is a range value. In a function in which the numbers represent x and y, for every x value, only one y value exists.

Which of the following relations is NOT a function?

(A) {(4, 8), (5, –1), (7, 6), (10, 4)}

(B) {(–2, 7), (–1, 2), (5, –4), (5, –4), (19, 0), (22, 7)}

(C) {(0, 1), (1, 2), (2, 3), (3, 4), (4, 5)}

(D) {(–5, 10), (0, 10), (5, 10), (10, 10)}

(E) {(2, 4), (4, 6), (6, 7), (2, 9), (7, 1)}

The correct answer is Choice (E). The domain number 2 is repeated and paired with both 4 and 9. Thus, 2 is paired with more than one range number. That means that the relation is not a function. Choice (A) is incorrect because no domain number is paired with more than one range number. Choice (B) is incorrect, because although the domain number 5 is repeated, 5 is only paired with –4. Choice (C) is incorrect because, although some numbers are used more than once, no domain number is paired with more than one range number. Choice (D) is incorrect because, although 10 is a range number three times, no domain number is paired with more than one range number.

Working with functions

Functions in the forms of equations often involve $f(x)$, or another letter followed by x, set equal to an expression that contains x. $f(x)$ is pronounced "f of x."

Consider the equation $f(x) = x + 5$. Any value that you put in for x will result in just one value of $f(x)$. A value that is to stand in for x will be represented in the parentheses next to f to show that the value takes the place of x. For the function $f(x) = x + 5$, you can determine the value of $f(12)$ by putting 12 in for x in $x + 5$. The result is $12 + 5$, or 17. 12 takes the place of x in $f(x)$, so 12 takes the place of x in $x + 5$. Understanding that principle is the key.

Since the letter next to the parentheses is *f*, the name of the function is *f*. Letters other than *f* are often used in function equations. For example, $g(x)$, $h(x)$, and $p(x)$ are commonly used.

If $g(x) = x^2 + 3$, what is the value of $g(5)$?

(A) 5

(B) 8

(C) 28

(D) 25

(E) 3

The correct answer is Choice (C). Because 5 takes the place of *x* in $g(x)$, 5 takes the place of *x* in $x^2 + 3$. Therefore, $g(5) = 5^2 + 3$, which is $25 + 3$, or 28. Choice (A) is just the number that replaces *x*. Choice (B) is the value of $5 + 3$ instead of $5^2 + 3$. Choice (D) is merely the value of 5^2. Choice (E) is just the number that is added to x^2 in the function.

The example involves replacing *x* with a number. Another possibility is replacing *x* with something like $f(x)$. For example, you can find the value of $g(f(x))$ if you have enough information. Suppose $g(x) = x + 1$ and $f(x) = x^3$. To find the value of $g(f(2))$, first find the value of $f(2)$, and then get *g* of that number. $f(2)$ is 2^3, which is 8, so $f(2) = 8$. Therefore, $g(f(2))$ is the same as $g(8)$. The value of $g(8)$ is $8 + 1$, or 9. Thus, the value of $g(f(2))$ is 9.

Thinking Outside the Algebra Box

The information reviewed so far in this chapter covers the basics of working algebra problems, but some of the problems in the Praxis Core math section require basic algebra skills plus an extra degree of critical thinking. Understanding patterns of relationships between quantities and the basic rules of reasoning will help you get the answers to such problems.

Recognizing relational patterns

For some problems, you need to determine how a pattern works and represent it algebraically. This is another example of translating English into mathematical language, but the translating isn't as direct as it may be in other situations.

If a word problem involves a number of 18-wheeler trucks and the question is how many wheels there are in all, you need to understand that there are 18 wheels for every truck. In other words, the number of trucks multiplied by 18 equals the number of wheels. This is an example of *direct variation*, which is a relationship pattern in which one quantity increases as another one increases, though they may increase at different rates. Every time a number of 18-wheeler trucks is increased by 1, the number of wheels increases by 18. As one quantity increases, so does the other. The number of wheels increases 18 times faster than the number of trucks. If the number of trucks is represented by *x*, the number of wheels needs to be represented by $18x$.

Inverse variation is a relationship pattern in which one quantity decreases as another one increases. The two quantities don't increase together, as they do with direct variation. With inverse variation, the greater one quantity is, the smaller the other one is. For example, the amount of time it takes to travel a certain distance decreases with increased rate. Suppose you're traveling a distance of 10 miles. The faster you travel, the less time it will take.

The distance formula is $d = rt$, in which d = distance, r = rate, and t = time. From that formula, it can be concluded that $r = d/t$ and $t = d/r$. The relationship between t and r is one of inverse variation.

Anytime a formula, such as $d = rt$, is used in algebra, simply write the formula with every variable's value filled in except for the variable that still has an unknown value. Then, solve for that variable. Word problems that require using formulas look more difficult than that on the surface, but they really are that simple.

Algebraic reasoning

Some of the math questions on the Praxis Core exam involve *conditional statements,* also known as "if-then statements." They state that if one given fact exists, another given fact exists. This is an example of a conditional statement:

If $p - 4 = 5$, then $p + 8 = 17$.

You may be asked whether a certain conditional statement is true. In many cases, you can solve an equation or inequality and then determine whether the conclusion is true. By solving either of the preceding equations, you can determine that $p = 9$. You can then put 9 in for p in the other equation and see whether the equation is true. In this example, it is. If p did not have the same value in both equations, the statement would be false.

If you're in doubt about how to figure out the full nature of a conditional statement, there's an effective method you can use. If you can come up with even one example of a situation where the conditional statement fails, the conditional statement is false. Think about this conditional statement:

If $y^2 > 64$, then $y > 8$.

All you have to do is look for one example of a number that makes the statement fail. If you can find any such number, the statement is false. When testing numbers, try using some positive integers, some negative integers, 0, and some fractions between 0 and 1. Sampling those sections of the number line goes a long way toward covering the numerical principles that need to be put to the test. Numbers that make both of the preceding inequalities true include all numbers that are greater than 8, but no number less than –8 works for both inequalities. If you put any number less than –8 in for y, you can see that it doesn't work. As soon as you find that one exception, you can truthfully conclude that the conditional statement is false.

Practice Questions about Algebra

These practice questions are similar to the algebra questions you'll encounter on the Praxis Core exam.

1. If $10x - 8 = 17$, what is the value of $7 + 4x$?

    (A) 17

    (B) 107

    (C) $10\frac{3}{5}$

    (D) 25

    (E) 41

2. What is the sum of $9j^3k^8m^{24}$ and $24j^3k^8m^{24}$?

    (A) $15j^3k^8m^{24}$

    (B) $33j^6k^{16}m^{48}$

    (C) $15jkm$

    (D) $33j^3k^8m^{24}$

    (E) $576j^9k^{64}m^{576}$

3. Which of the following is NOT a factor of $-54p^4q^7r^3u^{11}$?

    (A) $-6p^4q^7r^3u^{11}$

    (B) $9q^8r^3$

    (C) $-27u$

    (D) $-18pqr^{11}$

    (E) $2p^4q^7r^3u^{11}$

5. What is the solution to the inequality $-8x + 7 \geq 39$?

    (A) $x < -4$

    (B) $x \leq -5.75$

    (C) $x \leq -4$

    (D) $x > -5.75$

    (E) $x \geq -4$

4. What is the higher of the two even integers that have a sum of 42?

    (A) 20

    (B) 26

    (C) 18

    (D) 24

    (E) 22

Answers and Explanations

Use this answer key to score the practice algebra questions in this chapter.

1. **A. 17.** You can solve the first equation and determine the value of x.

$$10x - 8 = 17$$
$$10x = 25$$
$$\frac{10x}{10} = \frac{25}{10}$$
$$x = 2.5$$

Because the value of x is 2.5, you can substitute 2.5 for x in the expression $7 + 4x$ to determine the value the expression. $7 + 4(2.5) = 7 + 10$, or 17. Choice (B) is the value of $7 + 4(25)$, and 25 is the value of the right side of the equation before you divide both sides by 10. Choice (C) results from subtracting 8 from both sides instead of adding it. Choice (D) is the value of the right side of the equation after you add 8 to both sides. Choice (E) is just wrong.

2. **D. $33j^3k^8m^{24}$.** To add terms, add their coefficients and follow the sum with the same variables and accompanying exponents the added terms have. Choice (A) has a coefficient that is the difference of the coefficients of the added terms. Choice (B) has exponents that are the sums of the added terms' exponents. Choice (C) has a difference of the coefficients followed by the correct variables with false exponents, which are the differences of the added terms' exponents instead of the same exponents. Choice (E) incorrectly has the product of coefficients and the products of exponents.

3. **B. $9q^8r^3$.** The variable q has an exponent of 8, which is wrong because 8 is higher than the exponent of q in $-54p^4q^7r^3u^{11}$. All the other choices are factors because their coefficients are factors of -54 and they have the same coefficients with exponents that are whole numbers that aren't greater than the corresponding exponents in $-54p^4q^7r^3u^{11}$.

4. **E. 22.** You can use x to represent the first integer. Because the next number is the next even integer, it is 2 higher, so you can represent it with the expression $x + 2$. The sum of the two consecutive even integers is 42, so you can represent the situation with the equation $x + x + 2 = 42$.

$$x + x + 2 = 42$$
$$2x + 2 = 42$$
$$2x + 2 - 2 = 42 - 2$$
$$2x = 40$$
$$\frac{2x}{2} = \frac{40}{2}$$
$$x = 20$$

Because the value of x is 20, the first even integer is 20. The next one is 2 higher, so it's 22. Choice (A) is the lower of the two integers. The other choices are randomly incorrect.

5. **C. $x \leq -4$.** Solving this inequality involves flipping the sign because you have to divide by a negative number.

$$-8x + 7 \geq 39$$
$$-8x + 7 - 7 \geq 39 - 7$$
$$-8x \geq 32$$
$$\frac{-8x}{-8} \leq \frac{32}{-8}$$
$$x \leq -4$$

Choice (A) has the < symbol, not the ≤ symbol. Choice (B) results from adding 7 to both sides of the inequality instead of subtracting it. Choice (D) results from adding 7 to both sides of the inequality, not changing the direction of the inequality sign when dividing both sides by a negative number, and leaving out the "or equal to" mark. Choice (E) results from not changing the direction of the inequality sign when dividing both sides by a negative number.

Chapter 6

Grasping Geometry Concepts

The time has come for you to review America's favorite subject, geometry. Well, it's America's favorite subject according to a recent survey of one person — a geometry teacher. Okay, never mind that. Geometry is basically the study of the nature of shapes and where shapes exist. The subject begins with points and goes all the way to three-dimensional figures.

Like other areas of math, geometry involves principles from areas that typically precede its study. Algebraic expressions, for example, are commonly used in geometry, and using geometric principles to solve for variables is very common. So make sure you have a good grasp of geometry concepts because you never know when one may appear on the Praxis Core — or in real life. The math test of the Praxis exam is about 20 percent geometry. Because the math test has 56 questions, you'll have 11 or 12 geometry questions to answer.

Understanding the Building Blocks of Geometry

A few elements in geometry make up all the others, even the most complex geometric figures. You need to understand these elements to truly understand the more complicated figures and properties in geometry. The starting point for understanding geometric elements is the point. The starting point would automatically have to be a point. It's not a starting cylinder. And then you move onto lines, planes, and angles.

Getting to the point

The most basic building block of geometry is the *point*, which is an exact and infinitely small location. Points make up all the physical realities studied in geometry. Points are named by capital letters that are placed near them. These are Point A and Point B:

A   B
•   •

© John Wiley & Sons, Inc.

Points aren't always represented by dots. Dots are generally used when the location of a point would otherwise be unclear.

Defining lines and parts of lines

Any two points, anywhere in the universe, are on the same line. A *line* is a continuous set of an infinite number of points extending infinitely in two directions. Lines are one-dimensional.

A line can be named by any two points on it in any order, with a line symbol on top. Three of the points on the following line are labeled. The line can be called $\overleftrightarrow{AB}, \overleftrightarrow{AC}, \overleftrightarrow{BA}, \overleftrightarrow{BC}, \overleftrightarrow{CB}$, or $\overleftrightarrow{CA}$.

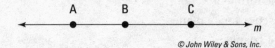

© John Wiley & Sons, Inc.

A line can also be named by a single italicized letter that is not a point on it. For example, the preceding line can be called line *m*.

Parts of lines that serve as building blocks of geometry include rays and segments. A *ray* is like a line, but it has one endpoint and extends infinitely in only one direction. A ray is named by its endpoint and any other point on it, with a ray symbol on top. The following ray can be called $\overrightarrow{DE}$ or $\overrightarrow{DF}$.

© John Wiley & Sons, Inc.

A line segment, more commonly called just a *segment,* is a part of a line with two endpoints. Segments are named by their two endpoints, in either order. A segment symbol can be placed on top of the letters, but it isn't necessary. This line segment is $\overline{PQ}$ or $\overline{QP}$ and can also be written as just PQ or QP:

© John Wiley & Sons, Inc.

Moving along planes in space

You have now entered the second dimension on a plane. A *plane* is a flat surface that is infinitely thin and goes forever in all directions. Any two lines exist on one plane. Planes are usually named by three points. They can also be named by a single italicized letter. The following plane can be named plane RST, but it can also be called plane *p*.

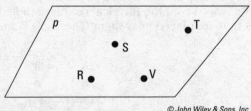

© John Wiley & Sons, Inc.

Getting the right angles on angles

An *angle* is a shape formed by two sides, with each side being either a line or part of a line. The point at which the two sides meet is called the *vertex*. An angle can be named by three points on it in the order of any point on either side, the vertex, and a point on the other side. If the vertex is presented as the vertex of just one angle, that angle can be named by the vertex alone. The following angle can be called ∠B, ∠ABC, ∠CBA, or ∠3.

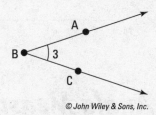

© John Wiley & Sons, Inc.

If a point is the vertex of more than one angle, you can't name the angle by the vertex. That would be confusing because the angle named would not be clearly identified. The name could apply to any of the angles with that vertex. In the following illustration, which angle would be ∠J? Nothing indicates which angle it is.

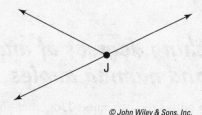

© John Wiley & Sons, Inc.

An angle named by three of its points must be named with the vertex in the middle. Otherwise, a different angle is indicated.

Recognizing congruence

Two segments or angles that have the same measures are *congruent*. The measure of a segment is the distance from one of its endpoints to the other, and the measure of an angle is the rate at which the sides separate as distance from the vertex increases. (I get more into angle measurement in the next section.) If two segments are congruent, they will have the same number of marks on them.

© John Wiley & Sons, Inc.

The congruence symbol is ≅. If AB has the same measure as CD, then AB ≅ CD. The single mark in each segment indicates that they're congruent. The congruence of EF and GH is also indicated, but they are not congruent to AB and CD, so they have two marks each.

Angles that have the same number of arcs are congruent. In the following illustration, ∠*J* is congruent to ∠*M*, but ∠*P* is not congruent to either.

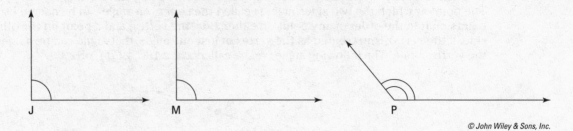

© John Wiley & Sons, Inc.

Understanding Angle Measures and Relationships

Angle sizes vary, so units are used to distinguish the different sizes. The unit of measure that's most commonly used — and the only one used on the Praxis Core exam — is the *degree,* and it is represented by the symbol °.

Distinguishing degrees of angle measure and naming angles

An angle in which both sides are merged together could be 0 degrees, or 0°, but if one side completes a full circle, the angle it forms with the other side is 360°. An angle in which the two sides are part of the same line is 180° because one side completes half a circle with the other side.

Angles are classified according to their general sizes. An angle that is between 0° and 90° is an *acute angle.* If an angle is exactly 90°, it's a *right angle.* An angle with a measure between 90° and 180° is an *obtuse angle,* and a 180° angle is a *straight angle.* Right angles are often symbolized by a small square near the vertex.

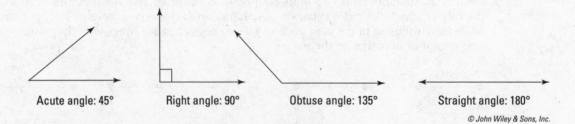

Acute angle: 45°   Right angle: 90°   Obtuse angle: 135°   Straight angle: 180°

© John Wiley & Sons, Inc.

Working with angle relationships

If two angles have measures that add up to 180°, they are *supplementary.* For example, a 130° angle and a 50° angle are supplementary. Because straight angles are 180°, two angles that share a side and form a straight angle together are automatically supplementary. They make what is called a *linear pair* because they are a pair of angles that together form a line.

Complementary angles are like supplementary angles, except two angles that are *complementary* have measures that add up to 90°. A 37° angle and a 53° angle are supplementary. Two angles that share a side and form a right angle together are complementary.

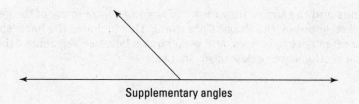

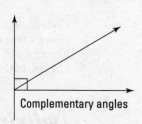

Supplementary angles

Complementary angles

© John Wiley & Sons, Inc.

Another major type of relationship is that of vertical angles, which are formed by two intersecting lines. Vertical angles are opposite each other, and if you have two intersecting lines, you always have four vertical angles. Vertical angles are always congruent; that is, they have the same measurement.

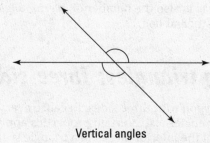

Vertical angles

© John Wiley & Sons, Inc.

The measure of ∠*ABD* is 168°. What is the measure of ∠*DBC*?

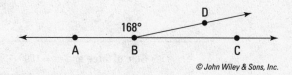

© John Wiley & Sons, Inc.

(A) 192°

(B) 168°

(C) 12°

(D) 180°

(E) 102°

The correct answer is Choice (C). ∠*ABD* and ∠*DBC* form a linear pair, so they are supplementary. That means their measures have a sum of 180°. 180 – 168 is 12, so the measure of ∠*DBC* is 12°. Choice (A) is the result of adding 12 to 180. Choice (B) is the same measure as that of ∠*ABD*, Choice (D) is merely the measure of a straight angle, and Choice (E) is the difference of 270° and 168°.

Knowing Common Shapes and Their Basic Properties

Understanding segments and the angles they form helps you analyze many of the geometric shapes you may be asked about on the Praxis Core exam. This includes the basic shapes like squares and other rectangles, triangles, and even circles because segments exist inside circles. In the following sections, we review basic shapes.

Defining polygons in general

A polygon is an enclosed figure formed on one plane by segments joined at their endpoints. Rectangles, triangles, and other shapes are types of polygons. The polygons primarily focused on in geometry — and more particularly on the Praxis Core exam — are *convex polygons,* which basically are polygons that don't point inward anywhere.

Polygons are also classified according to the number of sides they have. The number of sides a polygon has is also the number of *interior angles* (inside angles formed by sides that are next to each other) it has.

Analyzing triangles: Three-sided polygons

A *triangle* is a polygon with three sides. Because every triangle has three sides, each triangle has three interior angles also. Certain properties apply to all triangles. For example, the sum of the measures of the interior angles of a triangle is 180°. This fact is true for all triangles.

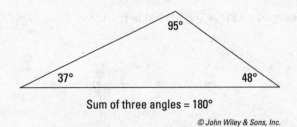

Sum of three angles = 180°

© John Wiley & Sons, Inc.

Another rule that applies to all triangles is that if two sides of a triangle are congruent, the angles opposite (across from) those sides are congruent. The rule also works in the other direction. If two angles of a triangle are congruent, the sides opposite those angles are congruent too.

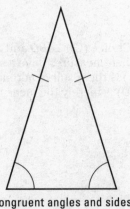

Congruent angles and sides

© John Wiley & Sons, Inc.

Questions on the Praxis Core exam can involve more than one rule regarding triangles and sometimes more basic rules in addition to them. You may need to use multiple rules to reach a conclusion. Many combinations of principles can be involved.

According to the diagram, what is the measure of ∠1?

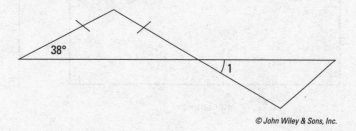

© John Wiley & Sons, Inc.

(A) 38°

(B) 1°

(C) 142°

(D) 322°

(E) 52°

The correct answer is Choice (A). Two sides of the triangle on the left are congruent, so the angles opposite them are congruent. They are therefore both 38°. ∠1 is vertical to a 38° angle, so it too is 38°. Choice (B) involves the name of the angle in question, but 1 is not given as the measure of the angle. It has no ° beside it. Choice (C) is the supplement of 38°. Choice (D) results from subtracting the given angle measure from 360°. Choice (E) is the complement of 38°.

Identifying facts about quadrilaterals

As triangles are three-sided polygons, quadrilaterals are four-sided polygons. Squares and other rectangles are quadrilaterals, but they are not the only types. The sum of the interior angles of a quadrilateral is always 360°.

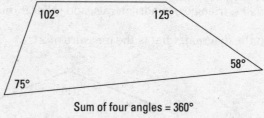

Sum of four angles = 360°

© John Wiley & Sons, Inc.

A quadrilateral in which both pairs of opposite sides are parallel is a *parallelogram*. For any parallelogram, both pairs of opposite sides are also congruent. Also, any quadrilateral in which both pairs of opposite sides are congruent is a parallelogram. A *rectangle* is a quadrilateral in which all four interior angles are right angles, and all rectangles are parallelograms, so their opposite sides are congruent. A *square* is a rectangle in which all four sides are congruent.

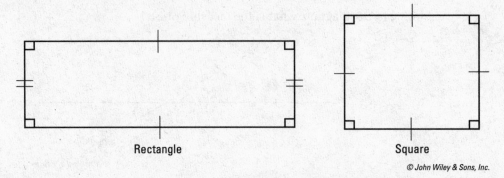

Rectangle   Square

© John Wiley & Sons, Inc.

A *trapezoid* is a quadrilateral that has just one pair of parallel sides. The two parallel sides are the *bases* of the trapezoid. The bases in the following trapezoid are indicated by arrows, which are used in geometry to suggest that lines and parts of lines are parallel.

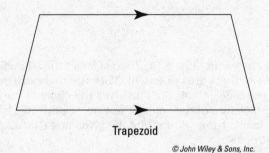

Trapezoid

© John Wiley & Sons, Inc.

Working with other types of polygons

No limit exists for the number of sides a polygon can have. Many names are used for types of polygons based on the number of sides they have. For example, a five-sided polygon is a *pentagon,* and an eight-sided polygon is an *octagon.* However, the Praxis Core exam doesn't focus on the major rules concerning polygons that have more than four sides. What you need to be able to do is recognize what is inside such polygons. Rules you need to know may apply to segments, angles, triangles, quadrilaterals, and other formations that are within them.

According to the diagram, what is the measure of ∠1?

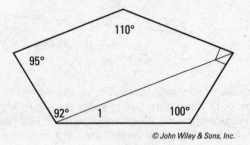

© John Wiley & Sons, Inc.

(A) 63°

(B) 27°

(C) 180°

(D) 88°

(E) 53°

The correct answer is Choice (E). The pentagon is divided into a quadrilateral and a triangle. Because the interior angle sum of a quadrilateral is 360°, the interior angle without a given measure in the quadrilateral is 63°. That angle is complementary to an angle in the triangle, so that angle in the triangle has a measure of 27°. Because another angle in the triangle is 100° and the interior angle sum of a triangle is 180°, ∠1 has to be 53°. The other choices can result from the wrong uses of formulas.

Knowing the basic facts about circles

A circle is a shape like the others covered so far, but a circle has no sides. A *circle* is the set of all points in one plane that are a given distance from a point called the *center*. The distance that all the points are from the center is the *radius* of the circle. A radius is also an actual segment that connects the center to a point on the circle. The *diameter* of a circle is the distance across the interior through the center, and it is also the name of a segment that covers the path. The diameter of a circle is always twice the radius. Because the radius of the following circle is 3 centimeters, the diameter is 6 centimeters. A circle is named by its center, so this circle is Circle K.

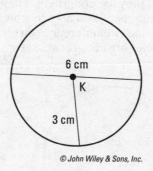

© John Wiley & Sons, Inc.

Working with Shapes that Are Alike

Polygons can be alike in certain ways, and so can circles. Polygons that have the same number of sides don't necessarily have the same shape, but they do if they are congruent or similar.

Forming conclusions about congruent shapes

When two polygons have the same number of sides and all of their corresponding (same position, different polygons) pairs of sides and corresponding pairs of angles are congruent, the polygons themselves are congruent. Also, if you are given the fact that two polygons are congruent, you have enough information to conclude that every pair of corresponding parts is congruent.

The two following triangles are congruent. Notice that every side and angle of one triangle is congruent to its corresponding part in the other triangle. They are the same triangle in two different places, exact copies of each other. As a result, all of their corresponding parts are congruent.

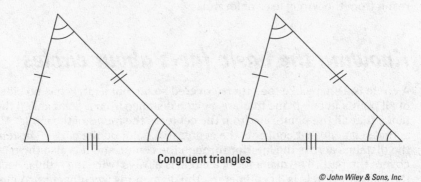

Congruent triangles

© John Wiley & Sons, Inc.

All other types of polygons can be congruent. Circles can be congruent too. If two circles have the same radius, they are congruent. They have the same diameter and other measures. I get into circumference and area in a bit, but for now it's enough to say that congruent circles have the same circumference (distance around the circle) and the same area. The following two circles are congruent.

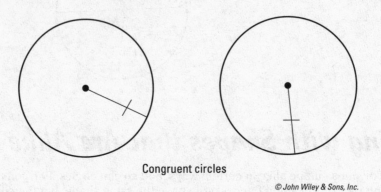

Congruent circles

© John Wiley & Sons, Inc.

Working with similar shapes

Similar shapes are exactly the same shape but not necessarily congruent. Imagine magnifying or reducing a picture of a quadrilateral. The resulting image would look identical to the original except that it would be a different size. The two shapes would be similar.

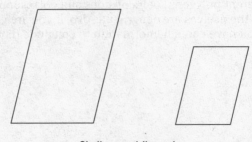

Similar quadrilaterals

© John Wiley & Sons, Inc.

Polygons that are similar have congruent corresponding angles. They also have side measures that are *proportional,* which means that the ratio of the measure of a side in one polygon to the measure of the side that corresponds to it in the other polygon is always the same ratio. Recall that a proportion is an equation in which one ratio is equal to another. The ratio of one side measure to its corresponding side measure is the *scale factor* of the similarity relationship. Scale factor depends on which figure is put first in the ratio, so two scale factors can exist between two figures. For the following two triangles, the scale factor is 2:1, or 2/1.

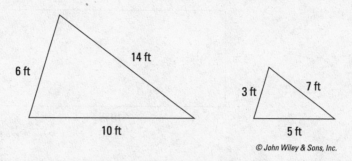

© John Wiley & Sons, Inc.

The way to determine the measure of a side of a polygon that's similar to another polygon is to determine the scale factor and use it as a ratio in a proportion. You can do that by writing a side measure over its corresponding side measure and setting it equal to another such ratio. Make sure you are consistent in the way you write the ratios. If you put the first polygon measure on top in one ratio, the first polygon measure has to go on top in the other ratio.

Suppose the triangle side that is 7 feet was of unknown measure, but the other measures were given. You could find the side measure by letting a variable represent it and solving a proportion involving it.

$$\frac{6}{3} = \frac{14}{x}$$
$$6x = 14(3)$$
$$6x = 42$$
$$\frac{6x}{6} = \frac{42}{6}$$
$$x = 7$$

Corresponding angles of similar polygons are congruent.

Figuring out Geometric Formulas

Geometric figures have certain properties, and the number of dimensions they have is part of what decides what other properties they have. Line segments have a distance that can be referred to as length, width, or height. Two-dimensional figures such as circles and triangles have area as well as parts with one-dimensional measurements. Three-dimensional geometric figures have the preceding properties plus volume. Formulas aren't provided on the Praxis Core, so you'll need to know the major area, surface area, and volume formulas.

Finding the perimeter

The perimeter of a two-dimensional figure is the distance around it. To determine the perimeter of a polygon, you can add all the side measures. The following rectangle has a perimeter of 28 meters.

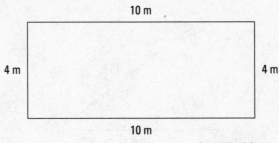

10 m

4 m   4 m

10 m

© John Wiley & Sons, Inc.

Because the opposite sides of a rectangle are congruent, a formula makes calculating the perimeter simpler than adding up all the side measures. Two of the sides have the length (l), and two sides have the width (w), so adding twice the length and twice the width gives the perimeter:

Perimeter of rectangle = $2l + 2w$

Because the length and width of a square are the same, you can get the perimeter by multiplying the measure of one side by 4.

Circling the circumference

The perimeter of a circle is the circle's *circumference*. The formula for circumference involves π, which is the ratio of a circle's circumference (C) divided by its diameter (d). Because all circles are similar, the ratio is the same for all circles.

$$\frac{C}{d} = \pi$$

π is an irrational number, so it never terminates or repeats in decimal form, but its value can be rounded to 3.14. Because circumference divided by diameter is π, circumference is diameter times π:

$$\frac{C}{d} = \pi$$
$$\frac{C}{d}(d) = \pi(d)$$
$$C = \pi d$$

The diameter of a circle is twice the radius, so $d = 2r$. Therefore, $C = \pi(2r)$. The formal way to write a term is with numbers before variables, and π is a number, so the official formula for the circumference is this:

$$C = 2\pi r$$

Remember that within a formula, any variable can represent an unknown in a problem. To find the value of the variable, fill every known number into the formula and solve for what is not yet known.

What is the radius of a circle with a circumference of 10π units?

(A) 10

(B) 5

(C) 100

(D) 5π

(E) 10π

The correct answer is Choice (B). You can use the formula for circumference and solve for r.

$$C = 2\pi r$$
$$10\pi = 2\pi r$$
$$\frac{10\pi}{2\pi} = \frac{2\pi r}{2\pi}$$
$$5 = r$$
$$r = 5$$

The other choices result from misuse of the circumference formula or using the wrong formula.

If getting the answer to a question involves the use of a formula with π in it, π may not appear as part of the answer choices. In that case, you need to use 3.14, the approximation for π, and do the calculation. 3.14 is not exactly π, but it's a close approximation.

Getting into the area

A two-dimensional figure exists on a plane. The area of a two-dimensional figure is the amount of plane in it. In other words, area is a measure of how much room is inside a two-dimensional shape. Different shapes have different area formulas.

The area of a parallelogram is its base times its height. The base can be any side, but the height has to be the measure of a segment that is perpendicular to it and its opposite side.

area of parallelogram = bh

The area of the following parallelogram is its base times its height, or (7 cm)(10 cm), or 70 cm^2.

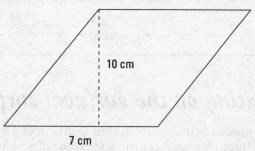

10 cm

7 cm

© John Wiley & Sons, Inc.

Any combination of base and height for a rectangle, which is a type of parallelogram, is a combination of length (l) and width (w), so the area of a rectangle is lw. Length and width are the same for a square because all four sides are congruent, so to get the area of a square, all you have to do is multiply a side measure by itself. In other words, square a side measure.

If a parallelogram is cut at the vertices, the result is two congruent triangles. Also, any triangle can be put together with a congruent triangle to form a parallelogram. Because of this, every triangle has half the area of the parallelogram that can be formed by putting the triangle with an exact copy of itself. Therefore, the area of a triangle is not base times height, but half that:

$$\text{area of triangle} = \frac{1}{2}bh$$

The area of the following triangle is $\frac{1}{2}bh$, or $\frac{1}{2}$ (8 ft) (11 ft), which is 44 ft².

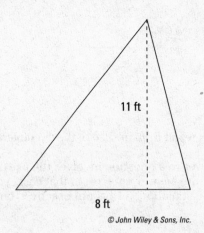

11 ft

8 ft

© John Wiley & Sons, Inc.

Table 6-1 shows the formulas for finding the areas of common shapes. Make sure you know these well because you'll probably be asked at least one question about area on the Praxis.

Table 6-1	Area Formulas for Common Shapes
Figure	**Area**
Parallelogram	bh
Rectangle	lw
Square	s^2
Triangle	$\frac{1}{2}bh$
Trapezoid	$\frac{1}{2}h(b_1 + b_2)$
Circle	πr^2

Calculating on the surface: surface area

Surface area applies to three-dimensional figures, and it's the total amount of area that is on a figure. Many three-dimensional figures are made of nothing but *faces* that are polygons. For example, a cube is composed of six square faces. To find the surface area of such a figure, you can get the area of each face and add all the areas. The sum is the surface area of the figure. However, formulas provide shortcuts.

To find the surface area of a cube or any other *right rectangular solid,* which is a three-dimensional figure with two bases (base faces, not base sides; you have entered the third dimension) connected by rectangles that are perpendicular to the bases, you can add twice the base area (because there are two bases) to the rest of the surface area, which is called the *lateral area.* The lateral area is found by multiplying the perimeter (P) of the base by the height of the figure. With right rectangular solids, any two opposite faces can be considered the bases, but the faces you choose determine what you must consider the height, which is the measure of a segment that is perpendicular to the bases. Put all of this together: The surface area of a right rectangular solid is $2B + Ph$. In the rectangular solid that follows, one base area you can use is 7 m · 8 m, which makes the height 5 m. The perimeter of that base is 30 m. The surface area is therefore (2)(7 m)(8 m) + (30 m)(5 m), or 262 m^2.

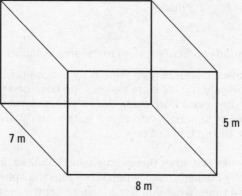

7 m

5 m

8 m

© John Wiley & Sons, Inc.

A cylinder is formed by two circular bases that are connected by a tube. The lateral area of a cylinder is the base circumference times the height of the cylinder. It's another case of base perimeter times height. A cylinder has two bases, so add $2B$ to the lateral area to get the surface area. Suppose the cylinder in the following diagram has a radius of 7 cm and a height of 15 cm. The surface area would be $2\pi(7)^2 + 2\pi(7)(15)$, or 98π cm^2 + 210π cm^2, which is 308π cm^2.

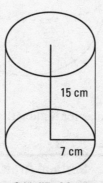

15 cm

7 cm

© John Wiley & Sons, Inc.

Some of the figures for which you may be asked to find the surface area on the Praxis Core exam don't involve exactly the formula used for rectangular solids. *Cones* and *pyramids,* for example, have only one base, and that changes things. Their surface area formulas involve *slant height,* which is the distance from the *apex,* or the top point, to the center of an edge of the base. A pyramid has one base that is some type of polygon, and a cone has a circular base. In the following figures, the dotted segments represent slant height.

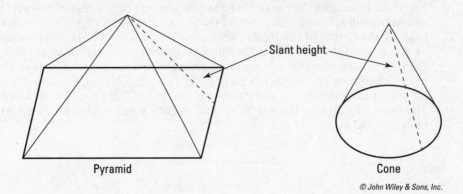

© John Wiley & Sons, Inc.

For both pyramids and cones, the lateral area is half the base perimeter, or $\frac{1}{2}P$, times the slant height. Slant height is represented by ℓ. Because the base of a cone is a circle, the base perimeter is $\pi r \ell$ and the base area is πr^2. The base of a pyramid can be that of any type of polygon (but the Praxis Core exam doesn't hassle you with areas of pyramid bases that aren't triangles or squares). Add just B to the lateral areas of pyramids and cones because they have one base each, not two.

A sphere isn't like the other three-dimensional figures. It has no bases. It's basically a ball. The circle really pushed things when it got into the sphere department. The surface area of a sphere is just 4 times what you would use to get the area of a circle, so it's $4\pi r^2$. By the way, the radius of a sphere is the distance from the center of the sphere to a point on the sphere.

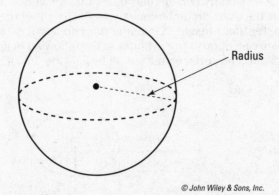

© John Wiley & Sons, Inc.

Table 6-2 shows the formulas for finding the surface area of common shapes.

Table 6-2	Surface Area Formulas for Common Shapes
Figure	**Surface Area**
Rectangular solid	$2B + Ph$
Cylinder	$2\pi r^2 + 2\pi rh$
Pyramid	$B + \frac{1}{2}P\ell$
Cone	$\pi r^2 + \pi r \ell$
Sphere	$4\pi r^2$

Finding the right volume

Volume is a three-dimensional measure. While surface area is the amount of plane on the surface of a three-dimensional figure, volume is the amount of space inside a three-dimensional figure. For rectangular solids and cylinders, the volume can be found by multiplying the base area by the height. For rectangular solids, the volume is more specifically *lwh* since *lw* is the base area. The volume of a pyramid is $\frac{1}{3}$ what the volume would be if the apex were a congruent base instead of a point, and a cone is $\frac{1}{3}$ the volume of what it would be if the apex were a congruent base instead of a point. That's why the volume of a pyramid or cone is $\frac{1}{3}Bh$ instead of *Bh*. Remember that the bases of cones and cylinders are circles.

The height of one of these figures is the measure of a segment that goes from an apex or a base perpendicular to the plane on which the base, or other base, lies. If you have a question about these figures on the Praxis Core exam, the height will most likely be the measure of a segment that is perpendicular to the actual base. In the following figures, the dotted segments represent height.

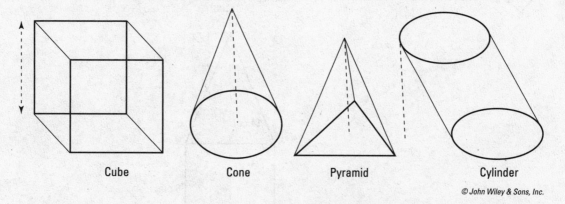

Cube   Cone   Pyramid   Cylinder

© John Wiley & Sons, Inc.

The formulas for the volumes of major three-dimensional figures are listed in Table 6-3.

Table 6-3	Volume Formulas for Common Shapes
Figure	**Volume**
Rectangular solid	*Bh* or *lwh*
Cylinder	$\pi r^2 h$
Pyramid	$\frac{1}{3}Bh$
Cone	$\frac{1}{3}\pi r^2 h$
Sphere	$\frac{4}{3}\pi r^3$

Combining Shapes

The Praxis Core exam may ask you about areas or volumes of figures created by joining figures of the types covered so far in this chapter. In some situations, the mergers of figures add area or volume, and in others, you may be asked for the area or volume of a shaded region that exists outside of another figure, in which cases area or volume is reduced.

Coming together: Shapes that have joined without an invasion

When shapes join without one intruding on the other, you can find the area or volume of the figure they form together by adding the areas or volumes of the figures that form it. For example, a triangle may share a side with a square, or a cone may share a base with a cylinder. Just add the areas or volumes of the figures to find the total area.

The figure shown has a height of 14 cm and is composed of a square and a triangle that share a side. What is the area of the figure that they form?

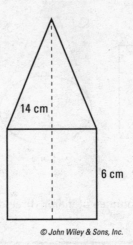

© John Wiley & Sons, Inc.

(A) 60 cm²

(B) 232 cm²

(C) 84 cm²

(D) 20 cm²

(E) 220 cm²

The correct answer is Choice (A). One side of the square is 6 cm, so all of its sides are 6 cm. That means the base of the triangle is also 6 cm. Because the height of the overall figure is 14 cm and a side of the square is 6 cm, the height of the triangle is 8 cm. The area of the square is s^2, or 36 cm², and the area of the triangle is $\frac{1}{2}bh$, or $\frac{1}{2}$ (6 cm)(8 cm), which is 24 cm².

The sum of the areas of the square and the triangle is 36 cm² + 24 cm², or 60 cm². The other choices can result from incorrect calculations involving measures in the diagram.

Preparing for invasion: When one shape invades another

If a question on the Praxis Core exam involves a shape that exists within another one and you're asked to find the area or volume of the shape region that is outside of the intruding shape, subtract the area or volume of the intruding shape from that of the shape upon which it is intruding.

To find the area of the shaded region of the rectangle that follows, you can get the area of the rectangle and then subtract the area of the triangle. The remaining area is the area of the shaded region. The area of the rectangle is (12 mi)(5 mi), or 60 mi². The height of the triangle is the same as the width of the rectangle, so the area of the triangle is $\frac{1}{2}$(12 mi)(5 mi), or 30 mi². 60 mi² – 30 mi² = 30 mi², so the remaining shaded region has an area of 30 mi².

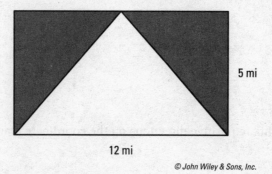

5 mi

12 mi

© John Wiley & Sons, Inc.

Knowing the Ways of the XY Coordinate Plane

The coordinate plane is a two-dimensional system of points that are named by their positions in regard to two intersecting number lines, the *x*-axis and the *y*-axis. The *x*-axis is horizontal, and the *y*-axis is vertical. Using the *xy* coordinate plane, you can find and name the locations of points, lines, parts of lines, graphs of equations and inequalities, and two-dimensional figures.

Naming coordinate pairs

Every point on the coordinate plane is named by two numbers, the first of which is an *x*-coordinate, which indicates a point's position along the *x*-axis, and the second of which is a *y*-coordinate, an indication of a point's position along the *y*-axis. The point of intersection of the *x* and *y* axes is called the *origin,* and its coordinates are (0, 0).

To determine the coordinates of a point, first locate the origin. Then determine which number on the *x*-axis the point is on or directly above or below. That is the *x*-coordinate of the point. Then determine the number on the *y*-axis the point is on or next to; that is the *y*-coordinate. To think about it another way, the number of horizontal units you move from the origin is the *x*-coordinate, and the number of vertical units you move from the origin is the *y*-coordinate. Several points and their corresponding ordered pairs are shown on the following coordinate plane.

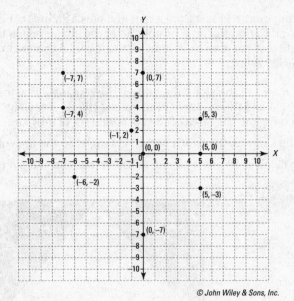

© John Wiley & Sons, Inc.

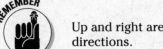

Up and right are positive directions on the coordinate plane, and down and left are negative directions.

Identifying linear equations and their graphs

Every line on the coordinate plane is the graph of a *linear equation*. Every point on a line represents an ordered pair that makes a linear equation true. In other words, if the *x*-coordinate is put in for *x* in the equation and the *y* value is put in for *y*, the equation is true. The graph therefore represents all the ordered pairs that make the equation work or that are solutions to the equation.

Not all equations are linear. Equations that are linear have certain characteristics. *x* and *y* are generally in linear equations, but sometimes other variables are used. Also, some linear equations have only one variable. At least one variable is necessary for the equation to be linear. Also, no variable has an exponent other than 1, which is generally understood and not shown. *x* and *y* are never exponents or multiplied by each other in linear equations. For example, $3x - 2y = 5$, $y = -7x + 4$, and $x = 12$ are all linear equations. The following graph represents $3x - 2y = 5$. Notice how every point on the graph represents an ordered pair that makes the equation true.

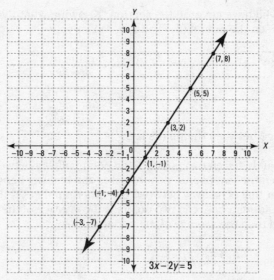

© John Wiley & Sons, Inc.

The *slope* of a line is an indication of the line's steepness and direction. It is a ratio of the rate of change in y to the rate of change in x. With any two points on a line on the coordinate plane, you can find the slope of the line. The change in y is the difference of the y-coordinates, and the change in x is the difference of the x coordinates.

$$\text{slope} = \frac{y_1 - y_2}{x_1 - x_2}$$

In the formula for slope, (x_1, y_1) is one point and (x_2, y_2) represents the other point. Which point you call which doesn't matter, but make sure you are consistent. In other words, subtract in the same direction both times.

Another way to determine the slope of a line is to write the equation in slope-intercept form, $y = mx + b$, where m represents slope and b represents y-intercept, which is the y-coordinate of the point where the line intersects the y-axis. For example, the equation $2y - 10 = 8x$ can be rewritten as $y = 4x + 5$, which shows that the slope of the graph is 4 because it is the coefficient of x when the equation is in slope-intercept form. Just get y by itself on the left side and put the x term first on the right side. (If you need a review of how to isolate variables, flip back to Chapter 5.) Once the equation is in that form, the coefficient of x is the slope of the graph of the line.

To determine whether a graph represents an equation, you can test the points on the graph. Every ordered pair represented by the graph must make the equation true. For a linear equation, testing two points is sufficient because only one line can pass through two points.

Using the distance and midpoint formulas

The distance between two points on the coordinate plane is given by the formula distance $= \sqrt{(x_1 - x_2)^2 + (y_1 - y_2)^2}$. The formula is based on x and y changes and the Pythagorean theorem, which we cover in the section "Knowing what Pythagoras discovered." The distance between the points (5, 7) and (9, 4) is

$$\sqrt{(5-9)^2+(7-4)^2}=\sqrt{(-4)^2+(3)^2}$$
$$=\sqrt{25}$$
$$=5$$

The distance between the points is 5.

The midpoint between two points is the point halfway between them. Its *x*-coordinate is halfway between the two points' *x*-coordinates and halfway between the two points' *y*-coordinates. The number that is halfway between two other numbers is the average of the two numbers. Thus, the midpoint between two points is the average of the *x*-coordinates followed by a comma and then the average of the *y*-coordinates.

Midpoint: $\left(\dfrac{x_1+x_2}{2}, \dfrac{y_1+y_2}{2}\right)$

The midpoint between (–2, 7) and (4, 3) is

$$\left(\frac{-2+4}{2}, \frac{7+3}{2}\right)=\left(\frac{2}{2}, \frac{10}{2}\right)$$
$$=(1, 5)$$

The distance between two points is a single number, while the midpoint between two points is a point, represented by an ordered pair.

Finding meaning in intersecting graphs

Because every point on the graph of an equation represents an ordered pair that is a solution to the equation, a point on two different equation graphs is a solution to both equations. Therefore, when two graphs intersect, their point of intersection represents a solution to both graphs' equations. The following graph represents the equations $x + y = 7$ and $2x - y = 8$. They intersect at (5, 2), so (5, 2) is the solution to both equations. In other words, if you put 5 in for *x* and 2 in for *y* in either equation, you get an equation that is true.

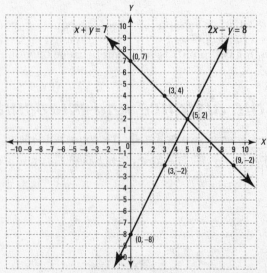

© John Wiley & Sons, Inc.

Transforming coordinate plane figures

Points on the coordinate plane can be the vertices of figures such as triangles and quadrilaterals.

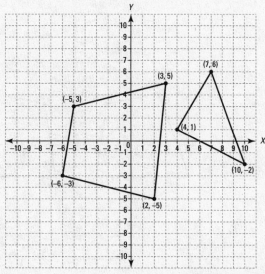

© John Wiley & Sons, Inc.

The figures can be altered in various ways by changing the locations of their vertices. Such changes are called *transformations.* Four major types of transformations can be covered on the Praxis Core exam. One type of transformation is a *translation,* which involves simply moving the figure from one location to another. Translating a figure involves moving it a number of units horizontally and a number of units vertically. The number can, of course, be 0 for one of the changes.

In the following graph, a triangle has vertices (–2, –3), (0, 0), and (4, –5). If it is translated 3 units left and 2 units up, 3 is subtracted from each *x*-coordinate and 2 is added to each *y*-coordinate to get the coordinates of the vertices of the new triangle. Thus, the new vertex coordinates are (–5, –1), (–3, 2) and (1, –3).

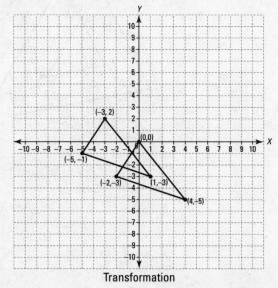

Transformation

© John Wiley & Sons, Inc.

Reflections involve flipping figures over an axis and creating new images that are like mirror reflections. To reflect a figure over the *x*-axis, change the *y*-coordinates of its points to their opposites. If the figure is a polygon, changing the vertices is enough. To reflect a figure over the *y*-axis, change the *x*-coordinates of the points to their opposites to get the new points. The following graph shows a reflection of a quadrilateral over the *y*-axis.

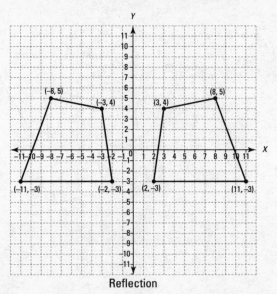

Reflection

© John Wiley & Sons, Inc.

Dilations are simply changes in the sizes of figures. To dilate a figure by a certain amount, multiply both coordinates of the points by the same number. The triangle in the graph that follows is dilated to 3 times its original size. This is achieved by multiplying all of its vertex coordinates by 3 to get the new coordinates.

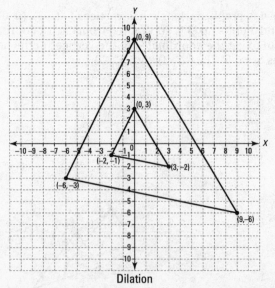

Dilation

© John Wiley & Sons, Inc.

Rotations involve the moving of figures along circular paths while the distance between every point and the center of the circular path stays the same. The types of rotations you are likely to see on the Praxis Core exam are 180° and 90° around the origin. Both are counterclockwise rotations. To rotate a figure 180° around the origin, get the opposite of each coordinate. Those will be the new coordinates. To rotate 90° around the origin, switch the coordinates of each point and get the opposite of the resulting *x*-coordinate. In the following figure, a line segment is rotated 90° and 180° about the origin.

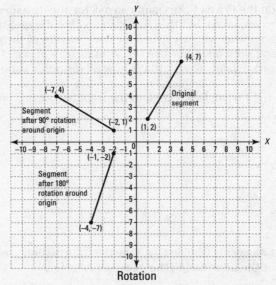

Rotation

© John Wiley & Sons, Inc.

Touching on Right Triangles

You can expect to see some questions about right triangles on the Praxis Core exam. A *right triangle* is a triangle with one right angle. A triangle can have no more than one right angle because the sum of the angles is 180°, and two right angles meet that number, not allowing for a third angle. The two sides of a right triangle that form the right angle are the *legs,* and the side across from the right angle is the *hypotenuse*.

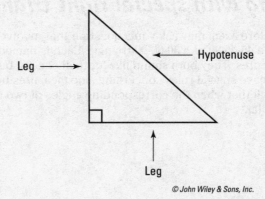

© John Wiley & Sons, Inc.

Knowing what Pythagoras discovered

Pythagoras was a Greek philosopher and mathematician who discovered a principle that became known as the Pythagorean theorem, which states that the sum of the squares of the two legs of a right triangle is equal to the square of the hypotenuse. The theorem is often represented by the equation $a^2 + b^2 = c^2$, where a and b are the measures of the legs of a right triangle and c is the measure of the hypotenuse.

Questions on the Praxis Core exam can ask for the measure of the hypotenuse when both leg measures are given, but they can also involve the measures of the hypotenuse and one leg being given when you are asked for the measure of the other leg. To determine the answer to any such question, use the formula $a^2 + b^2 = c^2$, fill in the known values, and solve for the unknown value. Really, that's how all formulas should be used.

If a leg of a right triangle is 3 cm and the hypotenuse is 5 cm, what is the measure of the other leg?

(A) 16 cm

(B) 8 cm

(C) 2 cm

(D) 4 cm

(E) 15 cm

The correct answer is Choice (D). Take the information you know, plug it into the theorem, and solve for the information the question asks for:

$$a^2 + b^2 = c^2$$
$$3^2 + b^2 = 5^2$$
$$9 + b^2 = 25$$
$$b^2 = 16$$
$$b = 4 \text{ cm}$$

If a geometric figure is described but not illustrated, draw the figure so you have a visual representation. That will make working the problem easier.

Working with special right triangles

The Praxis Core exam may ask you a question that involves one of two types of special right triangles — a 45-45-90 or a 30-60-90 triangle. Each is named after the combination of angle degree measures. They both sound like football cheers, but that wasn't the original idea. Both types have special rules concerning side measures because every example of each is similar. Recall that when the corresponding angles of two triangles are congruent, the triangles are similar.

All 45-45-90 triangles are *isosceles,* which means they have two congruent sides. A 60-60-60 triangle is *equilateral,* which means all three of its sides are congruent. All 45-45-90 triangles are similar, all 30-60-90 triangles are similar, and all 60-60-60 triangles are similar. However, 60-60-60 triangles are not right triangles. A right triangle has one 90° angle.

For every 45-45-90 triangle, the two legs are congruent because the angles opposite them are congruent. The hypotenuse is always $\sqrt{2}$ times the measure of a leg.

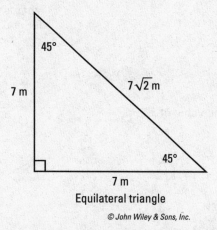

Equilateral triangle

© John Wiley & Sons, Inc.

For every 30-60-90 triangle, the hypotenuse measure is twice that of the shorter leg (which is opposite the 30° angle), and the longer leg is $\sqrt{3}$ times the measure of the shorter leg.

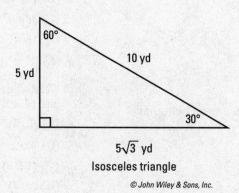

Isosceles triangle

© John Wiley & Sons, Inc.

Practice Questions about Geometry

These practice questions are similar to the geometry questions that you'll encounter on the Praxis.

1. The hypotenuse of a 30-60-90 triangle is 12 meters. What is the measure of the longer leg?

   (A) $6\sqrt{3}$ meters

   (B) 24 meters

   (C) $6\sqrt{2}$ meters

   (D) 6 meters

   (E) $12\sqrt{2}$ meters

2. In the diagram, what is the value of x?

   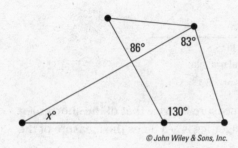

   © John Wiley & Sons, Inc.

   (A) 86°

   (B) 130°

   (C) 24°

   (D) 44°

   (E) 50°

3. What is the circumference of a circle that has an area of 25π cm²?

   (A) 5 cm

   (B) 12.5 cm

   (C) 12.5π cm

   (D) 10π cm

   (E) 10 cm

4. The following figure is composed of a cylinder with a height of 6 feet and a cone with a height of 6 feet. The cylinder and the cone share a base that has a radius of 3 feet. What is the volume of the figure the cylinder and cone compose?

   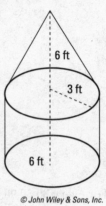

   © John Wiley & Sons, Inc.

   (A) 108π ft³

   (B) 72π ft³

   (C) 36π ft³

   (D) 18 ft³

   (E) 36 ft³

5. What is the midpoint between (8, 6) and (4, 2)?

   (A) (5, 5)

   (B) $4\sqrt{2}$

   (C) (12, 8)

   (D) (4, 4)

   (E) (6, 4)

Answers and Explanations

Use this answer key to score the practice geometry questions in this chapter.

1. **A. $6\sqrt{3}$.** The hypotenuse is 12, and the shorter leg is half that measure, or 6. The longer leg is the shorter leg measure times $\sqrt{3}$, so the measure of the longer leg is $6\sqrt{3}$. Choices (C) and (E) involve the use of $\sqrt{2}$, which is part of a formula for the measure of the hypotenuse of a 45-45-90 triangle. Be careful. Choices (B) and (D) can result from careless errors involving the given information.

2. **D. 44°.** The triangle that has an angle measure of $x°$ has an angle that is a vertical angle to an 86° angle, and vertical angles are congruent. The third angle of the same triangle is supplementary to a 130° angle because they form a linear pair, so that third angle is 50°. The sum of 86 and 50 is 136. The interior angle sum of a triangle is 180°, and 180° − 136° = 44°. Therefore, x is 44°. The other choices can result from using false principles involving the measurements in the diagram.

3. **D. 10π cm.** To solve this problem, you must use what you know to find the value of the radius, which is needed for the circumference formula. Because the area of a circle is πr^2, $r^2 = 25$. That means $r = 5$. The circumference of a circle is $2\pi r$. So $2\pi(5) = 10\pi$. The other choices can result from misuse of operations involved in the necessary steps.

4. **B. 72π ft³.** To solve this problem, you have to find the volumes of the separate shapes and add them together to get the volume of the overall shape. The volume of a cylinder is $\pi r^2 h$, and the volume of a cone is $\frac{1}{3}\pi r^2 h$. $\pi(3)^2(6) + \frac{1}{3}\pi(3)^2(6) = 54\pi + 18\pi = 72\pi$ ft³. Remember to multiply by $\left(\frac{1}{3}\right)$ when finding the volumes of cones and pyramids.

5. **E. (6, 4).** The midpoint between two points is $(\frac{x_1+x_2}{2}, \frac{y_1+y_2}{2})$, or the average of the x-coordinates and the average of the y-coordinates separated by a comma. The average of 8 and 4 is 6, and the average of 6 and 2 is 4, so the midpoint is (6, 4). The other choices can result from applying the wrong formula or errors involved in using the midpoint formula. Remember that a midpoint is a point, not a distance.

Chapter 7

Pinning Down Statistics and Probability

. . . .

. . . .

*T*he probability of you becoming a statistician after you finish this chapter is about one out of infinity; that is, it's not very likely to happen. Statistics is the study of simple, real-life facts and figures — like the number of students who passed or failed a math quiz or the number of people who access Facebook on their cellphone versus their computer. Statistical data can often be thought of as data that is analyzed, averaged, and displayed in tables and graphs.

The review in this chapter also focuses on probability, which deals with how likely something is to happen. So we can easily say that you are likely to be asked to solve probability problems on the Praxis Core exam, given that we know that there are at least 11 real-life questions on the exam that deal with statistics and probability.

Representing Data

It's time to plan a date with a collection of lots of pieces of information called *data*. On your date, you'll find that data is honest, true-life, and based on facts of everyday life. A collection of data is known as a *data set*.

As you get familiar with data, make a point of looking for patterns within the data. Looking for patterns allows you to predict what new data may come later on and then use it to make important real-life decisions.

For the Praxis Core exam, you need to become familiar with many ways to display or represent your data. Using lists, tables, graphs, charts, and plots to represent data is a surefire way to make sure you aren't tricked by the data. These methods of organizing data can also help you see patterns more readily. In the sections that follow, you become skilled at dissecting and interpreting different types of data representations.

Tables

When you have gobs of data about a particular subject, you can sort, analyze, and display your data in a table. Tables only work if you have at least two sets of data to be organized into columns and rows.

When working with tables, make sure to pay attention to the title of the table; it helps you understand what data to analyze. Next, notice the column and row titles.

In the following table, the data for the types of flowers and the number of each type of plant in Mary's flower bed are listed. Make sure to read your question carefully and dissect the data accordingly.

Which ratio compares the number of rose plants to the number of daffodil plants?

Mary's Flower Bed

Type of Flower	Number of Plants
Roses	8
Tulips	10
Daffodils	12
Total	**30**

© John Wiley & Sons, Inc.

(A) 3:2

(B) 2:3

(C) 4:3

(D) 5:6

(E) 3:4

The correct answer is Choice (B). The ratio of roses to daffodils is 8:12; when simplified, the ratio is 2:3. The Praxis Core exam will expect answers in the most reduced form.

Bar graphs and line graphs

A bar graph uses the length of vertical or horizontal bars to represent numbers and compare data. Bar graphs are good to use when your data is in categories. Bar graphs must contain a title, axis labels for the horizontal and vertical axis, scales, and bars that represent numbers.

The following bar graph shows the number of canned goods collected by homerooms at Cardozo Middle School.

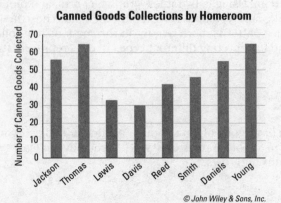

© John Wiley & Sons, Inc.

Mr. Smith's homeroom collected more cans than how many other homerooms?

(A) 3

(B) 4

(C) 5

(D) 6

(E) 7

The correct answer is Choice (A). Use the graph to compare the number of cans collected by each homeroom. According to the length of the vertical bars, Mr. Smith's homeroom collected more cans than Mr. Lewis, Mr. Davis, and Mrs. Reed's classes.

Line graphs are graphs that show data that is connected in some way over a period of time. Suppose you're preparing for a statistics test and each day you take a short, online quiz to see how you're progressing. These are the results:

Day 1	30%
Day 2	20%
Day 3	50%
Day 4	60%
Day 5	80%

After you've created a table from your results, display them in a line graph. You can then decide, based on your progress on the practice quizzes, how likely you are to pass your statistics test. What trends do you see in the following graph?

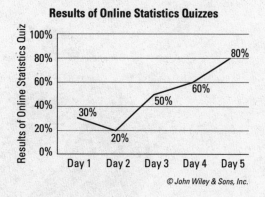

© John Wiley & Sons, Inc.

The graph indicates that as the days of practicing the online quizzes increase, your score increases; so you will, more than likely, pass your statistics test.

Pie charts

Are you ready for a slice of pie? Pie charts are also known as circle graphs. These graphs focus on a whole set of data that is divided into parts. To create a pie chart, follow these steps:

1. **Record the data in table format.**

2. **Convert each data value (the raw number) into a fraction.**

   Use the data value for the numerator and the total for the denominator.

3. **Convert the fraction to a decimal.**

   Divide the numerator by the denominator.

4. **Convert the decimal to a percent.**

   Move the decimal point two places to the right and add a percent symbol.

5. **Multiply the percent by 360 to get the number of degrees for that slice of your pie chart.**

6. **Display all the slices together in the pie chart.**

The following table shows the conversion of raw data to information that can be used to create a pie chart. The resulting pie chart is shown in the example question.

Favorite Fruit of 170 People					
Type of Fruit	Number	Fraction	Decimal	Percent	Degrees
Apples	45	$\frac{45}{170}$	0.26	26%	95
Bananas	20	$\frac{20}{170}$	0.12	12%	42
Strawberries	50	$\frac{50}{170}$	0.29	29%	106
Peaches	55	$\frac{55}{170}$	0.32	32%	116
Total	170	$\frac{170}{170}$	0.99*	99%*	360

*Due to rounding, amounts total less than 100 percent.

© John Wiley & Sons, Inc.

When reading a pie chart, the larger the value, the larger the piece of pie!

Use this graph to answer the following questions.

Favorite Fruit

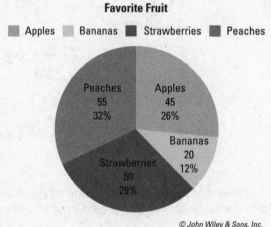

© John Wiley & Sons, Inc.

What are the two favorite fruits of the people surveyed?

(A) Strawberries and apples

(B) Peaches and strawberries

(C) Peaches and apples

(D) Strawberries and bananas

(E) Peaches and bananas

The correct answer is Choice (B). Out of 170 people, 55 chose peaches. When $\frac{55}{170}$ is converted to a decimal, it becomes 0.32 or 32%. Out of the same 170 people, 50 chose strawberries. When $\frac{50}{170}$ is converted to a decimal, it becomes 0.29, or 29%. These are the two largest pieces of the pie.

What percentage of the people liked strawberries and bananas?

(A) 53%

(B) 59%

(C) 41%

(D) 61%

(E) 47%

The correct answer is Choice (C). Out of 170 people, 50 chose strawberries. When $\frac{50}{170}$ is converted to a decimal, it becomes 0.29 or 29%. Out of the same 170 people, 20 chose bananas. When $\frac{20}{170}$ is converted to a decimal, it becomes 0.12, or 12%. Adding these percentages together, 29% + 12% = 41%.

Stem-and-leaf plots

A stem-and-leaf plot blossoms into a useful graph when analyzed properly. You usually use this type of graph when you have large amounts of data to analyze. You can analyze data sets such as classroom test results or scores of the basketball team using a stem-and-leaf plot.

Based on place value, each value in your data set is divided into a stem (tens) and leaf (ones). Draw a vertical line to separate the stem from the leaf. The leaf is always the last digit in the number. The stem represents all other digits to the left of the leaf. To divide 105 into stem-and-leaf format, you draw a line to separate the stem from the leaf, 10| 5 , which indicates a stem of 10 and a leaf of 5.

Say you have the following numbers:

50, 65, 65, 60, 50, 50, 55, 100, 55

The first step is to arrange your data in least to greatest order, as follows:

50, 50, 50, 55, 55, 60, 65, 65, 100

Now arrange these numbers vertically in a table:

Stem	Leaf
5	0
5	0
5	0
5	5
5	5
6	0
6	5
6	5
10	0

© John Wiley & Sons, Inc.

This arrangement allows you to quickly identify your stems. Your stems in the data set are 5, 6, and 10. You have five data values in the list in the 50s: 50, 50, 50, 55, and 55. The leaves that go along with the 5 stem are 0, 0, 0, 5, and 5. You have three data values in the 60s: 60, 65, and 65. The leaves that go with the 6 stem are 0, 5, and 5. Finally, you have one leaf with a data value of 0 to accompany the stem of 10.

Following is the stem-and-leaf plot of the data set. Make sure to give your stem-and-leaf plot a title and a key.

Math Test Results	
Stem	**Leaf**
5	0 0 0 5 5
6	0 5 5
10	0

Key: 5 0 means 50

© *John Wiley & Sons, Inc.*

When using a stem-and-leaf plot, you can quickly identify the least and greatest values in the data set (50 and 100), calculate the range (100 – 50 = 50), and calculate the median or middle number (55).

The results from Mrs. Davis's math test follow. Use the stem-and-leaf plot to answer the following questions.

Math Test Results	
Stem	**Leaf**
5	0 0 5 5
6	0 5
7	0
8	5 5 5
9	0 0 0 5 5

© *John Wiley & Sons, Inc.*

In which interval did most students score?

(A) 50–59

(B) 60–69

(C) 70–79

(D) 80–89

(E) 90–99

The correct answer is Choice (E). Five students scored in the 90s on the test.

What is the median score on the math test?

(A) 60

(B) 65

(C) 70

(D) 85

(E) 90

The correct answer is Choice (D). There are 15 students who took the exam with these scores: 50, 50, 55, 55, 60, 65, 70, 85, 85, 85, 90, 90, 90, 95, 95. The score in the center of the data set is 85. This is the median (for more on finding the median, see the later section "Measuring arithmetic mean, median, or mode").

What is the mode of the data set?

(A) 85

(B) 55

(C) 90

(D) 95

(E) 50

The correct answer is Choice (C). Three students scored a 90 on the test. The score in the data set that occurs the most is 90. This is the mode (for more on finding the mode, see the later section "Measuring arithmetic mean, median, or mode").

Box-and-whisker plots

Box-and-whisker plots, also known as box plots, show different parts of a data set using a line of numbers that are in order from least to greatest.

A box-and-whisker plot allows you to divide your data into four parts using *quartiles*. The *median,* or *middle quartile,* divides the data into the lower half and an upper half (for more on finding the median, see the later section "Measuring arithmetic mean, median, or mode"). The median of the lower half is *the lower quartile*. The median of the upper half is the *upper quartile*. Your data set will contain the following five parts:

- **The least value:** The smallest value in the data set.

- **The lower quartile:** The median of the lower half of the data set.

- **The median:** The median or middle quartile. This divides the data into a lower half and an upper half. The median is the number in the center. If two numbers are in the center, find the average of the two middle values.

- **The upper quartile:** The median of the upper half of the data set.

- **The greatest value:** The largest value in the data set.

The following diagram shows how data is dissected using a box-and-whisker plot. To create a box-and-whisker plot, follow the diagram below.

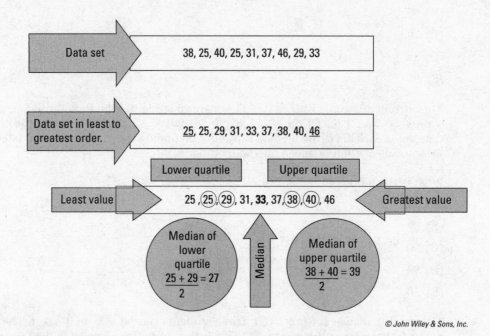

© John Wiley & Sons, Inc.

The diagram begins with the *data set*. The data set is then put in least to greatest order. Underline the *least value* and the *greatest value* in the data set. Then find the *median* of the entire data set. Remember, when calculating the median, if there are two values in the center of a data set, find their average. The median divides the data set into the *lower quartile* and the *upper quartile*. You must then find the median of the lower quartile and the median of the upper quartile.

After dissecting the data into the five values, graph the five values on a number line. Draw a box from the median of the lower quartile to the median of the upper quartile. Draw a vertical line inside the box at the median. The lines connecting the least and greatest values to the box are called the *whiskers*. You can think of your data in four quartiles, known as Q1, Q2, Q3, and Q4. Each quartile represents about 25 percent of the data set.

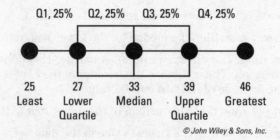

© John Wiley & Sons, Inc.

Use the following graph to answer the following questions.

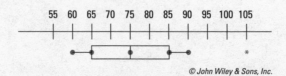

© John Wiley & Sons, Inc.

This box plot indicates the scores from yesterday's math test. How many students did not get above 65%?

(A) 25%

(B) 85%

(C) 75%

(D) 50%

(E) 65%

The correct answer is Choice (A). The box-and-whisker plot indicates that the lowest score on the test was 60. The median of the lower quartile is 65, so 25 percent of the students scored lower than 65.

What is the median test score from yesterday's math test?

(A) 25%

(B) 85%

(C) 75%

(D) 50%

(E) 65%

The correct answer is Choice (C). The median of the box-and-whisker plot is indicated by a line drawn through the center of the box. The value graphed at this point is 75.

Venn diagrams

"Venn" you need to picture relationships between different groups of things, use a Venn diagram. A *Venn diagram* is an illustration where individual data sets are represented using basic geometry shapes such as ovals, circles, or other shapes. Simply draw and label two or more overlapping circles to represent the sets you're comparing. The sets overlap in an area called the *intersection*. When an item is listed in both sets, it goes in the intersection. If an item doesn't fit in either set, it falls outside the circles.

Use the following graph to answer the following questions.

Favorite Sports of 50 Students

Football   Basketball

2   23   5   20

© John Wiley & Sons, Inc.

Football is the favorite sport of how many students in the Venn diagram?

(A) 23

(B) 48

(C) 25

(D) 50

(E) 5

The correct answer is Choice (A). In the Venn diagram, 23 students picked football as their favorite sport.

Football and basketball are the favorite sports of how many students?

(A) 25

(B) 23

(C) 48

(D) 2

(E) 5

The correct answer is Choice (E). Five students in the Venn diagram like football and basketball.

How many students do not like football or basketball?

(A) 25

(B) 23

(C) 5

(D) 48

(E) 2

The correct answer is Choice (E). There are two students who did not fall inside the Venn diagram; therefore, they like neither football nor basketball.

Scrambling around scatter plots

If you want to determine the strength of your relationship, use a scatter plot. Scatter plots are a graphical representation of two variables determining whether a positive, a negative, or no correlation exists. Data from two sets are plotted as ordered pairs (*x, y*). You can draw three conclusions from scatter plots:

✔ If the coordinates are close to forming a straight line that rises up from left to right, then a positive relationship or correlation exists.

✔ If the coordinates form a straight line with one variable increasing as the other decreases, then a negative relationship or correlation exists.

✔ If the coordinates don't form a line and are all over the place, then *no relationship or correlation exists!* Hence, the name scatter plot.

The three types of correlations are shown below.

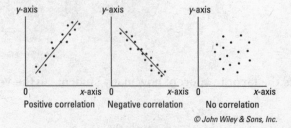

Positive correlation   Negative correlation   No correlation

© John Wiley & Sons, Inc.

Make sure to give your plot a title and make sure to label your axes when you create a scatter plot.

Loitering around line plots

If you want to see your mode (the value that occurs the most) pop up quickly, use a line plot. A line plot, also known as a dot plot, allows you to identify the range, mode, and outliers in your data set. Follow these simple steps:

1. **Put your data in order from least to greatest.**

2. **Arrange your data on a number line.**

3. **Mark each value in the data set with an *x* or a dot.**

Using the following line plot, what is the mode of the data set?

Mrs. Tates' test scores: 50, 50, 60, 90, 90, 50, 70, 90, 80, 90

Line Plot of Mrs. Tates' Test Scores

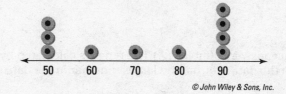

© John Wiley & Sons, Inc.

(A) 50

(B) 60

(C) 70

(D) 80

(E) 90

The correct answer is Choice (E). The score of 90 appears in the data set the most.

Analyzing Data

After you've created a visual representation of your data, the next phase is to analyze and interpret the data by making comparisons; calculating the mean, median, and mode; determining the range; and finding out what variables affect your data set. After you analyze, interpret, and display the pieces of information, you can use them to make important decisions. This section prepares you to analyze data sets in a variety of ways.

Combing through comparisons

When you're working data analysis problems on the Praxis Core exam, it's wise to comb your data set, looking for the smallest and largest values to calculate the range. Then you need to find the mean, median, or mode — or *measure of central tendency* — of the data set. A measure of central tendency tells you where the middle of a data set lies. You have to be clear on which measure is appropriate for the data you have. Then you can use your data analysis to make important, real-life decisions.

Homing in on the range

When preparing for the Praxis Core exam, you need to know how to calculate the range of a data set. The range is the difference between the largest (maximum) and smallest (minimum) values in your data set. If your range is small, most values in the data set are alike; however, if you have a large range, the values in the data set are different from each other. Whether you have 14 or 14,000 pieces of data in your set, simply take the difference between the largest and smallest values in the data set to find the range.

Brit went bowling with her classmates. She bowled five games with the following scores: 193, 190, 149, 146, and 183. What is the range of her bowling scores?

(A) 47

(B) 46

(C) 149

(D) 44

(E) 3

The correct answer is Choice (A) The range is calculated by subtracting the smallest number in the data set from the largest number in the data set: $193 - 146 = 47$.

Measuring arithmetic mean, median, or mode

Who do you think is the most popular in the measures of central tendency clique: mean, median, or mode? The measures of central tendency are all types of averages of data sets. When preparing for the Praxis Core exam, you need to be able to decide the value of a data set that best describes the entire data set.

Mastering the mean

For a data set with no high or low numbers, the mean, also known as the average, is the most popular measure of central tendency. To find the mean of a set of values, use the following formula:

$$\frac{\text{Sum of all values in the data set}}{\text{Number of values in the data set}}$$

Marking the middle with the median

When the data set has a couple of values higher or lower than the others, the median is the most popular measure of central tendency. When finding the median of a data set, you must first ensure that the data is in order from least to greatest. Use the crossout method to mark out values until you get to the center. If two values are left in the center, take the average of them.

$$\text{Median} = \cancel{45}, \cancel{65}, \cancel{65}, 70, 75, \cancel{77}, \cancel{80}, \cancel{250} = 70 + 75 = 145 \div 2 = 72.50$$

Making the most of the mode

When your data set is filled with the same data values, then the mode wins as the most popular value. In the following data set, the mode is 23 because it appears most often.

15, 20, **23**, **23**, **23**, 40, 45, 60

The table below contains Kelsey's Face Time usage for 1 week (in minutes).

Amount of Daily Face Time Usage for 1 Week (in minutes)						
Sun	Mon	Tue	Wed	Thur	Fri	Sat
65	250	75	65	45	77	80

© John Wiley & Sons, Inc.

Find the mean, median, and mode of the data set. Write your answers in the boxes provided. Which measure best describes the amount of time spent on Face Time?

Mean

Median

Mode

The mean (93.85) and mode (65) are close to only a few data points; the median (75) is close to most data points, so the best measure of central tendency for this data set is the median. You can say that Kelsey spends an average of 75 minutes per week on Face Time. Here's how to calculate each of the three measures of central tendency:

Mean $= 45 + 65 + 65 + 75 + 77 + 80 + 250 = 657 \div 7 = 93.85$

Median $= 45, 65, 65, 75, 77, 80, 250 = 75$

Mode $= 65$, because it appears most frequently in this set of data.

Variably affecting data

When working with data analysis, variables often affect the data. Did you ever have a test score that was exceedingly better or worse than your other scores? In statistics, this piece of data is known as the *outlier*, which drifts way out at the end of a data set. Outliers can affect how your data is interpreted.

You can tell whether your data set has outliers by putting your numbers in least to greatest (ascending) order. Check each number to see whether it's much less or much greater than the next number.

The following data set contains the math test scores for a student. Plot the data set on a line plot.

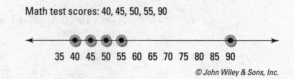

Math test scores: 40, 45, 50, 55, 90

© John Wiley & Sons, Inc.

Once you see the test data displayed on a line plot, you can see that 90 is a loner, or outlier, in the data set. To decide what best measure of central tendency to use, calculate the mean, median, and mode of the data set.

Scrutinizing samples for data analysis

What if you were collecting data about the favorite food of middle school students? It would be difficult to interview every student in the middle school group or population, so you'd take a *sample*, which is a depiction of the entire group.

The sample you choose must represent the whole group or population. You wouldn't collect data from only the football team or the math classes. An ideal sample would be to randomly select five students from each class period or to randomly select students from the school directory. From the sample, you can infer data about the entire population. If 10 kids out of 100 like pizza for lunch, then 100 kids out of 1,000 probably like pizza for lunch too.

A *random sample* is a select group that represents the entire population. If you're studying middle school students, you can't just survey your friends at middle school. You need to randomly select students from the middle school directory — including all ages and all grades taught at the school.

Interpreting linear models

You can use data in a table to make a graph. The graph and the table will both present the same data but in different ways. If the graph of the values in a table forms a line when graphed, then it can be called a *linear function*. First graph the data points, and then connect the points with a line. If you can connect them with a line, the relationship is linear.

Linear models simply use patterns to explore relationships. Say that the honor society is selling mugs as a fundraiser. The daily sales and income are recorded in a table. The mugs sell for $10 each.

First, identify your input (*x*) and output (*y*) variables. The income or money you make depends on how many mugs are sold, so the number of mugs you sell will determine how much money you make.

Next, record the mug sales in a table.

Number of Mugs Sold (x)	Income (10x)
1	10
5	50
10	100
30	300

Then plot your table value as a line graph. Now you're ready to analyze your data. Make sure you study the shape of the graph below; use your finger to trace the *x* and *y* values. You can say that the number of mugs sold (*x*) determines the income (*y*), or $10*x* = *y*. The more mugs sold, the more income made. The table shows if you sell one mug, you'll make $10; if you sell ten mugs, you'll make $100.

© John Wiley & Sons, Inc.

Calculating Probability

The review in this section focuses on probability of an event, also known as *P* (event), which deals with how likely something is to occur. You can record the probability of an event as a fraction, decimal, or percent.

A chance action, such as tossing a number cube, is also called an *experiment*. Each observation of the experiment is called a *trial,* and what happens at the end of the trial is the *outcome.* One or more outcomes are called *events*.

When you throw a single die, there are six possible outcomes: 1, 2, 3, 4, 5, or 6. The probability of any one of them occurring is 1/6.

Determining the likelihood of an event

When you throw a single die, there are six sides and six possible outcomes The table below indicates that the even outcomes are half and the not even outcomes are half; therefore, the likelihood of rolling an even number is as likely to happen or not — you have a 3/6 (read, three in six) or 50-50 chance.

Even	*Not Even*
2, 4, 6	1, 3, 5

What is the likelihood that you'll roll a 6 on the single die? When a single die is rolled, either a 6 will be rolled or it won't be rolled. There is only one 6 on the single die, so the likelihood that it will be rolled is 1 out of 6.

Using complements

Are you ready for a complement? The *complement* of an event is the set of all outcomes that are not the event. Analyze the situation that is occurring and find your total possible outcomes.

For example, you have 16 total marbles in a bag, and the marbles are different colors. Write each color as a fraction, decimal, or percent of the total number.

Blue: 8/16   **Red:** 5/16   **Green:** 2/16   **Black:** 1/16   **Total:** 16/16 or 1

The bag contains eight blue marbles, five red marbles, two green marbles, and one black marble. The probability of randomly picking a blue marble is 8/16. What is the probability of not drawing a blue marble? The probability of not picking a blue marble would be 8/16 or the sum of the remaining marbles in the bag. The (P) of not picking blue is the complement.

Pointing Out Scientific Notation Facts

Scientific notation is a shortcut for writing very large or very small numbers. The decimal point is moved about in such a way as to make the numbers easier to write and read.

The goal is to write the scientific notation number as a product of two factors: The first factor is a number equal to or greater than 1 but less than 10, and the second factor is a power of 10 (also called the *base*). So to write 3,000 in scientific notation, you'd write 3.0×10^3. All the focus is on the decimal point.

Exponents tell you how many times to use the base as a factor. A positive exponent indicates a large number (greater than 1), and a negative exponent indicates a very small number (less than 1, also known as a decimal).

Light travels 1 meter in 0.0000000025 seconds. Write the number in scientific notation.

```

```

The correct answer is 2.5×10^{-9}. Focus on the decimal point. You have to move the decimal point nine places to the right to reach 2.5. Why would you decide to stop the decimal at 2.5? Because that number is between 1 and 10. Write the number in scientific notation as 2.5×10^{-9}. Moving the decimal point to the right indicates a very small number and is written with a negative exponent.

Light travels 18,000,000,000 meters per minute. Write the number in scientific notation.

```

```

The correct answer is 1.8×10^{10}. Focus on the decimal point. Remember, if the decimal point isn't visible in the number, it's found at the end. Your task is to count how many places you have to move the decimal point to get to a number between 1 and 10. The number in the preceding example question written in scientific notation is 1.8×10^{10}.

Practice Questions about Probability and Statistics

These practice questions are similar to the questions about statistics and probability that you'll encounter on the Praxis.

1. There are 9 yellow counters and 15 red counters in a bag. What is the probability of picking a yellow counter from the bag?

    (A) 5/8

    (B) 1/2

    (C) 2/5

    (D) 2/3

    (E) 3/8

2. The following box plot represents the scores from a math test. What is the median of the scores?

    © John Wiley & Sons, Inc.

    (A) 60

    (B) 65

    (C) 75

    (D) 85

    (E) 90

3. There are 9 yellow counters and 15 red counters in a bag. What is the probability of NOT picking a yellow counter from the bag?

    (A) 5/8

    (B) 1/2

    (C) 2/5

    (D) 2/3

    (E) 3/8

4. Find the range, mean, median, and mode for the following data set:

    1, 3, 3, 3, 3, 4, 6, 6, 6, 8, 12

    Range

    Mean

    Median

    Mode

5. What is the median of the math test results?

Math Test Results	
Stem	**Leaf**
5	0 0 0 5 5
6	0 5 5
10	0

    Key: 5 0 means 50

    © John Wiley & Sons, Inc.

    (A) 50

    (B) 55

    (C) 60

    (D) 65

    (E) 100

6. Which of the following represents 57,590,000 in scientific notation?

    (A) 57.59×10^6

    (B) 5.759×10^{-7}

    (C) 57.59×10^{-7}

    (D) 5.759×10^7

    (E) 57.59×10^7

7. Which is the best way to survey a random sample of students from your school about their favorite radio station?

    (A) Survey 5 students in each first-period class.

    (B) Survey 12 students in the band.

    (C) Call 25 friends.

    (D) Survey each student in your math class.

    (E) Survey the football team.

Answers and Explanations

Use this answer key to score the practice statistics and probability questions in this chapter.

1. **E. 3/8.** There are 24 counters in the bag. Nine of the 24 counters, or 9/24, are yellow, which reduces to 3/8.

2. **C. 75.** The median of the box-and-whisker plot is identified by the line in the center of the box, which is plotted at 75.

3. **A. 5/8.** There are 24 counters in the bag. Nine of the counters or 9/24 are yellow and 15 counters, or 15/24 or 5/8, are red.

4. **Range, 11; mean, 5; median, 4; and mode, 3.** Using the data set 1, 3, 3, 3, 3, 4, 6, 6, 6, 8, 12, the range is $12 - 1 = 11$. You find the range by subtracting the smallest data value from the largest.

    The mean $= 55 \div 11 = 5$. You find the mean, also known as the average, by adding the numbers in the data set and dividing the total by the number of items in the data set.

    The median $= 4$. The median is the center or middle number in the data set. If there are two numbers in the center of the data set, find the average of them.

    The mode $= 3$. It is the number that occurs the most frequently in the data set.

5. **B. 55.** Extract the data from the stem-and-leaf plot and highlight the middle number: 50, 50, 50, 55, **55**, 60, 65, 65, 100

6. **D. 5.759×10^7.** 57,590,000 written in scientific notation is 5.759×10^7. Move your decimal point to the left until you reach a number between 1 and 10. It takes 7 places to reach 5.759; therefore, your answer should be 5.759×10^7.

7. **A. Survey 5 students in each first-period class.** Surveying five students in each first period class will give a more diverse sample than the other methods presented in the other answer choices.

Chapter 8

Test-Taking Strategies for Core Math

Mathematical knowledge and practice are very important for taking the Praxis Core exam's math section, but the arsenal you take into battle doesn't have to stop there. Test-taking strategies can make your weapons even more effective. What you know is extremely important, but so is what you do with what you know. This chapter is about making the best of the knowledge you have.

If you decide to use only one bit of advice on test-taking strategies, let it be this: Never stay on a question that looks like it will take an extreme amount of time to answer. This applies to any type of math question. You can write down the number of the question in the hope of going back to it later. Some people get so caught up in a challenge to answer a time-consuming question that they use up time they could have used to answer four or five other questions.

All the Praxis Core exam math questions are worth the same number of points, so make sure you don't treat any one of them as if it's more important than the others. Whether you're asked to solve a simple equation or find the volume of a remaining region of a cone, the question is worth as much as the other 55. Timing is part of the challenge, so use it well.

Using Helpful Shortcuts

Getting answers that are correct on the Praxis Core exam is really important. However, coming up with the right answers isn't your only concern. You must consider something else of major relevance: The exam is timed. You have two hours (120 minutes) to answer 56 problems. Any methods you can use to reduce the time you take to answer questions without sacrificing accuracy will help you. The methods we outline in the following sections are real, and they work. We encourage you to give them a trial run as you take the practice tests in Part V and online.

Solving equations versus determining what must be solved

You will almost definitely have word problems that require setting up and solving algebraic equations when you take the Praxis Core exam. Answering these problems requires more than the ability to solve equations. You also need to determine what information the problem is asking you for, that is, what needs to be solved. You can use a variable to represent the unknown quantity that must be determined.

If the problem has more than one unknown, see whether you can represent the others in terms of the first. For example, if Bob's score in bowling is in question and the problem says that Frank scored 10 points higher than Bob, you can use x to represent Bob's score and $x + 10$ to represent Frank's score.

The next step is to put the algebraic expressions into an equation and solve the equation. The solution to the equation will be the value of the first unknown. Once you know it, you can find the values of any other unknowns by putting the value of the variable for which you just solved into the expressions used to represent the variables for which you have not yet solved.

John is four years older than Adam. John was twice Adam's age 33 years ago. What is John's age now?

(A) 42

(B) 8

(C) 25

(D) 41

(E) 37

The correct answer is Choice (D). The question asks for John's age, so you can make John's age the first unknown and represent it with a variable, such as x. Because John is four years older than Adam, you can represent Adam's age with the expression $x - 4$. The next step is to write an equation with the two expressions. Just translate the information in the word problem into mathematical language. John was twice Adam's age 33 years ago. Their ages 33 years ago can be represented by subtracting 33 from their current ages:

John: $x - 33$

Adam: $x - 4 - 33$

"Twice Adam's age 33 years ago" can be represented by 2 multiplied by 33 less than Adam's current age.

Adam: $2(x - 4 - 33)$

Then set up an equation that shows their ages 33 years ago with John's being twice as much as Adam's:

$x - 33 = 2(x - 4 - 33)$

Notice the direct translation of worded information in that equation. It says exactly the same thing in a different way. The solution to the equation is 41. (For a review of how to solve algebraic equations, turn to Chapter 5.) John's age is therefore 41.

Be extremely careful in making sure you know precisely what question you are being asked. It's not always what you may assume it is. In the preceding example, for instance, you could have been asked Adam's current age or even the sum of John's and Adam's ages. Don't assume that the first unknown is the answer to the question. The need to use caution in identifying the exact question you're being asked is often even greater on geometry questions.

Using estimation and approximation

Estimation is the act of using known information to get a number that is close to the answer to a question although it may not be the actual answer. This can be helpful on the Praxis Core exam because most of the test is multiple choice. When you estimate, you have a good chance of getting the answer right by choosing the one that's closest to your estimate. Because the test is timed, estimation may be handy for a few last answers before time's up.

Estimation can also help you to eliminate choices that are definitely wrong, and it can help you make sure the answer you get is not something beyond the fringe of reason or the result of a miscalculation. However, don't spend too much time estimating for just that purpose. You'll be performing a juggling act with time and caution.

Approximation is using numbers that are very close to numbers given in a problem for the purpose of making calculating easier. This, too, can save you time when time is running short, and it can also help you eliminate wrong answers. If you have to make a wild guess, your chances of guessing the correct choice increase when you can eliminate some of the choices.

When you multiply with irrational numbers in decimal form, you often have to approximate. An *irrational number* is a number that can't be represented as a ratio of two integers. An irrational number in decimal form doesn't terminate or repeat. In other words, the digits after the decimal don't have a pattern and continue infinitely. Because you don't have time to calculate with an infinite number of digits, approximation can often help.

For example, the number 7.32960584965105. . . is an irrational number. You may come across a number like that when you use your calculator. Rounding such a number to four decimal places should be sufficient to get a correct result in almost all cases. Rounding also saves time, and time is precious on the Praxis Core exam.

Using the calculator

An on-screen calculator is provided for you on the math section of the Praxis Core exam. That makes computation easier and saves time over doing calculations on paper. The calculator's keypad includes keys for all the digits, the four basic operations (adding, subtracting, multiplying, and dividing), square roots, making numbers negative, a decimal, parentheses, memory, clearing, transfer display (which can transfer your answers to the answer box on constructed response questions), and, of course, the highly important equal sign. The calculator is also programmed to follow the order of operations. However, you still need to know the order of operations for solving variable equations.

Identifying calculations you can make in your head

We highly encourage caution when making calculations for the Praxis Core exam. That involves writing out work on scratch paper and using the calculator, but only when you actually have time to do those things. You should write and use the calculator even for the calculations you're sure you can do in your head when you're keeping a good pace, though we don't recommend using the calculator for calculations that can come from pure memory.

However, when time becomes a major issue, you need to know what more-complex calculations you can do in your head relatively safely. The first category to consider is problems for which writing and using the calculator don't actually help you figure out the answer. For these calculations, the paper and calculator will only help you avoid careless errors. Suppose you have to calculate 2 + 2. We recommend using paper even for that when you're good on time. Using paper allows you to write out every step of the calculations, better ensuring that you avoid careless errors. When you're way behind time, you should speed up by making such a calculation only in your head. Timing is important, but so is caution.

Make sure you can add and subtract all combinations of two single-digit numbers purely by memory. This will help you add numbers with more than one digit in your head when necessary. For example, if you know that $9 + 8 = 17$, you can quickly conclude that $59 + 8 = 67$. Also, make very sure that you know all the multiplication tables for 2 through 12.

While we believe in writing every step involved in answering a math question, we don't think the calculator should be used for every single calculation. The more you have in your brain's memory, the faster your pace will be.

The art of guessing as a last resort

If time really wears thin on the exam and you only have time to make wild guesses, go ahead and make nothing but wild guesses. A point may come where you don't even have time to estimate, approximate, or do quick calculations in your head. That's when you need to just start hitting answers as fast as you can.

If you make all of your choices randomly, you have some probability of getting all of them right. However, the flip side to that coin is that you have equal probability of getting all of them wrong. Still, you'll most likely get some right if you answer enough of them that way.

We recommend choosing the same option every time. The Praxis Core exam tends to distribute answer choices close to evenly. Because of this, if you pick the third choice every time, you'll almost surely get an answer right if you pick it enough times.

In the examples used in this book, the choices are lettered. That's only for the purpose of being able to easily identify the choices when discussing them. On the actual Praxis exam, the choices are not lettered. They have elliptical figures beside them. With that being the case, you should pick a certain number in the order of choices and stick with it when you're in wild guess mode. You could pick the first choice, second choice, third choice, and so on and stick with it every time. However, if you get a quick enough peek to have any reason at all to think any choice is even slightly better than the others, you should choose that one.

A small number of questions tell you that more than one answer choice may apply. If you notice one of those during a pure guessing phase, you should mark at least two answers of the three or four answer choices presented.

A few of the questions don't have choices presented with them. You should answer those last if you're in a guessing phase. When you get around to guessing on them, see how much time you have left. Quickly look at the problem and give the best guess you can give. If you still have a few more seconds to actually think about the answer, do all of the thinking you have time to do and then give the best answer you can.

Working backward

When you're in doubt about how to answer a math problem by using the conventional calculation methods, you can increase the probability of getting the correct answer by *working backward*. This approach can be used in various situations and in different ways. For example, if an end result is given and you're asked about what was involved in getting the result, you can start at the end and work toward the beginning. This technique can be used for age problems, problems concerning final amounts of money, final locations, and other types of problems. The technique is sometimes the only one that will work.

Robert went for a walk on a trail that runs north and south after getting a ride on a four-wheeler. At the end of his walk, he was 14 miles north of his campsite. He had previously walked 10 miles south, and before that he walked 20 miles north. How far north of his campsite was Robert when he began his walk?

(A) 24 miles

(B) 0 miles

(C) 4 miles

(D) 44 miles

(E) 6 miles

The correct answer is Choice (C). You can answer this problem by using positive and negative numbers and adding them, with north distances being positive and south distances being negative. However, you can also work backward from the final distance and trace Robert's travel back to the beginning of the hike. If Robert was 14 miles north and had previously walked 10 miles south, he was 24 miles from his campsite before the final part of the walk. If he got to that point by walking 20 miles north, he was 20 miles back, which is 4 miles from the campsite. Choice (A) is the distance Robert was from his campsite before changing directions, but not the initial distance. Choice (D) results from adding 20 to 24 instead of subtracting it.

Narrowing Down Answer Choices

You improve your chances of choosing the right answer — and choosing it quickly — by eliminating choices that you know are wrong. This narrows the set of choices to consider and helps lead you to the right answer. We discuss this earlier in this chapter to make a case for increasing the probability of getting the right answer, but another advantage is that it helps lead you to better considerations.

How to eliminate obviously wrong answer choices

If a choice is so outrageous that it couldn't possibly be the correct answer, you should eliminate it from consideration. For example, the length of a rectangle can never be greater than the rectangle's perimeter. A person's age years ago can't be greater than his or her current age. The mean of a set of data can never be greater than the highest number. These are just some examples of impossibilities you can readily notice.

If $3j = 90$, what is the value of j?

(A) 270

(B) 30

(C) 60

(D) 120

(E) 3

The correct answer is Choice (B). You can find the answer by solving the equation.

$$3j = 90$$

$$\frac{3j}{3} = \frac{90}{3}$$

$$j = 30$$

To help ensure you get the correct answer, you can eliminate Choices (A) and (D) because both of those choices are greater than 90. You have to multiply 3 by a positive number to get 90, and no positive number is greater than 3 times itself. Eliminating those choices leaves you with three choices to consider instead of five. Choices (C) and (E) are randomly incorrect.

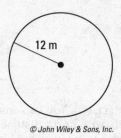

© John Wiley & Sons, Inc.

The radius of the preceding circle is 12 meters. What is the circumference of the circle?

(A) 24π meters

(B) 12π meters

(C) 12 meters

(D) 144π meters

(E) 6π meters

The correct answer is Choice (A). The formula for the circumference of a circle is C = 2πr. Substituting 12 m for r, you get 2π(12 m) = 24π m. You can eliminate Choice (C) right away because neither π nor a decimal number, which would result from multiplying 12 by a decimal approximation of π, is in the answer. Another reason Choice (C) can be eliminated is because the radius of a circle can't possibly equal the circle's circumference. Multiplying by 2π can never be the same as multiplying by 1; 2π is not equal to 1, and it never will be, as far as we know. Choice (B) can be eliminated because multiplying by π is not the same as multiplying by 2π. You can also eliminate Choice (E) because the number that precedes π in a representation of a circumference cannot be less than its radius unless different units are used. Multiplying a positive number by 2π has to result in an increase. The three eliminations leave you with Choices (A) and (D), and that puts you closer to the right answer. Choice (D) is incorrect because it is the area of the circle, not the circumference, except with m instead of m². If the unit were m², you could eliminate it right away because circumference is not properly expressed in square units.

Avoiding the most common wrong answers

Other choices to watch out for and be ready to eliminate are the ones that result from the most common calculation mistakes. Memorizing the rules for all the math topics you'll face on the Praxis is important for avoiding these common mistakes.

For geometry questions, some of the most common mistakes involve getting formulas confused, such as area and circumference. If you have a question about the area or circumference of a circle, you may have an answer choice that gives you the number involved in a measure about which you're not being asked. Be ready to avoid such answers.

Also remember the difference between the interior angle sums of triangles and quadrilaterals. Choices may be the result of using the wrong number. Confusion between supplementary and complementary angles is common, and so is confusion between formulas for surface area and volume. Forgetting that $\frac{1}{3}$ is in the formulas for the volume of pyramids and cones also happens often. (Take a spin through Chapter 6 if you need a refresher on any of these geometry topics.)

As for algebra and number and quantity questions, losing track of the fact that a number is negative is one of the most common mistakes. The distributive property is very frequently used improperly. Remember that the term right before the parentheses is supposed to be multiplied by every term in the parentheses, not just the first one. $5(x + 3)$ is equal to $5x + 15$, not $5x + 3$.

The rules for switching between decimals and percents can be easily confused. Keep in mind that moving a decimal two places to the right is multiplying by 100 and moving the decimal two places to the left is dividing by 100. Dropping a percent is multiplying by 100, and adding one is dividing by 100.

For statistics and probability questions, be careful about confusing mean, median, and mode. People often forget that the median of a set of data can be found only when the numbers are in order. When using scientific notation, be careful about the direction in which you move decimals. Numbers resulting from wrong decimal directions may be in the choices.

Which of the following has the same value as 35.937 percent?

(A) 3,593.7

(B) 3.5937

(C) 0.35937

(D) 35,937

(E) 0.035937

The correct answer is Choice (C). To convert a percent to a decimal number, drop the percent and move the decimal two places to the left. Choice (A) results from dropping the percent and moving the decimal two places to the right. The other choices result from moving the decimal numbers other than two places to the right or left. The lesson here is that Choice (A) can be reached through a very common mistake in converting percents to decimals. You want to avoid such wrong choices. They're lurking, so be ready.

45 17 90 28 17

What is the median of the preceding set of data?

(A) 28

(B) 90

(C) 17

(D) 39.4

(E) 45

The correct answer is Choice (A). When the numbers are in order, the middle number is 28. It is therefore the median. Interestingly, Choice (A) also happens to be the range of the set of data. Hopefully, you didn't reach the correct answer because you mistook median for range. Sometimes mistakes lead to the right answers, but we don't advise counting on that method. Choice (B) is the middle number in the set of data as it is presented, but not when the data is in order. Choice (C) is the mode and also the lowest number. Choice (D) is the mean. Choice (E) is just one of the numbers in the set of data.

Tackling the Constructed Response

Some of the questions on the Praxis Core exam's mathematics section are not multiple choice. You'll be asked to type the answer in a box for this type of question. These are called constructed response questions. You'll encounter only a handful of constructed response questions, but you should be familiar with how they work and what's expected in your answers. Because you won't have the benefit of being able to look at any answer choices, you need to be aware of the requirements for submitting answers in the correct forms.

Tips for preparing responses and answering questions

The first thing to make sure of before you submit a constructed response is that the answer you typed is the answer you actually got. Leaving out a decimal, a digit, π, or something else essential to a correct answer will result in a wrong answer and no points for that question. Figuring out a correct answer is not the final step in a constructed response question. Submitting the correct answer is the only thing that counts.

Also, make sure you're very clear on the instructions. A question might ask something like what measure of an angle is represented by $(2x + 3)°$, in which case you would have to figure out the value of a variable to determine the answer. For such a question, make sure your answer is the measure of the angle and not the value of the variable. That is one example of when paying close attention to the question is necessary.

You also need to be careful about subtle parts of instructions. A question may ask for an exact answer, an answer rounded to the nearest hundredth, or an answer in terms of π. If you're asked to answer in terms of π, your answer should have π in it. That means you do not want to use 3.14 in your calculation. 3.14 is not π; it is a rounded approximation of it. Neglecting to follow the instructions exactly can cause an answer to be incorrect.

Some constructed response questions ask for more than one answer. If you're given such a question, make sure you give all the required answers. People are so used to answering each question with one answer submission on a test that they can easily overlook the need for more than one answer to a constructed response question on the Praxis exam. Again, you need to follow instructions very closely.

Understanding the importance of avoiding careless errors

Careless errors are one of the major obstacles that stand between people and high levels of math success. The problem seems to apply especially to algebra students. To avoid careless errors, you must be cautious in all aspects of working through the math problem. Several methods can be used to defeat this menace:

✓ **Work every step of a problem on scratch paper.** Even if you feel like you can make a calculation correctly in your head, you should work it out completely so you have a visual account of what you are doing. This greatly helps you avoid going in a wrong direction.

✔ **Always be on the lookout for errors.** Try to catch them before they would otherwise happen. Think about how careful surgeons are when they perform surgery. One false move can be tragic. Missing a problem on the Praxis Core exam isn't quite as tragic, but it is unfortunate. Be careful and aware of potential mistakes, just like a surgeon.

✔ **Talk problems out in your head as you work them.** This process adds one more level of attention in addition to thinking about the problems and seeing them worked out on paper.

✔ **Go back over problems if you have time.** If you finish the test before your time runs out, don't pass up the opportunity to review your answers and possibly push up your score. Every minute you can spend reviewing your answers is valuable.

✔ **Be especially careful when working with negative numbers.** They are the number one area for careless errors. If you see a negative sign, think of it as a wet floor sign telling you to be extra cautious.

✔ **Don't assume that not noticing a careless error means you didn't make one.** Careless errors are sneaky. Most of them aren't caught in the act, but the damage they cause is almost always revealed.

Some proper ways of representing answers

The instructions for constructed response questions tell you how you're required to answer them if more than one possibility would otherwise exist. If an answer includes a unit of measurement, you need to submit it. If you're asked to answer something in terms of some kind of unit, variable, or other representation, including it in your answer is a must.

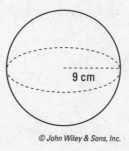

9 cm

© John Wiley & Sons, Inc.

What is the volume of a sphere that has a radius of 9 centimeters? Give your answer in terms of π.

The correct answer is 972π cm^3. The volume of a sphere is $\frac{4}{3}\pi r^3$.

$$\frac{4}{3}\pi(9 \text{ cm})^3 = \frac{4}{3}\pi(729 \text{ cm}^3)$$
$$= 972\pi \text{ cm}^3$$

The unit used for the radius is centimeters, so the unit used for volume must be cubed centimeters (cm^3). The answer to the problem has to involve a number times π and also cm^3. The proper answer is therefore 972π cm^3, not just 972π or the result of multiplying 972 by 3.14. You should force your constructed responses to pass a major inspection that you conduct.

Part III
Refining Your Reading Comprehension Skills

The four types of reading comprehension questions on the Praxis:

- Brief statements followed by one question; these may include visual representation questions
- Short passages of about 100 words, followed by two or three questions
- Long passages of about 200 words, followed by four to seven questions
- Paired passages of about 200 words total, followed by four to seven questions

 Change the way you think about reading passage questions with tips in the free article at www.dummies.com/extras/praxiscore.

In this part . . .

✔ Find out how to crack questions about main ideas, tone, argumentation, and graphs in everything from brief statements to long passages.

✔ Discover how to read test passages in the most efficient way, as well as how to quickly reject wrong answers and distinguish between a good answer and the best one.

Chapter 9

Reading Comprehension: Finding Meaning and Identifying Purpose

· ·

In This Chapter

▶ Surveying the parameters of the reading test

▶ Answering short-passage-based questions about the main idea, author's tone, and vocabulary

▶ Mastering paraphrased, argumentative, and "if" questions related to long passages

▶ Interpreting image-based questions

· ·

You already know that the so-called Praxis "writing" test is really just a grammar test, and that the point of that test is to make sure you have your grammatical rules straightened out. But why is there a Praxis reading test? After all, if you're even taking the test (or reading this book), then you obviously already know how to read. The answer is that, as Sherlock Holmes is so fond of telling people, there's a difference between *seeing* and *observing:* Anyone with a pair of eyes can look around a room and see what is there, but only a clever sleuth will discern the difference between what is an important clue and what is not.

ETS knows perfectly well that you can read all the words in the little paragraphs it gives you. What you're being tested on is whether you can pick out the details that are most important or relevant when it comes to answering a specific question.

Previewing the Praxis Reading Test

An important thing to keep in mind while taking the Praxis reading test is that you aren't being tested on prior or outside knowledge. The subject matter of the passages may be history, science, the arts, or anything at all, but the test isn't a history or a science or an art test. The information you need to answer the question correctly is always contained in the passage that precedes the question. In fact, outside knowledge of a particular subject could even be a *dis*advantage, because you're expected to answer the questions based *solely* on the arguments and details contained within the passages provided. This is why questions typically begin with the phrase *"According to the passage"* or *"According to the author"* (in the rare cases where the question doesn't specify this, remember to answer based solely on the passage anyway). You're expected to comprehend claims and follow arguments about a wide variety of topics; you're being tested on your comprehension ability, not your familiarity with those topics.

Knowing what the test contains

As the previous paragraph mentions, the passages on the test can be about absolutely anything. There's no point in worrying about what the subject matter will be, for a couple of reasons: One, there's no way to predict it, because every test is different, and two, it doesn't — and more importantly, it *shouldn't* — matter. If you walk into the Praxis reading test hoping that there will be passages about *this* or concerned that there may be passages about *that,* you're thinking about the test the wrong way. You want to train yourself to let go of the instinct to react to a passage by thinking "Yay! This one is about elephants, and I like elephants!" or "Oh, no! This one is about submarines, and I don't know the first thing about submarines!" You're only being tested on your ability to follow what the passage is saying, so it really doesn't matter what the passage is about.

The Praxis reading test lasts for 85 minutes (there will be a countdown clock in the upper-right corner of your computer screen to help you manage time), and in that time, you're given 56 multiple-choice questions. The Praxis reading test contains four types of questions, as follows:

- Paired passages of about 200 words total, followed by four to seven questions
- Long passages of about 200 words, followed by four to seven questions
- Short passages of about 100 words, followed by two or three questions
- Brief statements followed by one question; these may include visual representation questions

Technically, we suppose there are different question types on the Praxis reading test, but the way we see it, this is what philosophers would call "a distinction without a difference." Don't be discouraged or intimidated by a big, Goliath passage. Chop down the giant one sentence at a time. Aside from the visual-information questions, which are about charts and graphs, and the paired passages, on which you're expected to compare one author's argument to another's, the rest of the test is the same basic thing over and over: You read a paragraph, and you answer one or more questions about it. Sometimes the paragraph is a little shorter, and sometimes it's a little longer. Sometimes there's only one question about the paragraph, and sometimes there are three or four. But you never have to actually *do* anything differently based on these differences, so there's no point in worrying about them. On every single question, your mission is identical: Read the paragraph and answer the question(s) based on the information it contains. (And as for the intimidation factor of a "long" passage, this paragraph you're reading now contains about 200 words — did it seem terribly "long" to you?)

Applying a general strategy

Like most of the major standardized tests, the Praxis has one section about grammar and another section about reading comprehension. Grammar involves rules that can be memorized; reading comprehension is a bit trickier.

Because grammar is rule-based, even if you think you're bad at grammar, you can improve your skills quickly by memorizing a list of rules and practicing them (even if doing so isn't necessarily the most fun you've ever had).

But how do you study for the reading comprehension section of the test that's not so cut and dried? You apply strategies to correctly answer the questions. A strategy is basically just a rule that depends on circumstances. Whereas a rule says "Do this," a strategy says "*If* this happens, *then* do this." (I give you more details about these *if . . . then* concepts later in the chapter.)

No matter what the question asks, you're faced with exactly four wrong answers and one right answer (except on those "check all that apply" questions, of which there are usually only one or two). Concentrating on this simple idea is the most important step in becoming a whiz at reading comprehension tests. Just keep these points in mind:

- There are always four wrong answers and one right answer.
- A choice that isn't right is wrong, and a choice that isn't wrong is right.

✔ When you select an answer as right, you are *implicitly declaring that the other four are wrong*.

✔ If one of the other choices *isn't wrong*, then it *must be right*, so you should have picked that one instead.

✔ In short, you aren't looking for the *right* answer so much as you are looking for the *not-wrong* answer.

Mastering Short-Passage Questions

The most common type of question in the reading portion of the Praxis exam is what's called a short-passage question. You're given a selection of text usually only three or four sentences in length, and you're asked one question about it. The question is unique to the passage, and the passage is unique to the question.

In the following sections, I outline the types of information the questions focus on and give you pointers on how to figure out what the correct answer is.

Ferreting out the main idea

The most common — and the most straightforward — type of short-passage question is a "main idea" question. The wording of the question is usually along the lines of "The main idea of the passage is . . . " or "The primary purpose of the passage is . . . ", and your mission is to select the answer choice that best completes the sentence. Basically, phrases like "main idea" and "primary purpose" are just fancier ways of asking

✔ "What's this about?"

✔ "What's the point of this?"

✔ "What is this paragraph trying to say?"

Although such questions may seem easy after you've had a bit of practice with them, they can be difficult in the sense of being deceptively simple if you're not used to them. Questions like these try to trick you by making the wrong answers flashier or more attractive than the right one. They may have more details in them, or they may contain more exact words from the passage.

However, you're not looking for the statement about the passage that is the most detailed or the most specific — you're looking for the statement that is *true*. And there will be only one of those. The other four choices, for one reason or another, will be wrong. A common trick that the test-writers use on such questions is to make the right answer so vague or uninteresting that you barely notice it. The wrong answers stand out more. But never forget that all you're trying to do is pick the statement about the purpose of the passage that's *true* (in other words, *not wrong*) — no more and no less. Consider the following example question.

Anyone who paid attention in grade-school science class could tell you that the five classes of vertebrates are mammals, reptiles, amphibians, birds, and fish. For centuries, these categories made sense to scientists because they represented clear distinctions based on what we were able to observe about the animal kingdom. But now that we know more about evolutionary history, the borders between these traditional and visually "obvious" classes are not so clear. A crocodile looks more like a turtle than a penguin, but the common ancestor of the crocodile and the penguin actually lived more recently than did the common ancestor of the crocodile and the turtle.

The primary purpose of the passage is to

(A) explain how penguins evolved from crocodiles.

(B) dispute some recent theories in the field of evolutionary biology.

(C) correct a misconception common in grade-school science curricula.

(D) discuss how a biological concept is more complicated than it looks.

(E) summarize a disagreement about vertebrates between two schools of zoologists.

The correct answer is Choice (D). To understand why Choice (D) is correct, consider: *Does the passage "discuss how a biological concept is more complicated than it looks?"* Yes, it does. In fact, it *indisputably* does — in other words, there is no reasonable way to argue that the passage does *not* do this. So (D) is the right answer because it *cannot possibly be wrong.*

As for the others, by now you've figured out that they're all wrong. But look at what they have in common: All the wrong answers stand out by repeating specifics or key words from the passage — but they also twist those specifics so the statements are no longer true.

Choice (A) is wrong because the passage technically doesn't say that penguins evolved *from* crocodiles; it says that penguins and crocodiles *have a common ancestor.* And even if the passage did say this, it wouldn't be the primary purpose of the passage, because it's only one example given right at the end. The test-writers know that the example given at the end will be fresh in your mind, so they try to get you to jump the gun by making it the first choice!

Choice (B) is wrong because of the verb it uses. The author is indeed talking about "recent theories in the field of evolutionary biology," but he isn't *disputing* them, only *explaining* them (there is no indication that the author disagrees). Always remember that it only takes one false move to make an answer choice wrong!

Choice (C) is wrong because the passage technically never says that the vertebrate classes as explained in schools are incorrect (a "misconception"). The five classes of vertebrates are still mammals, amphibians, reptiles, birds, and fish. The passage discusses some interesting information that *seems as if* it *might lead* to scientists changing those categories somehow *in the future,* but it never says they've done so already!

As for Choice (E), did the passage say or imply anything about "two schools" of zoologists? No. The passage explains that zoologists (biologists that specifically study animals) nowadays have more information than zoologists did in the past, but it never hints at anything about a debate.

Discerning the author's tone and intent

The most common type of reading comprehension question students complain about — even *dread* — is *authorial intent* questions. "I can answer questions about the information in the passage," they say, "but how am I supposed to know what the author *intended* to do? What am I, a mind reader?" But you don't have to be a mind reader to answer this type of question. You answer it the same way you answer any other question on the Praxis reading test — four of the choices are wrong, and you pick the one that isn't.

Look at it this way: If I showed you a picture of a man carrying a guitar, and I asked you what he was on his way to do, you wouldn't know. He might be on his way to band practice, he might be returning the guitar to a friend, or he might be an actor who's portraying a musician in a play. All of those answers are plausible. *However,* if it were a *multiple-choice* question, all you'd have to do is eliminate the four implausible choices and select the one that remains. If the man were on his way to build a porch, he would have a toolbox rather than a guitar; if he were on his way to help put out a fire, he'd have a bucket of water instead of a guitar; and so forth.

That's how you answer an authorial-intent question without needing to be psychic. Four of the choices are implausible, and the right answer is the one that's left!

The frequent complaint by horror-movie fans that their favorite genre is discriminated against at the Academy Awards is difficult to assess. The data would seem to back it up: After all, in the 85-year history of cinema's top prizes, only one horror film — 1991's *The Silence of the Lambs* — has taken home the Oscar for Best Picture. On the other hand, many critically respected scary movies have simply had very bad luck: *Jaws* and *The Exorcist* almost certainly would have won had they not been up against Oscar-magnets *One Flew Over the Cuckoo's Nest* and *The Sting* in their respective years. Some critics have suggested that the "horror movies never win awards" objection is a self-fulfilling prophecy: When a movie wins many prestigious awards, we stop thinking of it as a "horror movie," no matter how scary it is.

In the preceding passage, the author's intent is to

(A) analyze the idea that horror movies are discriminated against at the Oscars.

(B) rebut the assertion that horror movies seldom win prestigious awards.

(C) persuade Academy Awards voters to stop overlooking deserving horror films.

(D) satirize a silly idea about "discrimination" against a certain genre of films.

(E) predict whether more horror movies will win Oscars in the near future.

The correct answer is Choice (A). Why? Because there's no way that the correct answer *can't* be Choice A. The passage is about the idea that horror movies seldom win Oscars, and the author is indisputably analyzing that idea. Remember, "analyze" is just a fancy word for "look at closely and thoroughly." Because this is all that Choice (A) asserts to be the case, there's no room for it to be wrong.

Choice (B) is wrong because the author is not *rebutting* anything (to "rebut" means to "offer a counterargument"). Choice (C) is wrong because the author isn't trying to *persuade* anyone to do anything, only presenting information. Choice (D) is wrong because the author isn't *satirizing* anything ("satirizing" means "making fun of" — did you laugh?). Choice (E) is wrong because the author doesn't say one single word about what may or may not happen in the future, so the passage doesn't contain any *predictions*.

If you have a knack for this sort of thing, you may have noticed that the *initial verb* in each answer choice was pretty much all you needed to eliminate the four wrong answers: The author is not *rebutting, persuading, satirizing,* or *predicting,* but he *is analyzing* (because hey, how could he *not* be analyzing?). And even if you didn't pick up on that, don't despair, because you've picked up on it now.

I certainly don't mean to imply that you should only look at portions of the answer choices. A cardinal rule of multiple-choice test-taking is that you should always read all the choices in their entirety before making a decision. What I'm saying is that sometimes the distinction between the right answer and the wrong ones doesn't depend equally on every single word the answers contain. It only takes one wrong word to make an answer choice wrong, so because Choices (B), (C), (D), and (E) are all wrong based on their first words, those first words are all you need to eliminate them, leaving only Choice (A), which must, therefore, be right.

As for questions about the author's tone, those are basically the same game. The only difference is that you deal with adjectives instead of verbs. For example, whereas the answer choices for an authorial intent question may begin with the words *analyze, rebut, persuade, satirize,* and *predicts,* the answer choices for a question about the author's tone may describe that tone alternately as *analytical, argumentative, persuasive, satirical,* or *speculative.* In either case, you should approach the question in the same way: Eliminate four wrong answers and pick the one that's left.

Putting vocabulary in context

Don't panic! Unlike the SAT, with its infamous vocabulary section in anticipation of which test-takers study endless lists of "big words," the Praxis reading test doesn't contain vocabulary questions in the traditional sense. By this I mean that you won't see any questions that ask you to fill in the blank with the right word and choices that are all fifty-cent words with which the average person is probably unfamiliar. Instead, the Praxis reading test throws you a few *vocabulary in context* questions, wherein five proposed synonyms for a given word from the passage are offered as choices, and you're expected to select the one that works best.

You can answer these questions correctly by using the intuitive method of plugging all five choices into the place of the given word and seeing which one works best. There are just a few things you'll want to be careful of, however, and I go over those right after this sample question.

Though conspiracy theorists like to think of themselves as rebels whose ideas are too shocking to be accepted, the charge leveled at them by mainstream historians is not one of disrespect but rather of wishful thinking: There is almost never any aspect of the event in question that the conspiracy theory is necessary to explain, and it is almost always far less plausible than any number of less titillating theories.

As used in Line 2, "charge" most nearly means

(A) credit

(B) attack

(C) accusation

(D) content

(E) responsibility

The correct answer is Choice (C), simply because *accusation* is the word that works best if you plug it into the passage in place of *charge* (an *accusation* of wishful thinking is leveled at the conspiracy theorists by mainstream historians). None of the other words make anywhere near as much sense as *accusation* when substituted for the word *charge.*

Now, notice that all the answer choices can function as synonyms for the word "charge" in different contexts: To *charge* something is to put it on *credit* if we're talking about shopping; a *charge* is an *attack* if we're talking about a battlefield; *charge* can mean *content* (the noun with the stress on the first syllable, not the adjective with the stress on the second) in physics, like whether a particle contains a positive or a negative charge; and a *charge* can be a *responsibility* in the sense that when you're in charge of something, you're responsible for it.

So the difficulty isn't that you may not know the meaning of the word in question. Rather, the difficulty is that you *do* know the words, all too well! The question is counting on the fact that most people will recognize all the choices as possible synonyms for *charge* under the right circumstances, and it's asking which one works as a synonym for it under *these particular* circumstances.

The trick, then, is to simply ignore the original word and everything you know about it. Don't think about what it means most of the time or attempt to psychoanalyze the question by determining what the "hardest" or "easiest" thing it might mean is. Just pretend that a blank exists instead of the original word and then pick the answer choice that works best in that blank. The original word doesn't even matter!

Looking at Long-Passage Questions

Though the Praxis reading test has many short-passage questions that pair very brief paragraphs with generally broad questions in a 1:1 ratio (that is, one question per passage), some of the test features long-passage questions, wherein several questions are asked about a single passage of two or three paragraphs in length.

Though there are no hard-and-fast rules about which types of questions can or will be asked about which types of passages (in other words, a "main point" or "vocabulary in context" question *could* be asked in reference to a long passage), certain types of questions are more commonly paired with the long passages. A question dealing with support for an argument, for example, is more likely to pop up in reference to a long passage, simply because the short passages are usually too brief to contain much in the way of detailed support for (or attacks on) an argument.

So, although there's no reason why a long passage couldn't contain any of the types of questions discussed in the "Mastering Short-Passage Questions" section, long passages are far more likely than short passages to contain the types of questions discussed in the following sections.

Purpose and paraphrase

If there's one thing you can expect from a series of long-passage questions, it's that there'll be at least one question that identifies a little detail or factoid from somewhere in the passage and asks you "What's the point of this?" The question won't be phrased that way, of course. It will be more drawn out, along the lines of one of the following:

- ✔ When the author writes that "this, that, or the other," he most nearly means that . . .

- ✔ It can be inferred that the author views the "such-and-such" as a type of . . .

- ✔ It is implied that the "blah blah blah" is significant because . . .

Although a "What's the point of this part?" question can be phrased in any number of ways, it always basically comes down to the same thing: The question quotes a portion of the passage (it may be an entire sentence or a small detail comprised of two or three words), and it essentially asks, "Why did the author mention this right here?"

This question type may sound similar to authorial intent and mind reading (see the section "Discerning the author's tone and intent" for more about that), but it's not. Just as with authorial-intent questions, the best method of answering a "What's the point of this part?" question is to eliminate wrong answers until only one choice is left.

In theory, an author may use a particular phrase or reference a particular detail for any number of reasons — just as a piece of writing may be about any topic under the sun or written with any of a host of intentions. In practice, however, Praxis reading questions tend to ask about only a finite number of points that a particular phrase may have. With reference to the types of questions referred to in the preceding bullet points, for example, the most likely explanations are as follows:

- ✔ If a question asks you "what the author most nearly means by" a particular phrase, you're simply being asked for a paraphrase of the quoted text. A good strategy is to rephrase the quotation to yourself in your own words before looking at the choices, and then pick the answer choice that is the closest to what you just said.

- ✔ If a question asks you to "infer how the author views" the quoted detail, the quoted detail is probably a particular example of some general category that is referenced elsewhere in the passage (for example, if the passage as a whole is about mythical animals and the author mentions Bigfoot, he does so because Bigfoot is a type of mythical animal).

- ✔ If the question asks "Why is this significant?" about a quoted detail, the point of the detail is likely that it impacts the meaning of something else. Perhaps it's an important example of some general principle that the passage is trying to prove or explain, or perhaps it's a notable exception to that principle.

Arguments and support

A typical *argumentation/support* question on the Praxis reading test quotes a statement from the passage back to you — usually a detail or factoid — and then asks you why the author made mention of that detail or factoid at that particular juncture. Usually, the detail in question is being used to support a particular assertion, and you're being asked what assertion or viewpoint it's being used to support.

The best analogy here is to the "vocabulary in context" questions (see the earlier section, "Putting vocabulary in context"). Why? Because there's no point in trying to answer the question without looking back at the passage. Just as the word in a Praxis vocabulary question is meaningless out of context, the detail in a Praxis argument/support question is meaningless out of context too.

Just as you should answer the vocabulary questions by plugging the five answer choices back into the passage to see which suggested word works as a synonym, you should approach the argument/support questions by plugging the five answer choices back into the passage to see which suggested concept *relates to* the context surrounding it.

After all, even though a piece of argumentative writing can be about anything, it's still going to be arranged in a logical fashion. You wouldn't offer a detail to support one idea when you're right in the middle of talking about something else!

Getting the hang of "If" questions

"If" questions (so called because they usually begin with "If it were found that . . . ") are like argument/support questions, only instead of asking how a detail from the passage is used to support the author's argument, they ask how a detail or fact that is *not* in the passage *would* affect the author's argument *if* it were found to be true. The point of such questions is that they demonstrate advanced logical thinking — that is, they show that the test-taker fully understands the weight and implications of the argument being made on an abstract level, rather than merely showing that the test-taker comprehends the passage's exact words.

For example, consider a question like "*If* it were found that the defendant in a murder trial has a twin brother, how badly would this weaken the prosecution's case?" The answer would be that the prosecution's case would be weakened if it relied solely on eyewitness testimony but that it would not be weakened if they had fingerprint evidence, because twins look alike but don't have identical fingerprints. Don't worry — questions on the test don't involve outside knowledge; they deal only with the information provided to you in the passage and the questions themselves. (So if, in the example given here, they wanted you to base your answer on the fact that twins don't have identical fingerprints, the passage would tell you this.) This is just an example of what is meant by an "if" question.

If you're good at logical reasoning, you may be excited about answering "if" questions. But if you're not so hot at logical reasoning, rest assured that there are simple, step-by-step ways to eliminate wrong answers to an "if" question, just as there are for the other types of questions.

"If" questions come in two basic types. In the first kind, the question gives you a detail, and the answer choices are possible ways that the detail may affect the argument. Keep in mind that there are only *three* ways in which a given detail can possibly affect an argument:

- ✔ It can support it.
- ✔ It can undermine it.
- ✔ It can have no effect.

However, the question needs to have *five* choices, so the choices can involve questions of degree: "The given fact completely proves the argument," "The given fact supports the argument slightly," "The given fact completely disproves the argument," "The given fact undermines the argument slightly," and "The given fact has no effect on the argument."

"If" questions also often pop up in reference to passages that compare excerpts from two authors, in which case the answer choices may be something like "The given fact supports the author of Passage 1," "The given fact undermines the author of Passage 1," "The given fact supports the author of Passage 2," "The given fact undermines the author of Passage 2," and "The given fact has no effect on the argument of either author."

The second type of "if" question reverses this dynamic. Instead of providing you with a single detail and giving you five choices about how the detail affects the argument, this type of "if" question asks you to identify which of five possible details supports or undermines the argument.

The way to approach such a *reverse if* question is to begin by understanding that a detail has to be *about the same thing* as the argument in order to have any effect on it one way or the other. So your first step is to eliminate all the choices that are unrelated (for example, if the author's argument is that Babe Ruth is the greatest baseball player of all time, then a factoid about basketball's Michael Jordan or football's Jerry Rice neither supports nor undermines it). After you've eliminated the answer choices that have no effect one way or the other (unless you're being asked to identify the detail that has *no* effect on the argument, which is rare, but possible), the next step is to look for points that are either *consistent with* or *mutually exclusive to* the author's viewpoint. A detail or factoid that is consistent with the author's viewpoint (a detail that would or could be true if the author is right) supports that argument, and a detail or factoid that is mutually exclusive to (that is, couldn't be true at the same time as) the author's viewpoint undermines it.

Sample questions for long passages

In this section, you get a chance to practice some "purpose" questions, "support" questions, and "if" questions by looking at a long passage followed by an example of each.

Line "Did King Arthur really exist?" may seem like a fairly straightforward question, but the only possible answer to it is "It depends on what you mean by 'King Arthur.'" Though virtually all adults now understand that the existence of a historical English king by the name of Arthur wouldn't involve his possessing a magical sword called Excalibur or being friends with a
(05) wizard named Merlin, far fewer people realize how tricky it would be to call him a king, or even to call him English.

Every first-millennium history book that makes mention of Arthur indicates that he lived during the late 5th and early 6th centuries and agrees that he played a role in the Battle of Badon in approximately 517. We know that the Battle of Badon was a real event, but what a
(10) historical Arthur might have done besides participate in this battle is anyone's guess. The earliest source that mentions Arthur, the *Historia Brittonum* of 828, links him with Badon but refers to him only as a *dux bellorum*, or war commander — not as a king (the fact that no British historical text composed between 517 and 828 mentions Arthur, even though they all mention Badon, is not terribly convenient for those who wish to believe in his existence).

(15) Indeed, there wouldn't even have been a "king" in that place at that time. The Roman Empire had only recently pulled out of Great Britain, and the power vacuum quickly reduced the region to a free-for-all of warring tribes. If Arthur held political power, it wasn't over very many people, and it certainly wasn't over all England. And as for the English? Ironically, those were the people he was fighting against. The people who spoke the language that became
(20) English and were the ancestors of the people we now think of as English were the Anglo-Saxons, who invaded Great Britain from mainland Europe during Arthur's purported lifetime. Arthur himself, if he existed, was a Briton, one of the original inhabitants who had been conquered by the Romans and subsequently resisted (unsuccessfully) the Anglo-Saxons. The descendants of Arthur's people would be today's Welsh, not the English.

When the author writes "We know that the Battle of Badon was a real event, but what a historical Arthur might have done besides participate in this battle is anyone's guess" (Line 9), he means to say that

(A) Arthur must have existed, because he is linked by multiple sources to a battle we know to have occurred.

(B) Arthur probably did not exist, because if he did, then he would have been mentioned in earlier sources about this battle.

(C) Although it is likely that Arthur fought at Badon, we don't know what rank he held or even which side he fought on.

(D) It is not impossible that there were two Arthurs, one who fought at Badon and another who was a king.

(E) Even if Arthur did exist, we don't know anything about him besides the fact that he supposedly fought in one battle.

The correct answer is Choice (E). The construction "*a* historical Arthur" (as opposed to "*the* historical Arthur") implies uncertainty about whether Arthur existed. Saying that what he "might have done besides participate in this battle is anyone's guess" is another way of saying that his participation in the Battle of Badon is the only fact about Arthur asserted by any of the primary historical texts. The pertinent information here is that Arthur may or may not have existed, and that if he did exist, all we know about him is that he fought at Badon. This is simply a paraphrase question, and Choice (E) is simply a paraphrase of the quoted sentence from the passage.

Choice (A) is wrong because, although both the quoted sentence and the passage as a whole indicate that *if* Arthur existed, *then* he fought at Badon, neither the quoted sentence nor the passage as a whole ever asserts that he *must have* existed.

Choice (B) is wrong because, although the passage as a whole does imply that Arthur's existence is unlikely based on his absence from texts composed shortly after Badon, this fact is not a paraphrase of the quoted sentence, which is what the question is asking for.

Choice (C) is wrong because the passage as a whole establishes which side Arthur fought on at Badon (if he existed), and because, in any case, this question is not what the quoted sentence is addressing (the question is asking for a paraphrase of the quoted sentence).

Choice (D) is wrong because, while it may be possible that there were two Arthurs, this is not what the quoted sentence is addressing, and the question is asking for a paraphrase of the quoted sentence.

When the author describes early 6th-century Britain as "a free-for-all of warring tribes" (Line 17), he most likely does this in order to support the idea that

(A) a historical Arthur almost certainly did not exist.

(B) a historical Arthur would not have spoken English.

(C) the historical Arthur probably didn't hold political power.

(D) a historical Arthur couldn't have been a king.

(E) Great Britain had formerly been controlled by the Romans.

The correct answer is Choice (D). The context makes it clear that what is in question here is the concept of Arthur as a "king." The characterization of early 6th-century Britain as "a free-for-all of warring tribes" is meant to support the assertion that the people were not all ruled by one man.

Choice (A) is wrong because, while the passage as a whole does seem to indicate that the existence of a historical Arthur is unlikely, the context of the quoted phrase concentrates specifically on the implausibility of anyone (be it Arthur or anybody else) being a "king" in any recognizable sense in this particular place and time.

Choice (B) is wrong because, while the passage as a whole definitely establishes that a historical Arthur would not have spoken English, the context of the quoted phrase concentrates specifically on the implausibility of anyone being a "king" in any recognizable sense in this particular place and time.

Choice (C) is wrong because, while the passage as a whole does cast doubt on the idea that Arthur held political power rather than merely a military rank, the context of the quoted phrase concentrates specifically on the implausibility of anyone being a "king" in any recognizable sense in this particular place and time. This section of the passage *doesn't* establish that Arthur couldn't have held *any* political office, just that he wasn't a king.

Choice (E) is wrong because, while the passage does state that Great Britain had been controlled by the Romans, this is not the assertion that the "free-for-all of warring tribes" concept is being used to support; we already know it is true, and the "free-for-all of warring tribes" is what happened afterwards.

Which of the following discoveries, if such a discovery were made, would provide the most compelling new evidence for the existence of a historical Arthur?

(A) A text composed in 855 that definitively calls him a king

(B) A text composed in 925 that states he was born in 482

(C) A text composed in 595 that says he fought at Badon, but was not a king

(D) A monument erected soon after Badon and dedicated to an unidentified king

(E) A painting from 835 that includes a figure clearly labeled as King Arthur

The correct answer is Choice (C). The question doesn't ask you to identify a finding that would support the existence of a historical *King* Arthur, just the existence of Arthur as a historical figure who lived at all (the passage already explains that it was virtually impossible for him to have been a king). The end of the second paragraph establishes that the biggest problem for historians who support the existence of a historical Arthur is that he is not mentioned in any source for about 300 years after he supposedly lived. A source that mentions Arthur and was written closer to his own lifetime would be a marvelous find for those who want to argue his existence (and a text from 595 would be much closer to Arthur's reputed lifetime than any text we currently have).

Choice (A) is wrong because the passage states that the earliest source we have that mentions Arthur is from 828, so a source from 855 would not be earlier (and therefore more persuasive). It would be interesting that it called him a king (because the text from 828 does not), but this wouldn't be very good evidence — it could easily be embellishment based on the 828 text.

Choice (B) is wrong because, while specifics like a birth year are good to have, the sudden assertion of a birth year in a text from 925 would be highly suspect. If no texts from the previous 400 years mentioned the year that Arthur was born, where would a writer in 925 suddenly have gotten this information?

Choice (D) is wrong because the mere existence of an early 6th-century monument to *some* king wouldn't mean that the king was Arthur.

Choice (E) is wrong because while a painting of "King Arthur" from 835 would be the earliest reference to Arthur as a king, it wouldn't be evidence that he existed. As with the hypothetical text from 855 in Choice (A), this rendering could just be an embellishment of the text from 828.

Visual-Information Questions

Questions about vocabulary and authorial intent are pretty normal stuff for any standardized reading comprehension test. The types of Praxis reading questions we've gone over so far probably aren't terribly different from what you remember encountering on tests you had to take in school. The most unusual thing about the Praxis reading test (don't worry — I said *unusual*, not *difficult*) is that it also includes what are referred to as *visual-information* questions, which is the Praxis's fancy term for questions about charts and graphs. Most reading and writing tests don't do this.

There aren't a ton of visual-information questions on the Praxis exam. There may only be two or three. Depending on the exam you happen to take, you may see three questions all about the same graph, or you may see one or two questions each about a couple of different graphs. But every point helps, so this section tells you about these questions.

Rethinking charts and graphs

If charts and graphs make you nervous because they seem more like math and science stuff than reading and writing stuff, the first step for you is to think about visual representation questions differently. The fact that visual-information questions are on the Praxis reading portion of the exam isn't a mistake or the result of someone's bizarre whim — it proves that, regardless of appearances, these questions really are reading comprehension questions at heart.

A graph — or any kind of picture — can be thought of as a visual depiction of information that could also be presented verbally. Just as you could *either* compose the sentence "A horse jumps over a fence" *or* you could draw a picture of a horse jumping over a fence to represent the same idea, a bar graph, line graph, pie chart, or any other type of chart or graph can be thought of as verbal information presented in pictorial form.

So relax. The visual-information questions *are* reading comprehension questions. They're just weird ones.

Getting graphs

The most common type of a graph is a line graph. A line graph represents the relationship between two variables: an independent variable plotted along the x (horizontal) axis and a dependent variable (a variable that *depends on* the first one) plotted along the y (vertical) axis. The line running through the quadrant formed by their intersection is what you look at to figure out what value for one variable equals what value for the other. So say you had a line graph that plotted the relationship between "hours spent studying" and "score on the Praxis reading test" (as though everyone who studied for the same amount of time got the exact same score, which would certainly be nice . . .). The "hours spent studying" would be plotted with hatch marks along the horizontal axis, and the various possible "scores on the Praxis reading test" would be plotted along the vertical axis, because this is the variable that depends on the other one. If you want to know the score someone would get who studied for, say, five hours, you'd just proceed upward from the 5-hour hatch mark on the bottom until you hit the line representing the actual data, then turn and go left until you hit the corresponding score on the side of the graph. (See Chapter 6 for more on line graphs.)

Another type of graph commonly found in Praxis visual-information questions is a bar graph. Rather than depicting the relationship between an independent and a dependent variable like a line graph does, a bar graph represents how different categories stack up against each other with respect to some particular idea. For example, you might use a bar graph to compare the number of World Series won by various baseball teams. The names of all the teams would be plotted along the horizontal with a bar above each name, and the heights of the bars would indicate the number of World Series each team had won, with the vertical axis of the graph hatch-marked to indicate how many championships were represented by a given bar height. The bar representing the New York Yankees would be very high (some might say unfairly high); the bars representing the St. Louis Cardinals, Oakland Athletics, and Boston Red Sox would be lower, but still respectably high; and the San Diego Padres and Texas Rangers wouldn't have bars over their names at all (at least not as of this writing, since neither team has yet won a World Series).

You could also plot that same information with another common type of graph called a pie chart. The difference between a pie chart and a bar graph is that a pie chart represents percentages of a total, so it looks like a circle with different-sized triangular pieces marked off inside it (hence its name). On a World Series pie chart, the Yankees' slice of the pie would be nearly one-fourth of the whole pie, as there have been 109 World Series and the Yankees have won 27 of them. The Cardinals' slice would be about one-tenth of the pie (11 World Series victories out of 109). Because a pie graph represents percentages of a total, the teams that have never won a World Series wouldn't appear on the pie at all.

But really, there's no sense in trying to memorize every type of chart or graph in the world. There are far too many ways to represent data visually for it to be in your interest to try and guess which types of charts or graphs will make an appearance when you take the exam.

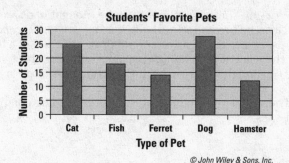

© John Wiley & Sons, Inc.

Based on the preceding graph, the biggest drop-off in popularity between consecutively ranked pets is between

(A) the most popular pet and the second-most-popular pet.

(B) the second-most-popular pet and the third-most-popular pet.

(C) the third-most-popular pet and the fourth-most-popular pet.

(D) the fourth-most-popular pet and the fifth-most-popular pet.

(E) The drop-offs in popularity between the first- and second-most-popular pets and between the third- and fourth-most-popular pets were equally large.

The correct answer is Choice (B). In order to answer this question correctly, you have to think about the pets in order of most popular to least popular — that is, rank them consecutively as the question states. The biggest drop-off in popularity between consecutively ranked pets by a fairly wide margin is between cats (the second-most-popular pet, chosen by 25 students) and fish (the third-most-popular pet, chosen by about 17 or 18 students), with a drop-off of 7 or 8 votes. Note that the bar graph doesn't allow you to judge perfectly how many students voted for fish, but that doesn't matter. Whether fish got 17 or 18 votes, the biggest drop-off in popularity is still between cats and fish.

Choice (A) is wrong because cats only got two or three fewer votes than dogs, so this isn't the biggest drop-off in popularity. Choice (C) is wrong because ferrets only got three or four fewer votes than fish, so this isn't the biggest drop-off in popularity. Choice (D) is wrong because hamsters only got one or two fewer votes than ferrets, so this isn't the biggest drop-off in popularity.

Choice (E) is wrong because, although it is *true* that the gap between dogs and cats and the gap between fish and ferrets are equally large, neither of them is the largest drop-off in popularity. It doesn't matter that they were equally large, because the question was asking for the largest drop-off! Be careful!

Practice Reading Comprehension Questions

These practice questions are similar to the reading comprehension questions that you'll encounter on the Praxis.

Questions 1 through 3 are based on the following passage.

Line Perhaps more so than that of any other man, his name is synonymous with incalculable brilliance in the hard sciences, and yet it is far from accurate to view Sir Isaac Newton as a model of
(05) rationalism. True, he invented calculus, laid the foundations for the science of optics, and — most famously — formulated the laws of motion and the principles of gravitation. Yet his myriad discoveries are more accurately seen as
(10) the byproducts of his boundless and obsessive mathematical mind than as the result of what today we would deem a scientific worldview: Privately, Newton spent as much time on alchemy and the search for the Philosopher's
(15) Stone as on legitimate empirical science, and he was consumed with efforts to calculate the date of Armageddon based on a supposed secret code in the Bible. Rather than being the human embodiment of the secular Enlightenment, Isaac
(20) Newton the man was a superstitious mystic whose awe-inspiring brain still managed to kick-start the scientifically modern world almost despite himself.

1. The central idea of the passage is to set up a contrast between

   (A) Newton's brilliant scientific successes and his embarrassing scientific failures.

   (B) Newton's secret private life and his false public image.

   (C) scientific methodology before Newton and scientific methodology after Newton.

   (D) Newton's scientific achievements and his unscientific worldview.

   (E) how Newton is viewed today and how he was viewed in his own time.

2. As it is used in context, the word "empirical" seems most nearly to mean

   (A) evidence-based.

   (B) mystical.

   (C) awe-inspiring.

   (D) outdated.

   (E) ironic.

3. It is fair to assume that part of the author's goal in composing the passage was to encourage his readers to consider the occasional disconnects between

   (A) our desire to celebrate "great" minds and our moral duty to tell the truth about them.

   (B) modern stereotypes of historical figures and their more complex real identities.

   (C) humanity's ability to reason and our dark and chaotic emotional lives.

   (D) what some people are mistakenly credited with doing and what they actually did.

   (E) the greatness of our modern scientific worldview and the horrors of our superstitious past.

Questions 4 through 6 are based on the following passage.

It has become a commonplace for the socially Line
conscious to complain about "gentrification," and yet it's difficult for many people to agree that the phenomenon is actually a problem, or even about what the term is precisely supposed to mean. We (05)
know the label is usually applied to people — usually young ones — from middle-class backgrounds moving into poorer neighborhoods in search of lower rents, slowly but surely driving up those rents in the process as more fashionable (10)
commercial interests follow them there. On the one hand, everybody likes low rent, but on the other, how can anyone realistically complain about a formerly undesirable neighborhood becoming less dangerous and more economically solvent? (15)

4. The passage presents the term "gentrification" as all of the following EXCEPT a

   (A) controversy.

   (B) buzzword.

   (C) euphemism.

   (D) paradox.

   (E) mixed blessing.

5. The passage frames the "socially conscious" people referred to in the opening sentence as people with a tendency to

   (A) deliberately define terms in unhelpfully vague ways.

   (B) oversimplify complex economic problems.

   (C) discriminate against young people for short-sighted reasons.

   (D) be disproportionately influenced by fashionable ideas.

   (E) take up causes that they may not have thought through.

6. Which of the following best describes the organization of the passage?

   (A) A loaded term is judiciously unpacked.

   (B) A traditional phrase is redefined for a new era.

   (C) A sarcastic label is reexamined in seriousness.

   (D) A theoretical concept is put into practice.

   (E) A careless mistake is mercilessly corrected.

Questions 7 through 9 are based on the following passage.

Line   After the Gadsden Purchase of 1853, the United States needed to find an efficient way of exploring the territory newly acquired from Mexico, much of which was desert. The idea of
(05) purchasing camels and forming a U.S. Army Camel Corps for the purpose was initially scoffed at, but finally approved in 1855, and a herd of 70 camels was subsequently amassed by Navy vessels sent off to Egypt and Turkey. Ironically, how-
(10) ever, the Camel Corps was stationed in Texas, a state that seceded from the Union upon the outbreak of the Civil War in 1861. With a war to fight and no need or desire to explore territory that now belonged to another nation, Texas simply
(15) set the camels free and shooed them off into the desert. The lucky camels thrived and bred, and a feral camel population survived in the southwestern United States until well into the 20th century, occasionally causing havoc when one or
(20) more camels would wander into a town and spark a riot among the horses. The last such incident recorded took place in 1941.

7. The author's tone in the passage can best be characterized as

   (A) primarily explanatory but subtly critical.

   (B) largely theoretical but consistently open-minded.

   (C) primarily informative and somewhat humorous.

   (D) largely analytical and mildly biased.

   (E) primarily skeptical but ultimately forgiving.

8. In context, the "another nation" referred to in line 14 is:

   (A) the United States

   (B) the Confederacy

   (C) Mexico

   (D) Egypt

   (E) Turkey

9. The primary purpose of the final sentence of the passage is presumably to

   (A) emphasize how large the population of feral camels eventually became.

   (B) surprise the reader by linking the content of the passage to living memory.

   (C) provide a hint about what finally killed off the wild camel population.

   (D) definitively answer a question posed at the beginning of the passage.

   (E) imply that some wild camels might still be alive in the American Southwest.

Questions 10 through 12 are based on the following passage.

Even the poorest of history students could   Line
tell you that it was Marie Antoinette who issued the oblivious response "Let them eat cake" upon being informed that the peasants had no bread — except that it wasn't. The famous anec- (05)
dote so frequently used to underscore how out-of-touch the very wealthy can be appears in Jean-Jacques Rousseau's *Confessions,* written in 1765, when the future and ill-fated queen of France was only nine years old and still living in (10)
her native Austria. Far from making any claims to historical accuracy, Rousseau attributes the pampered faux pas only to an anonymous "great princess" and presents it as a yarn that was old and corny even then. Presumably, the legend had (15)

Line been repeated about any number of European royal women for generations — but since Marie Antoinette ended up being the *last* queen of France, the version in which she says it was the
(20) one that stuck.

10. According to the passage, the most likely reason that the phrase "Let them eat cake" has become associated with Marie Antoinette is that

   (A) she may have actually said it, although this cannot be proven.

   (B) her life happened to overlap with that of Jean-Jacques Rousseau.

   (C) she was the final person to have her name inserted into an old joke.

   (D) food shortages among the peasants reached an apex during her reign.

   (E) she is the only queen of France that the average history student can name.

11. Which of the following questions is directly answered by the passage?

   (A) From what nation was Marie Antoinette originally?

   (B) In what nation did the "Let them eat cake" legend first start?

   (C) Who lived longer, Jean-Jacques Rousseau or Marie Antoinette?

   (D) Whom did Rousseau himself believe had said "Let them eat cake?"

   (E) What point was Rousseau trying to make with the "Let them eat cake" anecdote?

12. Which of the following phrases from the passage is used most nearly as a synonym for *oblivious,* as it appears in the first sentence?

   (A) "ill-fated"

   (B) "pampered"

   (C) "anonymous"

   (D) "old and corny"

   (E) "out-of-touch"

Answers and Explanations

Use this answer key to score the practice reading comprehension questions in this chapter.

1. **D. Newton's scientific achievements and his unscientific worldview.** The passage establishes that Isaac Newton was personally superstitious and a religious fanatic, and this "unscientific worldview" is contrasted with the brilliant scientific achievements he made despite this.

   The right answer is not Choice (A) because the passage never alludes to any "embarrassing scientific failures" of Newton — only to private beliefs and endeavors that were unscientific. The right answer is not Choice (B) because the passage never implies that Newton deliberately cultivated a "false public image," only that he privately believed superstitious things.

   The right answer is not Choice (C) because, although science after Newton was certainly different as a result of the many landmark innovations he made, the passage is concerned only with Newton himself, not with the difference in the sciences before and after him. The right answer is not Choice (E) because while the passage points out inaccuracies in the way Newton is often viewed today, it doesn't address how he was viewed in his own time.

2. **A. evidence-based.** Both in the passage and in most contexts, "empirical" means "evidence-based."

   The right answer is not Choice (B) because "empirical" doesn't mean "mystical," either in the passage or in most contexts (in fact, it means very nearly the opposite). The right answer is not Choice (C) because "empirical" doesn't mean "awe-inspiring" (this is just another unrelated phrase from the passage, used as a red herring).

The right answer is not Choice (D) because although the passage characterizes some of Newton's personal beliefs as "outdated," the word "empirical" does not mean or appear to mean "outdated" in context. The right answer is not Choice (E) because although the contrast between Newton's achievements and his personal beliefs is "ironic," this is not what the word "empirical" means or appears to mean in context.

3. **B. modern stereotypes of historical figures and their more complex real identities.** The passage is primarily — indeed, almost exclusively — concerned with highlighting the difference between our modern stereotype of Isaac Newton as an Enlightenment rationalist and the more complex truth of his status as a superstitious mystic.

The right answer is not Choice (A) because the passage doesn't hint at anything like a "moral duty to tell the truth" about famous figures like Newton; it corrects a misconception, but it's not an exposé as such. The right answer is not Choice (C) because the passage is about Newton specifically, not the human race in general, and it doesn't characterize Newton's private life as "dark and chaotic," only "superstitious."

The right answer is not Choice (D) because the passage never addresses anything that Newton is "mistakenly credited with doing." The right answer is not Choice (E) because while the passage characterizes Newton as superstitious, it never brings up anything resembling any collective "horrors" of the superstitious past of humanity in general.

4. **C. euphemism.** A "euphemism" is a polite term substituted for a vulgar or offensive one, and the passage never presents "gentrification" as such a term.

The right answer is not Choice (A) because the passage *does* present gentrification as a "controversy," insofar as it's a thing that people argue about. The right answer is not Choice (B) because the passage *does* present gentrification as a "buzzword," that is, a politically loaded term that is often used but poorly defined.

The right answer is not Choice (C) because the passage *does* present gentrification as a "paradox," insofar as it is difficult for people to decide whether it is a good thing or a bad thing. The right answer is not Choice (E) because the passage *does* present gentrification as a "mixed blessing," in other words, it is a phenomenon with both good and bad aspects.

5. **E. take up causes that they may not have thought through.** By highlighting some of the good things about gentrification, the passage implies that the "socially-conscious" people who "complain" about it may not have considered the situation fully before making up their minds.

The right answer is not Choice (A) because, though the passage does characterize the term "gentrification" as somewhat vague, it never accuses anyone of *deliberately* defining it poorly. The right answer is not Choice (B) because, though gentrification is an economic issue and the discussion about it is often oversimplified, the passage's point in referring to "socially conscious" people is that they take up causes prematurely in general, not that they specifically are reductionist about economics.

The right answer is not Choice (C) because, while the passage mentions that gentrification often involves young people, the point in context of the term "socially conscious" has nothing to do with discriminating against any particular group of people. The right answer is not Choice (D) because, while the passage mentions "fashionable" businesses moving into an area as an effect of gentrification, the point of the term "socially conscious" in context has nothing to do with what is or isn't fashionable.

6. **A. A loaded term is judiciously unpacked.** The passage establishes that "gentrification" is a "loaded" (in other words, a politically charged) term, and this term is subsequently "judiciously unpacked," or meticulously analyzed.

The right answer is not Choice (B) because the passage never implies that "gentrification" used to mean one thing but is now being used to mean another. The right answer is not Choice (C) because the passage never implies that "gentrification" is often — or ever — used in a sarcastic or unserious fashion.

The right answer is not Choice (D) because the passage makes no distinction between theory and practice; gentrification is a phenomenon from real life and is discussed as such. The right answer is not Choice (E) because, while the passage does seek to shed some light on a vague term, it doesn't identify a "careless mistake" and certainly can't be characterized as "merciless" in tone.

7. **C. primarily informative and somewhat humorous.** The passage is indisputably informative, and it is, on occasion, slightly humorous. Because both these things are true, there's no real way that this answer choice can be wrong.

The right answer is not Choice (A) because though the passage is explanatory, it's never critical. The right answer is not Choice (B) because the passage merely relates historical events; there's nothing "theoretical" about it, and "open-mindedness" isn't an issue.

The right answer is not Choice (D) because the passage merely relates information without analyzing anything; by extension, it can't be biased because it doesn't present an opinion. The right answer is not Choice (E) because the passage deals only with historical facts, not opinion or theory, so there's nothing for it to be either "skeptical" or "forgiving" about.

8. **A. the United States.** From Texas's point of view, the United States was "another nation" because Texas had seceded to join the Confederacy.

The fact that Texas itself was part of the Confederacy eliminates Choice (B). Mexico, Choice (C), is the nation to which the Gadsden Purchase land originally belonged. Egypt and Turkey, Choices (D) and (E), respectively, are merely nations from which the camels were purchased.

9. **B. surprise the reader by linking the content of the passage to living memory.** The author's intent in the last sentence is to shock and amuse the reader, who will presumably be surprised to hear that wild camel "incidents" were still taking place in the United States in 1941 (in other words, in "living memory" — a phrase used to mean "within the memory of at least some people who are still alive").

The right answer is not Choice (A) because the final sentence of the passage doesn't imply anything about the size of the wild camel herd at any point. The right answer is not Choice (C) because, although it presumably implies that the camels didn't survive too long past 1941, the final sentence of the passage doesn't imply anything about how they actually died.

The right answer is not Choice (D) because there is no question at the beginning of the passage that the final sentence answers. The right answer is not Choice (E) because the final sentence doesn't imply that some camels may have survived — if they had, there presumably would have been camel incidents after 1941.

10. **C. she was the final person to have her name inserted into an old joke.** The ending of the passage offers the theory that the "Let them eat cake" joke was repeated about royals for years, and that the version with Marie Antoinette's name is the version that "stuck" because there were no more French queens after her.

The right answer is not Choice (A) because the passage definitively establishes that Marie Antoinette couldn't have said "Let them eat cake" (the joke appears in a book written when she was a child). The right answer is not Choice (B) because, while it's true that the life of Marie Antoinette overlapped with that of Jean-Jacques Rousseau, the passage doesn't imply that this is the reason the "Let them eat cake" story is associated with her. (Why would it be?)

The right answer is not Choice (D) because, while it may be true that food shortages among the peasantry reached an apex during Marie Antoinette's reign, the passage does not state or imply that this is the main reason why the "Let them eat cake" story is associated with her. The right answer is not Choice (E) because, while it may be true that Marie Antoinette is the only queen of France that the average student can name (in America, at least), the passage doesn't state or imply that this is the main reason why the "Let them eat cake" story is associated with her.

11. **A. From what nation was Marie Antoinette originally?** The middle of the passage makes reference to Marie Antoinette's "native Austria."

The right answer is not Choice (B) because the passage never answers the question of what nation the "Let them eat cake" story originated in — it implies that the story was told about "any number of *European* royal women for generations." The right answer is not Choice (C) because the passage never states whether Jean-Jacques Rousseau or Marie Antoinette lived longer.

The right answer is not Choice (D) because the passage never implies that Rousseau had any belief about who "really" said "Let them eat cake"; if he presented the story as an old joke, then he likely believed that no one really said it. The right answer is not Choice (E) because, while the passage states that the "Let them eat cake" story is often used to emphasize the cluelessness of the rich, it never explains what point Rousseau himself was using it to make in the context of his *Confessions*.

12. **E. "out-of-touch."** In both the context of the passage and most of the time, "oblivious" means "clueless" or "out-of-touch."

It does not mean "ill-fated," "pampered," "anonymous," or "old and corny," either in the context of the passage or elsewhere, ruling out Choices (A), (B), (C), and (D), respectively.

Chapter 10

Test-Taking Strategies for Core Reading

Chapter 9 covers the structure of the Praxis reading test and the types of questions you can expect to see. But that chapter is principally an overview of the types of reading skills you'll want to hone before the exam. In this chapter, we take more of a "game theory" approach to the task at hand, helping you to crack the code of the test and earn a great score by any down-and-dirty means necessary (aside from cheating, of course).

Figuring Out Which to Read First: The Passage or the Question

The same question seems to arise first whenever the subject of answering questions about reading passages comes up: Should you read the passage first and then look at the question(s), or should you scan the question(s) first and then look back for the answers in the passage?

The majority of students who struggle with reading comprehension find that it's best to start by reading the passage.

So *why* is it better to read the passage first? Wouldn't a more commonsense approach be to glance at the question beforehand so you know what you're supposed to be looking for? That thinking is understandable, but the question-first method is less desirable for a few reasons.

On most reading tests, there are multiple questions about a single passage, so if you start with the questions and then look back, you end up reading certain bits and pieces of the passage over and over instead of reading the whole thing only once. Reading the passage once saves time.

Now, granted, the Praxis Reading test has a good number of "one-to-one pairings" — brief passages about which only one question is asked — and reading the questions first doesn't cause as many problems in these instances. However, because you encounter a variety of reading passages on the Praxis — long passages, short passages, one-to-one pairings — you don't want to continually change your strategy based on the type of question that pops up on the screen. Getting into the habit of reading the question first only on the brief passages means you have to switch up your strategy when a long passage with multiple questions appears. You run the risk of getting thrown off your game. (Whatever your method is, practicing it and sticking to it is always a good idea.)

When you look at the question before reading the passage, having the question on your mind while reading has a tendency to get in the way. You're unable to really consider what the passage is saying because you're mentally hearing the question over and over and nervously scanning the text for one sentence that explicitly states the answer. But right answers often aren't found in one particular sentence. Sometimes they involve making an inference based on considering several of the author's points together; other times, you may be dealing with a "tone" or "purpose" question that requires you to take a step back and consider the passage as a whole.

As a general rule, focusing on the task before you is always easier when nothing is distracting you. It's why you can easily walk across a balance beam that's one foot off the ground, whereas walking across the same beam when it's 50 feet off the ground is terrifying. Having the question running through your head while you're trying to make sense of the passage is like trying to walk the balance beam while you're freaking out about how high off the ground it is. Just take the passage on its own terms. If you do that well, when it comes time to look at a question, the answer should be obvious.

What about those questions that ask you what the author means by a specific phrase or give you a specific line number? You're just wasting time reading the whole passage if the question is only about one measly little line or sentence in it, right? Wrong! One of the most dangerous pitfalls of the question-first method is that it can instill you with a false sense of confidence about where you need to look. Just because the question asks you what the author means in Line 17 doesn't necessarily mean that the best way to answer the question is to jump straight to Line 17 and read it again and again. Often, the purpose of a given sentence is best clarified by contextual clues found elsewhere in the passage.

Having a good sense of what the passage as a whole means is always an advantage, even if the question ends up asking about only one specific part of the passage. Reading the whole passage before you see the question allows you to process the flow of the text as a whole, rather than as merely a series of statements and details, as you'd see it if you were scanning for one single point.

But the most important reason not to look at the question first is that looking at the question will probably also tempt you to look at the answer choices. And the answer choices were *designed* to confuse you.

Having the wording of the answer choices in your head while you're reading the passage is a recipe for disaster. The writers of the test design the wrong answer choices by taking details or groups of words from the passage that are memorable or seem important and then inserting them into answer choices that don't answer the question. So having those phrases in your mind while you read causes you to linger over red herrings, possibly ignoring the right answer in the process.

Examining Strategies for the Various Passages

Most people who take the Praxis don't mind brief statements that are accompanied by one question. Where folks get a little nervous is when they have to read a longer passage (100–200 or so words) and then answer a couple of questions about what they just read. Many people aren't too fond of the paired passages either, where they have to read two passages of about 200 words total and then answer a handful of questions.

In the following sections, I reveal what types of questions usually correspond to each type of passage. Armed with these details, you can face any passage with confidence.

Approaching long and short passages

When a new question first pops up on your computer screen, you can easily tell whether it's going to be a one-to-one pairing of a brief passage and a single question or a long passage about which there will be several questions. A one-to-one question appears as a centered paragraph with a question below it, whereas a long passage is narrower with the question (which is the first of several) off to the side. Often, the lines in the passage are also numbered so that questions can specifically refer to "Line 5" or "Line 13."

On the long passages, sticking to the method of reading the passage before the questions is doubly important, because repeatedly scanning a long passage for several answers that are only revealed one at a time adds up to a lot of time wasted. But aside from sticking to the system of reading the passage first, what *else* should you keep in mind while reading the long passage?

A long passage often asks about the meaning or purpose of specific details or sentences, as opposed to asking you about the tone or the purpose of the passage as a whole. Of course, the test *might* ask you about overall tone in a long passage, just as it might pair a vocabulary question with a short passage — there aren't really any rules stipulating that certain types of questions have to be paired with certain passage lengths. But the fact remains that certain types of questions are more commonly found on the long passages.

Questions for long passages often examine the relationship between the passage's main idea and its supporting points. So when you see a long passage pop up, be prepared for questions along the lines of "The author mentions [*some factoid*] in order to support the assertion that . . . " Long-passage questions tend to be about how the parts form the whole: The questions ask you about the parts, but getting the answers involves comprehending the whole.

Be careful of the trick where a minor detail from the end of a passage is purported to be the "main idea" or "primary purpose" of the passage in an early answer choice. The question writers do that to try and trick you into jumping on that answer merely because it's fresh in your mind. Remember, something that wasn't even brought up until the end of the passage is unlikely to be the main idea.

Short passages tend to ask more fact-based questions. When you see a short passage, be prepared to answer questions along the lines of "The passage is primarily concerned with [*some factoid*]" or "Which of the following is an unstated assumption made by the author of the passage?"

The long and the short passages really aren't that different. The long passages have more questions about them because, well, they're *longer,* so the test-writers have more text to ask questions about. But honestly, that's about it. Aside from the fact that a long passage is more likely to be argumentative (and therefore lend itself to questions about main and supporting points) whereas a short passage is more likely to be purely informative, you don't need to approach either one of them in some essentially "different" way. Answering four questions about four paragraphs is more-or-less the same as answering one question about one paragraph four times.

Approaching the paired passages

Some of the passages on the Praxis reading test involve a side-by-side comparison of two passages by two different authors on the same topic. They may explicitly disagree with each other and present two arguments that are mutually exclusive (that is, can't be true at the same time), or they may just analyze the same issue from two different angles. The questions concentrate on the differences between the two passages. (If this sounds like a pain, keep in mind that you *usually* see only one passage like this on a given Praxis reading test, although no rule says that there can't be more than one.)

You know you're facing a question like this when the first paragraph is designated as "Passage 1" and the second as "Passage 2" (they both pop up on your computer screen at the same time, one above the other). When you have a passage (or, I guess, passages) like this before you, expect to see questions about the differences between the two authors' viewpoints.

Now, the trick to successfully dealing with paired passages is to avoid going straight from reading the passage to reading the question like you would for other reading questions. Instead, take a few seconds to *anticipate* the question. Formulating an expectation in your head about what the question may be is actually a good idea, and when it comes to paired passages, it's a *very* good idea. After you've read the two paired passages, stop for a moment before looking at the question and ask yourself: *What is the difference between the two authors' viewpoints?*

Your goal with this approach is to look at two brief, mutually exclusive thesis-driven paragraphs and explain the difference between them in your own words. You probably wouldn't have any trouble writing a short sentence that would accurately explain the essence of the two authors' disagreement. However, when you're asked to choose from among five prospective explanations written by someone else, discerning the difference between the authors' points gets tricky.

The solution to this problem is easy: Consider what the difference is in your own words *before* you look at the question and the answer choices, and then pick the answer choice that presents the nearest paraphrase of what you just said.

Of course, "What is the difference between the two authors' arguments?" isn't the *only* question that the Praxis reading test can ask you about a set of paired passages. A version of this question is almost certain to be *one* of the questions that follows the paired passages, but there will be others too (as a type of "long passage," a paired passage is always followed by multiple questions). Another common question asks something along the lines of "Which of the following devices is used by the author of Passage 1 but not by the author of Passage 2?" The answer choices then present you with five options along the lines of rhetorical questions, similes, flashbacks, pop-culture references, and personification. There's really no shortcut to answering a question like this: You just have to look back at the passages and see which of the devices is used by the first author but not the second. (Don't worry — the two passages are brief enough that you can do this without eating up a whole lot of time.)

The real trick is not getting confused or turned around. When a question asks something like "Which of these devices is used by Author 1 but not Author 2?," there's often a wrong answer choice that names a device that is used *by Author 2 but not Author 1* to try and trip you up. So stay sharp and remember what the question asks! ("I got it backwards" is a common head-slapping exclamation on tests like this, so seriously, watch out.)

Approaching Questions about Charts and Graphs

As Chapter 9 explains, the visual-information questions are where the Praxis reading test breaks the mold of most reading comprehension tests. People simply aren't used to encountering charts and graphs on a reading test, so these questions can make even very sharp

English majors nervous because they seem like something that escaped from a math or science test. But the best way to think about the visual-information questions (of which you'll see only a few) is to remember that they *are,* in fact, reading comprehension questions — you just "read" pictures instead of words.

So, the good news about the charts and graphs questions is that they really aren't any harder than any of the other questions on the Praxis reading test. The bad news is that there's no trick for answering them correctly. You just have to read the question and then look at the chart or graph to find the answer.

Just because there isn't a trick, though, doesn't mean that there isn't an advantage that can be exploited. There's actually a big advantage ripe for exploitation on the visual-information questions, and that is the fact that they invariably appear toward the very end of the test. The Praxis reading exam usually has about 56 questions, and the visual-information questions usually appear in the late 40s or early 50s. So if you're the sort of person who gets nervous around charts and graphs, you'll at least be in a good position to calculate how much time it's wise to spend on them.

In short, the best advice about the visual-information questions for people who aren't comfortable around charts and graphs is to look at the clock, realize how much time you have, and be meticulous in selecting your answer. For example, rather than just reading the question and looking at the graph to see what you think the answer is, take the extra time to plug in the other four answer choices and make sure they're all wrong. Maybe you made a silly mistake on the first glance that this process will help you catch. (If you *don't,* in fact, have a lot of time left when you get to the visual-information questions, see the section "Tips for Slow Readers" at the end of this chapter.)

Eliminating Wrong Answers

When you're taking the Praxis reading test, remember a piece of advice that was actually the brainchild of a student many years ago: "Don't answer the questions; question the answers."

What in the world does that mean? Well, it all comes back to the advice from Chapter 9 about how there are always four wrong answers and one right answer, and any answer choice that isn't wrong must be right. No matter what kind of question you're looking at, no matter how long or short the passage is, you are always fundamentally dealing with the same situation: You're given five statements about the passage, and only one of them is 100 percent true. So look each answer choice straight in the eye and ask it "Are you 100 percent not wrong?" The answer can be "yes" to only one of them.

We can't stress this enough: You're not looking for the most interesting statement about the passage, the most detailed one, the one with the biggest words in it, the one that's the most different from the others, the longest one, or the shortest one. You are looking for the one that has nothing in it that isn't true. The right answer may be vague, boring, or unremarkable, but that doesn't matter. All that matters is that *everything in it is true*.

That's what *questioning the answers* means. If you train your test-taking head to examine the answer choices this way, you'll almost always be able to eliminate at least three of them pretty quickly. If you can eliminate four, well then, problem solved. But sometimes, you may find that the question-the-answers method leaves you with a 50/50 conundrum — two remaining choices that you can't seem to choose between because they both look plausible.

When that happens, ask yourself *Which of these statements about the passage could be true without the other one also automatically being true?* For example, if Choice (B) says "the passage is about an elephant" and Choice (D) says "the passage is about a mammal," the answer must be Choice (D). Why? Because elephants are mammals, so if Choice (B) is true, then so is Choice D! An animal can be a mammal without also being an elephant, but an animal can't be an elephant without also being a mammal.

The "Which of these statements can be true by itself?" method won't solve every 50/50 dilemma, but you'll be surprised by how many of them it does end up solving. If you do find yourself in a 50/50 bind that you just can't seem to crack, pick one, even if it's just a wild guess. Unlike on the SAT and many other standardized tests, you don't lose points for a wrong answer (as opposed to a blank one) on the Praxis. Because there's no difference between "blank" and "wrong," you have no reason not to guess.

If the true-by-itself razor doesn't help, try looking out for red-flag words such as "always" and "never" (pick the choice that doesn't have them). If this tip doesn't apply, then just pick the broader or less detailed of the two answers, on the grounds that an answer choice with less detail in it has a lesser chance of any of the details being wrong.

Tips for Slow Readers

This section deals with the complaint that so many standardized-test takers have, especially about reading comprehension tests: "I could get all the questions right if I had enough time, but I keep running out of time because I read slowly!"

If you're worried about running out of time on the Praxis reading test because you've had trouble with time management on other standardized tests in the past, keep in mind that time may not be a problem this time around. Although some of the questions on the Praxis can be tricky, most test-takers find it to be one of the more forgiving standardized tests where time is concerned (the time ratio ends up working out to more than 1.5 minutes per question, which almost everyone finds to be more than enough).

If anything, the more likely danger on the Praxis reading test is rushing because you *expect* to run out of time and making silly mistakes in your haste. Take some sample Praxis exams and time yourself. If you find that time *is* indeed likely to be a problem for you on this particular test, some of the following tips may help:

- ✔ **Skip the hard stuff.** If you come to a particular sentence or section of a passage that you don't fully understand, resist the urge to read it over and over. Just keep going. The "hard part" only matters if that's the part the question ends up being about, and it probably won't be, so don't worry about it unless it turns out that you have to after you see the question.

- ✔ **Eliminate the wrong answers.** If you find yourself stuck on a particular question, don't waste time reading the choices again and again, praying that one will suddenly jump out at you as correct. Get more proactive about eliminating wrong answers. Don't just *read* the answer choices — *do* something about them as you read, and you'll notice an improvement in your time.

- ✔ **Resist the urge to skim.** Letting your eyes rapidly glaze their way down the passage or using the old "first and last sentence of each paragraph" trick actually costs you more time than it ends up saving you, because most of the time you just end up having to read the passage again more carefully after you see the question. Read the whole passage *quickly* and *once,* without laboring over the parts that you don't fully get. It may *feel* like you're going slower than you would by skimming, but all things considered, you're actually not. Doing something right the first time is faster than doing it quickly but inefficiently the first time and then having to do it again.

✔ **Don't ponder skipping the question.** Although the computer-delivered Praxis exam *does* allow you to skip and return to questions, keep in mind that doing so — or even thinking about doing so — can eat up more time than it would to simply force yourself to answer all the questions the first time around. Ten seconds spent wondering about whether you should skip each question really adds up!

Part IV
Fine-Tuning Your Writing Skills

Tips for Crafting Each Paragraph in an Essay

- ✔ **First paragraph**
  - Craft a short introduction.
  - State your position, which is your thesis.
- ✔ **Middle paragraphs**
  - Begin with a topic sentence related to your thesis.
  - Provide specific examples, details, and/or experiences. Explain why these are important and how they relate to your thesis.
  - End each paragraph with a strong final sentence relating to the thesis.
- ✔ **Conclusion**
  - Tie up your ideas into one neat package.
  - Sum up the supporting details.
  - Drive your point home.

Get the lowdown on the big-five grammar rules in the free article at www.dummies.com/extras/praxiscore.

In this part . . .

✔ Discover the differences between the two essays you have to write, and get tips for writing a solid essay in just 30 minutes.

✔ Review the essential grammar rules you're tested on when you take the Praxis.

✔ Get insights on the most logical ways to approach sentence-correction, passage-revision, and research-skills questions.

Chapter 11

Acing the Essay

In your career as a teacher, success depends on your being clearly understood, not only by your students but also by their parents, your colleagues, the school administration, and your community. The Praxis tests this ability by requiring you to write two essays. One directs you to respond to a statement by writing an essay that agrees or disagrees with a particular point of view. This essay is referred to as the argumentative essay, and you draw on your own observations and opinions to complete this writing assignment.

The other essay gives you a statement about a general topic that's familiar to all adults and asks you to write an essay about that topic, using two provided sources. This is the informative/explanatory essay. You don't need any special knowledge to write the essay. In addition to using information from the source material, you can also support the topic with examples from your own personal experience and general knowledge.

You have 30 minutes to produce each essay, so the essays don't have to be long. But they do need to be organized, logical, and supportive of the main ideas. Additionally, in the informative/explanatory essay, you must demonstrate that you can extract information from the provided sources and cite the sources correctly.

This chapter gives you details about how to write a strong essay, explains how your essay will be scored, and gives you several essay prompts so you can practice your writing skills.

Perusing the Types of Prompts: "Picking a Side" versus "Exploring an Idea"

The Praxis presents a prompt for writing the essay, and this prompt directs you to address the topic in a particular manner. You're directed to write either an argumentative essay, in which you argue for or against the stated idea, or an informative/explanatory essay, in which you write about a topic and explain why it's important. Understanding the writing prompt is essential for writing a successful essay. Take time to analyze the prompt before you begin the drafting process. Restate the topic in your own words.

The following sections explain how to write an argumentative essay and how to write an informative/explanatory essay.

Writing persuasively

A persuasive essay is written to convince the reader to accept your view, or your opinion. A good persuasive essay is forceful, well-organized, and carefully reasoned.

The prompt may concern an issue about which you feel strongly. If so, your job in writing your essay is to persuade the reader to accept your view. Conversely, the prompt may be one about which you have no strong feelings. In this case, you can address the topic by exploring both sides of the idea. In either case, you must make your position clear. The scorer should not have to guess where you stand.

The directions for the first essay will be similar to these:

> Discuss the extent to which you agree or disagree with this opinion. Support your views with specific reasons and examples from your own experience, observations, or reading.

Read the prompt carefully. Think about it. Do you agree or disagree? Maybe you're not sure of your opinion. In that case, which stance is easier for you to take? For which side of the issue can you generate the most support? For which side of the issue can you produce the best essay? Take that side.

Sticking to the facts

The second essay requires you to read passages from two sources and draw on the information in both sources as well as your own experiences to write the essay. You must correctly cite the sources.

The directions for the second essay will be similar to these:

> The following assignment requires you to use information from two sources to discuss the most important concerns that relate to a specific issue. When paraphrasing or quoting from the sources, cite each source by referring to the author's last name, the title, or any other clear identifier.

The Praxis doesn't test the depth of your knowledge of a topic. The Praxis tests your ability to analyze information, write well, and incorporate outside sources while citing correctly. So you don't need to be a *Jeopardy!* champion to write this essay.

The Praxis scorers want just the facts in your essay. Don't waste their time and endanger your good score with unnecessary descriptions or comments that don't contribute to your main point, your *thesis*.

Creating a Solid Essay

The standard five-paragraph essay is an excellent way to organize an essay, and this method is the most frequently taught form of writing in the classroom. Even though this method isn't the only way to produce an essay, for most test-takers, the five-paragraph essay is a good choice for the Praxis essay. You may find, however, that only one or two middle paragraphs are sufficient to fully develop your thesis.

Making an outline: Essential or overrated?

Although a formal outline isn't necessary, getting organized is essential. After you've read the directions and the prompt, restate the prompt in your own words. Be sure you understand what the prompt is asking you to do.

If you're writing the argumentative essay, think about your viewpoint. If you're working on the informative/explanatory essay, read the source material. Then, for either essay, formulate a rough thesis. Next, take a mental inventory. What examples or experiences can you relate to the topic? Write them down. In what order will you arrange these supporting details? Number them. Reread the prompt. Are your supporting details relevant? Make adjustments and rewrite your thesis, if necessary. You should spend no more than five to seven minutes on these tasks.

A common maxim regarding essay writing is, "Tell them what you are going to tell them, tell them, and then tell them what you told them." Although a bit simplistic, this is still good advice to keep in mind when you're organizing your writing.

Looking at the sections of your essay

Keep in mind that good writing of any kind requires an excellent thesis, topic sentences, and well-organized supporting details as well as a strong conclusion.

Here's a breakdown of how to structure each paragraph in your essay:

✔ **First paragraph**

- Craft a short introduction.

- State your position, which is your thesis. (Here's your chance to make a good first impression. Best foot forward!)

✔ **Middle paragraphs**

- Begin with a topic sentence related to your thesis.

- Provide specific examples, details, and/or experiences. Explain why these are important and how they relate to your thesis. If you're working on the argumentative essay, what benefits can occur as a result of your point of view?

- End each paragraph with a strong final sentence relating to the thesis.

Read the prompt again to be sure everything you wrote relates to it! Remember: You don't want the thought "So what?" to enter the minds of your readers.

✔ **Conclusion**

- Put a bow on it! Tie up your ideas into one neat package. Avoid merely summarizing.

- Restate your position if this is the argumentative essay.

- Sum up the supporting details.

- Drive your point home.

✔ **Works Cited** (only for the essay requiring the use of sources)

- List the sources to which you refer in your essay.

- Be sure to format your sources properly.

After you have organized your thoughts, begin writing your essay. Be sure to save the last four or five minutes to proofread, correcting spelling and grammar.

Don't box yourself in: Theses aren't set in stone

After you've written your thesis and begun to develop it in your middle paragraphs, you may find that an adjustment is in order. You may discover while writing your examples or experiences that your thesis statement has evolved and could be better.

Write your revised statement. After you've completed your essay, revisit your revised thesis and reread the prompt. If your revised thesis is better, change it.

Citing the sources

When you write the informative/explanatory essay, you must cite any outside sources you quote or paraphrase. You can cite sources within the body of the text several different ways:

✔ You can cite a source by including the author's name in the sentence you are writing. Be sure to use quotation marks when quoting directly.

 • According to Mary Lucas, "Children learn best by doing."

If you paraphrase, you must still cite your source:

 • Mary Lucas believes that children can learn best by doing.

✔ You can cite a source by writing the last name of the author in parentheses at the end of the sentence before the period:

 • Children learn best by doing (Lucas).

At the end of your essay, include a "Works Cited" section. Generally, the works cited section should include the name of the author (last name, first name, and middle name or initial), the name of the article (if appropriate), the name of the publication, the city of publication, and the year of publication for each source used. The following list provides generic templates for various types of sources:

✔ **Books:** Author's last name, first name and middle name/initial. Title of Book. Place of publication: Publishing company, year of publication.

✔ **Encyclopedias:** Author's last name, first name and middle name/initial. "Article Name." Title of Encyclopedia. Year of edition.

✔ **Magazines:** Author's last name, first name and middle name/initial. "Article Name." Title of Magazine. Day of month (if applicable) Month year: page number(s) of article.

✔ **Websites:** Author's last name, first name and middle name/initial. "Title of Article/ Document." Title of Site. Ed. Name of editor (first name last name). Date of publication or most recent update. Name of organization associated with site. Date of when you accessed the document. <http://www.websiteaddress.com>

Checking out some additional writing pointers

Here are some general, but important, tips to keep in mind as you write your essays (see Chapter 13 for some additional strategies):

✔ Be careful to address only the assigned topic. Don't wander off course — no sudden left turns.

✔ Don't leave anything out. Address every point, but be concise. Be specific; make every word count.

✔ Provide clear support for your points. Imagine that for every point you make, someone asks, "So what?" Be sure you have an answer. Doing this keeps your writing relevant.

✔ Pay attention to grammar, usage, and mechanics. Errors here will cost you points.

✔ Use transitions to make your words flow from idea to idea and paragraph to paragraph.

✔ Vary the length and structure of your sentences.

✔ Avoid passive voice. Use active verbs whenever possible.

✔ Include correct citation, whether you paraphrase or quote directly from the source.

Turning a Good Essay into a Great One

The Praxis essay scorers are looking for the complete package. They want a well-written, interesting essay. If you want a top score, you need to do more than organize your essay well and have good support for your thesis. You should also provide anecdotes when applicable, choose your words carefully, and acknowledge the other side of the argument when writing a persuasive essay. The following sections touch on these tactics.

Adding interesting anecdotes

Experienced writers and speakers often relate an anecdote to make a point. An anecdote is a very short story and can be an excellent way to support your essay's thesis. Personal stories are particularly memorable and, consequently, make your point memorable, too.

Consider this prompt for an argumentative essay:

> "Because students have so many extracurricular activities and so little time outside the school day, the majority of school hours should be limited to academic courses only."

What could be better to support your view than a brief anecdote about your own experience in juggling extracurricular activities and academics?

The anecdote is simply a suggestion and not a requirement. It helps to illustrate your main ideas by using a real life situation.

Although the Praxis is no place to practice your stand-up comedy routine, an amusing anecdote to illustrate your point is certainly allowed and can add energy and personality to your essay. Just be sure that the anecdote clearly supports your thesis and doesn't distract the reader.

Painting a picture with words

The old saying "A picture is worth a thousand words" applies to the essay. Even though you can't literally place a picture into your essay, your words can paint a picture to support your point. Create an image, a "word picture," by being very specific. Consider the following descriptions:

Vague: a nice day

Specific: bright sunshine, marshmallow clouds in a brilliant blue sky

By revising the vague statement of a nice day, the specific, detailed adjectives and nouns create a detailed image of a nice day in the reader's brain.

Vague verbs are too weak to create an image. Instead, use strong, active verbs. For example, instead of "walk," use a more specific verb — "ambled," "strolled," or "trotted," for example.

Use specific words in your essay to appeal to the five senses: sight, hearing, touch, taste, and smell. Doing so gives the reader the sense that he is there and can experience what you're describing.

However, using specific words also comes with a caveat. You should know the words that you use. "Big words" won't earn you extra points.

The big word isn't necessarily preferable to the simple word nor is the unusual word preferable to the everyday word. Clarity is your goal. Don't confuse the reader by "overwriting." Big words used inappropriately can mean fewer points for your essay. Use words with which you are comfortable.

Finally, avoid jargon — language that is so specialized that it may be misunderstood. You may know, for example, the specialized language that computer "techies" use every day, but assume that your reader does not.

Anticipating objections against your position

When you write the argumentative essay, consider what could be said against your view and prepare a strong retort. Recognizing opposing views strengthens your own. By refuting the opposite view, you make yours much stronger.

Ignoring a major opposing view weakens your position. Suppose, for example, you are writing in favor of banning certain books in the school library. Think about the opposing views and decide how you can refute them.

Understanding How the Essay Is Scored

Your essay will be evaluated by two scorers. Each will assign a point value of 1 to 6. If the points vary widely, your essay will be reviewed by a third evaluator.

The scorers issue points based on the following factors:

- ✔ A 6-point essay demonstrates a high degree of competence. This is a winner! It takes into consideration all the advice given in this chapter. It doesn't have to be perfect, but it does make the writer's position clear, and it is well organized. In addition, a 6-point essay uses strong supporting details, displays sentence variety, and exhibits excellent grammar, competent word usage, and almost flawless mechanics.

- ✔ A 5-point essay is just a step below the 6. Although it's strong and displays some of the characteristics of the 6-point essay, the ideas don't flow as logically, the sentence variety isn't as effective, and the language use may not display as much facility.

- ✔ A 4-point essay demonstrates competence. Although it is adequate, it's not as well-written as higher-scoring essays. The thesis may not be stated as clearly as the higher scoring essays. Relevant supporting details, examples, and reasons are not as well explained.

✔ A 3-point essay is blemished but demonstrates some competence. The thesis and supporting ideas may only be implied instead of clearly stated. It may display errors in language use, grammar, and mechanics.

✔ A 2-point essay has serious flaws. The thesis may be weak or nonexistent. The organization may be weak with few supporting details. It may have frequent errors in grammar, word usage, and mechanics.

✔ A 1-point essay is sorely lacking coherence and development. No clear thesis or support is mentioned. This essay completely misses the mark.

The Praxis scorers are a diverse lot, but they have one thing in common: They're looking for good writing. They don't score essays based upon their own personal views, so don't worry about writing your essay based on what you think the scorers want to hear. Although you never want to write anything that could offend anyone, you need not concern yourself with taking a particular view to please the scorer. Praxis scores are holistic, based on an overall assessment of your work.

Checking Out Some Practice Prompts

To better prepare for the essay-writing section of the Praxis, try writing an essay using one or all of these practice prompts. Remember to organize first. Then write. Time yourself.

Prompts for argumentative essays

Directions: Discuss the extent to which you agree or disagree with this opinion. Support your views with specific reasons and examples from your own experience, observations, or reading.

"Because students have so many extracurricular activities and so little time outside the school day, the majority of school hours should be limited to academic courses only."

"The technology included in the latest model automobiles — weather reports, e-mail access, GPS, and so forth — distracts the driver and should be eliminated."

"Although learning to eat nutritious food is important, some leaders in our society have taken the matter of eating healthy too far."

"Television reporting of news in the United States has begun to rely too heavily on ratings, leading networks to strive for entertainment and sensationalism rather than unbiased reporting."

"All high school and college students should be required to take regular drug tests."

"Students with poor academic performance should be barred from all extracurricular activities."

Prompts for informative/explanatory essays

Prompt #1

Directions: The following assignment requires you to use information from two sources to discuss the most important concerns that relate to a specific issue. When paraphrasing or quoting from the sources, cite each source by referring to the author's last name, the title, or any other clear identifier.

Source 1:

Adapted from: Fitzpatrick, John R. "House and the Virtue of Eccentricity," *House and Philosophy*. Hoboken, NJ: John Wiley & Sons, Inc. 2009. Print.

Diogenes of Sinope (404–323 BCE) was the most famous of the cynics. He distrusted the written word, and if he did write anything, none of it survived. But he was influential enough for others to record his life and views. Diogenes's philosophy stressed living an ethical life, a life as nature intended. Thus, the conventional life of Athens was far too soft, and the polite life of civil society was far too dishonest. Diogenes believed that one's private persona and public persona should be identical — what one says and does in private should be what one says and does in public. Diogenes is perhaps best known for walking the streets with a lit torch "looking for an honest man." We are all aware of modern politicians who preach family values in public while privately divorcing their spouses, abandoning their children, or soliciting prostitutes. For Diogenes, if you're going to talk the talk, then you'd better walk the walk; only by "walking your talk" can you live ethically and happily.

Source 2:

Adapted from: Malloy, Daniel P. "Clark Kent Is Superman: The Ethics of Secrecy," *Superman and Philosophy: What Would the Man of Steel Do?* Hoboken, NJ: John Wiley & Sons, Inc. 2013. Print.

The essential difference between secrecy and privacy is that privacy is often thought of as a right, whereas secrecy is a method. There are certain things we all have a right to keep to ourselves that do not require secrecy. The right to privacy has been somewhat controversial. Legally, at least in America, it has been established through precedent and interpretation, but cannot actually be found anywhere in the U.S. Constitution. Contemporary philosopher Judith Jarvis Thompson, along with some other philosophers, has argued that the right to privacy isn't a moral right either. Instead, Thompson argues that what we take to be the right to privacy is actually an amalgam of rights that a person has over herself and her property. Still, privacy does have some moral grounding. Secrecy, on the other hand, is not morally grounded. We have no right to keep secrets. Secrecy, then, is morally neutral. It is not presumed to be immoral, as lying is. Nor is it presumed to be a moral right. Secrecy is a tool, and just like any other tool, its rightness or wrongness depends on the use to which it is put.

Prompt #2

Directions: The following assignment requires you to use information from two sources to discuss the most important concerns that relate to a specific issue. When paraphrasing or quoting from the sources, cite each source by referring to the author's last name, the title, or any other clear identifier.

Source 1:

Adapted from: Nielsen, Carsten Fogh. "World's Finest Philosophers," Superman and Philosophy: What Would the Man of Steel Do?. Hoboken, NJ: John Wiley & Sons, Inc. 2013. Print.

In Leviathan, one of the most influential books on political philosophy ever written, the British philosopher Thomas Hobbes claimed that human beings neither do nor should trust each other, and described the natural state of human association as a war "of every man against every man." Hobbes recognized that many people might not agree with this somewhat depressing analysis, and that some might claim that human beings are not nearly as bad as Hobbes portrays them. In response to this, Hobbes asked those who disagreed with him to take a closer look at how they themselves actually behave: "Let him therefore consider with himself, when taking a journey, he arms himself, and seeks to go well accompanied; when going to sleep, he locks his doors; when even in his house, he locks his chest . . . Does he not there as much accuse mankind by his actions as I do by my words?"

Source 2:

Adapted from: Finkelman, Leonard. "Superman and Man," Superman and Philosophy: What Would the Man of Steel Do? Hoboken, NJ: John Wiley & Sons, Inc. 2013. Print.

The human nature optimist believes that the essence of humanity is selflessness. To quote philosopher Jean-Jacques Rousseau (1712-1778), "men, being wild rather than wicked, and more intent to guard themselves against the mischief that might be done them, than to do mischief to others, were by no means subject to very perilous dissensions." [. . .] Rousseau wrote that mankind is "born free, and everywhere is in chains." In the state of nature, you have compassion for your neighbor; however, your desire for compassion from her will compel you toward vanity, or the attempt to elevate yourself and diminish others.

Reviewing a Sample Essay

Take a look at a highly competent essay based on the following prompt: "Because students have so many extracurricular activities and so little time outside the school day, the majority of school hours should be limited to academic courses only."

So much to do. So little time. The school day is packed with activity, much of it unrelated to academic coursework. Assemblies, pep rallies, class meetings, and the myriad of other activities packed into a school day break students' concentration and fragment the day. Even so, most of these activities provide students with valuable learning experiences and hours of fun. To better serve students, the school day should strictly separate academics and extracurricular activities.

A typical school day lasts from 8 a.m. until 3 p.m. During that school day, approximately five hours are devoted to academics, and those five hours are typically interrupted several times by nonacademic activities. For example, on a typical day at my school, the academic day is interrupted at least half a dozen times by announcements, guest speakers, club and class meetings, bake sales, pep rallies, assemblies . . . the list goes on and on. Consequently, students often lose their concentration and focus. Students are continuously shifting from academics to nonacademics and back.

In addition, the time that students spend dashing to and from the classroom to extracurricular activities in the gym, auditorium, or other areas is time that could be better spent. Separating academics from extracurricular by moving all extracurricular activities to the end of the day would reduce transition time and valuable minutes would be added to study. Any appointments or obligations students might need to schedule outside of school could be attended to during the nonacademic hours, further increasing the time devoted to study. Once the academic portion of the day has ended, students would be free to enjoy the other side of school life: socializing, building relationships, attending events, listening to speakers, and, in general, participating fully in the school community. Students could catch their breath, stretch, smile, and look forward to the next few hours with friends, knowing the day's most important work was behind them.

While five straight hours of academics would be quite grueling and certainly not the answer, these "academic hours" could be broken by short, nonstructured breaks and lunch. By placing uninterrupted academic study first, academics become top priority. With no extended interruptions and less time spent in transition, students would be more focused and academic performance would increase. Numerous studies show that emphasizing the importance of academics in the school day leads to increased student performance.

The typical school day can overwhelm students with the volume and variety of activities to which they must attend. They sprint from one activity to another, barely stopping to catch their breath or assimilate the impact of the last class. Simply rearranging and compartmentalizing the many activities will add productive time to the school day, increase students' concentration and focus, and lead not only to better academic performance but also to more enjoyment of extracurricular activities.

Here is why this essay would receive a score of 6:

- ✔ **Introduction:** The introduction catches the reader's attention: "So much to do. So little time." The introduction also sets the stage for what's to come by mentioning the many activities in a school day and why these activities are a problem. The paragraph ends with a strong statement, a thesis.

- ✔ **Middle paragraph 1:** Notice that the first paragraph begins to build the case for a separation of academic and nonacademic activities. The argument is strengthened through the use of a personal anecdote. Note the transition words like "for example" and "consequently" that move the reader smoothly through the paragraph.

- ✔ **Middle paragraph 2:** The second paragraph continues to build the argument by presenting another benefit to the separation of academic and nonacademic activities: time saved. This idea is presented in the first sentence, the topic sentence. Notice the active verb, "dashing." Notice the "word picture" created in the last sentence, "Students could catch their breath. . . ." Also notice that the final sentence is a strong one, further stressing the benefit.

- ✔ **Middle paragraph 3:** In this paragraph, the writer recognizes and addresses an opposing argument: Five hours of academics would be too grueling. The writer continues to present further benefits to his suggested plan and ends with a strong sentence.

- ✔ **Conclusion:** The conclusion sums up the argument, restates the thesis, and brings closure.

Evaluating Your Essay

After you have written your essay, use the following list to help you evaluate your writing.

- ✔ **Have you constructed a strong, narrow thesis that directly addresses the prompt?** Does your essay proceed logically from paragraph to paragraph and idea to idea? Does the introduction lead smoothly to the conclusion? If your thesis is not clear, you will lose points. If your essay contains anything that doesn't pertain to your thesis, you will lose points.

- ✔ **Does your introductory paragraph anticipate the rest of your essay?** Does it easily hook to the thesis statement and link to the supporting details?

- ✔ **Are your supporting details relevant to the topic and closely aligned to your thesis?** Be sure your evidence is specific. General, vague statements will cost you. Be sure each middle paragraph has a sentence (preferably at the end) that clearly connects to your thesis.

- ✔ **Do you use transitions to move logically from one idea to another?** Examples of transitions include "consequently," "in addition," "however," "conversely," "in contrast," and "similarly."

- ✔ **Is your essay well organized?** Make sure it contains an introduction, your thesis, supporting details, and a conclusion. It should consist of a clear beginning, middle, and end.

- ✔ **Have you paid attention to action verbs and specific language?** Is your language natural or have you tried to impress by using language with which you're not comfortable? Watch out for overuse of the verb "to be." Try to substitute strong, active verbs wherever possible. Create "word pictures" with specific language.

- ✔ **Have you used a variety of sentences?** Vary the length and structure. Use some short sentences and some long ones. Use some with introductory clauses and some without. Use simple sentences as well as complex and compound sentences.

✔ **Does your conclusion bring closure and drive your point home?** The reader should leave with a clear understanding of your position and should completely understand why you hold that position.

✔ **Have you used correct grammar, spelling, and punctuation?** Be sure you save a few minutes of the allotted time to proofread for careless errors. If you have two or three mistakes in punctuation, spelling, or grammar, they may cost you.

✔ **Have you correctly cited any outside sources?** Be careful to cite any sources, whether you quote directly or paraphrase. If you have any doubt about whether to cite or not, cite!

How many points does your essay deserve? Read your essay again, placing yourself in that scorer's shoes (refer to the section "Understanding How the Essay Is Scored" for more details on scoring).

Write, write, write. You *can* improve your score by practicing. Have others read your essay and make suggestions. The more you write, the more comfortable you'll be on test day. Read your essay out loud. Doing so will help you notice areas where your thoughts may not flow smoothly. If possible, use grammar/spell check to help you catch any errors and learn from them.

Chapter 12

Giving Grammar a Glance

In This Chapter

▶ Identifying the purposes of the parts of speech

▶ Understanding various sentence structures

▶ Reviewing the rules regarding punctuation and capitalization

▶ Watching out for misplaced modifiers, redundancy, and double negatives

▶ Homing in on homophones

You probably wince when you hear the word "grammar." That's okay; so do most people. Folks tend to run screaming when they hear the word because they imagine "grammar" as a set of "rules for the sake of rules" that some highfalutin' person imposes on them in an effort to force them to speak "properly."

Grammar rules aren't rules "because someone says so." Rather, grammar refers to the internal logic by which words in English — or any other language — connect to one another in speech or writing. This chapter reviews the rules you need to know to ace the Praxis Core exam by featuring multiple-choice questions that cover standard English usage, revision-in-context, and sentence correction.

Getting a Grip on the Parts of Speech

The parts of speech are the categories into which different words are organized. English has eight of them: nouns, verbs, adjectives, adverbs, pronouns, prepositions, conjunctions, and interjections. These terms probably sound familiar to you from elementary school (with the possible exception of "interjections," which refer to stand-alone exclamations like "Wow," but interjections don't come up on the Praxis, so this is the last time this book will mention them).

Like most grammar tests, the Praxis writing test doesn't ask you directly about the parts of speech — you aren't asked to identify what part of speech a particular word within a sentence is. But because it's impossible to discuss grammar without using the terms for the different parts of speech, we review them here. Along the way, we alert you to different types of Praxis questions that involve the various parts of speech, so you know what to look out for.

Bear in mind that a given word doesn't always act as the same part of speech. What part of speech a word is depends on its function in the sentence in which it appears. For example, "purple" is an adjective in the sentence "I like purple lollipops," but it's a noun in the sentence "Purple is my favorite color."

Finding nouns as subjects and objects

A noun is a person, place, or thing. It's important to clarify that "things" don't necessarily have to be physical objects — for our purposes here, concepts and ideas are also "things." Thus, words like "justice," "honor," "hunger," and "love" (when they're not acting as verbs, of course) are also nouns. Three types of objects that you may see on the Praxis that function as nouns are direct objects, which receive the action of action verbs; indirect objects, which receive the action of the verb when the sentence also contains a direct object; and objects of the preposition, which follow the preposition in a prepositional phrase. (I explain objects more in detail later in this chapter).

A noun (along with a verb) is one of the two parts of speech that every sentence has to have in order to be a complete sentence. (Commands that consist solely of verbs, such as "Help!" or "Stop!", are still complete sentences because the subject is implied to be whomever the speaker is addressing.)

Although nouns are the bedrock of any language, we don't need to talk too much about them, because the Praxis doesn't try to trip you up where nouns are concerned. There's really only one noun-related trick or difficulty that you need to watch out for: Although the subject of a sentence is always a noun, and you may be used to thinking of "the subject" as meaning "whoever or whatever the sentence is about," that's actually not the most efficient way to locate the subject of a sentence in grammatical terms. For example, in the sentence "One of my best friends is a lawyer," the subject isn't "friends" or "lawyer" — it's "one." (For more tips on this issue, consult the section "The sentence skeleton: Identifying the main subject and verb" later in this chapter.)

Putting verbs to work

Verbs are "action words." Along with nouns, they're one of the two parts of speech that you absolutely need in order to have a complete sentence (and in a command, a verb can be a complete sentence all by itself).

Making verbs agree with other words

The order of the day when it comes to verbs on the Praxis, or any other grammar test, is agreement. A verb has to *agree* with the noun that performs the action of the verb, as well as with the other verbs in the sentence.

As far as agreement between verbs and nouns is concerned, the main issue is number agreement, as in singular versus plural. A singular noun needs to govern a verb in its singular form (as in "the elephant dances"), and a plural noun needs to govern a verb in its plural form (as in "the elephants dance"). Number-agreement issues are easy to spot when the noun and verb are right next to each other, but a favorite trick of grammar tests is to give you a sentence where the noun and verb *aren't* right next to each other. (See the later section "The sentence skeleton: Identifying the subject and verb" in this chapter for more details about finding the subject and verb when they aren't side by side.)

The other type of agreement you need to look out for is *tense* agreement, which concerns the agreement of one verb with another verb. For example, you can't say "I *ran* to the store and *buy* cat food" or "I *run* to the store and *bought* cat food"; it has to be "I *ran* to the store and *bought* cat food." Just as with number agreement, problems with tense agreement are easy to spot when the words concerned are close to each other in the sentence, but the Praxis tries to trick you by writing a long sentence in which the words concerned are far apart.

You should also be aware that, under certain circumstances, every verb in a sentence doesn't have to be in the same tense: For example, it's just fine to say "I *ran* to the store *to buy* cat food" (this time, *buy* is in the infinitive, so it doesn't have to agree with the past-tense *ran*). Mixing verb tenses is also perfectly alright if the actions in question were performed at different times. For instance, in the sentence "I *got* a good grade on the test because I *had studied* that book in high school," the verb *got* is in the past tense and the verb *had studied* is in the past-perfect tense, but the sentence is correct because one action was performed more recently than the other.

You don't have to know the different tense names on the Praxis Core, but you should be familiar with their various forms. Check out the progression of the verb "to run" in the following list:

- **Present:** I run
- **Present progressive:** I am running
- **Present perfect:** I have run
- **Past:** I ran
- **Past progressive:** I was running
- **Past perfect:** I had run
- **Future:** I will run
- **Future progressive:** I will be running
- **Future perfect:** I will have run

Watch out for the trick where the test gives you a sentence containing a noun whose singular and plural forms are identical (such as "sheep" or "fish") or a verb whose present- and past-tense forms are identical (such as "read"). In these cases, look for context clues elsewhere in the sentence to determine the number intended for the noun or the tense intended for the verb.

Some verbs have *transitive* and *intransitive* forms: The verb is different depending on whether it takes an object. "Rise/raise" is a good example: Compare the sentences "I *rise* from my chair (no object = intransitive) and "I *raise* the window" (object = transitive). In the first sentence, you are *rising* yourself, and in the second, you are *raising* something else. This rule is the explanation to the allegedly difficult (but not really so difficult once you know the rule) "lie/lay" conundrum: "lie" is intransitive and "lay" is transitive, so it's "I *lie* down" but "I *lay* the book down on the table."

Parallel phrasing

If you just felt a heart attack coming on when you saw the word "parallel" because you remember it from math class rather than English class, don't worry — this rule doesn't involve any geometry (nor is it as difficult as parallel parking, in case what you just experienced what was actually a driver's ed flashback). *Parallel phrasing* simply means that when you have a sentence with multiple verb phrases, the verbs in those phrases all need to be in the same form. (And if you actually enjoyed geometry, then I hope we never meet. Get it? Parallel? "Never meet?" Oh, forget it!)

The most common verb forms that grammar tests like to mix up when creating parallel-phrasing questions are the *infinitive* (the form with "to" in front, like "to be" or "to go") and the *participial* (the form with "-ing" at the end, like "being" or "going"). Neither form is more correct than the other — they just have to match. So, for example, it's fine to say either "I like to swim and to bike" or "I like swimming and biking," but you can't say "I like to swim and biking" or "I like swimming and to bike."

There are other, less blatant violations of parallel phrasing as well. For example, the sentence "Nobody cares about what I say or my actions" should be revised to read either "Nobody cares about what I say or what I do," or "Nobody cares about my words or my actions." See how the second two sentences flow better? This sort of parallel phrasing, however, is more about style than grammar, so standardized tests almost always limit mix-ups to infinitives and participials.

Which of the following choices presents the *best* revision of the following sentence?

The time to compose outlines has passed, so you should begin writing your essay, making sure to use persuasive arguments and inspiring quotations.

(A) The time to compose outlines has passed, so you should begin writing your essay, making sure to use persuasive arguments and inspiring quotations.

(B) The time for composing outlines has passed, so you should begin to write your essay, to use persuasive arguments, and to inspire with quotations.

(C) The time to compose outlines has passed, so you should begin to write your essay, to be sure to use persuasive arguments and inspiring quotations.

(D) The time to compose outlines has passed, so you should begin to write your essay, in which you should use persuasive arguments and inspiring quotations.

(E) The time for composing outlines has passed, so you should begin writing your essay, making sure of using persuasive arguments and inspiring quotations.

The correct answer is Choice (D). The verbs in the first two clauses ("to compose" and "to write") are both in the infinitive, the infinitive/participial choice in the next clause is avoided through the use of an "in which" clause, and the word "inspiring" doesn't have anything to do with the parallel-phrasing issue, because it's being used as an adjective. Choice (A) is the best of the incorrect choices, but it could be better; the juxtaposition of the infinitive ("to compose") and the participial ("writing") in the first two clauses is a bit messy. Choice (B) seems like it might be right at first, because all the verbs are in the infinitive, but the list-like structure makes it seem as if writing the essay, using arguments, and using quotations are three *different* activities, when what the sentence *wants* to imply is that the second two are a part of the first (don't simply look at verb forms without paying attention to the flow of the sentence as a whole). Choice (C) is simply messy and confusing: The "to be" that opens the final clause makes it sound like a list is coming, but then the sentence stops short. Choice (E) may seem right at first, because all the verb forms are in the participial, but the alteration of "to use" to "of using" is extremely awkward — there is more at stake in a sentence than whether the verbs match.

Gerunds: Verb forms that acts as nouns

Some words may appear to be verbs but are actually nouns, and they're called gerunds. A *gerund* is a participial verb form (in other words, it has an "-ing" ending) that works as a concept in the sentence rather than as an action performed by a noun. Check out these examples:

> Boxing is a sport that has been around for a long time.

> Standing in a busy road is not wise.

> Looking for gerunds is fun.

None of the underlined words are verbs, though they can be used as verbs. They are nouns. In fact, they're the subjects of the sentences. A gerund doesn't always need to be the subject of a sentence, however. In the sentence "Dancing is fun," the gerund is the subject, but in the sentence "I like dancing," the gerund is the object. In short, the key to recognizing gerunds is to look out for participial ("-ing") verbs that are being *referred to as ideas,* rather than being *performed by nouns.*

There are other cases where a word that is normally a verb can be a noun, like *run* in the sentence "I'm going to go for a run" or *dance* in the sentence "The big dance raised a lot of money for the school," but these aren't examples of gerunds — they're just words that can be nouns as well as verbs. In general, there's a lot of overlap between nouns and verbs.

Because they are technically nouns, gerunds are grammatically possessions, so the noun that "owns" the gerund should be in the possessive: "*Nina's* singing is lovely," "I appreciate *your* answering the telephone," "Please excuse *my* spilling that drink," and so on.

Using adjectives to describe people, places, and things

Adjectives modify nouns and pronouns. You probably don't have too much difficulty spotting an adjective when you see one, and in any case, the Praxis doesn't ask you to simply pick out all the adjectives in a given sentence, so we can get right to discussing the adjective-related tricks that the test *does* use.

When it comes to the Praxis writing test, the most common adjective-related trick is to substitute an adjective for an adverb, or vice versa, in an effort to see whether you catch the mistake. Look out for this trick especially on those "no error" questions wherein four portions of a given sentence are underlined, and you have to indicate which portion contains an error or select "no error" if the sentence is correct. Anytime you see an adjective or an adverb underlined by itself on such a question, you should always double-check to insure that the word in question is being used correctly.

The reason this trick is possible to play, of course, is because most (but not all) adjectives can be turned into adverbs with the addition of "-ly." Examine, for example, the roles of the adjective *quick* and the adverb *quickly* in the similar sentences "The quick dog ran up the hill" and "The dog ran quickly up the hill." True to their respective functions, the adjective modifies a noun *(dog)*, and the adverb modifies a verb *(ran)*. The Praxis tries to trick you by giving you a sentence in which the words that are supposed to agree are not right next to each other. If, for example, you encountered the sentence "The dog ran up the hill quick," it may be less immediately noticeable that *quick* should be *quickly* (even though *quick* is next to the noun *hill,* the intent of the word is still to modify the verb; therefore, it must be an adverb, because adjectives cannot modify verbs).

And if the Praxis *really* wants to get tricky, it will throw a participial verb form into the mix, so that you have to figure out whether the "-ing" word is a noun (in which case it should be modified by an adjective) or a verb (in which case it should be modified by an adverb). Consider the differences between these two correct sentences:

> Constant dancing has worn out my shoes.

> My shoes are worn out because I am constantly dancing.

In the first sentence, *dancing* is a gerund (and the subject of the sentence), so it is modified with the adjective *constant.* In the second sentence, *dancing* is a verb in the present-progressive tense, so it's modified with the adverb *constantly.* Pretty sneaky, huh?

Not all adverbs end in "-ly," not all adjectives can be turned into adverbs by adding "-ly," and some words that end in "-ly" are adjectives (adverbs are discussed in more detail in the next section). Take adjectives of number, for example. *Five* is an adjective in the sentence "There are five cupcakes on the table" (it modifies a noun, after all), but there's no such word as *fively. Old* is an adjective in "The old forest is beautiful," but the forest can't do something *oldly*, because no such word exists. *Elderly* is a word, but guess what? It's an adjective — as is *elder*, making *elder/elderly* one of the few cases where a word and the same word with "-ly" attached are both adjectives, albeit ones with different meanings: The first is a comparative adjective meaning "old*er* (than someone else)," and the second just means "old." If that isn't enough to blow your mind, note that "beautiful" in the sentence about the forest is, of course, also an adjective, despite the fact that it comes next to the verb *is*.

Don't try to determine whether a word is (or should be) an adjective or an adverb based on how it's spelled or what it looks like. Instead, look at the job it is doing in the sentence — that is, whether it's modifying a noun/pronoun or a verb (unless the verb is a form of "to be").

The last bit of adjective-related funny business concerns punctuation. In the sentence "The three young French girls are charming," you may notice something odd: There are no commas in the sentence, even though the noun *girls* has three adjectives in front of it. You've presumably been taught that you need commas when multiple adjectives modify the same noun (as in "The hairy, hungry, faithful dog ran up the hill"), so what's going on here?

Certain types of adjectives don't need to be separated by commas when they appear in a series before a noun — in this case, our exceptions are "adjectives of number," "adjectives of age," and "adjectives of nationality." Adjectives of size are another exception: You wouldn't put a comma between *big* and *American* in "the big American ship," would you? (Nor, for example, would you ever say "the American big ship," because another convention dictates that adjectives of nationality must immediately precede the noun.)

Trust your ear. Although memorizing rules certainly has its place when it comes to grammar, it's not always the most efficient strategy. You may not have known that there were any rules about adjective order, but if you had heard someone say "the Japanese old five cars," it would have sounded wrong to you, right? You would have simply *sensed* that it should be "the five old Japanese cars," for some reason you couldn't explain. When you have an instinct like that, following it is usually more reliable than racking your brain for a rule. Speakers of a language — especially native speakers — often sense rules that may never have been explained to them. Cool, huh?

Calling on adverbs to describe actions and conditions

Adverbs can modify verbs, adjectives, or other adverbs — and they don't need to be anywhere near the words they modify to get the job done. All things considered, adverbs are probably the most versatile part of speech. They can look many different ways, they can perform many different jobs, and they can appear just about anywhere in the sentence. In short, whenever you find yourself looking at a word and wondering "What the heck part of speech is this word?" the safe bet is that it's an adverb.

Just consider the following three correct sentences:

I studied tirelessly all night. (*Tirelessly* is an adverb modifying the verb *studied*.)

The movie was very sad. (*Very* is an adverb modifying the adjective *sad*.)

I handled the dynamite extremely gently. (*Extremely* is an adverb modifying the other adverb *gently*, which is modifying the verb *handled*.)

In those examples, two of the adverbs end in "-ly," and the one that doesn't is still fairly easy to spot as an adverb, because *very* means the same thing as *extremely*.

But adverbs can disguise themselves much more confusingly than that. They can even look like nouns. For example, in the sentence "I'm going to a concert tonight," the word *tonight* is an adverb. Why? Because it is doing the job of an adverb. If I asked you to describe what the word *tonight* is doing in that sentence, you'd probably say that it's modifying (or adding more information to) the word *going* (namely, it answers the question of *when* the speaker is going). And because *going* is a verb, the word that modifies it must therefore be an adverb.

When it comes to adverbs, be aware that they are masters of disguise. Never try to pick out adverbs based on what they look like. Instead, look at what the word in question is modifying. If it's modifying a verb, an adjective, or another adverb, it's an adverb, no matter what it looks like.

In cases where the word looks so little like an adverb that you simply can't believe it is one, a good way to double-check is to substitute a word that *does* look like an adverb and see whether it can do the same job. For example, if you alter the sentence "I'm going to a concert tonight" to read "I'm going to a concert excitedly" or "I'm going to a concert cheerfully," you can see that all three sentences are grammatically correct and that *excitedly* and *cheerfully* are clearly adverbs. Therefore, *tonight* must be an adverb too, because it occupies the space in the sentence that needs to be occupied by an adverb.

Please indicate which, if any, of the underlined portions contains an error.

> We had a <u>rough</u> time trying to figure out which of the <u>generally</u> <u>quiet</u> children had been
>   A   B   C
>
> <u>constant</u> making noise. <u>No error</u>.
> D   E

The correct answer is Choice (D). *Making* is a verb, so it should be modified with an adverb instead of an adjective: *constantly* instead of *constant*. Choice (A) is wrong because *rough,* as an adjective, correctly modifies the noun *time.* Choice (B) is wrong because *generally,* as an adverb, correctly modifies the adjective *quiet.* Choice (C) is wrong because *quiet,* as an adjective, correctly modifies the noun *children.* Choice (E) is wrong because the sentence does, in fact, contain an error.

Getting the lowdown on pronouns

A *pronoun* is a word that takes the place of a noun. Pronouns were created to avoid repetition of nouns. Think about the repetitive nature of the following sentence:

> Richard went to the store and bought Richard some bread, and then Richard drove to another store where Richard often shops.

Now look at what pronouns can do:

> Richard went to the store and bought himself some bread, and then he drove to another store where he often shops.

The words "himself" and "he" are pronouns, and they take the place of the noun "Richard" three times in the preceding sentence. The most common pronouns — and the ones that are probably the most familiar to you — are the *personal pronouns.* Basically, personal pronouns represent specific people and things and work as substitutes for their specific names.

When it comes to pronouns on the Praxis, there are two tricks you have to watch out for: singular versus plural, and subjective case versus objective case. Table 12-1 summarizes these properties, and we go into these properties in more detail in the following sections.

Table 12-1	Pronouns and Their Properties			
	Subjective Case		**Objective Case**	
	Singular	**Plural**	**Singular**	**Plural**
First person	I	we	me	us
Second person	you	you	you	you
Third person	he, she, it	they	him, her, it	them

Singular versus plural pronouns

One of the most important issues with pronouns is that they agree in number with their antecedents (*antecedent* is the fancy word for "the noun that a pronoun takes the place of," but although the word literally means "comes before," it's important to note that a pronoun doesn't *always* come after the word it's standing in for in the sentence).

Take, for example, the following correct sentence:

If a student wants to drop a class, he or she must visit the Registrar's office.

You don't know who this hypothetical student is, but regardless, you still know there is only *one* hypothetical student, so you need a singular pronoun. Although it's now very common to use *they* in spoken English as a gender-neutral singular pronoun (to avoid the labor of constantly saying "he or she" or the sexism of just saying "he" when gender is unknown), be advised that the Praxis and virtually all grammar tests do *not* yet consider this to be correct. Inclusive and time-saving as it is, "they" is still plural and *only* plural as far as most tests are concerned.

However, because the writers of grammar tests know that test-takers are on the lookout for "they" as a wrong answer (when it should be "he or she"), question-writers will occasionally flip things around on you and use "they" correctly, hoping that you'll be fooled into instinctively changing it to "he or she." Consider the following correct sentence:

If students want to drop a class, they must visit the Registrar's office.

This time, of course, the pronoun's antecedent ("students") is actually plural, so *they* is correct. You only have to watch out for mismatches like the following:

Incorrect: If a *student* wants to drop a class, *they* must visit the Registrar's office.

Incorrect: If *students* want to drop a class, *he or she* must visit the Registrar's office.

Subjective versus objective pronouns

Aside from singular versus plural (see the preceding section), the most common pronoun-related trick that the Praxis uses involves subjective versus objective case. If those terms aren't familiar to you, don't worry: You already know what they mean, even if you don't know the fancy terms. The difference between subjective and objective case is the difference between "I" and "me," or "we" and "us," or "he/she" and "him/her," or "they" and "them." Namely, the difference is that you use the second word (the *objective* case) when the pronoun is the *object* of a verb or a preposition. A pronoun doesn't have to be the *subject* of the sentence for you to use the first word, or *subjective* case — you use it whenever the pronoun is *not* the object of anything.

Even if you've never heard the terms "subjective case" and "objective case" before, you probably still sense that it's wrong to say "He hit I" or "Throw the ball to I." As an English speaker, situations where you should say "me" instead of "I" (or "us" instead of "we," and so on) are simply something you sense — you've probably been using subjective and objective pronoun cases correctly 99 percent of the time for all your life, even if nobody has ever taught you the rule for doing so.

What you need to be concerned about for the Praxis is that 1 percent of cases where you *don't* automatically sense what the correct usage is. Also predictably, the way a test tries to trip you up with pronoun case is the same way it tries to trip you up with anything else: by putting other words in between the two words that are supposed to agree with each other.

Look at the following four sentences, all of which are incorrect, but some of which are more obviously incorrect than others:

> **Obviously incorrect:** Please take I home now.
>
> **Obviously incorrect:** Throw the ball to I.
>
> **Less obviously incorrect:** Please take Taryn and I home now.
>
> **Less obviously incorrect:** Throw the balls to my friends and I.

The error in all four of those sentences is that the pronoun should be in the objective case instead of the subjective case — in other words, it should be "me" instead of "I." In two of the sentences, the pronoun is the object of a verb ("take"), and in the other two, it is the object of a preposition ("to"). But putting another noun in between the verb or preposition and the pronoun makes it a lot less obvious that the wrong pronoun case is being used, doesn't it?

The verb "to be" doesn't take an objective case for its object, because the object of "to be" is the same person or thing as its subject: That's why it's correct to say "This is *she*" instead of "This is *her*" when you answer the telephone and someone asks to speak to you.

Which version of the underlined portion makes the sentence correct?

Before you take the photograph of <u>Deloris and I, let</u> us adjust our lights.

(A) Deloris and I, let

(B) Deloris and me, let

(C) Deloris and myself, let

(D) Deloris, and I let

(E) Deloris, and me let

The correct answer is Choice (B). The pronoun is one of the objects of the preposition *of,* so it should be the objective-case *me,* not the subjective-case *I.* The comma should be placed between that pronoun and the verb *let,* because that's the point at which the introductory subordinate clause ends and the main independent clause (which is a command) begins.

The right answer is not Choice (A) because the pronoun is one of the objects of the preposition *of,* so it should be the objective-case *me,* not the subjective-case *I.*

The right answer is not Choice (C) because the speaker has not yet appeared in the sentence and is not reflexively performing any verb upon himself, so there's no need to use *myself* instead of *me*.

The right answer is not Choice (D) because the pronoun is one of the objects of the preposition *of*, so it should be the objective-case *me*, not the subjective-case *I*. Additionally, the comma should be placed between that pronoun and the verb *let*, because that's the point at which the introductory subordinate clause ends and the main independent clause (which is a command) begins.

The right answer is not Choice (E) because the comma should be placed between the pronoun and the verb *let*, because that's the point at which the introductory subordinate clause ends and the main independent clause (which is a command) begins.

The dreaded "whom" made easy

Perhaps no single word in the English language strikes more terror into the hearts of those who are about to take a grammar test than *whom*. Hardly anyone who isn't an English teacher has any confidence whatsoever in his or her ability to use it correctly, and most people just avoid using it altogether. But believe it or not, *whom*'s bark is much worse than its bite. Its usage is really not all that difficult to understand.

Just as "me" is the objective case of "I" or "us" is the objective case of "we," "whom" is simply the objective case of "who." The rules for *who/whom* are no different from the rules for *I/me, he/him, we/us,* or *they/them*. So where did its fearsome reputation come from? Well, *who/whom* is made a bit more complicated than the other pronouns by the fact that *who* is frequently used as an *interrogative* pronoun, meaning that it's used to ask questions. The arrangement of words in a question is different from the arrangement of words in a statement. For example, in a question, the pronoun may be the first word, whereas the verb of which it is the object may be the last word. So a question like "*Who* do you love?" should actually be "*Whom* do you love?" because the pronoun is the object of the verb *love*.

Most of the time, if a question on the Praxis involves *whom*, it employs *whom* as a relative pronoun rather than an interrogative one. Consider the following sentence, which uses *whom* correctly but as a relative pronoun (that is, it's used to link clauses rather than to ask a question):

My grandmother, from whom I inherited my green eyes, lives in Wisconsin.

You remember the simple grade-school rule about how you're supposed to use *who* when you're talking about a person, but *that* or *which* when you're talking about an animal or a thing, right? Okay, so the sentence you just examined is no different from saying:

This book, from which I learned grammar, was well worth the price.

In both cases, the relative pronoun is right next to the preposition *from*, so it's easy to spot as the object. In the first sentence, you use *who/whom* instead of *which*, because you're talking about a person, and the form is *whom* instead of *who* because it's the object of a preposition. If *whom* comes up on the Praxis, it will probably be in a situation like that.

Considering conjunctions

Conjunctions link parts of a sentence together (think *conjoin*), be they individual words (as in "I bought bread *and* eggs") or entire clauses (as in "I went cycling on Saturday, *and* I went swimming on Sunday"). In addition to the "big three" conjunctions — *and*, *but*, and *or* — some other common ones are *so, yet,* and *nor*. (*For* can also be a conjunction, but most of the time, *for* is a preposition, as in "The telephone call was *for* you.")

The seven words discussed in the preceding paragraph are the only seven *coordinating* conjunctions, which you can remember with the mnemonic FANBOYS (**f**or, **a**nd, **n**or, **b**ut, **o**r, **y**et, **s**o). But there are many more *subordinating* conjunctions (*because, since, although, when, unless, while,* and *until* are just a few).

So what's the difference? When two clauses are linked with a coordinating conjunction, the conjunction can *only* go in the middle, whereas a subordinating conjunction may appear at the beginning of a sentence or between two clauses in a sentence.

In terms of taking the Praxis writing test, why do you need to know this? The answer is "commas." Questions on the Praxis writing exam expect you to know where commas do or don't go. In fact, in the questions that underline four portions of a sentence and instruct you to pick the portion that contains an error (or select "no error" if there are no errors), occasionally *a single comma by itself* is underlined as one of the four choices, so you need to know whether a comma belongs in that spot. And knowledge of conjunction rules plays a big part in knowing where commas should or shouldn't go.

So, say you have two independent clauses: "I studied hard" and "I aced the test." Now say you want to link them with a conjunction. If you want to link them with a coordinating conjunction, there's only one way to do that: Put the coordinating conjunction in the middle and place a comma before the conjunction ("I studied hard, so I aced the test"). Keep in mind that if you don't have the comma, or if you have the comma but not the conjunction, the sentence is incorrect.

It is incorrect to place a comma before a coordinating conjunction unless the coordinating conjunction links two independent clauses (compare "I like watching TV and playing video games" and "I like watching TV, and I like playing video games") or precedes the last item in a series (compare "I invited James, Tom, Scott, and Brian").

If, on the other hand, you feel like linking the two clauses with a subordinating conjunction, you have two options: Either put the subordinate clause second and don't use a comma, or put the subordinate clause first and use a comma (either "I aced the test because I studied hard" or "Because I studied hard, I aced the test). Keep in mind that if you include the comma when the subordinate clause comes second or omit the comma when the subordinate clause comes first, the sentence is incorrect.

Perusing prepositions

You hear a lot about prepositions in the section on pronouns, because it talks about how pronouns should be in the objective case when they're the object of either a verb or a preposition. Of course, that knowledge isn't much help if you don't know a preposition when you see one.

So what is a *preposition?* It's a word that provides information about the relationship of words to each other in time and space: *before* and *after* are prepositions, for example, as are *over* and *under.* (The "time and space" rule is not absolute, however. *About* is one example of a preposition that does not relate to relationships in time and space, as in "The movie was *about* skateboarders." Oh, and be aware that *about* can also be an adverb meaning *approximately,* as in "The movie was *about* two hours long.")

There are too many prepositions for you to simply memorize all of them, but a handy, short list includes the following: *aboard, about, above, around, at, before, behind, below, beneath, beside, between, beyond, but* (when used like *except,* as in "I want everything *but* anchovies on the pizza"; the rest of the time, it's a conjunction), *by, down, during, except, for, from, in, inside, into, like* (when used to mean *similarly to* or *such as,* as in "He looks *like* my cousin" or "Some countries, *like* Switzerland, are landlocked"), *near, of, off, on, over, past, since* (when used to signify the last time something occurred, as in "I haven't seen him *since* Monday"), *through, throughout, to, towards, under, underneath, until, up, upon, with, within,* and *without.*

Many people find it helpful to refer to prepositions as "squirrel words," meaning that they represent things a squirrel can do: The squirrel ran *around* the room; the squirrel ran *under* the table; the squirrel jumped *over* the chair; the squirrel crawled *inside* my desk; the squirrel ran *down* the hallway, *past* the water fountain, and *through* the door; and so on.

Most preposition-related questions on the Praxis writing exam involve determining whether the pronoun should be in the subjective or objective case. The only other common type of preposition question on the Praxis concerns preposition selection itself. Occasionally, a "no error" question will have a preposition underlined by itself, and you're expected to know whether the preposition is being used correctly in that context or whether another preposition would be better. Consider these examples:

> **Correct:** "I'm obsessed *with* grammar."
>
> **Incorrect:** "I'm obsessed *on* grammar."
>
> **Correct:** "The movie was based *on* the book."
>
> **Incorrect:** "The movie was based *about* the book."

So whenever you see a preposition underlined by itself on a "no error" question, make sure it's the best one to use in that context. Unfortunately, preposition usage in English is largely *idiomatic,* which is the fancy word for "you say it that way because you just do." Think about it: Why do you say "*in* the morning" but "*at* night?" or "get *in* the car" but "get *on* the plane?" You just do.

Many prepositions can also function as other parts of speech, so the mere presence of a word that, in some instances, can be a preposition doesn't necessarily mean that the pronoun following it should be in the objective case. (Compare "I get to use the bike *after* him," in which *after* is a preposition, to "*After* he is done using it, I get the bike," in which *after* is a subordinating conjunction.) As mentioned earlier, *but* and *since* are two more words that can be either prepositions or conjunctions, and the incredibly versatile word *like* can actually function as any part of speech except a pronoun!

If you want to memorize many of the most common prepositions, do an Internet search for "prepositions Jingle Bells." There's a song setting a list of prepositions to the tune of "Jingle Bells" that's incredibly helpful and quite easy to memorize.

Making Sense of Sentence Structure

Now that you've reviewed the parts of speech and how to put them together (see the preceding sections), it's time to brush up on how groups of words fit together to make sentences. When it comes to "groups of words," there are two types: *clauses* and *phrases*. Without getting unnecessarily technical, the difference is that a *clause* has both a subject and a verb whereas a *phrase* does not.

Now, you probably know that the definition of a *sentence* is that it has both a subject and a verb. So you're probably wondering what the difference is between a *clause* and a *sentence*. Well, the best analogy is that it's like the difference between a home and a building. If you live in a house, then your home and your building are the same thing. But if you live in an apartment, then your building contains other homes in addition to yours. To qualify as a home, a given space needs to contain a few essential elements: a bedroom and a bathroom, for example. A big, fancy house may have multiple bedrooms and bathrooms, but it's still just one home. Conversely, an apartment building can contain many bedrooms and bathrooms but be divided up into many different homes, each of which contains one bedroom and one bathroom.

A sentence, then, may only contain one clause — in this case, the clause and the sentence are the same thing. A longer sentence, on the other hand, can contain multiple clauses. It also may contain one or more *phrases* — bits of extra information that are nice to have, but not necessary to make a complete sentence. To continue with the "home" analogy, you can say that a phrase is like a den: It's nice to have a den in your home, but you don't need to have one for your home to count as a home; at the same time, a den all by itself cannot be said to constitute a home.

To turn now to punctuation, you can say that punctuation marks are like walls. Periods are the outer walls that separate your home from other people's homes, and commas (or semicolons, dashes, and so forth) are the inner walls that separate the rooms in your home from one another. Sometimes these inner walls are absolutely necessary (it would certainly be odd if your bathroom were not separated from the other rooms by any walls), and other times, they're not (the kitchen and the dining room may just be two separate areas within one big room). Most of the time, clauses and phrases are separated from one another by punctuation marks such as commas, but under certain circumstances, they may not be. We review punctuation later in the chapter. This section focuses on sentence structure.

Independent clauses versus everything else

Independent clause is the fancy name for "a group of words that can stand as a complete sentence by itself." Some sentences consist of a single independent clause, while others consist of an independent clause joined to one or more other types of clauses or phrases. Still others consist of two or more independent clauses joined to one another, or of two or more independent clauses joined to one or more other types of clauses or phrases, and so on. From a strictly grammatical standpoint, you can combine as many clauses and phrases as you like into a single sentence, as long as you combine them according to the rules.

Take the sentence "I eat popcorn." It is both an independent clause and a complete sentence. But say you want to make this sentence a little more interesting, so you change it to "I eat popcorn at the movies." *At the movies* is a prepositional phrase (which you can tell by the fact that *at* is a preposition). It's not divided from your initial independent clause with commas, and you can say that it's now part of your independent clause, even though it's not an essential part — you can get rid of it and still have a complete sentence. Now suppose you expand the sentence yet again, to read "Every Tuesday, I eat popcorn at the movies."

Now you have an *adverbial phrase* at the beginning, followed by a comma, because it precedes the independent clause. Now say you expand the sentence even further, to read "Every Tuesday, if I'm hungry, I eat popcorn at the movies." This time, you've added a *dependent clause:* "I'm hungry" *could* be a complete sentence by itself, but here, it's bonded to the subordinating conjunction *if*, so the clause is dependent. You now have multiple subjects and verbs in the sentence, but the main subject and verb of the whole sentence are still "I eat," from your initial independent clause. Anything that isn't an independent clause is considered a fragment, which doesn't generate a complete thought.

The sentence skeleton: Identifying the main subject and verb

Don't worry: You don't actually need to know the difference between a clause and a phrase or between one type of phrase and another to answer any questions on the Praxis writing test. You *do*, however, need to be pretty good at quickly identifying the main subject and verb of a sentence. The ability to do this is useful when it comes to answering all sorts of grammar questions, and being familiar with the terms *independent clauses, dependent clauses,* and *phrases* makes the task easier (the preceding section gives you the lowdown on these terms).

In other words, you *don't* technically need to know the fancy names for all the different types of "extra stuff" that can be in a sentence, but you *do* need to be able to tell the difference between the things that need to be there in order to have a complete sentence and the things that don't.

So, okay, say you're asked to identify the main subject and verb of this sentence:

> According to biologists, one of the most endangered animals is the Javan rhinoceros.

If you correctly discerned that the subject is *one* and the verb is *is*, good job! The nouns in the sentence that jumped out at you were probably *biologists, animals,* and *Javan rhinoceros,* but none of these is the main subject. Why not? Well, *biologists* can't be the subject of the sentence because it's part of an introductory phrase rather than the main independent clause. *Animals* can't be the subject because it's part of a prepositional phrase (specifically, the one governed by *of*). And *Javan rhinoceros* can't be the subject because it's the object. That leaves you with *one, the singular pronoun which serves as the subject of the sentence.*

The use of the word *one,* can sometimes be confusing in this case, as it is sometimes used as a numerical expression. However, *one* is an indefinite pronoun in the sentence, which is a predicate nominative for *Javan rhinoceros.* Other indefinite pronouns, such as *all, many, or some* could be substituted in its place and the sentence would still make sense.

As for the verb, not only is *is* the main verb, but it's actually the *only* verb in the whole sentence! *According to* is an expression that works like a preposition, and *endangered* here is an adjective modifying *animals.*

No matter what sort of grammar question you're dealing with, it's always a good idea to ground yourself by first identifying the main subject and verb — what I call the "sentence skeleton," because everything else in the sentence is constructed around it. You can get rid of everything in a sentence except the main independent clause (or, for that matter, the subject and verb of the main independent clause) and still have a complete sentence. The sentence won't be as informative, but it will still be grammatically correct. And no word that's located in one of the parts of the sentence you can get rid of can possibly be the main subject or main verb. For example, if you were to take all the prepositional phrases and clauses from the preceding sentence, you'd be left with the sentence, *One is a Javan Rhinoceros.*

Run-ons and comma splices

Although you probably remember the term *run-on* from school, you may not be 100 percent sure what it means. Many people mistakenly believe that a run-on sentence is just a sentence that is too long, but that's not actually what the term means.

A run-on sentence is a sentence wherein two (or more, in especially messy cases) independent clauses have been placed next to each other without being properly joined. Just as the bones in your body need to be connected to one another with ligaments, independent clauses must be connected to one another with the proper combination of conjunctions and/or punctuation.

The run-on sentence's ugly cousin is the comma splice. The *comma splice* is a run-on sentence that attempts to join two independent clauses with only a comma, when more than just a comma is necessary.

In short, both run-ons and comma splices are grammatical errors, and very similar ones — the difference is that a comma splice has a comma in it and a run-on doesn't.

In case all that was about as clear as mud, here are some examples. Start by examining the correct, complete sentence "Shakespeare is my favorite writer, because his characters are the most memorable." This sentence consists of two independent clauses ("Shakespeare is my favorite writer" and "his characters are the most memorable"), joined with the conjunction *because* and a comma before the conjunction. Using a comma and a conjunction is the most common way to correctly join two independent clauses. A comma splice is when the writer puts in just the comma without the conjunction, and a run-on is when the writer puts nothing at all between the two clauses, as in these sentences:

- ✔ **Comma splice:** "Shakespeare is my favorite writer, his characters are the most memorable."
- ✔ **Run-On:** "Shakespeare is my favorite writer his characters are the most memorable."

Most grammar tests for older students or adults don't bother throwing in too many run-ons, because they're easy to spot. But test-writers just *love* to throw comma splices at you! Learn to spot a comma splice from a mile away, and your score will shoot up significantly solely due to your acquiring that one skill!

Which of the following sentences is *not* grammatically correct?

(A) Before your friends get here, we should pick up some snacks.

(B) That movie was too long, I almost fell asleep.

(C) If I don't get this question right, I'm going to be deeply ashamed.

(D) I'm afraid of that dog, so I'm going to walk the long way home.

(E) The sun is warm, the sky is blue, and I'm happy.

The correct answer is Choice (B). That sentence presents two independent clauses joined with only a comma, making it a comma splice and the only one of the five choices that is *not* a correct sentence. Choice (A) presents an independent clause preceded by a dependent clause, with a comma between the two, which is correct. Choice (C) links two independent clauses by placing a comma between them and the subordinating conjunction "if" at the beginning of the first clause, which is correct. Choice (D) links two independent clauses with a comma and a coordinating conjunction, which is correct. Choice (E) presents three independent clauses, and although there is only a comma between the first two, there's a comma and a conjunction between the second and third, so that choice is correct as well.

Appositives: Interruptions to the independent clause

So far, we've been talking about independent clauses and other types of clauses and phrases that can be added onto the root independent clause. But in addition to all the non-independent clauses and phrases that can be added *around* the main independent clause, there's one other type of extra information that can be added to a sentence, and it's extra-tricky because it gets inserted *into* the main independent clause. It's called an *appositive*.

Based on the information in the preceding sections, you may have been under the impression that the main subject and verb of a sentence — which may not be right next to each other — won't be separated from each other by any commas, because commas are used to separate all the extra clauses and phrases from the central independent clause. And that's true, *unless* the sentence contains an appositive. The good news is that, although they fall into an inconvenient location within the sentence, appositives at least have the decency to be set off with punctuation.

Examine the following sentences, in which the main subjects and main verbs appear in boldface:

> **Jack**, my youngest cousin, **is** a carpenter.
>
> The **movie**, though it wasn't completely faithful to the book, **made** interesting choices.
>
> **Most** of the restaurants in this neighborhood, while they may not deliver or stay open very late, **pride** themselves on their affordability.

In all three examples, an additional descriptive phrase — an appositive — is inserted into the middle of the independent clause, between the subject and the verb. Appositives are usually set off with a pair of commas, though they can also be set off with a pair of dashes, as in the first sentence of this paragraph. Think of an appositive as being similar to a parenthetical remark but not quite inconsequential enough to actually appear in parentheses. It's also worth noting that an appositive often (though not always) could easily have been placed elsewhere in the sentence: The first example sentence could just as easily have read "My youngest cousin Jack is a carpenter" as "Jack, my youngest cousin, is a carpenter." But either way, the subject is still *Jack* and the verb is still *is*.

When you're searching for the main subject and verb of a sentence, you may also have to lift out an appositive that *splits* the independent clause, in addition to brushing away all the other types of extra clauses and phrases that come *before and after* the independent clause.

Pondering Punctuation

Just as road signs or traffic signals are placed wherever streets intersect with one another, punctuation marks appear at the junctures where different parts of a sentence come together. Now that you know all about phrases and clauses, it's time to review how punctuation marks are used to mark their intersections. You already know that a period comes at the end of a sentence (or a question mark or exclamation point), so we don't need to talk about periods. Instead, this section is mainly concerned with commas, as well as with the other, less common, punctuation marks that may come up on the Praxis writing test.

Commas

It may be a little gross, but you may find it helpful to think of commas as the scars that are left when a sentence is operated on. The "operation" may be a "transplant," wherein a portion of the sentence is moved elsewhere (for example, placing a subordinate clause before the main independent clause instead of after it), or it may be a "graft," wherein two elements of a sentence are spliced together (for example, making two independent clauses into one sentence or adding extra information to an independent clause).

Comma placement is determined by what is happening at a given point in the sentence. There are six situations in which commas are necessary, which we outline in the following sections.

Joining two or more independent clauses

A comma is always necessary if there is more than one independent clause in the sentence (unless another punctuation mark, such as a semicolon, colon, or dash, does the job). For example, when combining the independent clauses "There was no school" and "I went to the beach," you end up with "There was no school, so I went to the beach." Note that a coordinating conjunction is absolutely required after the comma. In cases where more than two independent clauses are being combined, a comma is still required after each one, but the coordinating conjunction is only necessary before the last, as in "Ben plays guitar, Brian plays bass, and Scott plays drums."

Following an introductory clause

When the sentence opens with a non-independent clause or phrase, a comma is required after the introductory clause/phrase and the subsequent independent clause. For example, "In order to pass the test, you must study."

Whether a clause is independent or non-independent, as well as whether a comma is required, has nothing to do with the length of the sentence. You can have a long independent clause preceded by an introductory clause as brief as a single word in length ("Relieved, he called his friends and family to tell them how well he did on the test"), or you can have a brief independent clause preceded by a fairly lengthy dependent one ("Saddened by all the sorrow and confusion in this crazy, modern world of ours, he wept").

Before an "afterthought" clause

An "afterthought" clause is like an introductory clause, but it comes after the independent clause instead of before it. Be aware, however, that a dependent clause beginning with a subordinating conjunction is *not* an afterthought clause and does *not* need to be preceded by a comma (although it *does* need to be followed by one if it comes first). Examples of sentences with afterthought clauses include "I don't need a tune-up, just an oil change" and "I saw my two favorite animals at the zoo, lemurs and red pandas."

On both sides of an appositive/"interrupting" clause

When a non-independent clause or phrase comes in the middle of an independent clause, it needs to be set off with commas on both sides. For example, the second sentence in the afterthought-clause section could also have taken the form of "I saw my two favorite animals, lemurs and red pandas, at the zoo."

There's no rhyme or reason to which part of the sentence *has* to be the appositive; it all depends on how you feel like writing it: You can say either "Abraham Lincoln, the 16th president, was the first president with a beard" or "The 16th president, Abraham Lincoln, was the first president with a beard."

Although, for the sake of your sanity, this book avoids using all the fancy names for the many types of interrupting clauses, there are some other types of interrupting clauses that aren't technically appositives but still need to be set off with commas. A *which* clause is a good example, as in "Halloween, which was called Samhain by the Celts, is my favorite holiday." Certain types of interrupting clauses or phrases can be as short as one or two words, like *for example* or *however* (as in "This sentence, for example, has a very short interrupting clause in the middle" or "This sentence, however, has an even shorter one").

Whenever any type of phrase or clause falls in the middle of a single independent clause, it needs to have commas on both sides.

Separating items in a list

When listing words or phrases, commas are used to separate the items in the list. You may be listing individual words ("I bought cheese, milk, bread, pasta sauce, and fireworks"), or you may be listing phrases or concepts several words long ("I bought a book with a green cover, an umbrella with purple stripes, six leopards that can dance the tango, and fireworks with which to scare the leopards if they won't stop dancing").

The comma preceding the *and* before the last item in the list — the so-called *Oxford comma* — is considered optional by grammarians. It is correct either to include or omit it, and the Praxis doesn't ask you questions about this rule.

Separating multiple adjectives before a single noun

"The brave, popular, wizened, sleepy, jocular elephant taught the leopards to tango" is an example of a sentence containing multiple adjectives that all modify the same noun. Accordingly, they are separated by commas. As explained in the section on adjectives earlier in this chapter, certain types of adjectives don't require commas even when they appear in series, but grammar tests very rarely test on this.

Semicolons

As far as the Praxis writing and virtually all other grammar tests are concerned, semicolons do one thing and one thing only: Namely, they separate two independent clauses within a single sentence. We've already talked about how two independent clauses can be joined by a comma and a coordinating conjunction; the semicolon takes the place of both the comma and the coordinating conjunction. So you can write either of the following sentences:

I fed the cats, and now they like me.

I fed the cats; now they like me.

When it comes to semicolons, that's about it. If you see a semicolon on the test, check to make sure that the words both before and after it constitute independent clauses. If they do, the semicolon is being used correctly; if they don't, it isn't. (This doesn't necessarily mean that an answer choice that uses a semicolon correctly is the right answer, because it may be wrong for some other reason — just that the reason it's wrong isn't because of the semicolon).

Apostrophes

Unlike the other punctuation marks discussed in this section, apostrophes don't separate parts of a sentence. Rather, they're used within individual words for two reasons: to show contraction (as in "cannot" becoming "can't") and to indicate possession (as in "that is my friend's car"). When it comes to contractions, the apostrophe goes where the missing letter or letters would be. The only tricky thing about this is distinguishing certain contractions from similar-sounding words that don't have apostrophes (we discuss that in the upcoming section on homophones).

As for using apostrophes to indicate possession, that's a little more complicated, but not exactly difficult. Here's what you need to know:

- To make a singular word (not ending in "s") possessive, add both an apostrophe and an "s," with the apostrophe coming before the "s," as in "I borrowed my cousin's guitar."

- To make a plural word ending in "s" possessive, add an apostrophe after the "s," as in "My parents' house is in the suburbs."

- To make a plural word that does not end in "s" possessive, add both an apostrophe and an "s," with the apostrophe coming before the "s," as in: "That room is where we keep the children's toys."

Perhaps the most important apostrophe rule concerns what apostrophes are *not* used to do: Namely, they are *never* used to indicate pluralization. So remember, it is *not* "My friend's brought their guitar's," because *friends* and *guitars* in that sentence are simply plural and not possessive. Yes, the friends own the guitars, but the words themselves are not indicating possession from a grammatical perspective.

Misplaced Modifiers

Depending on when you went to school, you may be familiar with the rules in this section under a different name. Once upon a time, misplaced modifiers were called *dangling participles.* Then they were called *dangling modifiers* for a while. Then someone decided that the "dangling" business just sounded silly, so now grammarians call them *misplaced modifiers*.

A *modifying* clause is a dependent clause that opens a sentence and provides descriptive information about the subject of the subsequent independent clause. You can tell where one clause ends and the other begins because there's always a comma between the dependent and independent clauses when the dependent clause comes first.

For example, take the sentence "After growing tired of the parade, Taryn went home." The second clause is the main independent clause, and the first (a descriptive, dependent clause) provides more information about the subject, Taryn, and why she went home. The rule for such situations is that the noun being described by the dependent clause *has to come right after the comma,* and a sentence that violates this rule is said to contain a misplaced modifier.

The sentence in the preceding paragraph is correct, but if someone were to write "After growing tired of the parade, we found out that Taryn went home," that would be an example of a misplaced modifier. A reader might be able to intuit from the context that Taryn is the one who left, but as written, the sentence means that *we* are the ones who got tired of the parade rather than Taryn, because *we* is the (pro)noun that immediately follows the modifying clause (and is the subject of the independent clause).

Which of the following sentences is correct?

(A) Needing to make an urgent call, Megan's search for her phone charger was frantic.

(B) While playing football in the house, the lamp was broken.

(C) Confused by the directions, the gang drove around aimlessly.

(D) Never having met him before, I'm amazed you got along so well with Danny.

(E) Unlike some people, you can always depend on Gabriel.

The correct answer is Choice (C). "The gang" is who or what was "confused," so this sentence places its subject in correct relation to its modifier (the fact that "the" precedes "gang" doesn't matter). Choice (A) is wrong because, although the name "Megan" comes right after the comma, it is possessive, so the entire noun phrase is "Megan's search" — and Megan's *search* didn't need to make a call; Megan *herself* did. Choice (B) is wrong because, although what the writer means to say is clear, the sentence as written means that the *lamp* was playing football, which it obviously wasn't doing. Choice (D) is wrong because it's clear from context that the person being addressed is the one who has never met Danny before, not the speaker, so "I'm" should not immediately follow the comma. Choice (E) is wrong because, although it's clear from the context that reliable Gabriel is the one who is "unlike some people," the sentence as written means that the person being addressed is the one who is "unlike some people," which is presumably not what the speaker means to say.

Redundancy and Double Negatives

You should never repeat yourself or say the same thing twice. In other words, you should avoid doing what the previous sentence just did! In the grammar game, that's known as *redundancy.* Redundancy can take the form of an entire phrase that repeats information provided by an earlier phrase (as in the little joke that opened this paragraph), or it can come down to something as simple as an unnecessary adjective, as in "the tree-filled forest" (by definition, a forest is filled with trees, so pointing this is out is hardly necessary).

Grammar tests like to throw in some redundancy questions now and then because the test-writers know that most people are too concerned with grammar to stop and think about what a sentence actually *means.* (The first sentence in this section, for example, is *grammatically* correct in the sense that it doesn't break any rules about clauses, agreement, punctuation, or anything like that, but it's still undesirable, because you could chop the sentence in half and each half would mean the same thing.)

Double negatives are a special type of redundancy that occurs when two words that both indicate the negation of an idea are inserted into a sentence when only one is necessary, as in the sentence "Nobody gave me nothing." Either "Nobody gave me anything" or "People gave me nothing" would be correct, but you don't need to use a "negating" word twice. Singing "I can't get no satisfaction" made the Rolling Stones a lot of money, but it wouldn't have been a correct response on the Praxis or any other test.

Which of the following sentences contains an example of redundancy?

(A) The brisk wind swept across the hard surface of the frozen lake.

(B) Nobody had better tell me what I can't do.

(C) I now see that the right time is now.

(D) Children will act the way that children will act.

(E) None of the above

The correct answer is Choice (E). None of the first four choices actually contains an example of redundancy. Choice (A) isn't redundant because none of the adjectives are unnecessary: Not all winds are brisk, so adding that detail is fine; not all surfaces are hard, so this detail is fine to add; and not all lakes are frozen, so it's fine to specify that this one is. Choice (B) isn't redundant because, despite the presence of both *nobody* and *can't,* it isn't actually a double negative: The speaker doesn't want anyone to tell her that she isn't able (or permitted) to do something, so "*Nobody* had better tell me what I *can't* do" is exactly what she means. Choice (C) isn't redundant because the two uses of "now" don't refer to the same thing: The right time is now (as opposed to some other time), and the speaker has only just realized this (as opposed to realizing it at some other time). Choice (D) isn't redundant because the speaker is presumably pointing out that some situation involving some rambunctious children is out of anyone's control and that he doesn't have a good explanation for why children act the way they do — in terms of logic, the sentence is a *tautology,* but a tautology isn't the same thing as redundancy in a grammatical sense.

Homophones: "They're in there with their bear"

As you probably remember from elementary school, *homophones* are words that sound the same but are spelled differently. Two things about homophones are likely to trip you up when you take the Praxis: the differences between words that are spelled the same, but one has an apostrophe; and the meaning of words that sound the same but have different spellings.

Which one has the apostrophe?

The types of homophones that give the average person the most trouble are the ones where one word is a contraction (that is, it has an apostrophe) and the other word is a possessive pronoun — for example, "it's/its," "you're/your," "they're/their (and there)," and "who's/whose." In all of those cases, the one with the apostrophe is the contraction.

This concept is confusing because the first thing you learn about apostrophes is that they show possession, and now suddenly the word without the apostrophe is the possessive one. But hey, that's the rule (don't look at me — I didn't invent the English language).

The easiest way to keep all this straight (and get the questions right on the Praxis) is simply to get in the habit of reading the words with the apostrophes as though they were two separate words: "it's" means "it is," so say/think "it is" whenever you see "it's." Say "you are" whenever you see "you're," say "they are" whenever you see "they're," say "who is" whenever you see "who's," and so on. If the sentence no longer makes sense, then the word in question should be the one *without* the apostrophe.

TIP

If the homophone you have trouble with is *their* versus *there,* you can remember that *their* is the possessive because it contains the word *heir,* and that *there* is the one about places because it contains the word *here* (that's not actually *why* the words are spelled that way; it's just a good way to remember which is which).

Spelled and used differently, but sound the same

When it comes to homophone trouble in cases where neither word has an apostrophe, here are the most common pairs of words that give people grief and how to remember which is which:

✔ **Then/than:** *Then* is an adverb indicating order ("I aced the test, and *then* I went straight to the bar"), and *than* is a subordinating conjunction used for comparison ("I know grammar better *than* my friends do, thanks to this book"). Getting into the habit of pronouncing them differently helps a lot, but if there's no time for that, then just use the "e" and "a" themselves as clues, and think *then = order* and *than = comparison.*

✔ **Affect/effect:** Ninety-nine percent of the time, the difference is that *affect* is a verb and *effect* is a noun: "His insults did not *affect* me" versus "His insults had no *effect* on me." Unfortunately, there's more. *Effect* can also be a verb meaning "to bring about," as in "You'll need to do more than sign petitions if you really want to *effect* change." And just to make sure your day is completely ruined, *affect* can also be a noun — but you'll probably never see it unless you're a psych major, since *affect* as a noun is only used in scientific contexts to signify the behavioral trait that's being studied in a psych experiment (so feel free to forget I ever told you that). So for the purposes of the Praxis, just remember that *affect* is a verb and *effect* is a noun, unless the verb means "to bring about," in which case it's *effect.*

✔ **To/too:** *To* is a preposition that can be used in all sorts of ways. *Too* is an adverb that can mean either "extremely" or "unacceptably" ("The music is *too* loud"), or "also" ("I'm coming *too*"). The best method for keeping them straight is to remember that one word is used *way* more than the other: There probably isn't a single paragraph in this book that doesn't use *to.* So rather than trying to memorize the million different things that *to* can do, just remember that if it means "unacceptably/very" or "also," it's *too,* and if not, then it's *to.*" (There's also *two,* which means the number between one and three, but most people don't have any trouble with that.)

✔ **Compliment/complement:** The one with the "i" means saying something nice about somebody, and the one with the "e" means that two things go together well ("He *complimented* me on the fact that my shoes *complement* my dress").

✔ **Whether/weather:** The first one means that something is in question, and the second one refers to what it's like when you go outside ("I don't know *whether* the *weather* will improve"). As with *than/then,* it helps to get into the habit of pronouncing them differently. Your friends may think it's obnoxious of you to start pronouncing the "h" in "whether," but you can stop after the test.

✔ **Farther/further:** These words aren't technically homonyms, because they're pronounced differently, but they still give people a lot of trouble. The difference is that *farther* relates to actual physical distance, whereas *further* indicates the extent to which you feel like doing something ("I don't want to have any *further* discussion about whether you can long-jump *farther* than I can").

Capitalization: What You Need to Know

When you first began looking into what is or isn't tested on the Praxis writing exam, your reaction to finding out that there were questions about capitalization was probably something like "There are questions about *capitalization* on this test?! What am I, in third grade?"

Yes, you almost certainly already know that the first letters of the first words of sentences are capitalized, as are people's names; the names of proper places like cities, states, or countries; the names of companies like "Facebook"; the names of sports teams and bands; and the words in the titles of books, movies, and so on.

You may not, however, know some of the trickier rules about capitalization, and those are the ones that the Praxis writing test will ask about. Here's a rundown of the most common capitalization-related tricks:

- ✔ **Titles, like "president":** Titles, such as "president," "mayor," and so forth, are only capitalized when they are placed before the name of, or used to indicate, a *specific* president or mayor or what-have-you. So you should write "Abraham Lincoln was the 16th president," but "Everyone knows that President Lincoln wore a stovepipe hat." If you're talking about the *current* president (or mayor, or whoever), you capitalize the word even if the person's name doesn't appear in the sentence, because you're still indicating a specific person: "The President held a press conference this morning."

  The same rule applies for God versus a god: You capitalize "God" when referring to a/the actual, specific God, but not when you're talking about deities in general: "I prayed to God that I would pass the test" versus "Apollo was one of the Greek gods."

- ✔ **The names of seasons:** Many people are unclear about this, but the rule is that the names of seasons are only capitalized if you are addressing the season directly, as you might in a poem. So you say "I love the way the leaves change color in the fall," but "Oh, my beloved Fall, how I love it when your leaves change color!"

- ✔ **The names of specific regions, even if they are not actual countries:** You should capitalize the names of all proper nouns, and that includes geographical areas that are not technically specific countries, cities, and the like: "My uncle frequently travels to the Far East." You should *not,* however, capitalize the names of cardinal directions when they're just used to indicate a direction rather than an area: "My uncle has to fly east to get to the Far East." You should also not capitalize the "cardinal direction" part of a name when a suffix is attached to it, because that involves a comparison rather than a proper name, with the exception of cases where the cardinal direction with a comparative suffix is part of an actual proper noun: "Many people don't realize that northern Brazil lies in the Northern Hemisphere."

- ✔ **Specific eras in history:** The title of a specific period in history, even a slang or unofficial one, is a proper noun and should be capitalized accordingly: "The Disco Era was mercifully short-lived."

Practice Questions about Grammar

These practice questions are similar to the questions about grammar that you'll encounter on the Praxis.

1. Which version of the following sentence is correct?

   The childrens' toys, are all over the floor, so you'd better watch your step.

   (A) The childrens' toys, are all over the floor, so you'd better watch your step.

   (B) The childrens' toys are all over the floor, so you'd better watch you're step.

   (C) The children's toys, are all over the floor, so you'd better watch you're step.

   (D) The children's toys are all over the floor, so you'd better watch your step.

   (E) The childrens toys, are all over the floor, so you'd better watch your step.

2. Which version of the following sentence is correct?

   I wouldn't eat that sandwich if I were you, I'm not sure how long its been in the refrigerator.

   (A) I wouldn't eat that sandwich if I were you, I'm not sure how long its been in the refrigerator.

   (B) I wouldn't eat that sandwich if I were you, I'm not sure how long it's been in the refrigerator.

   (C) I wouldn't eat that sandwich if I were you; I'm not sure how long its been in the refrigerator.

   (D) I wouldn't eat that sandwich if I were you, I'm not sure how long; it's been in the refrigerator.

   (E) I wouldn't eat that sandwich if I were you; I'm not sure how long it's been in the refrigerator.

3. Which version of the following sentence is correct?

   That hotdog restaurant, was a village landmark, I can't believe it closed!

   (A) That hotdog restaurant, was a village landmark, I can't believe it closed!

   (B) That hotdog restaurant, it was a village landmark, and I can't believe it closed!

   (C) That hotdog restaurant — as a village landmark — I can't believe it closed!

   (D) That hotdog restaurant was a village landmark — I can't believe it closed!

   (E) That hotdog restaurant being a village landmark, so I can't believe it closed!

4. Which version of the following sentence is correct?

   The album containing all my birthday pictures is missing!

   (A) The album containing all my birthday pictures is missing!

   (B) The album containing all my birthday pictures are missing!

   (C) The album contains all my birthday pictures are missing!

   (D) The album contains all my birthday pictures is missing!

   (E) The album containing all my birthday pictures, which is missing!

5. Which version of the following sentence is correct?

   She was running late for work, Megan locked herself out of her apartment.

   (A) She was running late for work, Megan locked herself out of her apartment.

   (B) Because she was running late for work, and Megan locked herself out of her apartment.

   (C) Running late for work, Megan locked herself out of her apartment.

   (D) Running late for work, and Megan locked herself out of her apartment.

   (E) Running late for work; Megan locked herself out of her apartment.

6. Which version of the underlined portion makes the sentence correct?

   Although we've had a rough couple of <u>seasons, because I think</u> this might be our year.

   (A) seasons, because I think

   (B) seasons, I think

   (C) seasons, but I think

   (D) seasons, however, I think

   (E) seasons: I think

7. Which version of the following sentence is correct?

   The affects of the anesthesia has begun to wear off.

   (A) The affects of the anesthesia has begun to wear off.

   (B) The affects of the anesthesia have begun to wear off.

   (C) The effects of the anesthesia have begun to wear off.

   (D) The effects of the anesthesia has began to wear off.

   (E) The effects of the anesthesia have began to wear off.

8. How many commas are needed to correctly punctuate the following sentence?

   The fastest two-legged animal the ostrich may be found in Australia and zoos all over the world.

   (A) None

   (B) One

   (C) Two

   (D) Three

   (E) Four

9. Which version of the underlined portion makes the sentence correct?

   When I was young, I won <u>a year supply</u> of pretzels in a radio contest.

   (A) a year supply

   (B) a year's supply

   (C) a years' supply

   (D) yearly a supply

   (E) a year of supplies

10. The problem with the following sentence is that it contains a

    As someone whom I have known for years, I'd expect you not to take his side over mine.

    (A) comma splice.

    (B) misplaced modifier.

    (C) parallel-phrasing error.

    (D) redundancy.

    (E) misuse of "whom."

11. Which version of the underlined portion makes the sentence correct?

    Don't let any of the cats' toys slide under the <u>stove, it</u> will whine all night.

    (A) stove, it

    (B) stove, or it

    (C) stove, they

    (D) stove, or they

    (E) stove; it

12. How many of the words in the following sentence are capitalized when they should *not* be?

    Neither my Father nor I could believe that Coach Collins wanted me to start in center field for the Brooklyn Beavers this Spring.

    (A) None

    (B) One

    (C) Two

    (D) Three

    (E) Four

13. Which version of the underlined portion makes the sentence correct?

    <u>It's going to take more than</u> one person to get this couch upstairs.

    (A) It's going to take more than

    (B) Its going to take more then

    (C) It's going to takes more than

    (D) Its going to takes more then

    (E) It's going to take more then

14. Which version of the underlined portion makes the sentence correct?

    Before you take the picture of <u>Sam and I, let</u> us fix our hair.

    (A) Sam and I, let

    (B) Sam and me, let

    (C) Sam and myself, let

    (D) Sam, and I let

    (E) Sam, and me let

15. A sentence that contains a colon is definitely grammatically incorrect *if*

    (A) the colon does not precede a list or quotation.

    (B) the sentence does not also have a comma in it.

    (C) the portion of the sentence after the colon is longer than the portion before it.

    (D) the colon is not preceded by an independent clause.

    (E) the colon is not both preceded by and followed by independent clauses.

Answers and Explanations

Use this answer key to score the practice grammar questions in this chapter.

1. **D. The children's toys are all over the floor, so you'd better watch your step.** The sentence is two independent clauses joined by the coordinating conjunction "so," so you need only one comma, placed right before the conjunction. The plural of the word *children* is *children's,* and the possessive second-person pronoun is *your.*

   The right answer is not Choice (A) because there's no such word as *childrens'* (with the apostrophe after the "s"), and because no comma is needed between the subject and the verb. The right answer is not Choice (B) because there's no such word as *childrens'* (with the apostrophe after the "s"), and because the possessive form is *your,* not *you're.*

   The right answer is not Choice (C) because no comma is needed between the subject and the verb, and because the possessive form is *your,* not *you're.* The right answer is not Choice (E) because there's no such word as *childrens* (with no apostrophe), and because no comma is needed between the subject and the verb.

2. **E. I wouldn't eat that sandwich if I were you; I'm not sure how long it's been in the refrigerator.** The two independent clauses are correctly separated by a semicolon, and the correct *it's* (the one with the apostrophe, which means *it is,* or in this case, *it has*) is used.

   The right answer is not Choice (A) because this sentence contains a comma splice, and because the wrong *its* is used (you need the one with the apostrophe, which means *it is*). The right answer is not Choice (B) because this sentence contains a comma splice.

   The right answer is not Choice (C) because the wrong *its* is used (you need the one with the apostrophe, which means *it is* or *it has*). The right answer is not Choice (D) because the punctuation is misplaced: You need a semicolon in place of that comma, and no punctuation at all in the place where the semicolon currently appears.

3. **D. That hotdog restaurant was a village landmark — I can't believe it closed!** This sentence correctly presents two independent clauses separated by a single dash (a semicolon would also have been correct, but that's not one of the options).

   The right answer is not Choice (A) because the first comma, which appears between the subject and the verb, is unnecessary, and because the second comma results in a comma splice.

   The right answer is not Choice (B) because there's no need to repeat the subject by inserting a comma and a pronoun *(it)* before the verb. That portion of the sentence should simply read "restaurant was," rather than "restaurant, it was." (The inclusion of *and* after the second comma avoids creating a comma splice, but the sentence is already incorrect for the aforementioned reason.)

The right answer is not Choice (C) because double dashes are only appropriate when the portions of the sentence outside the dashes work together to form a complete sentence (in other words, the dashes work like parentheses). The right answer is not Choice (E) because *being* can't work here as the main verb of the sentence; it should say *was*.

4. **A. The album containing all my birthday pictures is missing!** The main verb of the sentence is the singular *is* (because the subject is the singular *album*), and the word *containing* functions as a preposition here.

The right answer is not Choice (B) because the subject of the sentence is *album,* so the verb should be the singular *is,* not the plural *are.* The right answer is not Choice (C) because *contain* is not the verb; it works as a preposition here, so you need *containing,* not *contains.* Additionally, the subject of the sentence is *album,* so the verb should be the singular *is,* not the plural *are.*

The right answer is not Choice (D) because *contain* is not the verb; it works as a preposition here, so you need *containing,* not *contains.* The right answer is not Choice (E) because the sentence has no main verb. The subordination of *is* to *which* means that the sentence would have to keep going after the *which* clause (to form a main verb clause).

5. **C. Running late for work, Megan locked herself out of her apartment.** This sentence correctly presents an independent clause preceded by a dependent modifying clause and a comma.

The right answer is not Choice (A) because this is a comma splice. The right answer is not Choice (B) because neither clause is independent, as the first begins with *because* and the second begins with *and* (omit either of those words, and the sentence would be correct).

The right answer is not Choice (D) because the second clause is the independent clause, and no conjunction is necessary. The right answer is not Choice (E) because the first clause is not independent, so you need a comma instead of a semicolon.

6. **B. seasons, I think.** The presence of the subordinating conjunction *although* means that the first clause is not independent, so the second of the two clauses should be an independent clause with no conjunction (this is the "although trick").

The right answer is not Choice (A) because the presence of both *although* and *because* means that both clauses are subordinate — in other words, the sentence contains no independent clause. The right answer is not Choice (C) because, although the sentence would be correct with *either* "although" in the first clause *or* "but" in the second, it is incorrect to include both.

The right answer is not Choice (D) because *however* with commas on either side properly interrupts a single independent clause; it doesn't join two clauses (in other words, *however* is not a conjunction). In any case, the presence of *although* in the first clause means that this sentence would still be incorrect even if *however* were a conjunction.

The right answer is not Choice (E) because the clause that precedes a colon must be independent (which this clause is not, because it is subordinated to *although*).

7. **C. The effects of the anesthesia have begun to wear off.** *Effects* is the subject of the sentence and a noun, so it should be spelled with an "e." It is also plural, so the verb should be *have,* not *has.* Finally, the present perfect plural form of *begin* is *have begun,* not *have began.*

The right answer is not Choice (A) because *effects* is the subject of the sentence and a noun, so it should be spelled with an "e." It's also plural, so the verb should be *have,* not *has.* The right answer is not Choice (B) because *effects* is the subject of the sentence and a noun, so it should be spelled with an "e."

The right answer is not Choice (D) because *effects* is plural, so the verb should be *have,* not *has,* and because the present perfect plural form of *begin* is *have begun,* not *have began.* The right answer is not Choice (E) because the present perfect plural form of *begin* is *have begun,* not *have began.*

8. **C. Two.** Only two commas are needed, one on either side of the appositive clause *the ostrich*. The main sentence works as a single independent clause if *the ostrich* is lifted out. No comma is needed for the series of adjectives that precede *animal,* because they limit or modify each other. And no comma is needed before the *and,* because the verb *found* extends to both places.

The right answer is not Choice (A) because commas are definitely needed in this sentence. The right answer is not Choice (B) because more than one comma is needed in this sentence.

The right answer is not Choice (D) because fewer than three commas are needed in this sentence. The right answer is not Choice (E) because fewer than four commas are needed in this sentence.

9. **B. a year's supply.** Even though the pretzels belong to the speaker and not literally to the year, the word *year* must still be possessive: "a *year's* supply," "a *year's* worth," and so on.

The right answer is not Choice (A) because the word *year* must be possessive. The right answer is not Choice (C) because you are talking about one year's supply of pretzels, so you need the singular possessive (with the apostrophe before the "s"), not the plural possessive.

The right answer is not Choice (D) because it's difficult to discern what this sentence is trying to say; the syntax is awkward in a way that impedes comprehension. The right answer is not Choice (E) because, although it is possible to discern what the sentence means to say, it's unnecessarily wordy. Why say "a year of supplies of pretzels" rather than simply "a year's supply of pretzels"?

10. **B. misplaced modifier.** The sentence contains a misplaced modifier. The initial modifying clause reads "As someone whom I've known for years," which means that a word referring to the person whom the speaker knows (either a proper name or pronoun) must immediately follow the comma.

The right answer is not Choice (A) because both clauses are not independent, so the sentence doesn't contain a comma splice. The right answer is not Choice (C) because there's no parallel-phrasing issue with this sentence.

The right answer is not Choice (D) because there's no example of redundancy in this sentence. The right answer is not Choice (E) because *whom* is used correctly in this sentence (the pronoun is the object of *known,* so it should be in the objective case).

11. **D. stove, or they.** The plural possessive form *cats'* in the non-underlined portion of the sentence establishes that you are dealing with more than one cat, so the pronoun should be *they* rather than *it*. A conjunction (in this case, *or*) is also needed to avoid a comma splice.

The right answer is not Choice (A) because it's a comma splice, and because the pronoun should be *they,* not *it*. The right answer is not Choice (B) because the pronoun should be *they,* not *it*.

The right answer is not Choice (C) because it's a comma splice. The right answer is not Choice (E) because the pronoun should be *they,* not *it*.

12. **C. Two.** Neither *father* nor *spring* should be capitalized, because they're not being directly addressed. The other capitalized terms, *Coach Collins* and *Brooklyn Beavers,* are proper nouns and are appropriately capitalized.

The right answer is not Choice (A) because there are words in the sentence that are incorrectly capitalized. The right answer is not Choice (B) because more than one word in the sentence is incorrectly capitalized.

The right answer is not Choice (D) because fewer than three words in the sentence are incorrectly capitalized. The right answer is not Choice (E) because fewer than four words in the sentence are incorrectly capitalized.

13. **A. It's going to take more than.** The sentence is correct as it is, because it appropriately includes the contraction *it's* (for *it is*), the infinitive *to take,* and the comparative conjunction *than* (spelled with an "a").

   The right answer is not Choice (B) because you need the contraction *it's* (for *it is*), not the possessive *its,* and because you need the conjunction *than,* not the adverb *then.* The right answer is not Choice (C) because you need the infinitive *to take,* not *takes.*

   The right answer is not Choice (D) because you need the contraction *it's* (for *it is*), not the possessive *its;* the infinitive *to take,* not *takes;* and the conjunction *than,* not the adverb *then.* The right answer is not Choice (E) because you need the conjunction *than,* not the adverb *then.*

14. **B. Sam and me, let.** The pronoun is one of the objects of the preposition *of,* so it should be the objective-case *me,* not the subjective-case *I.* The comma should be placed between that pronoun and the verb *let,* because that's the point at which the introductory subordinate clause ends and the main independent clause (which is a command) begins.

   The right answer is not Choice (A) because the pronoun is one of the objects of the preposition *of,* so it should be the objective-case *me,* not the subjective-case *I.* The right answer is not Choice (C) because the speaker has not yet appeared in the sentence and is not reflexively performing any verb upon himself, so there's no need to use *myself* instead of *me.*

   The right answer is not Choice (D) because the pronoun is one of the objects of the preposition *of,* so it should be the objective-case *me,* not the subjective-case *I.* Additionally, the comma should be placed between that pronoun and the verb *let,* because that's the point at which the introductory subordinate clause ends and the main independent clause (which is a command) begins.

   The right answer is not Choice (E) because the comma should be placed between the pronoun and the verb *let,* because that's the point at which the introductory subordinate clause ends and the main independent clause (which is a command) begins.

15. **D. the colon is not preceded by an independent clause.** The one hard-and-fast rule for colons is that the portion of the sentence preceding the colon must contain an independent clause.

   The right answer is not Choice (A) because a colon doesn't necessarily have to precede either a list or a quotation. Those are just the most common uses for colons. The right answer is not Choice (B) because there's no rule about any kind of relationship between the presence of a colon and the presence of commas.

   The right answer is not Choice (C) because there's no rule about whether the portion of the sentence before or after the colon has to be longer. The right answer is not Choice (E) because a colon isn't used to link *two* independent clauses — that's the rule for a *semicolon.*

Chapter 13

Test-Taking Strategies for Core Writing

In This Chapter

▶ Surveying the four types of multiple-choice questions

▶ Figuring out what's wrong and how to fix it

▶ Acing essay writing

Do you have the writing skills you need for a successful career in education? The Praxis Core writing test is meant to determine exactly that. Whether you feel pretty confident about your writing skills or you're just starting to gear up for the Praxis, this chapter gives you the strategies you need to tackle the writing section.

Knowing the Types of Multiple-Choice Writing Questions

The multiple-choice portion of the Praxis writing test contains 40 questions with a 40-minute time limit. Some of the questions consist of a sentence or two followed by choices. Other questions involve reading a longer passage and selecting such choices as the best revision, best conclusion, or best version.

These questions address usage, research skills, sentence correction, and revision in context:

✔ **Usage:** The usage questions require you to recognize a variety of errors regarding mechanics, structure, grammatical relationships, and word choice. The questions test your ability to find errors in using adjectives and adverbs, subject and verb agreement, pronoun and antecedent agreement, verb tense, pronoun case, and the use of intensive pronouns. You're also expected to identify errors in punctuation and capitalization.

✔ **Research skills:** The questions concerning research test your ability to use reliable research strategies, to recognize the parts of a citation, and to judge the credibility and relevance of research sources.

✔ **Sentence correction:** In addressing questions concerning sentence correction, you choose the answer that best revises or restates a phrase or sentence using standard written English. For some questions, you select Choice (A) if the sentence is correct as written. Errors you may encounter include problems with parallelism, run-on sentences, fragments, misplaced and dangling modifiers, coordinating and subordinating conjunctions, and errors in the placement of phrases and clauses.

✔ **Revision in context:** The revision-in-context questions test your ability to recognize the best way to improve a passage or a portion of a passage. These questions may address many different aspects: organization, word choice (precise and effective words), consistency in style and tone, and correct grammatical conventions. Some questions test your ability to recognize that some passages or portions thereof need no improvement.

The multiple-choice section of the writing test is scored separately from the essay section. Keep in mind:

- ✔ Only one choice is correct. No questions have more than one right answer.
- ✔ Read the question carefully. Try putting the question into your own words, if possible.
- ✔ Read all the answer choices before making your choice.
- ✔ Avoid reading too much into the questions. There are no "trick" questions.
- ✔ Skip questions that are difficult for you and come back to them later.
- ✔ Pay attention to time. Remember to leave a few minutes to go back to the questions you skipped and to check your work. For unanswered questions, try to narrow your choices. If necessary, guess.

Type 1: Answering usage questions

Some of the multiple-choice questions consist of a sentence with underlined portions. You must decide whether any one of the underlined portions has an error in grammar, sentence construction, word use, punctuation, or capitalization. If so, you select the underlined portion that contains the error. If the sentence is correct as written, you select "No error." No sentence has more than one error.

You know you're looking at a usage question when one of the answer choices is "No error." The first thing to do in this situation is to read the question without paying attention to the underlined portions. You may find the error immediately. If you don't, look carefully at each underlined portion. Still nothing? Then, mark "No error."

Put on your grammar policing outfit and watch out for these errors:

- ✔ Incorrect punctuation, particularly commas, semicolons, and apostrophes
- ✔ Pronoun usage, particularly pronoun/antecedent errors or vague pronouns
- ✔ Verb tense
- ✔ Subject/verb agreement errors
- ✔ Word choice, particularly words like *affect* and *effect*, which are often confused

Each of the following questions consists of a sentence with four underlined portions. Read each question and decide whether any of the underlined parts contains an element that would be considered incorrect or inappropriate in carefully written English. The error or concern may be in grammatical construction, word use, capitalization, or punctuation. Select the underlined portion that should be revised. If there are no errors, select "No error."

Because <u>writing a novel is</u> a long and involved process <u>requiring a great deal of patience</u> and
     A   B

perseverance, <u>the aspiring novelist must have</u> a quiet place to <u>work; a noisy environment is</u>
                       C   D

<u>not conducive</u> to thought and creativity. <u>No error</u>.
     E

Because the example question represents no problems in usage, structure, or word choice, Choice (E) is the correct answer.

When someone gives a speech, however informative it may be, they must be sure to
⎯⎯⎯⎯⎯⎯⎯⎯⎯⎯⎯⎯⎯⎯⎯   ⎯⎯⎯⎯⎯⎯⎯⎯⎯⎯
            A   B
engage the audience for its entire duration. No error.
⎯⎯⎯⎯⎯⎯⎯⎯⎯⎯   ⎯⎯⎯⎯⎯⎯⎯⎯⎯⎯⎯   ⎯⎯⎯⎯⎯⎯
          C   D   E

The correct answer is Choice (B). The plural pronoun "they" refers to the pronoun "some-one," which is singular. The error, then, is a disagreement between the pronoun and its antecedent.

My parents have been living in Europe before I was born, but they came to America in 1998
⎯⎯⎯⎯⎯⎯⎯⎯⎯⎯⎯⎯⎯⎯⎯   ⎯⎯⎯⎯⎯⎯⎯⎯⎯⎯   ⎯⎯⎯⎯⎯⎯⎯⎯⎯⎯⎯⎯⎯⎯
                 A   B   C
to join my uncle's business. No error.
          ⎯⎯⎯⎯⎯⎯⎯   ⎯⎯⎯⎯⎯⎯⎯
              D   E

The correct answer is Choice (A). The verb phrase "have been living" is present-perfect tense, which indicates something that began in the past and continues in the present. Because the parents no longer live in Europe, the correct verb should be past tense, "lived."

My best friend, as well as my many associates at work, think that the local library is both
⎯⎯⎯⎯⎯⎯⎯⎯⎯⎯⎯⎯⎯⎯⎯⎯   ⎯⎯⎯⎯⎯⎯⎯⎯⎯⎯⎯⎯⎯   ⎯⎯⎯⎯⎯⎯
              A   B   C
poorly staffed and utterly inefficiently managed. No error.
⎯⎯⎯⎯⎯⎯   ⎯⎯⎯⎯⎯⎯⎯⎯⎯⎯⎯⎯⎯⎯   ⎯⎯⎯⎯⎯⎯⎯
    D   E

The correct answer is Choice (B). The subject of the sentence is "friend," a singular noun. Therefore, a singular verb, "thinks," is correct. Remember that subjects and verbs must agree in number. The intervening phase, "as well as my many associates at work," does not affect the number of the subject. "Friend" is still singular.

Type 2: Showing your research skills

Some questions on the Praxis test your knowledge of basic research skills. Your task is to choose the best answer from the choices given. You should be ready to answer questions about correct citation, relevance and credibility of sources, and appropriate research strategies.

Smith, S. "Making Hay While the Sun Shines." *Hobbies*. 12 May 2002: 51–52.

In the preceding citation, which of the following is cited?

(A) A magazine article

(B) A book

(C) An interview

(D) A newspaper article

(E) A website

The correct answer is Choice (A). Citations are arranged in a specific order, and various elements of the citation clue you in to the fact that the source cited is a magazine article. For example, there are two titles, one in quotation marks (the title of the article) and one in italics (the title of the magazine itself). The fact that the date of publication includes a month and day, as opposed to just a year, is also evidence that this is a citation for a magazine article.

Which of the following is a secondary source on John Adams?

(A) A biography of John Adams

(B) A letter written by John Adams to his father

(C) A photograph of John Adams and his son

(D) A copy of a speech delivered by John Adams

(E) An essay written by John Adams

The correct answer is Choice (A). A secondary source contains information that has been interpreted by another scholar, as opposed to being an original discovery. The other choices represent primary sources because they are firsthand, original information that hasn't been subjected to interpretation.

Type 3: Making sentence corrections

In questions involving sentence correction, the Praxis presents a sentence in which some part of the sentence or the entire sentence is underlined. You're given five choices for rewriting the underlined section of the sentence (or the entire sentence). The first choice makes no changes; the other four are different ways of writing the sentence. Choose the first choice if you believe no change is necessary. Otherwise, indicate which of the remaining choices is best.

The correct answer will be clearly written and will most effectively express the idea presented in the original sentence. Be particularly mindful of word choice, sentence construction, correct grammar, and punctuation.

<u>Annie, who won the blue ribbon for her apple pie, is a better cook than any contestant in the contest</u>.

(A) Annie, who won the blue ribbon for her apple pie, is a better cook than any contestant in the contest.

(B) Annie won the blue ribbon for her apple pie; and is the best cook.

(C) Annie, who won the blue ribbon for her apple pie, had been better in comparison to anyone in the contest.

(D) Annie, who won the blue ribbon for her apple pie, is a better cook than any other contestant in the contest.

(E) Annie won the blue ribbon for her apple pie, she is a better cook than any other contestant.

The correct answer is Choice (D). Using the words "any other" is necessary so Annie (who is a contestant) isn't compared to herself.

Choice (A) compares Annie to herself. Because she is one of the contestants, she can't be better than herself. Choice (B) uses a semicolon incorrectly. Choice (C) omits the word "other" and also has an error in verb tense. The verb "had been" creates inconsistent verb tense. Choice (E) contains a comma splice.

My best friend Jacob lately discovered that <u>neither new clothes nor having the right kind of car</u> would get him a date with Sophia.

(A) neither new clothes nor having the right kind of car

(B) neither how good his clothes were nor his car

(C) neither the right clothes or securing the right car

(D) neither new clothes and getting the right car

(E) neither new clothes nor the right car

The correct choice is (E). The correlative conjunctions "neither/nor" must link similar grammatical elements. Choice (E) links a noun, "clothes" to another noun, "car." Choices (A) and (B) both contain parallel-phrasing errors, and Choices (C) and (D) use incorrect conjunctions instead of using "neither's" partner, "nor."

Type 4: Regarding revision-in-context questions

Revision-in-context questions ask that you edit or revise a passage to make it better. The problem may be a clumsy or incorrect sentence or a portion of a sentence. Your job is to make the choice that best improves the sentence. Improving the passage may require a change in word choice, style, tone, grammar, or organization. For some passages, no revision is necessary.

 Think of the passage as your first draft of an assigned essay. Imagine that this essay will mean the difference between a "B" and a "C" as your final grade in the course (and your grade point average really could use a "B"). How can you make it better? Try to imagine what comments your instructor would make.

For each of the following three example questions, choose the best answer based on this passage:

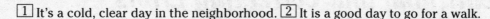

1 It's a cold, clear day in the neighborhood. 2 It is a good day to go for a walk.

3 I like walking because it is good exercise. 4 It is a time to notice the change in seasons.

5 It is a good time to stop and visit with neighbors. 6 My dog really likes to walk with me,

too. 7 He doesn't know about exercise, he just likes the companionship.

 Which would be the best revision, if any, of Sentences 1 and 2?

(A) It's a cold, clear day in the neighborhood, a good day for a walk.

(B) Being cold and clear, I like to walk.

(C) Walking is good on a cold, clear day.

(D) It's a cold, clear day in the neighborhood, and it is a good day to go for a walk.

(E) It's a cold and clear day, I feel like going for a walk around the neighborhood.

The correct answer is Choice (A). Because both sentences are short, joining them improves the passage. While all the choices join the sentences, only Choice (A) preserves the original context and is also concise. Choice (B) contains a misplaced modifier. "Being cold and clear" appears to modify "I." Choice (C) leaves out the idea of walking in a neighborhood (which is important to the rest of the passage). Choice (D) joins the sentences but is less concise. Choice (E) contains a comma splice.

 Which would be the best revision, if any, of Sentences 3, 4, and 5?

(A) No change.

(B) I like to exercise and to notice the change in seasons and visit the neighbors when I walk.

(C) Not only is walking good exercise, but walking also provides the opportunity to notice the change in seasons and to visit with neighbors.

(D) I can exercise, look at the change of season, and visit with neighbors while I walk.

(E) Walking is good because it makes me exercise. I can also notice the seasons and visit with neighbors.

The correct answer is Choice (C). This choice effectively uses the correlative conjunctions "not only" and "but also" to provide a transition and to link ideas concisely. The other choices provide no transition and are less effective in linking ideas. Always think about conciseness — using the fewest words to express the same information or ideas.

Which would be the best revision, if any, of Sentences 6 and 7?

(A) No change.

(B) Another benefit to a neighborhood walk is the chance to take my dog; he enjoys the walk and the companionship even though he knows nothing about exercise.

(C) My dog likes the walk. He enjoys the companionship.

(D) My dog likes the walk, he enjoys the companionship.

(E) However, my dog enjoys the walk and the companionship.

The correct answer is Choice (B). It uses a transition: "Another benefit. . . ." to tie ideas together and also combines the sentences effectively with a semicolon. Choice (C) creates two choppy sentences. Choice (D) incorrectly joins clauses with a comma. Choice (E) uses an illogical transition, "however."

Identifying and Correcting Errors in Multiple-Choice Items

Correctly answering multiple-choice items on the writing portion of the Praxis requires that you read each question carefully. Where possible, put the question into your own words. Be sure to read every choice before you make your selection.

Eliminating the obviously wrong choices

The process of elimination can help you choose the correct answer in a multiple-choice question. Start by crossing off the answers that couldn't be right. Then spend your time focusing on the possible correct choices before selecting your answer. Doing so greatly increases the odds of your choosing correctly.

Pay special attention to answers that contain these words: *none, never, all, more, always,* and *only.* These words indicate that the answer is an undisputed fact and, consequently, isn't likely to be the correct choice. Conditional words like *usually* or *probably* make the answer more likely.

Be particularly careful of multiple-choice questions using the words *not, least,* and *except.* These questions usually ask you to select the choice that doesn't fit. Stay alert! It's easy to misread these questions.

Don't be afraid to say it's right the way it is

Although it may seem counterintuitive, if a sentence is correct as written, choose Choice (A) or "No error." Fear not: This choice is the correct answer for some of the questions. Just be sure to consider all the choices before making your decision.

The art of guessing as a last resort

Your score is based on the number of correct answers. You're not penalized for incorrect answers. For this reason, you should answer every question.

If you face a difficult question, narrow your choices as much as possible and, if necessary, guess! Don't spend too much time considering a difficult question. Mark the question and come back to it. Answer the easy questions first.

You're not expected to answer all the questions correctly. In order to pass the Praxis, you must simply achieve the minimum passing score for your state.

A word of advice about "trusting your ear"

If you grew up in a family of English teachers who corrected your every incorrect utterance, complete with an accompanying grammar lesson, it's probably pretty safe for you to "trust your ear"; that is, whatever sounds right to you is likely to be right. However, if you're like most people, you grew up in a family that was considerably less interested in your grammar. Language that sounds right to you is simply language you're accustomed to hearing and may very well be incorrect. Play it safe and analyze the sentence carefully. It's easy to make a mistake when "trusting the ear." Consider some examples.

> Neither the boys nor the girl (is/are) paying attention.

While "are" may sound right, the correct answer is "is." The verb agrees with the closest subject when subjects are compound.

> I will split the cost between you and (I/me).

You probably hear someone use the incorrect construction of "between you and I" pretty often. Just because you hear it spoken, though, doesn't mean it's correct grammar. Objects of the preposition must be objective case, so "me" is the pronoun to use here.

> You and (I/me) should see that new movie.

In this example, the personal pronoun is being used as one of the subjects of the sentence. Subjects must be nominative case, so "I" is the correct choice here.

Mastering the Essay

The Praxis requires you to write two essays. One is an *argumentative essay,* which means you must support a particular position, giving clear and specific examples and reasons. The second essay, the *informative/explanatory essay,* requires you to read articles from two different sources, identify the main ideas and issues of both, and use them to construct your own essay. You have 30 minutes to write each essay.

Although you don't need any specific knowledge of the topics you're given, you are expected to draw from your own experience and observation to write an effective essay using appropriate organization, development, tone, style, word choice, and standard written English. Above all, write clearly and stay on topic. Be careful to address all the points presented.

For the informative/explanatory essay, it's important to use information from both sources and correctly cite the source. Read the source material carefully and organize your thoughts before you begin to write. You're judged according to how well you synthesize the source material.

Your essay should be clear, consistent, and forceful with careful attention to mechanics and usage as well as diction and syntax. Keep the following pointers in mind:

✔ Establish your point quickly. Make a strong first impression.

✔ Avoid long introductions.

✔ Organize each body paragraph around a strong topic sentence.

✔ Be sure every paragraph supports the thesis.

✔ Pay attention to word choice: strong verbs, precise nouns.

✔ Use a variety of sentence types and lengths.

✔ Use clear transitions to aid the flow of your essay.

✔ Be concise.

✔ Strive for a strong conclusion that delivers a final punch!

Outlining your thoughts and managing your time

You are not expected to have a formal outline for your essays. You must, however, organize your thoughts before you begin to write.

Read the prompt carefully. Think about what you must do to adequately address the prompt. Take a position. Then write down examples, observations, and reasoning that support your position. Number these in the order they should appear in your essay.

After you've organized your thoughts, write your thesis sentence.

Breathe! Taking time to collect your thoughts pays off. Now you're ready to begin writing your essay.

You have 30 minutes to write each essay. The first 5 to 7 minutes should be used to analyze the prompt and organize your thoughts. Keep your eye on the time and save the last 5 to 7 minutes to review and proofread your work. In the time that's left — 16 to 20 minutes — write the body of your essay according to the numbered points you jotted down.

Arm yourself with versatile examples

Support for your thesis should include examples from your own experiences, reading, and observations. If these examples are too similar or too general, they merely restate and, thus, lose their strength. Strive for versatile, specific examples and avoid general statements as much as possible.

If you're armed with impressive examples from deep philosophical works or scientific journals (that everyone else somehow missed), good for you! But it doesn't really matter to the evaluator of your essay whether your examples are erudite or "down home." He is looking for good, solid, versatile examples that stay on target and make your point.

Practicing ahead of time

How can you best prepare for essays? Write, write, write. For the argumentative essay, practice taking a side in a current issue you have read or heard about. How will you support your opinion? How will you organize? For the informative/informational essay, read about a topic from two or three sources and practice using this information in an essay. Regardless of what type of essay you're writing, make sure you do the following:

- Practice writing sentences with dependent clauses, and be sure that the sentences you write are clear, concise, and punctuated correctly.

- Using the punctuation section in Chapter 12 as a guide, practice writing sentences similar to the ones used in the explanations. Doing so will help you remember the punctuation rules.

- Using the homophone section in Chapter 12 as a guide, write sentences using the example homophones correctly.

- Practice! Clear your desk. Grab a pen and paper and write. Read your essay with a critical eye. Ask friends and/or family to read your essay and make suggestions. The more you write, the more comfortable you'll feel on test day.

- Go to your bookshelf or library and use the material there to practice writing correct citations for books, encyclopedias, magazines, and websites. Remember that materials like magazines and websites are the most appropriate sources for recent information on a topic, while books provide more detailed, in-depth information. Be sure you know which sources are most appropriate for different topics.

Part V
Tackling Praxis Core Practice Tests

What to Do the Night Before the Test

- ✔ **Gather everything you need:** Make sure you have the directions to the test center, your picture ID, your admission ticket, and your lucky shoes.

- ✔ **Get a good night's sleep.** Wait until you get your passing scores to celebrate with your friends.

- ✔ **Avoid junk food.** Salty and sugary foods are the enemy and will drain your energy. Eat fruits and vegetables for fuel that will see you through the test.

Find out how to make the most of the practice tests with the free article at www.dummies.com/extras/praxiscore.

In this part . . .

✔ Discover your areas of strength and weakness by taking a full-length Praxis Core practice test (or two).

✔ Score your test quickly with an answer key.

✔ Determine where you went wrong (or right) by reading through answer explanations for all practice test questions.

Chapter 14

Practice Exam 1

. . . .

*N*ow it's time to audition for the starring role in "Acing the Praxis Core." It's your chance to see how well you can perform on the practice exam in a mock test setting. Remember, Praxis makes perfect . . . I mean, "practice makes perfect."

When you take the following practice test, try your best to create a setting that's similar to the one in which you'll take the real Praxis. That means

- ✔ De-gadgetize! No cellphone, tablet, TV remote, and so on. However, you have access to an on-screen, four-function calculator when you take the Praxis Math, so you can keep a calculator handy when you reach the math practice test in this chapter.
- ✔ Find a quiet place to take the practice test — somewhere free from disruptions.

After you've created a testing environment, adjust your mind-set:

- ✔ Make sure you're aware of the amount of time allowed for each section so you don't spend too much time on one question.
- ✔ Focus on the concept that you're being tested on and turn your radar on to identify key words that indicate the operation you need to solve the problem.
- ✔ Don't leave any answers blank.
- ✔ Stay focused on your goal — to ace the Praxis Core. Have self-confidence because now is your opportunity to shine!

When you finish this audition, there shouldn't be a need to call in an understudy. Make sure to go through the detailed explanations of the answers in Chapter 15. Pay close attention to the questions you missed. Go back and review the question, and then review the answer to make sure you understand it.

If you want to practice taking the test electronically, as you'll do on test day, go to `learn.dummies.com` where we've put this practice test online. This online practice is included with the book. There, you can answer the questions digitally, and the software records which questions you answered correctly and incorrectly. This summary provides you with a snapshot of which areas you excel in and which areas you may need additional review in.

Answer Sheet for Practice Exam 1

Reading

1. Ⓐ Ⓑ Ⓒ Ⓓ Ⓔ
2. Ⓐ Ⓑ Ⓒ Ⓓ Ⓔ
3. Ⓐ Ⓑ Ⓒ Ⓓ Ⓔ
4. Ⓐ Ⓑ Ⓒ Ⓓ Ⓔ
5. Ⓐ Ⓑ Ⓒ Ⓓ Ⓔ
6. Ⓐ Ⓑ Ⓒ Ⓓ Ⓔ
7. Ⓐ Ⓑ Ⓒ Ⓓ Ⓔ
8. Ⓐ Ⓑ Ⓒ Ⓓ Ⓔ
9. Ⓐ Ⓑ Ⓒ Ⓓ Ⓔ
10. Ⓐ Ⓑ Ⓒ Ⓓ Ⓔ
11. Ⓐ Ⓑ Ⓒ Ⓓ Ⓔ
12. Ⓐ Ⓑ Ⓒ Ⓓ Ⓔ
13. Ⓐ Ⓑ Ⓒ Ⓓ Ⓔ
14. Ⓐ Ⓑ Ⓒ Ⓓ Ⓔ
15. Ⓐ Ⓑ Ⓒ Ⓓ Ⓔ
16. Ⓐ Ⓑ Ⓒ Ⓓ Ⓔ
17. Ⓐ Ⓑ Ⓒ Ⓓ Ⓔ
18. Ⓐ Ⓑ Ⓒ Ⓓ Ⓔ
19. Ⓐ Ⓑ Ⓒ Ⓓ Ⓔ
20. Ⓐ Ⓑ Ⓒ Ⓓ Ⓔ
21. Ⓐ Ⓑ Ⓒ Ⓓ Ⓔ
22. Ⓐ Ⓑ Ⓒ Ⓓ Ⓔ
23. Ⓐ Ⓑ Ⓒ Ⓓ Ⓔ
24. Ⓐ Ⓑ Ⓒ Ⓓ Ⓔ
25. Ⓐ Ⓑ Ⓒ Ⓓ Ⓔ
26. Ⓐ Ⓑ Ⓒ Ⓓ Ⓔ
27. Ⓐ Ⓑ Ⓒ Ⓓ Ⓔ
28. Ⓐ Ⓑ Ⓒ Ⓓ Ⓔ
29. Ⓐ Ⓑ Ⓒ Ⓓ Ⓔ
30. Ⓐ Ⓑ Ⓒ Ⓓ Ⓔ
31. Ⓐ Ⓑ Ⓒ Ⓓ Ⓔ
32. Ⓐ Ⓑ Ⓒ Ⓓ Ⓔ
33. Ⓐ Ⓑ Ⓒ Ⓓ Ⓔ
34. Ⓐ Ⓑ Ⓒ Ⓓ Ⓔ
35. Ⓐ Ⓑ Ⓒ Ⓓ Ⓔ
36. Ⓐ Ⓑ Ⓒ Ⓓ Ⓔ
37. Ⓐ Ⓑ Ⓒ Ⓓ Ⓔ
38. Ⓐ Ⓑ Ⓒ Ⓓ Ⓔ
39. Ⓐ Ⓑ Ⓒ Ⓓ Ⓔ
40. Ⓐ Ⓑ Ⓒ Ⓓ Ⓔ
41. Ⓐ Ⓑ Ⓒ Ⓓ Ⓔ
42. Ⓐ Ⓑ Ⓒ Ⓓ Ⓔ
43. Ⓐ Ⓑ Ⓒ Ⓓ Ⓔ
44. Ⓐ Ⓑ Ⓒ Ⓓ Ⓔ
45. Ⓐ Ⓑ Ⓒ Ⓓ Ⓔ
46. Ⓐ Ⓑ Ⓒ Ⓓ Ⓔ
47. Ⓐ Ⓑ Ⓒ Ⓓ Ⓔ
48. Ⓐ Ⓑ Ⓒ Ⓓ Ⓔ
49. Ⓐ Ⓑ Ⓒ
50. Ⓐ Ⓑ Ⓒ Ⓓ Ⓔ
51. Ⓐ Ⓑ Ⓒ Ⓓ Ⓔ
52. Ⓐ Ⓑ Ⓒ Ⓓ Ⓔ
53. Ⓐ Ⓑ Ⓒ Ⓓ Ⓔ
54. Ⓐ Ⓑ Ⓒ Ⓓ Ⓔ
55. Ⓐ Ⓑ Ⓒ Ⓓ Ⓔ
56. Ⓐ Ⓑ Ⓒ Ⓓ Ⓔ

Writing

1. Ⓐ Ⓑ Ⓒ Ⓓ Ⓔ
2. Ⓐ Ⓑ Ⓒ Ⓓ Ⓔ
3. Ⓐ Ⓑ Ⓒ Ⓓ Ⓔ
4. Ⓐ Ⓑ Ⓒ Ⓓ Ⓔ
5. Ⓐ Ⓑ Ⓒ Ⓓ Ⓔ
6. Ⓐ Ⓑ Ⓒ Ⓓ Ⓔ
7. Ⓐ Ⓑ Ⓒ Ⓓ Ⓔ
8. Ⓐ Ⓑ Ⓒ Ⓓ Ⓔ
9. Ⓐ Ⓑ Ⓒ Ⓓ Ⓔ
10. Ⓐ Ⓑ Ⓒ Ⓓ Ⓔ
11. Ⓐ Ⓑ Ⓒ Ⓓ Ⓔ
12. Ⓐ Ⓑ Ⓒ Ⓓ Ⓔ
13. Ⓐ Ⓑ Ⓒ Ⓓ Ⓔ
14. Ⓐ Ⓑ Ⓒ Ⓓ Ⓔ
15. Ⓐ Ⓑ Ⓒ Ⓓ Ⓔ
16. Ⓐ Ⓑ Ⓒ Ⓓ Ⓔ
17. Ⓐ Ⓑ Ⓒ Ⓓ Ⓔ
18. Ⓐ Ⓑ Ⓒ Ⓓ Ⓔ
19. Ⓐ Ⓑ Ⓒ Ⓓ Ⓔ
20. Ⓐ Ⓑ Ⓒ Ⓓ Ⓔ
21. Ⓐ Ⓑ Ⓒ Ⓓ Ⓔ
22. Ⓐ Ⓑ Ⓒ Ⓓ Ⓔ
23. Ⓐ Ⓑ Ⓒ Ⓓ Ⓔ
24. Ⓐ Ⓑ Ⓒ Ⓓ Ⓔ
25. Ⓐ Ⓑ Ⓒ Ⓓ Ⓔ
26. Ⓐ Ⓑ Ⓒ Ⓓ Ⓔ
27. Ⓐ Ⓑ Ⓒ Ⓓ Ⓔ
28. Ⓐ Ⓑ Ⓒ Ⓓ Ⓔ
29. Ⓐ Ⓑ Ⓒ Ⓓ Ⓔ
30. Ⓐ Ⓑ Ⓒ Ⓓ Ⓔ
31. Ⓐ Ⓑ Ⓒ Ⓓ Ⓔ
32. Ⓐ Ⓑ Ⓒ Ⓓ Ⓔ
33. Ⓐ Ⓑ Ⓒ Ⓓ Ⓔ
34. Ⓐ Ⓑ Ⓒ Ⓓ Ⓔ
35. Ⓐ Ⓑ Ⓒ Ⓓ Ⓔ
36. Ⓐ Ⓑ Ⓒ Ⓓ Ⓔ
37. Ⓐ Ⓑ Ⓒ Ⓓ Ⓔ
38. Ⓐ Ⓑ Ⓒ Ⓓ Ⓔ
39. Ⓐ Ⓑ Ⓒ Ⓓ Ⓔ
40. Ⓐ Ⓑ Ⓒ Ⓓ Ⓔ

Math

1. Ⓐ Ⓑ Ⓒ Ⓓ Ⓔ
2. Ⓐ Ⓑ Ⓒ Ⓓ Ⓔ
3. Ⓐ Ⓑ Ⓒ Ⓓ Ⓔ
4. Ⓐ Ⓑ Ⓒ Ⓓ Ⓔ
5. Ⓐ Ⓑ Ⓒ Ⓓ Ⓔ
6. Ⓐ Ⓑ Ⓒ Ⓓ Ⓔ
7. Ⓐ Ⓑ Ⓒ Ⓓ Ⓔ
8. Ⓐ Ⓑ Ⓒ Ⓓ Ⓔ
9. Ⓐ Ⓑ Ⓒ Ⓓ Ⓔ
10. Ⓐ Ⓑ Ⓒ Ⓓ Ⓔ
11. Ⓐ Ⓑ Ⓒ Ⓓ Ⓔ
12. Ⓐ Ⓑ Ⓒ Ⓓ Ⓔ
13. Ⓐ Ⓑ Ⓒ Ⓓ Ⓔ
14. Ⓐ Ⓑ Ⓒ Ⓓ Ⓔ
15. Ⓐ Ⓑ Ⓒ Ⓓ Ⓔ
16. Ⓐ Ⓑ Ⓒ Ⓓ Ⓔ
17. Ⓐ Ⓑ Ⓒ Ⓓ Ⓔ
18. Ⓐ Ⓑ Ⓒ Ⓓ Ⓔ
19. Ⓐ Ⓑ Ⓒ Ⓓ Ⓔ
20. Ⓐ Ⓑ Ⓒ Ⓓ Ⓔ
21. Ⓐ Ⓑ Ⓒ Ⓓ Ⓔ
22. Ⓐ Ⓑ Ⓒ Ⓓ Ⓔ
23. Ⓐ Ⓑ Ⓒ Ⓓ Ⓔ
24. Ⓐ Ⓑ Ⓒ Ⓓ Ⓔ
25. Ⓐ Ⓑ Ⓒ Ⓓ Ⓔ
26. Ⓐ Ⓑ Ⓒ Ⓓ Ⓔ
27. Ⓐ Ⓑ Ⓒ Ⓓ Ⓔ
28. Ⓐ Ⓑ Ⓒ Ⓓ Ⓔ
29. Ⓐ Ⓑ Ⓒ Ⓓ Ⓔ
30. Ⓐ Ⓑ Ⓒ Ⓓ Ⓔ
31. Ⓐ Ⓑ Ⓒ Ⓓ Ⓔ
32. Ⓐ Ⓑ Ⓒ Ⓓ Ⓔ
33. Ⓐ Ⓑ Ⓒ Ⓓ Ⓔ
34. Ⓐ Ⓑ Ⓒ Ⓓ Ⓔ
35. Ⓐ Ⓑ Ⓒ Ⓓ Ⓔ
36. Ⓐ Ⓑ Ⓒ Ⓓ Ⓔ
37. Ⓐ Ⓑ Ⓒ Ⓓ Ⓔ
38. Ⓐ Ⓑ Ⓒ Ⓓ Ⓔ
39. Ⓐ Ⓑ Ⓒ Ⓓ Ⓔ
40. Ⓐ Ⓑ Ⓒ Ⓓ Ⓔ
41. Ⓐ Ⓑ Ⓒ Ⓓ Ⓔ
42. Ⓐ Ⓑ Ⓒ Ⓓ Ⓔ
43. Ⓐ Ⓑ Ⓒ Ⓓ Ⓔ
44. Ⓐ Ⓑ Ⓒ Ⓓ Ⓔ
45. Ⓐ Ⓑ Ⓒ Ⓓ Ⓔ
46. Ⓐ Ⓑ Ⓒ Ⓓ Ⓔ
47. Ⓐ Ⓑ Ⓒ Ⓓ Ⓔ
48. Ⓐ Ⓑ Ⓒ Ⓓ Ⓔ
49. Ⓐ Ⓑ Ⓒ Ⓓ Ⓔ
50. Ⓐ Ⓑ Ⓒ Ⓓ Ⓔ
51. Ⓐ Ⓑ Ⓒ Ⓓ Ⓔ
52. Ⓐ Ⓑ Ⓒ Ⓓ Ⓔ
53. Ⓐ Ⓑ Ⓒ Ⓓ Ⓔ
54. Ⓐ Ⓑ Ⓒ Ⓓ Ⓔ
55. Ⓐ Ⓑ Ⓒ Ⓓ Ⓔ
56. Ⓐ Ⓑ Ⓒ Ⓓ Ⓔ

Part 1

Reading

> **Time:** 85 minutes for 56 questions
>
> **Directions:** Each statement or passage in this test is followed by a question or questions based on its content. After reading a statement or passage, choose the best answer to each question from among the five choices given. Answer all questions following a statement or passage on the basis of what is *stated* or *implied* in that statement or passage; you are not expected to have any previous knowledge of the topics treated in the statements and passages. Remember, try to answer every question.

The ABC hit drama *Lost* speaks to our deepest fear: the fear of being cut off from everything we know and love, left to fend for ourselves in a strange land. This fear is a philosophical fear, because it speaks to the human condition. It forces us to confront profound questions about ourselves and the world: Why am I here? Does my life matter? Do I have a special purpose? Can I make a difference?

1. In this passage, the author implies that a "philosophical fear" is one that

   (A) concerns how we affect other people, instead of only ourselves.

   (B) is inspired by interpretations of art, as opposed to direct experiences.

   (C) frightens us more than do non-philosophical fears.

   (D) has at its roots uncertainty about the meaning of life.

   (E) is centered on what happens after death, instead of with daily life.

Line *X-Men* comics were one of the first Marvel series to feature female characters as the leads in multiple story lines. X-Women are shown as strong and powerful, equal to the men around (05) them. *X-Men* comics also developed a diverse population of mutant superheroes that included African characters such as Storm, Native Americans like Dani Moonstar and Thunderbird, and Asian characters such as Jubilee and Lady (10) Deathstrike. Originally, Stan Lee named the comic "The Mutants," a less gender-specific title, but his editor thought the audience wouldn't understand what or who a mutant was, so Lee suggested *X-Men* because the main characters (15) had "extra" powers and were led by a man named Professor X. That was also a rather new concept: having a handicapped leader in

Professor X, who, despite being wheelchair-bound, is still one of the most powerful, influential heroes in the *X-Men* series. Here, too, we can (20) see the underlying philosophical spirit of the X-Verse: All of our traditional hierarchies are scrutinized, questioned, and reimagined.

2. In analyzing comic books about the *X-Men*, the author's main concern is

   (A) the ways in which the series' origins are at odds with its current manifestation.

   (B) the unique place of women characters in this particular comic-book universe.

   (C) ascertaining what *X-Men* writer Stan Lee was or was not directly responsible for creating.

   (D) the extent to which *X-Men* has influenced other popular comic-book series.

   (E) how the comics encourage readers to question traditional notions about power.

There are serious problems with the idea that God dictates the meaning of our lives. Think of great scientists, who better our lives with their discoveries. Or humanitarians, who tirelessly work to improve the world. Or entertainers even, who make our lives more enjoyable. Do we really want to say that if there's no God, then these accomplishments and goods don't count?

Go on to next page ▷

3. The author of this passage is primarily concerned with

   (A) arguing that God does not actually exist.

   (B) challenging religious people who disrespect the accomplishments of science.

   (C) pointing out that people can do good even when not motivated by religious faith.

   (D) questioning the viewpoint that all meaning must derive from a God.

   (E) encouraging people who do not believe in God to examine the implications of their arguments.

Questions 4 through 6 are based on the following passage.

Line   Myths abound about Shakespeare in part because of half-remembered or out-of-date scholarship from schooldays; because Shakespeare the man is such an elusive and charismatic cul-
(05) tural property; and because interventions in Shakespeare studies, particularly biographical and theatrical ones, make headline news: Witness the "authorship question" or speculation about Shakespeare's sexuality. Put simply, myths are
(10) told and retold about Shakespeare because no other writer matters as much to the world: Nineteenth-century Germany had a flourishing academic Shakespeare criticism before England did; India had a Shakespeare Society before
(15) England; Shakespeare is regularly performed at amateur and professional levels, in translation, worldwide. Shakespeare is not just English. Thus myths about Shakespeare go some way toward telling us stories about ourselves.

4. This passage is primarily concerned with

   (A) determining precisely what it is that Shakespeare's works tell us about ourselves.

   (B) correcting out-of-date scholarship.

   (C) examining the reasons why arguments about Shakespeare fascinate us.

   (D) satirizing some of the more outlandish recent suppositions about Shakespeare.

   (E) analyzing the theory that Shakespeare may not have been who he claimed to be.

5. The author most probably uses the phrase "interventions in" in Line 5 to mean

   (A) interference with

   (B) appraisals of

   (C) obstacles to

   (D) unexpected collaborations regarding

   (E) new approaches to

6. By using the phrase "Shakespeare the man is such an elusive and charismatic cultural property," the author means to say that

   (A) Shakespeare's works have been co-opted by those in power to such an extent that we have lost sight of his original intentions.

   (B) there is more controversy over which culture interprets the plays of Shakespeare correctly than there is about the works of other artists.

   (C) scholars and journalists deliberately spread misinformation about Shakespeare because there is so much money to be made from arguing about him.

   (D) largely because he is so shrouded in mystery as a human being, the prospect of claiming symbolic kinship with Shakespeare is both daunting and enticing.

   (E) the perceived "greatness" of Shakespeare's writing does not originate from a property of the works themselves, but is instead the result of society turning Shakespeare himself into a symbol of something.

Questions 7 through 11 are based on the following passage.

    One popular website in which users ask and   Line answer each other's questions poses this question: "Was Shakespeare popular in his day?" The entire answer posted by a reader states "Yes, he was Shakespeare!" It's a fair summary of general (05) assumptions: How could Shakespeare be Shakespeare — read and performed 400 years after his death and translated across languages, media, and hemispheres — had he not been popular in his own time? But the questions of how (10) we define popularity and whether the evidence about Shakespeare confirms this myth need a

Go on to next page ⟶

little more probing, and we need also to separate popularity in the theater from popularity in print.

(15)   First, to the theater. From 1594 onwards, when he joined the Lord Chamberlain's Men as both sharer (part-owner) and resident play-wright, Shakespeare's own popularity is intrinsi-cally related to that of the company. Thus, while

(20) the development of the Chamberlain's Men and the company's increasing dominance in the London theater economy cannot be solely attrib-uted to Shakespeare's plays, nor can it be sepa-rated from them. The Globe theater, built by the

(25) Chamberlain's Men in 1599, could take over 3,000 spectators; in 1608 the company opened an addi-tional indoor theater, Blackfriars, for winter per-formances. In 1603 it received the patronage of the new king, James, becoming the King's

(30) Men and performing regularly at court. Shakespeare's own wealth also grew over this period: In 1596 his family acquired a coat of arms and with it the right to be styled "gentlemen"; a year later he bought a large house in Stratford-

(35) upon-Avon, reputedly the town's second-largest. All these economic and prestige indicators sug-gest that the company and its house dramatist were thriving, and this in turn suggests that Shakespeare's works, like the plays the company

(40) performed by other dramatists including Thomas Middleton and Ben Jonson, were popular.

It is, however, harder to be more specific. The only sustained details we have about the econom-ics of the Elizabethan theater come from the rival

(45) company the Admiral's Men and from papers associated with their entrepreneurial manager Philip Henslowe. These papers suggest that Christopher Marlowe's *The Jew of Malta,* with its dynamic and amoral central character Barabas,

(50) was among the most frequently performed plays, with a schedule including ten performances in six months, far in excess of records for any Shakespeare play. When Thomas Middleton's *A Game at Chess,* a sharp satire on Anglo-Spanish

(55) relations, hit the Globe in 1624, it was such a sen-sation that it played for nine consecutive perfor-mances: No play of Shakespeare's can claim anything like that box-office success. While our iconic reference point for classical literary drama

(60) is probably the image of Hamlet holding the skull of the jester Yorick, for the early modern period the most instantly recognizable drama was not Shakespeare, but the bloody revenge tragedy by Thomas Kyd, *The Spanish Tragedy.* Kyd's play

(65) spawned a prequel, a ballad version; was reworked by later playwrights to extend its stage life; and was quoted, parodied, and generally riffed upon by writers up to the closing of the the-aters. There is no contemporary evidence that

(70) any of Shakespeare's plays had this reach.

7. The passage states that we definitively know which of the following to be true?

(A) Shakespeare's plays were consistently less popular than those of Thomas Kyd.

(B) Audiences of Shakespeare's time were more entertained by amoral characters than moral ones.

(C) All schoolchildren today are taught that Shakespeare was popular in his day, regardless of whether this was in fact true.

(D) King James encouraged his subjects to read the plays of Shakespeare.

(E) Shakespeare himself, for whatever reason, was indisputably financially successful.

8. Which of the following best describes the organization of the passage?

(A) A popular misconception is identified and then disproved with evidence.

(B) An ongoing debate is summarized from an impartial perspective.

(C) New findings are announced and the methodology used to uncover them is explained.

(D) A complex question is analyzed from more than one point of view.

(E) Dramatists of Shakespeare's time are ranked by popularity, based on exhaus-tive research.

9. Which of the following is presented by the passage as a key question that cannot be answered?

(A) Did people see Shakespeare's plays because they liked the writing, or the acting?

(B) How are Shakespeare's main characters different from those of Christopher Marlowe?

(C) Why has the image of Hamlet become our reference point for classical literary drama?

(D) Did Shakespeare make most of his money from writing plays, or by some other means?

(E) Were people in Shakespeare's own cul-ture as concerned with popularity as we are today?

Go on to next page

10. Which of the following does the author NOT discuss as a possible indicator of artistic popularity?

    (A) Whether the author of the work makes money from it

    (B) Whether a play is well-received by less educated audience members, as well as educated ones

    (C) Whether a play runs for a high number of performances

    (D) Whether an artistic work is referenced in or alluded to by other subsequent artistic works

    (E) Whether a work of literature ends up being regularly translated into other languages

11. Presumably, the author alludes briefly to the content of the plays by Marlowe, Middleton, and Kyd that the passage mentions in order to

    (A) prevent the audience from confusing them with plays that are by Shakespeare.

    (B) distinguish between authors who may have influenced Shakespeare and those who did not.

    (C) provide some indication of the sort of content that was a "box-office draw" in Shakespeare's time.

    (D) introduce an examination of why plays dealing with ethnic differences were so common then.

    (E) support the earlier assertion that Shakespeare was not the only writer of his day to mix comedy with more serious concerns.

Questions 12 through 14 are based on the following passage.

Line   Claude Nicolet has described the Roman Principate as a significant stage on the road to the modern state. On the other hand, several features that marked this new version of the impe-
(05)   rial order seem to undermine this claim. The autocratic power center was adapted to republican institutions in ingenious and effective ways but, by the same token, suffered from a certain under-institutionalization of its more innovative
(10)   aspects — hence the overpowering emphasis on the person of the ruler and a corresponding weakness of the foundations for continuous and impersonal statehood.

12. Which of the following best describes the organization of the passage?

    (A) It raises a historical question and then discusses possible answers to that question.

    (B) It identifies a misconception and then analyzes why it is so widespread.

    (C) It defines a sociological term and then illustrates it with a series of analogies.

    (D) It compares and contrasts the two sides of an ongoing controversy.

    (E) It challenges a previous assessment regarding the extent of an influence.

13. As it is discussed in this passage, the central contrast of ancient Imperial Rome was that it

    (A) was as politically powerful as a modern nation but was run more like a cult than a country.

    (B) adopted cosmetic autocratic trappings but never abandoned republican bureaucracy.

    (C) invented new ideas more quickly than its neighbors but inevitably changed them for the worse.

    (D) eventually became so efficiently run that no one cared who was in charge.

    (E) paradoxically blended military might with the veneration of scientific knowledge.

14. The implied relationship between Imperial Rome's "emphasis on the person of the ruler" and the concept of "continuous and impersonal statehood" is that

    (A) fighting over the Imperial succession disastrously interfered with the business of governance.

    (B) the fact that Rome was symbolized by one man prevented it from being seen as an idea.

    (C) Rome's reluctance to separate church and state made it powerful at first, but also made its eventual downfall inevitable.

    (D) the fact that the Emperor's decisions were often biased was an insoluble problem.

    (E) because the Emperor kept so many innovations secret, the other branches of Roman government were not able to function effectively.

Go on to next page

If deciding and acting don't change the future, what about changing the past? Although the difference between eternalism and presentism divides philosophers into two heavily armed camps, the question of whether the past can be changed is, relatively speaking, a side issue. Almost all philosophers are in agreement: No, sir, it cannot. Aristotle regarded the past as necessary, and St. Augustine (354-430 C.E.) thought that not even God can change the past. Surprisingly for philosophy, almost everyone who has thought about the matter has followed suit.

15. The author begins the last sentence with the word "surprisingly" in order to imply that

   (A) the idea being examined is, in his opinion, implausible.

   (B) philosophers were skeptical of the assertion at first, and were then surprised when they agreed.

   (C) philosophers were surprised when average people turned out to agree with them.

   (D) it is decidedly a rarity for the vast majority of philosophers to be in agreement about something.

   (E) he would have expected people trained in philosophy to be more original.

Though it is the most famous and most cherished of the rights guaranteed by the U.S. Constitution, freedom of speech is quite possibly also the most misunderstood. When a celebrity or other (5) public figure lands in hot water over controversial comments, his or her supporters will inevitably take up the cry of "free speech" — but such a reaction bespeaks a fundamental misunderstanding of both constitutional law and the Founding Fathers' (10) intent. Freedom of speech does not, and was never intended to, mean that no one is allowed to criticize you for what you say, only that the government is not allowed to imprison you for it. Far from being something it intended to prevent, heated (15) debate among the citizenry is the very outcome that the First Amendment was designed to ensure.

16. The passage is primarily concerned with

   (A) lamenting the fact that the half-baked comments of celebrities make news.

   (B) attempting to explain why U.S. citizens are more reluctant to debate than they once were.

   (C) correcting what appears to be a common misconception about U.S. law.

   (D) excoriating the vanity of people who seem to think that no one may disagree with them.

   (E) arguing that freedom of speech is not as important as other constitutional rights that are less famous.

Though King Richard I of England — famously known as "the Lionheart" — remains popular in the U.K. and is one of the few Medieval British monarchs whose name is widely known even in America, his golden reputation is based more on (5) romantic wishful thinking than historical fact. He wasn't a bad king, but this is mainly because he wasn't much of a king at all. During the ten years of Richard's reign, he spent only six months in England and most of his time acting as a military (10) commander in the Crusades, rather than concerning himself with the business of government. The idealization of Richard largely comes courtesy of the fact that his inept younger brother John — the sinister "Prince John" of so many Robin Hood (15) films — watched over England in Richard's absence, and so Richard's popularity skyrocketed based on little aside from the fact that he was not John. Perhaps the greatest irony is that this archetypal English King, born less than a century after (20) the Norman Conquest, spoke no English, a fact that popular culture understandably glosses over. After all, it simply wouldn't do to have Good King Richard return at the end of the Robin Hood movie and speak French. (25)

Go on to next page

17. The author logically implies which of the following about King Richard the Lionheart?

    (A) He might not have been such a beloved king if he had spent more time actually acting as king.

    (B) He was far less effective as a military commander than most people like to imagine.

    (C) It was both unusual and shameful that he spoke no English.

    (D) He deserves to be widely known in America less than do most other Medieval British Monarchs.

    (E) His depiction in popular culture is embarrassingly inaccurate and should be corrected.

> *Questions 18 through 20 are based on the following passage.*

Line   Teenage students who ask their English teachers to recommend some great young poets are invariably disappointed. There are, of course, a number of truly great bards who did their
(05) finest work in their mid-20s (John Keats or Percy Shelley, for example), an age that certainly seems "young" enough to a teacher, but a teenager who says "young" means another teenager. This leads to the awkward — and, from the student's point
(10) of view, biased — acknowledgment of the plain fact that, in the entire history of poetry, virtually no teenage poets have managed to produce anything of merit, the lone and significant exception being the 19th-century French symbolist Arthur
(15) Rimbaud. The usual explanation for this is that, unlike in other art forms such as music, where "prodigies" like Mozart can compose symphonies at the age of eight, the composition of a truly great poem requires at least as much life
(20) experience as inborn aptitude, and the concerns of a teenager are inevitably silly, no matter how much technical skill he or she might possess. And yet, the question remains: If it was possible for Rimbaud to write poetry of undeniable genius
(25) at the age of 15, then why has no one else managed to do so?

18. The central paradox raised by the passage concerns the question of

    (A) why many adults, such as teachers and literary critics, are biased against the poetry of teenagers.

    (B) why students and teachers, even fairly young teachers, have different definitions of "young."

    (C) why musicians usually develop mature skill levels at younger ages than do writers.

    (D) why teenagers tend to be suspicious of literature written by people they consider "old."

    (E) why, since there has been one great teenage poet, there haven't been more.

19. Which of the following best describes the organization of the passage?

    (A) It criticizes a common error, before eventually admitting that the error is excusable.

    (B) It describes a typical situation, then uses it as a springboard for critical inquiry.

    (C) It offers an example of relativism, before turning to examine an objective question.

    (D) It prefaces a criticism of immaturity with a lighthearted anecdote.

    (E) It satirizes the biases of teenagers, before grudgingly acknowledging the biases of adults.

20. According to the passage, teenage students would probably respond to the characterization of a 30-year-old poet as "young" with

    (A) relief.

    (B) sarcasm.

    (C) hostility.

    (D) accusations.

    (E) fear.

Go on to next page

Questions 21 through 24 are based on the following passage.

Line The existential philosopher Jean-Paul Sartre (1905–1980) is well known for his cynical account of interpersonal relationships, as manifested in both his philosophy and his literary works.
(05) Known for his declaration "Hell is other people," Sartre highlights the anxiety that our relationships with others elicit and the way those relationships can inhibit personal autonomy. While Sartre regards interpersonal relations as tremen-
(10) dous sources of conflict and concern, he is also emphatic that these relationships are essential to our being. Sartre's theory of others is conveyed in his principal philosophic work *Being and Nothingness* and in his play *No Exit.*
(15) Sartre's account of social relationships contrasts with that of his contemporary and fellow existentialist Martin Heidegger (1889–1976). While both Sartre and Heidegger regard humans as fundamentally social beings, Heidegger
(20) emphasizes the sense of connection people experience. In contrast, Sartre emphasizes how others frequently irritate and impede us, and he asserts that the relations that exist between individuals are fundamentally ones of "conflict." He
(25) attributes the ambivalence we experience toward others to three main causes. The first reason that others arouse negative feelings in us is that they represent potential obstacles to our freedom. According to Sartre, without interfer-
(30) ence from others, individuals are typically absorbed in existence, particularly in the task of obtaining the things that they need and desire from the environment. Rather than thinking about their experience, they are immersed in it.
(35) They act without reflecting. As Sartre explains, the appearance of another person pulls the individual out of this original state of absorption. The appearance of another comes not only as a surprise, but also as a threat.

21. According to the passage, Sartre believed that the natural human condition is characterized by

   (A) obsequiousness.

   (B) mendacity.

   (C) cupidity.

   (D) diffidence.

   (E) solipsism.

22. In Line 35, "reflecting" is used most nearly to mean

   (A) considering the consequences.

   (B) gathering information from past experience.

   (C) examining how others might see them.

   (D) fearing punishment.

   (E) deliberately courting a reaction.

23. In the passage as a whole, the tone adopted by the author with regard to the works of Jean-Paul Sartre is one of

   (A) dispassionate explication.

   (B) grudging admiration.

   (C) qualified optimism.

   (D) respectful pity.

   (E) playful mockery.

24. Based on the passage, the most likely assumption is that Jean-Paul Sartre would have advised people to do which of the following?

   (A) Admit that society is a competition and figure out how to get what you want from people.

   (B) Learn to see yourself as others do early in life, so that others' opinions will come as less of a shock.

   (C) Abandon your desires, so that others will not be able to hurt you.

   (D) Spend as little time around others as possible until you are sure that your identity is stable.

   (E) Accept the necessity of human relationships, but do not lose all sense of personal freedom.

Questions 25 through 27 are based on the following passage.

Though the declaration once seemed overdra- Line matic and premature, the idea that Kurt Cobain, the singer and songwriter from the grunge band Nirvana who committed suicide in 1994, was the "last rock star" has come to appear increasingly (05) prescient — not because of any permanent, shattering impact that Cobain's career had on rock as an art form, but rather because of cultural and technological changes that happened to occur in

Go on to next page

(10) the wake of his death. Purely by coincidence, Cobain was the final rock frontman whose apotheosis predated the mainstreaming of the Internet, a technological sea-change that had massive effects on youth culture and the music industry:
(15) Increasingly porous barriers between youth communities helped hip-hop and dance music displace rock as the best-selling and most visible genre, and the era of downloading meant that record companies could market directly to a vari-
(20) ety of audiences at once and make just as much money without creating unfellowed megastars. Though the ominous title of "last rock star" was originally intended to imply that no one could follow Cobain, it ended up coming true because
(25) the World Wide Web made rock stars themselves obsolete.

25. The passage is primarily concerned with

   (A) aesthetically comparing the music of the pre-Internet age and the music of the Internet age.

   (B) analyzing a specific effect that technology appears to have had on youth culture.

   (C) criticizing people who make silly predictions involving sweeping generalizations.

   (D) suggesting that hip-hop would be less popular today if Cobain hadn't died when he did.

   (E) providing examples of predictions that came true in ironic ways.

26. According to the passage, the music industry of today differs from the music industry of the early 1990s in that

   (A) it considers hip-hop more relevant and innovative than rock and promotes it accordingly.

   (B) it is making far less money, thanks to downloading, so it cannot promote megastars the way it used to.

   (C) the most successful artists become successful by coincidence, rather than as the result of deliberate marketing.

   (D) the average music consumer is younger, and the music those consumers buy is happier in tone.

   (E) it is based on making a multiplicity of artists slightly famous, rather than making a few artists incredibly famous.

27. The author's attitude toward the subject matter most nearly appears to be one of

   (A) rueful reflection.

   (B) bittersweet nostalgia.

   (C) firm conviction.

   (D) satisfied gloating.

   (E) indignant incredulousness.

In the third X-Men movie, *The Last Stand*, a "cure" is discovered that suppresses the activity of the mutant gene, turning mutants into ordinary humans. Storm, the weather-controller, reacts by asking, "Who would want this cure? I mean, what kind of coward would take it just to fit in?" Meanwhile, Rogue — whose touch can sap the life, energy, and abilities of other people — is already preparing her trip to the pharmaceutical clinic.

28. It can be inferred from the passage that Rogue would agree with which of the following statements?

   (A) Bravery is just as vain as a desire to fit in.

   (B) People have a responsibility to try and fit in if their differences make them dangerous.

   (C) The decision to be like others is braver than the desire to be different from them.

   (D) The desire to be more like others is not always a sign of cowardice.

   (E) Scientific modifications to nature are generally superior to nature.

Line Though popular culture often still regards them as the quintessential aspect of the test, analogies were actually removed from the SAT in 2005. The decision to axe the series of questions
(5) that simultaneously tested vocabulary knowledge and critical-thinking skills (for example, "cat is to kitten as goose is to . . . ") was a relief to many, but a cause for outrage and suspicion to others. Though the College Board never
(10) issued a full explanation for the decision, education insiders indicated that the analogies were dumped in response to complaints that logical reasoning was an inborn skill that couldn't be studied (meaning that these questions rewarded
(15) natural aptitude rather than diligent preparation) and that the vocabulary words were biased

Go on to next page ⇒

towards certain ethnic or socioeconomic groups. (One recent question had infamously employed the word *regatta,* a type of sailing race.) Fans of
(20) the analogies section countered that the entire point of the test was for smart kids to do well, and that students of any ethnic group or socio-economic class could have learned a word from reading, regardless of their life experience.

29. The passage directly answers which of the following questions?

    (A) What was the official explanation for the removal of analogies from the SAT?

    (B) What are the criteria used to determine whether a certain vocabulary word is biased?

    (C) What were some of the complaints people had traditionally made about the SAT analogies section?

    (D) What is the primary purpose of standardized tests such as the SAT?

    (E) Do more people learn difficult words from reading or from life experience?

Questions 30 through 32 are based on the following passage.

Line   The fact that Europa, a moon of the planet Jupiter, spins on its axis at a rate faster than that at which it orbits the planet probably wouldn't cause many people to leap from their chairs with
(05) excitement. But perhaps it should: Such an orbital eccentricity indicates that Europa is likely to have a sizeable layer of liquid between its frozen outer crust and dense core, and the fact that the liquid in question is almost certainly
(10) water means that Europa is now the top candidate in our solar system for an extraterrestrial body that contains life. A subsurface ocean would receive little if any of the sunlight that was long thought to be a prerequisite for life, but sci-
(15) entists now know that life can originate in and be supported by the chemical disequilibrium created by undersea volcanoes, a feature that Europa's hidden sea is likely to contain. We may find out conclusively in our lifetimes, though we
(20) will have to have a bit of patience: The Jupiter Icy Moon Explorer (JUICE) satellite will launch in 2022 and reach the Jupiter system in 2030.

30. Which of the following, if true, would increase the probability of life on Europa?

    (A) The discovery that life can originate in liquid substances other than water

    (B) The discovery of other moons that spin more quickly than they orbit

    (C) Indications that an even greater number of earthly life-forms originated from undersea volcanoes

    (D) Proof that Europa is the oldest of Jupiter's moons

    (E) Proof that Europa's frozen crust is, in fact, entirely comprised of water ice

31. The author most likely includes the sentence about undersea volcanoes in order to

    (A) draw a more exact comparison between Europa and Earth.

    (B) appeal to younger readers and get them interested in space exploration.

    (C) address an anticipated objection from more-informed readers.

    (D) establish that Europa's subsurface ocean is warm.

    (E) provide a definition for the term "chemical disequilibrium."

32. The passage directly answers which of the following questions?

    (A) What other extraterrestrial bodies in our solar system might contain life?

    (B) How do we know that Europa probably contains a liquid layer?

    (C) Why do most life-forms require sunlight to originate?

    (D) Of what substances is Europa's core comprised?

    (E) In what year will we know for certain whether Europa contains life?

Go on to next page

Questions 33 through 38 are based on the following passages.

Passage 1

Line   Even among people who comprehend and accept the basics of the theory of evolution, a common misunderstanding involves the belief that evolution is *goal-oriented* or somehow "des-
(05) tined" to arrive at one and only one "right" outcome — for example, the belief that mice are *supposed to be* fast, or that wolves are *supposed to be* vicious, or that human beings are *supposed to be* intelligent. Although it is indisputably true that
(10) the traits of speed, aggression, and intelligence have *thus far* been beneficial adaptations for the animals that became mice, wolves, and humans, we must not fall victim to the fallacy of *retrospective determinism* — that is, the idea that, just
(15) because something *did* happen, it must have been *meant* to, and must therefore *always* be that way.

Passage 2

Line   Pop sociologists love to talk about how factors like matchmaking websites or the troubled economy are affecting people's love lives, but those minor changes are nothing compared to the
(05) "dating revolution" that's been recently observed in the African elephant population. For untold generations, the male elephant with the biggest, baddest set of tusks has been the elephant equivalent of the captain of the football team, calling the
(10) shots among males and making all the lady elephants swoon. In comparatively recent history, of course, tusks are also a liability, as any elephant with an impressive pair is a target for human ivory poachers. And although we're still not sure
(15) whether an elephant "never forgets," it now appears clear that an elephant — a female one, anyway — is smart enough to understand both the motivation behind poaching and a little bit of genetics as well. In what could only be the result
(20) of an effort to keep her eventual offspring from becoming the victims of poachers, female elephants are now seeking out smaller-tusked or entirely tuskless males, a phenomenon that has been jokingly but not inaccurately described as
(25) the biggest "Revenge of the Nerds" ever witnessed in the animal kingdom.

33. Which best describes the relationship between Passage 1 and Passage 2?

   (A) Passage 2 provides an example of a correction made by Passage 1.

   (B) Passage 2 issues a counterargument to a viewpoint presented in Passage 1.

   (C) Passage 2 falls victim to a fallacy that is warned against in Passage 1.

   (D) Passage 2 provides an alternate explanation for a phenomenon observed in Passage 1.

   (E) The arguments of Passage 1 and Passage 2 are largely unrelated.

34. In the context in which it appears in Passage 2, "untold" in Line 6 most nearly means

   (A) "infinite."

   (B) "successive."

   (C) "an immaterial number of."

   (D) "a disputed number of."

   (E) "many."

35. The humorous reference to the elephants' "Revenge of the Nerds" in Passage 2 accomplishes which of the following with regard to the content of Passage 1?

   (A) It provides an illustration of why retrospective determinism is fallacious.

   (B) It offers an explanation of why so many people misunderstand evolutionary theory.

   (C) It raises a paradox about whether evolution can be goal-oriented.

   (D) It questions whether a phenomenon that involves human interference is truly evolutionary.

   (E) It dismisses the concerns of Passage 1 in favor of a viewpoint that is more inclusive.

36. Compared with Passage 1, the purpose and tone of Passage 2 is

   (A) equally concerned, but more exhortatory.

   (B) equally open-minded, but more skeptical.

   (C) equally educated, but less scientific.

   (D) equally analytical, but more jocose.

   (E) equally angry, but more forgiving.

Go on to next page

37. Both authors do which of the following?

    (A) Define scientific terms for a general audience.

    (B) Reference terms and phrases from popular culture.

    (C) Make reference to examples of desirable evolutionary traits.

    (D) Discuss recent changes to evolutionary theory.

    (E) Gently mock those who disagree with the main thesis.

38. Both passages are primarily concerned with

    (A) disputing common objections to evolutionary theory.

    (B) dispelling common misconceptions about evolutionary theory.

    (C) establishing the author's authority to address the subject.

    (D) explaining scientific facts and principles to a general audience.

    (E) expanding general interest in science by entertaining the reader.

Entering the Church of All Saints in the small town of Sedlec in the Czech Republic might well be the creepiest experience imaginable if you didn't know what to expect (and possibly even if you did know). Artistically arranged human bones, predominantly skulls, line every surface within the small chapel. There's even a chandelier made entirely of bones that includes at least one of every bone in the human body. What kind of lunatic designed this nightmarish place? The Sedlec Ossuary, as it is known, was actually given its unique décor over many centuries by Catholic monks. Soil from the Holy Land was brought to its tiny cemetery in the 13th century, and so many Christians desired their remains to be interred there. Eventually, the monks simply ran out of room and had to get creative.

39. The author uses the rhetorical question in Line 9 to

    (A) establish that the design of the Sedlec Ossuary is a mystery.

    (B) criticize the monks for using the bones as they did.

    (C) instill an expectation in the reader that is then ironicized.

    (D) set up an inside joke about something the reader already knows.

    (E) provide a transition between two separate ideas.

A good trivia question isn't just about stumping people. It's easy to simply ask people something they won't know. What makes trivia fun is when people feel as if they *should* know the answer, but somehow don't. "What's the population of Butte, Montana?" is a terrible question because there's no reason why anyone should know that, even if he or she is *from* Butte, Montana. But a question like "Who was the last U.S. president with a beard?" gets people interested. We all saw a poster on the wall with the presidents' pictures on it in school, and we know that many of them had beards, but we don't necessarily remember which ones. The fact that people feel as if they *should* know is what makes it fun to guess. (The answer, if you're wondering, is Benjamin Harrison, the 23rd president.)

40. The author suggests that "Who was the last U.S. President with a beard?" is an example of a good trivia question because

    (A) it's about an important subject, as opposed to a completely useless one.

    (B) it has an answer that the majority of people will figure out eventually.

    (C) it's actually impossible to get right, but it seems possible at first.

    (D) it deals with a subject that most people learn about in school.

    (E) it has an answer that people have been exposed to but can't recall.

Though most people believe that the famous British monument of Stonehenge was built by the druids as a site for their mysterious rituals, this idea is wrong on several fronts. First of all, we now know that Stonehenge is much older than was long supposed. The first megaliths were raised sometime between 3000 and 2500 BCE, meaning that Stonehenge considerably predates the druids and may even be older that the Great Pyramid of Egypt. As for what Stonehenge was used for, the answer may very well be "nothing." Most anthropologists now believe it was a sacred *necropolis,* or "city of the dead," which stood on lands believed to be occupied by the spirits and strictly forbidden to the living.

Go on to next page

41. Which of the following discoveries would suggest an alternative to the theory that Stonehenge was forbidden to the living?

   (A) The discovery of tool fragments beneath the megaliths.

   (B) The discovery that the tallest stone lines up directly with the sun on the summer solstice.

   (C) The discovery of trivial, everyday personal items in the topsoil.

   (D) The discovery of trace evidence of human blood on many of the megaliths.

   (E) Soil analysis indicating periodic widespread fires on the plain.

> *Questions 42 through 46 are based on the following passage.*

Line   When the Frankish king Charlemagne was crowned emperor on Christmas Day, 800, this was the final step in a century-long process during which the Franks assumed Rome's inheri-
(05) tance in Western Europe. Ever since they made their first historical appearance in northeastern Gaul, the Franks had been in close contact with the *Imperium Romanum,* and after the collapse of its western half in 476, they had conquered large
(10) parts of northern, central, and finally southern Europe. Already in the sixth century, their kingdom had become the dominant power in the West (Geary 1988; Wood 1994). Despite several crises, it succeeded in maintaining this position
(15) until the end of the seventh century, and moved on to further expansion during the eighth.
     The Franks were Rome's heirs not only in a geographical sense but also concerning the internal constitution of their realm. Their kings were
(20) not the only ones in the former imperial territories to imitate the Roman mode of rule, but especially in religious matters they adapted much more thoroughly, and from the beginning, to the Roman population majority than did any of the
(25) other German states. Apart from a favorable geographical position at a safe distance from Byzantium and the Arabs, this was the main reason why the Frankish realm survived its many inner crises and proved capable of extending its
(30) power to Italy, including Rome.

42. The primary purpose of the first paragraph of the passage is to

   (A) explain how the Franks assumed Rome's inheritance in Western Europe.

   (B) establish that Charlemagne was the most influential of the early Medieval European rulers.

   (C) raise the question of why the western half of the Roman Empire collapsed.

   (D) introduce a historical situation that subsequent paragraphs will go on to analyze.

   (E) inform the reader that the Frankish Empire survived several crises.

43. Which of the following best describes the relationship between the two paragraphs in the passage?

   (A) The first paragraph describes a misconception that the second goes on to correct.

   (B) The first paragraph introduces a general idea, and the second supports it with specifics.

   (C) The first paragraph raises several questions that the second attempts to answer.

   (D) Both paragraphs present slightly different perspectives on a single issue.

   (E) Both paragraphs attempt to rebut objections to a single theory, but in different ways.

44. The author of the passage mentions "Byzantium" and "the Arabs" in Line 27 in order to establish that these societies were

   (A) other dominant political powers of the time.

   (B) key influences on the Franks, in addition to Rome.

   (C) the traditional enemies of the collapsed Western Roman Empire.

   (D) envious of the Franks' favorable geographical position.

   (E) considered German states at the time.

Go on to next page

45. The first sentence of the passage suggests that which of the following is true of Charlemagne?

    (A) He was the first ruler to see himself as truly Frankish, as opposed to Roman.

    (B) He played a key role in the collapse of the Western Roman Empire.

    (C) He was actually less important than other Frankish kings, despite being the most famous.

    (D) His religious beliefs were more popular than those of previous Frankish kings had been.

    (E) His accession represented the full transfer of status from Ancient Rome to the Franks.

46. The author would most likely agree with which of the following about the Franks?

    (A) They outcompeted the Roman Empire by being more in touch with the common people.

    (B) They applied the Roman model of government to an altogether different geographical area.

    (C) They learned from the Romans, and the transfer of power was slow but nearly inevitable.

    (D) It was clear from the beginning that the Frankish Empire would not last as long as had the Roman.

    (E) The Franks emerged as the dominant power due to an improbable series of lucky coincidences.

Questions 47 through 49 are based on the following chart.

Following is a chart showing the most common types of Internet purchases for seven different nations.

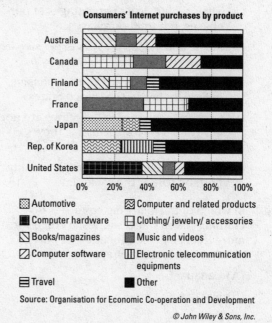

Consumers' Internet purchases by product

Source: Organisation for Economic Co-operation and Development

© John Wiley & Sons, Inc.

47. What is the only country included on the graph in which automotive products account for a significant percentage of Internet-based sales?

    (A) Finland

    (B) France

    (C) Japan

    (D) Republic of Korea

    (E) United States

48. If it were found to be true that consumers in the United States actually bought more music and videos via the Internet than did consumers in France, what would be the most plausible explanation for the apparent discrepancy between this statement and the graph?

    (A) The graph reflects percentages of purchases, not total purchases.

    (B) Music and videos are less expensive in France than in the United States.

    (C) Music and videos are more expensive in France than in the United States.

    (D) Consumers in the United States are not always paying for the music they download.

    (E) This statement and the graph cannot both be true at the same time.

49. In which of the following countries do clothing/jewelry/accessories account for more than 20 percent of Internet purchases? (Select all that apply.)

    (A) Canada

    (B) Finland

    (C) France

Questions 50 through 53 are based on the following passage.

Line   Generally, in Shakespeare's romantic comedies of the 1590s, the young women are much better at knowing themselves than are the young men. The women are plucky, patient, and good-
(05) humoured. They seem to enjoy teasing their young men, but do so knowing that they will submit themselves finally to their wooers. Marriage will put women in a subordinate position. They are aware of this, and accept the con-
(10) ditions of a patriarchal culture. They are intent on marriage, and generally know right away whom it is that they will marry. Although the men nominally take the lead in proposing marriage, the women are better aware of what is at stake. The
(15) women seem smarter and more self-possessed. They are wittier and blessed with an ironic sense of humour that serves them well in dealing with masculine frailty. They are ultimately forgiving. The men, conversely, seem woefully lacking in a
(20) sensible perspective on their own desires. They flee ineffectually from romantic attachments, or mistrust the women to whom they are attracted despite themselves, or are fickle in their choices. They seem far more sensitive to the judgement of

their male friends than are the women to the (25) judgement of their female peers. Their male egos are painfully insecure. A cutting remark from a woman, or a jeering laugh from a male friend, can unnerve the men utterly. Because they understand themselves so little, Shakespeare's young (30) men can often seem absurd, even while we are invited to be sympathetic. They are their own worst enemies.

50. Based on the passage, it would seem that, when it came to representing gender roles in his romantic comedies, Shakespeare usually employed which of the following templates?

    (A) The male characters take the social initiative, but the female characters are more emotionally sensitive.

    (B) The male characters form closer bonds with their friends of the same gender than do the female characters.

    (C) The broad view of society is patriarchal, but the individual female characters are smarter than the male characters.

    (D) The female characters are generally presented as morally superior to the male characters.

    (E) The female characters are more interested in marriage, whereas the male characters are more interested in sex.

51. It can be inferred that the author would be inclined to make what criticism of the presentation of gender roles in Shakespeare's comedies?

    (A) It is often difficult for the audience to genuinely like the male characters.

    (B) The rigid gender roles can make Shakespeare's plays predictable.

    (C) It is unimaginative that romantic relationships inevitably lead to marriage.

    (D) The female characters are too forgiving of the male characters.

    (E) It is unrealistic that the male characters have so little power.

Go on to next page

52. Based on the passage, with which of the following modern media creations do Shakespeare's romantic comedies appear to have the most in common?

    (A) Commercials that ironicize conventional gender roles — for example, where women are shown playing tackle football or men are shown getting manicures

    (B) TV dramas centered on strong female characters with magic or supernatural powers

    (C) Sitcoms where the juvenile husband's antics drive the plot but the wife always turns out to be right at the end

    (D) Game shows or reality shows that pit teams of men against teams of women

    (E) Popular music that preaches messages of female empowerment but is sung by women who are conventionally attractive

53. Based on the passage, the most likely assumption is that Shakespeare employed this depiction of gender roles in his plays because it allowed him to

    (A) make political statements without being taken seriously.

    (B) question religion without too many people noticing.

    (C) write more female parts than were usually found in other people's plays.

    (D) encourage men to be more sensitive to people's judgments.

    (E) create humorously unusual situations without seeming too subversive.

John Locke worked outside academia and wrote for the general educated reader. The relative accessibility of his prose is consistent with a strong antiauthoritarian streak that runs through his thinking. He is considered a founder, respectively, of two individualistic movements: empiricism in epistemology and liberalism in political philosophy.

54. Which of the following could be substituted for the term "accessibility" in the second sentence with the least change in meaning?

    (A) Opacity

    (B) Bluntness

    (C) Brevity

    (D) Completeness

    (E) Simplicity

Stephen Hawking is a theoretical physicist working in the fields of cosmology and quantum gravity. His work with Roger Penrose showed that time and space began with the Big Bang and will end in black holes. He also discovered that black (05) holes emit radiation and eventually disappear — this radiation is now known as Hawking Radiation. Because Hawking is a scientist who deals with big pictures and laws of the universe, he's done a fair amount of thinking about philosophical (10) topics such as free will. Hawking has written that if — and this is a big *if* — a theory could perfectly predict behavior, it would disprove free will. Such a theory is virtually impossible, however, because there are too many details for it to (15) account for. Moreover, even if we knew it was true, we could not live by it.

55. Which of the following accurately describes Stephen Hawking's career and views?

    (A) He is a scientific positivist who does not believe in the existence of free will.

    (B) He discovered black holes, and he occasionally writes about philosophy.

    (C) He has made important scientific discoveries, but he believes that science and ethics must remain separate.

    (D) He is an expert in black holes who has also given serious thought to the human condition.

    (E) He believes that a complete scientific description of the universe would probably disprove free will.

Go on to next page

Line After returning to the United States from India, Ram Dass wrote his best-known book, *Remember, Be Here Now,* which was required reading for the counterculture of the seventies
(05) and in which he presented a vision of how to expand consciousness by using history's various spiritual traditions instead of drugs. The book emphasizes the importance of remaining in the present moment. Past and future exist only in
(10) our minds, and by focusing on them, we cause ourselves to suffer more than we do when our attention is in the present moment.

56. In the first sentence, the phrase "required reading" is intended to imply that

(A) the book was frequently taught in schools.

(B) the book was a best-seller.

(C) the book is now considered out-of-style.

(D) the book was extremely complicated.

(E) the book was considered "cool."

STOP DO NOT TURN THE PAGE UNTIL TOLD TO DO SO.
DO NOT RETURN TO A PREVIOUS TEST.

Part 2
Writing

> **Time:** 40 minutes for 40 multiple-choice questions
>
> **Directions:** Choose the best answer to each question. Mark the corresponding oval on the answer sheet.
>
> **Directions:** The following passage is a draft of an essay. Some portions of the passage need to be strengthened through editing and revision. Read the passage and choose the best answers for the questions that follow. Some questions ask you to improve particular sentences or portions of sentences. In some cases, the indicated portion of the passage will be most effective as it is already expressed and thus will require no changes. In choosing answers, consider development, organization, word choice, style, and tone, and follow the requirements of standard written English. Remember, try to answer every question.

1 One of the traditional aspects of successful art is that people take it for real. 2 Pliny describes a famous painting competition between Zeuxis and Parrhasius in the fifth century BCE. 3 Zeuxis unveiled his painting of a still life in which the grapes were so tempting that a bird came to peck at them. 4 Zeuxis then asked Parrhasius to draw the curtain to reveal his painting. 5 Parrhasius explained that the curtain was itself a painting.

6 When Sir Thomas More's *Utopia* was published in the 16th century, a priest asked his bishop to send him to Utopia (Utopia is a fictional island — its name in Greek means "no place" — but the characters in the book share their names with real people and so perhaps *are* real, and one describes his visit to Utopia). 7 On his deathbed Balzac called for Dr. Bianchon, being one of his fictional creations. 8 Before Freud had a sizable body of patients on which to base case studies, he turned to realist drama — Shakespeare, Ibsen, Greek tragedy — to analyze its characters. 9 It may sound odd to talk of Greek drama with its masks and formal choruses as "realistic," but Freud was responding to the plays' emotional realism.

10 "Lifelike" and "realistic" are always compliments, the barometers by which we judge how (or whether) a performance has worked. 11 But increasing numbers of literary critics are questioning whether this should be so. 12 In the U.K. of the 1950s, the queen's Christmas Day broadcasts undoubtedly seemed lifelike to viewers, but in 2012 they seem stilted, not at all related to anything we recognize as natural. 13 As Edward Pechter points out, questions about what is lifelike in Renaissance drama confuse means and effects. 14 The actor Thomas Betterton "may have chanted — that is, have sounded like chanting to us if we were able to travel back in time to the Theatre Royal in the late 17th century — but to his audience, tuned to a different frequency, his performance might have seemed like life itself."

Go on to next page ➡

1. Which word would be the best replacement for aspects as it is used in Sentence 1 (reproduced below)?

   One of the traditional <u>aspects</u> of successful art is that people take it for real.

   (A) prizes

   (B) hallmarks

   (C) aspirations

   (D) pitfalls

   (E) emanations

2. Which is the best way to revise and combine Sentences 4 and 5 (reproduced below) at the underlined portion?

   Zeuxis then asked Parrhasius to draw the curtain to reveal his <u>painting. Parrhasius explained</u> that the curtain was itself a painting.

   (A) painting; therefore, Parrhasius explained

   (B) painting; unfortunately, Parrhasius explained

   (C) painting; in fact, Parrhasius explained

   (D) painting; on the other hand, Parrhasius explained

   (E) painting; Parrhasius explained

3. In context, which sentence provides the best introduction to the second paragraph?

   (A) Analogous stories occur in the realm of literature.

   (B) Opinions about this classic tale vary considerably.

   (C) As the centuries progressed, controversies over realism only got more heated.

   (D) And that was just the tip of the iceberg.

   (E) Zeuxis wasn't the only one who was fooled.

4. In context, which is the best version of the underlined portion of Sentence 7?

   On his deathbed Balzac called for <u>Dr. Bianchon, being one</u> of his fictional creations.

   (A) Dr. Bianchon, being one

   (B) Dr. Bianchon, among one

   (C) Dr. Bianchon, one

   (D) Dr. Bianchon, he was one

   (E) Dr. Bianchon was one

5. If a word in Sentence 9 (reproduced below) were to be placed in italics, the most logical word to italicize would be

   It may sound odd to talk of Greek drama with its masks and formal choruses as "realistic," but Freud was responding to the plays' emotional realism.

   (A) *sound,* in order to emphasize the fact that not everything that sounds odd is actually odd.

   (B) *Greek,* in order to heighten the differences between Greek drama and other dramatic traditions.

   (C) *"realistic,"* in order to emphasize that word even more than the quotation marks do alone.

   (D) *responding,* in order to highlight the fact that Freud was only calling attention to elements of the plays that were already present.

   (E) *emotional,* in order to emphasize the idea that there is more than one type of realism.

6. In context, the version of Sentence 11 (reproduced and underlined below) that provides the best transition between Sentences 10 and 12 would be:

   "Lifelike" and "realistic" are always compliments, the barometers by which we judge how (or whether) a performance has worked. <u>But increasing numbers of literary critics are questioning whether this should be so.</u> In the U.K. of the 1950s, the queen's Christmas Day broadcasts undoubtedly seemed lifelike to viewers, but in 2012 they seem stilted, not at all related to anything we recognize as natural.

   (A) But increasing numbers of literary critics are questioning whether this should be so.

   (B) But what is so great about real life, that we should be judging art by comparison to it?

   (C) But lifelike at one point in history does not mean the same thing as lifelike at another.

   (D) Some people even care more about realistic plots than they do about whether the actors are any good.

   (E) But all of this changed suddenly in the middle of the 20th century.

Go on to next page

7. If the author wanted to change the expression *tuned to a different frequency* in Sentence 14 (reproduced below) to a less metaphoric and more straightforward phrase, the best paraphrase would be

   The actor Thomas Betterton "may have chanted — that is, have sounded like chanting to us if we were able to travel back in time to the Theatre Royal in the late 17th century — but to his audience, <u>tuned to a different frequency</u>, his performance might have seemed like life itself."

   (A) responding differently from how a modern audience would.

   (B) simultaneously paying attention to something other than the play.

   (C) unable to understand the play in the same way the actors did.

   (D) used to hearing people speak a different way in everyday life.

   (E) less jaded by exposure to many different types of art than are modern audiences.

8. In context, which sentence provides the best conclusion to the last paragraph?

   (A) To the majority of people throughout history, artists and politicians may not have seemed quite so different as they do to us today.

   (B) Audiences have undoubtedly become more sophisticated over the course of the last few centuries.

   (C) Science would almost certainly not have made so many advances in the 20th century if it had not been preceded by equally brilliant literature.

   (D) So analyzing this idea is tricky because it involves a concept — lifelike/realistic — which is not constant.

   (E) The question of when to apply the word "realistic" to a work of literature is much more difficult than the question of when to apply it to a painting.

Directions: In each of the following sentences, some part of the sentence or the entire sentence is underlined. Beneath each sentence you will find five ways of writing the underlined part. The first of these repeats the original, but the other four are all different. If you think the original sentence is better than any of the suggested changes, you should select the first answer choice; otherwise you should select one of the other choices.

This is a test of correctness and effectiveness of expression. In choosing answers, follow the requirements of standard written English; i.e., pay attention to acceptable usage in grammar, diction (choice of words), sentence construction, and punctuation. Choose the answer that expresses most effectively what is presented in the original sentence; this answer should be clear and exact, without awkwardness, ambiguity, or redundancy. Remember, try to answer every question.

9. Although Tom has an unusual sense of humor, he is <u>nevertheless extreme polite.</u>

   (A) nevertheless extreme polite.

   (B) nevertheless extremely politely.

   (C) nevertheless extremely polite.

   (D) nevertheless extreme politely.

   (E) never less extreme than polite.

10. <u>I have never driven there before last week,</u> but I managed to find the restaurant in time.

    (A) I have never driven there before last week

    (B) I had never driven there before last week

    (C) Although I have never driven there before last week

    (D) Although I had never driven there before last week

    (E) Seeing as how I'd never driven there before last week

Go on to next page

11. If students need to drop or add a class, or have any questions about scheduling, then they are encouraged to visit the Registrar's office.

    (A) they are encouraged to visit

    (B) he or she is encouraged to visit

    (C) one is visiting

    (D) that student should be encouraged to visit

    (E) remember to visit

12. It's just between you and I, I don't think the team has a chance of making the playoffs this year.

    (A) It's just between you and I

    (B) It's just between you and me

    (C) Please keep this between you and myself

    (D) Just between you and I

    (E) Just between you and me

13. Since Jim had spent the entire afternoon bragging about how good he is at poker, and so everyone found it hilarious that he ended up being the first player eliminated from the game.

    (A) and so everyone found it hilarious that

    (B) so everyone found it to be hilarious when

    (C) therefore, everyone found it hilarious because

    (D) everyone found it hilarious when

    (E) everyone found it so hilariously that

14. Each year, the affectionate group of old friends met annually to tell old stories and catch up on what had been happening in their lives.

    (A) Each year, the affectionate group of old friends met annually

    (B) Annually and affectionately, the group of old friends met each year

    (C) Affectionately, it was on an annual basis that the group of old friends met each year

    (D) Meeting annually, the affectionate group of old friends

    (E) Each year, the affectionate group of old friends would meet

15. When they heard the first loud peal of thunder, the kids ran towards the house, none of them knowing when the downpour would begin.

    (A) none of them knowing when the downpour would begin

    (B) and not a one of them knowing when the downpour was to begin

    (C) none of them had known that a downpour was to begin

    (D) without one of their knowing when the downpour would begin

    (E) and none of them had known the downpour to begin

16. I turned the volume down on your cellphone because its constantly buzzing and was driving me crazy.

    (A) its constantly buzzing and was

    (B) its buzzing was constant

    (C) it's buzzing constantly was

    (D) its constant buzzing was

    (E) it's constantly was buzzing and

17. Discouraged by the fact that the old-fashioned coach discouraged controversial subject matter, Samantha's decision to quit the speech team was final.

    (A) Discouraged by the fact that the old-fashioned coach discouraged controversial subject matter, Samantha's decision to quit the speech team was final.

    (B) Discouraged by the fact that the old-fashioned coach discouraged controversial subject matter, Samantha decided to quit the speech team.

    (C) She was discouraged by the fact that the old-fashioned coach discouraged controversial subject matter, Samantha decided to quit the speech team.

    (D) As she was discouraged by the fact that the old-fashioned coach discouraged controversial subject matter, a decision to quit the speech team was made by Samantha.

    (E) Being discouraged by the fact that the old-fashioned coach discouraged controversial subject matter, the speech team was quit by Samantha.

Go on to next page

18. Some of the homeowners who lived right on the park were opposed to the construction of a new playground, but <u>none of they're arguments had any affect</u> on the excited parents.

    (A) none of they're arguments had any affect

    (B) none of there arguments had any affect

    (C) none of their arguments had any effect

    (D) none of they're arguments had any effect

    (E) none of their arguments had any affect

Directions: Each of the following questions consists of a sentence that contains four underlined portions. Read each sentence and decide whether any of the underlined parts contains a grammatical construction, a word use, or an instance of incorrect or omitted punctuation or capitalization that would be inappropriate in carefully written English. If so, select the underlined portion that must be revised to produce a correct sentence. If there are no errors in the sentence as written, select "No error." **No sentence has more than one error.**

---

19. The town and its nearby lake <u>are</u> beautiful,
    A
    but <u>unfortunately</u>, we have <u>to get up</u> early
    B   C
    for work tomorrow, so please take Chris

    <u>and I</u> home now. <u>No error</u>.
    D   E

20. The style of grammatical instruction used by the charter school is <u>quite rigorous</u>, but it
    A
    was modeled <u>by</u> a program <u>that got fantastic</u>
    B   C
    results <u>back in</u> the 1980s. <u>No error</u>.
    D   E

21. <u>Having spent nearly</u> an hour searching for
    A
    it everywhere, Megan was <u>both relieved</u>
    B
    <u>and more than</u> a little confused when she
    B
    finally <u>found that her</u> other shoe <u>had been</u>
    C   D
    inside the refrigerator for some reason.

    <u>No error</u>.
    E

22. <u>All of us</u> here at the camp <u>have become</u>
    A   B
    experts in hiking and canoeing, <u>and although</u>
    C
    it rained more often than <u>we would have</u>
    <u>liked</u>, the bad weather made for some
    D
    amusing stories. <u>No error</u>.
    E

23. <u>In contrast to</u> the debut record, which had
    A
    pleased the critics and <u>been especially hailed</u>
    B
    for its <u>originality and innovativeness</u>, the
    C
    band's second album was <u>dubbed repeti-</u>
    <u>tively</u>. <u>No error</u>.
    D   E

Directions: Read each of the following sentences. The answer choices present five ways of writing the sentence. The first of these repeats the original, but the other four are all different. If you think the original sentence is better than any of the suggested changes, you should select the first answer choice; otherwise, you should select one of the other choices.

This is a test of correctness and effectiveness of expression. In choosing answers, follow the requirements of standard written English; i.e., pay attention to acceptable usage in grammar, diction (choice of words), sentence construction, and punctuation. Choose the answer that expresses most effectively what is presented in the original sentence; this answer should be clear and exact without awkwardness, ambiguity, or redundancy.

---

24. Richard Nixon, the 37th President, was the first to visit the far east while in office.

    (A) Richard Nixon, the 37th President, was the first to visit the far east while in office.

    (B) Richard Nixon, the 37th President was the first to visit the Far East while in office.

    (C) Richard Nixon, the 37th president was the first to visit the far east while in office.

    (D) Richard Nixon the 37th president, was the first to visit the Far East while in office.

    (E) Richard Nixon, the 37th president, was the first to visit the Far East while in office.

Go on to next page

25. You should be careful, the childrens' toy cars are all over the floor.

    (A) You should be careful, the childrens' toy cars are all over the floor.

    (B) You should be careful; the children's toy cars are all over the floor.

    (C) You should be careful, the children's toy cars' are all over the floor.

    (D) You should be careful — the childrens' toy car's are all over the floor.

    (E) You should be careful; the childrens toy car's are all over the floor.

26. This past summer I learned that, although most people assume it is the elephant, the most expensive animal for zoos to keep is actually the panda.

    (A) This past summer I learned that, although most people assume it is the elephant, the most expensive animal for zoos to keep is actually the panda.

    (B) This past Summer I learned, that although most people assume it is the elephant the most expensive animal for zoos to keep, is actually the panda.

    (C) This past summer I learned that although most people assume it is the Elephant, the most expensive animal for zoos to keep is actually the Panda.

    (D) This past Summer I learned that although most people assume it is the elephant; the most expensive animal for zoos to keep is actually the panda.

    (E) This past Summer I learned that, although most people assume it is the Elephant, the most expensive animal for zoos to keep is actually the Panda.

27. Your friend just called to ask which of his albums it was you wanted to borrow.

    (A) Your friend just called to ask which of his albums it was you wanted to borrow.

    (B) You're friend just called to ask, which of his albums it was you wanted to borrow.

    (C) Your friend just called, to ask which of his album's it was you wanted to borrow.

    (D) You're friend just called to ask which of his albums it was; you wanted to borrow.

    (E) Your friend just called to ask, which of his album's it was, you wanted to borrow.

28. Which of the following versions of the following sentence is not grammatically correct?

    Although a posted sign said that no guests were permitted in the hotel pool after 10 p.m., we went for a swim anyway.

    (A) Although a posted sign said that no guests were permitted in the hotel pool after 10 p.m., we went for a swim anyway.

    (B) A posted sign said that no guests were permitted in the hotel pool after 10 p.m.; we went for a swim anyway.

    (C) A posted sign said that no guests were permitted in the hotel pool after 10 p.m., however, we went for a swim anyway.

    (D) A posted sign said that no guests were permitted in the hotel pool after 10 p.m. — however, we went for a swim anyway.

    (E) Despite the posted sign, which said that no guests were permitted in the hotel pool after 10 p.m., we went for a swim.

Directions: Each of the following questions consists of a sentence that contains four underlined portions. Read each sentence and decide whether any of the underlined parts contains a grammatical construction, a word use, or an instance of incorrect or omitted punctuation or capitalization that would be inappropriate in carefully written English. If so, select the underlined portion that must be revised to produce a correct sentence. If there are no errors in the sentence as written, select "No error." **No sentence has more than one error.**

---

29. Before the group entered the White House,
                                        A
    the tour guide reminded Laura and her
        B
    friends to keep careful track of which cam-
                                   C
    eras were their's. No error.
         C   D   E

30. It's never pleasant to have a losing season;
    A   A
    but all the members of the Springfield Lions
    B   C
    were confident that they'd do better next
         D
    year. No error.
          E

Go on to next page

31. Because so many of the <u>people who</u>
      A
    attended the barbeque <u>were</u> vegetarian,
      B
    <u>Taryn and Rebecca's</u> spicy <u>cream cheese</u>
      C D
    <u>and cucumber rolls</u> were a big hit. <u>No error</u>.
      D   E

32. Though nearly all of her <u>Facebook friends</u>
      A
    always make a big deal out of <u>Valentine's</u>
    <u>Day, Emily</u> considers it a manufactured <u>hol-</u>
      B
    <u>iday, and</u> barely notices it, regardless of
      C
    whether <u>she's single or</u> in a relationship.
      D
    <u>No error</u>.
      E

33. While it may sound unnecessarily fancy by
    <u>today's standards, but the</u> fact is that
      A
    <u>President Lincoln's</u> opening the <u>Gettysburg</u>
      B
    <u>Address</u> with the <u>odd but now famous phrase</u>
      C   D
    "four score and seven years ago" sounded
    endearingly folksy at the time. <u>No error</u>.
                                      E

> **Directions:** The following questions are a test of your familiarity with basic research skills. For each question, choose the best answer. Remember, try to answer every question.

34. The two citation formats that are standard for thesis papers in American schools are
    (A) UDA and MLA style citations.
    (B) MLA and APA style citations.
    (C) APA and IRL style citations.
    (D) IRL and SDS style citations.
    (E) SDS and UDA style citations.

35. Assuming that all have been consulted while writing the paper, which of the following types of sources do NOT need to be listed in a Works Cited page?
    (A) secondary sources
    (B) YouTube videos
    (C) dictionaries used to look up words in primary sources
    (D) noncopyrighted blogs
    (E) any sources from which the author did not quote directly

36. When an in-text quotation exceeds four lines in length, it is to be set off from the main text as a separate paragraph, single-spaced, with additional indentation and no quotation marks, and is often presented in a different or a smaller font. This practice is known as
    (A) double quoting.
    (B) Chicago quoting.
    (C) ghost quoting.
    (D) hyperquoting.
    (E) block quoting.

37. When a cited text has six or more authors, the in-text citation should include only the first author's last name, followed by which of the following Latin phrases (and the year of publication or page number)?
    (A) *ibid.*
    (B) *et al.*
    (C) *id est*
    (D) *populusque*
    (E) *ex urbe*

38. Which of the following should appear in quotation marks as opposed to italics?
    (A) The title of a poem
    (B) The title of a music album
    (C) The title of a TV show
    (D) The title of a film
    (E) The name of a newspaper

Go on to next page

39. The brief overview that typically appears at the beginning of a published research paper, containing the thesis statement plus some remarks on the methodology and conclusions, is known as the

    (A) impression.

    (B) opinion.

    (C) assessment.

    (D) abstract.

    (E) cornerstone.

40. In a formal research paper, all of the following are discouraged EXCEPT for

    (A) employment of the first-person point of view.

    (B) employment of the second-person point of view.

    (C) the usage of contractions.

    (D) the retention of profanity in direct quotations.

    (E) opening the paper by quoting from a dictionary.

STOP DO NOT TURN THE PAGE UNTIL TOLD TO DO SO.
DO NOT RETURN TO A PREVIOUS TEST.

Argumentative Essay

Time: 30 minutes

Directions: Read the opinion that follows.

"Epicureanism, the school of philosophy derived from the teachings of the Greek philosopher Epicurus (341–270 BCE), holds that the meaning of life is simply to experience pleasure. This philosophy opposes the teachings of the metaphysical philosopher Plato (428–327 BCE), who believed that the point of life was to discern and achieve moral good as established by the gods. Sadly, Epicureanism is more popular today, and this is why society is falling apart."

Discuss the extent to which you agree or disagree with this point of view. Support your position with specific reasons and examples from your own experience, observations, or reading.

STOP DO NOT TURN THE PAGE UNTIL TOLD TO DO SO.
DO NOT RETURN TO A PREVIOUS TEST.

Source-Based Essay

Time: 30 minutes

Directions: Both of the following sources address methods of reasoning about morality. Read the two passages carefully and then write an essay in which you identify the most important concerns regarding the issue and explain why they are important. Your essay must draw on information from *both* of the sources. In addition, you may draw upon your own experience, observations, or reading. Be sure to *cite* the sources, whether you are paraphrasing or directly quoting.

When paraphrasing or quoting from the sources, cite each source by referring to the author's last name, the title of the source, or any other clear identifier.

Source 1

Adapted from: White, Mark D. "Why Doesn't Batman Kill the Joker?" *Batman and Philosophy: The Dark Knight of the Soul.* Ed. Mark D. White and Robert Arp. Princeton, NJ: John Wiley & Sons, Inc. 2008. Print.

Utilitarianism [is] a system of ethics that requires us to maximize the total happiness or well-being resulting from our actions. Saving many lives at the cost of just one would represent a net increase in well-being or utility, and while it would be a tragic choice, utilitarians would generally endorse it.

While utilitarians would generally endorse killing one person to prevent killing more, members of the school of ethics known as *deontology* would not. Deontologists judge the morality of an act based on features intrinsic to the act itself, regardless of the consequences stemming from the act. To deontologists, the end never justifies the means, but rather the means must be justifiable on their own merits. So the fact that the killing would prevent future killings is irrelevant — the only relevant factor is that killing is wrong, period. But even for the strictest deontologist, there are exceptions — for instance, killing in self-defense would generally be allowed by deontologists.

Source 2

Adapted from: Kershnar, Stephen, "Batman's Virtuous Hatred." *Batman and Philosophy: The Dark Knight of the Soul.* Ed. Mark D. White and Robert Arp. Princeton, NJ: John Wiley & Sons, Inc. 2008. Print.

In judging whether persons are good or bad, we can use the ideas of virtue and vice, which form a central part of the moral philosophy known as *virtue ethics.* Virtue ethics concerns what sort of a person one should be, differing from other schools of ethics that focus on how someone should act and on how to evaluate the consequences of an act. The philosopher Aristotle (384–322 BCE) put forth the most famous view of virtue ethics. In his view, moral virtues are the most appropriate character traits of a person that make him good and, thus, allow him to make the right decisions. According to Aristotle, persons themselves are primarily virtuous. A person is virtuous when he tends to do the right thing, and that action is virtuous only if it's the kind of thing that a virtuous person would do.

Virtue ethics has been criticized for a couple of reasons. First, one could argue that it's circular in that "virtue" is defined as the tendency to do good things, while at the same time "good things" is defined in terms of what virtuous people tend to do. Second, virtue ethics has been criticized for being impractical because it provides no guidance when two or more virtues conflict. For example, justice and mercy have a tendency to conflict with one another on a regular basis when people try to make moral decisions about an appropriate punishment for a crime.

Part 3
Mathematics

Time: 85 minutes for 56 multiple-choice questions

Directions: Choose the best answer to each question. Mark the corresponding oval on the answer sheet. Remember, try to answer every question.

1. If Jan is x years old and Frank is 7 years older than twice Jan's age, which of the following expressions represents Frank's age 2 years ago?

    (A) $2x - 2$

    (B) $2x + 7$

    (C) $2x + 9$

    (D) $2x + 5$

    (E) $2x$

4. If David's test scores for the current term are 83, 72, 94, 100, and 68, what will he need to make on his next test to have an average test score of 85?

    (A) 93

    (B) 85

    (C) 83.4

    (D) 70

    (E) 94

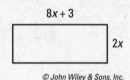

© John Wiley & Sons, Inc.

2. If the preceding rectangle has a perimeter of 46 units, what is the area of the rectangle?

    (A) 2

    (B) 76

    (C) 23

    (D) 22

    (E) 26

5. If the measure of ∠1 in the preceding diagram is 118 degrees, what is the measure of ∠2?

    (A) 45 degrees

    (B) 28 degrees

    (C) 180 degrees

    (D) 62 degrees

    (E) 28 degrees

3. Which of the following has the numbers $5, -2, 1\frac{1}{2}, -7.53,$ and $\frac{11}{3}$ in order of magnitude from least to greatest?

    (A) $-7.53, 5, \frac{11}{3}, -2, 1\frac{1}{2}$

    (B) $5, -2, 1\frac{1}{2}, -7.53, \frac{11}{3}$

    (C) $1\frac{1}{2}, -2, \frac{11}{3}, 5, -7.53$

    (D) $5, \frac{11}{3}, 1\frac{1}{2}, -2, -7.53$

    (E) $\frac{11}{3}, -7.53, -2, 1\frac{1}{2}, 5$

6. What is the sum of $9a, 3b, -5b,$ and $-12a$?

    (A) $3a - 2b$

    (B) $-5ab$

    (C) $3a + 2b$

    (D) $-21a - 8b$

    (E) $-3a - 2b$

Go on to next page

7. Which of the following is the greatest common factor of 40 and 60?

   (A) 12

   (B) 20

   (C) 1

   (D) 10

   (E) 5

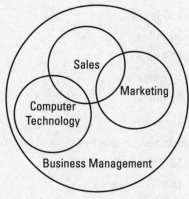

© John Wiley & Sons, Inc.

8. The preceding diagram represents areas of expertise of executives at a business. According to the diagram, which of the following statements is true?

   (A) Not all of the marketing experts are business management experts.

   (B) None of the sales experts are computer technology experts.

   (C) None of the marketing experts are computer technology experts.

   (D) None of the sales experts are marketing experts.

   (E) All of the marketing experts are computer technology experts.

9. Which of the following is the simplified form of $\dfrac{p^2+2p-15}{p^2-2p-35}$?

   (A) $\dfrac{p-3}{p-7}$

   (B) $p-5$

   (C) $p+3$

   (D) $\dfrac{p^2+2p-15}{p^2-2p-35}$

   (E) $\dfrac{p-7}{p-3}$

> Any number that is 1 greater than the square of an integer is a prime number.

10. Which of the following numbers is a counterexample to the preceding statement?

    (A) 65

    (B) 37

    (C) 17

    (D) 101

    (E) 2

11. What is the greatest common factor of 42 and 28?

    (A) 1

    (B) 21

    (C) 2

    (D) 7

    (E) 14

12. If $3x - 7 = 17$, then what is the value of $-8x + 21$?

    (A) 115

    (B) –3

    (C) 85

    (D) –85

    (E) –43

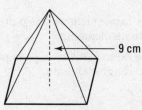

© John Wiley & Sons, Inc.

13. The preceding pyramid has a square base, a height of 9 cm, and a volume of 432 cm³. What is the surface area of the pyramid rounded to the nearest whole number?

    (A) 108 cm³

    (B) 135 cm³

    (C) 2,808 cm³

    (D) 260 cm³

    (E) 520 cm³

Go on to next page ⟹

14. What is the simplified form of the expression $26 - [(9 \cdot 12 - 9 \cdot 11)^2 - 5] + 20$?

    (A) 75

    (B) 80

    (C) –30

    (D) –35

    (E) 35

23 41 78 83 41 54 85 92 76

15. Which statement about the preceding set of data is false?

    (A) The mean is greater than the median.

    (B) The median is greater than the mean.

    (C) The mean is greater than the mode.

    (D) The mode is less than the median.

    (E) The mean and the median are greater than the mode.

$$\{(-4, -2), (-1, 3), (3, 9), (4, 5), (-1, 9)\}$$

16. Why is the preceding relation NOT a function?

    (A) The range element –2 is followed by a domain element 1 greater than itself in the next ordered pair.

    (B) 3 is paired with its square.

    (C) 3 is an element of both the domain and range.

    (D) The range element 9 is paired with two domain elements.

    (E) The domain element –1 is paired with two range elements.

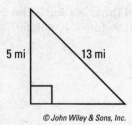
© John Wiley & Sons, Inc.

17. What is the perimeter of the preceding right triangle?

    (A) 186 miles

    (B) 30 miles

    (C) 338 miles

    (D) 12 miles

    (E) 60 miles

18. What is the product of 2, –1, 4, –3, and 6?

    (A) 12

    (B) 144

    (C) –144

    (D) 24

    (E) –48

Stem	Leaf
2	1 3 5
3	0 2
4	4 5 7
5	0 1 3 4 8
6	1 2 5

3 | 2 represents 32.

© John Wiley & Sons, Inc.

19. Which number is not represented in the preceding stem-and-leaf plot?

    (A) 30

    (B) 23

    (C) 60

    (D) 51

    (E) 45

Go on to next page

20. 27 is 75 percent of what number?

 (A) 36

 (B) 20.25

 (C) 277.7

 (D) 0.36

 (E) 2.025

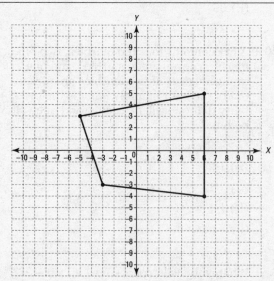

© John Wiley & Sons, Inc.

21. If the preceding quadrilateral is translated 7 units up and 4 units left, what will be the coordinates of the new vertices?

 (A) (3, –3), (5, 3), (–6, –4), and (–6, 5)

 (B) (–10, 1), (–12, 7), (–1, 0), (–1, 9)

 (C) (7, 4), (9, 10), (–2, 3), and (–2, 12)

 (D) (–7, 4), (–9, 10), (2, 3), and (2, 12)

 (E) (4, –7), (10, –9), (3, 2), and (12, 2)

22. If Adam eats $\frac{1}{4}$ of a pie and Wade eats half as much of the pie as Adam eats, what fraction of the pie does Wade eat?

 (A) $\frac{1}{4}$

 (B) $\frac{1}{8}$

 (C) $\frac{3}{4}$

 (D) $\frac{1}{16}$

 (E) $\frac{1}{6}$

23. If $3q + 5 = 35$, what is the value of q?

 (A) $\frac{40}{3}$

 (B) 30

 (C) 35

 (D) $\frac{1}{16}$

 (E) 10

Favorite Food by National Origin	Percent
Italian	17%
Mexican	24%
Indian	5%
Greek	8%
Chinese	17%
Japanese	14%
Other	15%

© John Wiley & Sons, Inc.

24. The preceding table shows the percentages of categories chosen, in terms of national origin, as favorites in a poll of members of a volunteer service organization. If 500 members were polled, how many more members chose Mexican than Greek and Japanese combined?

 (A) 10

 (B) 2

 (C) 4

 (D) 24

 (E) 120

25. If $j = -3$, $k = 5$, and $m = 10$, what is the value of $\dfrac{8m - 4(j+k)^2}{11+j}$?

 (A) 9

 (B) –8

 (C) 8

 (D) –1

 (E) 64

Go on to next page

26. A polling company plans to poll workers of a large corporation on an issue not concerning the corporation. Which of the following methods would most likely involve polling an unbiased sample?

 (A) Asking the president of the company questions and using his answers to represent the company

 (B) Asking questions of every tenth worker who walks through the main entrance for work

 (C) Polling every third cafeteria worker who enters the cafeteria for work

 (D) Asking people questions as they stand in the lobby awaiting an executive meeting

 (E) Conducting interviews of people who work in the mailroom

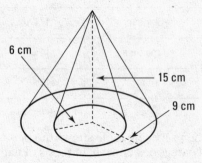

6 cm

15 cm

9 cm

© John Wiley & Sons, Inc.

27. In the preceding diagram, two cones share a center and an apex. The larger cone has a radius of 9 centimeters and the smaller cone has a radius of 6 centimeters. Both cones have a height of 15 centimeters. To the nearest whole number, how much of the volume of the larger cone exists outside of the smaller cone?

 (A) 39π cm^3

 (B) 585π cm^3

 (C) 27π cm^3

 (D) 15π cm^3

 (E) 225π cm^3

28. How many centimeters are in 27.3 decameters?

 (A) 2,730

 (B) 0.027

 (C) 0.27

 (D) 27,300

 (E) 2.7

29. Natasha is 9 times Eric's age. In 10 years, the sum of their ages will be 50. What is Natasha's age now?

 (A) 50

 (B) 14

 (C) 46

 (D) 4

 (E) 36

30. A hat contains four red marbles, two blue marbles, seven green marbles, and one orange marble. If two marbles are picked out of the hat randomly, what is the probability that one will be orange and one will be blue?

 (A) 98 percent

 (B) 1/98

 (C) 3/14

 (D) 1/7

 (E) 3 percent

31. What is the value of $5 + 7 + (-6) - 5 + 22$?

 (A) 33

 (B) 35

 (C) 23

 (D) 45

 (E) –45

$$\frac{21}{7} = \frac{12}{x}$$

32. In the preceding proportion, what is the value of x?

 (A) 33

 (B) 96

 (C) 4

 (D) 3

 (E) $\frac{1}{3}$

Go on to next page

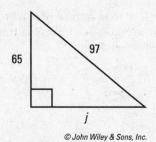

© John Wiley & Sons, Inc.

33. For the preceding right triangle, what is the value of *j*?

(A) 65

(B) 32

(C) 9,409

(D) 72

(E) 5,184

34. Which of the following numbers is between $-\frac{19}{4}$ and -3.71?

(A) $-3\frac{3}{4}$

(B) $-3\frac{71}{100}$

(C) $-4\frac{13}{16}$

(D) -3.7

(E) -5

437   12   37   858   1   218

35. What is the median of the preceding set of data?

(A) 127.5

(B) 447.5

(C) 37

(D) 858

(E) 260.5

36. Evaluate $\dfrac{(x-4)^2+8}{x+12}$ if $x = 6$

(A) $\frac{5}{9}$

(B) $\frac{14}{9}$

(C) $\frac{2}{3}$

(D) 6

(E) $\frac{7}{9}$

 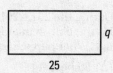

© John Wiley & Sons, Inc.

37. The two preceding rectangles are similar. What is the value of *q*?

(A) 2.5

(B) $\frac{5}{2}$

(C) 10

(D) –11

(E) 11

38. If $7k - 2k + 28 = 10k + 3$, what is the value of $-8k - 17$?

(A) –5

(B) –57

(C) 10

(D) 5

(E) 57

39. If *x* is 20 less than *y* and *y* is 14 more than *z*, how much greater than *x* is *z*?

(A) –6

(B) –34

(C) 34

(D) 6

(E) 40

40. If a coin is flipped four times, what is the probability that it will land on heads all four times?

(A) 1/16

(B) 1/2

(C) 1/8

(D) 1/4

(E) 1/1

Go on to next page

41. During the 2013–2014 baseball season, Mark hit the ball 48 out of 60 times he was up at bat. What percentage did Mark strike out?

    (A) 80 percent

    (B) 20 percent

    (C) 50 percent

    (D) 30 percent

    (E) 60 percent

42. What is the value of $\left(9\frac{2}{3}\right)\left(-7\frac{5}{8}\right)\left(8\frac{1}{4}\right)$?

    (A) $-608\frac{1}{10}$

    (B) $608\frac{3}{32}$

    (C) $-608\frac{3}{32}$

    (D) $608\frac{1}{10}$

    (E) -609

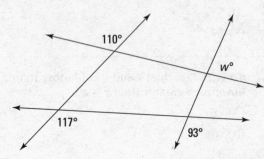

© John Wiley & Sons, Inc.

43. In the preceding diagram, what is the value of w?

    (A) 94

    (B) 86

    (C) 46

    (D) 100

    (E) 40

2 5 7 9 100 100 101

44. What is the range of the preceding set of data?

    (A) 101

    (B) 2

    (C) 100

    (D) 9

    (E) 99

45. 22 is p less than a third of r. Which of the following equations indicates the relationship between p and r?

    (A) $22 - p = \frac{r}{3}$

    (B) $\frac{r}{3} - p = 22$

    (C) $\frac{p}{3} - r = 22$

    (D) $p - 22 = \frac{r}{3}$

    (E) $\frac{r}{3} - 22 = -p$

2, 8, 32, 128...

46. What is the 8th term of the preceding sequence?

    (A) 131,072

    (B) 32,768

    (C) 8,192

    (D) 4

    (E) 256

47. A circle has an area of 25π. What is the circumference of the circle?

    (A) 10π

    (B) 5

    (C) 5π

    (D) 10

    (E) 25

$$3x - 2y = -2$$
$$2x - 3y = -13$$

48. What is the solution to the preceding system of equations?

    (A) (0, 0)

    (B) (4, 7)

    (C) (11, 15.5)

    (D) (7, 4)

    (E) (0, 11)

Go on to next page

49. Ware's scores in a gymnastics competition were 7, 9, 5, 10, 9, and 4. What is the mode of his set of scores?

    (A) 4

    (B) 10

    (C) 9

    (D) 8

    (E) 7.3

50. What is $\frac{18}{81}$ in simplest form?

    (A) $\frac{1}{7}$

    (B) $\frac{2}{9}$

    (C) $\frac{1}{9}$

    (D) 9

    (E) $\frac{9}{2}$

$$7h - 4 < 10h - 19$$

51. What is the solution to the preceding inequality?

    (A) $h > -\frac{23}{3}$

    (B) $h > -5$

    (C) $h < 5$

    (D) $h > 15$

    (E) $h > 5$

52. Which of the following is NOT a multiple of 12?

    (A) 84

    (B) 6

    (C) 132

    (D) 108

    (E) 12

$$5451.38 \cdot 10^7$$

53. What can be done to the preceding expression to change it to scientific notation?

    (A) Move the decimal three places to the left and make the exponent three higher.

    (B) Move the decimal three places to the left and make the exponent three lower.

    (C) Move the decimal two places to the left and make the exponent two higher.

    (D) Move the decimal two places to the left and make the exponent two higher.

    (E) Move the decimal four places to the left and make the exponent one higher.

54. What is the least common multiple of 20 and 5?

    (A) 60

    (B) 1

    (C) 5

    (D) 20

    (E) 40

$$30x - 8 \le 142$$

55. What is the solution to the preceding inequality?

    (A) $x \ge 5$

    (B) $x \le 150$

    (C) $x \le \frac{67}{30}$

    (D) $x \le 5$

    (E) $x \ge \frac{67}{30}$

Go on to next page

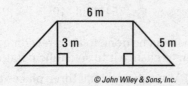

© John Wiley & Sons, Inc.

56. The preceding figure is formed by a rectangle and two congruent right triangles, each with a hypotenuse of 5 meters. The length of the rectangle is 6 meters, and the width of the rectangle is 3 meters. What is the area of the figure formed by the rectangle and two triangles?

(A) 48 m²

(B) 42 m²

(C) 24 m²

(D) 20 m²

(E) 30 m²

STOP DO NOT TURN THE PAGE UNTIL TOLD TO DO SO.
DO NOT RETURN TO A PREVIOUS TEST.

Chapter 15

Practice Exam 1: Answers and Explanations

· ·

You've taken Practice Exam 1 in Chapter 14. How do you think you did? Use the answers and explanations in this chapter to see how well you performed and to understand where you might have gone wrong on the answers you missed. Remember, the practice exam can help you determine where you need to focus your studies in preparation for the real Praxis Core. If you want to score your test quickly, flip to the end of the chapter, where the "Answer Key" gives only the letters of the correct answers.

Don't forget that you can access three additional practice tests at learn.dummies.com. You can practice taking the test on a computer, review answers and explanations, and get a personalized summary of your simulated test results.

Part 1: Reading

1. **D. has at its roots uncertainty about the meaning of life.**

   The second sentence draws a cause-and-effect relationship ("because") by explaining that a "philosophical fear" is one that "speaks to the human condition." The passage goes on to link such fears with questions like "Why am I here?" and "Does my life matter?" The accurate paraphrase of all this is that a philosophical fear involves "uncertainty about the meaning of life."

   The right answer is not Choice (A) because, although the word "ourselves" does appear in the passage, the passage is not drawing a contrast between altruism and selfishness.

   The right answer is not Choice (B) because, although *the passage itself* is an interpretation of art (a TV show), it doesn't say that a philosophical fear involves this.

   The right answer is not Choice (C) because, although it may certainly be *possible* that the author of the passage would agree with the idea that philosophical fears are the most frightening, this is pure speculation, as the passage neither states nor implies this.

   The right answer is not Choice (E) because, although people do often seek to assuage philosophical fears by theorizing about an afterlife, the passage doesn't say that such fears are about an afterlife. The rhetorical questions at the end of the passage are about this world, not the next one.

2. **E. how the comics encourage readers to question traditional notions about power.**

   The end of the passage, in what is clearly an attempt to sum up the main idea, refers to these comics causing readers to "scrutinize" and "question" the "traditional hierarchies" (*hierarchies* are power structures).

   The right answer is not Choice (A) because the passage doesn't really address the current state of the series at all, much less draw contrasts between current *X-Men* comics and the classic issues.

   The right answer is not Choice (B) because, although the passage discusses the place of female characters in the *X-Men* comics in some detail, women are only *one* example in the passage's larger point about how the comics are inclusive of traditionally marginalized groups (ethnic minorities and the differently abled are also discussed, in addition to women).

The right answer is not Choice (C) because, although the passage refers to Stan Lee creating the X-Men, the passage is mainly concerned with analyzing the comics' effect on readers, not with figuring out whose ideas were whose with respect to the writers.

The right answer is not Choice (D) because, though the passage refers to X-Men leader Professor X as "influential," and though it can be safely assumed that *X-Men* is indeed an influential comic book, this is not the main concern of the passage.

3. **D. questioning the viewpoint that all meaning must derive from a God.**

The passage closes by examining the notion that there must be a God in order for what human beings do to "count" — in other words, the idea that *meaning* can only derive from some sort of deity.

The right answer is not Choice (A) because the author is only challenging the idea that *all meaning* can *only* derive from the existence of a God, not necessarily that such a God exists. Whether there is or isn't a God is irrelevant to the concerns of the passage.

The right answer is not Choice (B) because the author mentions scientists as *one example* of a type of person who does things that could still be called "meaningful" even in the absence of a God, not to set up an argument pitting science against religion.

The right answer is not Choice (C) because, while the author presumably does believe that it's possible for people to do good based on motivations other than spiritual ones, this is not the point he is trying to make. The passage is about whether others see such deeds as meaningful, not about what motivated the people who performed them (which is never explained one way or the other).

The right answer is not Choice (E) because there is no indication that the passage is aimed specifically at people who don't believe in God or, for that matter, those who do. You can safely assume that the passage is aimed at readers in general, not at a specific type of reader.

4. **C. examining the reasons why arguments about Shakespeare fascinate us.**

The passage brings up many things, but the one constant theme is that people all over the world have long been interested in talking about Shakespeare and his works. This answer choice, the broadest of the choices, states this without adding anything else that might make the statement incorrect.

The right answer is not Choice (A) because, while the passage addresses people's belief that Shakespeare's works tell us about ourselves, the goal of the passage is not to *determine precisely what* this is, only to refer to the fact that people want to find out.

The right answer is not Choice (B) because, though the passage refers early on to "out-of-date scholarship," the point of the passage is not to correct it. It goes on to talk about other things.

The right answer is not Choice (D) because, while it is certainly possible that the author considers certain theories about Shakespeare to be "outlandish," the passage is not *satirizing* them, but merely alluding to them.

The right answer is not Choice (E) because, while the passage refers to the "authorship question"— the belief of certain conspiracy theorists that Shakespeare was a front for someone else or that he didn't exist — this is not the author's position or even the main topic he is addressing. He mentions the "authorship question" as one of many aspects of Shakespeare studies.

5. **E. new approaches to**

"New approaches to" is the only phrase among the choices given that can be plugged in for "interventions in" without changing the meaning of the sentence. In context, it's clear that the author means to discuss new ways of looking at or interpreting Shakespeare.

The right answer is not Choice (A) because, while some purists may consider certain new approaches to Shakespeare as "interference," the author is not making a value judgment.

The right answer is not Choice (B) because "*appraisals of* Shakespeare studies" would mean evaluations of the worth of such studies, not simply applying new methods to the studies.

The right answer is not Choice (C) because this section of the passage is not talking about things that are preventing or getting in the way of Shakespeare studies, so *obstacles* is the wrong word.

The right answer is not Choice (D) because, while new ways of thinking about or presenting Shakespeare may involve "unexpected collaborations" (in other words, people working together who seem unlikely to do so), they don't have to. The phrase is a possible example, not a synonym.

6. **D. largely because he is so shrouded in mystery as a human being, the prospect of claiming symbolic kinship with Shakespeare is both daunting and enticing.**

The phrase "cultural property" invokes the idea of societies ascertaining their relationship with Shakespeare and his works. Because *elusive* means "hard to pin down" and *charismatic* means "charming and/or attractive," the paraphrase of the whole idea is that communities want to feel attached or close to Shakespeare, but the facts that little is known about him as a person and that there is disagreement about the meaning of his works make it difficult for people to feel secure in this respect.

The right answer is not Choice (A) because, though many people believe this to be a true statement, it is not a paraphrase of the quoted sentence specifically.

The right answer is not Choice (B) because, while arguments about Shakespeare are generally seen as more important than arguments about other artists, the quoted sentence does not specifically pit one culture against another. The phrase *cultural property* is meant to invoke the idea of a society's relationship to a work of art, not a competition over *which* culture something belongs to.

The right answer is not Choice (C) because, while the passage goes on to imply that such an idea may not exactly be improbable, the quoted sentence itself only involves the idea that communities want to feel a kinship with Shakespeare, and not any implications about scholarly dishonesty.

The right answer is not Choice (E) because, while there have been some radical critics who have argued things to this effect, this idea is wholly unrelated to the phrase quoted in the question.

7. **E. Shakespeare himself, for whatever reason, was indisputably financially successful.**

The last half of the second paragraph provides evidence that Shakespeare was definitely personally financially successful.

The right answer is not Choice (A) because the passage (in the last paragraph) only establishes that *one* specific play by Kyd was the most successful individual play of Shakespeare's era. It never says or implies that all or most of Kyd's plays were more successful than all or most of Shakespeare's.

The right answer is not Choice (B) because, though the last paragraph mentions a popular play of Marlowe's with an "amoral" central character, the passage does not say or imply that *all* plays with amoral main characters were popular.

The right answer is not Choice (C) because, while the first paragraph implies that many contemporary people believe Shakespeare to have been the most popular writer of his day, the passage never says that *all* schoolchildren are taught this.

The right answer is not Choice (D) because, though the middle of the second paragraph explains that Shakespeare's company received the patronage of King James, it doesn't say that James encouraged the people to read Shakespeare.

8. **D. A complex question is analyzed from more than one point of view.**

The first paragraph closes by raising "the question of how we define popularity," and the passage then goes on to examine how artistic "popularity" can be defined in many different ways.

The right answer is not Choice (A) because, while the passage admits that the idea that Shakespeare was "popular" is *up for debate,* it doesn't go so far as to call it a *misconception,* and it certainly doesn't go on to *disprove* it.

The right answer is not Choice (B) because the author of the passage is analyzing a question himself, not merely summarizing a debate between other people.

The right answer is not Choice (C) because the passage never presents any information that is *new.* It talks about some things that most people don't know, so the information may be new to them, but it was not recently discovered.

The right answer is not Choice (D) because the passage doesn't exactly *rank* Elizabethan and/or Jacobean dramatists by popularity. Indeed, the passage seems to support the idea that such a ranking would be impossible, because popularity is such a subjective concern.

9. **A. Did people see Shakespeare's plays because they liked the writing, or the acting?**

The beginning of the second paragraph discusses how Shakespeare's popularity can't be separated from the popularity of the acting troupe he wrote for — in other words, there is no way to know whether most people at the time went to those plays because they liked Shakespeare's writing, because the actors were popular actors, or because of a combination of these factors.

The right answer is not Choice (B) because, although the passage doesn't go into great detail about this subject, common sense dictates that we could easily discuss the ways in which Shakespeare's characters are different from those of Marlowe, because we can still *read* their plays.

The right answer is not Choice (C) because, though the passage does not seek to explain *why* Hamlet has become our "reference point for classical literary drama," it also never implies that this question *cannot in principle* be answered.

The right answer is not Choice (D) because the second paragraph implies that Shakespeare's financial success came from the theater, and no part of the passage indicates that there is any reason to assume it actually came from elsewhere.

The right answer is not Choice (E) because the passage simply never addresses one way or the other the question of whether people in Shakespeare's day cared as much as we do about popularity. But just because the passage never brings up a question, that doesn't mean it's saying that it *cannot* be answered.

10. **B. Whether a play is well-received by less educated audience members, as well as educated ones**

The passage never addresses any kind of rift between popularity among educated audience members and popularity among less educated ones. Although it is fair to assume that opinions about Shakespeare and other playwrights of his day differed among the educated and the uneducated, the fact remains that the passage doesn't talk about this.

The right answer is not Choice (A) because the second paragraph devotes quite a bit of space to examining Shakespeare's financial success.

The right answer is not Choice (C) because the last paragraph explicitly addresses the question of how many performances a play runs for, apropos of Thomas Middleton's *A Game at Chess.*

The right answer is not Choice (D) because the last paragraph explicitly addresses the question of how often a play is referenced by later artists, apropos of Thomas Kyd's *Spanish Tragedy.*

The right answer is not Choice (E) because the first paragraph brings up the fact that Shakespeare is translated into nearly every modern language as evidence of his *current* popularity.

11. **C. provide some indication of the sort of content that was a "box-office draw" in Shakespeare's time.**

The entire passage is about whether Shakespeare, in comparison with other dramatists, was "popular" — or, in modern language, a "box-office draw" — in his time. Every other writer whose work is mentioned is brought up in service of this general idea.

The right answer is not Choice (A) because there's no reason to assume that the works by Marlowe, Kyd, and so on would be confused for Shakespeare plays by readers, and the passage isn't written as if it considers this a danger.

The right answer is not Choice (B) because, while some of the other authors mentioned may or may not have influenced Shakespeare, the question of who influenced Shakespeare is not what the passage is about, and none of the other authors are brought up with this question in mind.

The right answer is not Choice (D) because, though a couple of the plays by other authors that are mentioned are described as involving themes of ethnicity, the passage does not explicitly (or even implicitly) tie this fact in with the question of their popularity. It could easily be a coincidence.

The right answer is not Choice (E) because, though it is true that Shakespeare mixed comedy with other themes and that he was not the only writer who did this, the passage doesn't discuss this or bring up the other writers to support a point about it.

12. **E. It challenges a previous assessment regarding the extent of an influence.**

The "previous assessment" is that of Claude Nicolet, to the effect that the Roman Principate was *a significant stage on the road to the modern state*. The passage then discusses certain elements of Imperial Rome that would seem to "undermine this claim."

The right answer is not Choice (A) because the passage does not open by raising a question, but rather by challenging a prior assertion.

The right answer is not Choice (B) because, though the passage does characterize the idea of Imperial Rome's influence on the modern state as a misconception, it doesn't characterize this misconception as widespread — rather, it attributes it to one historian named Claude Nicolet.

The right answer is not Choice (C) because the passage neither defines a term nor offers any analogies.

The right answer is not Choice (D) because, while the passage does discuss two mutually exclusive opinions, it doesn't present them neatly as "two sides" in an "ongoing controversy."

13. **A. was as politically powerful as a modern nation but was run more like a cult than a country.**

The passage describes Imperial Rome as "effective" (that is, powerful), but the "overpowering emphasis on the person of the ruler" it alluded to can be taken to mean that the society was "run more like a cult than a country."

The right answer is not Choice (B) because, though the passage states that the prior "republican institutions" were retained during Rome's imperial period, it also establishes that the autocratic nature of the Empire was more than "cosmetic" (or on the surface).

The right answer is not Choice (C) because, while the passage praises Imperial Roman government as "ingenious" (or innovative), it never says that these new ideas were inevitably changed for the worse.

The right answer is not Choice (D) because, far from implying that "no one cared who was in charge" in Imperial Rome, the passage implies that people were in fact far *too* concerned with the ruler as a person.

The right answer is not Choice (E) because the passage never says anything about the "veneration of scientific knowledge" in Imperial Rome. The Romans may or may not have praised scientific knowledge or may have praised it during certain periods but not during others.

14. **B. the fact that Rome was symbolized by one man prevented it from being seen as an idea.**

This choice is essentially an exact paraphrase of the quoted phrases: The fact that government centered on the emperor being personally worshiped prevented people from seeing Rome as a fluid nation in an "impersonal" way.

The right answer is not Choice (A) because, though there certainly was frequent infighting over the succession in Imperial Rome, the passage never talks about this.

The right answer is not Choice (C) because, though the implication that the emperor was more or less worshiped would seem to imply that Rome did not, in fact, separate church and state, the passage never implies that this had anything to do with Rome's eventual downfall.

The right answer is not Choice (D) because, though it was probably the case that the emperor's decisions were often biased (as is the case in any dictatorship), the passage never talks about this.

The right answer is not Choice (E) because, though the passage alludes to Imperial Roman government being "innovative" and to the "weakening" of certain impersonal bureaucratic aspects of government, it never says anything about the emperor keeping secrets from the other branches of government.

15. **D. it is decidedly a rarity for the vast majority of philosophers to be in agreement about something.**

The adverb "surprisingly" modifies the idea that "almost everyone . . . has followed suit." The implication is that it is rare for philosophers to all agree about something.

The right answer is not Choice (A) because the author never says that he disagrees with the majority opinion.

The right answer is not Choice (B) because the sentence doesn't mean that the philosophers *themselves* were surprised — rather, it means that *it is surprising* (to anyone) when philosophers all agree.

The right answer is not Choice (C) because the sentence doesn't mean that the philosophers *themselves* were surprised, about whether regular people agreed, or about anything else — rather, it means that *it is surprising* (to anyone) when philosophers all agree.

The right answer is not Choice (E) because "surprisingly" is not used here to indicate disappointment or disapproval on the author's part. The author doesn't think it is "unoriginal" to believe that the past cannot be changed (after all, sometimes people all agree for a good reason).

16. **C. correcting what appears to be a common misconception about U.S. law.**

The fact that the first sentence alludes to the First Amendment being "misunderstood," and that the last two sentences both make corrections about what it *doesn't* mean, all point to the idea that the point of the passage is to correct a misconception.

The right answer is not Choice (A) because the so-called "half-baked comments of celebrities" are used in the passage as an example of something that people misunderstand the law's relationship to; the point of the passage is about the law itself, not the comments.

The right answer is not Choice (B) because, although it could conceivably be assumed based on the passage that U.S. citizens are more reluctant to debate than they once were, this is not the main point of the passage (though it may be an *effect* of the misconception that *is* the main point).

The right answer is not Choice (D) because, while the author is concerned with the inaccurate interpretation of the First Amendment as meaning that "no one is allowed to disagree," he discusses this as a simple matter of people not having done their homework, not as the result of vanity.

The right answer is not Choice (E) because the passage doesn't compare Freedom of Speech to other constitutional rights — it only discusses what Freedom of Speech does or does not mean.

17. **A. He might not have been such a beloved king if he had spent more time actually acting as king.**

The passage mentions that Richard only spent six months in England, and later suggests that he was popular mainly because he was not his unpopular brother. The logical gloss of all this is that Richard might not have been as popular if he had actually been the one running the country while he was king (in other words, people would not have been able to idealize him, as they did in his absence).

The right answer is not Choice (B) because the passage never says that Richard was less effective than is supposed as a military commander — just that he was far more a military commander than he was a king in any administrative sense.

The right answer is not Choice (C) because, while it is mildly embarrassing to some nowadays that the quintessential English king spoke French, the passage never says this was "shameful," and certainly never says it was "unusual."

The right answer is not Choice (D) because, while the passage does seem to imply that Richard's level of fame is possibly undeserved, it never compares him to any other monarchs who are allegedly more deserving.

The right answer is not Choice (E) because, while the passage does say that Richard's depiction in popular culture is inaccurate, it doesn't seem to think that this is any huge problem in need of rectification.

18. **E. why, since there has been one great teenage poet, there haven't been more.**

Though it doesn't open with this as some kind of thesis statement, the passage does eventually arrive at a paradox: Rimbaud proves that it is humanly possible to write great poetry as a teenager, so why hasn't anyone else done so?

The right answer is not Choice (A) because the passage doesn't agree that teachers and critics are "biased" against the poetry of teenagers — on the contrary, it appears to agree with the notion that the poetry of teenagers is generally pretty bad.

The right answer is not Choice (B) because the passage doesn't see the fact that teenagers and adults have different definitions of "young" as a paradox — it's pretty obvious why they do.

The right answer is not Choice (C) because the passage offers an explanation of why it is more common for musicians to be prodigies than for poets.

The right answer is not Choice (D) because the passage doesn't really get into analyzing *why* teenagers are mistrustful of the poetry of (allegedly) "old" people.

19. **B. It describes a typical situation, then uses it as a springboard for critical inquiry.**

The grousing of the teenage student is our "typical situation," and from there the passage arrives at (in other words, "springboards to") a legitimately interesting question: "Why has there been only one good teenage poet?"

The right answer is not Choice (A) because the complaint of the teenage student at the beginning is more an example of short-sightedness than a factual error, and the passage doesn't go on to say it is "excusable" so much as notice that it raises an interesting question.

The right answer is not Choice (C) because, while the opening anecdote involves two people seeing something differently, it is not "an example of relativism" exactly, because the implication is that the student is simply wrong.

The right answer is not Choice (D) because, though the anecdote about the student is not exactly heavy, it's not altogether "lighthearted" either. And the point of the passage as a whole is not that it is a "criticism of immaturity."

The right answer is not Choice (E) because, though the passage is somewhat sardonic, it would be hyperbole to call it a "satire," and nothing about the "biases of adults" is ever acknowledged.

20. **B. sarcasm.**

The passage's assertion that "a teenager who says 'young' means another teenager" seems to imply that someone who refers to a 30-year-old as "young" in front of a teenager is likely to meet with sarcasm.

The right answer is not Choice (A) because there's no indication in the passage that teenagers would be relieved to hear a 30-year-old described as "young." Indeed, they would dispute such a characterization.

The right answer is not Choice (C) because, though the passage establishes that teenagers would disagree with the characterization of a 30-year-old as "young," the safe decision based on the choices is that simple *sarcasm* is more likely than outright *hostility*.

The right answer is not Choice (D) because, though the passage establishes that teenagers would disagree with the characterization of a 30-year-old as "young," the safe decision based on the choices is that simple *sarcasm* is more likely than some sort of unspecified *accusations*.

The right answer is not Choice (E) because, though the passage establishes that teenagers would disagree with the characterization of a 30-year-old as "young," there's no indication that such a statement would make them *afraid*.

21. **E. solipsism**

This is just a vocabulary question. *Solipsism* is a fancy word for the belief that there is nothing (or at least nothing important) outside of the self. The reference to the "original state of absorption" makes it clear that this word is the right choice.

The right answer is not Choice (A) because *obsequiousness* means fawning over or flattering others. The passage describes the philosophy of Sartre as implying that the natural condition of people is to do just the opposite.

The right answer is not Choice (B) because *mendacity* means dishonesty; the passage never really talks about dishonesty.

The right answer is not Choice (C) because *cupidity* means greed. While the passage does describe humans as being essentially self-absorbed, a word meaning "greed" is not the best of the choices (because another one of the choices means self-absorption).

The right answer is not Choice (D) because *diffidence* means shyness. The passage does imply that people (in Sartre's opinion) don't really want other people around, but it's not because they're shy.

22. **C. examining how others might see them.**

The phrase "rather than thinking about their experience, they are immersed in it" makes it clear that *reflecting* (in this context) means being compelled to see yourself as others do; becoming self-conscious rather than self-absorbed.

The right answer is not Choice (A) because, although the sentence "They act without reflecting" may seem to mean "they act without considering the consequences" if read out of context, in context it clearly has more to do with self-consciousness.

The right answer is not Choice (B) because, although *reflecting* is often used to mean "remembering the past," in this context it has more to do with self-consciousness in the presence of others.

The right answer is not Choice (D) because in context, *reflecting* is used more to indicate the idea of mere self-consciousness in the presence of others, in the moment, rather than having to do with punishment or consequences in the future.

The right answer is not Choice (E) because, although self-consciousness in the presence of others may eventually lead to "courting a reaction" (either as a defense mechanism, or out of spite), in this context it simply refers to self-consciousness itself.

23. **A. dispassionate explication.**

The fact that the author doesn't appear to have much of a "tone" at all is a clue to the answer: He is simply explaining something (the philosophy of Sartre) without much emotion.

The right answer is not Choice (B) because, although it's safe to assume that the author admires the philosophy of Sartre, there's no indication that the admiration is *grudging* (that is, that the author *doesn't want to* admire Sartre).

The right answer is not Choice (C) because the author is being neither optimistic nor pessimistic about anything — he is merely explaining the philosophy of Sartre, not speculating about how something will turn out.

The right answer is not Choice (D) because there is no indication that the author pities Sartre or anyone else — he is merely explaining the philosophy of Sartre in an unemotional way.

The right answer is not Choice (E) because the passage is neither humorous nor making fun of anything.

24. **E. Accept the necessity of human relationships, but do not lose all sense of personal freedom.**

The first paragraph mentions that Sartre admitted personal relationships were "essential to our being," and the second paragraph as a whole shows that Sartre was primarily concerned with personal freedom. The logical gloss is that he would have advised accepting the inevitability of interpersonal relations while prioritizing your own freedom.

The right answer is not Choice (A) because, while the passage does imply that Sartre saw human interaction as fundamentally a competition, there's no indication that he advised manipulating people.

The right answer is not Choice (B) because, while the passage does imply that Sartre saw interaction with others as carrying the possibility of egotistical "shock," there's no indication that he would have advised people to adopt or conform to — or even care about — the views of others, early in life or at any other time.

The right answer is not Choice (C) because, although Sartre did see human existence as being characterized by desires and other people as being in the way of those desires, there's no indication that he would have advised people to renounce their desires.

The right answer is not Choice (D) because the first paragraph mentions Sartre admitting that personal relationships were "essential to our being," so there's no indication that he even would have thought it *possible* to avoid other people until your identity is stable.

25. **B. analyzing a specific effect that technology appears to have had on youth culture.**

Though the passage begins and ends as though the main point were about Kurt Cobain himself, Cobain essentially works as a framing device for an analysis the passage makes about youth and music culture — that is, that the Internet age has diminished the need that the music industry once had to create "rock stars" in the traditional sense.

The right answer is not Choice (A) because, while the type of music that was popular in the pre-Internet age is contrasted with the type of music that is popular in the Internet age, the two styles of music are not compared aesthetically — in other words, the passage is not a critical assessment of the music itself.

The right answer is not Choice (C) because, while a sort of "prediction" involving Kurt Cobain is used to frame the passage, the point of the passage is not to criticize people who make predictions.

The right answer is not Choice (D) because the passage attributes the increased popularity of hip-hop to the Internet, not directly to Cobain's death. Presumably, the ascendancy of hip-hop would have happened even if Cobain hadn't died, because the Internet would have been invented either way.

The right answer is not Choice (E) because the passage only gives *one* example of a prediction that came true in an ironic way, not several.

26. **E. it is based on making a multiplicity of artists slightly famous, rather than making a few artists incredibly famous.**

The penultimate sentence of the passage explains that the Internet allowed the music industry to micromarket different artists to various niche groups of music fans all at once, rather than having to market certain "huge" artists to everyone, as it once did.

The right answer is not Choice (A) because the passage doesn't attribute the popularity of hip-hop to the fact that the music industry itself prizes it more highly — it says that hip-hop became popular because of the Internet, rather than because of something the industry did on purpose.

The right answer is not Choice (B) because, although it is true that the music industry is making less money because of illegal downloading, the passage doesn't discuss this or attribute anything to it.

The right answer is not Choice (C) because the passage doesn't say that marketing plays no role in which artists get popular anymore — it says that marketing is done differently, not that it isn't done.

The right answer is not Choice (D) because, while it may well be true that the average music consumer is now younger and that the music such consumers buy is happier than the music of the '90s, the passage doesn't talk about this.

27. **B. bittersweet nostalgia.**

The passage is looking back on something, so it is *nostalgic,* and it does so with a fond but somewhat sad tone, so it is *bittersweet.* (Even if this is not abundantly clear, the other four choices are clearly wrong.)

The right answer is not Choice (A) because *rueful* means "full of regret," and the author of the passage does not regret anything. He doesn't even make reference to himself personally.

The right answer is not Choice (C) because the author is not discussing his own personal beliefs, so his level of *conviction* is not an issue.

The right answer is not Choice (D) because the author is not *gloating* about anything. The passage does refer to a prediction coming true, but it wasn't the author's prediction.

The right answer is not Choice (E) because *indignant* means "offended," and *incredulousness* means "the quality of not being able to believe something." The author is not offended, and he never alludes to being unable to accept the truth of something.

28. **D. The desire to be more like others is not always a sign of cowardice.**

Storm proceeds from the assumption that anyone who wants the mutant cure is a "coward." Rogue, who apparently wants the cure based on the fact that her mutation carries a more considerable downside (she can never touch anyone) than does Storm's, presumably disagrees.

The right answer is not Choice (A) because there's no indication that Rogue somehow considers bravery to be vain, nor is there any logical reason why she would think this — the more logical interpretation is that she simply doesn't consider the desire to fit in to be cowardly.

The right answer is not Choice (B) because, while it's *possible* that Rogue (or anyone else) *might* think this, there is no reason why she *has* to, based on the passage. She is making a decision for herself, not a sweeping pronouncement about what others should do.

The right answer is not Choice (C) because it's not logically necessary for Rogue to think that wanting to fit in is braver, only that it's not necessarily cowardly. The statement is more ambitious than it needs to be, especially when compared with Choice (D).

The right answer is not Choice (E) because there's no reason why Rogue's actions would need to be underpinned by a sweeping statement about science versus nature. She is making a decision that affects only herself, with regard to one specific situation.

29. **C. What were some of the complaints people had traditionally made about the SAT analogies section?**

The middle of the passage mentions two specific complaints that people had traditionally had about SAT analogies. The passage doesn't confirm that these complaints are definitely the reason analogies were removed, but the passage still answers the question of what people's complaints were.

The right answer is not Choice (A) because the passage states that "the College Board never issued an official explanation" for the removal of the analogies. People were left to speculate about the reasons.

The right answer is not Choice (B) because, although one example of a supposedly biased vocabulary word is given, the passage never expands on any criteria used to determine whether words are biased in general.

The right answer is not Choice (D) because the passage never mentions what the primary purpose of standardized tests is.

The right answer is not Choice (E) because, although the passage alludes to the fact that people can learn vocabulary from life experience or from reading, it never attempts to answer the question of which way is more common.

30. **E. Proof that Europa's frozen crust is, in fact, entirely comprised of water ice.**

The passage says that there's a decent chance life exists on Europa because the subsurface ocean is "almost certainly water." If it were found that the ocean was definitely water, then this would improve the chances even more, and the ocean would have to be water if it were found that the frozen surface was water ice.

The right answer is not Choice (A) because even if life could originate in substances other than water, that wouldn't be relevant unless Europa's ocean were found to be one of those substances.

The right answer is not Choice (B) because the discovery of other moons that spin faster than they orbit would indicate that they might have liquid oceans too, but it wouldn't change anything about the possibility of life on Europa.

The right answer is not Choice (C) because the discovery that more life-forms *on Earth* than previously thought had originated from volcanoes wouldn't change anything about the possibility of life on Europa. Scientists already know it's possible for life to originate from volcanoes, so how many species on Earth did or didn't is beside the point.

The right answer is not Choice (D) because how old Europa is, and whether any of Jupiter's other moons are older, doesn't change anything about what we currently know to be true of Europa regarding the possibility of life on it.

31. **C. address an anticipated objection from more-informed readers.**

In the vicinity of the statement about volcanoes, the passage alludes to the fact that sunlight was once believed to be a prerequisite for life. If any readers remembered learning this (in school, or from reading on their own), then they would be confused by the assertion that a subsurface ocean with no sunlight could support life, so the passage clarifies that the theory has been recently revised.

The right answer is not Choice (A) because the mention of undersea volcanoes wouldn't "draw a comparison" between Europa and Earth unless we knew for a fact that Europa had such volcanoes — at this point, we can only say that it *might*.

The right answer is not Choice (B) because, although younger readers may well think that undersea volcanoes are cool, this is not why the fact was included. There's no reason to believe that the passage is aimed at younger readers.

The right answer is not Choice (D) because, although undersea volcanoes would indeed warm up their portion of the ocean, temperature is not the most crucial issue in context.

The right answer is not Choice (E) because the passage *doesn't*, in fact, define "chemical disequilibrium."

32. **B. How do we know that Europa probably contains a liquid layer?**

The opening sentence about how Europa rotates faster than it revolves explains that this proves the existence of a liquid layer.

The right answer is not Choice (A) because the passage never addresses the question of whether any other bodies in our solar system (other than Europa and Earth) might contain life.

The right answer is not Choice (C) because the passage never explains why most life-forms need sunlight to originate; it just states that they do (so far as we know).

The right answer is not Choice (D) because the passage never states what Europa's core is comprised of.

The right answer is not Choice (E) because the passage never states when we will know for sure whether Europa contains life. It says what year the satellite will be launched and when it will reach the vicinity of Jupiter, but not how long it will be there or when the information it obtains will get back to us.

33. **A. Passage 2 provides an example of a correction made by Passage 1.**

Passage 1 explains that, despite a common misconception, evolution does not move toward a specific goal, but only responds to the environment (which includes other animals, like humans) as it changes. Passage 2 provides an example of evolution doing this. Therefore, Passage 2 provides an example of a correction made by Passage 1. The two passages agree, but Passage 2 discusses an example, whereas Passage 1 speaks generally.

The right answer is not Choice (B) because Passage 2 doesn't disagree with Passage 1.

The right answer is not Choice (C) because Passage 2 does not make the mistake warned against in Passage 1.

The right answer is not Choice (D) because Passage 2 does not offer a different explanation from Passage 1.

The right answer is not Choice (E) because the two passages are, in fact, discussing the same idea (that evolution does not move toward a specific goal, but only responds to the environment).

34. **E. "many."**

Untold simply means "many" in a context where the exact number is not known, but the number is known to be high. The substitution of "many" for "untold" would not be quite as poetic, but it would mean the same thing.

The right answer is not Choice (A) because, although *untold* does mean "a lot of," it doesn't quite mean "infinite" (there hasn't been an *infinite* number of generations of elephants, just a lot).

The right answer is not Choice (B) because *untold* doesn't mean that things have come in a row (in other words, successively).

The right answer is not Choice (C) because "immaterial" means that something doesn't matter. The passage isn't saying that the number of generations of elephants doesn't matter, but rather that there have been a lot of generations of elephants.

The right answer is not Choice (D) because the idea here is not that the number of generations of elephants is in dispute, just that there have been a lot of generations of elephants.

35. **A. It provides an illustration of why retrospective determinism is fallacious.**

The fact that there can be a biological "Revenge of the Nerds"— that is, that a trait once considered unattractive in mates can come to be considered attractive if the environment changes — nicely illustrates why the fallacy of retrospective determinism (the idea that evolution has specific traits in mind as the "right" ones) mentioned in Passage 1 is fallacious.

The right answer is not Choice (B) because the "Revenge of the Nerds" quip is not an explanation of why people misunderstand evolutionary theory; it's a characterization of a specific example of the correct understanding.

The right answer is not Choice (C) because the "Revenge of the Nerds" quip does not challenge the idea that evolution doesn't have a specific goal in mind — on the contrary, it helps to illustrate the fact that it does not.

The right answer is not Choice (D) because the "Revenge of the Nerds" quip doesn't challenge the idea that humans can play a role in evolutionary pressure (of course they can; they are part of the environment).

The right answer is not Choice (E) because nothing about Passage 2, including the "Revenge of the Nerds" quip, dismisses the concerns of Passage 1. The two passages agree with each other.

36. **D. equally analytical, but more jocose.**

Both Passage 1 and Passage 2 are explaining a scientific theory, but Passage 2 attempts to do so in a more humorous and entertaining fashion, whereas Passage 1 is comparatively dry.

The right answer is not Choice (A) because neither passage demonstrates "concern" (except perhaps for the accurate understanding of science), and neither passage is "exhortatory" (which means "trying to convince people to do something").

The right answer is not Choice (B) because Passage 2 is not "skeptical" of anything. It provides an example to support an idea, but it doesn't dispute anything.

The right answer is not Choice (C) because Passage 2 is just as scientific as Passage 2. It's more humorous in tone, but it's still discussing science.

The right answer is not Choice (E) because neither passage is angry in tone, and Passage 2 doesn't "forgive" anyone for anything. It simply explains an interesting phenomenon.

37. **C. Make reference to examples of desirable evolutionary traits.**

Both passages make reference to examples of desirable evolutionary traits. Passage 1 mentions speed in mice, aggression in wolves, and intelligence in humans, and Passage 2 mentions tusks — either big or small ones, depending on the time in history — in elephants.

The right answer is not Choice (A) because only Passage 1 defines a scientific term; Passage 2 does not.

The right answer is not Choice (B) because only Passage 2 makes reference to pop culture; Passage 1 does not.

The right answer is not Choice (D) because neither passage discusses changes to evolutionary theory. They correct misconceptions about it.

The right answer is not Choice (E) because neither passage "mocks" anyone. Passage 1 rather bluntly corrects people, but that's hardly the same thing as mockery.

38. **D. explaining scientific facts and principles to a general audience.**

Both passages explain scientific principles to a general audience. Because that is all that this answer choice asserts, there's no way it can be wrong.

The right answer is not Choice (A) because neither passage addresses *objections* to evolutionary theory. Passage 1 addresses *misunderstandings* of it, but that's all.

The right answer is not Choice (B) because only Passage 1 seeks to dispel a misconception about evolutionary theory. Passage 2 supports the correction made in Passage 1, but it doesn't bring up any misconceptions itself.

The right answer is not Choice (C) because neither passage spends any time establishing the author's qualifications.

The right answer is not Choice (E) because only Passage 2 seeks to be entertaining. Passage 1 is only trying to be informative. (It is well-written, but that's not the same thing as entertaining.)

39. **C. instill an expectation in the reader that is then ironicized.**

The idea that the "nightmarish" place was designed by a "lunatic" is ironicized when the passage reveals that it was designed by monks, for a religious purpose, at the request of the people whose bones appear there.

The right answer is not Choice (A) because the design of the Sedlec Ossuary is not a mystery — the passage explains it.

The right answer is not Choice (B) because the passage reserves moral judgment about the design of the ossuary. It simply provides information.

The right answer is not Choice (D) because the reader does not in fact know the explanation for the Sedlec Ossuary's unusual décor at this point in the passage. The passage goes on to explain it.

The right answer is not Choice (E) because the passage does not discuss two separate ideas. It is about the Sedlec Ossuary the whole time.

40. **E. it has an answer that people have been exposed to but can't recall.**

The passage explains that a trivia question is fun when people enjoy guessing because they feel as if they should know the answer, even though they usually won't. Choice (E) is a paraphrase of this.

The right answer is not Choice (A) because the passage never says or implies that a trivia question has to be about something "important."

The right answer is not Choice (B) because there is no reason to assume, based on either the passage or common sense, that the majority of people would somehow "eventually figure out" such a question.

The right answer is not Choice (C) because the question is not, in fact, impossible to get right. Assuming someone knows the names of the presidents, he or she can make a lucky guess.

The right answer is not Choice (D) because the passage never implies that all good trivia questions need to deal with subjects people learned about in school. The fact that people feel like they should remember the answer is the issue, and in this case it *just so happens* that people may remember what the presidents looked like from seeing a poster in school.

41. **C. The discovery of trivial, everyday personal items in the topsoil.**

If "everyday, personal items" were discovered in the ground all around Stonehenge, then that would indicate that people milled around there in normal day-to-day life, rather than never going there or only going there for certain ritualistic purposes on special occasions.

The right answer is not Choice (A) because obviously people had to be at Stonehenge to build it in the first place, so finding tool fragments would not be unexpected.

The right answer is not Choice (B) because Stonehenge could still have been oriented towards the sun in a certain symbolic way even if living people were not supposed to go there once it was built.

The right answer is not Choice (D) because it's likely that people would have hurt themselves, perhaps badly, while either erecting the stones or bringing them there in the first place. Blood traces wouldn't mean that people hung around at Stonehenge after it was built.

The right answer is not Choice (E) because widespread fires could have occurred naturally. Even if people aren't allowed to go somewhere, there can still be a fire there from time to time.

42. **D. introduce a historical situation that subsequent paragraphs will go on to analyze.**

The first paragraph introduces the idea that the Frankish Empire was the heir to the Roman Empire, and then the second paragraph goes into more detail about why this was.

The right answer is not Choice (A) because the first paragraph doesn't explain how the Franks assumed Rome's inheritance — the second paragraph does.

The right answer is not Choice (B) because Charlemagne is not compared to any other Medieval monarchs.

The right answer is not Choice (C) because the passage never addresses the question of why the Western Roman Empire collapsed — it just states the fact that it did.

The right answer is not Choice (E) because, although both paragraphs allude in closing to Frankish "crises," these crises are not the main point of either paragraph.

43. **B. The first paragraph introduces a general idea, and the second supports it with specifics.**

The first paragraph describes a general phenomenon, and the second supports it with details and explanations.

The right answer is not Choice (A) because the first paragraph never brings up a misconception, and the second paragraph never corrects one.

The right answer is not Choice (C) because the first paragraph doesn't raise any questions. It only states facts.

The right answer is not Choice (D) because the two paragraphs do not present competing viewpoints — they're a continuation of a single idea.

The right answer is not Choice (E) because neither paragraph rebuts any other theories; they both explain things on their own terms, rather than responding to someone else.

44. **A. other dominant political powers of the time.**

The allusion to the Franks being at a "safe distance" from Byzantium and the Arabs implies that these were other powerful cultures of the day.

The right answer is not Choice (B) because there's no indication that the Byzantines and Arabs were influences on the Franks — the passage seems to imply that they were contemporary, competing empires.

The right answer is not Choice (C) because, although Byzantium and the Arabs could have been enemies of the bygone Western Roman Empire, the right answer doesn't need to be this ambitious.

The right answer is not Choice (D) because the "favorable geographical position" is only "favorable" because it's far away from the Byzantines and Arabs.

The right answer is not Choice (E) because there's no contextual reason to assume that the "other German states" alluded to earlier in the passage include the Byzantines and Arabs. This sentence is making a separate point.

45. **E. His accession represented the full transfer of status from Ancient Rome to the Franks.**

The opening sentence refers to the crowning of Charlemagne as the "final step" in a long process of power and prestige being transferred from the Western Roman Empire to the Frankish Empire. The implication is that the crowning of Charlemagne made this process officially complete.

The right answer is not Choice (A) because the passage never implies that Frankish kings before Charlemagne saw themselves as Roman. They would have seen themselves as Frankish; they just weren't as powerful as Charlemagne would become.

The right answer is not Choice (B) because the passage mentions that Charlemagne was crowned in 800, whereas the Western Roman Empire collapsed in 476.

The right answer is not Choice (C) because, although the opening sentence does imply that other Frankish rulers played a role in the process, it never implies that any one of them was actually more important than Charlemagne.

The right answer is not Choice (D) because the first sentence says nothing about Charlemagne's religious beliefs. The second paragraph says that the Franks were more in line with Roman religion than were competing German states, but that's all, and it doesn't mean the same thing.

46. **C. They learned from the Romans, and the transfer of power was slow but nearly inevitable.**

The passages establish that the Franks learned from the Romans and that the transfer of power took a long time, but was never really in doubt. Because this is all that this answer choice asserts, there's no way it can be wrong.

The right answer is not Choice (A) because the passage doesn't say that the Franks were in competition with the Romans — it establishes that they came along later.

The right answer is not Choice (B) because the passage alludes to the Franks being Rome's heirs in a geographical sense — meaning that they controlled roughly the same territory, not an "altogether different" area.

The right answer is not Choice (D) because the passage never addresses the question of how long the Frankish Empire lasted and whether the duration of its power was predictable or not.

The right answer is not Choice (E) because the passage, particularly in the second paragraph, explains that the succession of the Franks to a Roman level of power was a slow and steady process, not a "series of lucky coincidences" at all.

47. **C. Japan**

The key shows that automotive sales are represented by the white field filled with tiny black dots, and only the bar representing Japan is visibly filled in with that pattern to any extent.

Choices (A), (B), (D), and (E) are not right because the bars for Finland, France, the Republic of Korea, and the United States don't show automotive sales as represented by the white field filled with tiny black dots.

48. **A. The graph reflects percentages of purchases, not total purchases.**

The x-axis of the graph clearly shows that it illustrates percentages, not total purchases. In other words, the idea is not whether U.S. consumers buy more or less total music and videos than French consumers; the idea is what percentage of the total purchases made by consumers in each country are accounted for by purchases of music and videos.

The right answer is not Choice (B) or Choice (C) because the respective prices of music and video products in France and the U.S. wouldn't affect what respective *percentages* of total sales for each country were accounted for by sales of those products — the graph is charting the number of sales, not revenue.

The right answer is not Choice (D) because stolen products wouldn't show up on a graph about purchases.

The right answer is not Choice (E) because the statement and the graph can easily both be true. The graph reflects percentages, not total sales.

49. **A, C. Canada and France**

Purchases of clothing/jewelry/accessories are represented by the white field with thin black horizontal and vertical stripes. The bars with that pattern take up more than 20 percent of the space in the bars for Canada and France, but not in the bar for Finland. The bar with that pattern goes past the 20 percent mark in the bar for Finland, but only because it comes after the top-left diagonal striped bar representing books/magazines; the clothing/jewelry/accessories bar itself does not take up greater than 20 percent of the space on the Finland bar. When you answer this type of question on the Praxis, you would click the bubbles for "Canada" and "France," but NOT the bubble for "Finland."

50. **C. The broad view of society is patriarchal, but the individual female characters are smarter than the male characters.**

The passage explains that the inevitability of marriage reaffirms the patriarchal societal structure of the time, but it also clearly states that individual female characters in the comedies are almost always smarter than their eventual husbands.

The right answer is not Choice (A) because the passage states that the men in Shakespeare's comedies are actually more sensitive (to the judgments of their friends, as well as to the comments of women).

The right answer is not Choice (B) because the passage doesn't really address the question of whether male or female characters are closer with their same-sex friends. It says that the men are more sensitive to the judgments of their friends, but that's not the same thing.

The right answer is not Choice (D) because the passage never addresses "moral superiority" one way or the other.

The right answer is not Choice (E) because the passage implies that both male and female characters are interested in marriage, and it doesn't even mention sex.

51. **A. It is often difficult for the audience to genuinely like the male characters.**

The statement that the male characters "can often seem absurd, even while we are invited to be sympathetic" is as close as the passage comes to an actual criticism (in the pejorative sense) of Shakespeare's art.

The right answer is not Choice (B) because the passage never implies that the plays are predictable (it mentions that they end with marriage, but that is common in comedies, and in any case, it has nothing to do with "rigid gender roles").

The right answer is not Choice (C) because the passage doesn't seem to think it is a negative that the plays usually end with marriage. That was simply a common trope in romantic comedies of the time (and even today).

The right answer is not Choice (D) because the passage does say that the female characters are *more* forgiving, but not that they are *too* forgiving.

The right answer is not Choice (E) because the passage doesn't seem to think it negatively affects the plays for the men to be weak or sensitive. (It's what makes the plots possible, after all.)

52. **C. Sitcoms where the juvenile husband's antics drive the plot but the wife always turns out to be right at the end**

The passage mentions that, in Shakespeare's comedies, men "nominally take the lead," but the women are "better aware" and "seem smarter." This convention survives today in stereotypical mainstream sitcoms where the husband's actions typically cause the plot to happen, but the women set things right at the end.

The right answer is not Choice (A) because the passage does not say that gender roles are completely *reversed* in Shakespeare's comedies (women sometimes temporarily disguise themselves as men, but that's not the same thing).

The right answer is not Choice (B) because, although the passage does say that Shakespeare's women are intelligent, they are not self-sufficient in the sense that a "strong woman character" would be today (they still depend on marriage), and certainly not to the point of having superhuman abilities.

The right answer is not Choice (D) because the passage does not imply that men team up to compete against women, and vice versa, in Shakespeare's comedies.

The right answer is not Choice (E) because nothing resembling the relationship between messages of female empowerment and physical attractiveness is alluded to anywhere in the passage.

53. **E. create humorously unusual situations without seeming too subversive.**

The fact that the men are zany or insecure and the women are smarter allows comedy to happen, but the fact that the plays end with marriage reaffirms the dominant social order (in other words, they're *not* "subversive").

The right answer is not Choice (A) because nothing about "political statements" is alluded to in the passage.

The right answer is not Choice (B) because nothing in the passage indicates that Shakespeare intended to "question religion" in his work.

The right answer is not Choice (C) because the passage never says that Shakespeare's plays contained *more* female parts than did the plays of his contemporaries.

The right answer is not Choice (D) because, although the passage does say that the men in Shakespeare's plays are atypically sensitive to people's judgments, it doesn't say that Shakespeare's goal was to try and make men more like this in real life. If anything, the implication is that it was played for laughs.

54. **E. simplicity**

If something is "accessible," then most people can understand it. So, in this context, *accessibility* simply means *simplicity* (in terms of Locke's language, not his ideas).

The right answer is not Choice (A) because *opacity* means that something is unclear — the exact opposite of *accessibility*.

The right answer is not Choice (B) because *bluntness* means that something is straightforward in terms of its message, not necessarily that the writing itself is clear to a wide audience (which is what *accessible* means).

The right answer is not Choice (C) because *brevity* means that something is short, not that it is clear.

The right answer is not Choice (D) because *completeness* means that something is thorough, not necessarily that it's clear.

55. **D. He is an expert in black holes who has also given serious thought to the human condition.**

The multiple mentions of Hawking's discoveries about black holes surely qualify him as an "expert," and the fact that he theorizes about free will means that he has given thought to the human condition, even if it isn't his main job. Because those are the only things this answer choice asserts, there is no way it can be wrong.

The right answer is not Choice (A) because the passage does not say that Hawking doesn't believe in free will — just that he wouldn't *if* a theory could be devised that predicted everything. There's no indication that he thinks such a theory is likely to be devised.

The right answer is not Choice (B) because the passage never says that Hawking *discovered* black holes. He clearly knows a lot about them, but he is not their discoverer.

The right answer is not Choice (C) because the passage never implies that Hawking thinks that science and ethics have nothing to do with each other. Indeed, his statements about free will would seem to indicate that he thinks they are related to an extent.

The right answer is not Choice (E) because the passage states that Hawking thinks a theory that would *predict the future* accurately would disprove free will, not that a complete description of the universe *as it currently exists* would do so.

56. **E. the book was considered "cool."**

Referring to Das's book as "required reading for the counterculture" is a way of saying that people needed to read it to be considered hip or "in the know."

The right answer is not Choice (A) because, in this context, "required reading" is being used as a figure of speech, and not to refer literally to school curricula.

The right answer is not Choice (B) because calling something "required reading" means that it was considered important by certain people, not necessarily that it was a best-seller.

The right answer is not Choice (C) because the fact that a book was cool in the 1970s doesn't necessarily mean that it's unhip now.

The right answer is not Choice (D) because the expression "required reading" has nothing to do with how complicated a book is, one way or the other.

Part 2: Writing

1. **B. hallmarks**

The vague and overused word *aspects* could stand to be replaced with another word here (it is not incorrect, but a better word could be used). What you need is a term that means something like *characterizations,* and it would be nice if it also had a noble ring to it, because the passage is talking about "successful art." *Hallmarks* works perfectly.

The right answer is not Choice (A) because the passage isn't actually talking about *prizes* being given to any art, just about some quality that is recognizable in the art.

The right answer is not Choice (C) because *aspirations* means *hopes.* Because the passage is talking about art that is *already* "successful," rather than about art that merely hopes to be so, this term doesn't work.

The right answer is not Choice (D) because *pitfalls,* which means *possible dangers,* doesn't make sense in this context. You're looking for a positive word here, not a negative one.

The right answer is not Choice (E) because *emanations* means something like the slang term "vibes"— a quality that is given off by or exudes from the art. It simply doesn't make sense in this context.

2. **E. painting; Parrhasius explained**

You're being asked to combine two complete sentences (in other words, two independent clauses). All the choices correctly employ a semicolon to do this, but the matter at hand is whether you also need a transition word or phrase and, if so, which one. Although using *any* transition phrase isn't automatically wrong, none of the offered choices makes sense in context. So the smart move is to select the choice with no transition phrase at all (remember, only employ a transition phrase when doing so is clearly *better* than not doing so).

The right answer is not Choice (A) because *therefore,* which means "as a result of this," is not necessary in context. Parrhasius's explanation was technically a "result" of Zeuxis's request, but it was a surprise, not the expected logical next step.

The right answer is not Choice (B) because it isn't "unfortunate" that Parrhasius gave this explanation. Tricking people into thinking the curtain was real was precisely what he intended to do!

The right answer is not Choice (C) because *in fact* is used when a previous statement is being added onto and amplified — the second clause agrees with the first or continues in the same vein. The relationship between these two sentences is one of irony or surprise, so *in fact* doesn't fit.

The right answer is not Choice (D). *On the other hand* is used for contrasts, and these two clauses do contrast each other in that the second is a surprise in relation to the first. But what you have here is a case of the truth being revealed after someone has been mistaken about it, not a counterpoint to a previous statement in a "debate" or "weighing the options" sense.

3. **A. Analogous stories occur in the realm of literature.**

All you have to do with a "which sentence should introduce the paragraph?" question is ask yourself what the ensuing paragraph is generally about. Here, you see that the subject is being changed to literature (from visual art, which was discussed in the previous paragraph), and that all the examples in this paragraph concern literature. So the logical choice is to pick the sentence that basically says "Now we will look at some examples from the literary world."

The right answer is not Choice (B) because the ensuing paragraph does not present any opinions about the previous story — in fact, it doesn't refer back to it at all.

The right answer is not Choice (C) because "controversy" is not the right word for either the story related in the first paragraph or any of the anecdotes related in the second.

The right answer is not Choice (D) because although the expression "tip of the iceberg" does basically imply that "there is way more to this than what we were just talking about," it's a little vague in this context. Because all of the ensuing paragraph examines literature, a sentence that means "Now we will consider examples from literature" is clearly better than one that merely means "Now I will say some more stuff about this."

The right answer is not Choice (E) because the ensuing paragraph doesn't go on to talk about any other people besides Zeuxis that Parrhasius fooled with his curtain trick.

4. **C. Dr. Bianchon, one**

This answer choice correctly uses a comma to separate an initial independent clause from a subsequent afterthought clause (an afterthought clause is like an appositive clause that comes at the end of the sentence instead of in the middle).

The right answer is not Choice (A) because you don't need the word *being* in there. The gerund is not necessary at the start of an afterthought clause — the subject *one* works by itself. (Always watch out for the word *being* — it's frequently used as a trick on grammar tests!)

The right answer is not Choice (B) because, grammatically, it makes no sense to say "among one." You can only be "among" *several* things.

The right answer is not Choice (D) because this creates a comma splice (two independent clauses joined by only a comma), a serious grammatical error.

The right answer is not Choice (E) because this choice smashes up two separate clauses into one long nonsense clause where "Dr. Bianchon" is both the object of the first clause and the subject of the second.

5. **E. *emotional*, in order to emphasize the idea that there is more than one type of realism.**

What are being distinguished here (and indeed, in the passage as a whole) are different ways of looking at the idea of "realism." Because the point of the sentence is that Freud was thinking of a different type of realism from the type we normally mean when we use that word today, the logical word to italicize (for emphasis) is *emotional*, the adjective modifying the noun *realism* as Freud thought of it. (Just think of which word you would emphasize with pronunciation if you were speaking the sentence aloud.)

The right answer is not Choice (A) because there would be no reason to especially emphasize the word *sound*.

The right answer is not Choice (B) because no other type of drama besides the Greek is discussed in the sentence.

The right answer is not Choice (C) because to both place a word in quotation marks *and* italicize it is generally considered a stylistic error.

The right answer is not Choice (D) because you already know that Freud was *responding* to the texts.

6. **C. But lifelike at one point in history does not mean the same thing as lifelike at another.**

The sentence preceding the one in question establishes that we typically use "lifelike" and "realistic" as compliments, and the subsequent sentence offers a specific example of how concepts of realism can change over time. So the logical sentence to place between them is a sentence that *explicitly states* how concepts of realism can change over time — in other words, a sentence stating the assertion of which the next sentence offers an example.

The right answer is not Choice (A) because, although a literary critic is mentioned a few sentences later, the paragraph does not say that any literary critics are arguing that the words "lifelike" and "realistic" should never be used as compliments.

The right answer is not Choice (B) because, like Choice (A), this choice implies that using the words "lifelike" and "realistic" as compliments is a bad thing, when that's not the point of the paragraph. It's only suggesting that we have to be careful when doing so, because terms like *realistic* are subjective.

The right answer is not Choice (D) because, although this statement may be true, it doesn't work in this context. The ensuing sentences talk about how concepts of realism can change, not about audiences who prefer realistic stories to skill at acting.

The right answer is not Choice (E) because, although the example offered in Sentence 12 is indeed from the 20th century, the paragraph does not imply that ideas about realism changed suddenly at that specific time — rather, the implication is that such ideas are *always* changing.

7. **A. responding differently from how a modern audience would**

The question is simply pointing out that the author is using a figure of speech and asking what the figure of speech literally means. By "tuned to a different frequency," Pechter means to say that audiences in Betterton's time were used to seeing different styles in the art of their day, so an artistic style that might be jarring to us would not be jarring to them.

The right answer is not Choice (B) because the point of the sentence is not that audiences in Betterton's time were more distracted than modern audiences, but rather that they were accustomed to different things.

The right answer is not Choice (C) because the point is not that the audiences didn't understand the play, but rather that they expected different things from it than a modern audience would.

The right answer is not Choice (D) because, although audiences in Betterton's time *would* in fact have been used to hearing people speak a different way in daily life, that's not the reason why they would have been less alienated by his performance than modern people would be.

The right answer is not Choice (E) because, although there *are* more types of art today, that's not the reason why Betterton's audience would have considered his style more "realistic" than modern audiences might consider it. They would have considered it realistic because they were used to it, just like audiences do today, no matter how many different types of art there are.

8. **D. So analyzing this idea is tricky because it involves a concept — lifelike/realistic — which is not constant.**

The conclusion to the last paragraph is necessarily also the conclusion to the passage as a whole, so you should pick the sentence that speaks to the main theme of the entire passage — and the main theme of the entire passage is that ideas about what is "lifelike/realistic" change over time.

The right answer is not Choice (A) because the main theme of the entire passage has nothing to do with a comparison between artists and politicians.

The right answer is not Choice (B) because the passage never implies that our ideas about realism today are better or more accurate than past ideas — only that they are different.

The right answer is not Choice (C) because, although the second paragraph mentions Freud, a scientist who was inspired by literature, the passage as a whole is not about a relationship between art and science — it is just about art.

The right answer is not Choice (E) because, although examples from the worlds of both painting and literature are discussed, the passage as a whole is not about painting *versus* literature in any way — it is just about concepts of realism in art of all kinds.

9. **C. nevertheless extremely polite**

"Polite" is an adjective, and adjectives get modified by adverbs. Tom is *extremely* (adverb) *polite* (adjective). *Nevertheless,* another adverb meaning "despite this," is added to modify *extremely,* because Tom's politeness is presented as a surprising contrast to his unusual sense of humor.

The right answer is not Choice (A) because adjectives need to be modified by adverbs, not other adjectives, so saying *extreme polite* doesn't work because *extreme* and *polite* are both adjectives.

The right answer is not Choice (B) because the fact that the verb is "to be" means that you need an adjective, which in turn is modified by an adverb rather than two adverbs, as you might need with another verb.

The right answer is not Choice (D) because things are backwards here: You need an adjective being modified by an adverb, not an adverb being modified by an adjective.

The right answer is not Choice (E) because, although this is *grammatically* a correct sentence, it doesn't make any sense in context. (Watch out for that trick!)

10. **B. I had never driven there before last week**

The speaker of the sentence apparently drove to the restaurant last week (the past tense). The speaker is also stating that he hadn't ever done so prior to that time, so for that you need the *past perfect* tense (for actions that were already performed as of a certain point in the past — the "past of the past," if you will). He *had never driven* there (past perfect tense) before that specific time when he *drove* there (past tense). The fact that the action had *not* been performed doesn't change anything about the tense; it just means you add the word *never* (so *had driven* becomes *had never driven*).

The right answer is not Choice (A) because *have driven* is in the *present perfect tense,* which denotes actions that are presently in the state of being completed ("Yes, I have eaten lunch already").

The right answer is not Choice (C) for two reasons. Firstly, the problem of the present perfect tense from Choice (A) is still there. Secondly, the fact that *although* precedes the first clause and *but* precedes the second means that *both* clauses are dependent, so the sentence is grammatically wrong no matter what tense it's in (you can have *although* before the first clause or *but* before the second, but not both).

The right answer is not Choice (D) because, while the tense (the past perfect) is correct, the fact that *although* precedes the first clause and *but* precedes the second means that *both* clauses are dependent, so the sentence is grammatically wrong (you can have *although* before the first clause or *but* before the second, but not both).

The right answer is not Choice (E) for two reasons. First, the sentence is grammatically wrong because it doesn't contain an independent clause. Second, it doesn't make sense. *Seeing as how* implies causality: How would the fact that you've never driven somewhere before *cause* you to find it in time?

11. **A. they are encouraged to visit**

This is sort of a trick question, but not really. You are so used to being told to say "he or she" in place of "they" *as a singular pronoun* that you may sometimes forget that "they" is, of course, correct when the subject of the sentence *is,* in fact, plural. The subject of this sentence is *students,* which is plural, so *they* is the correct pronoun.

The right answer is not Choice (B) because, although *he or she* would be correct if the subject of the sentence were singular and of unspecified gender, the subject of this sentence is *students,* which is plural.

The right answer is not Choice (C) for two reasons. Firstly, the subject of the sentence is *students,* which is plural, so the singular *one* doesn't agree with it. Secondly, the tense doesn't match: *is visiting* is in the present continuous tense, but the "if/then" structure of the sentence ("If students need to . . . ") implies a future visit, so the student or students would not *already be* visiting the office.

The right answer is not Choice (D) because the subject of the sentence is *students,* which is plural, so *that student,* which is singular, does not agree with it.

The right answer is not Choice (E) because the sentence starts off in the third person ("If students . . . "), so it shouldn't suddenly switch to the second person at the end (a command like "remember to visit" is in the second person, because the reader is being addressed).

12. **E. Just between you and me**

Although some people are in the habit of saying "just between you and I" to try and sound correct, "just between you and me" is actually correct. *Between* is a preposition, and a pronoun that is the object of a preposition should be in the objective case.

The right answer is not Choice (A) for two reasons. Firstly, because *between* is a preposition, the object pronoun should be *me,* not *I.* Secondly, the presence of *it's* (a subject and verb) at the beginning of the first clause makes that clause independent. So the sentence is a comma splice (two independent clauses joined with only a comma), a very serious grammatical error.

The right answer is not Choice (B) because the presence of *it's* (a subject and verb) at the beginning of the first clause makes that clause independent. So the sentence is a comma splice.

The right answer is not Choice (C) for two reasons. Firstly, the speaker has not already been mentioned in the sentence, so there's no reason to use *myself* instead of *me.* Secondly, both clauses are independent (the first clause is a command, but a command is an independent clause), so the sentence is a comma splice.

The right answer is not Choice (D) because *between* is a preposition, so the object pronoun should be *me,* not *I.*

13. **D. everyone found it hilarious when**

The fact that the first clause begins with *since* renders it dependent, so the second clause (the part after the comma) should be independent. You don't need a coordinating conjunction (like *and* or *so*) before the second clause if you already have a subordinating conjunction (like *since* or *although*) before the first one. Oh, and it doesn't matter whether you use *when* or *that* at the end — either is acceptable, so that part of the question is just a red herring.

The right answer is not Choice (A) because it has both a subordinating conjunction *(since)* before the first clause and a coordinating conjunction before the second, so neither clause is independent, which means it's not a complete correct sentence (whether you say *and so* or just *so* doesn't make a difference).

The right answer is not Choice (B) because it has both a subordinating conjunction *(since)* before the first clause and a coordinating conjunction before the second, so neither clause is independent, which means it's not a complete, correct sentence.

The right answer is not Choice (C) because *therefore* is an adverb, not a coordinating conjunction. It can't join two independent clauses without creating a comma splice. If it precedes an independent clause, then *therefore* should begin a new sentence.

The right answer is not Choice (E) because it should be *found it hilarious,* not *found it hilariously.* The first means that in their opinion, it was funny. The second means that the way in which they found it was funny itself.

14. **E. Each year, the affectionate group of old friends would meet**

This is the only answer choice that is both a complete, correct sentence and not redundant (saying both *each year* and *annually* is redundant, because they mean the same thing).

The right answer is not Choice (A) because it is redundant. *Each year* and *annually* mean the same thing, so you don't need to say both.

The right answer is not Choice (B) because it is redundant. (Switching *affectionate* as an adjective modifying *group* to *affectionately* as an adverb modifying *met* is just a distraction — it makes no difference.)

The right answer is not Choice (C) because it is redundant.

The right answer is not Choice (D) because, although it's the only one of the wrong answer choices that's not redundant, it isn't a complete, correct sentence: *the group of old friends to tell* is not a coherent independent clause (the subject and verb do not agree).

15. **A. none of them knowing when the downpour would begin**

This answer choice correctly follows an independent clause with a dependent "afterthought clause" that describes the subject of the independent clause (an afterthought clause is like an appositive, but it comes at the end of the sentence instead of in the middle).

The right answer is not Choice (B) because the final clause is not independent, so you don't need a conjunction after the comma.

The right answer is not Choice (C) because this is an independent clause, as was the clause right before it, so this answer choice creates a comma splice (a very serious grammatical error).

The right answer is not Choice (D) because, although preceding a gerund with a possessive is correct in the proper context (as in "I appreciate *your answering* the telephone"), in this particular context, it doesn't make sense. It's preceded by *without one of,* and the phrase that follows would need to be plural.

The right answer is not Choice (E) because, although this is a *grammatically* correct sentence, it doesn't make sense. (Watch out for that trick!)

16. **D. its constant buzzing was**

Buzzing is a gerund, which means it functions as a noun here, with *constant* as the adjective modifying it. The possessive *its* is the one without the apostrophe (the one with the apostrophe means *it is*), and the possessive *its* is the correct one to use because the phone possesses the buzzing.

The right answer is not Choice (A) because an adverb can't be possessed, so using the possessive *its* before an adverb doesn't work.

The right answer is not Choice (B) because, although the correct version of *its* (the possessive) is used, it's incorrect to say *the buzzing was constant driving me crazy.*

The right answer is not Choice (C) because the *it's* with the apostrophe means *it is.* The possessive is the one without the apostrophe.

The right answer is not Choice (E) because the *it's* with the apostrophe means *it is,* and the phrase *it is constantly was buzzing* doesn't make sense. It combines the present and past tenses in a way that renders it nonsensical.

17. **B. Discouraged by the fact that the old-fashioned coach discouraged controversial subject matter, Samantha decided to quit the speech team.**

This is a "misplaced modifier" question. When there is an initial dependent descriptive clause, the noun that is being described has to begin the subsequent independent clause. *Samantha* is who or what was *discouraged,* so this choice is correct because *Samantha* is the noun that begins the second clause.

The right answer is not Choice (A) because, although the word *Samantha* appears to open the independent clause, it's possessive, so the subject of the independent clause here is actually *Samantha's decision.* Her *decision* wasn't what was *discouraged* — Samantha herself was — so this is a misplaced modifier.

The right answer is not Choice (C) because it's a comma splice, a very serious grammatical error. You can't have two independent clauses joined with only a comma and no conjunction.

The right answer is not Choice (D) for two reasons. First and most importantly, the sentence contains a misplaced modifier, because *a decision* was not who or what was *discouraged* (Samantha herself was). Secondly, the independent clause is in the passive voice, which is considered awkward: Why would you say *a decision was made by Samantha* instead of *Samantha decided?*

The right answer is not Choice (E) for three reasons. Firstly, the word *being* is unnecessary and can simply be omitted. Secondly, the sentence contains a misplaced modifier, because *the speech team* is not who or what was *discouraged* (Samantha was). Thirdly, the independent clause is in the passive voice: Why would you say *the speech team was quit by Samantha* instead of *Samantha quit the speech team?*

18. **C. none of their arguments had any effect**

The third-person plural possessive pronoun is spelled *their,* and the noun that means "result" is spelled *effect.*

The right answer is not Choice (A) because *they're* means "they are," and because *affect* (with an "a") is a verb.

The right answer is not Choice (B) because *there* is the noun for a place, not the possessive, and because *affect* (with an "a") is a verb.

The right answer is not Choice (D) because *they're* means "they are."

The right answer is not Choice (E) because *affect* (with an "a") is a verb.

19. **D. and I**

It should be *take Chris and me home,* because *take* is a verb, and both Chris and the speaker are objects of the verb.

The right answer is not Choice (A) because two things are beautiful (the town and the lake), so the plural *are* is correct.

The right answer is not Choice (B) because the adverb *unfortunately* is correctly used here to describe a state of affairs that the speaker laments (having to get up early).

The right answer is not Choice (C) because *we have to get up early* is perfectly correct. The "no error" questions will frequently underline infinitives, because people are often suspicious of them, but that doesn't mean they're always wrong.

The right answer is not Choice (E) because there is, in fact, an error in the sentence.

20. **B. by**

This is a preposition-choice question. You can say "modeled on" or "modeled after" in this context, but "modeled by" means something else (namely, that the program from the 1980s *itself* modeled the later school's style).

The right answer is not Choice (A) because the adverb *quite* (which is an adverb despite the fact that it doesn't end in "-ly," like *very*) is correctly used to modify the adjective *rigorous*.

The right answer is not Choice (C) because the adjective *fantastic* is correctly used to modify the noun *results,* and this portion of the sentence points out that the earlier program is who or what got these "fantastic results."

The right answer is not Choice (D) because nothing is grammatically incorrect about the construction "back in the 1980s." It may sound a little informal, but it's not wrong.

The right answer is not Choice (E) because there is, in fact, an error in the sentence.

21. **E. No error.**

Believe it or not, there is no error in this sentence. It is grammatically complex, which raises suspicions, but it is, in fact, correct.

The right answer is not Choice (A) because the subsequent independent clause begins with the noun *Megan,* who is, in fact, who or what had *spent nearly an hour,* so there is no misplaced modifier.

The right answer is not Choice (B) because you can say that someone was *relieved,* and you can say that someone was *more than a little confused.* This sentence says both things about Megan, and it says them correctly.

The right answer is not Choice (C) because, although you might think at first that the *that* shouldn't be there, it actually should. When you read the entire sentence, it becomes clear that Megan didn't just *find her shoe;* rather, she *found that her shoe had been in the refrigerator.*

The right answer is not Choice (D) because the bulk of the sentence is in the past tense, but this part of the sentence wants to indicate a *continuous* past, and so it uses *had been.* Yes, you could also say *was* and it wouldn't be wrong, but the fact that you *could also* say it a different way doesn't necessarily mean that the way it's said is incorrect — sometimes, two or more ways of putting something are acceptable.

22. **E. No error.**

Believe it or not, there is no error in this sentence. It is grammatically complex, raising suspicions, but it is, in fact, correct.

The right answer is not Choice (A) because, although *we* is the subjective case, the construction *all of us* means that the subject noun is technically *all*, and that *we* becomes *us* because it is the object of the preposition *of*.

The right answer is not Choice (B) because the speaker is using the first-person plural (referring to herself and others), so the plural *have become* is correct.

The right answer is not Choice (C) because there are three clauses in the sentence: The first and third are independent, and the middle is dependent. The *although* is what renders the middle clause dependent, and the *and* is what connects the first clause to the rest of the sentence.

The right answer is not Choice (D) because, while the construction *it rained more often than we would have liked* may sound a little more formal than the way you would expect a presumably young person to talk, it's not wrong.

23. **D. dubbed repetitively**

Because you're probably used to seeing adverbs follow verbs, this question tries to trick you by creating a situation where that adverb should actually be an adjective. Remember that *dubbed* is a synonym for *called*: People *dubbed* the second album *repetitive*. Convert that to the passive voice (which is necessary here because the subject of the verb is not identified), and you get *the second album was dubbed repetitive*.

The right answer is not Choice (A) because *in contrast to* is the correct construction here.

The right answer is not Choice (B) because *it had been especially hailed* is an acceptable construction, if a little complicated.

The right answer is not Choice (C) because *originality* and *innovativeness* are both nouns, qualities said to belong to the first record. There's nothing wrong with this part of the sentence.

The right answer is not Choice (E) because there is, in fact, an error in the sentence.

24. **E. Richard Nixon, the 37th president, was the first to visit the Far East while in office.**

This question is testing you on three things: where the commas (if any) should go, whether the word *president* needs to be capitalized, and whether the term *Far East* needs to be capitalized. Firstly, as an appositive, *the 37th president* needs to be set off with a pair of commas. Secondly, because it's not being used as a title (in other words, it doesn't precede the name), *president* doesn't need to be capitalized here. Thirdly, *Far East* does need to be capitalized, because it refers to a specific region of the globe rather than to a relative cardinal direction.

The right answer is not Choice (A) because *president* should not be capitalized and *Far East* should.

The right answer is not Choice (B) because *president* should not be capitalized, and because the sentence is missing the necessary comma after the appositive clause.

The right answer is not Choice (C) because *Far East* should be capitalized, and because the sentence is missing the necessary comma after the appositive clause.

The right answer is not Choice (D) because the sentence is missing the necessary comma preceding the appositive clause.

25. **B. You should be careful; the children's toy cars are all over the floor.**

You have two independent clauses, so they can't be separated with just a comma. Either a semicolon *or* a dash is correct, but not a comma. As for the apostrophes, *children's* needs an apostrophe (before the "s," because the word *children* is already plural).

The right answer is not Choice (A) because it's a comma splice, and because the apostrophe in *children's* should be before the "s."

The right answer is not Choice (C) because it's a comma splice, and because *cars* doesn't need an apostrophe.

The right answer is not Choice (D) because the apostrophe in *children's* should be before the "s," and because *cars* doesn't need an apostrophe.

The right answer is not Choice (E) because *children's* needs an apostrophe (before the "s") and *cars* should not have one.

26. **A. This past summer I learned that, although most people assume it is the elephant, the most expensive animal for zoos to keep is actually the panda.**

This question is testing you on three things: the placement of the commas, whether the names of animals should be capitalized, and whether the names of seasons should be capitalized. The correct answers are that neither the names of animals (unless they are the proper names of specific animals, like "Jumbo") nor those of seasons should be capitalized, and that the "although" clause should be set off with a pair of commas, because it's inserted into the middle of the independent clause.

The right answer is not Choice (B) because *summer* should not be capitalized, because the first comma should follow the word *that* rather than precede it, and because the comma after *elephant* is omitted.

The right answer is not Choice (C) because the comma that should precede *although* is omitted, and because *elephant* and *panda* should not be capitalized.

The right answer is not Choice (D) because *summer* should not be capitalized, because the comma that should precede *although* is omitted, and because the punctuation mark after *elephant* should be another comma, not a semicolon.

The right answer is not Choice (E) because the words *summer, elephant,* and *panda* should all be lowercase rather than capitalized.

27. **A. Your friend just called to ask which of his albums it was you wanted to borrow.**

The sentence is a single, uninterrupted, independent clause, so no commas are necessary. The possessive pronoun *your* should be used (as opposed to *you're,* which means *you are*), and none of the words in the sentence require apostrophes.

The right answer is not Choice (B) because *you're* is a contraction of "you are" and is not the possessive pronoun, and because you don't need a comma before *which.* Although an "extra information" *which* clause does need to be preceded by a comma, in this case the *which* simply means "which one," rather than indicating a new clause.

The right answer is not Choice (C) because the prepositional phrase (beginning with *to*) doesn't need to be preceded by a comma, and because *albums* doesn't need an apostrophe, as it is not possessive.

The right answer is not Choice (D) because *you're* is a contraction of "you are" and is not the possessive pronoun, and because there's no reason to insert a semicolon (or any other punctuation mark) anywhere in the sentence.

The right answer is not Choice (E) because *albums* doesn't need an apostrophe, as it is not possessive. There also doesn't need to be a comma before *which.* Finally, you don't need a comma between *was* and *you.*

28. **C. A posted sign said that no guests were permitted in the hotel pool after 10 p.m., however, we went for a swim anyway.**

Choice (C) creates a comma splice. Although *however* should be set off with a pair of commas when it interrupts a single independent clause, it cannot be used to join two independent clauses, no matter how many commas are used. This is the one answer choice that is *not* acceptable; the others are all correct.

The right answer is not Choice (A) because this choice correctly uses a single comma to link a dependent "although" clause with a subsequent independent clause.

The right answer is not Choice (B) because this choice correctly joins two independent clauses with a semicolon.

The right answer is not Choice (D) because this choice correctly separates two independent clauses with a single dash (which works like a semicolon here). The second of the two independent clauses begins with *however,* which is followed by a single comma.

The right answer is not Choice (E) because this choice correctly presents a single independent clause that is interrupted by a non-limiting, "extra information" *which* clause, which is set off by a pair of commas.

29. **D. their's**

The possessive adjective *theirs* does not require an apostrophe.

The right answer is not Choice (A) because capitalizing *White House* is correct, as it is the name of a specific place.

The right answer is not Choice (B) because capitalizing *tour guide* isn't necessary, as it's the name of a job and not a specific proper noun.

The right answer is not Choice (C) because no commas or any other changes are necessary in this portion of the sentence. It is correct as it is.

The right answer is not Choice (E) because there is, in fact, an error in this sentence.

30. **B. season; but**

The punctuation between *season* and *but* should be a comma, not a semicolon. A comma links two independent clauses when the second independent clause opens with a conjunction; a semicolon is used when there is no conjunction.

The right answer is not Choice (A) because this is the correct version of *it's* (the one with the apostrophe, which means "it is").

The right answer is not Choice (C) because it's correct to capitalize both *Springfield,* as it is the name of a city or town, and *Lions,* because here it is the name of a sports team and not the type of animal.

The right answer is not Choice (D) because *they'd* is an acceptable contraction for "they would."

The right answer is not Choice (E) because there is, in fact, an error in this sentence.

31. **E. No error.**

There are no errors in the sentence, in terms of either word choice or punctuation.

The right answer is not Choice (A) because this *who* clause is a limiting one that provides essential distinguishing information (as opposed to an "extra information" clause), so no comma is necessary before it.

The right answer is not Choice (B) because *people* is plural, so the plural *were* is correct.

The right answer is not Choice (C) because when two people both possess something, the convention is to make only the second of the two names possessive.

The right answer is not Choice (D) because the *cream cheese and cucumber rolls* are a single item, so no comma is needed before the word *and.*

32. **C. holiday, and**

The noun *Emily* is performing both the verb *considers* and the verb *notices;* because a single subject is performing both verbs, a comma should not separate the two verb phrases.

The right answer is not Choice (A) because *Facebook* should indeed be capitalized, as it's the proper name of a company.

The right answer is not Choice (B) because *Valentine's Day* (which includes an apostrophe) and *Emily* are all proper nouns and should indeed be capitalized.

The right answer is not Choice (D) because, as a contraction for "she is," *she's* needs an apostrophe, and because no comma is necessary before the conjunction *or,* as it precedes neither a new independent clause nor a complement.

The right answer is not Choice (E) because there is, in fact, an error in the sentence.

33. **A. today's standards, but the**

This is that common trick about "doubling up" on conjunctions. There is a subordinating conjunction *(while)* before the first independent clause and a coordinating conjunction *(and)* before the second, which is incorrect. You need one or the other, but not both.

The right answer is not Choice (B) because *President* does need to be capitalized here, as it precedes a specific president's name.

The right answer is not Choice (C) because, as a proper noun, *Gettysburg Address* does need to be capitalized.

The right answer is not Choice (D) because "odd but now famous" is a single adjectival phrase; the conjunction *but* does not precede an independent clause or a complement, so no comma is needed before it.

The right answer is not Choice (E) because there is, in fact, an error in the sentence.

34. **B. MLA and APA style citations.**

MLA (for *Modern Language Association*) format and APA (for *American Psychological Association*) format are the two citation formats generally used in American schools.

The right answer is not Choice (A) because, although MLA is correct, UDA is a trick (it stands for *Ulster Defence Association,* a royalist vigilante squad that operated in Northern Ireland in the 1970s).

The right answer is not Choice (C) because, although APA is correct, IRL is a trick (it stands for *In Real Life,* an acronym used on the Internet to refer to events taking place in the non-Internet world).

The right answer is not Choice (D) because IRL stands for *In Real Life,* and because SDS stands for *Students for a Democratic Society,* a left-wing protest organization from the 1960s. Neither acronym refers to a citation format.

The right answer is not Choice (E) because neither acronym refers to a citation format.

35. **C. dictionaries used to look up words in primary sources**

Students are not required to list dictionaries that they merely used to look up words in a Works Cited page. Technically, you should list a dictionary in the Works Cited page if you quoted directly from the dictionary, but instructors generally dissuade students from quoting the dictionary in papers.

The right answer is not Choice (A) because *secondary sources* refers to all the sources consulted aside from the primary text that the paper is about — so you sure had better list those!

The right answer is not Choice (B) because, even though they're on the Internet (and often silly), if you did indeed use YouTube videos as sources, then you need to list them in the Works Cited page like any other source.

The right answer is not Choice (D) because sources still need to be cited even if they're not copyrighted. As for the fact that they are *blogs,* citation format doesn't discriminate against the Internet — sources are sources.

The right answer is not Choice (E) because you need to list all consulted sources in the Works Cited page, regardless of whether you quoted from them directly. Only quoted sources would end up with in-text citations, but quoted and nonquoted sources alike belong in the Works Cited page.

36. **E. block quoting.**

The convention described is known as *block quoting*.

The other answer choices are not right because *double quoting, Chicago quoting, ghost quoting,* and *hyperquoting* don't exist. They're simply made-up terms.

37. **B. *et al.***

The abbreviation *et al.* is short for *et alii*, or "and others."

The right answer is not Choice (A) because *ibid.* (short for *ibidem*, or "in the same place") is the abbreviation used in footnotes to signify that the source is the same as that of the previous footnote.

The right answer is not Choice (C) because *id est* means "that is." It's what the common abbreviation *i.e.* stands for (not to be confused with *e.g.*, which stands for *exempli gratia*, or "for example").

The right answer is not Choice (D) because *populusque* means "and the people."

The right answer is not Choice (E) because *ex urbe* means "from out of the city."

38. **A. the title of a poem.**

The convention is that the title of an entire or whole work should be in italics, whereas the title of a part of a whole should be in quotation marks. Because an individual poem is one part of a book of poems, the title of a poem is in quotation marks (and the title of the entire poetry collection is in italics).

The right answer is not Choice (B) because the title of an album should be in italics (and the title of a song from that album should be in quotation marks).

The right answer is not Choice (C) because the title of a TV show should be in italics (and the title of an episode of that show should be in quotation marks).

The right answer is not Choice (D) because the title of a film should be in italics.

The right answer is not Choice (E) because the title of a newspaper should be in italics (and the title of a single article or editorial from that newspaper should be in quotation marks).

39. **D. abstract.**

The overview that appears at the beginning of a research paper is called the *abstract*.

The other choices are not right because nothing in academic writing is called the *impression,* the *opinion,* the *assessment,* or the *cornerstone.* They're just made-up terms.

40. **D. the retention of profanity in direct quotations.**

Research can be done about absolutely any topic under the sun, and direct quotes are direct quotes. If the person you are quoting used profanity and you have a good reason to quote that person, then the profanity stays.

The right answer is not Choice (A) because writing from the first-person point of view (that is, using the first-person pronoun "I" or making reference to oneself) is generally considered unacceptable in a research paper.

The right answer is not Choice (B) because employing the second-person (that is, addressing the reader, as in "If *you* were to . . . ") is generally considered unacceptable in a research paper.

The right answer is not Choice (C) because the rule against using contractions in formal writing (such as a research paper) is still generally observed.

The right answer is not Choice (E) because, while there's no "rule" against it as such, every professor strongly discourages the "middle-school" move of opening a paper by quoting from the dictionary.

Argumentative Essay

Take a look at the following essay written in response to the opinion that's presented in Chapter 14. To score your own essay, flip back to Chapter 11, where you can find a checklist to help you evaluate your own writing.

I have sympathy for the opinion expressed, because I can see how someone who misunderstood Epicureanism could come to the conclusion that it is a selfish philosophy that can be blamed for the supposed collapse of modern society — but the fact is that the person who wrote this condemnation has clearly misunderstood Epicurus and his philosophy.

Based on a simple description, it might seem that Epicureanism simply amounts to saying, "if it feels good, do it." But this is not what the philosophy means. When Epicureans talk about "pleasure," they don't simply mean short-term physical joy of the sort one might obtain by partying all the time with no thought for tomorrow or the feelings of others. Rather, "pleasure" in this sense means true happiness, which often involves both planning for the future and being kind to others. For example, although spending all your money at the bar might bring you happiness today, you wouldn't be very happy in another few weeks when you were unable to pay your rent; as for being good to others, this is the only way of making and keeping friends, and almost everyone agrees that friendship and the good opinion of others are necessary for a happy life.

Many people feel as if someone who says, "I just want to be happy" is being unintellectual or even selfish, but why should that be? After all, if you ask any parent what he or she wants out of life for his or her child, that parent will almost certainly say that he or she wants the child to be happy. Certainly, it is safe to assume that a loving parent inherently wants what is best for their child — and if that's almost always identified as "happiness," then why on earth should we feel as if this goal is silly?

Though the word "pleasure" conjures up stereotypical images of sex, drugs, and rock 'n' roll for many people, all it really means is the avoidance of pain. I don't believe that anyone in the world genuinely wants pain for himself or for others unless he has been philosophically corrupted by some political or religious system that teaches him to hate. Every just political system that has ever been developed is concerned with the life satisfaction of the citizenry, so if "the pursuit of happiness" was good enough for Thomas Jefferson in the Declaration of Independence, then why shouldn't it be good enough for us today? Many religious people look upon pleasure-based philosophies with suspicion, but even Jesus spends most of his time in the gospels telling people to love and be good to one another, and presumably, this is so people will be happy.

The fact that Epicureanism is an entirely responsible philosophy becomes very clear when we define pleasure as the absence of pain. I certainly don't have a better idea than to say that the primary moral duty in life is to avoid making other people suffer. Granted, different philosophical and religious schools have different ideas about what causes suffering: A Buddhist thinks that suffering is caused by attachment to worldly things, and a Platonist thinks that suffering is caused by ignorance of divinely inspired right action. But they are still in agreement that suffering is bad. If suffering is bad, then the opposite of suffering is good, and the opposite of suffering is happiness. I think if everyone took a step back now and then to remember that, no matter our philosophical or political backgrounds, we are all trying to create a just world in which people will be free to pursue their own personal fulfillment, then we might not fight so much (fighting, after all, causes suffering).

Even the Hippocratic Oath that doctors take begins with the words "First, do no harm." That sounds like a pretty solid philosophical starting point to me, no matter what you do for a living. An individual might believe in one god, or many gods, or no god, but as far as I can tell, no god or gods would prefer a world with more suffering in it to one with more happiness in it — and so, from this perspective, Epicureanism isn't even incompatible with Platonism. All one has to do to resolve the two is to suggest that the nature of metaphysical goodness at the center of Platonic philosophy *is* happiness itself. I certainly don't have a better suggestion, do you?

Source-Based Essay

Take a look at the following essay written about methods of reasoning about morality. To score your own essay, flip back to Chapter 11, where you can find a checklist to help you evaluate your own writing.

Both passages address a fairly simple question, but one that has confounded philosophers for as long as philosophers have existed: In cases where the answer is not obvious, how are human beings to distinguish right from wrong (or perhaps, right from less right)? Unlike scientific truths, arguments about morality cannot be proven in the traditional sense, so even as humanity's technical knowledge about the world has increased, our relationship to this question has remained the same.

Most people, of course, are satisfied with the idea that murder or theft is wrong, but what about the question of whether a wealthy person — or even an average person — is morally obligated to give to charity? As Mark White explains it, a utilitarian philosopher might argue that he is, on the grounds that his donations would increase the amount of happiness (or reduce the amount of suffering) in the world (White, 2008). The homeless people who are saved from starvation by the meals that his donations buy them benefit more from the money than the wealthy man would if he kept it, so if the wealthy man is a utilitarian, then he must give. But the question of how much he should give is still up in the air. Is he obligated to give away money until he is no richer than the average person?

People who are uncomfortable with the gray areas of utilitarianism might decide to become deontologists, whom White describes as strict adherents to some objective list of "good actions" and "bad actions." But White admits that, even for deontologists, there are exceptions, such as "killing in self-defense" (White, 2008). We might also include the traditional example of the man who steals in order to feed his starving family. But exceptions like this make deontology fall apart — if there are exceptions to moral absolutes, then who gets to decide what the exceptions are? Absolutes with exceptions aren't really absolutes anymore, are they?

The ancient idea of "virtue ethics" as outlined by Aristotle and explained by Stephen Kershnar might be a way around this. Rather than attempting to make moral decisions by weighing external factors, such as a utilitarian would do in appealing to aggregate happiness or as a deontologist might do in appealing to "objective" lists of good and bad actions, a virtue ethicist would imagine a stereotypically "good" person and ask himself how this person would behave in such-and-such a situation (Kershnar, 2008). Someone who asks, for example, "What would Mahatma Gandhi have done in this situation?" is using virtue ethics. The system could work just as well with a fictional character as with a historical figure; a comic-book fan, for instance, might ask himself, "What would Superman do?" But the way I see it, there are pitfalls with virtue ethics as well. Can a regular person reasonably be expected always to act in the way that someone as virtuous as Gandhi would have? And of course, nobody really has the powers and abilities of Superman — he would risk nothing by flying into a burning building to save people, but I stand a good chance of losing my life if I attempt to do so. Am I morally obligated to act the same way as someone who would be risking far less than I would by performing the same good deed?

These readings, and the questions they prompt us to ask ourselves, outline the fundamental problem with moral reasoning and the ways in which it is very different from scientific reasoning. We can now say we know for a fact that force equals mass times acceleration or that the earth is 90 million miles from the sun, but we are no closer to knowing when — if ever — it is acceptable to tell a lie than we were thousands of years ago. To the vast majority of people, it somehow feels less wrong to download a song without paying for it than to shoplift a CD from a store, and yet we can't fully explain what the difference is. We probably shouldn't simply shrug our shoulders and say that morality is just a subjective matter of our feelings — after all, the fact that mean people don't have the same feelings as nice people is how we tell the difference between mean and nice people — and yet, even though they have been trying for centuries, some of the smartest people in history have been unable to come up with a better idea.

Part 3: Mathematics

1. **D. $2x + 5$**

   Twice Jan's age is $2x$, and 7 more than that is $2x + 7$, which represents Frank's current age. Frank's age 2 years ago is 2 less than that, or $2x + 5$.

2. **B. 76**

$$8x + 3 + 2x + 8x + 3 + 2x = 20x + 6$$
$$20x + 6 = 46$$
$$20x = 40$$
$$x = 2$$
$$length = 8(2) + 3 = 19$$
$$width = 2(2) = 4$$
$$A = lw$$
$$A = (19)(4)$$
$$A = 76$$

   By adding the four side measures in terms of x, you get the expression $20x + 6$ for the perimeter. If you set that equal to 46 and solve the equation, you can determine that $x = 2$. Then, you can put 2 in for x in the length and width expressions to find that the length is 19 and the width is 4. Because the area of a rectangle is length times width, the area of this rectangle is $A = (19)(4)$, which is 76.

3. **C. $1\frac{1}{2}$, -2, $\frac{11}{3}$, 5, -7.53**

   Magnitude is the same as absolute value, or positive distance from 0. You can get the absolute values of all the numbers by dropping the negative signs from the negative numbers and leaving the positive numbers positive. If you convert all the numbers to the same form, such as decimals or improper fractions, you can more easily see the order of the magnitudes from least to greatest.

4. **A. 93**

   Because a mean is the sum of all items of data divided by the number of items of data, you can add all the test scores and a variable representing the missing test score and then divide that sum by the number of test scores, which is 6. If you set that ratio equal to 85 and solve for the variable, you can determine that the missing test score is 93.

$$\frac{(83 + 72 + 94 + 100 + 68 + x)}{6} = 85$$
$$\frac{417 + x}{6} = 85$$
$$417 + x = 510$$
$$417 + x - 417 = 510 - 417$$
$$x = 93$$

5. **D. 62 degrees**

   $\angle 1$ and $\angle 2$ form a linear pair, so they are supplementary and therefore have measures with a sum of 180 degrees. Because $\angle 1$ is 118 degrees, $\angle 2$ must be 62 degrees because $180 - 118$ is 62.

6. **E. –3a – 2b**

   Only like terms can be combined. $9a$ and $-12a$ are like terms because they have exactly the same variable with the same exponent, which is understood to be 1, and their sum is $-3a$. $3b$ and $-5b$ are like terms with a sum of $-2b$. $-3a$ and $-2b$ are not like terms, so they cannot be combined into a single term.

7. **A. 20**

   You can determine the factors of 40 and 60 by writing each as a product of factors and writing each of those factors as products of factors, and so forth, until each is written as a product of prime factors. By multiplying every possible combination of prime factors for each, you can find all the factors of each number. Of the choices given, the greatest common factor of 40 and 60 is 20.

8. **C. None of the marketing experts are computer technology experts.**

   In the Venn diagram, the figures representing marketing and computer technology do not overlap. That means none of the marketing experts are also computer experts. None of the other statements express correct situations concerning overlapping areas of expertise.

9. **A. $\dfrac{p-3}{p-7}$**

   By using reverse FOIL for the top and bottom expressions, you can see that the top is $(p + 5)(p - 3)$ and the bottom expression is $(p + 5)(p - 7)$. Because $p + 5$ is a factor of both the top and bottom expressions, it can be cancelled, leaving $\dfrac{p-3}{p-7}$.

10. **A. 65**

    65 is 1 greater than 64, which is the square of the integer 8. 65 is not a prime number. All of the other choices are 1 greater than the square of an integer, but they are prime numbers.

11. **E. 14**

    By writing each number as a product of factors and writing each of those factors as products of factors where possible, and continuing the process until both 42 and 28 are written as products of all prime factors, you can multiply every possible combination of prime factors to find the other factors. Then, look for the common factors of 42 and 28 and find the largest of them. It is 14. Choices (A), (C), and (D) are factors of 42 and 28, but none of them are greater than 14. Choice (B) is not a common factor of 42 and 28 because it is not a factor of 28.

12. **E. –43**

    By solving the first equation, you can see that $x = 8$. If you put 8 in for x in the second equation, the equation has a value of –43.

    $$3x - 7 = 17$$
    $$+7 = +7$$
    $$3x = 24$$
    $$x = 8$$
    $$-8x + 21$$
    $$-8(8) + 21$$
    $$-64 + 21$$
    $$-43$$

13. **D. 260 cm³**

    This problem requires you to take what you know and use it to work your way to what you don't know.

The formula for the volume of a pyramid is $\frac{1}{3}Bh$. The volume and height of the pyramid are given, so you can put those values into the formula and solve for B, base area. This process reveals that the base area is 144 cm².

The base is a square, so the sides have equal measures. The measure of a side times itself gives the area of the square, so a side is equal to the square root of the area. The square root of 144 is 12, so each side is 12 cm.

That means the distance from the center of the square base to the midpoint of one of its sides is 6 cm. The center-midpoint segment, the segment representing the height of the pyramid, and a segment representing the slant height of the pyramid form a right triangle. By using the Pythagorean theorem, $a^2 + b^2 = c^2$, you can determine that the slant height of the pyramid is approximately 10.8 cm.

With the information gathered so far, you have what you need to use the formula for the surface area of a pyramid, which is $\frac{1}{2}$ times perimeter times slant height. By putting the known values into the formula, you can conclude that the surface area of the pyramid, to the nearest whole number, is 260 cm³.

14. **C. –30**

By following the order of operations, or GEMDAS (grouping symbols, exponents, multiplication and division from left to right, addition and subtraction from left to right), you start with the innermost grouping symbols, the parentheses. You must follow GEMDAS within them by multiplying before you subtract. The value within the parentheses is 9. Then you must use the exponent by squaring 9 to get 81. Next, subtract 5 from 81 to get 76. At this point, the value within the brackets has been determined. $26 - 76 = -50$, and $-50 + 20 = -30$. The other choices can be reached through uses of false orders of operations.

$$26 - \left[(9 \cdot 12 - 9 \cdot 11)^2 - 5\right] + 20$$
$$26 - \left[(108 - 99)^2 - 5\right] + 20$$
$$26 - \left[(9)^2 - 5\right] + 20$$
$$26 - \left[(81) - 5\right] + 20$$
$$26 - 76 + 20$$
$$-50 + 20$$
$$-30$$

15. **A. The mean is greater than the median.**

The mean can be determined by adding all the data figures and then dividing by the number of data figures. The mean is 63.666 . . .

The median is found by putting the data in order from least to greatest and determining the middle number or the average of two middle numbers. In this case, it is a single middle number, 76.

The mode is the number that appears the highest number of times in the set. That number is 41.

Using the exact numbers for mean, median, and mode, you can compare them and determine that the only false statement is Choice (A). The mean is 63.666. . ., which is not greater than the median, 76. All of the other statements are true.

16. **E. The domain element –1 is paired with two range elements.**

A relation is a function as long as every domain element is paired with only one range element. The relation here has the domain element –1 paired with both 3 and 9. That's why the relation isn't a function. None of the other choices concern a domain element being paired with more than one range element.

17. **B. 30 miles**

By using the Pythagorean theorem, $a^2 + b^2 = c^2$, you can determine that the missing side measure is 12 miles. Then you can add the side measures to get the perimeter, which is 30 miles.

$$a^2 + b^2 = c^2$$
$$5^2 + b^2 = 13^2$$
$$25 + b^2 = 169$$
$$b^2 = 169 - 25$$
$$b^2 = 144$$
$$b = \sqrt{144}$$
$$b = 12$$
$$5 + 12 + 13 = 30$$

18. **B. 144**

Because two of the factors are negative and 2 is an even number, the answer is positive. The product of the absolute values is 144. The answer is therefore 144. Choice (C) involves the false conclusion that the answer is negative. The other choices involve miscalculations in multiplying absolute values, and Choice (E) also involves the wrong sign.

19. **C. 60**

Because the stem numbers represent tens and the leaf numbers represent ones, according to the key, all of the choices are numbers represented in the stem-and-leaf plot except 60. No 0 is a leaf where 6 is the stem.

20. **A. 36**

By translating the sentence into mathematical language, you can get the equation $27 = 0.75x$, where x represents the unknown. Solving the equation reveals that x is 36. The other choices can result from incorrect translations of the question.

21. **D. (–7, 4), (–9, 10), (2, 3), and (2, 12)**

The vertices of the quadrilateral before the translation are (–3, –3), (–5, 3), (6, –4), and (6, 5). To translate the quadrilateral 7 units up and 4 units left, add 7 to each y-coordinate and subtract 4 from each x-coordinate. The resulting coordinates are (–7, 4), (–9, 10), (2, 3), and (2, 12). The other choices can result from performing the wrong operations on the original coordinates or placing them in incorrect orders, or both.

22. **B. $\frac{1}{8}$**

A fraction of a number is equal to the fraction times that number. Wade eats $\frac{1}{2}$ of $\frac{1}{4}$ of the pie, so he eats $\frac{1}{2} \cdot \frac{1}{4}$. The product of those fractions is the product of the numerators over the product of the denominators, so the product is $\frac{1}{8}$. That is the fraction of the pie eaten by Wade. Choice (A) results from subtracting $\frac{1}{4}$ from $\frac{1}{2}$. Choice (C) results from adding the fractions.

23. **E. 10**

To solve the equation, get the variable by itself on one side of the equal sign. You can do this by undoing everything being done to the variable by doing the opposite. You can subtract 5 from both sides to undo adding 5 and then divide both sides by 3 to undo multiplying by 3. The result is the equation $q = 10$, which tells you the value of q. You can check the solution by putting 10 into the equation in place of q and seeing that the result is a true equation.

$$3q + 5 = 35$$
$$-5 = -5$$
$$\frac{3q}{3} = \frac{30}{3}$$
$$q = 10$$

24. **A. 10**

The sum of the Japanese and Greek percentages is 22 percent. That figure subtracted from the percentage for Mexican (24 percent) is 2 percent. Two percent of 500 is 0.02(500), which is 10. You could find the numbers of people represented by each percentage first, but finding the difference of the percentages first is probably easier.

25. **C. 8**

By placing each variable value into the equation in place of the variable, you get an equation without variables. From there, you can follow the order of operations. A fraction bar is a grouping symbol, so the parentheses on top are within a grouped part of the fraction. The value within the parentheses is 2, the square of which is 4. The product of 4 and 4 is 16, and 8(10) – 16, or 80 – 16, is 64. Therefore, the value of the numerator is 64. The denominator is 11 + (–3), so the value of the denominator is 8. A fraction represents the numerator divided by the denominator: $\frac{64}{8} = 8$.

$$\frac{8(10) - 4(-3+5)^2}{11 + (-3)} = \frac{80 - 4(2)^2}{8} = \frac{80 - 16}{8} = \frac{64}{8} = 8$$

The other choices represent numbers that can be reached as a result of using wrong orders of operations and miscalculations.

26. **B. Asking questions of every tenth worker who walks through the main entrance for work**

Asking questions of every tenth person who walks through the main entrance would most likely result in answers from people of varying departments and other categories that may affect poll results. The other choices involve samples that lack diversity and could therefore cause biased results.

27. **E. 225π cm^3**

The formula for the volume of a cone is $\frac{1}{3}Bh$, where B represents base area and h represents the height of the cone. The base of a cone is a circle, so the base area of a cone is πr^2, with r representing the radius of the base. Using the formula, you can determine that the volume of the bigger cone is 405π cm^3, and the volume of the smaller cone is 180π cm^3. The volume of the larger cone minus the volume of the smaller cone is therefore 225π cm^3.

$$\text{Larger} = \frac{1}{3}\pi r^2 h$$

$$\frac{1}{3}\pi(9)^2 15 = \frac{1,215\pi}{3} = 405\pi \ cm^3$$

$$\text{Smaller} = \frac{1}{3}\pi r^2 h$$

$$\frac{1}{3}\pi(6)^2 15 = \frac{540\pi}{3} = 180\pi \ cm^3$$

$$405\pi \ cm^3 - 180\pi \ cm^3 = 225\pi \ cm^3$$

28. **D. 27,300**

Because "deca" is three places in the larger direction from "centi" on the list of metric prefixes, you can move the decimal three places to the right to get the answer. All of the other choices involve moving the decimal incorrectly.

29. **E. 36**

You can use a variable to represent Eric's age and 9 times that variable to represent Natasha's age. Then you can write an equation based on the situation described. The sum of their ages in 10 years can be represented by $x + 10 + 9x + 10$, which is equal to 60. By solving the equation $x + 10 + 9x + 10 = 60$, you can determine that x is 4, so Natasha's age is 9(4), or 36. Choice (A) is the sum of their ages in 10 years, Choice (B) is Eric's age in 10 years, Choice (C) is Natasha's age in 10 years, and Choice (D) is Eric's current age.

$$\text{Eric} = x$$
$$\text{Natasha} = 9x$$
$$x + 10 + 9x + 10 = 60$$
$$10x + 20 = 60$$
$$10x + 20 - 20 = 60 - 20$$
$$10x = 40$$
$$\frac{10x}{10} = \frac{40}{10}$$
$$x = 4$$
$$\text{Eric} = 4$$
$$\text{Natasha} = 9(4) = 36$$

30. **B. 1/98**

The hat contains 14 marbles, 2 of which are blue and 1 of which is orange. Because probability is determined by dividing the number of qualifying outcomes over the number of possible outcomes, the probability of picking a blue marble is 2/14, or 1/7. The probability of picking an orange marble is 1/14. The probability of picking both is the product of the two fractions, or 1/98. Choice (C) results from adding the probabilities instead of multiplying them. Choice (D) is merely the probability of choosing a blue marble.

31. **C. 23**

The answer can be reached by adding the numbers from left to right, or really in any order. You can treat the subtraction of 5 as the addition of –5. They're the same thing. Also, adding –6 is the same as subtracting 6.

$$5 + 7 + (-6) - 5 + 22 = 12 + (-6) - 5 + 22$$
$$= 6 - 5 + 22$$
$$= 1 + 22$$
$$= 23$$

32. **C. 4**

To solve a proportion, you can cross multiply and use the resulting equation. In this case, the resulting equation is $21x = 7(12)$.

$$21x = 7(12)$$
$$21x = 84$$
$$\frac{21x}{21} = \frac{84}{21}$$
$$x = 4$$

33. **D. 72**

Using the Pythagorean theorem, the legs have measures of 65 and j because the legs of a right triangle form the right angle. By adding the squares of those measures, you get the square of the measure of the other side, the hypotenuse. This can be expressed in an equation. If you solve the equation for j, you find the value of j, which is 72. The other choices involve miscalculations that can result when solving the equation.

$$a^2 + b^2 = c^2$$
$$65^2 + b^2 = 97^2$$
$$4225 + b^2 = 9409$$
$$b^2 = 9409 - 4225$$
$$b^2 = 5184$$
$$b = \sqrt{5184}$$
$$b = 72$$

34. **A.** $-3\frac{3}{4}$

$-\frac{19}{4}$, -3.71, and all the answer choices can be written as improper fractions, mixed numbers, or decimals. When they're all in the same form, you can see which numbers are greater than others. For example, $-3\frac{3}{4}$ is the only choice that is between $-\frac{19}{4}$ and -3.71, which can be written as $-4\frac{3}{4}$ and $-3\frac{71}{100}$ by converting to mixed numbers.

35. **A. 127.5**

The set of data doesn't have just one middle number; it has two middle numbers. When the numbers are in order from least to greatest, the two middle numbers are 37 and 218. The mean of those two numbers is the median of the set of data, and that mean is 127.5, so 127.5 is the median of the set of data.

Choice (B) is the mean of the two numbers that are in the middle before the set of data is placed in order. Choice (C) is one of the two middle numbers, but because there are two, it can't be the median. The same is true of Choice (D). Choice (E) is the mean of the set of data.

36. **C.** $\frac{2}{3}$

Replace x with 6 in the rational expression.

$$\frac{(6-4)^2 + 8}{6+12} = \frac{(2)^2 + 8}{18} = \frac{4+8}{18} = \frac{12}{18} \div \frac{6}{6} = \frac{2}{3}$$

By using the order of operations and simplifying the resulting fraction, you can conclude that if $x = 6$, the expression $= \frac{2}{3}$. The other choices result from using incorrect orders of operations.

37. **C. 10**

Because the rectangles are similar, their lengths and widths are in proportion. You can set up a proportion involving ratios of corresponding sides. You have several options for this. One proportion you can use is $\frac{10}{25} = \frac{4}{q}$. The solution to the proportion is the value of q, which is 10.

$$\frac{10}{25} = \frac{4}{q}$$
$$10q = (25)(4)$$
$$10q = 100$$
$$q = 10$$

38. **B. –57**

By solving the first equation, you can find that the value of k is 5. Then you can put 5 in for k in the second equation to get –57.

$$7k - 2k + 28 = 10k + 3$$
$$5k + 28 = 10k + 3$$
$$5k - 10k + 28 = 10k - 10k + 3$$
$$-5k + 28 = 3$$
$$-5k + 28 - 28 = 3 - 28$$
$$-5k = -25$$
$$\frac{-5k}{-5} = \frac{-25}{-5}$$
$$k = 5$$
$$-8k - 17$$
$$-8(5) - 17$$
$$-40 - 17$$
$$-57$$

39. **D. 6**

    x is 20 less than y, or $y - 20$.

    z is 14 less than y, or $y - 14$.

    The issue is how $y - 20$ compares to $y - 14$. You can subtract one from the other to find out.

    $y - 14 - (y - 20) = -14 - (-20)$, or $-14 + 20$, which is 6.

    Because $z - x$ is 6, z is 6 greater than x.

40. **A. 1/16**

    Every time a coin with heads and tails is flipped, the probability that it will land on heads is 1/2. The probability of multiple events is the product of the probabilities of the individual events. $\left(\frac{1}{2}\right)\left(\frac{1}{2}\right)\left(\frac{1}{2}\right)\left(\frac{1}{2}\right) = \left(\frac{1}{16}\right)$. Choices (B), (C), and (D) result from multiplying 1/2 by itself incorrect numbers of times. Choice (D) results from multiplying 1/2 by 2.

41. **B. 20 percent**

    Mark hit the ball 48 out of 60 times he was up at bat, which converts to 80 percent. If Mark hit the ball 80 percent of the time, then he struck out 20 percent of the time he was up at bat.

42. **C. $-608\frac{3}{32}$**

    The best way to multiply mixed numbers is to convert them to improper fractions. To multiply fractions, put the product of the numerators over the product of the denominators. You can then convert the result to a mixed number if necessary. The answer in this case is $-608\frac{3}{32}$. The answer is negative because an odd number of negative numbers are factors in the multiplication.

    $$\left(9\frac{2}{3}\right)\left(-7\frac{5}{8}\right)\left(8\frac{1}{4}\right) =$$
    $$\left(\frac{29}{3}\right)\left(\frac{-61}{8}\right)\left(\frac{33}{4}\right) = \frac{-58,377}{96} = -608\frac{3}{32}$$

43. **A. 94**

    The angle that is w degrees is a vertical angle to an angle in the quadrilateral, as is the 110-degree angle. All vertical angles are congruent, so those are the measures of two of the angles of the quadrilateral. The 117-degree angle is supplementary to another angle in the quadrilateral, and the 93-degree angle is vertical to the remaining one. The interior angles of a quadrilateral have a sum of 360 degrees. By adding the angle measures of the quadrilateral and setting the sum equal to 360 degrees, you can solve for w. The result is 94 degrees. The other choices result from combinations of mixing the rules of supplementary angles with those of vertical angles.

44. E. 99

The range can be determined by subtracting the lowest number from the highest number. In this case, that's 101 – 2, or 99. Choice (A) is the highest number, Choice (B) is the lowest number, Choice (C) is the mode, and Choice (D) is the median.

45. B. $\frac{r}{3} - p = 22$

A third of r can be written as $\frac{r}{3}$ and p less than that as $\frac{r}{3} - p$. All of the other choices involve false representations of those expressions.

46. B. 32,768

The sequence is geometric, which means that every number in the sequence is multiplied by the same number to get the next one. For this sequence, the number multiplied by each time is 4. By picking up at 128 and multiplying by 4 another 4 times (to reach the 8th term), you get 32,768.

2, 8, 32, 128, 512, 2,048, 8,192, 32,768, 131,072

Choice (A) is the 9th term in the sequence, and Choice (C) is the 7th term in the sequence. Choice (D) is the number you need to multiply by each time, and Choice (E) is 128 multiplied by 2.

47. A. 10π

Using the formula for the area of a circle, $A = \pi r^2$, you can determine that the radius of the circle is 5. From there, you can use the formula for the circumference of a circle, $C = 2\pi r$, to determine that the circumference of the circle is 10π. The other choices can result from using formulas with slight errors.

48. B. (4, 7)

x is 4, and y is 7. One method you can use to find the solution is elimination. By multiplying both sides of the top equation by 2 and both sides of the bottom equation by –3, you get two equations in which the coefficient of x is the same.

$$3x - 2y = -2$$
$$2(3x - 2y) = 2(-2)$$
$$6x - 4y = -4$$

$$2x - 3y = -13$$
$$-3(2x - 3y) = -3(-13)$$
$$-6x + 9y = 39$$

You can subtract the resulting bottom equation from the top one to get rid of x.

$$6x - 4y = -4$$
$$-6x + 9y = 39$$
$$\overline{\hspace{2cm}}$$
$$5y = 35$$

Then solve for y, which is 7.

$$\frac{5y}{5} = \frac{35}{5}$$
$$y = 7$$

You can then put 7 in for y to determine that x is 4.

$$3x - 2(7) = -2$$
$$3x - 14 = -2$$
$$3x = -2 + 14$$
$$3x = 12$$
$$x = 4$$

You can put the solution into both equations to see that it works for them.

49. **C. 9**

The mode is the number that is in the set of data the highest number of times. That number is 9. Choice (A) is the lowest number, Choice (B) is the highest number, Choice (D) is the median, and Choice (E) is the mean.

50. **B. $\frac{2}{9}$**

To simplify a fraction, determine the greatest common factor of the numerator and denominator. For $\frac{18}{81}$, it is 9. Next, put the number of times the greatest common factor goes into the numerator over the number of times it goes into the denominator. 9 goes into 18 two times and 81 nine times. The simplified form of $\frac{18}{81}$ is therefore $\frac{2}{9}$.

51. **E. $h > 5$**

To solve an inequality, follow the rules of solving equations. However, the inequality sign must change directions if you switch the sides or multiply or divide both sides by a negative number.

$$7h - 4 < 10h - 19$$
$$7h - 4 - 7h < 10h - 19 - 7h$$
$$-4 < 3h - 19$$
$$-4 + 19 < 3h - 19 + 19$$
$$15 < 3h$$
$$\frac{15}{3} < \frac{3h}{3}$$
$$5 < h$$
$$h > 5$$

52. **B. 6**

Although 6 is a factor of 12, 6 is not a multiple of 12. A multiple of a number is a product of the number and a whole number. The remaining choices are all multiples of 12.

53. **A. Move the decimal three places to the left and make the exponent three higher.**

Scientific notation consists of a number in which a single digit is followed by a decimal point and multiplied by 10 with an exponent. The number in the question has four digits after the decimal, so the decimal must be moved three places to the left. To keep the original value, the exponent of 10 has to increase by three to make up for moving the decimal three places to the left.

$$5451.38 \cdot 10^7 = 5.45138 \cdot 10^{10}$$

54. **D. 20**

You can list several multiples of 5 and 20 until you find a common multiple. If it's the lowest of all the common multiples, it's the least common multiple. That lowest common multiple is 20. Choices (A) and (E) are common multiples of 5 and 20, but Choice (D) is lower than both. Choices (B) and (C) are factors of both numbers, but not multiples of either.

55. **D.** $x \leq 5$

By adding 8 to both sides and then dividing both sides by 30, you get the variable by itself on one side, which is the goal. The result is $x \leq 5$.

56. **E. 30 m²**

The width of the rectangle, 3 meters, is also the measure of a leg of each triangle. Because the triangles are congruent, each one has a hypotenuse of 5 meters. With those measures, you can use the Pythagorean theorem to determine that the other leg of each triangle has a measure of 4 meters. Using the formulas for rectangle area ($A = lw$) and triangle area $\left(A = \frac{1}{2}bh\right)$, you can determine that the area of the rectangle is 18 m², and the area of each triangle is 6 m². The sum of the areas of the triangles and the area of the rectangle is the area of the overall figure, and that area is 30 m².

Triangle 1	Triangle 2	Rectangle
$a^2 + b^2 = c^2$	$a^2 + b^2 = c^2$	$A = lw$
$3^2 + b^2 = 5^2$	$3^2 + b^2 = 5^2$	$A = 6(3)$
$9 + b^2 = 25$	$9 + b^2 = 25$	$A = 18m^2$
$b^2 = 25 - 9$	$b^2 = 25 - 9$	
$b^2 = 16$	$b^2 = 16$	
$b = \sqrt{16}$	$b = \sqrt{16}$	
$b = 4$	$b = 4$	
$A = \dfrac{4(3)}{2} = 6m^2$	$A = \dfrac{4(3)}{2} = 6m^2$	

Answer Key

Part 1: Reading

1. D	13. A	25. B	37. C	49. A, C
2. E	14. B	26. E	38. D	50. C
3. D	15. D	27. B	39. C	51. A
4. C	16. C	28. D	40. E	52. C
5. E	17. A	29. C	41. C	53. E
6. D	18. E	30. E	42. D	54. E
7. E	19. B	31. C	43. B	55. D
8. D	20. B	32. B	44. A	56. E
9. A	21. E	33. A	45. E	
10. B	22. C	34. E	46. C	
11. C	23. A	35. A	47. C	
12. E	24. E	36. D	48. A	

Part 2: Writing

1. B	11. A	21. E	31. E
2. E	12. E	22. E	32. C
3. A	13. D	23. D	33. A
4. C	14. E	24. E	34. B
5. E	15. A	25. B	35. C
6. C	16. D	26. A	36. E
7. A	17. B	27. A	37. B
8. D	18. C	28. C	38. A
9. C	19. D	29. D	39. D
10. B	20. B	30. B	40. D

Part 3: Mathematics

1. D	13. D	25. C	37. C	49. C
2. B	14. C	26. B	38. B	50. B
3. C	15. A	27. E	39. D	51. E
4. A	16. E	28. D	40. A	52. B
5. D	17. B	29. E	41. B	53. A
6. E	18. B	30. B	42. C	54. D
7. A	19. C	31. C	43. A	55. D
8. C	20. A	32. C	44. E	56. E
9. A	21. D	33. D	45. B	
10. A	22. B	34. A	46. B	
11. E	23. E	35. A	47. A	
12. E	24. A	36. C	48. B	

Chapter 16

Practice Exam 2

● ●

*I*f you didn't get the starring role in "Acing the Praxis Core" when you took the practice exam in Chapter 14, you have a second chance here. Refocus, reexamine, review, and reassess the areas where you didn't score so well!

✔ Refocus by redefining your goal — to ace the Praxis Core.

✔ Reexamine the questions you missed on the first practice exam.

✔ Review concepts that you weren't clear on during the first practice test.

✔ Reassess — prepare to take the next practice test.

You must remember that this is a timed test. De-gadgetizing (setting aside your cellphone, the TV remote, and other such gadgets) is still a must — although you may use a calculator when you reach the math practice test. Make sure you're aware of the amount of time allowed for each section so you don't spend too much time on one question. Don't leave any answers blank. Stay focused on your goal — to ace the Praxis Core.

This practice test is available online at learn.dummies.com. After you answer the questions, you can review a summary of your performance on this test and any other tests you've taken. (We've included three unique tests online that aren't printed in the pages of this book.) This summary provides you with a snapshot of your strengths and weaknesses so you know where you need to spend more time studying.

Answer Sheet for Practice Exam 2

Reading

1. Ⓐ Ⓑ Ⓒ Ⓓ Ⓔ
2. Ⓐ Ⓑ Ⓒ Ⓓ Ⓔ
3. Ⓐ Ⓑ Ⓒ Ⓓ Ⓔ
4. Ⓐ Ⓑ Ⓒ Ⓓ Ⓔ
5. Ⓐ Ⓑ Ⓒ Ⓓ Ⓔ
6. Ⓐ Ⓑ Ⓒ Ⓓ Ⓔ
7. Ⓐ Ⓑ Ⓒ Ⓓ Ⓔ
8. Ⓐ Ⓑ Ⓒ Ⓓ Ⓔ
9. Ⓐ Ⓑ Ⓒ Ⓓ Ⓔ
10. Ⓐ Ⓑ Ⓒ Ⓓ Ⓔ
11. Ⓐ Ⓑ Ⓒ Ⓓ Ⓔ
12. Ⓐ Ⓑ Ⓒ Ⓓ Ⓔ
13. Ⓐ Ⓑ Ⓒ Ⓓ Ⓔ
14. Ⓐ Ⓑ Ⓒ Ⓓ Ⓔ
15. Ⓐ Ⓑ Ⓒ Ⓓ Ⓔ
16. Ⓐ Ⓑ Ⓒ Ⓓ Ⓔ
17. Ⓐ Ⓑ Ⓒ Ⓓ Ⓔ
18. Ⓐ Ⓑ Ⓒ Ⓓ Ⓔ
19. Ⓐ Ⓑ Ⓒ Ⓓ Ⓔ
20. Ⓐ Ⓑ Ⓒ Ⓓ Ⓔ
21. Ⓐ Ⓑ Ⓒ Ⓓ Ⓔ
22. Ⓐ Ⓑ Ⓒ Ⓓ Ⓔ
23. Ⓐ Ⓑ Ⓒ Ⓓ Ⓔ
24. Ⓐ Ⓑ Ⓒ Ⓓ Ⓔ
25. Ⓐ Ⓑ Ⓒ Ⓓ Ⓔ
26. Ⓐ Ⓑ Ⓒ Ⓓ Ⓔ
27. Ⓐ Ⓑ Ⓒ Ⓓ Ⓔ
28. Ⓐ Ⓑ Ⓒ Ⓓ Ⓔ
29. Ⓐ Ⓑ Ⓒ Ⓓ Ⓔ
30. Ⓐ Ⓑ Ⓒ Ⓓ Ⓔ
31. Ⓐ Ⓑ Ⓒ Ⓓ Ⓔ
32. Ⓐ Ⓑ Ⓒ Ⓓ Ⓔ
33. Ⓐ Ⓑ Ⓒ Ⓓ Ⓔ
34. Ⓐ Ⓑ Ⓒ Ⓓ Ⓔ
35. Ⓐ Ⓑ Ⓒ Ⓓ Ⓔ
36. Ⓐ Ⓑ Ⓒ Ⓓ Ⓔ
37. Ⓐ Ⓑ Ⓒ Ⓓ Ⓔ
38. Ⓐ Ⓑ Ⓒ Ⓓ Ⓔ
39. Ⓐ Ⓑ Ⓒ Ⓓ Ⓔ
40. Ⓐ Ⓑ Ⓒ Ⓓ Ⓔ
41. Ⓐ Ⓑ Ⓒ Ⓓ Ⓔ
42. Ⓐ Ⓑ Ⓒ Ⓓ Ⓔ
43. Ⓐ Ⓑ Ⓒ Ⓓ Ⓔ
44. Ⓐ Ⓑ Ⓒ Ⓓ Ⓔ
45. Ⓐ Ⓑ Ⓒ Ⓓ Ⓔ
46. Ⓐ Ⓑ Ⓒ Ⓓ Ⓔ
47. Ⓐ Ⓑ Ⓒ Ⓓ Ⓔ
48. Ⓐ Ⓑ Ⓒ Ⓓ Ⓔ
49. Ⓐ Ⓑ Ⓒ Ⓓ Ⓔ
50. Ⓐ Ⓑ Ⓒ Ⓓ Ⓔ
51. Ⓐ Ⓑ Ⓒ Ⓓ Ⓔ
52. Ⓐ Ⓑ Ⓒ Ⓓ Ⓔ
53. Ⓐ Ⓑ Ⓒ Ⓓ Ⓔ
54. Ⓐ Ⓑ Ⓒ Ⓓ Ⓔ
55. Ⓐ Ⓑ Ⓒ Ⓓ Ⓔ
56. Ⓐ Ⓑ Ⓒ Ⓓ Ⓔ

Writing

1. Ⓐ Ⓑ Ⓒ Ⓓ Ⓔ
2. Ⓐ Ⓑ Ⓒ Ⓓ Ⓔ
3. Ⓐ Ⓑ Ⓒ Ⓓ Ⓔ
4. Ⓐ Ⓑ Ⓒ Ⓓ Ⓔ
5. Ⓐ Ⓑ Ⓒ Ⓓ Ⓔ
6. Ⓐ Ⓑ Ⓒ Ⓓ Ⓔ
7. Ⓐ Ⓑ Ⓒ Ⓓ Ⓔ
8. Ⓐ Ⓑ Ⓒ Ⓓ Ⓔ
9. Ⓐ Ⓑ Ⓒ Ⓓ Ⓔ
10. Ⓐ Ⓑ Ⓒ Ⓓ Ⓔ
11. Ⓐ Ⓑ Ⓒ Ⓓ Ⓔ
12. Ⓐ Ⓑ Ⓒ Ⓓ Ⓔ
13. Ⓐ Ⓑ Ⓒ Ⓓ Ⓔ
14. Ⓐ Ⓑ Ⓒ Ⓓ Ⓔ
15. Ⓐ Ⓑ Ⓒ Ⓓ Ⓔ
16. Ⓐ Ⓑ Ⓒ Ⓓ Ⓔ
17. Ⓐ Ⓑ Ⓒ Ⓓ Ⓔ
18. Ⓐ Ⓑ Ⓒ Ⓓ Ⓔ
19. Ⓐ Ⓑ Ⓒ Ⓓ Ⓔ
20. Ⓐ Ⓑ Ⓒ Ⓓ Ⓔ
21. Ⓐ Ⓑ Ⓒ Ⓓ Ⓔ
22. Ⓐ Ⓑ Ⓒ Ⓓ Ⓔ
23. Ⓐ Ⓑ Ⓒ Ⓓ Ⓔ
24. Ⓐ Ⓑ Ⓒ Ⓓ Ⓔ
25. Ⓐ Ⓑ Ⓒ Ⓓ Ⓔ
26. Ⓐ Ⓑ Ⓒ Ⓓ Ⓔ
27. Ⓐ Ⓑ Ⓒ Ⓓ Ⓔ
28. Ⓐ Ⓑ Ⓒ Ⓓ Ⓔ
29. Ⓐ Ⓑ Ⓒ Ⓓ Ⓔ
30. Ⓐ Ⓑ Ⓒ Ⓓ Ⓔ
31. Ⓐ Ⓑ Ⓒ Ⓓ Ⓔ
32. Ⓐ Ⓑ Ⓒ Ⓓ Ⓔ
33. Ⓐ Ⓑ Ⓒ Ⓓ Ⓔ
34. Ⓐ Ⓑ Ⓒ Ⓓ Ⓔ
35. Ⓐ Ⓑ Ⓒ Ⓓ Ⓔ
36. Ⓐ Ⓑ Ⓒ Ⓓ Ⓔ
37. Ⓐ Ⓑ Ⓒ Ⓓ Ⓔ
38. Ⓐ Ⓑ Ⓒ Ⓓ Ⓔ
39. Ⓐ Ⓑ Ⓒ Ⓓ Ⓔ
40. Ⓐ Ⓑ Ⓒ Ⓓ Ⓔ

Math

1. Ⓐ Ⓑ Ⓒ Ⓓ Ⓔ
2. Ⓐ Ⓑ Ⓒ Ⓓ Ⓔ
3. Ⓐ Ⓑ Ⓒ Ⓓ Ⓔ
4. Ⓐ Ⓑ Ⓒ Ⓓ Ⓔ
5. Ⓐ Ⓑ Ⓒ Ⓓ Ⓔ
6. Ⓐ Ⓑ Ⓒ Ⓓ Ⓔ
7. Ⓐ Ⓑ Ⓒ Ⓓ Ⓔ
8. Ⓐ Ⓑ Ⓒ Ⓓ Ⓔ
9. Ⓐ Ⓑ Ⓒ Ⓓ Ⓔ
10. Ⓐ Ⓑ Ⓒ Ⓓ Ⓔ
11. Ⓐ Ⓑ Ⓒ Ⓓ Ⓔ
12. Ⓐ Ⓑ Ⓒ Ⓓ Ⓔ
13. Ⓐ Ⓑ Ⓒ Ⓓ Ⓔ
14. Ⓐ Ⓑ Ⓒ Ⓓ Ⓔ
15. Ⓐ Ⓑ Ⓒ Ⓓ Ⓔ
16. Ⓐ Ⓑ Ⓒ Ⓓ Ⓔ
17. Ⓐ Ⓑ Ⓒ Ⓓ Ⓔ
18. Ⓐ Ⓑ Ⓒ Ⓓ Ⓔ
19. Ⓐ Ⓑ Ⓒ Ⓓ Ⓔ
20. Ⓐ Ⓑ Ⓒ Ⓓ Ⓔ
21. Ⓐ Ⓑ Ⓒ Ⓓ Ⓔ
22. Ⓐ Ⓑ Ⓒ Ⓓ Ⓔ
23. Ⓐ Ⓑ Ⓒ Ⓓ Ⓔ
24. Ⓐ Ⓑ Ⓒ Ⓓ Ⓔ
25. Ⓐ Ⓑ Ⓒ Ⓓ Ⓔ
26. Ⓐ Ⓑ Ⓒ Ⓓ Ⓔ
27. Ⓐ Ⓑ Ⓒ Ⓓ Ⓔ
28. Ⓐ Ⓑ Ⓒ Ⓓ Ⓔ
29. Ⓐ Ⓑ Ⓒ Ⓓ Ⓔ
30. Ⓐ Ⓑ Ⓒ Ⓓ Ⓔ
31. Ⓐ Ⓑ Ⓒ Ⓓ Ⓔ
32. Ⓐ Ⓑ Ⓒ Ⓓ Ⓔ
33. Ⓐ Ⓑ Ⓒ Ⓓ Ⓔ
34. Ⓐ Ⓑ Ⓒ Ⓓ Ⓔ
35. Ⓐ Ⓑ Ⓒ Ⓓ Ⓔ
36. Ⓐ Ⓑ Ⓒ Ⓓ Ⓔ
37. Ⓐ Ⓑ Ⓒ Ⓓ Ⓔ
38. Ⓐ Ⓑ Ⓒ Ⓓ Ⓔ
39. Ⓐ Ⓑ Ⓒ Ⓓ Ⓔ
40. Ⓐ Ⓑ Ⓒ Ⓓ Ⓔ
41. Ⓐ Ⓑ Ⓒ Ⓓ Ⓔ
42. Ⓐ Ⓑ Ⓒ Ⓓ Ⓔ
43. Ⓐ Ⓑ Ⓒ Ⓓ Ⓔ
44. Ⓐ Ⓑ Ⓒ Ⓓ Ⓔ
45. Ⓐ Ⓑ Ⓒ Ⓓ Ⓔ
46. Ⓐ Ⓑ Ⓒ Ⓓ Ⓔ
47. Ⓐ Ⓑ Ⓒ Ⓓ Ⓔ
48. Ⓐ Ⓑ Ⓒ Ⓓ Ⓔ
49. Ⓐ Ⓑ Ⓒ Ⓓ Ⓔ
50. Ⓐ Ⓑ Ⓒ Ⓓ Ⓔ
51. Ⓐ Ⓑ Ⓒ Ⓓ Ⓔ
52. Ⓐ Ⓑ Ⓒ Ⓓ Ⓔ
53. Ⓐ Ⓑ Ⓒ Ⓓ Ⓔ
54. Ⓐ Ⓑ Ⓒ Ⓓ Ⓔ
55. Ⓐ Ⓑ Ⓒ Ⓓ Ⓔ
56. Ⓐ Ⓑ Ⓒ Ⓓ Ⓔ

Part 1
Reading

Time: 85 minutes for 56 questions

Directions: Each statement or passage in this test is followed by a question or questions based on its content. After reading a statement or passage, choose the best answer to each question from among the five choices given. Answer all questions following a statement or passage on the basis of what is *stated* or *implied* in that statement or passage; you are not expected to have any previous knowledge of the topics treated in the statements and passages. Remember, try to answer every question.

Line   People often comment on the irony of the fact that Alfred Nobel, the man who endowed the famous Nobel Prizes, spent his life inventing military explosives (including dynamite). Fewer

(05)   people, however, know how directly related Nobel's two legacies actually are: When a French newspaper believed him dead and mistakenly printed his obituary in 1888, Nobel was horrified to see himself referred to as "the merchant of

(10)   death." In an effort to make amends for the harm his inventions had caused, he changed his will, leaving nearly his entire estate to endow the famous prizes in Peace, Literature, and various natural sciences that now bear his name.

1. According to the passage, Alfred Nobel endowed the Nobel Prizes in an effort to

   (A) make more money.

   (B) prolong his life.

   (C) conceal other things he had done.

   (D) ensure that his name would live forever.

   (E) change his legacy.

Line   It's certainly an exciting time for killer whales, or at least for the marine biologists who study them. Only in the last couple of decades has genetic testing revealed killer whales to be a

(05)   large species of dolphin, much more closely related to those cute fellows than to the larger whales. We've also learned that at least three, and possibly as many as six, subspecies of killer whales diverged from one another around two

(10)   million years ago, and all have distinct markings, diets, and systems of communication. Even the name *killer whale* is falling out of fashion; most scientists now prefer to use the term *orca*.

2. The primary purpose of the passage is to

   (A) explain how killer whale subspecies diverged from one another.

   (B) explore the ways in which scientists and the general public see killer whales differently.

   (C) report on new and exciting discoveries about killer whales.

   (D) argue that people should use the term *orca* instead of *killer whale*.

   (E) humorously humanize killer whales for an audience of schoolchildren.

Line   The archaeological excavation of Göbekli Tepe in southeastern Turkey in the 1990s revolutionized our knowledge about early human civilization. The site's stone pillars are not only larger

(05)   and heavier than those at the more famous Stonehenge in England but also have meticulous artworks carved into them that are clearly the work of specialist craftsmen. The place was obviously labored over in a highly organized fashion

(10)   for many years, beginning around 10,000 BCE, and yet it contains no residences or any evidence of permanent human habitation; humans had not yet invented agriculture and were still nomadic, so Göbekli Tepe must have been a

(15)   place of worship to which people returned at important times of the year. This is the first confirmation that early humans built elaborate structures for their gods before they even built permanent homes for themselves.

Go on to next page

3. According to the passage, the theory that Göbekli Tepe was a religious site rests primarily on

    (A) the fact that it is so large.

    (B) the elaborate nature of its artwork.

    (C) evidence that nobody actually lived there.

    (D) the close resemblance it bears to Stonehenge.

    (E) its role in the invention of agriculture.

Questions 4 through 6 are based on the following passage.

Line   Often named as one of the greatest female sculptors of all time, Malvina Hoffman was born in New York City in 1887. Early in her career, she studied under the famous Auguste Rodin, as well
(05) as with Gutzon Borglum, the Danish-American who would go on to create Mount Rushmore. Hoffman's crowning achievement was a series of bronze sculptures, commissioned by the Field Museum of Natural History in Chicago, exploring
(10) physical and cultural differences among humans. She traveled extensively in order to study her subjects in life and eventually produced 105 spectacularly detailed and lifelike pieces depicting people from all over the world. Hoffman's sculptures were
(15) a centerpiece of the 1933 Chicago World's Fair, and an entire hall at the Field Museum was dedicated to their subsequent display. By the 1960s, however, the notion of physical differences among various types of humans had become a touchy
(20) subject; some argued that Hoffman's work was racist. Three years after her death in 1966, the Field Museum moved most of Hoffman's work into basement storage. A few pieces remain displayed without fanfare in select corners of the museum,
(25) but the vast majority of the masterpiece collection of this pioneering female artistic genius has not been seen in nearly 50 years.

4. The principal intent of the passage is to

    (A) offer a professional and personal biography of Malvina Hoffman.

    (B) argue that it was wrong of the Field Museum to move Hoffman's work into storage.

    (C) explain why some people were offended by Hoffman's sculptures.

    (D) inform readers about Hoffman and the controversy surrounding her work.

    (E) raise questions about why there aren't more famous female sculptors.

5. The author most probably uses the word *pioneering* in the final sentence to mean

    (A) trailblazing

    (B) controversial

    (C) rebellious

    (D) perceptive

    (E) hardworking

6. The paradox raised by the passage concerns the need to balance

    (A) the cultural values of the past with those of the future.

    (B) multicultural sensitivity with celebration of the achievements of women.

    (C) scientific approaches to deep questions with artistic approaches to them.

    (D) intentionalist artistic criticism with interpretive artistic criticism.

    (E) the mission of a museum with the values of the public.

Questions 7 through 11 are based on the following passage.

    Everyone knows that the Renaissance was   Line
an explosion of artistic brilliance and scientific
advancement in the Europe of the 15th and 16th
centuries and that it was especially welcome
after the preceding centuries of ignorance and   (05)
violent political oppression now referred to as
the Dark Ages. But why did the Renaissance
happen when it did? For that matter, why did it
happen at all? Believe it or not, this European
golden age we call the Renaissance may simply   (10)
be the term we've given to the direct aftereffects
of Europe's worst nightmare: the Black Plague.
    Originating in the plains of central Asia, the
Black Death hit Europe in 1347, when merchant
ships laden with Asian goods landed in southern   (15)
Italy, unwittingly bringing along the rats whose
fleas carried the deadly plague bacteria. By the
end of the century, more than 50 percent of
Europe's total population had died. This time
must have been indescribably horrific to live   (20)
through, but those who did were changed by the
experience: Desperation to stop the devastation
had gotten people thinking seriously about science and medicine, and daily confrontation with
so much death focused their hearts and minds   (25)
on the human experience and the things that
made life worth living. Perhaps most importantly,

Go on to next page

the Black Death meant the collapse of the feudal
system. The masses of commoners who had
(30) been bound to work the lands of their lords as
serfs had been too badly annihilated for the
arrangement to remain feasible. The survivors
were allowed to buy their freedom and go into
business for themselves as skilled tradesmen,
(35) leading to the emergence of a middle class and
the birth of our modern free-market economic
system. In a multitude of ways, human life was
suddenly more valuable than ever before.

7. Which of the following best describes the
purpose and organization of the passage?

   (A) It examines a familiar concept from an
   unorthodox viewpoint.

   (B) It challenges a traditional explanation
   via a conspiracy theory.

   (C) It walks a fine line between the two
   sides of a controversy.

   (D) It compares and contrasts the art of
   two different periods.

   (E) It scientifically analyzes the origins of
   an epidemic.

8. When the author says in Line 25 that the
Black Death "focused their hearts and
minds on the human experience," he is
likely alluding to which phenomenon mentioned in the first paragraph?

   (A) "artistic brilliance"

   (B) "scientific advancement"

   (C) "violent political oppression"

   (D) "this European golden age"

   (E) "Europe's worst nightmare"

9. As it's used in Line 32, "feasible" most
nearly means

   (A) lucrative

   (B) legal

   (C) ethical

   (D) comprehensible

   (E) coherent

10. According to the passage, the reason that
the feudal economic system of the Middle
Ages collapsed was because

   (A) new philosophies led people in power
   to consider issues of social justice.

   (B) scientific discoveries led to a wider
   range of job options for the middle class.

   (C) laborers became so scarce that they
   were in a better bargaining position.

   (D) trade between Asia and the
   Mediterranean led to increased
   mechanization.

   (E) the Black Death prompted feudal lords
   to flee their castles and abandon their
   lands.

11. When the author suggests that the
Renaissance "may simply be the term
we've given to the aftereffects of" the Black
Plague, he means to suggest that

   (A) the Renaissance did not actually happen.

   (B) the Renaissance was the inevitable
   result of the vastly reduced population.

   (C) the Renaissance actually started in central Asia.

   (D) the Renaissance is a modern concept
   we have projected onto the wrong historical period.

   (E) "the Renaissance" is a dishonest euphemism for a much darker idea.

*Questions 12 through 14 are based on the fol-
lowing passage.*

Perhaps no term that has entered mainstream
discourse via the language of philosophy is more
misunderstood than *nihilism*. The word conjures
up images of melancholy iconoclasts dressed in
black, and it is doubtlessly largely for that reason (05)
that it has become something of a byword among
rebellious youngsters. Even more serious and educated people frequently seem to believe that nihilism is a philosophy built around the idea that life
is meaningless and that there is therefore no such (10)
thing as morality. But in actuality, *nihilism* doesn't
mean that and isn't even a term for a school of philosophy at all. All the philosophers who have used
the term *nihilism* — even Friedrich Nietzsche, with
whom it is most closely associated — have not (15)
espoused it themselves, but rather used it

Go on to next page

pejoratively to describe other philosophies with which they disagreed. Used properly, *nihilistic* is an insult for a philosophical viewpoint that (in the (20) speaker's opinion) sucks all the significance out of life due to some massive flaw or contradiction. Though certain philosophers such as Nietzsche and Kierkegaard claimed that they welcomed nihilism, they did so because they saw nihilism not as (25) an end in itself but rather as a necessary step on the path toward creating greater significance.

12. In writing the passage, the author's intention was presumably to

   (A) espouse a particular philosophy.

   (B) correct a widespread misconception.

   (C) take sides in a philosophical debate.

   (D) suggest a new take on an old idea.

   (E) defend an unpopular viewpoint.

13. According to the passage, *nihilism* is a term that

   (A) is not used by any actual philosophers.

   (B) is used by different philosophers to mean different things.

   (C) philosophers use to describe others' work rather than their own.

   (D) was only popular among philosophers during one specific period.

   (E) young people often deliberately misuse.

14. The tone of the passage can best be described as

   (A) sardonic.

   (B) condescending.

   (C) jovial.

   (D) dispassionate.

   (E) apprehensive.

Line   ASMR, or *Autonomous Sensory Meridian Response,* is a pleasant, trancelike state that some people claim to experience as a result of exposure to auditory *triggers* such as the sounds of whisper-
(05) ing, nail tapping, paper crinkling, or gum chewing. In the last year or so, hundreds of ASMR videos designed to help viewers fall asleep or reduce stress have popped up on YouTube; some of the more prolific and creative *ASMRtists* have become
(10) minor Internet celebrities. Professional psychologists have largely declined to comment on whether

there is a scientific basis for the effects that ASMR enthusiasts, known as *tingleheads,* are purported to experience, but by the standards of pop psychology, the ASMR movement is one of the most (15) coherent and fast-growing we're seen in years.

15. Certain terms in the passage are placed in italics because they are examples of

   (A) irony.

   (B) emphasis.

   (C) proper nouns.

   (D) misused terms.

   (E) jargon.

      The tiny dunnart of Australia is casually   Line referred to as a "marsupial mouse," but of course, it isn't really a mouse at all. As a marsupial, it is necessarily more closely related to all other marsupials — to the kangaroo, for example, or   (05) to the koala or Tasmanian devil — than it is to any non-marsupial mammal, such as a mouse. So why does it look exactly like a mouse? Because of a process called *convergent evolution.* The fact is that there are good reasons for animals to have   (10) the forms that they have. A mammal that is the size of a mouse and fulfills a mouselike niche will likely also have a stocky body, big ears, a longish snout, and so forth. In other words, it will end up looking like a mouse even though it isn't one.   (15)

16. The purpose of the passage is to

   (A) explain the differences between marsupials and non-marsupials.

   (B) define what does or doesn't count as a mouse.

   (C) use a specific animal as an example to explain a particular term.

   (D) excoriate people who use a certain scientific term incorrectly.

   (E) pinpoint why the dunnart is so important to evolutionary theory.

      As far as the public is concerned, 1941's   Line *Chaplinksy v. New Hampshire* might well be the most misunderstood Supreme Court case of all time. While it's true that *Chaplinksy* established the famous "fighting words" doctrine, it's also   (05) true that this doctrine doesn't mean what many people appear to think it means. The decision is often taken to mean that a citizen has the right to physically assault another citizen who gravely insults him, but anyone who tries to use that   (10)

Go on to next page

defense in court will be in for a rude awakening. All the Supreme Court actually did in that decision was uphold the right of a police officer to arrest a citizen who had verbally abused him, in

(15) accordance with a New Hampshire state law that the defendant subsequently tried to argue was unconstitutional. Ironically, in light of the fact that *Chaplinksy* has come to be known as "the 'fighting words' decision," no fight actually took place, and

(20) no one has ever successfully used *Chaplinsky* as a defense for a violent response to an insult.

17. The author suggests which of the following about *Chaplinsky v. New Hampshire?*

    (A) No one is sure what the decision actually means.

    (B) It has been rendered inconsequential by subsequent Supreme Court decisions.

    (C) It does not in fact provide a legal excuse for violence.

    (D) The state law it upheld was probably unconstitutional.

    (E) None of the above.

Questions 18 through 20 are based on the following passage.

Line   He is arguably the most famous and influential fictional character ever created, so it usually surprises people to learn that the world's greatest detective, the peerless Sherlock Holmes, was

(05) essentially a rip-off. Years before Arthur Conan Doyle published the first Sherlock Holmes adventure in 1887, the American master of horror, Edgar Allan Poe, published a trilogy of short stories featuring his own detective character, Auguste

(10) Dupin. Debuting in 1841's "The Murders in the Rue Morgue," Dupin shares many similarities with the later and far more famous Holmes beyond the simple fact that he is a master amateur sleuth whom the police consult when they are baffled: He

(15) smokes a pipe, he lives with a best friend who narrates his adventures, and he has a tendency to go on at length about logic in a condescending and socially oblivious manner. Doyle himself always admitted the obvious influence and gave Poe

(20) credit for inventing the detective genre, but the question remains: Why did Sherlock Holmes immediately become a popular literary phenomenon, when a nearly identical character who debuted nearly half a century earlier did not? Perhaps Poe

(25) and his Dupin were simply ahead of their time.

18. The primary purpose of the passage is to

    (A) accuse Arthur Conan Doyle of plagiarism.

    (B) argue that Poe's detective stories were better than Doyle's.

    (C) explain that a very famous character was heavily based on a lesser-known one.

    (D) cast doubt on the traditional explanation of who invented the detective story.

    (E) clear up confusion about the differences between Sherlock Holmes and Auguste Dupin.

19. In the concluding sentence of the passage, the author is using

    (A) conjecture.

    (B) foreshadowing.

    (C) synecdoche.

    (D) allusion.

    (E) poetic license.

20. By the phrase "socially oblivious" in Line 18, the author most nearly means

    (A) newfangled.

    (B) gauche.

    (C) egomaniacal.

    (D) iconoclastic.

    (E) smarmy.

Questions 21 through 24 are based on the following passage.

Line   The current rule of thumb in English departments of American colleges when it comes to the teaching of "freshman comp" — the introductory writing courses that virtually all incoming stu-

(05) dents are required to take — is that instructors are supposed to grade and correct student work based on the students' writing alone, without attempting to change or influence the students' opinions. This is a polite notion, and for that

(10) reason it is popular with administrators, whose primary motivation is to avoid controversy. But there are more than a few problems with this nice-sounding idea. The first is that, in practice, it's impossible, rather like the paradox from the

(15) climax of Shakespeare's *The Merchant of Venice*, where Shylock is challenged by the disguised

Go on to next page

Portia to take a pound of flesh without spilling a drop of blood. If a student's opinion, or any of the supposed facts cited in support of it, is (20) objectively false, then how can the organization of the argument be analyzed as a discrete aspect of the paper?

More importantly and more dangerously, such a yardstick carries the implication that (25) *everything* is simply a matter of opinion, which of course is not true. Although it might well lead to more tension in the classroom and more hurt feelings on the parts of some students, the inescapable fact is that there are simply better rea- (30) sons to believe some things than there are to believe other things. If politeness dictates that this fact cannot be acknowledged, even at the college level, then the students are being taught far less than they could or should be, and the (35) function of the professor is demoted to that of a simple proofreader.

21. The author's attitude toward the "rule of thumb" mentioned in the first paragraph and analyzed throughout the passage as a whole can best be described as one of

    (A) intellectual disdain.

    (B) shocked cynicism.

    (C) melancholy regret.

    (D) paranoid alarm.

    (E) droll dismissiveness.

22. In Line 21, "a discrete aspect of the paper" refers to an element of the paper that is

    (A) comprehensible.

    (B) scientifically expressible.

    (C) well done.

    (D) vague or confusing.

    (E) self-contained.

23. In the passage, the author suggests that the standard under discussion was put in place at the behest of

    (A) lazy teachers.

    (B) offended students.

    (C) naïve administrators.

    (D) poorly trained scientists.

    (E) angry parents.

24. Based on the passage, the author would most likely suggest that college composition instructors should

    (A) deliberately offend students as a test of their argumentative skills.

    (B) draw the line at respecting opinions that are demonstrably untrue.

    (C) be free to teach their own personal opinions without administrative interference.

    (D) place more emphasis on grammar, mechanics, and eloquence than on logic.

    (E) find excuses to flunk students whose general knowledge is woefully insufficient.

Questions 25 through 27 are based on the following passage.

It's the most famous series of words ever composed in the English language. Everyone has heard of it, and most people even know a little bit of it by heart, regardless of whether they ever made a deliberate effort to commit it to memory. (05) And virtually everyone, including many English teachers and a fair number of the actors who have delivered it on stage, is dead wrong about what it means. The plain fact is that Hamlet's "To be or not to be" soliloquy is *not* about whether (10) to commit suicide. Hamlet already flatly ruled out suicide on ethical grounds in his first soliloquy back in act one. The immortal showstopper from act three is about something much more complex and much more deeply related to the (15) grander themes of the play than that. When the melancholy prince asks "Whether 'tis nobler in the mind to suffer/The slings and arrow of outrageous fortune/Or to take arms against a sea of troubles," he is not simply debating whether to (20) cash in his chips, but instead pondering an eternal paradox of morality: Should a good person "turn the other cheek" in the face of evil, as scripture advises? Or should he attempt to make the world a better place by actively combating (25) the wicked, running the risk not only of dying in the process, but — even more troublingly — of becoming just as bad as the people he seeks to oppose?

Line

Go on to next page

25. The author's argument is that the "To be or not to be" soliloquy is actually about

    (A) whether it is better to go on living or to die.

    (B) whether there is really a God.

    (C) whether to retreat from the world or try to improve it.

    (D) whether it is wiser to fight evil openly or to use subterfuge.

    (E) something so complex that it is nearly impossible to grasp.

26. According to the passage, Hamlet's viewpoint on suicide is that it's

    (A) preferable to unethical action.

    (B) an eternal paradox of morality.

    (C) attractive but frightening.

    (D) inevitable.

    (E) unacceptable.

27. The author's goal in composing the passage is presumably to

    (A) take an ethical stand.

    (B) simplify a complex issue.

    (C) issue a warning about the future.

    (D) correct a misreading.

    (E) apologize for a mistake.

Founded in 1994 by philosophers Peter Singer and Paola Cavalieri, the Great Ape Project is an international organization that lobbies for a United Nations Declaration of the Rights of Great Apes. These proposed rights would include not only life but also liberty, meaning that great apes could no longer be experimented upon or even kept in zoos. The reasoning goes that, because great apes are intelligent enough to understand their status as captives in a zoo, keeping them in one is morally equivalent to imprisoning a human who has committed no crime.

28. The passage provides information for answering most fully which of the following questions?

    (A) Why should great apes have rights similar to human rights?

    (B) What is the difference between a great ape and a monkey?

    (C) Who are the most famous supporters of the Great Ape Project?

    (D) Are more great apes used in scientific research or zoo exhibitions?

    (E) How is intelligence in great apes measured?

The words "rabbit" and "hare" are often used interchangeably (especially in the titles of Bugs Bunny cartoons), but the two animals are quite different. Hares live and bear their young in nests, not in underground burrows like rabbits do, and (05) those young are born already furred and able to see, as opposed to blind and hairless like newborn rabbits. Unlike rabbits, who live in groups, hares are loners. A hare has 48 chromosomes to the rabbit's 44, and its jointed skull is unique (10) among mammals. Hares and rabbits really aren't that difficult to tell apart if you know what to look for, although it doesn't help that the animal known as a jackrabbit is actually a hare, and that the pet breed called a Belgian hare is really a (15) rabbit.

29. According to the passage, which of the following is true of hares?

    (A) They are the only animal with a jointed skull.

    (B) They have fewer chromosomes than do rabbits.

    (C) They are born blind and hairless.

    (D) They do not make use of underground burrows.

    (E) They live in groups.

Go on to next page

Questions 30 through 32 are based on the following passage.

Line Are time machines and time travel possible? Many physicists, including the great Stephen Hawking, now say yes. But before you get too excited, understand that there is a lot of fine print.
(05) Firstly, virtually all authorities on the subject agree that time travel to the past is an impossibility. Traveling backward in time would open the door to all sorts of insoluble conundrums, like the famous Grandfather Paradox ("What if you went
(10) back in time and killed your own grandfather, thereby preventing yourself from ever existing in the first place?"). As Hawking succinctly explains, when it comes to physics, things that would create paradoxes tend not to happen — not directly
(15) because they would create the paradoxes, but because they must be impossible for some other reason. Time travel to the future, however, is eminently possible, even if the process is less exciting than in the movies. All you'd have to do is move
(20) really fast.

As Einstein discovered, time slows down for moving objects as they approach the speed of light. A traveler in a spaceship moving at half the speed of light would only experience the passing
(25) of one day for every two days that passed on Earth. Get up to 99 percent of the speed of light, and a year would pass on earth for every day on the ship. So if you want to travel through time, all you have to do is build a spaceship that can
(30) go really fast and then hang around in space for a while, going really fast. When you come back to Earth, you will have traveled into the future, simply because less time will have passed for you than for everyone else. A "time machine,"
(35) then, is just anything that can move fast enough to function as one.

30. Which of the following, if true, would resolve an objection made in the passage?

(A) It's possible to exceed the speed of light.

(B) It's not possible to exceed the speed of light.

(C) Matter can be sent into the past, but not living beings.

(D) The past exists currently, but in another dimension.

(E) Time as it passes on Earth is not the most accurate definition of "time."

31. The author uses the phrase "fine print" in Line 4 to most nearly mean

(A) complicated explanations.

(B) exceptions and qualifications.

(C) dangerous possibilities.

(D) missing information.

(E) unexpected tricks.

32. The passage indicates which of the following about time travel to the future?

(A) We have achieved it already without realizing that we had.

(B) It would automatically resolve whatever paradoxes it creates.

(C) It's an illusion, but an extraordinarily convincing one.

(D) It's a natural consequence of the relationship between speed and time.

(E) Technically, everything constitutes time travel to the future.

Questions 33 through 38 are based on the following passages.

Passage 1

Line The theory that the Cretaceous-Paleogene Event — the mass extinction 65 million years ago that is most famous for having killed the dinosaurs, although many other species disappeared
(05) as well — was caused by an asteroid impact is now so widely accepted that it can be hard to believe the idea was little more than a rogue hypothesis until fairly recently. Although paleontologists had previously realized that the extinc-
(10) tion would be compatible with an asteroid impact, there was no hard evidence for one until 1980, when Luis Alvarez and his team discovered that the geologic record contains massive levels of iridium, an element rare on Earth but plentiful
(15) in asteroids, at the Cretaceous-Paleogene Boundary. The fact that the actual location of the impact was the Chicxulub Crater in Mexico's Yucatan Peninsula wasn't established until 1990.

Passage 2

Line Increasing numbers of paleontologists are leaning toward the idea that the scientific community was too hasty in ascribing the extinction of the dinosaurs solely to an asteroid impact.
(05) After all, doing so involves writing off the idea

Go on to next page

that any role in the mass dying was played by the Deccan Traps, a nearly 200,000 square-mile grouping of volcanic flood basalts in what is now India. We know that they formed between 60 and

(10) 68 million years ago, releasing huge amounts of lava and toxic gases in the process. No one is denying that the Chicxulub asteroid impact did in fact occur, and that it almost certainly played a substantial role in the extinction, but there is

(15) also no good reason to insist that the Cretaceous-Paleogene Event had only a single cause.

33. Which best describes the relationship between Passage 1 and Passage 2?

   (A) Passage 1 and Passage 2 present two mutually exclusive scientific theories.

   (B) Passage 1 and Passage 2 examine the same theory from two different angles.

   (C) Passage 2 presents a new theory that has replaced the theory in Passage 1.

   (D) Passage 1 explains the origin of a theory that Passage 2 then modifies.

   (E) Passage 1 presents raw data, and Passage 2 forms a theory based on those data.

34. As it's used in Passage 2, Line 5, the phrase "writing off" most nearly means

   (A) ignoring.

   (B) misrepresenting.

   (C) obscuring.

   (D) exaggerating.

   (E) plagiarizing.

35. How do the two authors differ in their viewpoints concerning the Chicxulub asteroid?

   (A) One author believes it killed the dinosaurs, and the other does not.

   (B) Both authors agree that it killed the dinosaurs, but they disagree about when it hit Earth.

   (C) One author believes it killed the dinosaurs, and the other believes it was one of multiple causes.

   (D) Both authors believe it killed the dinosaurs, but they disagree about its chemical composition.

   (E) Both authors agree that it's a plausible extinction theory, but neither is 100 percent sure it's correct.

36. Which of the following is an accurate statement about a difference between the two passages?

   (A) Passage 1 bases its argument on chemistry, and Passage 2 bases its argument on physics.

   (B) Passage 1 argues that dinosaurs lived in North America, and Passage 2 argues that they lived in Asia.

   (C) Passage 1 is written for a scientific audience, and Passage 2 is written for a general audience.

   (D) Passage 1 analyzes an older theory, whereas Passage 2 suggests an original one.

   (E) Passage 1 explains the history of its theory, whereas Passage 2 does not.

37. The attitude of the author of Passage 2 toward the content of Passage 1 is that it's

   (A) false.

   (B) limited.

   (C) outdated.

   (D) self-contradictory.

   (E) elitist.

38. Both passages are primarily concerned with determining

   (A) when dinosaurs lived.

   (B) whether all dinosaurs went extinct at the same time.

   (C) whether an asteroid struck Earth 65 million years ago.

   (D) the causes of an agreed-upon event.

   (E) the reasons for the popularity of a particular theory.

Go on to next page

Ask any schoolchild (or virtually any adult) to draw a picture of a medieval knight, and the odds are that you'll wind up with a depiction of someone encased from head to foot in a suit of armor. This is one of the most widespread misconceptions about history. The iconic "suit of armor" that we now associate so closely with the period actually didn't develop until the tail end of the Middle Ages, and it didn't become common on the battlefield until well into what we now call the Renaissance. European warriors of the true Medieval period, even the wealthier and more aristocratic ones such as knights, would have worn scattered pieces of plate armor over chain-mail suits, but not "suits of armor" as we now picture them.

39. The passage relies on drawing a sharp distinction between

   (A) what children know and what adults know.

   (B) armor and everyday clothing.

   (C) the Medieval Period and the Renaissance.

   (D) European warriors and non-European warriors.

   (E) wealthy warriors and less wealthy warriors.

People often prickle at evolutionary or instinctual explanations for human behavior based on the idea that it's been a long time since humans lived in a state of nature. But this depends upon a rather sizeable misapplication of the phrase "a long time." When people speak of "human civilization" — meaning the existence of permanent settlements, agriculture, some rudimentary form of government — they're talking about things that only appeared about 10,000 years ago. Conversely, the first humans — members of the genus *Homo* — reared their heads just over two million years ago. Humans were evolving for a heck of a long time before they were "civilized."

40. The primary implication made by the passage is that

   (A) human civilization arose much later than most people believe.

   (B) the development of agriculture and government marked a sharp turn in human genetics.

   (C) civilization hasn't existed long enough to substantially alter human instinct.

   (D) human evolution stopped when humans organized the first civilizations.

   (E) experts disagree about the timescale of human evolution.

The title of "the southernmost city in the world" is valuable bait when it comes to attracting tourists, but the question of which burg — and, accordingly, which nation — can boast it is not such an easy matter to settle. It all comes down to the fact that there is no hard-and-fast definition of what counts as a "city." Ushuaia, the southernmost city in Argentina, has a population of 64,000. Just across the Beagle Channel, however, lies Chile's Puerto Williams. The latter is farther south, but it has a population of only about 3,000. Does that make it populous enough to count as a city? Unsurprisingly, Chile says yes, and Argentina says no.

41. The author's primary goal in writing the passage was most likely to call attention to the fact that

   (A) geography is a more complex matter than people realize.

   (B) apparently straightforward questions can be muddled by vague definitions.

   (C) nations will argue over silly things when money is at stake.

   (D) Chile's claim to the southernmost city is better than Argentina's.

   (E) Argentina's claim to the southernmost city is better than Chile's.

Go on to next page

Questions 42 through 46 are based on the following passage.

Line
You don't hear the name of William Tyndale every day, but if you speak English, he probably had a greater influence on the words that come out of your mouth than anyone besides William

(05) Shakespeare. An English Protestant reformer of the early 1500s, Tyndale was the first since the invention of the printing press to translate the Bible into English (John Wycliffe's handwritten translations of the 1300s were quickly banned

(10) and easily destroyed by authorities because the process of producing them was so laborious). Translating the Bible was an act punishable by death, as the ability of the common man to read scripture in his own language would weaken the

(15) power of the Church, so Tyndale had to do his work in hiding on continental Europe.

He was captured in 1535 and executed the following year, but ironically, Tyndale's Bible became the standard in England soon afterward,

(20) when Henry VIII broke with Rome. The more famous King James Bible of 1611, finalized by a committee of scholars, is largely just a revision of Tyndale's single-handed work, which established the tone and conventions of literary Early

(25) Modern English. As the formulator of such famous idioms as "eat, drink, and be merry," "fight the good fight," and "salt of the earth," Tyndale is surpassed in the coining of English expressions only by Shakespeare, who devel-

(30) oped his own ear for literary English by reading Tyndale's Bible as a schoolboy.

42. Which of the following best describes the relationship between the two paragraphs of the passage?

(A) The first paragraph concentrates on the history of English-language Bibles in general, and the second concentrates specifically on William Tyndale's translation.

(B) The first paragraph mainly presents details of William Tyndale's life, and the second deals more closely with his influence.

(C) The first paragraph explains the influence of William Tyndale's Bible, and the second concentrates on the influence of the King James Version.

(D) The first paragraph deals with William Shakespeare's influence on the English language, and the second with William Tyndale's influence on Shakespeare.

(E) The first paragraph discusses English translations of the Bible made before the invention of the printing press, and the second discusses those translations done after its invention.

43. The passage repeatedly invokes the name of William Shakespeare primarily in order to

(A) use him as the standard by which influence on the English language is measured.

(B) argue that the greatest influence on Shakespeare himself was William Tyndale.

(C) set up a comparison between the language of Tyndale's Bible and Shakespeare's plays.

(D) distinguish idioms coined by Tyndale from those coined by Shakespeare.

(E) compare the political constraints on Shakespeare's work to those on Tyndale's.

Go on to next page

44. The author would most likely agree with which of the following statements?

    (A) The plays of William Shakespeare were more influenced by religion than many realize.

    (B) William Tyndale's translation of the Bible was politically superior to later translations.

    (C) William Tyndale should be given more credit for Henry VIII's break with Rome.

    (D) Translations done by individuals are generally superior to those done by committees.

    (E) The character of modern literary English was largely established in the 16th century.

45. The passage brings up John Wycliffe as an example of someone

    (A) whose work had a considerable degree of influence on William Tyndale's.

    (B) whose politics were more extreme than Tyndale's, but whose talent was equal.

    (C) who attempted a similar project to Tyndale's but was thwarted.

    (D) whose influence on the English language is harder to measure than Tyndale's.

    (E) who was more earnestly religious but less talented than Tyndale.

46. The metaphoric use of the phrase "ear for" in the final sentence is roughly synonymous with

    (A) appreciation of.

    (B) interest in.

    (C) consumption by.

    (D) knack for.

    (E) recognition of.

> *Questions 47 through 49 are based on the following chart.*

Following is a chart showing the change in Oregon's wolf populations between 2009 and 2012.

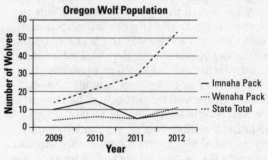

© John Wiley & Sons, Inc.

47. The year in which there was the greatest disparity between the populations of the Imnaha and Wenaha wolf packs was

    (A) 2009.

    (B) 2010.

    (C) 2011.

    (D) 2012.

    (E) The graph does not reveal this information.

48. The year or years in which there were apparently other wolf packs in the state of Oregon besides the Imnaha and Wenaha packs were

    (A) 2009 and 2010.

    (B) 2010 and 2011.

    (C) 2011 and 2012.

    (D) 2010 only.

    (E) 2012 only.

49. The year in which the wolves of the Imnaha pack comprised the greatest percentage of the total number of wolves in the state of Oregon was

    (A) 2009.

    (B) 2010.

    (C) 2011.

    (D) 2012.

    (E) The graph does not reveal this information.

Go on to next page

> *Questions 50 through 53 are based on the following passage.*

What, if anything, is the actual difference between a *psychopath* and a *sociopath?* The average person's confusion on this point is forgivable, because the fact is that psychologists and neurologists themselves disagree: Some consider the terms interchangeable, others favor dispensing with both in favor of the more modern diagnosis of *antisocial personality disorder* (which fits in more neatly with the spectrum of other personality disorders), and even the professionals who favor the continued and distinct use of both terms cannot form an agreement about what the difference is. Adding to the confusion is the fact that psychopaths and/or sociopaths are notably hard to study. For obvious reasons, an individual being screened for psychopathy is likely to lie, so only a highly skilled professional can make such a diagnosis concerning a living person. Diagnosing psychopathy and/or sociopathy postmortem is comparatively simpler, as there is agreement that the conditions involve observable differences in brain structure, but an autopsy cannot reveal whether such differences were present at birth or acquired. Nor can it say very much about the individual's subjective experience of the condition, and most agree the difference between psychopathy and sociopathy probably lies in this subjective experience. At the moment, the viewpoint that a psychopath has *no* sense of morality, whereas a sociopath has a *twisted* one, is gaining traction. In other words, although both psychopaths and sociopaths have highly reduced capacities for empathy, a psychopath does not know or care whether his or her actions are right or wrong; a sociopath, meanwhile, believes his or her actions to be right but has a definition of "right" that the average person would find horrifying.

50. You can infer from the passage that the majority of psychological and neurological professionals agree about which of the following statements?

(A) Both psychopathy and sociopathy are observable via brain autopsy.

(B) Both psychopathy and sociopathy are synonymous with antisocial personality disorder.

(C) Psychopathy and sociopathy are two different things.

(D) Neither psychopaths nor sociopaths know the difference between right and wrong.

(E) Neither psychopathy nor sociopathy is detectable via psychological examination.

51. The author's motivation in writing the passage is most likely which of the following?

(A) A desire to criticize the psychological community.

(B) A desire to voice a personal opinion about psychopaths.

(C) A desire to diagnose a particular person as either a psychopath or a sociopath.

(D) A desire to warn professionals about means used by psychopaths to evade detection.

(E) A desire to clear up confusion on the parts of general readers.

52. As it's used in Line 3, *forgivable* most nearly means

(A) morally excusable.

(B) initially confusing.

(C) logically expectable.

(D) disturbingly amusing.

(E) only mildly annoying.

53. The closing sentences suggest that sociopaths have a definition of right and wrong that is

(A) ineffable.

(B) idiosyncratic.

(C) inextricable.

(D) remunerative.

(E) eleemosynary.

The poetry of William Butler Yeats, who in 1923 became the first Irishman to receive the Nobel Prize for Literature, went through so many distinct phases during his long career that to read him is almost to read several different poets. The mystical and deliberately archaic-sounding verse of his early books borders on psychedelic; the strident political poems he produced at the time of World War I are awe-inspiring in their scope and confidence; and the lonely reflections on old age he published in his last years are as different from the first two phases as they are from each other.

Go on to next page

54. The passage suggests that the poetry of William Butler Yeats can accurately be described as

    (A) exclusionary.

    (B) impudent.

    (C) indeterminate.

    (D) multifaceted.

    (E) lugubrious.

Line
        Popular tradition holds that celebrities die in groups, but all superstition aside, the truth is that sometimes one famous individual is too lightly mourned solely because of having passed
(05) away in too close proximity to another celebrity. Perhaps no great American ever received a more insufficient send-off than show-business legend Groucho Marx, who happened to leave us on August 19, 1977, only three days after the death
(10) of Elvis Presley. Granted, Presley's death was both untimely and mysterious, whereas Groucho was an elderly man; still, the fact that the national hysteria over the King of Rock-and-Roll should have prevented the King of Comedy from
(15) getting his due is lamentable.

55. The relationship of the first sentence to the rest of the passage is that of

    (A) the general to the specific.

    (B) superstition to fact.

    (C) the rhetorical to the logical.

    (D) data to interpretation.

    (E) cause to effect.

The etymology of vulgar or profane words is a subject of both frustration and amusement for linguists. Because "dirty" words tend to be used in speech for a considerable length of time before they are ever used in print, their origins are often a subject of controversy. Often, urban legend will hold that a particular four-letter word originated as an acronym, but such after-the-fact explanations — jokingly dubbed "backronyms" — are inevitably spurious.

56. The passage suggests that the etymology of "dirty" words is often in doubt because

    (A) linguists are reluctant to study them.

    (B) deliberate disinformation is spread about them.

    (C) they are absent from preserved records.

    (D) their meanings change so rapidly.

    (E) they frequently originate as acronyms.

STOP DO NOT TURN THE PAGE UNTIL TOLD TO DO SO.
DO NOT RETURN TO A PREVIOUS TEST.

Part 2
Writing

Time: 40 minutes for 40 multiple-choice questions

Directions: Choose the best answer to each question. Mark the corresponding oval on the answer sheet.

Directions: Each of the following questions consists of a sentence that contains four underlined portions. Read each sentence and decide whether any of the underlined parts contains a grammatical construction, a word use, or an instance of incorrect or omitted punctuation or capitalization that would be inappropriate in carefully written English. If so, select the underlined portion that must be revised to produce a correct sentence. If there are no errors in the sentence as written, select "No error." **No sentence has more than one error.**

1. Some people drink coffee for <u>its</u> taste,
   A
   <u>whereas</u> many others <u>simply use</u> it as a
   B   C
   delivery system for the caffeine <u>it contains</u>.
   D
   <u>No error</u>.
   E

2. Although many films inspired by books are
   <u>well made and considered</u> cinematic clas-
   A
   sics, it's rare <u>for a film</u> to flesh out its char-
   B
   acters as fully <u>as did</u> the book <u>by which</u> it
   C   D
   was based. <u>No error</u>.
   E

3. Many <u>people who believe</u> the platypus
   A
   <u>to be a marsupial</u> because it's weird-looking
   B
   and lives in Australia, but it's actually a
   monotreme and <u>more closely related</u> to pla-
   C
   cental mammals like humans <u>than it is</u> to
   D
   the marsupials. <u>No error</u>.
   E

4. Turk Edwards <u>was a star lineman</u> for the
   A
   Washington Redskins in the 1930s <u>whom was</u>
   B
   eventually inducted into the Football Hall of
   Fame <u>but, ironically, his</u> career ended when
   C

he injured his knee <u>while walking</u> away from
                     D
a pre-game coin toss. <u>No error</u>.
                        E

5. While we don't know exactly how life <u>arose</u>
   <u>on Earth</u>, we can say that <u>what distinguishes</u>
   A   B
   a living organism from mere "chemical
   soup" <u>is their</u> ability to replicate in a manner
   C
   <u>that passes on</u> genes. <u>No error</u>.
   D   E

6. <u>Should you</u> have any questions about
   A
   what the <u>data represent</u>, please don't hesi-
   B
   tate <u>to ask</u> either Amy or <u>myself</u>. <u>No error</u>.
   C   D   E

7. The award-winning film *Braveheart*
   <u>depicts its</u> central characters <u>as wearing</u>
   A   B
   kilts, but in actuality the <u>Scots</u> did not wear
   C
   kilts until four centuries <u>after the time</u> of
   D
   William Wallace. <u>No error</u>.
   E

Go on to next page ➡

8. The children's museum is further away than
   A   B   C
   the waterpark, but it will presumably be
   both more educational and less crowded.
                             D
   No error.
   E

9. It didn't sell very many copies, but
                  A
   I thought the album was one of the
   best-produced musical endeavors in which
   B   C
   I have ever heard. No error.
   D   E

10. If you really want to effect change, then you
                         A   B
    should make sure your arguments affect
                                    C
    people's opinions, rather than merely
                            D
    shouting them into silence. No error.
                                E

11. Olympus Mons, being a shield volcano on
                   A
    the planet Mars with six calderas, dwarfs
        B   C
    Mount Everest, as it's nearly three times
                       D
    taller. No error.
            E

12. The treasurer of the society devoted to the
                        A
    upkeep and preservation of historic disc-
    golf courses were delighted by, but unsure
                 B
    of how best to allocate, the sudden influx of
    C   D
    donations. No error.
               E

13. I realize you've been searching frantically
               A
    for him all evening, but if Danny had been
                                         B
    here earlier, I certainly didn't see him.
         C   D
    No error.
    E

14. Because we still had half a day's travel
    A   B
    before us, we stopped for the night, but the
                                        C
    weather forecast failed to make us optimis-
    tic of the remainder of the trip. No error.
        D   E

15. The principle reason most students give for
        A   B
    opposing a tuition hike is suspicion that
    C   D
    most of the money will just be used on the
    sports teams. No error.
                  E

16. The theory that visual and auditory halluci-
    nations caused by infrasound are actually
                                 A
    the real explanation behind most reports of
                         B
    hauntings is gaining credibly among scien-
             C   D
    tists. No error.
           E

17. Though his short lyric poems have often
                                A
    been dismissed by critics as overly
                               B
    sentimental, Lord Byron has more recently
                                C
    been given credit for the immense influ-
    ence that his long narrative poems
    have had for novelists. No error.
    D   E

18. The question of which British Kings and
                   A   B
    Queens have been "great" since the power
    of the monarch was limited after the
    Glorious Revolution of 1688 is a tricky one,
    C
    as symbolic moral leadership is obviously
    harder to evaluate than are executive deci-
                         D
    sions. No error.
          E

19. Though they are often depicted alongside
            A   B
    dinosaurs in paintings or cartoon shows,
    the *Dimetrodon* was actually not a dinosaur
    at all, but rather a mammalian ancestor
    C   D
    called a *synapsid.* No error.
                        E

Go on to next page

Directions: In each of the following sentences, some part of the sentence or the entire sentence is underlined. Beneath each sentence you will find five ways of writing the underlined part. The first of these repeats the original, but the other four are all different. If you think the original sentence is better than any of the suggested changes, you should select the first answer choice; otherwise, you should select one of the other choices.

This is a test of correctness and effectiveness of expression. In choosing answers, follow the requirements of standard written English; i.e., pay attention to acceptable usage in grammar, diction (choice of words), sentence construction, and punctuation. Choose the answer that expresses most effectively what is presented in the original sentence; this answer should be clear and exact, without awkwardness, ambiguity, or redundancy. Remember, try to answer every question.

20. Students may not enjoy learning grammar, but a teacher who doesn't teach grammar <u>is not doing their job</u>.

   (A) is not doing their job
   (B) is not doing their jobs
   (C) are not doing their jobs
   (D) is not doing his or her job
   (E) are not doing his or her job

21. There are actually six different species of giraffe, <u>all with</u> distinctive spot patterns.

   (A) all with
   (B) in which all have
   (C) all of whom having
   (D) they all have
   (E) each one has

22. Although he is widely considered the greatest novelist of the 20th <u>century, but James Joyce</u> never won the Nobel Prize for Literature.

   (A) century, but James Joyce
   (B) century, seeing that
   (C) century, James Joyce
   (D) century; James Joyce
   (E) century, however, James Joyce

23. The late Christopher Hitchens had the capacity both to delight with the force of his learning and <u>wit, but was also shocking in</u> his iconoclasm and bluntness.

   (A) wit, but was also shocking in
   (B) wit, while also being shocking by
   (C) wit, he also shocked with
   (D) wit but also to shock with
   (E) wit and to shock with

24. <u>Having spotted the skyline in the distance, an attempt was made to</u> reach town without making any more stops.

   (A) Having spotted the skyline in the distance, an attempt was made to
   (B) Having spotted the skyline in the distance, and we attempted to
   (C) Having spotted the skyline in the distance, we decided to try and
   (D) We spotted the skyline in the distance, therefore we attempted to
   (E) Spotting the skyline in the distance and trying to

25. Nineteenth-century Hungarian composer Franz Liszt was the first artist <u>who female fans showed their appreciation for throwing</u> their undergarments onto the stage.

   (A) who female fans showed their appreciation for throwing
   (B) who female fans were showing their appreciation for and throwing
   (C) to whom female fans to show their appreciation by throwing
   (D) for whom female fans showed their appreciation by throwing
   (E) to whom female fans showed their appreciation to throw

Go on to next page ⇒

26. In about 6 billion years, the Sun will exhaust its supply of hydrogen and expand into a red giant, <u>and consume all the planets of our solar system, then collapse</u> into a white dwarf.

    (A) and consume all the planets of our solar system, then collapse

    (B) it will consume all the planets of our solar system and then collapse

    (C) and it will consume all the planets of our solar system; then collapse

    (D) consuming all the planets of our solar system and then it will collapse

    (E) consuming all the planets of our solar system before collapsing

27. Madagascar, an island off the western coast of <u>Africa, a biodiversity hotspot, and over 90 percent of its wildlife is found</u> nowhere else on the planet.

    (A) Africa, a biodiversity hotspot, and over 90 percent of its wildlife is found

    (B) Africa, is a biodiversity hotspot, with over 90 percent of its wildlife being found

    (C) Africa, being a biodiversity hotspot, over 90 percent of its wildlife found

    (D) Africa and a biodiversity hotspot, with over 90 percent of its wildlife found

    (E) Africa, it is a biodiversity hotspot, and over 90 percent of its wildlife is found

28. I have decided that I'm ready to take the test <u>now, however the rest of you may</u> delay for as long as you like.

    (A) now, however the rest of you may

    (B) now, however, the rest of you may

    (C) now; the rest of you, however, may

    (D) now; the rest of you however may

    (E) now, the rest of you, however, may

29. Though he was unappreciated in his time, today the works of Vincent van Gogh are more celebrated <u>than are those of</u> any other Post-Impressionist painter.

    (A) than are those of

    (B) than

    (C) compared to

    (D) compared with

    (E) compared than

30. It may look cool when people do it in the movies, but <u>the truth of it is firing</u> two guns at the same time is a very effective way of not hitting anything.

    (A) the truth of it is firing

    (B) the truth is that firing

    (C) the truth is, if one is firing

    (D) truly, if one is to fire

    (E) truly to fire

Directions: The following passage is a draft of an essay. Some portions of the passage need to be strengthened through editing and revision. Read the passage and choose the best answers for the questions that follow. Some questions ask you to improve particular sentences or portions of sentences. In some cases, the indicated portion of the passage will be most effective as it is already expressed and thus will require no changes. In choosing answers, consider development, organization, word choice, style, and tone, and follow the requirements of standard written English. Remember, try to answer every question.

⬛1 The state of poetry in contemporary America really depends on whom you ask. ⬛2 A certain type of person is likely to tell you that poetry is read by hardly anyone. ⬛3 He will add that the few people who do read it comprise an insular cadre of specialists, which is ignored by the culture at large. ⬛4 Another person may well say that we are living in a new golden age of American verse, one in which poetry events pack coffeehouses and even auditoriums with excited young people in numbers never seen before. ⬛5 The explanation is that these two respondents are talking about two very different things when they say "poetry."

⬛6 For centuries, the obvious definition of "poetry" has been that it is a genre of published

Go on to next page

Go on to next page

literature, written by writers, submitted for publication in journals and anthologies, and read by poetry lovers in thoughtful solitude. ⑦ In recent decades, however, a populist subgenre of poetry called "slam" has been challenging that definition, just as definitions are often challenged. ⑧ At slam events, poets take the stage in rapid succession for three to five minutes at a time, with the winners of each round being determined by applause and a single winner being crowned at the end of the night. ⑨ Unlike more traditional poets, many of whom have advanced degrees in poetry, slammers memorize their poems and act them out with gestures, impressions, and even sound effects, moving all about the stage in an effort to keep the crowd's attention. ⑩ This is a difficult task with any crowd.

⑪ Slam poets often argue that traditionalists — or, as they call them, "page" poets — are clinging to an outdated concept of poetry for the sake of elitism. ⑫ More traditional versifiers counter that slam poets — who are often ignorant of poetic history and cite popular songwriters or even stand-up comics as their primary influences — are simply crowd-pleasers who perform humorous, titillating, or shocking monologues and presume to call it poetry, with those who read more slowly or thoughtfully often getting booed off the stage for not putting on

enough of a show. ⑬ Each camp sincerely believes that it is being "oppressed" by the other: Slammers think that page poets are privileged, closed-minded, and exclusionary, whereas page poets see slammers as the "cool kids" trying to turn poetry into a popularity contest.

31. In context, what is the best way to combine Sentences 2 and 3 (reproduced here)?

    A certain type of person is likely to tell you that poetry is read by hardly anyone. He will add that the few people who do read it comprise an insular cadre of specialists, which is ignored by the culture at large.

    (A) A certain type of person is likely to tell you that poetry is read by hardly anyone except a few people who do read it and comprise an insular cadre of specialists, and that these people are ignored by the culture at large.

    (B) A certain type of person is likely to tell you that poetry is read by hardly anyone, and that the few people who do read it comprise an insular cadre of specialists ignored by the culture at large.

    (C) A certain type of person is likely to tell you that poetry is read by hardly anyone, only an insular cadre of specialists that is also ignored by the culture at large.

    (D) A certain type of person is likely to tell you that poetry is read by hardly anyone who does not comprise an insular cadre of specialists ignored by the culture at large.

    (E) A certain type of person is likely to tell you that poetry is read by hardly anyone, adding that the few people who do read it comprise an insular cadre of specialists, and specifying that they are ignored by the culture at large.

32. In context, what is best to do with Sentence 5 (reproduced here)?

    The explanation is that these two respondents are talking about two very different things when they say "poetry."

    (A) Leave it as it is.

    (B) Take the word *poetry* out of quotation marks and put the word *very* in italics.

    (C) Begin the sentence with "On the other hand."

    (D) Make it the second sentence of the subsequent paragraph.

    (E) Insert the word "however" between *respondents* and *are*.

33. In context, what is the best revision of the underlined portion of Sentence 7 (reproduced here)?

    In recent decades, however, a populist subgenre of poetry called "slam" has been challenging that definition, just as definitions are often challenged.

    (A) just as definitions are often challenged

    (B) and you're about to find out how and why.

    (C) with varying degrees of success.

    (D) to the delight of some and the consternation of others.

    (E) with methods as devious as they were unexpected.

34. In context, which is the best way to modify the underlined portion of Sentence 9 (reproduced here)?

    Unlike more traditional poets, many of whom have advanced degrees in poetry, slammers memorize their poems and act them out with gestures, impressions, and even sound effects, moving all about the stage in an effort to keep the crowd's attention.

    (A) many of whom have advanced degrees in poetry

    (B) who come from just as wide a range of backgrounds as do slammers

    (C) who are not necessarily any older than the slammers are

    (D) who are often more shy than slammers are, despite being more well-read

    (E) who typically stand at lecterns and read from notes or a published book during recitals

35. Which version of Sentence 10 (reproduced here) would make the best conclusion to the second paragraph?

    (A) This is a difficult task with any crowd.

    (B) Some of them even burst into song, though usually not very skillfully.

    (C) Their work is designed to be seen in performance rather than read.

    (D) Can the use of props among slammers be far behind?

    (E) The venues that host slams can't complain, because they always make money.

36. In context, which is the best transitional phrase to add at the beginning of Sentence 13 (reproduced here)?

    Each camp sincerely believes that it is being "oppressed" by the other: Slammers think that page poets are privileged, closed-minded, and exclusionary, whereas page poets see slammers as the "cool kids" trying to turn poetry into a popularity contest.

    (A) Ironically

    (B) Therefore

    (C) Undeniably

    (D) On the other hand

    (E) In conclusion

Directions: The following questions are a test of your familiarity with basic research skills. For each question, choose the best answer. Remember, try to answer every question.

---

37. Downing, Thomas. (2012, April). "The Standardized-Test Conundrum." *Education*, 76, 93–99.

    In the citation shown, which of the following is cited?

    (A) a book

    (B) a magazine article

    (C) a newspaper article

    (D) a blog entry

    (E) a speech

Go on to next page ⇒

38. In terms of research, the technical distinction between a primary source and a secondary source is that

    (A) a secondary source yields less important information than a primary source.

    (B) a primary source is quoted from directly, whereas a secondary source is not.

    (C) a primary source represents original research, whereas a secondary source contains information already compiled by someone else.

    (D) a primary source is a published work with an ISBN, whereas a secondary source might not have been published or even copyrighted.

    (E) a primary source is the text or texts that the paper is about, and a secondary source is anything else.

39. When an author includes a quotation (from a poem, for example) below the title of the essay and above the text, the quotation is called an

    (A) epigram.

    (B) epigraph.

    (C) epistle.

    (D) epithelium.

    (E) epitaxy.

40. The difference between a Works Cited page and a Bibliography is that

    (A) *Bibliography* is the term used in high school, and *Works Cited page* is the term used in college.

    (B) a Works Cited page lists only cited sources, whereas a Bibliography lists every source consulted.

    (C) a Bibliography lists only books, whereas a Works Cited Page lists all types of sources.

    (D) *Bibliography* is the term used in an unpublished paper, whereas *Works Cited page* is the term used in a published paper.

    (E) *Works Cited page* is the preferred term in APA style, whereas *Bibliography* is the preferred term in MLA style.

STOP DO NOT TURN THE PAGE UNTIL TOLD TO DO SO.
DO NOT RETURN TO A PREVIOUS TEST.

Argumentative Essay

Time: 30 minutes

Directions: Read the opinion that follows.

"Because most students are not really interested in becoming published writers, but are instead looking to vent about personal problems, high-school and college creative writing classes should seek to foster an emotionally nurturing environment above emphasizing the development of technical skill."

Discuss the extent to which you agree or disagree with this point of view. Support your position with specific reasons and examples from your own experience, observations, or reading.

STOP DO NOT TURN THE PAGE UNTIL TOLD TO DO SO. DO NOT RETURN TO A PREVIOUS TEST.

Source-Based Essay

Time: 30 minutes

Directions: Both of the following sources address the philosophical paradox of the desire to see things as they are versus the need to appreciate them in a manner that makes emotional sense to us. Read the two passages carefully and then write an essay in which you identify the most important concerns regarding the issue and explain why they are important. Your essay must draw on information from *both* of the sources. In addition, you may draw upon your own experience, observations, or reading. Be sure to *cite* the sources, whether you are paraphrasing or directly quoting.

When paraphrasing or quoting from the sources, cite each source by referring to the author's last name, the title of the source, or any other clear identifier.

Source 1

Adapted from: Wisnewski, Jeremy J. "Mutant Phenomenology." *X-Men and Philosophy: Astonishing Insight and Uncanny Argument in the Mutant X-verse.* Hoboken, NJ: John Wiley & Sons, Inc. 2009. Print.

Phenomenology is a philosophical movement that has its roots in late-nineteenth- and early-twentieth-century thought, in thinkers such as Edmund Husserl (1859–1938) and Martin Heidegger (1889–1976). It is a systematic investigation into phenomena — that is, into the way things present themselves to us in experience. Both Husserl and Heidegger thought that things present themselves as they really are in our experiences, but that we often distort the truth that experience presents. We impose particular theories onto phenomena and insist that they conform to our preconceived notions about how the world is. To do phenomenology is to try and set aside our preconceptions and to uncover the actual *being* of things as they reveal themselves to us. In a way, it is to see past our preconceptions into the heart of things.

Source 2

Adapted from: Tschner, George. "High-Tech Mythology in X-Men." *X-Men and Philosophy: Astonishing Insight and Uncanny Argument in the Mutant X-verse.* Hoboken, NJ: John Wiley & Sons, Inc. 2009. Print.

Creating and believing in mythical heroes and heroic deeds are ways that human consciousness conceptualizes major forces and conflicts. The ancient Greeks satisfied the need to understand the how, the why, the origin of things, and the destiny of human beings beyond social and biological life through an elaborate polytheism that invested divinities with powers and personalities beyond the human. Mythology is a figurative and metaphorical way the human intellect grasps its world and answers and resolves some of the most fundamental questions. Unlike ancient Greece, today's society faces one of its most pressing issues in the relationship between humanity and technology. Contemporary technology has created the machine, which has dwarfed the natural abilities of the human body. The native capacities of the human mind are slow and meager compared to the speed and processing power of the computer. The major events of the nineteenth and twentieth centuries have been shaped by the use and development of the machine in manufacturing, war, transportation, and scientific research.

STOP DO NOT TURN THE PAGE UNTIL TOLD TO DO SO.
DO NOT RETURN TO A PREVIOUS TEST.

Part 3
Mathematics

Time: 85 minutes for 56 multiple-choice questions

Directions: Choose the best answer to each question. Mark the corresponding oval on the answer sheet. Remember, try to answer every question.

1. Mary hid 25 Easter eggs. Six are yellow, six are green, eight are blue, and the rest are orange. If Sue found all the orange eggs, what fraction shows how many eggs she found? Show your answer in simplest form.

    (A) $\frac{20}{25}$

    (B) $\frac{4}{5}$

    (C) $\frac{1}{5}$

    (D) $\frac{1}{2}$

    (E) $\frac{3}{5}$

© John Wiley & Sons, Inc.

2. This diagram represents merit badges earned by Boy Scouts in a troop at summer camp. According to the diagram, which statement is NOT true about the scouts in the troop?

    (A) Some of the kids who earned hiking merit badges earned hunting merit badges.

    (B) All the scouts earned swimming merit badges.

    (C) None of the scouts who earned hunting merit badges earned swimming merit badges.

    (D) None of the scouts who earned pottery merit badges earned hiking merit badges.

    (E) All the scouts earned hunting merit badges.

Go on to next page

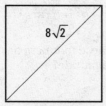

© John Wiley & Sons, Inc.

3. This square has a diagonal with a measure of $8\sqrt{2}$. What is the perimeter of the square?

(A) 32

(B) 64

(C) 8

(D) 16

(E) 128

$$8x - 2y = 48$$
$$-3x - 4y = 1$$

4. What is the solution to this system of equations?

(A) (3, 7)

(B) (–5, 4)

(C) (5, –4)

(D) (2, 3)

(E) (–10, –7)

5. Which of the following does NOT have the same value as $3\frac{2}{5}$?

(A) 3.4

(B) $\frac{17}{5}$

(C) $3\frac{4}{10}$

(D) $\frac{68}{20}$

(E) 3.04

6. Which of the following is a like term with $8x^{10}y^4z^7$?

(A) $8x^{10}y^6z^7$

(B) $17x^{10}y^4z^4$

(C) $-4x^{11}y^4z^7$

(D) $54x^{10}y^3z^7$

(E) $-3x^{10}y^4z^7$

> No number that is 1 more than a number divisible by 4 is divisible by 5.

© John Wiley & Sons, Inc.

7. Which of the following is a counterexample to this statement?

(A) 17

(B) 13

(C) 29

(D) 25

(E) 33

Stem	Leaf
2	0 0 4 8
4	3 5 7
7	0 1 9

2 | 4 = 240

© John Wiley & Sons, Inc.

8. Which of the following numbers is represented in this stem-and-leaf plot?

(A) 204

(B) 450

(C) 79

(D) 73

(E) 15

$$p - |-34| = 72$$

9. What is the solution to this equation?

(A) 106

(B) 38

(C) 102

(D) 42

(E) 36

10. If $\angle ABC$ is complementary to $\angle DEF$ and the measure of $\angle ABC$ is 34°, what is the measure of $\angle DEF$?

(A) 146°

(B) 326°

(C) 54°

(D) 56°

(E) 154°

Go on to next page

11. Which of the following is NOT a factor of 120?

    (A) 12

    (B) 14

    (C) 10

    (D) 5

    (E) 20

12. The sum of two consecutive even integers is 16 less than 3 times the higher integer. What is the lower of the two integers?

    (A) 2

    (B) 42

    (C) 12

    (D) 26

    (E) 14

    Week 1: 52

    Week 2: 64

    Week 3: 28

    Week 4: ?

13. The given record shows the number of pies sold by a bakery each of the first three weeks of the year. How many pies must the bakery sell in the fourth week for the mean number of pies sold per week to be 48?

    (A) 192

    (B) 48

    (C) 144

    (D) 42

    (E) 49

© John Wiley & Sons, Inc.

14. In this diagram, two congruent circles share a point, and each shares three points with the rectangle. The radius of each circle is 2 centimeters. What is the area of the shaded region, rounded to the nearest hundredth?

    (A) 32.00 cm²

    (B) 25.13 cm²

    (C) 57.13 cm²

    (D) 15.43 cm²

    (E) 6.87 cm²

$$17.7, \ -17.77, \ -\frac{54}{3}, \ 17\frac{4}{5}, \ 17\frac{2}{3}, \ -17\frac{5}{6}$$

15. Which of these numbers has the fourth-highest magnitude?

    (A) 17.7

    (B) $-17\frac{5}{6}$

    (C) -17.77

    (D) $-\frac{54}{3}$

    (E) $17\frac{4}{5}$

16. What is the sum of $3a^2b^5$ and $6a^2b^5$?

    (A) $9a^4b^{10}$

    (B) $3a^2b^5$

    (C) $18a^2b^5$

    (D) $9a^2b^5$

    (E) $9ab$

17. Aden ran 9 miles in 57 minutes and 14 seconds. He then immediately ran back to his starting point at a slower speed. What was Aden's average speed for the full trip?

    Which of the following would give you enough information to answer this question?

    (A) Aden's fastest mile

    (B) The amount of time Aden took to run the second half of the distance back to the starting point

    (C) The total distance Aden ran

    (D) The total amount of time Aden ran downhill

    (E) The amount of time Aden took to run back to the starting point

    3, 7, 11, 15, 19, 23 …

18. What is the 11th number in this sequence?

    (A) 43

    (B) 39

    (C) 47

    (D) 46

    (E) 51

Go on to next page

$$8j + 10 = 90 - 8j$$

19. What is the solution to this equation?

    (A) 10

    (B) All real numbers

    (C) 5

    (D) No solution

    (E) 0

20. If (–5, 8) is reflected over the x-axis, what is the resulting image point?

    (A) (5, 8)

    (B) (–5, –8)

    (C) (5, –8)

    (D) (8, 5)

    (E) (–8, 5)

$$\frac{x^2 + 9x + 20}{x^2 - x - 20}$$

21. Which of the following is the simplest form of the given rational expression?

    (A) $\dfrac{x^2 + 9x + 20}{x^2 - x - 20}$

    (B) –1

    (C) $\dfrac{x - 5}{x + 5}$

    (D) $\dfrac{x + 5}{x - 5}$

    (E) $-\dfrac{4}{5}$

22. Venus has two oatmeal cookies, five chocolate cookies, and one peanut butter cookie in a bag. If he reaches into the bag and randomly pulls out one cookie, what is the probability that it will be an oatmeal or peanut butter cookie?

    (A) $\dfrac{3}{5}$

    (B) $\dfrac{1}{32}$

    (C) $\dfrac{5}{8}$

    (D) $\dfrac{1}{4}$

    (E) $\dfrac{3}{8}$

23. Which of the following is the prime factorization of 210?

    (A) $2 \cdot 5 \cdot 7 \cdot 11$

    (B) $3 \cdot 5 \cdot 7$

    (C) $2 \cdot 15 \cdot 7$

    (D) $2 \cdot 3 \cdot 5 \cdot 7$

    (E) $2 \cdot 3 \cdot 35$

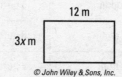

© John Wiley & Sons, Inc.

24. If the area of the given rectangle is 72 m², what is the value of x?

    (A) 4

    (B) 2

    (C) 1

    (D) 72

    (E) 6

25. What is the sum of $8x$, $12y$, $-3x$, and $5y$?

    (A) $5x - 17y$

    (B) $28xy$

    (C) $5x + 17y$

    (D) $22xy$

    (E) $11x + 17y$

26. Which of the following has a value equal to $28\frac{3}{5}$?

    (A) $\dfrac{144}{5}$

    (B) 28.3

    (C) 28.6

    (D) 286 percent

    (E) 28.7

Go on to next page

Favorite Dessert	Percentage of Respondents
Ice Cream	32 percent
Pie	24 percent
Cake	21 percent
Pudding	15 percent
Gelatin	6 percent
Other	2 percent

© John Wiley & Sons, Inc.

27. Three hundred people were asked to name their favorite dessert. This table shows the results of the survey. According to the table, which of the following statements is NOT true?

(A) The number of people who chose cake is 18 more than the number of people who chose pudding.

(B) The number of people who chose gelatin is 45 less than the number of people who chose cake.

(C) 6 people chose something in the "other" category.

(D) The number of people who chose pie is 24 less than the number of people who chose ice cream.

(E) The sum of the number of people who chose pie and the number of people who chose pudding is 9 greater than the number of people who chose ice cream.

28. If $f(x) = 3x^2 - 4x + 11$, what is the value of $f(7)$?

(A) 130

(B) 4

(C) 186

(D) 154

(E) 10

29. What is the greatest common factor of 250 and 450?

(A) 5

(B) 10

(C) 25

(D) 15

(E) 50

3 3 3 1 3 3 3

30. What is the mode of the given set of data?

(A) 3

(B) 1

(C) 4

(D) 19

(E) $\frac{19}{7}$

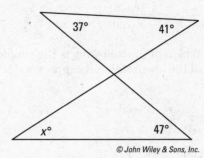

© John Wiley & Sons, Inc.

31. In this diagram, what is the value of x?

(A) 31°

(B) 30°

(C) 102°

(D) 78°

(E) 43°

32. If $2w - 6 = 10$, what is $-4w + 12$?

(A) 4

(B) 20

(C) –10

(D) –20

(E) 5

Go on to next page

33. Which of the following is 147.83 percent in decimal form?

    (A) 1.4783

    (B) 14,783.0

    (C) 14.783

    (D) 147,830

    (E) 1,478.3

34. Which of the following relations is a function?

    (A) {(1, 2), (1, 3), (1, 4), (1, 5)}

    (B) {(1, 7), (2, 4), (7, 5), (2, 8)}

    (C) {(–2, 9), (0, 4), (3, –5), (0, 6)}

    (D) {(2, 6), (4, 2), (8, 7), (10, 2)}

    (E) {(8, –11), (9, 10), (11, 8), (8, 12)}

35. What is $\frac{3}{7}$ of $\frac{9}{20}$?

    (A) $\frac{4}{9}$

    (B) $\frac{27}{140}$

    (C) $\frac{20}{21}$

    (D) $\frac{6}{13}$

    (E) $\frac{21}{20}$

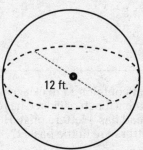

© John Wiley & Sons, Inc.

36. The diameter of the given sphere is 7 feet. What is the surface area of the sphere?

    (A) 36π ft.^{2}

    (B) 576π ft.^{2}

    (C) 144π ft.^{2}

    (D) 48π ft.^{2}

    (E) 24π ft.^{2}

37. Brian is 11 times older than Bitty. The sum of their ages is 48. How old was Bitty 2 years ago?

    (A) 42

    (B) 1

    (C) 12

    (D) 4

    (E) 2

38. Which of the following is 938,425 in scientific notation?

    (A) 9.38425×10^5

    (B) 9.38425×10^{-5}

    (C) 93.8425×10^4

    (D) 93.8425×10^{-4}

    (E) 9.38425×10^4

39. Which of the following is NOT a multiple of 12?

    (A) 12

    (B) 24

    (C) 132

    (D) 6

    (E) 1,212

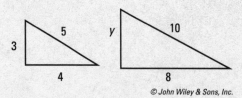

© John Wiley & Sons, Inc.

40. If the given triangles are similar, what is the value of *y*?

    (A) 1.5

    (B) 6

    (C) 4

    (D) 7

    (E) 5

Go on to next page

41. What is the sum of 17 and –19?

    (A) 2

    (B) –2

    (C) 36

    (D) –36

    (E) 8

42. A specific pie chart represents the 238,456 people who live in a city; one of the sectors of the pie chart has a central angle of 45 degrees. How many people does that sector represent?

    (A) 29,807

    (B) 8

    (C) 59,614

    (D) 45

    (E) 1,907,648

43. If Ace walks 724.26 decameters down a trail and then walks back to his starting point, how many kilometers does he walk on the way back to the starting point?

    (A) 7,242.6

    (B) 72.426

    (C) 7.2426

    (D) 724.26

    (E) 0.72426

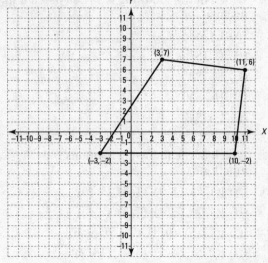

© John Wiley & Sons, Inc.

44. Which of the following is NOT an ordered pair of coordinates of a vertex of the given quadrilateral after a 90-degree rotation counterclockwise about the origin?

    (A) (6, –11)

    (B) (7, –3)

    (C) (–6, 11)

    (D) (–2, 3)

    (E) (–2, –10)

45. What is the solution to –4k + 9 < –15?

    (A) k < 6

    (B) k > –1.5

    (C) k < 1.5

    (D) k > 6

    (E) k > 1.5

46. A basket contains 14 necklaces and no other items. Each necklace has 26 beads. Each bead has 4 letters on it. How many total letters are in the basket?

    (A) 1,456

    (B) 44

    (C) 91

    (D) 1,526

    (E) 2,114

Go on to next page

47. If Kat drives 70 miles in 2 hours, what is her average speed for the drive?

    (A) 70 miles per hour

    (B) 35 miles per hour

    (C) 140 miles per hour

    (D) 210 miles per hour

    (E) 7 miles per hour

48. 42 is what percent of 105?

    (A) 44.1

    (B) 2.5

    (C) 47

    (D) 0.4

    (E) 40

12 24 32 54 8 0

49. What is the median of the given set of data?

    (A) 43

    (B) 21.67

    (C) 18

    (D) 54

    (E) 0

$$4\frac{1}{7}+9\frac{2}{3}+\left(-3\frac{5}{6}\right)=$$

50. Find the sum; don't simplify.

    (A) $\frac{1}{3}$

    (B) $\frac{35}{6}$

    (C) $\frac{35}{42}$

    (D) $\frac{419}{42}$

    (E) 10

$$\frac{12}{m}=\frac{36}{12}$$

51. What is the solution to the given proportion?

    (A) 4

    (B) 6

    (C) 2

    (D) 8

    (E) 3

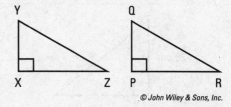

© John Wiley & Sons, Inc.

52. $\triangle XYZ$ and $\triangle PQR$ are congruent right triangles. If the measure of $\angle R$ is 38°, what is the measure of $\angle Y$?

    (A) 38°

    (B) 42°

    (C) 142°

    (D) 128°

    (E) 52°

53. Aggie has a $\frac{1}{5}$ probability of being picked to participate on the game show *Price of Fortune*. If she gets on the show, she will have a $\frac{1}{3}$ probability of winning a brand new car. What is the probability that Aggie will get on *Price of Fortune* and win a brand new car?

    (A) $\frac{1}{8}$

    (B) $\frac{8}{15}$

    (C) $\frac{1}{15}$

    (D) $\frac{3}{5}$

    (E) $\frac{3}{8}$

Go on to next page

> All numbers that are not prime are even.

54. Which of the following is NOT a counter-example to the given statement?

    (A) 45
    (B) 27
    (C) 11
    (D) 33
    (E) 9

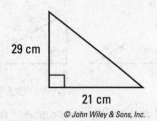

© John Wiley & Sons, Inc.

55. What is the area of the given right triangle?

    (A) 609 cm²
    (B) 290 cm²
    (C) 304.5 cm²
    (D) 210 cm²
    (E) 192 cm²

56. If John's age is represented by xy and Mike's age is represented by xyz, which of the following represents the product of John and Mike's ages?

    (A) x^2y^2z
    (B) xyz^2
    (C) $2xyz$
    (D) $2xy + z$
    (E) x^4yz

STOP DO NOT TURN THE PAGE UNTIL TOLD TO DO SO.
DO NOT RETURN TO A PREVIOUS TEST.

Chapter 17

Practice Exam 2: Answers and Explanations

• •

*I*f this is the second practice exam you've taken, we hope you've improved your scores and are feeling more confident about taking the Praxis Core. Use the answers and explanations in this chapter to see how well you performed and to understand where you might have gone wrong on the answers you missed. Remember, the practice exam can help you determine where you need to focus your studies in preparation for the real Praxis Core. If you want to score your test quickly, flip to the end of the chapter, where the "Answer Key" gives only the letters of the correct answers.

If you want even more preparation for taking the Praxis, head to learn.dummies.com. There you can take three more practice tests, review the answers and explanations, and get a personalized summary of your performance.

Part 1: Reading

1. **E. change his legacy.**

   The passage explains that Nobel was dismayed by seeing himself referred to as "the merchant of death" in a newspaper. He didn't want to be remembered that way, so he endowed the Nobel Prizes so that he would be remembered for something else. In other words, he wanted to change his legacy.

   The right answer is not Choice (A) because the passage never indicates that Nobel made any money from the Nobel Prizes; on the contrary, he devoted the fortune he had made through other means to their establishment.

   The right answer is not Choice (B) because there's no indication that Nobel thought he would actually live longer as a result of endowing the Nobel Prizes. The idea was to be remembered differently, not to live longer.

   The right answer is not Choice (C) because, though Nobel did want the prizes to draw attention away from other things he had done, he wasn't specifically trying to cover those things up. People would still know that he had invented explosives; he would just be *more* famous for something else.

   The right answer is not Choice (D) because the passage doesn't indicate that Nobel's motivation was to be famous forever as a result of endowing the Prizes. He was already famous, but he wanted to be remembered for doing a good thing instead of causing destruction.

2. **C. report on new and exciting discoveries about killer whales.**

   The passage reports on recent discoveries about killer whales. As is often the case with such questions, the broadest answer is the correct one.

   The right answer is not Choice (A) because, although the passage mentions that there are killer whale subspecies, it doesn't explain how they diverged or even focus entirely on the subspecies topic.

The right answer is not Choice (B) because the passage never implies any sort of disagreement between scientists and the general public.

The right answer is not Choice (D) because even though the passage closes by mentioning that most scientists now use the term *orca*, the passage as a whole is not an argument about proper terminology.

The right answer is not Choice (E) because the passage is not particularly humorous and, although it's not written for an audience of experts, there's no indication that it's aimed specifically at children.

3. **C. evidence that nobody actually lived there.**

The middle of the passage not only mentions the lack of evidence that Göbekli Tepe was residential but also establishes that the site dates from before humans established permanent residences at all. Therefore, its purpose must have been ceremonial.

The right answer is not Choice (A) because there's no reason to assume that an archaeological site was religious just because it's large. Religious structures are often large, but so are other types of structures.

The right answer is not Choice (B) because, while the passage explains that Göbekli Tepe had elaborate artwork, that fact in and of itself is not the primary evidence that it was a religious site.

The right answer is not Choice (D) because, though the passage does briefly compare Göbekli Tepe to Stonehenge, it doesn't imply a "close resemblance."

The right answer is not Choice (E) because the passage doesn't say that Göbekli Tepe played a role in the invention of agriculture; it mentions that people hadn't developed agriculture when Göbekli Tepe was built, as support for the conclusion that the structure could not have been a permanent residence.

4. **D. inform readers about Hoffman and the controversy surrounding her work.**

The best answer here is Choice (D) because the passage does inform readers about Hoffman and about the controversy surrounding her work. Other answers may be close, but Choice (D) is the most accurate description of the overall passage content.

The right answer is not Choice (A) because, while the passage does include details about Hoffman's life and work, it doesn't include enough personal detail to be called "a personal biography."

The right answer is not Choice (B) because the passage doesn't argue a specific viewpoint on the Field Museum's decision.

The right answer is not Choice (C) because the passage as a whole is about Hoffman and her work. It mentions that some people were offended by Hoffman's work and establishes what their reasoning was, but that doesn't serve as the basis of the passage.

The right answer is not Choice (E) because, although the passage establishes that there haven't been many famous female sculptors, that point isn't the main topic.

5. **A. trailblazing.**

Pioneering is a synonym for *trailblazing* — breaking new ground in a certain area (in Hoffman's case, being among the first famous female sculptors).

None of the other choices is correct because they aren't what *pioneering* means in this context. Many of them may be words that accurately describe Hoffman or her work, but they don't fit what the question is asking for.

6. **B. multicultural sensitivity with celebration of the achievements of women.** The thorny paradox raised by the passage is that, although Hoffman's work was potentially offensive from a multiculturalist perspective, the same sensitivity that demands we address this also encourages us to celebrate the work of important women in the arts.

The right answer is not Choice (A) because how would we even know what the cultural values of the future are? The passage does not make any predictions.

The right answer is not Choice (C) because the passage doesn't set up any kind of paradox that pits science against art; rather, it pits the duty to honor women artists against the duty to respect the views of people who might object to her work.

The right answer is not Choice (D) because the passage doesn't pit intentionalist criticism (that is, approaching works of art from the perspective of the artist's original intentions) against interpretive criticism (prioritizing that art's effects on the audience). Even if you didn't recognize these terms, it should still be possible to eliminate this answer choice. It was there to try to trick people who automatically gravitate towards the most confusing answer choice.

The right answer is not Choice (E) because the passage doesn't really get into what the mission of a museum is. You can reasonably infer that the Field Museum decided to hide the sculptures because of public opinion, but the passage is about Hoffman's work itself, not the museum and its mission.

7. **A. It examines a familiar concept from an unorthodox viewpoint.**

The familiar concept is the Renaissance, and the unorthodox viewpoint is the notion that it was caused by the preceding Black Plague.

The right answer is not Choice (B) because the passage doesn't address or imply any conspiracy theory.

The right answer is not Choice (C) because the passage never brings up a two-sided controversy.

The right answer is not Choice (D) because the passage discusses only one artistic period — the Renaissance — not two.

The right answer is not Choice (E) because, though the passage mentions how the Black Plague came to Europe, it doesn't scientifically analyze the origins of the epidemic.

8. **A. "artistic brilliance"**

The preoccupation with the "human experience" mentioned in the second paragraph led to the "artistic brilliance" mentioned in the first. The Renaissance is primarily associated with the arts, and the other part of the sentence in the second paragraph clearly alludes to the "scientific advancement" previously mentioned, so the rest of the sentence is presumably about the arts.

The right answer is not Choice (B) because the first half of the sentence ("desperation to stop the devastation had gotten people thinking . . ."), not the second, is what alludes to the "scientific advancement" mentioned in the first paragraph.

The right answer is not Choice (C) because the first paragraph mentions "violent political oppression" as a characteristic of the Dark Ages, not of the Renaissance.

The right answer is not Choice (D) because the "European golden age" indicates the Renaissance as a whole, not specifically the artistic side of it.

The right answer is not Choice (E) because "Europe's worst nightmare" refers to the Black Plague itself, not to the effect it had on people's relationship to art.

9. **E. coherent**

The feudal system collapsed after the Plague, so it was no longer *feasible* or *coherent* (it couldn't "cohere" or "hold together").

None of the other choices is correct because none gives a correct definition of *feasible*.

10. **C. laborers became so scarce that they were in a better bargaining position.**

    The passage explains that the peasant population was so devastated by the Plague that laborers were suddenly in a better position simply because there were fewer of them.

    The right answer is not Choice (A) because, although advances in ethical philosophy were made during the Renaissance, those advances aren't why feudalism ended. The collapse of feudalism was an immediate effect of the Plague, and the advancements of the Renaissance were an eventual effect.

    The right answer is not Choice (B) because scientific discoveries aren't what gave the emergent middle class a wider range of job options in the early Renaissance. The opportunities occurred because so many commoners died during the Plague.

    The right answer is not Choice (D) because trade between Asia and the Mediterranean is mentioned in the passage as contributing to the outbreak of the Plague in Europe, not as having led to "increased mechanization."

    The right answer is not Choice (E) because the passage doesn't mention feudal lords fleeing their castles and abandoning their lands. They stayed in their castles, but there weren't enough peasants left to farm their lands anymore.

11. **B. the Renaissance was the inevitable result of the vastly reduced population.**

    The meaning of the given phrase, and the point of the passage as a whole, is that the Renaissance came about more or less because Europe's population was thinned out by the Plague.

    The right answer is not Choice (A) because the passage never implies that the Renaissance didn't happen. The passage just makes an argument about what caused it.

    The right answer is not Choice (C) because the passage says that the Black Plague, not the Renaissance, started in central Asia.

    The right answer is not Choice (D) because the passage never implies that the Renaissance actually happened at a different time from when it reportedly did; it just makes an interesting argument about its causes.

    The right answer is not Choice (E) because, though the passage does indeed offer a dark explanation for the causes of the Renaissance, it doesn't suggest that the term "Renaissance" itself is a euphemistic (whitewashed) expression signifying something else.

12. **B. correct a widespread misconception.**

    The author starts off by calling a term "misunderstood" and then goes on to explain what it means "in actuality." The goal is clearly to correct a widespread misconception.

    The right answer is not Choice (A) because the passage is not espousing (arguing for) a particular philosophy; it's correcting the erroneous usage of a particular term. Simply pointing out a correct definition is not the same as making an argument for a certain viewpoint.

    The right answer is not Choice (C) because the author is not taking sides in a philosophical debate; no "debate" exists here. A popular misunderstanding is not a philosophical debate.

    The right answer is not Choice (D) because the author is not suggesting a new definition, just explaining what the original definition actually is.

    The right answer is not Choice (E) because the correct usage of a term is not an "unpopular viewpoint." Even if most people misunderstand the term, the simple correction of a definition is not a debate.

13. **C. philosophers use to describe others' work, rather than their own.**

    The author explains that actual philosophers always use the term *nihilism* pejoratively, as an insult for others' work, not as a description of their own.

    The right answer is not Choice (A) because the author explains that philosophers do in fact use the term *nihilism;* they just do so as an insult.

The right answer is not Choice (B) because among actual philosophers, the term *nihilism* always means the same thing. Non-philosophers are the people who use it incorrectly.

The right answer is not Choice (D) because the passage never implies that philosophers used the term *nihilism* during one particular era of philosophy only.

The right answer is not Choice (E) because the passage establishes that young people accidentally misuse the term *nihilism,* which directly refutes the idea that they misuse it deliberately.

14. **D. dispassionate.**

The author is simply explaining something in an unemotional fashion. The term for that sort of tone is *dispassionate*.

The right answer is not Choice (A) because the author is not using irony or cracking jokes at anyone's expense, so calling the tone sardonic isn't accurate.

The right answer is not Choice (B) because the author is not talking down to anyone, so the tone isn't *condescending*.

The right answer is not Choice (C) because the author doesn't seem to be particularly merry or gleeful, so the tone doesn't qualify as *jovial*.

The right answer is not Choice (E) because the author doesn't seem to be frightened, wary, or paranoid about anything, so the tone isn't *apprehensive*.

15. **E. jargon.**

The word *jargon* refers to any language that would be used by the members of a certain group among themselves but not recognized by outsiders without an explanation, so to call these terms *jargon* is accurate.

The right answer is not Choice (A) because the terms aren't being used ironically; the definitions given are what they actually mean to people in the ASMR community.

The right answer is not Choice (B) because the words in italics aren't being emphasized more than others; they have special formatting because they are unfamiliar.

The right answer is not Choice (C) because even though some of the terms are in fact proper nouns, the italics don't identify that characteristic. The term YouTube is a proper noun, and it isn't italicized in the passage.

The right answer is not Choice (D) because the terms aren't being misused. They may be unfamiliar to most people, but they are being used to mean what they actually mean.

16. **C. use a specific animal as an example to explain a particular term.**

The passage begins by talking about the dunnart, but it then becomes clear that it's using the dunnart just as a springboard to talk about the larger concept of convergent evolution. So this reading is one of those "specific example to general principle" passages that are such a common presence on tests like the Praxis.

The right answer is not Choice (A) because, even though the passage briefly compares a particular marsupial to a particular non-marsupial, the purpose of the passage as a whole is not to distinguish between marsupials and non-marsupials. (If it were, the passage would have explained the difference.)

The right answer is not Choice (B) because, although the passage does specify that dunnarts aren't mice, the passage as a whole is about convergent evolution, not specifically about mice.

The right answer is not Choice (D) because, while the passage does correct people, it would be a bit much to say it *excoriates* them. To *excoriate* is to severely and angrily criticize, so this would be a wild exaggeration of the passage's tone.

The right answer is not Choice (E) because the passage doesn't say or imply that the dunnart itself is key to evolutionary theory; it's an example of convergent evolution, which is an important concept, but lots of animals are examples of this process.

17. **C. It does not in fact provide a legal excuse for violence.**

This answer choice is essentially a paraphrase of the final sentence of the passage, so it's definitely a point that the passage makes.

The right answer is not Choice (A) because the passage implies that lots of people don't know what the *Chaplinsky* decision means, not that no one does.

The right answer is not Choice (B) because the passage never mentions anything about *Chaplinsky* being affected in any way by subsequent Supreme Court decisions.

The right answer is not Choice (D) because, although the defendant claimed the law was unconstitutional, the passage never takes a stance on this issue.

The right answer is not Choice (E) because one of the answer choices was in fact correct.

18. **C. explain that a very famous character was heavily based on a lesser-known one.**

The passage does in fact explain that a famous fictional detective (Sherlock Holmes) was based on a lesser-known one (Auguste Dupin); that's all the passage does, so Choice (C) is the correct answer. In general, answer choices that use broad terms such as *explain* are more likely to be correct than answer choices that use more specific words such as *argue* or *accuse*.

The right answer is not Choice (A) because the passage specifies that Arthur Conan Doyle "admitted the obvious influence and gave Poe credit," so plagiarism isn't an issue.

The right answer is not Choice (B) because the passage doesn't get into whose stories were better from a critical perspective.

The right answer is not Choice (D) because the traditional explanation has always acknowledged, as did Conan Doyle himself, that Poe invented the detective story. Poe's stories aren't as broadly famous as Conan Doyle's, but critics have always known that Poe's came first.

The right answer is not Choice (E) because the passage doesn't address any confusion about Holmes and Dupin. It says that most people have heard of Holmes but not Dupin, not that people confuse the two.

19. **A. conjecture.**

The fact that the sentence begins with "perhaps" is a clue that the final sentence of the passage is *conjecture* — a guess or hypothesis.

The right answer is not Choice (B) because the final sentence is not a clue to what comes later, so it's not *foreshadowing*.

The right answer is not Choice (C) because *synecdoche* means "using a part to symbolize a whole," as in when you refer to your car as your "wheels." This figure of speech doesn't occur in the final sentence. (Don't be fooled into picking an answer just because it's a fancy word; these options are often tricks.)

The right answer is not Choice (D) because an *allusion* is a reference, and the final sentence doesn't contain a reference to anything.

The right answer is not Choice (E) because *poetic license* refers to an author describing something in an inaccurate or ungrammatical way for the sake of aesthetics, and the final sentence doesn't do this.

20. **B. gauche.**

"Socially oblivious" in this context means "rude" or "unmannerly," and *gauche* is a fancy synonym for such terms.

None of the other choices is correct because none presents a close synonym of "socially oblivious."

21. **A. intellectual disdain.**

The author spends the rest of the passage explaining why the "rule of thumb" alluded to at the outset is a stupid idea, so you can fairly say that the author has "intellectual disdain" for it. (*Disdain* means "contempt" or "revulsion.")

The right answer is not Choice (B) because the author may be cynical but doesn't appear to be *shocked* by anything.

The right answer is not Choice (C) because the author doesn't regret anything or seem to be melancholy.

The right answer is not Choice (D) because the author is discussing a problem that exists, not delusionally imagining one.

The right answer is not Choice (E) because, while the author is *dismissing* the idea that he criticizes, he is not being *dismissive*. He wants to combat the problem, not ignore it.

22. **E. self-contained.**

Discrete means "separate," so the best answer is Choice (E), self-contained. (Remember, don't confuse *discrete* with *discreet,* meaning "secret.")

None of the other answers is correct because none is the definition of *discrete*.

23. **C. naïve administrators.**

The second sentence of the passage lays the blame on administrators, and the passage in general explains why their policy is naïve.

None of the other choices is correct because the second sentence of the passage establishes that the author blames administrators. Nowhere does the passage indicate that the author blames teachers, students, scientists, or parents. It never mentions scientists or parents at all.

24. **B. draw the line at respecting opinions that are demonstrably untrue.**

The last sentence of the first paragraph and the first two sentences of the second are the places where the passage most clearly states that the author's complaint is with professors being obliged to respect ideas that aren't true.

The right answer is not Choice (A) because the author never says or implies that professors should deliberately offend students. The point is that offense is sometimes unavoidable in education, not that it's desirable.

The right answer is not Choice (C) because the author's point is that facts need to be respected over opinions; the passage never suggests that professors should simply teach their own personal opinions.

The right answer is not Choice (D) because this statement is nearly the opposite of the author's point; the passage argues that professors *should* correct students' opinions and *not* merely their mechanics.

The right answer is not Choice (E) because the author never implies that professors should go out of their ways to flunk students who appear unknowledgeable. The passage simply says that correcting students' general knowledge should be part of a professor's job.

25. **C. whether to retreat from the world or try to improve it.**

Choice (C) is a clear paraphrase of the line from the passage that says "should a good person 'turn the other cheek' in the face of evil . . . . or should he attempt to make the world a better place by actively combating the wicked."

The right answer is not Choice (A) because early on, the author flatly states that the famous soliloquy is "*not* about whether to commit suicide."

The right answer is not Choice (B) because, although the author explains that the paradox Hamlet confronts involves whether to take a certain piece of scriptural advice, the passage never indicates that the question is about God's existence itself.

The right answer is not Choice (D) because the author explains that the speech is about whether to fight evil at all or to passively ignore it, not about the methods one may use to fight it.

The right answer is not Choice (E) because the passage doesn't imply that "To be or not to be" is about something incomprehensible; the author explains one possible meaning.

26. **E. unacceptable.**

The author states that "Hamlet already flatly ruled out suicide on ethical grounds" — that is, he decided suicide is unacceptable.

The right answer is not Choice (A) because the author states that Hamlet "flatly ruled out suicide on ethical grounds," which would indicate that suicide itself is unethical. And there's no indication Hamlet considers suicide the lesser of two evils.

The right answer is not Choice (B) because the "eternal paradox of morality" referred to in the passage is about whether to be active or passive in the face of evil, not about suicide.

The right answer is not Choice (C) because, although the idea that suicide is "attractive but frightening" is the common interpretation of the speech, the passage establishes early on that the author believes that interpretation to be wrong.

The right answer is not Choice (D) because nothing in the passage points to this answer.

27. **D. correct a misreading.**

In the third sentence, the author states that "virtually everyone . . . is dead wrong about what [the speech] means" and then goes on to explain why. This establishes that the author's goal is to "correct a misreading."

The right answer is not Choice (A) because the author explains that Hamlet is wondering about whether to take an ethical stand; it's not the author's own goal in writing the passage.

The right answer is not Choice (B) because the author is trying to explain a complex piece of literature, not to simplify a complex issue. If anything, the author's reading of the speech is more complex than the common one.

The right answer is not Choice (C) because the author never warns about anything that might happen in the future.

The right answer is not Choice (E) because the author explains that other people often make a mistake in explaining the "to be or not to be" speech; the passage never indicates the author made a mistake or apologizes for having made one.

28. **A. Why should great apes have rights similar to human rights?**

The final sentence, which begins with "The reasoning goes that . . .", is where the passage does indeed answer the question of why great apes should have rights similar to human rights.

The right answer is not Choice (B) because the passage never fully explains the difference between a great ape and a monkey. Monkeys are never mentioned.

The right answer is not Choice (C) because, although the passage mentions that the founders of the Great Ape Project are Peter Singer and Paola Cavalieri, it never says that they're its most famous supporters. There may be more famous supporters whom the passage simply never mentions.

The right answer is not Choice (D) because the passage mentions that great apes are both exhibited in zoos and used in scientific research, but it never says which purpose more great apes are used for.

The right answer is not Choice (E) because, although the passage mentions that great apes are intelligent, it never explains how researchers know this or how apes' intelligence is measured.

29. **D. They do not make use of underground burrows.**

The second sentence of the passage states that hares live in nests and that rabbits are the ones who live in burrows.

The right answer is not Choice (A) because that passage says that the hare is the only *mammal* with a jointed skull, not that it's the only *animal* with one.

The right answer is not Choice (B), (C), or (E) because all these statements are true of rabbits, not hares.

30. **C. Matter can be sent into the past, but not living beings.**

The passage objects to the idea of time-travel to the past by explaining that a human traveling to the past may cause a paradox. The idea that inanimate matter could be sent to the past, but not living beings, would get around the paradox, and thus resolve the objection.

The right answer is not Choice (A) because, though physicists do indeed believe exceeding the speed of light to be impossible, the passage doesn't raise any objection to a time-travel theory based on this issue. So a discovery that surpassing the speed of light is somehow possible would not resolve an objection made in the passage.

The right answer is not Choice (B) because physicists already believe that exceeding the speed of light is impossible, so a confirmation of this fact wouldn't explain anything.

The right answer is not Choice (D) because the passage never mentions other dimensions, so the discovery would be irrelevant to the claims of the passage.

The right answer is not Choice (E) because the passage doesn't present any definitions of *time,* so the discovery would be irrelevant to the claims of the passage.

31. **B. exceptions and qualifications.**

The expression *fine print* (like the words in small font at the bottom of a contract, where most of the catches are hidden) usually means something like "exceptions and qualifications," and that's what it means in this context as well; time travel is possible, but not in the way you probably think.

None of the other choices is correct because none is the definition of *fine print* as it's used in the passage.

32. **D. It's a natural consequence of the relationship between speed and time.**

The passage closes by saying that a time machine could be anything that goes fast enough — that is, that time travel is a natural consequence of the relationship between speed and time.

The right answer is not Choice (A) because the passage never says that humans have already achieved time travel.

The right answer is not Choice (B) because the passage never says that time travel to the future would resolve its own paradoxes, just that it wouldn't create any.

The right answer is not Choice (C) because, although the passage does explain that time travel to the future is to some extent a matter of perspective, that statement doesn't make time travel the same as an illusion. (It's actually happening, but only happening relative to something else.)

The right answer is not Choice (E) because, though the simple passage of time does technically constitute time travel to the future (in other words, you're traveling to the future right now because time is passing), that topic isn't addressed in the passage.

33. **D. Passage 1 explains the origin of a theory that Passage 2 then modifies.**

   Passage 1 explains where the asteroid theory came from, and Passage 2 then adds *to* the asteroid theory, rather than presenting a competing theory.

   The right answer is not Choice (A) because the theories presented in the two passages aren't in fact *mutually exclusive* (a term meaning they can't be true at the same time). Passage 2 admits that the asteroid impact happened; it just argues that other things happened too.

   The right answer is not Choice (B) because, though Passage 2 admits that the asteroid impact happened, that doesn't mean that the two passages are exploring the same theory from different angles. Passage 1 concerns the theory that the dinosaurs were killed by just an asteroid, and Passage 2 concerns the theory that they were killed by an asteroid and other events as well.

   The right answer is not Choice (C) because the theory in Passage 2 doesn't seek to replace the theory in Passage 1, just to modify it. Besides, to say that it has replaced the theory in Passage 1 would be incorrect because the readings establish that the theory from Passage 1 is still more popular.

   The right answer is not Choice (E) because Passage 1 and Passage 2 present two (marginally) different theories, not the data and the conclusions for one single theory.

34. **A. ignoring.**

   When Passage 2 says that attributing the extinction solely to an asteroid would involve "writing off" the Deccan traps, the best paraphrase is to say it would involve *ignoring* the Deccan Traps role in the extinction.

   The right answer is not Choice (B) because the objection made by Passage 2 is that the asteroid theory involves believing that the Deccan Traps played no role in the extinction — that is, that the Deccan Traps are being ignored, not misrepresented.

   The right answer is not Choice (C) because Passage 2 doesn't indicate that the theory from Passage 1 is *obscuring* (covering up or hiding) the role played by the Deccan Traps. It means that the theory from Passage 1 simply doesn't account for the Deccan Traps having played a role.

   The right answer is not Choice (D) because the complaint of Passage 2 is that the Deccan Traps aren't being credited with enough of a role in the extinction, which is the opposite of saying that their role is being exaggerated.

   The right answer is not Choice (E) because Passage 2 isn't accusing anyone of plagiarizing anything; it's saying that important data is being ignored, not stolen.

35. **C. One author believes it killed the dinosaurs, and the other believes it was one of multiple causes.**

   Passage 1 concerns the theory that the asteroid killed the dinosaurs, and Passage 2 concerns the theory that at least one other cause may have been involved. The place to confirm this answer is the final sentence of Passage 2 ("No one is denying . . .").

   The right answer is not Choice (A) because saying that the author of Passage 2 doesn't believe an asteroid killed the dinosaurs is going too far.

   The right answer is not Choice (B) because both authors agree about the timing of the asteroid impact.

   The right answer is not Choice (D) because the author of Passage 1 characterizes the asteroid as being heavily composed of iridium, and the author of Passage 2 never challenges this description.

   The right answer is not Choice (E) because the author of Passage 1 never appears to doubt that the asteroid theory is correct.

36. E. Passage 1 explains the history of its theory, whereas Passage 2 does not.

Much of Passage 1 consists of an explanation of when and how the asteroid theory was developed and supported. Passage 2 never gets into the history of the idea that the Deccan Traps played a role.

The right answer is not Choice (A) because the two passages aren't each based on a different scientific discipline. They both involve both chemistry and physics. (Also, keep in mind that an answer choice that would require you to have outside knowledge of the topic is extremely unlikely to be correct; this is a reading test, not a science test.)

The right answer is not Choice (B) because, although the passages establish that the asteroid hit what is now North America and the Deccan Traps formed in what is now Asia, neither passage says that either of these locations is the only place dinosaurs lived.

The right answer is not Choice (C) because the two passages are very similar in tone and reading level, so there's no reason to assume that they were composed with different audiences in mind.

The right answer is not Choice (D) because there's no indication that the author of Passage 2 formulated the Deccan Traps theory, so it's not an original (to the author) theory.

37. B. limited.

The theory from Passage 1 suggests one cause, and the theory from Passage 2 puts forth multiple causes that include the cause from Passage 1. Therefore, Passage 2 sees Passage 1 as limited — that is, true but incomplete.

The right answer is not Choice (A) because Passage 2 admits that the asteroid impact happened and played a role.

The right answer is not Choice (C) because Passage 2 never implies that the theory in Passage 1 is old and that its own idea is newer.

The right answer is not Choice (D) because Passage 2 never implies that the theory in Passage 1 is contradicting itself somehow.

The right answer is not Choice (E) because there's no indication that the author of Passage 2 sees the theory from Passage 1 as *elitist* (somehow snobbish or exclusionary).

38. D. the causes of an agreed-upon event.

The "agreed-upon event" is the extinction of the dinosaurs, and both passages discuss its possible causes.

The right answer is not Choice (A) because the two authors agree about when dinosaurs lived, which you can tell by the fact that they're both discussing the extinction as having happened at the same time.

The right answer is not Choice (B) because neither author ever says anything about some dinosaurs disappearing at different times from other dinosaurs.

The right answer is not Choice (C) because the author of Passage 2 concedes that the asteroid struck earth, and that it did so at the time that the theory in Passage 1 claims.

The right answer is not Choice (E) because neither author ever addresses the question of why one theory or another is popular, or even talks much about which theory is more popular.

39. C. the Medieval Period and the Renaissance.

The Middle Ages and *the Medieval period* are two terms for the same time in history, and the Renaissance came after it. The correction the passage makes is that suits of armor are actually from the Renaissance, not from the Medieval period.

The right answer is not Choice (A) because, although the passage begins by mentioning that most children would be mistaken about when suits of armor were actually worn, it also says that most adults would, too.

The right answer is not Choice (B) because the passage doesn't distinguish between armor and regular clothing; it distinguishes between the armor of two time periods.

The right answer is not Choice (D) because, although the passage establishes that European warriors were the ones who wore suits of armor, the passage doesn't involve comparing them to warriors from other places.

The right answer is not Choice (E) because the passage actually compares wealthy and less wealthy warriors, saying essentially that all Medieval warriors would have worn plate-and-mail suits.

40. **C. civilization hasn't existed long enough to substantially alter human instinct.**

The point of the passage as a whole, as stated most clearly in the last two sentences, is that human instinct and genetics were formed for millions of years, and that civilization hasn't existed for nearly long enough to have substantially altered these things.

The right answer is not Choice (A) because the passage never suggests that common people are broadly wrong about how long civilization has been around; rather, the point is that most people don't know how long humans were evolving before that time.

The right answer is not Choice (B) because the point of the passage is that the development of civilization (government, agriculture, and so on) *didn't* substantially affect human genetics, simply because it happened too recently to have done so yet.

The right answer is not Choice (D) because the passage certainly doesn't say that human evolution stopped when civilization began, just that the previous evolutionary trajectory hasn't yet been significantly altered by civilization.

The right answer is not Choice (E) because the passage never implies that experts disagree about any of this information; it says that laypeople misunderstand it.

41. **B. apparently straightforward questions can be muddled by vague definitions.**

Ultimately, the point of the passage is to call attention to the fact that the apparently straightforward question "What is the southernmost city in the world?" is not so easy to answer because it depends on what counts as a city.

The right answer is not Choice (A) because the point of the passage is not that geography is complex. The problem at hand is how many people a community needs in order to count as a city, which is not a geographic question.

The right answer is not Choice (C) because the passage never implies that the argument is silly. The author appears to think that the question is valid and interesting, though apparently unsolvable.

The right answer is not Choice (D) or Choice (E) because the passage never takes one country's side over the other's; it just explains the nature of the dispute.

42. **B. The first paragraph mainly presents details of William Tyndale's life, and the second deals more closely with his influence.**

The first paragraph is mainly about Tyndale's life, and the second paragraph is mainly about his influence, so Choice (B) is clearly the best description.

The right answer is not Choice (A) because both paragraphs are mainly about Tyndale, not just the second one.

The right answer is not Choice (C) because the first paragraph is about Tyndale's life, not the influence of his Bible.

The right answer is not Choice (D) because the first paragraph is much more about Tyndale and only briefly mentions Shakespeare. Though the second paragraph does allude to Tyndale's influence on Shakespeare, that's not the main point of the paragraph.

The right answer is not Choice (E) because the first paragraph is mainly about Tyndale, not other Bible translations done before the invention of the printing press. (It only briefly alludes to Wycliffe's translation.) Furthermore, the second paragraph is specifically about Tyndale's Bible, not printed Bible translations in general.

43. **A. use him as the standard by which influence on the English language is measured.**

Both allusions to Shakespeare invoke him as the greatest influence on the English language, in order to praise Tyndale by establishing his influence on both the language and on Shakespeare himself.

The right answer is not Choice (B) because only the second paragraph discusses Tyndale's influence on Shakespeare himself, and even then, it never says that Tyndale was the greatest influence on Shakespeare, just a major influence (don't pick a choice that goes further than you need it to).

The right answer is not Choice (C) because the passage never directly compares Tyndale's language to Shakespeare's.

The right answer is not Choice (D) because the passage never implies that people confuse figures of speech coined by Tyndale with those coined by Shakespeare.

The right answer is not Choice (E) because, although the passage certainly elaborates on the political constraints on Tyndale's work, it never mentions anything about political constraints on Shakespeare's.

44. **E. The character of modern literary English was largely established in the 16th century.**

The passage cites Shakespeare and Tyndale as the two greatest influences on the form of literary English, and it establishes that they both did their work in the 16th century.

The right answer is not Choice (A) because the passage says that Shakespeare was influenced by Tyndale's use of language in his translation of religious texts, not necessarily by religion itself.

The right answer is not Choice (B) because the passage never addresses the question of political differences among various English translations of the Bible.

The right answer is not Choice (C) because nothing in the passage implies that Tyndale's Bible caused Henry VIII's break with Rome. The passage merely explains that the Roman Catholic Church was against English translations of the Bible, and that such translations (like Tyndale's, even though he was already dead) became acceptable in England after the king broke with the Catholic Church.

The right answer is not Choice (D) because the passage never says that translations done by individuals are generally superior to those done by committees.

45. **C. who attempted a similar project to Tyndale's but was thwarted.**

The lone mention of Wycliffe explains that, like Tyndale, he tried to translate the Bible into English, but was thwarted because his handwritten translations made it much easier for the state to seize and destroy most of the copies.

The right answer is not Choice (A) because the passage never says that Tyndale was directly inspired by Wycliffe, just that they both tried to do the same thing.

The right answer is not Choice (B) because the passage never says Wycliffe was as talented as Tyndale or mentions anything about Wycliffe's politics.

The right answer is not Choice (D) because the passage doesn't say that Wycliffe's influence on English is harder to measure than Tyndale's; on the contrary, you can safely assume that Wycliffe's influence was much smaller because his Bibles were destroyed.

The right answer is not Choice (E) because, the passage never says Wycliffe was more religious than Tyndale.

46. **D. knack for.**

To have an "ear for" something, in music or in writing, is to be finely attuned to its capacity for aesthetic beauty — that is, to have a knack for it.

None of the other choices is correct because, in this context, no other answer is an appropriate synonym for the phrase "ear for."

47. **B. 2010.**

All you need to do is look for the year above which the bottom and the middle lines are farthest apart. That's 2010, when there were apparently about 6 wolves in the Wenaha pack and 15 in the Imnaha pack.

The right answer is not Choice (A), (C), or (D) because the bottom and the middle lines aren't farthest apart in those years.

The right answer is not Choice (E) because the graph does reveal the information requested.

48. **C. 2011 and 2012.**

In the years 2009 and 2010, the numbers indicated by the bottom and middle lines seem to add up to the number indicated by the top line — that is, the Wenaha and Imnaha wolf packs' populations added up to the total wolf population of the state. For the years 2011 and 2012, however, the number indicated by the top line is greater than the sum of the numbers indicated by the bottom and middle lines, indicating that wolves that belonged to packs other than the Wenaha and Imnaha were in the state.

The right answer is not Choice (A) because in both 2009 and 2010, the numbers indicated by the bottom and middle lines seem to add up the number indicated by the top line.

The right answer is not Choice (B) because, although 2011 is correct, in 2010, the numbers indicated by the bottom and middle lines seem to add up the number indicated by the top line.

The right answer is not Choice (D) because 2010 is not a right answer; the numbers indicated by the bottom and middle lines seem to add up the number indicated by the top line.

The right answer is not Choice (E) because 2012 isn't the only correct answer; 2011 also fits.

49. **B. 2010.**

This question is a tricky one; you have to look at the closeness of the middle and top lines, but you also have to consider percentages. In 2009, there looked to be about 15 wolves total (top line) and 10 in the Imnaha pack, so that means that 2/3 of the wolves in the state, or about 67 percent, were from the Imnaha pack. In 2010, the top and middle lines are also close together, but there look to be roughly 20 wolves total and 15 in the Imnaha pack, which means that 3/4 of the wolves in the state, or about 75 percent, were from the Imnaha pack. The answer is 2010, because 75 percent is more than 67 percent.

The right answer is not Choice (A), (C), or (D) because the percentage of total wolves that were from the Imnaha pack in those years is not the highest of the yearly percentages.

The right answer is not Choice (E) because the graph does in fact reveal the requested information.

50. **A. Both psychopathy and sociopathy are observable via brain autopsy.**

The middle of the passage states that, concerning both psychopathy and sociopathy, "there is agreement that the conditions involve observable differences in brain structure."

The right answer is not Choice (B) because the passage states that only *some* professionals think that both psychopathy and sociopathy are synonymous with antisocial personality disorder.

The right answer is not Choice (C) because the passage states that only some professionals use the terms *psychopath* and *sociopath* interchangeably.

The right answer is not Choice (D) because the passage establishes (at the end) that, according to how an increasing number of professionals use the term, only psychopaths genuinely have no sense of right and wrong.

The right answer is not Choice (E) because the passage states that psychopathy and sociopathy are difficult, but not impossible, to detect via psychological examination.

51. **E. A desire to clear up confusion on the parts of general readers.**

The passage aims merely to distinguish the ways that psychological professionals currently use the terms *psychopath* and *sociopath*.

The right answer is not Choice (A) because the passage is explanatory and informative, not critical — it never says that anyone is wrong.

The right answer is not Choice (B) because the passage never expresses a personal opinion; the author only explains what other people think.

The right answer is not Choice (C) because the passage never mentions any particular person; it's just about the terms *psychopath* and *sociopath* in general.

The right answer is not Choice (D) because, though the passage mentions that psychopaths often try to evade detection, the goal is not to warn professionals about this fact; the passage establishes that professionals already know it.

52. **C. logically expectable.**

When the passage describes the average person's confusion as "forgivable," it does so as a way of introducing the idea that many professionals use the terms psychopath and sociopath in different ways. The idea is that the layperson's confusion is unavoidable and understandable, so the most correct answer is Choice (C).

The right answer is not Choice (A) because, although the term *forgivable* sometimes means "morally excusable," the passage doesn't regard the average person's confusion as a moral issue, so Choice (A) is not the best of the choices in context.

The right answer is not Choice (B) because the passage doesn't say that the average person's confusion is confusing itself. This choice is trying to fool you by repeating words.

The right answer is not Choice (D) because the passage never indicates that the author regards people's confusion as either disturbing or amusing.

The right answer is not Choice (E) because the passage never says or implies that the author considers the layperson's confusion annoying.

53. **B. idiosyncratic.**

This is just a vocabulary question. The passage explains (at the end) that sociopaths have a sense of right and wrong that is massively out of line with most people's sense of these things. The fancy word for "different from other people" is *idiosyncratic*.

None of the other choices is correct because none of the other words means "different from other people. *Ineffable* means "inexpressible." *Inextricable* means "impossible to separate." *Remunerative* means "yielding money or reward." *Eleemosynary* means "related to or depending on charity."

54. **D. multifaceted.**

The point of the passage is that Yeats's poetry went through many different phases and had many different sides to it. The fancy word for "having many dimensions or aspects" is *multifaceted*.

None of the other choices is correct because none represents the "having many dimensions or aspects" concept.

55. **A. the general to the specific.**

The first sentence states a widespread principle or truism, and the rest of the passage talks about a specific example of it.

The right answer is not Choice (B) because, although the first sentence of the passage does make reference to a superstition, the point of the passage as a whole is not to distinguish superstition and fact.

The right answer is not Choice (C) because the passage is not divided between rhetoric (attempts at eloquence or persuasion) and logic.

The right answer is not Choice (D) because the first sentence of the passage doesn't provide data that the rest of the passage subsequently interprets.

The right answer is not Choice (E) because the first sentence of the passage doesn't state a cause with the rest of the passage then delineating its effects.

56. **C. they are absent from preserved records.**

The second sentence of the passage explains that "dirty" words are usually used in speech for a long time before they're written down in any way that survives to be studied. This gap is what makes pinning down their etymologies difficult.

The right answer is not Choice (A) because the passage never says that linguists are reluctant to study "dirty" words; on the contrary, it says that doing so is a source of "amusement" for them.

The right answer is not Choice (B) because, while the final sentence of the passage states that misinformation often circulates about the origins of "dirty" words, it explains that people do this mistakenly rather than deliberately.

The right answer is not Choice (D) because the passage never says or implies that the meanings of "dirty" words change more often than those of other words do.

The right answer is not Choice (E) because the passage explains that "dirty" words actually don't usually originate as acronyms, although urban legends often claim that they do.

Part 2: Writing

1. **E. No error**

The sentence does not contain an error.

The right answer is not Choice (A) because the *its* without the apostrophe is the possessive, so it's correct in this context.

The right answer is not Choice (B) because the conjunction *whereas* means something like "while on the other hand," so it's used correctly here.

The right answer is not Choice (C) because the sentence uses the adverb *simply* (meaning "merely") to clearly and correctly modify the verb *use*.

The right answer is not Choice (D) because this phrasing is grammatically correct as written. You may have picked this answer thinking it was missing the word *that;* although the phrase "that it contains" would also be correct, the omission of *that* doesn't create an error.

2. **D. by which**

A movie is based *on* a book, not *by* a book, so "on which" is the correct prepositional construction here.

The right answer is not Choice (A) because the movies in question are both "well made" and "considered cinematic classics." The construction is clear and correct, and no commas or other punctuation are necessary.

The right answer is not Choice (B) because *for* is the correct preposition in this context.

The right answer is not Choice (C) because saying that a movie didn't do something "as well as did the book" (as opposed to "as well as the book did") is perfectly correct even though it's a bit more formal than everyday speech.

The right answer is not Choice (E) because there is, in fact, an error in the sentence.

3. **A. people who believe**

The word *who* should be omitted, because the first clause needs to be independent ("people believe" is an independent subject and verb, whereas "people *who* believe" subordinates the verb to a pronoun, resulting in an incomplete sentence).

The right answer is not Choice (B) because this phrase correctly uses the infinitive.

The right answer is not Choice (C) because this is a clear and correct usage of an adverb modifying an adverb that is modifying an adjective.

The right answer is not Choice (D) because *than* (not *then*) is the word used for comparisons.

The right answer is not Choice (E) because there is, in fact, an error in the sentence.

4. **B. whom was**

The pronoun is the subject of a subordinate clause, so *who* is correct.

The right answer is not Choice (A) because the regular past tense is fine here.

The right answer is not Choice (C) because using a comma after a conjunction is acceptable when the sentence is interrupted by a modifying clause (such as "ironically") at that point.

The right answer is not Choice (D) because the participial verb form is fine here.

The right answer is not Choice (E) because there is, in fact, an error in the sentence.

5. **C. is their**

The antecedent of the pronoun is singular ("a living organism"), so you need the singular possessive pronoun *its* rather than the plural *their* here.

The right answer is not Choice (A) because the past tense *arose* is perfectly correct here.

The right answer is not Choice (B) because the third-person singular *distinguishes* is correct here.

The right answer is not Choice (D) because the subject of the verb in question is *manner*, so the third-person singular *passes on* (meaning "transmits") is correct.

The right answer is not Choice (E) because there is, in fact, an error in the sentence.

6. **D. myself**

The speaker is not performing a verb reflexively with herself as the object, so *myself* is incorrect. She should simply have said *me*.

The right answer is not Choice (A) because *should you* is a correct construction here (to mean "If you should . . .").

The right answer is not Choice (B) because, although data is often used as a singular noun, it's actually plural, so *data represent* is correct.

The right answer is not Choice (C) because the infinitive is correct in this context.

The right answer is not Choice (E) because there is, in fact, an error in the sentence.

7. **E. No error**

This sentence doesn't contain any errors.

The right answer is not Choice (A) because the *its* without an apostrophe is the possessive, so it's correct in this context. (*It's* with an apostrophe is the contraction for *it is*.)

The right answer is not Choice (B) because although the *as* isn't necessary here, including it's not wrong. In fact, including it is more formal and correct.

The right answer is not Choice (C) because *Scots* (Scottish people) is a proper noun and should be capitalized.

The right answer is not Choice (D) because *after the time* (meaning after the time in which he lived) is perfectly clear and correct in this context.

8. **B. further**

Because the sentence is discussing physical distance, *farther* is the correct adjective.

The right answer is not Choice (A) because the word *children* should indeed be possessive here (even though the museum doesn't literally belong to actual children), and the apostrophe is in the right place.

The right answer is not Choice (C) because *than* (not *then*) is the word used for comparisons.

The right answer is not Choice (D) because *less* is correct here (as opposed to *fewer*, which would be used for countable quantities).

The right answer is not Choice (E) because there is, in fact, an error in the sentence.

9. **C. in which**

You don't hear *in* an album; you just *hear* an album, so the addition of *in* is unnecessary and incorrect. Plus, *which* is used incorrectly here; the phrase should read "*that* I have ever heard."

The right answer is not Choice (A) because *very many* is a perfectly clear and correct instance of an adverb modifying an adjective.

The right answer is not Choice (B) because *best-produced* forms a two-word adjective here (in which the first word is not an adverb), so it should be hyphenated.

The right answer is not Choice (D) because present-perfect *have ever heard* is correct in this context.

The right answer is not Choice (E) because there is, in fact, an error in the sentence.

10. **E. No error**

This sentence contains no error.

The right answer is not Choice (A) because the word *effect* can also be a verb meaning "to bring about."

The right answer is not Choice (B) because *then* (not *than*) is the word used for conditional statements ("if/then"), so it's correct here.

The right answer is not Choice (C) because *affect* is a verb meaning "to change," so it's correct here.

The right answer is not Choice (D) because *than* (not *then*) is the word used for comparisons, so it's correct here.

11. **A. being**

The word *being* is pointlessly inserted into the appositive clause; the convention is for an appositive clause to limit itself to the definition without the gerund.

The right answer is not Choice (B) because *planet* doesn't need to be capitalized.

The right answer is not Choice (C) because *dwarfs* is used correctly here as a verb meaning "to make something else seem small by comparison."

The right answer is not Choice (D) because *it's* (with an apostrophe) is the contraction for "it is," so it's correct in this context.

The right answer is not Choice (E) because there is, in fact, an error in the sentence.

12. **B. were**

The subject is *treasurer*, which is singular, so the verb should be *was*, not *were*.

The right answer is not Choice (A) because "devoted to the upkeep . . ." is an adjectival phrase modifying *society*, so this construction is correct.

The right answer is not Choice (C) because "unsure of how best to allocate" is perfectly correct even though it may be a bit more formal than everyday speech.

The right answer is not Choice (D) because the infinitive is correct in this context.

The right answer is not Choice (E) because there is, in fact, an error in this sentence.

13. **B. had been**

The speaker is unsure of whether Danny ever actually arrived, so the hypothetical *was* ("if he *was* here") is correct, not the past-perfect *had been*.

The right answer is not Choice (A) because *you've been* — a contraction of the present-perfect *you have been* — is perfectly correct in this context.

The right answer is not Choice (C) because *earlier* (meaning "before now") is correct here.

The right answer is not Choice (D) because the regular past tense *didn't see* ("did not see") is correct here.

The right answer is not Choice (E) because there is, in fact, an error in the sentence.

14. **D. of**

Of is the wrong preposition here; correct options include *optimistic about* or possibly *optimistic for,* but not *optimistic of.*

The right answer is not Choice (A) because beginning a sentence with a subordinate *because* clause is fine as long as the clause is followed by a comma and an independent clause.

The right answer is not Choice (B) because the possessive *half a day's travel* (meaning "half a day's *worth of* travel") is a correct construction.

The right answer is not Choice (C) because the clause preceding it is independent, so the clause in Choice (C) must begin with a conjunction.

The right answer is not Choice (E) because there is, in fact, an error in the sentence.

15. **A. principle**

The words *principle* and *principal* are commonly confused. When the word means "primary or leading," as it does in this sentence, *principal* is correct.

The right answer is not Choice (B) because *students give* is correct subject/verb agreement.

The right answer is not Choice (C) because the participial verb form is correct here.

The right answer is not Choice (D) because the noun *suspicion* is used correctly in this context: "the reason is suspicion . . ."

The right answer is not Choice (E) because there is, in fact, an error in the sentence.

16. **D. credibly**

The proper word here is the noun *credibility,* not the adverb *credibly.*

The right answer is not Choice (A) because the noun performing the verb is *hallucinations,* which is plural, so the plural verb *are* is correct.

The right answer is not Choice (B) because *behind* is used correctly ("the explanation behind . . ."). You could also use *of* or *for,* but having other viable options doesn't automatically make the given wording wrong.

The right answer is not Choice (C) because the noun performing the verb is *theory,* which is singular, so the singular verb *is* is correct.

The right answer is not Choice (E) because there is, in fact, an error in the sentence.

17. **D. have had for**

The sentence uses the wrong preposition here. It should say that the poems had an influence *on* other writers, not an influence *for* them.

The right answer is not Choice (A) because the present perfect *have often been dismissed* is the correct tense in this context.

The right answer is not Choice (B) because *overly sentimental* is a correct instance of an adverb modifying an adjective.

The right answer is not Choice (C) because, although it's interrupted by modifying words, the present perfect *has more recently been given credit* is correct.

The right answer is not Choice (E) because there is, in fact, an error in the sentence.

18. **B. Kings and Queens**

The words *kings* and *queens* should not be capitalized here because they're used in the abstract rather than as titles before the names of specific people.

The right answer is not Choice (A) because "the question of which" is the correct construction here.

The right answer is not Choice (C) because *Glorious Revolution* is a proper noun referring to a specific historical event, so it should be capitalized.

The right answer is not Choice (D) because *than* (not *then*) is the word used for comparisons, so it's correct here. As for the placement of the verb *are*, it's correct either before or after "executive decisions."

The right answer is not Choice (E) because there is, in fact, an error in the sentence.

19. **A. they are**

As the rest of the sentence shows, the *Dimetrodon* is being discussed in the singular, so you need the singular *it is* here rather than the plural *they are*.

The right answer is not Choice (B) because *alongside* is used correctly in this context.

The right answer is not Choice (C) because using *at all* for the sake of emphasis is perfectly fine (though not necessary).

The right answer is not Choice (D) because "rather a" is a correct construction in this context. You could also add *was* ("was rather a"), but omitting it is acceptable.

The right answer is not Choice (E) because there is, in fact, an error in the sentence.

20. **D. is not doing his or her job**

The teacher in the sentence is singular ("a teacher"), so you need a singular verb *(is)*, pronoun *(his or her)*, and direct object *(job)*. The other choices are incorrect because they use plural versions of one or more of these items.

21. **A. all with**

The sentence is correct the way it is.

The right answer is not Choice (B) because the addition of the word *in* is incorrect; *which all have* would be acceptable, but not *in which all have*.

The right answer is not Choice (C) because you need *have* in this context, not the participial form *having.* (Also, *which* is preferable to *whom* in this case because the subject is an animal rather than a person.)

The right answer is not Choice (D) because it forms a comma splice.

The right answer is not Choice (E) because it forms a comma splice.

22. **C. century, James Joyce**

This choice is a correct example of an introductory subordinate clause (*although* is a subordinating conjunction) followed by a comma and an independent clause.

The right answer is not Choice (A) because the sentence doesn't need both the subordinating conjunction *although* before the first clause and the coordinating conjunction *but* before the second clause. Using one or the other would be correct, but not both.

The right answer is not Choice (B) because neither clause is independent.

The right answer is not Choice (D) because a semicolon here would not separate two independent clauses (an *although* clause is subordinate).

The right answer is not Choice (E) because although and however are doing the same job, so you don't need both of them (and if only *however* were there, you'd need to add a semi-colon or to start a new sentence).

23. **E. wit and to shock with**

This sentence presents a parallel-phrasing issue. The *both* is a clue that the sentence needs two verbs, both in the infinitive and not separated by a comma: *the capacity both to delight . . . and to shock. . . .* The only answer that accomplishes that is Choice (E).

The right answer is not Choice (A) because the *both* is a clue that the two verbs (*to delight* and *to shock*) should be in the infinitive and not separated by a comma.

The right answer is not Choice (B) because the *both* is a clue that the two verbs (*to delight* and *to shock*) should be in the infinitive and not separated by a comma.

The right answer is not Choice (C) because this forms a comma splice (and a nonsensical one at that, since the first independent clause says *both* but only includes one verb).

The right answer is not Choice (D) because the *both* is a clue that you need *and* rather than *but*.

24. **C. Having spotted the skyline in the distance, we decided to try and**

This sentence is a misplaced-modifier question. The modifier needs to attach to who or what spotted the skyline; as written, that subject is "attempt," and clearly an attempt can't spot something. The sentence is written in the second-person plural (we/us) point of view, so opening the independent clause with "we" makes sense.

The right answer is not Choice (A) because the "attempt" isn't who or what spotted the skyline, so the modifier is misplaced.

The right answer is not Choice (B) because neither clause is independent.

The right answer is not Choice (D) because this answer is a comma splice (because *therefore* is not a conjunction).

The right answer is not Choice (E) because it's a long participial phrase, not a complete sentence.

25. **D. for whom female fans showed their appreciation by throwing**

Choice (D) is the only answer choice in which all the prepositions and verb forms agree: Liszt was the artist *for whom* female fans showed their appreciation *by throwing* their undergarments. Remember, all the verbs in a sentence don't always have to be in the same form.

The right answer is not Choice (A) because it's constructed to imply that the fans had an appreciation for the act of throwing undergarments itself rather than an appreciation for Liszt.

The right answer is not Choice (B) because the past-progressive form *were showing* rather than the regular past tense *showed* is both awkward and unnecessary.

The right answer is not Choice (C) because using the infinitive *to show* in place of the past-tense *showed* is nonsensical in context.

The right answer is not Choice (E) because the fans showed their appreciation *by throwing* their undergarments (it was the *means by which* they showed appreciation), so you need *by throwing* rather than *to throw*.

26. **E. consuming all the planets of our solar system before collapsing**

The participial forms *consuming* and *collapsing* are appropriate to the afterthought clause that ends the sentence.

The right answer is not Choice (A) because the *and* should not have a comma before it (even if it didn't, the sentence as phrased would still be awkward).

The right answer is not Choice (B) because it forms a comma splice.

The right answer is not Choice (C) because a semicolon here would not separate two independent clauses (the *then* clause is not independent).

The right answer is not Choice (D) because the afterthought clause's structure isn't parallel.

27. B. Africa, is a biodiversity hotspot, with over 90 percent of its wildlife being found

The subject of the sentence is *Madagascar,* and the verb is *is;* this choice sets it up so that the subject and verb are separated by an appositive clause, and the sentence ends with a prepositional afterthought clause.

The right answer is not Choice (A) because it's not a complete sentence (it has no main verb).

The right answer is not Choice (C) because this is not a complete sentence (*being* can't be the main verb).

The right answer is not Choice (D) because it's not a complete sentence (it has no main verb).

The right answer is not Choice (E) because the inclusion of *it* gives the sentence two subjects, so it doesn't grammatically agree.

28. C. now; the rest of you, however, may

This choice correctly joins two independent clauses with a semicolon (the second of which contains the adverb *however,* correctly set off with a pair of commas).

The right answer is not Choice (A) because it forms a comma splice (*however* is not a conjunction).

The right answer is not Choice (B) because it also forms a comma splice (*however* is not a conjunction).

The right answer is not Choice (D) because, although the semicolon is correct, the *however* in the second independent clause would need to be set off with two commas.

The right answer is not Choice (E) because it forms a comma splice (between *now* and *the*).

29. A. than are those of

The sentence is correct as it is. The construction may be a little more formal than you're used to hearing in speech, but it isn't wrong.

The right answer is not Choice (B) because you're comparing *the works of* van Gogh to *the works of* other painters, not to the painters themselves, so you need to say *than are those of* (meaning the works of) any other, rather than simply *than* any other.

The right answer is not Choice (C) or Choice (D) because the *more* is a clue that you need *than,* rather than *compared* (the preposition you use after it — *to* or *with* — doesn't matter, because *compared* itself is wrong).

The right answer is not Choice (E) because you need *than* instead of *compared,* not both words.

30. B. the truth is that firing

This is the only choice that forms a coherent, correct sentence.

The right answer is not Choice (A) because the construction "the truth of it is" would require a comma afterwards, in place of the omitted "that."

The right answer is not Choice (C) or Choice (D) because the presence of the word *is* later in the sentence causes those phrasings to become nonsensical. (Always read the whole sentence to determine whether a choice makes sense in context.)

The right answer is not Choice (E) because it needs a comma after *truly* (and even then, it's extremely awkward).

31. **B. A certain type of person is likely to tell you that poetry is read by hardly anyone, and that the few people who do read it comprise an insular cadre of specialists ignored by the culture at large.**

   None of the choices is incorrect from a technical standpoint, but Choice (B) is the most concise and efficient of the answer choices.

   The right answer is not Choice (A) because this sentence is unnecessarily repetitive and could be more concise by eliminating "and that these people are."

   The right answer is not Choice (C) because it's unnecessarily repetitive and could be more concise in the "only an . . ." and "that is also . . ." portions.

   The right answer is not Choice (D) because it's terribly awkward, particularly the phrase "hardly anyone who does not comprise."

   The right answer is not Choice (E) because it's unnecessarily repetitive and could be more concise in the "adding that . . ." and "specifying that . . ." portions.

32. **A. Leave it as it is.**

   The sentence makes perfect sense exactly where it is and as it's written.

   The right answer is not Choice (B) because the word "poetry" belongs in quotation marks; the sentence refers to the act of saying it. Plus, there's no particular reason to italicize the word *very*.

   The right answer is not Choice (C) because beginning the sentence with "on the other hand" would make no sense; Sentence 5 doesn't present a counterpoint to the previous sentence.

   The right answer is not Choice (D) because this sentence would be out of place as the second sentence of the next paragraph; the explanation it alludes to would have already been begun.

   The right answer is not Choice (E) because the sentence doesn't present a counterpoint to the previous sentence, so you don't need to insert the word *however*.

33. **D. to the delight of some and the consternation of others.**

   The point of the paragraph is that slam poetry has both its supporters and its detractors, so the phrase "to the delight of some and the consternation of others" makes the most sense in context.

   The right answer is not Choice (A) because although definitions are often challenged, that isn't the most relevant statement to be made about the specific topic under discussion here.

   The right answer is not Choice (B) because simply announcing that something is about to be explained is usually an unnecessary rhetorical move; another answer choice is clearly more necessary.

   The right answer is not Choice (C) because the paragraph as a whole doesn't address any "varying degrees of success" on the part of slam poets. Another choice makes more sense in context.

   The right answer is not Choice (E) because the passage doesn't refer to slam poets employing any "devious" or "unexpected" methods. The reference makes no sense in context.

34. **E. who typically stand at lecterns and read from notes or a published book during recitals.**

   Because the rest of the sentence describes the performance style of slam poets, the best choice for the underlined portion is the phrase that contrasts this style with the style of traditional poets.

   None of the other answer choices is correct because none addresses the true subject of the sentence as a whole, which seeks to contrast the *styles* of traditional and slam poets.

35. **C. Their work is designed to be seen in performance rather than read.**

   The concluding sentence aims at a characterization of the slammers' work as a whole, and to say that it "is designed to be seen in performance rather than read" sums it up nicely.

   The right answer is not Choice (A) because this vague and obvious statement adds very little to the paragraph. It is true, but it could just as well not be there, which isn't what you want from a conclusion.

   The right answer is not Choice (B) because, though true, it's a minor, unnecessary detail. Another answer choice performs a much more logical function in this context.

   The right answer is not Choice (D) because speculation about slammers using props in the future is an odd tangent and not the most effective way to end the paragraph and transition into the next.

   The right answer is not Choice (E) because changing the subject to slammers making money for their venues is a tangent that is never addressed elsewhere.

36. **A. Ironically**

   The fact that each group thinks it's being oppressed by the other is ironic, so "Ironically" is a perfectly logical way to begin the sentence.

   The right answer is not Choice (B) because the sentence is not a result of what was being discussed immediately prior, so "Therefore" doesn't make sense as a transition word.

   The right answer is not Choice (C) because the emphatic "Undeniably" adds little in this context. This portion of the passage is not weighing evidence and/or attempting to persuade the reader.

   The right answer is not Choice (D) because the sentence is not a counterpoint to the previous one, so "on the other hand" doesn't make sense as a transition.

   The right answer is not Choice (E) because you don't need to say "In conclusion" just because it's the last sentence. It would seem out of place here.

37. **B. a magazine article**

   You can tell this citation is for a magazine article because it includes a month in the publication date, it lists two titles (the article in quotation marks, followed by the title of the publication itself in italics), and it notes an issue number and the page numbers of the article.

   The right answer is not Choice (A) because the inclusion of a month in the publication date, as well as the two titles, is a clue that the cited work is not a book.

   The right answer is not Choice (C) because newspapers come out daily, not monthly, so a magazine is more likely.

   The right answer is not Choice (D) because blogs don't have page numbers.

   The right answer is not Choice (E) because the lack of a specific date (day instead of just month), the presence of two titles, and the inclusion of page numbers are all clues that the cited work is not a speech.

38. **C. a primary source represents original research, whereas a secondary source contains information already compiled by someone else.**

   These are the correct definitions of "primary source" and "secondary source."

   None of the other choices is the correct definition of _primary source_ and _secondary source_.

39. **B. epigraph.**

   A quotation below the title and above the main body of the text is called an _epigraph_.

   The right answer is not Choice (A) because an _epigram_ is any saying or proverb.

The right answer is not Choice (C) because *epistle* is a fancy word for a letter (the kind you mail).

The right answer is not Choice (D) because *epithelium* is a type of animal tissue in biology.

The right answer is not Choice (E) because *epitaxy* refers to the deposition of crystal in geology.

40. **B. a Works Cited page lists only cited sources, whereas a Bibliography lists every source consulted.**

These are the correct definitions of *Bibliography* and *Works Cited page*.

None of the other answers give the correct definitions of *Bibliography* and *Works Cited page*.

Argumentative Essay

Take a look at the following essay written in response to the opinion that's presented in Chapter 16. To score your own essay, flip back to Chapter 11, where you can find a checklist to help you evaluate your own writing.

The idea that "high-school and college creative-writing classes should seek to foster an emotionally nurturing environment above emphasizing the development of technical skill" is the kind of recommendation that almost anyone would want to support when he or she first hears it. It pits kindness and sensitivity against elitism, and who would want to appear to be on the side of the elitists? The problem with it, however, is the same as the problem with many statements: It oversimplifies a complex issue into a simple either/or problem, and it fails to consider that not everyone who works with young people has the same job to do.

Would most young people who sign up for creative-writing classes prefer to vent about personal problems than to be nitpicked about whether their work is good enough for publication? Of course they would. But young people would probably rather vent about personal problems in math class instead of doing math too — that's just what young people are like. Yes, creative work certainly has more to do with personal expression than math does, but a class in school is still a class in school, and the students are in the class because there's something they're supposed to be learning. It may make a teacher feel like a great guy to tell everybody that his or her poem or story is fantastic just the way it is and then let the class use discussion time simply to share their feelings, but nobody learns anything that way.

A lot of young people struggle with issues in their lives, and it would help them to talk about those issues in a supportive environment. But that's what a therapist is for. Therapy is great, and many kids could benefit from it, but that doesn't mean it's the teacher's job. The writing teacher isn't obligated to be everyone's therapist instead of teaching writing, any more than it's the job of the math teacher or the science teacher to be a therapist instead of teaching math or science. If the writing teacher would rather help kids work out their problems than teach them how to write, then she should get a degree in psychology and become a therapist. And more importantly, a kid with a serious problem should be seeking help from someone who is specifically trained to address it instead of assuming that the English teacher is qualified to do so.

Perhaps most troubling is the fact that the question lumps together "high-school and college creative-writing classes" as though they are the same thing. A ninth-grader and a college student aren't taught the same things in the same way in any other subject, so why should they be taught writing in the same way? There's a world of difference between a 15-year-old and a 20-year-old, and what seems sensitive and encouraging to the former might seem patronizing and pointless to the latter. High-school freshmen may sign up for a creative-writing elective because it seems like an easy class, but a young adult who registers for a college course in the same subject may be considering a career as a writer and looking for tough and honest feedback. If the teacher just smiles and praises this student instead of helping him hone his skills as much as possible, then the college is essentially stealing his money, because he isn't learning what he paid to learn.

This isn't to say that writing teachers should be insensitive. Nobody is a brilliant writer right off the bat, and it often takes years of encouragement about work that isn't truly very good before a young person manages to pen anything worthwhile. But it's still the students' work that should be discussed in the classroom, rather than their personal lives.

Source-Based Essay

Take a look at the following essay written about the paradox of wanting to see things as how they are versus appreciating them in a way that makes emotional sense. To score your own essay, flip back to Chapter 11 and use the checklist to help you evaluate your own writing.

To a great extent, the history of human civilization has been a battle between those who seek to comprehend the natural world as it really is and those who are more concerned with the feelings, experiences, and behavior of the human beings who live in it. This conflict could be said to have reached its apex in the 20th century, during which science and technology advanced by breathtaking leaps and bounds even as human suffering and existential despair were exasperated by countless wars of unprecedented scale. Now, in the early years of the 21st century, we understand the world more clearly than ever before from a scientific and philosophical perspective, but we also feel more lost in that world than we ever have.

According to Jeremy Wisnewski, the philosophical discipline of phenomenology, as developed by such thinkers as Edmund Husserl and Martin Heidegger, is an attempt to "set aside our preconceptions and to uncover the actual *being* of things as they reveal themselves to us" and "to see past our preconceptions into the heart of things" (Wisnewski, 2009). No thinking person could argue that this is not, in theory, an admirable goal. Many of the people we love would not be here today had science not succeeded in doing this to a significant extent. No one with a friend or relative whose life was saved by modern medical science could wish for a return to the days when human beings interpreted even everyday events like illness in personalized terms of spells and demons instead of in a coldly objective — and therefore effective — manner.

On the other hand, however, people want to enjoy their lives, not merely to stay alive for the sake of doing so. We evolved our capacities for reason and intellect so we could bond and live in harmony with one another, not because we had some pressing need to figure out what is going on in the middle of a black hole. There is a wide range of subjective human experiences of existence, and what is fascinating to a philosopher or a physicist might well be frightening to the average person. As George Tschner pointed out, "mythology is a figurative and metaphorical way the human intellect grasps its world and answers and resolves some of the most fundamental questions" (Tschner, 2009). The tales of Odysseus's decade-long attempt to return home or of Orpheus's descent into the underworld in search of his lost bride will never help us cure a disease or colonize an alien planet, but they were never intended to do so. A viewpoint that constitutes a wrong answer to one question may be the right answer to another.

To return to Wisnewski's words, yes, we humans do "impose particular theories onto phenomena and insist that they conform to our preconceived notions about how the world is" (Wisnewski, 2009). But this is not a moral or an intellectual failing so much as it is something we evolved to do for a reason — and that reason is that it keeps our awareness of the cold, vast, unfeeling "reality" of existence from driving us to despair and madness. The scientific and philosophical methods are not a model for how everyone should live, and science and philosophy admit as much by reminding us that their disciplines are concerned with reality and results rather than with ethics and emotions. Objectivity and reason are not wrong, of course, and more spiritually inclined people would do well to stop fearing and demonizing them, but just because they are not wrong, that doesn't mean that they are how everyone should think all the time. The scientific method is a means to certain ends, and the mythological method is a means to certain other ends. Both missions are admirable and necessary, and both ways of seeing the world are therefore respectable.

Part 3: Mathematics

1. **C.** $\frac{1}{5}$

   Mary hid 25 eggs. By adding the number of yellow, green, and blue eggs ($6 + 6 + 8 = 20$) and subtracting that number from the total, you find that 5 of the 25 eggs were orange ($25 - 20 = 5$). The fraction of orange eggs found is $\frac{5}{25}$ or $\frac{1}{5}$ in simplest form.

   If you picked Choice (A), you probably added the yellow, green, and blue eggs only and forgot the orange eggs. The answer is not in simplest form. Choice (B) is answer Choice (A) in simplest form.

2. **C. None of the scouts who earned hunting merit badges earned swimming merit badges.**

   The Venn diagram shows that some of the scouts who earned hunting merit badges earned swimming merit badges, so Choice (C) is a false statement. The other four statements are true according to the diagram.

3. **A. 32**

   Because the figure is a square, each of its interior angles is 90 degrees. Every square is a rhombus, so the diagonals bisect the interior angles. That means the acute angles of each right triangle formed by the diagonal are 45 degrees, and each triangle is a 45-45-90 triangle. Therefore, each leg of the triangle has a measure of 8. The legs of the triangles are also sides of the square, so each side of the square has a measure of 8, and the sum of the side measures is thus 32. Choice (B) is the area of the square; Choice (C) is the measure of each side of the square; Choice (D) is half the square's perimeter; and Choice (E) is twice the square's area.

4. **C. (5, −4)**

   You can use either elimination or substitution to solve the system. Using elimination, you must line up the like terms. You can then multiply the top equation by −2 and add the equations to get rid of y and then solve for x, which has a value of 5.

   $$-2(8x - 2y) = 48(-2)$$
   $$-3x - 4y = 1$$
   $$-16x + 4y = -96$$
   $$-3x - 4y = 1$$
   $$-19x = -95$$
   $$\frac{-9x}{-19} = \frac{-95}{-19}$$
   $$x = 5$$

   Once you have the value of one variable, you can put it in place of the variable and solve for the other variable. The value of y is −4.

   $$-3(5) - 4y = 1$$
   $$-15 - 4y = 1$$
   $$-4y + 15 - 15 = 1 + 15$$
   $$-4y = 16$$
   $$y = -4$$
   $$(5, -4)$$

   Using substitution, you can find the value of x or y in terms of the other variable, substitute the resulting expression in for that variable in the other equation, and solve the resulting one-variable equation.

   Both methods come to the same answer (assuming you do them correctly, of course). Choice (B) has the negative signs of the correct answer switched.

5. **E. 3.04**

   Choices (B), (C), and (D) can all be simplified to $3\frac{2}{5}$, so you can rule them out. When you convert Choice (A) to fraction form, you get $3\frac{4}{10}$, which is equal to Choice (C). (0.4 is the same as $\frac{4}{10}$.) 3.04 is equal to $3\frac{1}{25}$, which isn't equal to $3\frac{2}{5}$. The other choices in fraction form are $3\frac{2}{5}$, so they're equal to it.

6. **E. $-3x^{10}y^4z^7$**

   The correct answer is Choice (E), which is the only choice with $x^{10}y^4z^7$ after the coefficient. All the other choices have the same variables but different exponent combinations.

7. **D. 25**

   If you subtract 1 from 25, you get 24, which is divisible by 4. 25 is also divisible by 5. All the other choices are 1 more than a number that is divisible by 4, but none of the other choices is divisible by 5.

8. **B. 450**

   The stems represent hundreds, and the leaves represent tens, as indicated below the plot. One of the stems represents 400, and one of its leaves represents 50. That number matches Choice (B). None of the other choices appears in the diagram.

9. **A. 106**

   $|-34|$ represents the absolute value of -34, which is 34. The equation is the equivalent of $p - 34 = 72$, which you can solve by adding 34 to both sides. $p = 72 + 34 = 106$. Choice (B) results from subtracting 34 from both sides instead of adding it.

   $$p - |-34| = 72$$
   $$p - 34 = 72$$
   $$p - 34 + 34 = 72 + 34$$
   $$p = 106$$

10. **D. 56°**

    The measures of complementary angles have a sum of 90°, so subtract the given angle of 34° from 90 to find the other angle: $90 - 34 = 56$. Choice (A) is the measure of an angle supplementary to a 34° angle (supplementary angles add to 180°). Adding Choice (B) to the given angle would give you 360°.

11. **B. 14**

    120 isn't divisible by 14, so the correct answer is Choice (B). 120 is divisible by all the other choices. **Remember:** Any number you can get by multiplying numbers in the prime factorization of 120 is a factor of 120.

12. **C. 12**

    Let x represent the lower of the consecutive even integers and $x + 2$ represent the higher integer. Now set up an equation based on the given information:

    $$x + (x + 2) = 3(x + 2) - 16$$
    $$x + (x + 2) = 3x + 6 - 16$$
    $$2x + 2 = 3x - 10$$
    $$2x - 3x + 2 = 3x - 3x - 10$$
    $$-x + 2 = -10$$
    $$-x + 2 - 2 = -10 - 2$$
    $$-x = -12$$
    $$x = 12$$

The solution is $x = 12$, so the lower integer is 12 and the higher integer is 2 more, or 14. Choice (A) is just the difference between the two integers, Choice (B) is 3 times the higher integer, Choice (D) is the sum of the integers, and Choice (E) is the higher integer.

13. **B. 48**

The mean (average) number of pies sold per week is the sum of all the weekly totals divided by the number of weeks. Let x equal the unknown Week 4 total, and set up an equation:

$$\frac{52 + 64 + 28 + x}{4} = 48$$
$$\frac{144 + x}{4} = 48$$
$$144 + x = 192$$
$$144 + x - 144 = 192 - 144$$
$$x = 48$$

Choice (A) is the sum you'd get in the numerator of the fraction if you put 48 in for x. Choice (C) is the sum of the given numbers that go into the numerator. Choice (D) is the mean of the given numbers.

14. **E. 6.87 cm²**

The radius of each circle is half the diameter. The two diameters cover the length of the rectangle, and one diameter covers the width. The area of the rectangle is found using the formula $l(w)$; therefore 8 cm by 4 cm is 32 cm². The area of a circle is πr^2, so each circle in the diagram has an area of 4π cm². The area of the shaded region is the area of the rectangle minus the area of the two circles, so it's 32 cm² – 8π cm². To the nearest hundredth, that is 6.87 cm². The other choices are miscalculations you can get from using the formulas.

15. **A. 17.7**

The magnitude of a number is its absolute value, which is always positive. You can drop all negative signs and put the resulting numbers in decimal form:

17.70, –17.77, –18.00, –17.80, 17.67, –17.83

Then put the numbers in order from greatest to least:

18.00, 17.83, 17.80. 17.77, 17.70, 17.67

The fourth number in the order is 17.7 in decimal form. The other choices correspond to numbers in different places in the order.

16. **D. $9a^2b^5$**

$3a^2b^5$ and $6a^2b^5$ are like terms, so to add them, just add their coefficients and keep the variables and exponents the same. The result is $9a^2b^5$. Choice (A) adds the coefficients correctly but also adds the exponents. Choice (B) results from subtracting the lower coefficient from the higher one. Choice (C) comes from multiplying the coefficients rather than adding. Choice (E) has the right coefficient but no variable exponents.

17. **E. The amount of time Aden took to run back to the starting point**

Speed is distance divided by time. You can calculate the total distance by adding 9 miles to 9 miles. If the trip to a point is 9 miles, the trip back is 9 miles. The total time, however, isn't given. Only the time to the turnaround point is given. With the time of the return trip, you could calculate the total time and then the overall speed. The other choices would not give you that necessary information.

18. **A. 43**

The sequence is arithmetic, and each number is 4 more than the previous one. Use the following formula to find any term of an arithmetic sequence:

$a_n = a_1 + (n - 1)d$

In the sequence, a_n stands for the number of the term to find, a_1 is the first term of the sequence, and d is the common difference between each term.

$$a_{11} = 3 + (11-1)4$$
$$a_{11} = 3 + (10)4$$
$$a_{11} = 3 + 40$$
$$a_{11} = 43$$

23 is the 6th term, so the 11th term is 4(5) greater. It is therefore 43. Choice (B) is the 10th term; Choice (C) is the 12th term; Choice (D) is 1 less than the 12th term; and Choice (E) is the 13th term in the sequence.

19. **C. 5**

Work the equation to isolate j:

$$8j + 10 = 90 - 8j$$
$$8j + 10 + 8j = 90 - 8j + 8j$$
$$16j + 10 = 90$$
$$16j + 10 - 10 = 90 - 10$$
$$16j = 80$$
$$\frac{16j}{16} = \frac{80}{16}$$
$$j = 5$$

20. **B. (–5, –8)**

A point's reflection over the x-axis involves changing only the sign of the y-coordinate. (Although the x-axis is horizontal, a reflection over it is a vertical change, so the y-coordinate is what changes.) Choice (A) results from changing the sign of the x-coordinate. Choice (C) comes from changing the signs of both coordinates. Choice (D) is just the reverse of the original coordinates, and Choice (E) reverses the original coordinates and changes the sign on the x-coordinate.

21. **D.** $\frac{x+5}{x-5}$

Using reverse FOIL, you can rewrite the rational expression as $\frac{(x+5)(x+4)}{(x-5)(x+4)}$. Because $x + 4$ is a factor of the numerator and the denominator, you can cancel it. What is left is $\frac{x+5}{x-5}$. Only Choice (D) is an expression of that in any form.

22. **E.** $\frac{3}{8}$

Because this question is an "or" probability problem, you have to add the probability of getting an oatmeal cookie to the probability of getting a peanut butter cookie. The probability that Venus will randomly pull an oatmeal cookie is $\frac{2}{8}$ because he has 2 oatmeal cookies out of a total of 8 cookies. The probability he will pull a peanut butter cookie is $\frac{1}{8}$, so $\frac{2}{8} + \frac{1}{8} = \frac{3}{8}$. Choice (A) has the wrong denominator; Choice (B) results from multiplying the probabilities; Choice (C) has the wrong numerator; and Choice (D) simplifies $\frac{2}{8}$ but fails to account for the peanut butter cookie.

23. **D.** $2 \cdot 3 \cdot 5 \cdot 7$

You can write 210 as a product of factors and break down those factors into products of factors. If you continue the process until all factors are prime, you get the prime factorization, which is $2 \cdot 3 \cdot 5 \cdot 7$. Choice (A) is incorrect because 11 isn't a factor of 210. Choice (B) doesn't list the factor 2. Choices (C) and (E) are factorizations but not the prime factorization.

24. **B. 2**

    The area of a rectangle is length times width. That means 12 m · 3x m is 72 m².

    $$\frac{12 \cdot 3x}{12} = \frac{72}{12}$$
    $$3x = 6$$
    $$\frac{3x}{3} = \frac{6}{3}$$
    $$x = 2$$

    The other choices can result from miscalculations when solving equations.

25. **C. 5x + 17y**

    8x and –3x are like terms, so you can combine them to get 5x. Similarly, you can combine 12y and 5y to get 17y. The sum of the four terms is therefore 5x + 17y. (x and y aren't like terms, so you can't combine the expression further.) Choice (A) uses the wrong sign between the terms. Choices (B) and (D) have the wrong coefficient and multiply the variables rather than adding them. Choice (E) results from adding 8x and 3x instead of 8x and –3x.

26. **C. 28.6**

    You can write all the answer choices in simplified mixed number form. 28.6 in mixed number form is $28\frac{6}{10}$, which can be simplified as $28\frac{3}{5}$. None of the other choices can be correctly written in that form.

27. **E. The sum of the number of people who chose pie and the number of people who chose pudding is 9 greater than the number of people who chose ice cream.**

    First, multiply each percentage by 300 to find out how many people chose each option, and then use those numbers to evaluate each statement. All the statements are true except Choice (E). 24 percent of those surveyed chose pie, and 15 percent chose pudding. 24 percent of 300 is 72, and 15 percent of 300 is 45. 72 + 45 = 117. 32 percent chose ice cream, and 32 percent of 300 is 96. 117 – 96 = 21, not 9, so the statement in Choice (E) is incorrect.

28. **A. 130**

    To solve f(7), substitute 7 for x in the equation: 3(7)² – 4(7) +11. The value of f(7) is therefore 130.

29. **E. 50**

    You can find all the factors of a number by multiplying the various combinations of numbers in its prime factorization. Because this test is multiple-choice, you can also test each number to see whether it's a factor of both numbers in the question. All the choices are factors of 250 and 450 except Choice (D). Of the four choices that are factors of both 250 and 450, 50 is the greatest.

30. **A. 3**

    The mode of a set of data is the number that is represented the highest number of times. For the given set of data, the number that appears the most is 3. Choice (B) is the number that appears the least number of times. Choice (C) is just the sum of the only two numbers that appear in the data. Choice (D) is the sum of the data. Choice (E) is the mean of the set of data.

31. **A. 31°**

    The sum of the interior angle measures of a triangle is 180°. The missing angle measure for the top triangle is therefore 102°. That angle is vertical to the top angle of the bottom triangle; vertical angles are always congruent, so the top angle of the bottom triangle is also 102°. 102° + 47° = 149°, and 180° – 149° is 31°. x is therefore 31°.

32. **D. –20**

The solution to the first equation is 8. If you put 8 in for w in $-4w + 12$, you get –20. The other choices result from putting incorrect values in for w.

33. **A. 1.4783**

To convert a percent to a decimal, drop the percent symbol and move the decimal two places to the left. ***Remember:*** Dropping the percent sign is the same as multiplying by 100. To keep the same value, you must also divide by 100, which you can do by moving the decimal two places to the left. The other choices result from moving the decimal incorrectly.

34. **D. {(2, 6), (4, 2), (8, 7), (10, 2)}**

In a function, each x value is used only once. Choice (D) is the only choice in which no x value is paired with more than one y value.

35. **B. $\frac{27}{140}$**

$\frac{3}{7}$ of $\frac{9}{20}$ is the same as $\frac{3}{7}$ times $\frac{9}{20}$. To find the product, multiply the numerators and multiply the denominators. $\frac{3}{7} \cdot \frac{9}{20} = \frac{27}{140}$. The fraction is already simplified.

36. **C. 144π ft.^{2}**

The surface area of a sphere is $4\pi r^2$. In this case, that is $4\pi(6)^2$ because a circle's radius is half its diameter. $4\pi(6)^2 = 4\pi(36)$, or 144π. The surface area of the sphere is therefore 144π ft.^{2}. Choices (A), (D), and (E) result from using a formula other than $4\pi r^2$. If you got Choice (B), you likely used 12 ft. as the radius rather than the diameter.

37. **E. 2**

Bitty's current age is unknown, so let x represent it. Brian's current age is 11 times greater, or $11x$. You know that the sum of their ages is 48, so set up an equation.

$$x + 11x = 48$$
$$12x = 48$$
$$x = 4$$

A correct equation using those terms shows that Bitty's current age is 4, which is Choice (D). But the question asks for her age 2 years ago, so subtract $4 - 2$ to get 2. Choice (A) shows Brian's age 2 years ago.

38. **A. 9.38425×10^5**

A number expressed in scientific notation has exactly one digit before the decimal. To fit 938,425 into this setup, move the decimal point five places to the left. Beyond that, the problem is just a matter of figuring out what exponent to use. Because you moved the decimal to the left, the exponent is the number of places moved. (When you move the decimal to the right, you put a negative sign on the exponent.) The other choices involve moving the decimal incorrectly or attaching the wrong exponent.

39. **D. 6**

A multiple of a number is that number times an integer, so a multiple is always greater than or equal to the number in question. That rules out 6 as a multiple of 12. (It's a factor of 12, but factors and multiples are two different beasts.) All the other choices are multiples of 12, which you can check by dividing each by 12 on your calculator.

40. **B. 6**

Similar triangles have congruent angles and proportional sides. You can figure out what each measure in the left triangle must be multiplied by to get the measure of the corresponding side in the other triangle. That number is 2. You can therefore multiply 3 by 2 to get the missing side measure. The other choices can result from various math errors.

41. **B. –2**

You can use a calculator to get the answer. If you happen to be anti-calculator, remember that when you add a negative number, you're actually subtracting that number. So $17 + -19$ is really $17 - 19$. The result is –2. The other choices result from various math errors.

42. **A. 29,807**

The central angle of a sector in a pie chart can tell you what portion of the pie chart a sector covers. Simply divide the central angle by 360: $\frac{45}{360}$ is $\frac{1}{8}$ (or 0.125), so the sector covers $\frac{1}{8}$ of the pie chart. The pie chart represents 238,456 people, so take $\frac{1}{8}$ of that number. The sector represents 29,807 people. Choice (B) is the number of 45-degree sectors a pie chart can have. Choice (C) is $\frac{1}{4}$ of the number of people represented by the pie chart, not $\frac{1}{8}$. Choice (D) is the number of degrees in the sector. Choice (E) results from multiplying 238,456 by 8 instead of $\frac{1}{8}$ (or 0.125).

43. **C. 7.2426**

The distance back to the starting point is the same as the distance from the starting point. The distance back is therefore 724.26 decameters. The next question is what that is in terms of kilometers. One kilometer contains 100 decameters, so divide the number of decameters by 100. $724.26 \div 100 = 7.2426$. (Dividing by 100 is the same as moving the decimal point two places to the left.) The other choices result from moving the decimal incorrectly.

44. **C. (–6, 11)**

The coordinates of the given image are (3, 7), (11, 6), (10, –2), and (–3, –2). To find the new coordinates after a 90-degree rotation counterclockwise about the origin, swap the order of the coordinates in each pair (making the *x*-coordinate the *y*-coordinate and vice versa) and find the opposite of the new *y*-coordinate. The coordinates in this case become (7, –3), (6, –11), (–2, –10), and (–2, 3). You can rule out the answer choices that contain any of these coordinates, leaving Choice (C).

45. **D. $k > 6$**

$$-4k + 9 < -15$$
$$-4k + 9 - 9 < -15 - 9$$
$$-4k < -24$$
$$\frac{-4k}{-4} > \frac{-24}{-4}$$
$$k > 6$$

Remember that when you divide both sides by a negative number, the direction of the inequality sign must be switched. Choice (A) results from not doing that. The other choices result from errors in the solving process.

46. **A. 1,456**

Each of the 14 necklaces has 26 beads, so the number of beads is $14 \cdot 26$, or 364. Each bead has 4 letters, so the number of letters is $364 \cdot 4$, or 1,456.

47. **B. 35 miles per hour**

Speed is distance divided by time, so divide 70 miles by 2 hours: $70 \div 2 = 35$, so Kat's speed is 35 miles per hour. The other answers come from various math errors.

48. **E. 40**

You can translate the question directly into mathematical language with the equation $\frac{42}{1} = \left(\frac{x}{100}\right)\left(\frac{105}{1}\right)$.

The solution to the equation is 40. Choice (B) is what you have to multiply 40 percent by to get 100 percent. Choice (D) is 40 percent in decimal form, but the question asks for a percent.

49. C. 18

The median of a set of data is the middle number or the mean of the two middle numbers *when the numbers are in order.* When the numbers from the question are in order, the two middle numbers are 12 and 24. The mean of 12 and 24 is 18, so 18 is the median of the set of data. Choice (B) is the mean (average) of the set of data rounded to the nearest hundredth. Choice (D) is the range. Choice (E) is just the lowest number.

50. D. $\frac{419}{42}$

All the added numbers are mixed numbers. The best way to add mixed numbers is to write them in improper fraction form and then get a common denominator and add the numerators. You can rewrite this problem as $\frac{174}{42} + \frac{406}{42} + \left(\frac{-161}{42}\right)$. The sum is 419/42. Choice (E) results from simplifying $\frac{420}{42}$.

51. A. 4

The problem involves solving a proportion because the equation is a fraction set equal to a fraction. By setting the cross products equal to each other, which you can always do with a proportion, you get $144 = 36m$, the solution to which is 4.

52. E. 52 degrees

$\angle R$ corresponds to $\angle Z$, so $\angle Z$ is also 38 degrees because the triangles are congruent. $\angle X$ is 90 degrees. The sum of the measures of $\angle Z$ and $\angle X$ is 128 degrees. That leaves 52 degrees for $\angle Y$ because 180 degrees – 128 degrees = 52 degrees. Choice (A) is the measure of $\angle R$ and $\angle Z$. Choice (B) is one digit off from the correct answer. Choice (C) is 180 degrees – 38 degrees. Choice (D) is the sum of the measures of $\angle Z$ and $\angle X$ and also the sum of the measures of $\angle R$ and $\angle P$.

53. C. $\frac{1}{15}$

You can find the probability of two events happening by multiplying the probabilities of each event. $\frac{1}{3} \cdot \frac{1}{5} = \frac{1}{15}$. Choice (B) results from adding the probabilities instead of multiplying them (which you'd do only if this problem were an "or" problem).

54. C. 11

For a number to work as a counterexample, it would have to be not prime and not even. The number 11 isn't even, but it's prime. All the other choices are counterexamples of the statement, so they don't fit what the question asks.

55. C. 304.5 cm²

Because the legs of the triangle are perpendicular, they can be treated as base and height. The formula for the area of a triangle is $A = \frac{1}{2}bh$.

$$\left(\frac{1}{2}\right)(21)(29) = 304.5 \text{ cm}^2$$

56. A. x^2y^2z

John's age times Mike's age can be represented by $(xy)(xyz)$, the product of which is x^2y^2z. The other choices result from incorrectly multiplying $(xy)(xyz)$. Remember that when you're multiplying variables with exponents, you add the exponents of the same variable; if no exponent is given, you know it's 1.

Answer Key

Part 1: Reading

1. E	13. C	25. C	37. B	49. B
2. C	14. D	26. E	38. D	50. A
3. C	15. E	27. D	39. C	51. E
4. D	16. C	28. A	40. C	52. C
5. A	17. C	29. D	41. B	53. B
6. B	18. C	30. C	42. B	54. D
7. A	19. A	31. B	43. A	55. A
8. A	20. B	32. D	44. E	56. C
9. E	21. A	33. D	45. C	
10. C	22. E	34. A	46. D	
11. B	23. C	35. C	47. B	
12. B	24. B	36. E	48. C	

Part 2: Writing

1. E	9. C	17. D	25. D	33. D
2. D	10. E	18. B	26. E	34. E
3. A	11. A	19. A	27. B	35. C
4. B	12. B	20. D	28. C	36. A
5. C	13. B	21. A	29. A	37. B
6. D	14. D	22. C	30. B	38. C
7. E	15. A	23. E	31. B	39. B
8. B	16. D	24. C	32. A	40. B

Part 3: Mathematics

1. C	13. B	25. C	37. E	49. C
2. C	14. E	26. C	38. A	50. D
3. A	15. A	27. E	39. D	51. A
4. C	16. D	28. A	40. B	52. E
5. E	17. E	29. E	41. B	53. C
6. E	18. A	30. A	42. A	54. C
7. D	19. C	31. A	43. C	55. C
8. B	20. B	32. D	44. C	56. A
9. A	21. D	33. A	45. D	
10. D	22. E	34. D	46. A	
11. B	23. D	35. B	47. B	
12. C	24. B	36. C	48. E	

Part VI
The Part of Tens

A free article at www.dummies.com/extras/praxiscore reviews ten points to keep in mind while taking the Praxis.

In this part . . .

✔ When working math problems on the Praxis, you need to be careful of more than just careless calculation errors. Check out ten common math errors to avoid.

✔ Reading and writing questions can trip you up if you don't pay attention to what the question is asking for. Know what to be on the lookout for, and discover how your own instincts may trip you up.

Chapter 18

Ten Common Math Errors to Avoid

In This Chapter

▶ Overlooking signs

▶ Confusing similar formulas and terms

▶ Freaking out over fractions

Knowing how to perform certain types of math operations is a big part of solving problems correctly, but it isn't everything. Caution is also important. Avoiding common math errors involves both. Think back to times when you saw what you missed on math tests and thought, "Oh yeah, I had this mixed up with that!" This chapter helps you avoid that exact situation. Errors are always a threat. Don't let them get you.

Misusing Negative Signs

In our observations, math mistakes occur most frequently when negatives are involved. Negatives are to math problems what land mines are to war zones, except they're only dangerous to math scores. That's the good news. When you see a negative sign, you should turn your level of caution up a notch or two. Such a small symbol has so much power to transform a quantity. Imagine being told that you have $1 million in a bank account and then being told, "Oh, I'm sorry. I didn't see the negative sign. You have –$1 million. You are that much in debt." It's a completely different picture. One misuse of a negative sign will usually wreck an entire answer. See Chapter 4 for the lowdown on negative numbers.

Multiplying by an odd number of negative factors results in a negative product, and multiplying by an even number of negative factors results in a positive product. Also keep in mind that the sum of two negatives is a negative and the sum of a negative and a positive has the sign of the number with the greater absolute value.

You will have a calculator to use on the Praxis Core exam. When you work with negative numbers, you should use the calculator even when you feel like you don't need it. Safety is a big issue in math.

Confusing Perimeter and Area

Many people mix up the formulas for perimeter and area. Remember that perimeter is the distance around something. If it is expressed in units, it's expressed in one-dimensional units, such as meters (m), centimeters (cm), feet (ft.), and inches (in.). Area is two-dimensional. It is the amount of a plane inside a two-dimensional figure. When area is expressed in units, the units are two-dimensional and have an exponent of 2. Such units include m^2, cm^2, $ft.^2$, and $in.^2$. For more details on calculating perimeter and area, turn to Chapter 6.

The perimeter of a circle is also called the circumference. Mixing up the formula for circumference with the formula for the area of a circle is common. Both formulas involve only π, r, and 2, but in different arrangements. The formula for the circumference of a circle is $C = 2\pi r$. The formula for the area of a circle is $A = \pi r^2$. So you see how they're especially easy to confuse — it happens all the time. Be very careful with the formulas for area and perimeter.

Incorrectly Combining Like Terms

Only like terms can be combined, and terms have to meet certain conditions to be like terms. They have to either have no variables or have exactly the same variables with the same exponent per corresponding variable. Remember that when no variable is shown with an exponent, its understood exponent is 1. $5xyz$ and $4xyz$ can be added to get $9xyz$, and $4x^2y^3z^4$ can be subtracted from $5x^2y^3z^4$ to get $x^2y^3z^4$. However, $5x^2y^3z^4 + 4x^2y^3z^5$ can't be simplified because the two terms are not like terms. z does not have the same exponent in both terms. Take a look at Chapter 4 for a review of exponents and Chapter 5 to see how they work in algebraic terms and equations.

Messing Up when Moving Decimals

Some really common math errors involve calculations and rewritings that require moving a decimal to the right or left. The two major areas of math that entail decimal movement are using scientific notation and converting between decimals and percents. Both involve doing something and then making up for it by undoing it. You can do this smoothly if you keep in mind that multiplying by a multiple of 10 can be done by moving a decimal to the right and dividing by a multiple of 10 can be accomplished by moving a decimal to the left. Decimals and percents are reviewed in Chapter 4.

Not Solving for the Actual Variable

Solving an equation or inequality involves stating what a variable equals or could equal. A mistake people commonly make is saying what something that almost looks like a variable could equal. For example, you may think an equation is solved by the conclusion $-x = 15$. That's not a solution. It shows a value for the opposite of the variable. To solve for x, you need a statement about x at the end, not $-x$. Solving for x (or any other variable) is all about the value of x (or whatever the variable is). Your final statement must be about what x equals, not about what $3x$, or $1/x$, equals, for example. Chapter 5 tells you everything you need to know about solving for variables.

Misrepresenting "Less Than" in Word Problems

When an operation is described with English words instead of mathematical symbols, part of your challenge is to represent the operation correctly. The most common mistake made in doing that is incorrectly representing a certain amount less than a number. The quantities are often falsely reversed. For example, "6 less than a number" can be represented by $x - 6$, but it cannot be represented by $6 - x$. The latter represents a certain amount less than 6, not 6 less than a certain amount. Check out Chapter 5 for a more detailed review of this concept.

The confusion that commonly exists here results from the fact that the subtracted quantity is mentioned in the description before the quantity from which it is subtracted. Be careful with that. 4 less than 7 is 7 – 4, not 4 – 7.

Mixing Up Supplementary and Complementary Angles

The words "supplementary" and "complementary" are often confused. Preparing ahead of time to avoid that confusion will help keep your work safer. Complementary angles have measures that add up to 90°, and supplementary angles have measures that add up to 180°. Here's a silly but effective mnemonic statement to help you remember the difference: *If you live to be 90, you deserve a complement. If you live to be 180, you are super.* You can find out all about angles in Chapter 6.

Finding the Wrong Median

The most common mistake that happens in finding a median of a set of data is failing to put the data in order. The median is the middle number or mean of the two middle numbers of a set of data *when the data is in order*. Getting that for a set of data that is not in order is not very likely to result in the actual median. Get the lowdown on determining the median, mean, and mode in Chapter 7.

Fearing Fractions

So "fearing fractions" isn't a specific mistake, but fraction problems create all sorts of opportunities for errors, and that scares people.

 Common denominators are necessary for adding and subtracting fractions, not for multiplying or dividing them. The distinction is extremely important.

Multiplying fractions involves multiplying the numerators and multiplying the denominators, and dividing by a fraction is the same as multiplying by its reciprocal. Adding and subtracting fractions involves getting a common denominator and then operating with only the numerators. The denominator doesn't change unless the sum or difference has to be simplified. You can review computing with fractions in Chapter 4.

Forgetting about Fractions in Formulas

Some of the formulas you need to know have 1/2 in them, and the 1/2 is often neglected. That can wreck your answer. For example, the formula for the area of a triangle is $A = (1/2)bh$. That is half of bh, so calculating just bh won't give you the area of a triangle. The area of a parallelogram is bh because a parallelogram can be split into two congruent triangles. The topic of area is covered in Chapter 6.

Chapter 19

Ten Mistakes to Avoid on the Praxis Reading and Writing Exams

In This Chapter

▶ Unlearning instincts for the reading and writing tests

▶ Understanding what the graders of the essays *aren't* looking for

▶ Taking care not to outsmart yourself

*W*e have instincts for a reason, but they don't always serve us well in every context. If you've ever played baseball or softball, you probably learned that "an outfielder's first step is always back" — this is an example of a rule that players have to internalize in order to help them *unlearn* their natural instinct to run forward when the ball is hit. Running toward the ball is what your mind *wants* you to do, but by doing so, you run the risk of misjudging the ball and watching it sail over your head.

Just like sports, test taking is an arena where your mind sometimes encourages you to do the wrong thing, and in those situations, you have to learn *not* to follow your instincts. This chapter helps you steer clear of common errors that test-takers make on the writing and reading portions of the Praxis Core.

Avoiding Mistakes Common to the Writing and Reading Tests

Before we turn to specific pieces of advice about the writing and reading tests, here are a couple of tips to keep in mind on both of them.

Don't look for patterns in the answers

The human brain has evolved to see patterns in everything. This capability is helpful when a pattern really is at work, but it can trip you up when you're confronting something truly random. For example, the fact that the ball of a roulette wheel has landed on an even number three times in a row doesn't mean that an odd number is due to come up next. Perhaps the biggest mistake that a test-taker can make on the Praxis is to look for a pattern in the answers. It's a waste of time and energy, and it won't help you get any more of the answers correct — in fact, it will probably cause you to select *wrong* answers that you wouldn't otherwise have picked.

Say you've eliminated three of the answer choices on a particular question, and now you're down to a 50/50 split between Choices (B) and (D). There are many logical ways to proceed, depending on what sort of question it is, but one thing you should never do is base your answer on how many (B)s or (D)s you've selected so far or which answer letter you selected most recently. The fact that you chose (B) for two of the previous three questions doesn't mean that the right answer to this question is any less likely to be (B) than (D) (and even if it did, you may have been wrong on one of the previous questions).

Where this instinct *really* has a tendency to trip up even very good test-takers is on those questions in the Writing test that offer the choice "No Error." It's easy to feel paranoid about whether you've selected "No Error" too many or too few times. But the best thing to do with that nagging little voice is ignore it. Even though it seems like a "special" answer, "No Error" is statistically no more or less likely to be right than any other answer. Every test is different, and the Praxis writing test you take may have a lot of correct "No Error" responses, or it may have only a couple. The best method is always to mark the answer you think is correct for each individual question on a case-by-case basis, paying absolutely no attention to how many or how few times you've selected the same answer choice previously.

Remember, this goes for "in-a-row" logic too: The fact that it seems unlikely that the correct answer would be Choice (C) three times in a row is no reason *not* to choose (C) if you genuinely think it's the right answer. There are few guarantees in life, but one thing you can take to the bank is the fact that looking for patterns on the Praxis Core is *always* a bad idea.

Don't change answers merely for the sake of changing them

The computer-delivered Praxis test allows you to skip and return to questions or even to look back over questions you've already answered. But just because you're allowed to do it doesn't necessarily mean it's a good idea!

The trickiest question to answer as a test-prep tutor is when students ask us, "Should I go back and check over my answers if I have time left over?" There's no one right answer to that question, because every student is different. Some test-takers tend to actually catch their careless mistakes when they look back, and others tend to get nervous and change answers that were right the first time.

To see which type of test-taker you are, go back over one of the practice tests in this book after you finish (but before you check your answers) and see whether you tend to catch real mistakes and improve your score when you go back and change answers, or whether you tend to outsmart yourself and change answers that were right the first time.

If you *do* end up deciding to go back and change an answer, you should be thinking more about whether the first answer you put is wrong than about whether the other answer you're considering seems right. It's common for more than one answer choice to seem right, and the way to avoid the problems this can cause is *never* to change an answer unless you can articulate to yourself *a reason why it's wrong*. "If it ain't broke, don't fix it" is an expression for a reason!

Sidestepping Mistakes on the Writing Test

Now that you've heard some general pointers about multiple-choice tests as a whole (see the preceding section), this section turns your attention specifically to the Praxis writing exam. The first two tips are about the multiple-choice questions, and the second two pertain to the essays.

Don't equate different with wrong

Quick! Which is correct: to say "I walked *down* the street" or "I walked *along* the street?" Well, based on the title of this section, you probably correctly guessed that either one is perfectly acceptable. Keep that in mind when you're taking the Praxis writing test: Just because you can think of a way to phrase something other than the way the question phrases it doesn't necessarily mean that the phrasing in the question is grammatically incorrect. There's often more than one correct way to say something.

This is a problem for a lot of test-takers on questions with the "No Error" answer choice. The fact that you can think of another word or phrase that could be substituted for under-lined portion (B) doesn't mean that underlined portion (B) is an error. The sentence may have no errors, or portion (B) may be distracting you from another underlined portion that really *does* contain an error.

Those questions aren't asking whether anything about the sentence *could be different* — they're asking whether anything about the sentence is *wrong*. You're supposed to be on the lookout for broken rules, not arbitrary stylistic matters.

Don't assume something must be correct just because it sounds fancier or more complex

Are you familiar with the term *overcorrection?* It's a mistake that occurs as a result of trying extra-hard to be right, and it's a common pitfall in grammar. An example is saying, "Just between you and *I*," even though "Just between you and *me*" is actually correct. Most people are insecure about their grammar, and grammatically stressful situations — such as taking a test or having a conversation with an English professor — can exacerbate that insecurity and cause people to say things in a way they wouldn't normally say them, even if the way they'd normally say them is fine.

Perhaps no single word in the English language pops up unnecessarily as a result of over-correction than *whom*. Nervous students writing essays may slap unneeded m's onto the end of the interrogative pronoun right and left. They're so nervous about saying *who* when they should say *whom* that they end up saying *whom* when they should say *who*. (See Chapter 12 for a review of when to use "who" and when to use "whom.")

Verb tenses are another area where you'll want to watch out for overcorrection. If "I *drove* to the store yesterday" sounds perfectly fine in context, resist the urge to select "I *had driven* to the store yesterday" just because the past-perfect tense sounds more complex than the regular past tense.

Fancy words like *whom* or fancy tenses like the perfect tenses aren't right *all* the time or even *most* of the time — they're right when they're right. So trust your ear and select the answer choices that sound correct in context, rather than always going for the fancy ones.

Don't turn the essay into a thesaurus explosion

Deploying ostentatious diction due merely to the fact that your extemporaneous prosody is slated for appraisal is egregiously unadvisable.

Does the preceding sentence sound good to you? Or would you rather read "Using big words just because you're taking an essay test isn't a good idea"? That's what we thought.

The idea that you get extra points for big words is probably the most persistent urban legend about standardized tests. Nevertheless, you should ignore the urge to use a fifty-cent synonym for each everyday word that pops into your head.

Stopping to think of big words you wouldn't normally use eats up precious time, and it won't make your score go up anyway, because — contrary to popular belief — the graders don't "count big words." If anything, adopting an unnatural style will probably make your score go *down,* because it sounds robotic and obnoxious (and if you don't normally use those words, chances are pretty good that you're using the big words incorrectly anyway).

The graders of the essay look for a sense of ease with written communication. You want to sound thoughtful, personable, persuasive, and, above all, as if you think writing is fun. If it seems like your main concern is trying to work in as many big words as you can, you'll end up looking like you're trying to disguise the fact that you're uncomfortable with the writing process.

Don't paint yourself into a corner with a rigid thesis

The first of the two essays on the Praxis writing test is thesis-driven; it asks you to adopt a stance on an issue or defend a viewpoint. You want to carve out a clear position and sound like you believe in what you're saying, of course, but it's not a good idea to start off by asserting your thesis so stringently that you won't be able to acknowledge an exception or gray area that occurs to you, for fear of appearing to contradict yourself.

When it comes to theses, you don't get extra points for extremism. If you think each side of the issue has some valid points, it's entirely okay to say so. You're graded on how well you write, not on your opinion. You want to steer clear of the dreaded essay-test dead end where you think of something bright and interesting to say halfway through your writing process but feel as if you can't say it because it doesn't fit in with your uncompromising thesis statement.

This doesn't mean you have to hem and haw. You can state your opinion clearly up-front and add an "on the other hand, I can understand why someone might think . . ." later. That way, if an exception to your thesis pops into your head, you can say so. This strategy not only helps you out when it comes to length, but it also gets you points for what essay graders call *anticipating objections* — demonstrating that you're able to see the issue from the other side's point of view, even though you don't agree with it. That's a sign of philosophical maturity (and it earns you points).

Evading Mistakes on the Reading Test

Reading comprehension is not as rule-based as grammar, but there are still a few definite traps you want to avoid falling into on the Praxis reading exam.

Don't rule out the "too obvious"

No one's saying the Praxis is easy, but there's no point in making things tougher on yourself by expecting it to be harder than it is. We can't tell you how many times we see students about to circle the correct answer, only to change it at the last second. When asked why, they often say that the first (and correct) answer was "too obvious."

So, we can't stress this enough: There is no such thing as "too obvious." There's only *right* or *wrong*.

The "too obvious" mistake is really a confidence problem: You expect the test to be hard, so when a question seems easy, you assume you must have missed something and question your (good) instincts. Some students even say they whittle the answer choices down to 50/50 and then pick the one they think is *wrong*, because they're so sure that there must be some trick that they're missing!

One of the answer choices will be right, and the other four will be wrong. There's no such thing as a question with an easy right answer or a hard right one. When a right answer seems obvious to you, give yourself some credit and assume that you're getting pretty good at this rather than being tricked.

Don't word-match

Do you know what students who don't speak English very well do when they have to take a multiple-choice test in English? They look for the answer choice that has the greatest number of words from the passage in it and pick that one. The people who write multiple-choice standardized tests like the Praxis reading test know this, and they use it to try to trick you. Inserting a string of matching words from the passage into one of the wrong answer choices as bait for people whose reading comprehension is weak is a common method that test-writers use to compose the wrong answer choices.

We're not saying that you should *always* pick the answer choice that has the *fewest* number of words in common with the passage, of course. We're just saying that you shouldn't base your answer on anything to do with how many words or phrases from the passage appear in a particular choice.

Don't ignore your outside knowledge

Unlike the writing exam, for which you need to know as many grammar rules as you can cram into your head, the Praxis reading exam doesn't test you on outside knowledge. A passage presents you with some information, and then you answer the question you're asked based solely on the information in the passage. For example, if a passage is about economics, you don't have to know anything about economics in order to get the question right — the passage is designed to tell you everything you need to know.

But just because you don't *need* to know anything other than what the passages tell you in order to correctly answer the questions, you shouldn't ignore or forget about things that you *happen* to know from real life. Now, we're *not* saying you should try to select *right* answers based on what you think is true in real life — when the question says "according to the author" or "according to the passage," it means that you are to identify what the text says, not give your personal opinion. However, outside knowledge is frequently useful when it comes to eliminating *wrong* answers.

Many of the passages may involve unsettled matters of opinion, but none of the authors is ever out-and-out *wrong* about anything. You may see a passage by a scientist who thinks life exists on the moon of Jupiter known as Europa, or you may see a passage by a scientist who thinks such life doesn't exist. According to current scientific thought, either opinion is plausible. But you'll never see a passage by a scientist who thinks there are panda bears on Mars, because that's just crazy! So although you're not supposed to select right answers based on your own knowledge or opinions, if you see an answer choice that you happen to know is *definitely, factually false,* you can cross it off immediately.

Don't try to answer more than the question asks you to

"Answer the questions" probably seems like unnecessarily obvious advice. Of course you're supposed to answer the questions — you're taking a test! But you'd be surprised how many test-takers forget to follow that advice. The question following a passage may ask something like "Which of the following claims is explicitly made in the passage?" You may see an answer choice that does indeed paraphrase a claim that was explicitly made in the passage, but then avoid picking it because the claim wasn't the author's main point. Huh?! The question didn't ask you what the author's main point was — it *just* asked you which of the claims was explicitly made in the passage. So answer *that* specific question and that specific question *alone.*

The same confusion can even occur with a simple vocabulary question. When the question says "The author is using this word most nearly to mean . . . ," it isn't asking you what that word means most of the time or for the fanciest thing it could possibly mean in another context. It's just asking you what the author used it to mean in one specific place, so *just answer that question.*

Index

Notes

Notes

Notes

About the Authors

Carla Kirkland is a lifelong educator who has served as a math teacher, curriculum specialist, and educational consultant. From Common Core State Standard workshops to Praxis tutorial reviews to K–12 subject area test remediation, her invigorating presentations speak to the hearts of math teachers and students throughout the southern United States. As founder and CEO of the Kirkland Group, an educational consulting firm headquartered in Ridgeland, Mississippi, Ms. Kirkland has provided online and face-to-face technical assistance and standardized test preparation to school districts for more than 20 years. She has facilitated numerous regional and national mathematics workshops.

Chan Cleveland has taught English on all K–12 levels and worked in several capacities at the Mississippi Department of Education. He has reviewed, revised, and developed language arts standard documents for many school districts and education organizations. Mr. Cleveland has assisted students and teachers with attaining positive results on the Praxis, ACT, and K–12 English subject area exams. He currently serves as an educational consultant and executive vice president of the Kirkland Group. Mr. Cleveland holds English degrees from Jackson State University and Mississippi College.

Dedication

This book is dedicated to our parents, Elaine Cleveland and the late Cornelius Cleveland, who died in 1992. Thanks for giving us the vision, courage, and wisdom to step out on faith and do what we love.

Authors' Acknowledgments

First of all we would like to thank God for the opportunity to write *Praxis Core For Dummies*. This book would not have been possible without the written contributions of Christopher Cook, Spencer Powers, and Dr. Cindy Thomas. Ginger Harris and Sarah Douglas also assisted us with the writing and revising process. We are grateful to James Giovannini for his sound advice.

We appreciate the school districts throughout the state of Mississippi and beyond that allowed us the opportunity to train their staff and students for the ACT, SAT, Praxis, MCT2, and SATP2. Some of our clients have been loyal for all 17 years of our existence in this business.

Finally, we want to add a special thanks to Lindsey Lefevere, Erin Mooney, and Vicki Adang of Wiley Publishing for facilitating this long process. All of the staff at Wiley Publishing is top of the line. Feel free to e-mail questions, critiques, and comments to info@kirklandgroup.org.

Publisher's Acknowledgments

Acquisitions Editor: Erin Calligan Mooney

Senior Project Editor: Victoria M. Adang

Copy Editor: Christine Pingleton

Technical Editor: Andrea Malmont, EdD

Project Coordinator: Sheree Montgomery

Project Manager: Laura Moss-Hollister

Cover Image: ©iStockphoto.com/DNY59

Apple & Mac

iPad For Dummies, 6th Edition
978-1-118-72306-7

iPhone For Dummies, 7th Edition
978-1-118-69083-3

Macs All-in-One For Dummies,
4th Edition
978-1-118-82210-4

OS X Mavericks For Dummies
978-1-118-69188-5

Blogging & Social Media

Facebook For Dummies, 5th Edition
978-1-118-63312-0

Social Media Engagement For Dummies
978-1-118-53019-1

WordPress For Dummies, 6th Edition
978-1-118-79161-5

Business

Stock Investing For Dummies,
4th Edition
978-1-118-37678-2

Investing For Dummies, 6th Edition
978-0-470-90545-6

Personal Finance For Dummies,
7th Edition
978-1-118-11785-9

QuickBooks 2014 For Dummies
978-1-118-72005-9

Small Business Marketing Kit
For Dummies, 3rd Edition
978-1-118-31183-7

Careers

Job Interviews For Dummies, 4th Edition
978-1-118-11290-8

Job Searching with Social Media
For Dummies, 2nd Edition
978-1-118-67856-5

Personal Branding For Dummies
978-1-118-11792-7

Resumes For Dummies, 6th Edition
978-0-470-87361-8

Starting an Etsy Business For Dummies,
2nd Edition
978-1-118-59024-9

Diet & Nutrition

Belly Fat Diet For Dummies
978-1-118-34585-6

Mediterranean Diet For Dummies
978-1-118-71525-3

Nutrition For Dummies, 5th Edition
978-0-470-93231-5

Digital Photography

Digital SLR Photography All-in-One
For Dummies, 2nd Edition
978-1-118-59082-9

Digital SLR Video & Filmmaking
For Dummies
978-1-118-36598-4

Photoshop Elements 12 For Dummies
978-1-118-72714-0

Gardening

Herb Gardening For Dummies,
2nd Edition
978-0-470-61778-6

Gardening with Free-Range Chickens
For Dummies
978-1-118-54754-0

Health

Boosting Your Immunity For Dummies
978-1-118-40200-9

Diabetes For Dummies, 4th Edition
978-1-118-29447-5

Living Paleo For Dummies
978-1-118-29405-5

Big Data

Big Data For Dummies
978-1-118-50422-2

Data Visualization For Dummies
978-1-118-50289-1

Hadoop For Dummies
978-1-118-60755-8

Language & Foreign Language

500 Spanish Verbs For Dummies
978-1-118-02382-2

English Grammar For Dummies,
2nd Edition
978-0-470-54664-2

French All-in-One For Dummies
978-1-118-22815-9

German Essentials For Dummies
978-1-118-18422-6

Italian For Dummies, 2nd Edition
978-1-118-00465-4

Math & Science

Algebra I For Dummies, 2nd Edition
978-0-470-55964-2

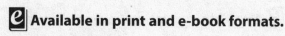 **Available in print and e-book formats.**

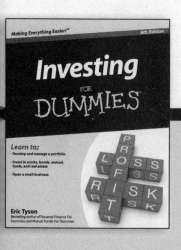
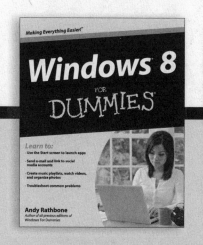

Available wherever books are sold. **For more information or to order direct visit www.dummies.com**

Anatomy and Physiology For Dummies, 2nd Edition
978-0-470-92326-9

Astronomy For Dummies, 3rd Edition
978-1-118-37697-3

Biology For Dummies, 2nd Edition
978-0-470-59875-7

Chemistry For Dummies, 2nd Edition
978-1-118-00730-3

1001 Algebra II Practice Problems
For Dummies
978-1-118-44662-1

Microsoft Office

Excel 2013 For Dummies
978-1-118-51012-4

Office 2013 All-in-One For Dummies
978-1-118-51636-2

PowerPoint 2013 For Dummies
978-1-118-50253-2

Word 2013 For Dummies
978-1-118-49123-2

Music

Blues Harmonica For Dummies
978-1-118-25269-7

Guitar For Dummies, 3rd Edition
978-1-118-11554-1

iPod & iTunes For Dummies, 10th Edition
978-1-118-50864-0

Programming

Beginning Programming with C
For Dummies
978-1-118-73763-7

Excel VBA Programming For Dummies,
3rd Edition
978-1-118-49037-2

Java For Dummies, 6th Edition
978-1-118-40780-6

Religion & Inspiration

The Bible For Dummies
978-0-7645-5296-0

Buddhism For Dummies, 2nd Edition
978-1-118-02379-2

Catholicism For Dummies, 2nd Edition
978-1-118-07778-8

Self-Help & Relationships

Beating Sugar Addiction For Dummies
978-1-118-54645-1

Meditation For Dummies, 3rd Edition
978-1-118-29144-3

Seniors

Laptops For Seniors For Dummies,
3rd Edition
978-1-118-71105-7

Computers For Seniors For Dummies,
3rd Edition
978-1-118-11553-4

iPad For Seniors For Dummies,
6th Edition
978-1-118-72826-0

Social Security For Dummies
978-1-118-20573-0

Smartphones & Tablets

Android Phones For Dummies,
2nd Edition
978-1-118-72030-1

Nexus Tablets For Dummies
978-1-118-77243-0

Samsung Galaxy S 4 For Dummies
978-1-118-64222-1

Samsung Galaxy Tabs For Dummies
978-1-118-77294-2

Test Prep

ACT For Dummies, 5th Edition
978-1-118-01259-8

ASVAB For Dummies, 3rd Edition
978-0-470-63760-9

GRE For Dummies, 7th Edition
978-0-470-88921-3

Officer Candidate Tests For Dummies
978-0-470-59876-4

Physician's Assistant Exam For Dummies
978-1-118-11556-5

Series 7 Exam For Dummies
978-0-470-09932-2

Windows 8

Windows 8.1 All-in-One For Dummies
978-1-118-82087-2

Windows 8.1 For Dummies
978-1-118-82121-3

Windows 8.1 For Dummies, Book + DVD
Bundle
978-1-118-82107-7

Available in print and e-book formats.

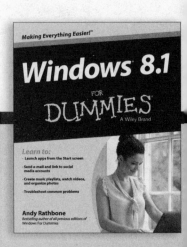

Available wherever books are sold. **For more information or to order direct visit www.dummies.com**

Take Dummies with you everywhere you go!

Whether you are excited about e-books, want more from the web, must have your mobile apps, or are swept up in social media, Dummies makes everything easier.

Visit Us

bit.ly/JE0O

Like Us

on.fb.me/1f1ThNu

Follow Us

bit.ly/ZDytkR

Watch Us

bit.ly/gbOQHn

Join Us

linkd.in/1gurkMm

Pin Us

bit.ly/16caOLd

Circle Us

bit.ly/1aQTuDQ

Shop Us

bit.ly/4dEp9

Leverage the Power

For Dummies is the global leader in the reference category and one of the most trusted and highly regarded brands in the world. No longer just focused on books, customers now have access to the For Dummies content they need in the format they want. Let us help you develop a solution that will fit your brand and help you connect with your customers.

Advertising & Sponsorships

Connect with an engaged audience on a powerful multimedia site, and position your message alongside expert how-to content.

Targeted ads • Video • Email marketing • Microsites • Sweepstakes sponsorship

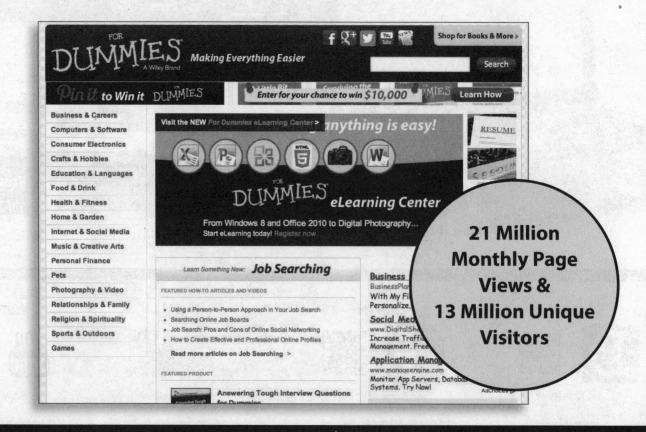

21 Million Monthly Page Views & 13 Million Unique Visitors

For Dummies is a registered trademark of John Wiley & Sons, Inc.

Custom Publishing

Reach a global audience in any language by creating a solution that will differentiate you from competitors, amplify your message, and encourage customers to make a buying decision.

Apps • Books • eBooks • Video • Audio • Webinars

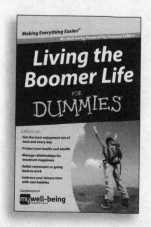

Brand Licensing & Content

Leverage the strength of the world's most popular reference brand to reach new audiences and channels of distribution.

For more information, visit www.Dummies.com/biz

FOR
DUMMIES®
A Wiley Brand

Dummies products make life easier!

- DIY
- Consumer Electronics
- Crafts

- Software
- Cookware
- Hobbies

- Videos
- Music
- Games
- and More!

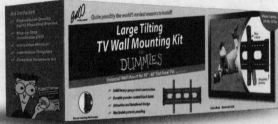

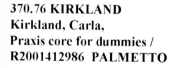

370.76 KIRKLAND
Kirkland, Carla,
Praxis core for dummies /
R2001412986 PALMETTO

ODC

Atlanta-Fulton Public Library

For Dummies is a registered trademark of J

A Wiley Bra

P9-DFZ-611

Great Weather Activities

BY MARY KAY CARSON

SCHOLASTIC
PROFESSIONAL BOOKS

NEW YORK • TORONTO • LONDON • AUCKLAND • SYDNEY

MEXICO CITY • NEW DELHI • HONG KONG

Dedication

To the blowing wind, warm sun, and fluffy snow

that makes us wonder about the mysteries of weather and

draws our attention to the natural world around us.

Acknowledgments

Thanks to Deborah Schecter for being such an encouraging and
faithful editor and to Tracey West for her magical editing.

Scholastic Inc. grants teachers permission to
photocopy the student activity pages in this book
for classroom use. No other part of this publication
can be reproduced in whole or in part, or stored in
a retrieval system, or transmitted in any form or by
any means, electronic, mechanical, photocopying,
recording, or otherwise, without written permission
of the publisher. For information regarding permission,
write to Scholastic Inc., 555 Broadway, New York, NY 10012.

Cover design by Pamela Simmons
Interior design by Imagination Ink
Interior illustration by Doug Horne
Science Consultant: H. Michael Mogil, Weather Educator,
How the Weatherworks

ISBN 0-590-22181-7

Copyright © 2000 by Mary Kay Carson
All rights reserved. Printed in the U.S.A.

Contents

Activities with this symbol
have student reproducibles.

Introduction

Weather is the perfect earth science topic for young students. Weather is something all children experience firsthand every day. They know and can talk about the temperature, rain, and sunshine. Real experiences with the weather make wonderful avenues that can lead students into a deeper knowledge and understanding of the world around them. And while weather is as accessible as cloud gazing, it can also be as mysterious as a tornado. Children are fascinated by weather's many mysteries.

About this Book

A quick look at the table of contents on page 3 tells you that this book is divided into four chapters: "The Sun and the Seasons"; "Air and Wind"; "Clouds, Rain, Sleet, and Snow"; and "Stormy Weather." The chapters and activities in this book do not need to be used in any particular order. In fact, they are interrelated. After all, it's the sun (Chapter 1) that drives wind (Chapter 2), and what would a thunderstorm (Chapter 4) be without rain (Chapter 3)? Feel free to integrate the information and activities in this book into your own weather unit to best serve your students' needs.

EACH CHAPTER INCLUDES:

Information

BACKGROUND INFORMATION: Each chapter starts with a few pages of background information briefly covering that chapter's need-to-know facts and scientific principles.

WORDS TO KNOW: You'll find key words and their definitions at a glance at the end of each background section.

WISE WEATHER FACTS: You'll want to share these fun, fascinating facts with your students.

Activities

ACTIVITIES: The activities in this book allow students to explore weather firsthand. They cover a number of curriculum areas, which are noted after the activity titles. Most activities are followed by one or more cross-curricular extension activities. These extensions are full of ideas and specific activities to further learning. Throughout the book you'll also find Measure the Weather activities, which show you how you and your students can build weather instruments that really work.

BOOK BREAKS: There are many wonderful books you can use to teach weather topics. Each Book Break recommends a book and suggests an activity to go with it.

ONLINE LINKS: Find out what the best weather websites are, and get suggestions for using each website with your unit.

REPRODUCIBLES: After each Activities section, you'll find several reproducible pages to use with the activities.

ADDITIONAL RESOURCES

At the very end of this book you'll find recommendations for books for teachers, more useful websites, and additional books for students.

National Science Education Content Standards

The information and accompanying hands-on experiments and lessons featured in this book meet many of the National Science Education standards, the set of criteria intended to guide the quality of science teaching and learning in this country. The standards outline key science content areas and support a hands-on, inquiry-based approach to learning. The following list shows how weather-related topics in this book correlate with the National Science Content Standards for Grades K-4:

The sun provides the light and heat necessary to maintain the temperature of the earth.

Objects in the sky—such as the sun—have patterns of movement that change their path over the seasons.

Weather changes from day to day and throughout the seasons.

Weather can be measured in quantities such as temperature, wind speed and direction, and precipitation.

Note that the Science Standards emphasize observing, measuring, identifying, and communicating weather patterns and elements for students in this age group. Understanding the intricacies of the underlying causes of weather—such as air pressure and worldwide currents—is more appropriate study for older students.

Getting Started and Keeping It Going

Here are a few ideas for launching—and sustaining—your class' unit on weather.

1 Invite students to help guide your weather investigations. Start the unit with a brainstorming session about weather to find out what most interests your students. Do they want to know about tornadoes or snowstorms? why the wind blows or what clouds are made of? Making a *K-W-L* chart is a great way to organize those thoughts and to chart progress. *K-W-L* stands for what we Know, what we Want to know, and what we've Learned. Divide a bulletin board into three sections and label each section with one of these headings. Give students squares of paper (or raindrop-, cloud-, or sun-shaped paper) and invite them to write weather questions or facts on them. As a class, decide where to tape or pin the questions on the bulletin board–under "What We Know" or "What We Want to Know." As your weather unit progresses, add more questions or facts as they arise, and move some questions to the "What We've Learned" section when you and your students feel you are ready to do so.

2 Consider setting up a weather learning center in a corner of your classroom. The center can incorporate a weather library full of resource books and weather-related storybooks. (You'll find lots of

recommendations throughout the book.) Decorate the center with the weather artwork created during the unit. Display students' poems about weather. The space will not only whet students' appetites for weather knowledge, it will provide a focused place for them to go and do independent investigations.

3 Set up a classroom weather station (or integrate it into the learning center) for measuring weather elements. You can use the instruments you make using the instructions in this book, professional instruments, or a combination of both. Have student groups take turns using the instruments to record and report the weather for the class daily. Challenge students to chart the weather conditions over a week or more using the reproducible Week of Weather chart on page 16.

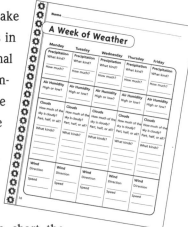

4 Designate a section of bulletin board or wall (or again, integrate it into the learning center) for displaying daily weather information such as a weather map from the day's paper, or the predicted temperature or wind direction. Students can take turns bringing in this information from home.

5 Invite students to keep a weather science journal while you're studying weather. It's a place to note words and terms they learn as the unit progresses, record observations and data from activities, and keep the reproducibles from this book. A science journal is a great way for students to build confidence about what they've learned and can help with assessment.

6 Videotape the weather on the morning news at home and watch the tape with your students. Consider watching the same forecast repeatedly throughout the unit, so students can see how much more they understand as they learn.

7 Invite a meteorologist to visit your class and talk about weather careers.

8 Plan a weather party to celebrate all the things that students have learned about weather. Make a production of the play *Maui Traps the Sun* (page 15) part of the day's events. Decorate the classroom with artwork from the unit and invite students to read weather poems they've written. Serve food with weather themes, like sun shakes (1 1/2 cups orange juice, 3/4 cup milk, and 1/2 teaspoon vanilla) or sugar cookies shaped like raindrops, clouds, or tornadoes.

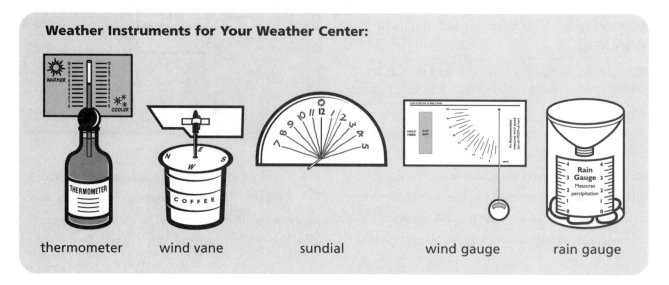

Weather Instruments for Your Weather Center:

thermometer   wind vane   sundial   wind gauge   rain gauge

CHAPTER 1

The Sun and the Seasons

WEATHER IS SOLAR POWERED

Weather is the condition of the air in a particular place at a specific time. Temperature and moisture in the air are mixed and churned by wind and pressure to make the weather sunny, cloudy, windy, stormy, or clear. The engine driving these weather variables is the sun—it fuels our weather. Our sun is a medium-sized and middle-aged star of average brightness that is powered by the nuclear fusion of hydrogen into helium. The sun bathes Earth in solar energy, including the light and heat that maintains the earth's temperature.

But the sun does not heat the earth evenly. Differences in terrain, latitude, and the time of year result in an uneven heating of the earth's surface, which in turn creates uneven heating of the air above it. It's hot during the summer, but cold during the winter; hot at the equator, but cold at the poles; colder atop a mountain than in the valley, etc. These global and local temperature differences drive the weather engine on our planet by creating air masses of different temperatures which yield pressure systems, fronts, and wind.

Wise Weather Fact

Verhoyansk in northeast Siberia has the world's most extreme temperature range. It can get down to -90°F (-68°C) during the winter and up to 98°F (37°C) during the summer.

Wise Weather Fact

Earth wobbles a bit on its tilted axis. The tilt varies over the centuries, but hovers near 23 1/2 degrees.

Words to Know

hemisphere: one half of Earth. On a globe, the Northern Hemisphere is the area above the equator, and the Southern Hemisphere is the area below the equator.

latitude: lines on the globe that measure distance from the equator

molecule: the smallest part of a substance that contains all of the chemical properties of that substance

temperature: a measure of the warmth or coldness of something

thermometer: an instrument that measures temperature

The Seasons

The main reason many parts of the globe receive different amounts of heat is that Earth rotates on a tilted axis. It's why we have seasons. If Earth rotated in an upright position, all the latitudes would receive the same amount of sunlight year-round. But because of the tilt, the Northern and Southern Hemispheres receive different amounts of sunlight throughout the year.

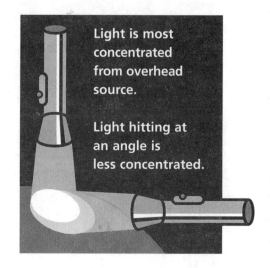

Light is most concentrated from overhead source.

Light hitting at an angle is less concentrated.

The Northern Hemisphere is tilted toward the sun during the summer which means that the sun rises higher in the sky, shining its light directly down on the surface–greatly heating it. In contrast, during winter the Northern Hemisphere is tilted away from the sun, so the sun is lower in the sky and its light reaches the surface at an indirect angle. The light is spread out over a greater area, so it is less concentrated and heats less. (This is easily seen by holding a flashlight at direct and indirect angles on a globe.) In addition, because the sun's arc is so low in the sky during winter, it makes a much shorter path. This is why the day is shorter, which means even less exposure to sunlight.

Temperature

Sunlight heats land and water which in turn heats the air above them. Temperature is the measure of how hot that air is. Temperature is actually a measure of the speed that air molecules are moving–the faster the molecules move, the higher the temperature. The temperature on the earth's surface averages about 60°F (16°C). But it ranges from about -100° to 125°F (-73° to 52°C) depending on the season, latitude, elevation, and time of day. The hottest time of day is usually mid-afternoon and the coldest is around dawn. The terrain greatly influences temperature because soil, water, and vegetation all absorb and release heat differently. Land cools and warms quickly, whereas water does not. So on a summer day, a lake's water can remain chilly even if its sandy beach is scorching hot. Dark areas absorb more heat than light areas, too. A dark green forest absorbs heat and warms up while a white snow-covered hill reflects sunlight and remains cool, for example. Differences in temperature at the earth's surface and up though the atmosphere are what drive weather on the planet.

What Warms More?

Different substances heat and cool differently. Land heats and cools faster than water, for example, and dark objects hold more heat than light ones. This principle leads to the uneven heating of the earth's surface and air masses that drive weather systems. In this activity students will use their thermometer-reading skills to compare the absorption of heat by soil, water, and air.

Directions

1 Divide the class into three or four groups and provide each group with a copy of page 17 and the materials above. Allow students time to get comfortable reading the thermometers. They can place them in their palms to warm them and then let them get cool, reading the changes. Check that all students know how to correctly read the thermometers. If the thermometers have both Celsius and Fahrenheit readings, decide which will be used in the activity. There's a place to note this on the data sheet.

2 Have students fill one carton with two cups of water and one with 2 cups of soil. The last container remains empty. Place a thermometer in each container. The thermometer bulb needs to go down into the soil an inch or two, not just sit on top.

3 Have students note the starting time on their data sheets at zero minutes and record a starting temperature for all three containers.

4 Set the containers under a lamp. Make sure all the containers are equally exposed to the light. They can be close together, but shouldn't touch.

5 Encourage students to add five minutes onto the starting time and write that time in the five minutes box. They can do this all the way across to help them know when it's time to take temperatures.

6 Have students continue to record the temperatures at five minute intervals. You may want to encourage one student in the group to be the temperature reader and another to be the recorder.

7 After the temperatures have been collected, invite students to answer the questions at the bottom of the sheet.

Extension

What *Else* Warms More? (Science) Challenge students to test the heat absorbing power of other "land" substances by substituting rocks, wet soil, dry leaves, or green leaves for the soil. Have them compare the results.

Materials

(for each group)

three clean quart-sized milk cartons with tops cut off (any identical containers that hold water will do)

soil

gallon jugs or pails of room-temperature water

three thermometers

lamp

reproducible page 17

watch

measuring cup

Note Set the soil and water in the room ahead of time so they are at a similar temperature.

MEASURE THE WEATHER:
Make a Thermometer
SCIENCE

Materials

(for each group)

16-oz. glass bottle

two white or clear plastic straws

water

food coloring

modeling clay

reproducible pages 18-19

glue

index card

scissors

gallon jugs or pails of room-temperature-water

eyedropper (optional)

Invite your students to measure temperature with a thermometer they make themselves. This easy-to-make thermometer works on the same principle that a "real" thermometer does. The liquid (water) expands as it heats up, forcing its way up the straw. The hotter the temperature, the more the liquid expands, and the farther it's pushed up.

Note that the scale used to measure the temperature on these thermometers is not a Celsius or Fahrenheit scale, but a simple scale designed to illustrate the basic principle of temperatures rising and falling. If you wish, you can help students calibrate their thermometers using a Celsius or Fahrenheit thermometer. Another thing to remember is that the units on the scale will not be accurate near or below freezing because water becomes more dense as it approaches freezing and frozen water (ice) expands.

Directions

Divide the class into three or four groups. Have students follow these directions:

1 Roll the clay into a ball. Its diameter needs to be slightly larger than the mouth of the bottle.

2 Set the clay ball on a table or desk. Cut one of the straws in half. Use the cut straw to poke a hole through the center of the ball of clay. Try to make the hole as straight and as clean as possible. Once the hole goes completely through the clay ball, pull out the straw. (Younger students may need help with this step. You can pre-poke the clay balls with straws if necessary.)

3 Carefully push a new straw into the hole made in step 2. Push it until about two inches of straw is sticking out of the bottom of the clay. Pinch and pat the clay around the straw on both sides to make a tight seal.

4 Fill the bottle to the top with room-temperature water and add a few drops of food coloring (so the water is easier to see as it travels up the straw).

5 Place the longer end of the straw into the bottle. Firmly press down on the ball of clay at the bottle's mouth to make an airtight seal. (This is a good time to check your students' thermometers for leakage and water level in the straw. The colored water should rise up into the straw beyond the mouth of the bottle. If it doesn't, use an eyedropper to add a little extra colored water into the top of the straw. If the water doesn't stay in the straw, there's a leak in the seal. Help students seal leaks as necessary.)

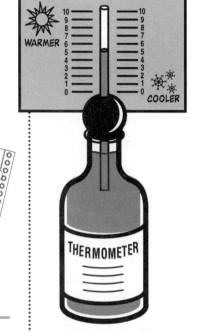

6 Glue the scale on page 18 onto an index card and cut it out. Carefully slide the card into the clay just behind the straw. A little glue will help keep it there.

7 Cut out the label on page 18, wrap it around the front of the bottle, and secure with tape.

8 Have students read the scale on their thermometers. Where is the water now? Then invite students to check the reading of their thermometers in some "extreme" conditions such as in the refrigerator, near a heat vent, or in a sunny window. What happens to the water in colder places? in warmer places? Have students use the chart on page 19 to record temperatures over a number of days and record their findings in a science journal.

Extensions

Temperature Graphs (Math) Challenge students to use their thermometers to record the outside temperature at the same time over a week and then make a bar graph of the results. Older students can make line graphs with the data and then compare it to a similar graph made with the week's worth of high temperatures from the newspaper. Is the shape of the graphs similar? Why?

A Different Kind of Thermometer (Science) Encourage students to think of a thermometer—an instrument that measures temperature—in broader terms. Challenge them to design their own ways of gauging temperature based on what they know about temperature's effect, such as melting chocolate, how many people are wearing coats, whether outdoor cats prefer to stay inside, whether the class goes outside for gym, etc.

Wise Weather Fact

Some kinds of crickets can serve as pretty good thermometers. Counting the number of chirps one of these crickets makes for 14 seconds and adding 40 gives an estimate of the temperature in degrees Fahrenheit.

What's the Time, Sun?

SCIENCE, SOCIAL STUDIES

The sun's power to heat varies throughout the day as it travels across the sky. At noon, direct sunlight gives rise to warmer temperatures than at dawn, when sunlight is indirect and less concentrated, for example. This variance in temperatures throughout the day effects the weather we experience. Noting the sun's daily journey across the sky is also a way to tell time. The sundial, an ancient instrument for tracking the sun, was the most common timepiece until clocks and watches became common in the eighteenth century. In a sundial a gnomon (NO-muhn), or marker, casts a shadow on a sundial plate that has been calibrated with lines for a particular latitude. In this activity, students will assemble a sundial and use it to tell time.

Materials

(for the whole class)

reproducible page 20

cardboard

glue

large paper clip

tape

ruler

Note: Sundials do not account for daylight savings time, which begins the first Sunday in April and ends the last Sunday in October. If you make the sundial when it's not daylight savings time, your sundial will be one hour *behind* the actual time between April and October. If you make your sundial during those months, you will need to readjust it when daylight savings time is over.

Directions

1 Glue or paste page 20 onto cardboard.

2 Open up the paper clip until it makes a long L-shape, as shown.

3 Using the paper clip, poke a hole in the sundial where the lines intersect at a dot on the bottom.

4 Insert the clip's short end into the hole. Turn the sundial over and tape the paper clip to the bottom. The paper clip is your gnomon.

5 With the sundial upright, make sure the gnomon is straight. Use some tape on both sides as support, if needed.

6 Begin just before noon on a sunny day. Set the sundial in an open area away from trees or buildings that will cast a shadow during the day. When it is exactly 12:00, orient the 12 on the sundial so that the shadow cast by the gnomon lines up exactly.

7 Every hour, on the hour, return to the sundial. Have a student trace the shadow line created by the gnomon, using the ruler to help draw a straight line. (Finish making the sundial the next sunny morning.)

8 At various times during the unit, visit the sundial as a class. How accurate is the sundial at telling time?

Extension

Sun Prints (Art) The sun isn't only good for telling time, it can also be used to make art! Students can infer the strength of sunlight by watching how colored construction paper fades. Have students arrange small heavy objects such as coins, erasers, and cups onto pieces of colored construction paper. Set the papers on a sunny windowsill and leave for a week or more. Then invite students to remove the objects and see the shapes left behind. The paper's dyes break down when exposed to sunlight, so the paper exposed to light will appear lighter than the paper covered by the object.

The Reason for Seasons

SCIENCE, GEOGRAPHY

Earth's tilted axis causes different latitudes to receive varying amounts of sunlight throughout the year. The result is the seasons. In this activity students will model the sunlight falling on different parts of the planet during Earth's rotation around the sun.

Materials

(for the whole class)

·····················

globe

lamp without a shade

Directions

1 Use the globe to review the Northern and Southern hemispheres, the poles, the equator, and the tilted axis. Ask: *Does Earth spin around straight like a top or is it tilted?* (tilted) *Where is it really cold?* (poles) *really hot?* (around the equator)

2 Set the lamp on a desk or table in the center of a dimly lit or darkened room.

3 Ask one student to hold the globe and stand a few feet away from the lamp. The student will need to hold it slightly away from his or her body and by the stand on the bottom so that light will hit the globe as the student walks around the lamp. The position of the globe in the student's hands should remain the same.

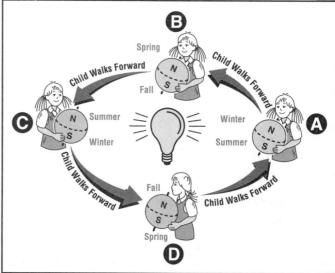

4 Start with the globe tilted, so that the Southern Hemisphere receives the most light. (See A above.) Ask: *What part of the globe is receiving the most sun?* (Southern Hemisphere) *What season is it there?* (summer) *What season is it in North America?* (winter) *Why is winter colder?* (less direct sunlight) Spin the globe so students can see that the entire Northern Hemisphere experiences winter at the same time. Ask: *What is one spin of the globe?* (a day)

5 Ask the student to move to position B, keeping the position of the globe steady. Ask: *What part of the globe is receiving the most light, now?* (equator) *What season is it in the Northern Hemisphere?* (spring) *What season is it in the Southern Hemisphere?* (fall) *Which hemisphere is receiving more light?* (both are equal)

6 Tell the student to move to position C, still keeping the globe steady. Ask: *What part of the globe is receiving the most sun?* (Northern Hemisphere) *What season is it there?* (summer) *Why is summer warmer?* (more direct sunlight) *What season is it in South America?* (winter)

7 Have the student move to position D, still keeping the globe steady. Ask: *What part of the globe is receiving the most light now?* (equator) *What season is it in the Northern Hemisphere?* (fall) *What season is it in the Southern Hemisphere?* (spring) *Which hemisphere is receiving more light?* (both are equal)

8 Complete the circle by asking the student to return to position A.

Read a Weather Map

SCIENCE, GEOGRAPHY

Materials

(for each student)

reproducible page 21

**colored pencils
(gray, purple, blue,
green, yellow, orange,
and red) or crayons**

Ⓔ ONLINE Ⓛ
L I N K

**www.usatoday.com/
weather**

Each day, the opening
page of USA Today's
weather site shows a
shaded temperature map
similar to the one in this
activity. Assign one stu-
dent each day to read
the map and then give a
short weather report to
the class, telling what
the temperature will be
in different parts of the
country.

M any weather maps today show temperatures as bands of varying color. A key at the bottom of the map identifies the colors with specific temperatures. There are lines of equal temperature separating these different areas. In this activity students color in areas of similar temperature on a weather map. They read the map to determine the temperature in different cities in the United States.

Directions

1 Photocopy and distribute page 21 to each student.

2 Explain that the numbers are temperatures in degrees Fahrenheit. Point out that the areas between the lines show ranges of temperature. For example, in the area between the 20°F line and the 30°F line, the temperature is in the 20s and will be colored purple.

3 Have students color in the temperature areas as instructed in steps 1 and 2. Check for understanding of the map by asking: *What's the temperature of the yellow area?* (50s) *the green area?* (40s)

4 Ask students to answer the questions at the bottom of the page, reminding them that their answers are temperature ranges—60s, 30s, etc. Consider doing question 1 as a class. Have students find Houston on the map. Ask: *What color is the temperature area for Houston?* (orange) Ask: *In the key, what temperature is orange?* (60s) *So what's the temperature in Houston?* (60s)

5 Challenge older students to use another map to find their own town and report the local temperature.

Answers: 1. 60s 2. 20s 3. 40s 4. 40s 5. 30s 6. Philadelphia

Book Break

Take students on a year-round weather forecasting tour by reading Gail Gibbons's book *Weather Forecasting* (Four Winds Press, 1987). It follows the workings of a weather station through all four seasons. Follow the reading by asking students what kind of weather forecasters are on the lookout for during winter, spring, summer, and fall.

Critters Through the Seasons
SCIENCE, LANGUAGE ARTS

Animals are adapted to deal with the changing seasons. Migration, hibernation, changing coat color, storing food, or putting on fat are all ways that animals cope with the changes in temperatures and the availability of water and food. Invite students to pick a favorite animal and create a mini-book illustrating how it spends the seasons. Students can choose an animal that lives in a climate with four seasons or one that lives where there is only a wet and dry season—like the Tropics or southern California. Encourage students to include what sort of home it lives in, what it eats, and how it warms or cools itself.

ACTIVITY

READ-ALOUD PLAY
Maui Traps the Sun
LANGUAGE ARTS, DRAMA

On pages 22-23 is a read-aloud play that retells a Hawaiian legend about why the sun shines more in the summertime. In it, a god named Maui (MOU-wee) forces the sun to shine for extra hours so his beloved mother can have more time to dry her bark cloth called *tapa.*

Materials

(for each student)

reproducible pages 22-23

Directions

Before reading the play aloud, review any vocabulary words— *snare, fibers, canoe,* etc.—that your students might be unfamiliar with. Allow students to take turns reading the parts. Students can also act out the play adding props they create, such as a rope snare made out of clothesline and a club made out of oaktag.

Book Break

The tale of how the Babylonian goddess of creation, Ishtar, made a deal with the ruler of the underworld in order to rescue her son Tammuz and how the seasons resulted is nicely retold in *Ishtar and Tammuz* by Christopher Moore (Kingfisher, 1996). The Greek myth of Demeter and Persephone, as retold in *Persephone and the Pomegranate* by Kris Waldherr (Dial Books, 1993), is another example of a myth that explains the origin of the seasons. Challenge students to write their own legends or plays explaining how the seasons came to be.

Name _____

A Week of Weather

Monday	Tuesday	Wednesday	Thursday	Friday
Precipitation What kind? _____ How much? _____	**Precipitation** What kind? _____ How much? _____	**Precipitation** What kind? _____ How much? _____	**Precipitation** What kind? _____ How much? _____	**Precipitation** What kind? _____ How much? _____
Air Humidity High or low? _____	**Air Humidity** High or low? _____	**Air Humidity** High or low? _____	**Air Humidity** High or low? _____	**Air Humidity** High or low? _____
Clouds How much of the sky is cloudy? Part, half, or all? _____ What kinds? _____ _____ _____ _____	**Clouds** How much of the sky is cloudy? Part, half, or all? _____ What kinds? _____ _____ _____ _____	**Clouds** How much of the sky is cloudy? Part, half, or all? _____ What kinds? _____ _____ _____ _____	**Clouds** How much of the sky is cloudy? Part, half, or all? _____ What kinds? _____ _____ _____ _____	**Clouds** How much of the sky is cloudy? Part, half, or all? _____ What kinds? _____ _____ _____ _____
Wind Direction _____ Speed _____	**Wind** Direction _____ Speed _____	**Wind** Direction _____ Speed _____	**Wind** Direction _____ Speed _____	**Wind** Direction _____ Speed _____

   Great Weather Activities Scholastic Professional Books

Group _____

What Warms More?

Temperature in °F/°C (circle one)

	0 minutes Time _____	5 minutes Time _____	10 minutes Time _____	15 minutes Time _____
Soil				
Water				
Air				

Questions

1. How many degrees did the soil heat up? _____

2. How many degrees did the water heat up? _____

3. How many degrees did the air heat up? _____

4. What heated up the most? _____

   _____

5. What heated up the least? _____

   _____

Bonus:

Which do you think cools fastest? _____

Why? _____

How could you test it? _____

_____

Make a Thermometer

Cut out the label.

Tape the label to the bottle.

Attach the scale to a card and stick it into the clay ball.

Thermometer
(thuh-MOM-uh-ter)
measures temperature

WARMER

10
9
8
7
6
5
4
3
2
1
0

10
9
8
7
6
5
4
3
2
1
0

COOLER

Measure the Weather:

Make a Thermometer

Date	Time	Temperature Reading	Where is the thermometer?

What's the Time, Sun?

Use this blank template to make a sundial plate.

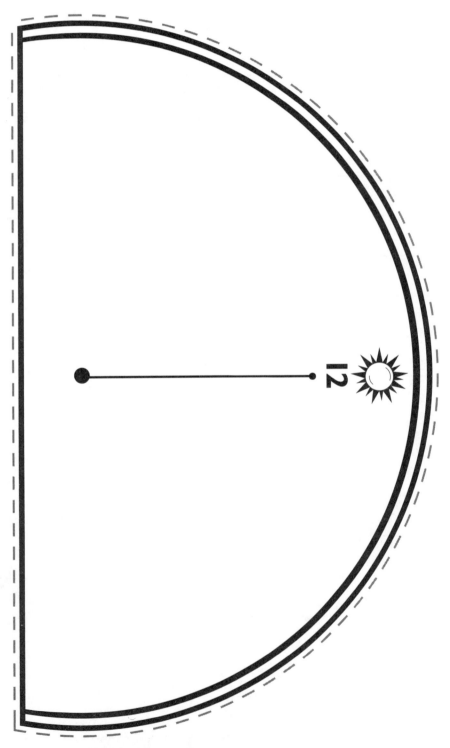

12

Name _____

Read a Weather Map

Color in the spaces between the lines. The key will tell you which colors to use.

To find the temperature of a city, find it on the map. What color is it?

Find the color in the key. That's the temperature!

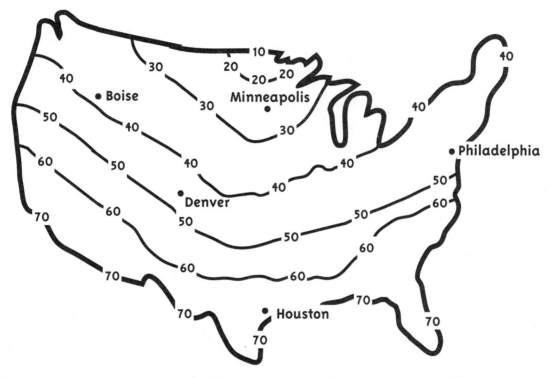

Key	10°F-20°F = gray	20°F-30°F = purple	30°F-40°F = blue
	40°F-50°F = green	50°F-60°F = yellow	60°F-70°F = orange

Questions

1. What's the temperature in Houston? _____

2. What's the temperature in Minneapolis? _____

3. What's the temperature in Philadelphia? _____

4. What's the temperature in Denver? _____

5. What's the temperature in Boise? _____

6. Which city is warmer, Boise or Philadelphia? _____

Maui Traps the Sun

A Hawaiian Legend

Characters

Narrator 1	Narrator 2	Narrator 3
Maui, Hina's son	**the Sun**	**Hina (HEE-nuh),** a Hawaiian goddess

Narrator 1: The god Maui loved his mother very much. He always helped her in any way he could.

Narrator 2: His mother was named Hina.

Narrator 3: Every day Hina worked very hard making tapa. Tapa is a special cloth made from the bark of the mulberry tree.

Narrator 1: Hina gathered the bark all by herself. Then she soaked the bark in seawater and pounded it on her tapa log.

Hina: There is never enough sunlight to make tapa! Already the Sun has turned toward the west. My tapa will never dry before it's dark!

Maui: The Sun travels too fast! I shall find him and tell him to move more slowly!

Hina: But, Maui, the Sun has great powers. No one has ever gotten close to the Sun and lived!

Maui: Then I shall be the first! I shall catch the Sun and make him go more slowly.

Narrator 2: Maui began making snares by twisting coconut fibers into eight strong ropes. At the end of each rope he tied a loop.

Narrator 3: He placed the eight snares and his magic club into his canoe. Then he traveled by river to the top of a dead volcano.

Narrator 1: Maui knew the Sun was asleep under a blanket of clouds on top of the volcano. Maui climbed the steep side of the volcano to the House-of-Sun. He laid out his snares.

Narrator 2: Then Maui hid behind some rocks and slept through the night. Maui awoke before daybreak.

Narrator 3: Maui watched as the Sun's longest leg came over the edge of the volcano's top. The Sun's leg created the first rays of the sunrise. The Sun's leg stepped into Maui's snare. Maui pulled the rope tight and tied it to a rock.

Sun: What are you doing?

Maui: My mother Hina needs more sunlight to dry her tapas. I will not let you go until you promise to travel more slowly in the sky.

Sun: Tapas! I have no time for tapas! I want my night's rest to be longer, not shorter!

Narrator 1: Maui picked up his magic club and swung the club against the Sun's longest leg, breaking off a piece. The Sun screamed in pain and anger.

Narrator 2: The Sun tried to get three more legs over the edge of the crater. Maui trapped each leg in a snare.

Narrator 3: Four more legs crawled over the crater and were trapped in the snares. The Sun became frightened. The more he struggled, the tighter he was trapped.

Sun: Don't hurt me! Without my light the plants and trees and people will die!

Maui: If you promise to travel more slowly through the sky part of the time, I will let you go.

Narrator 1: The Sun agreed, and Maui set the Sun free. After that, for part of the year the Sun traveled as he always did.

Narrator 2: But the rest of the year the Sun traveled more slowly. These days were longer and filled with sunshine and Hina was able to dry her tapas.

Narrator 3: Whenever the Sun was tempted to break his promise, his one broken ray reminded him of the strength and courage of Maui.

The End

CHAPTER 2

Air and Wind

WEIGHTY AIR

The atmosphere is the blanket of air that surrounds our planet. It's made up of gases—mostly nitrogen and oxygen with small amounts of water vapor, carbon dioxide, and a few other trace gases. Air may seem like nothing, but all those molecules of gas have weight (mass) and take up space (volume). The weight of the air pushes on the earth's surface, just like a stack of blankets on a table. This pushing force, or air pressure, is about 14.7 pounds per square inch (1 kg/cm^2) at sea level. Air pressure lessens with height, however, so there's less air pressure on top of a mountain than at sea level.

An area (or system) of air that has a higher pressure than its surroundings is called a high-pressure center or system, or simply a high. The sinking air of a high-pressure center stops air from moving upward. Because upward moving air is needed for clouds and precipitation to develop, fair weather often accompanie n area of high pressure. In contrast, a system of low pressure (or a low) has rising air, which encourages cloud and precipitation development. Cloudy weather and precipitation are often associated with an area of low pressure. The formation and movement of high- and low-pressure areas in the atmosphere drive much of the weather around the globe.

Wise Weather Fact

The air inside your classroom probably weighs as much as two or three of your students!

24

Why the Winds Blow

Wind is air on the move. Winds can vary from a gentle breeze to a hurricane force wind, but all wind results from temperature differences in the atmosphere. Because the sun unevenly heats the earth's surface—the equator gets more solar heating than the poles, for example—the air above the surface in turn receives varying amounts of heat depending on latitude, season, and geographical features such as mountains or oceans. Air above warm areas expands and rises, and cooler air flows in to replace it. That rising and falling air is wind.

Warm air rising over the equator and being replaced by cooler air from higher latitudes creates global, or prevailing, winds. These winds are responsible for the general circulation of the atmosphere. If Earth stood still, these winds would blow in a straight line. But the planet is spinning, so winds curve as they blow.

Winds are named for the direction from which they blow. This graphic shows the prevailing wind belts in the Northern and Southern Hemispheres.

Although the wind belts are semipermanent, they do shift somewhat from season to season and can change a bit from year to year. Nonetheless, these global winds play a very important part in determining the climate of an area.

Whereas prevailing winds play an important role in determining climate, the winds brought by highs and lows drive day-to-day weather. Synoptic-scale winds are winds moving around areas of high and low pressure in the atmosphere. Air flows toward a low-pressure area. Because of a force that scientists call the Coriolis effect, winds blow counterclockwise around a low. Alternately, air flows away from a high-pressure area (high), so winds blow clockwise around a high. In simple terms, this means that if you stand with your back to the wind in the Northern Hemisphere, a low-pressure area is at your left and a high-pressure area at your right.

Local winds are winds that blow only in a specific place. Sea or lake breezes between land and water are a common type of local wind. Land heats and cools faster than water, so in warmer months of the year, warm air over land rises and cooler air over the ocean or a lake blows in to replace it during the day. The reverse can happen at night as the land cools faster than the water. Mountains can create a similar situation as high mountain slopes heat up during the day. The rising warm air above them pulls cooler air up from the valleys. As the slopes cool at night, the heavy cool air flows down into the valley.

Finally, there are winds in upper levels of the atmosphere. These winds generally blow from west to east. However, a change in season, the location, or a nearby storm system can cause these winds to blow in almost any direction.

Easterlies
Westerlies
NE Trade Winds
SE Trade Winds
Westerlies
Easterlies

Wise Weather Fact

In the Northern Hemisphere, Earth's rotation makes winds blow clockwise around a high-pressure area as they move towards lower pressure. In the Southern Hemisphere, Earth's rotation makes winds blow counter-clockwise around a high-pressure area.

Words to Know

gale: a very strong wind, with a speed of 32-63 mph

mass: the amount of physical matter that something contains

volume: the amount of space that something takes up

wind: moving air

wind gauge: an instrument (also called an anemometer) that measures the speed at which wind is moving

wind vane: an instrument that shows the direction of the wind

Balloon Balance

SCIENCE

Materials

(for each pair of students)

two identical balloons

four 4-inch strips of tape

2- to 3-foot-long thin dowel or yardstick

straight pin

string

W eather is the condition of the air in a particular place at a specific time. But air is a combination of invisible gases, so its existence can be difficult for students to comprehend. Your students will discover that air takes up space (has volume) and has weight (mass) when they do this activity.

Directions

Divide the class into pairs and provide each pair with a set of materials. Start students thinking about air by having them simply fill and empty their balloons. Ask: *What's inside the filled balloon?* (air) *Does air take up space?* (yes) *Do you think it weighs something?* (yes) Then have students follow these instructions:

1 Blow up your balloons to equal size, tie them closed, and tape them onto the ends of the dowel using two strips of tape on each balloon. (You may need to help some students blow up their balloons.)

2 Tie the string near the center of the dowel. One student should hold the string away from his or her partner while the other slides the dowel back and forth until the balloons balance. Ask: *Which balloon is heavier?* (They are equal.)

3 Put a small piece of tape on one of the balloons. While the student holding the string stands still, the other student *carefully* punctures one of the balloons with the straight pin by sticking it through the taped area. (This will keep the balloon from exploding; the air will seep out slowly instead.)

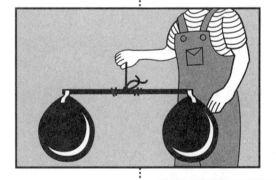

4 Ask: *What happened?* (The air escaped from the popped balloon and the full balloon dropped.) *Which side is heavier?* (the full balloon) *Why?* (The air inside the balloon has weight.)

5 Tape and puncture the other balloon and see if the two sides balance.

Extension

Paper Flyers (Science, Art) Flight—by animals or humans—is dependent on the fact that air has mass and volume. Wings create lift by "pushing" on air. Allow students to experiment with how wings use air to create lift. Have them drop sheets of crumbled and flat paper. Ask them to compare what happens. Ask: *Why does the open sheet "ride" the air?* (more air pushes on its greater surface area) Challenge students to make and decorate their own paper-airplane designs and test them for flying distance or height.

Wind Whirler

SCIENCE, ART

Hot air rises, often causing cooler air to rush in and replace it. This creates wind. In this activity students make a fun sunflower with petals that whirl as hot air rises.

Directions

1 Copy and hand out page 32 to students. Invite students to color their flowers, if desired.

2 Have students cut out the flowers along the dark lines. Ask them to fold the petals downward along the dotted lines. Help students use a pencil tip to carefully poke a small hole in the dot in the flower's center.

3 Push the yarn through the hole from the top and knot it underneath. Make a double or triple knot if the hole is much wider than the yarn. (Try to avoid taping the yarn because this makes the flower more difficult to spin.) It's done!

4 Ask students to dangle their flowers by the yarn. Have them hold their flowers about two feet over a bowl of ice and then about two feet over a heat source. Ask: *What happens?* (Nothing happens over the bowl of ice; the flower spins over the heat source.) *Why?* (Hot air rises, creating a wind that spins the flower's petals.)

5 Invite students to hang their spinning flowers in different parts of the room and observe whether or not they spin. Students can also design their own spinners. The key is to create a "wind-catching" shape.

Materials

(for each student)

reproducible page 32

scissors

12-inch length of yarn or string

tape

sharpened pencil

safe heat source such as a radiator or heat vent

large bowl of ice

colored pencils, markers, or crayons (optional)

Extensions

Windy Socks (Art) Kites are another fun wind-powered creation. Kites shaped like wind socks are easy to make and fly. Make a copy of reproducible page 33 and cut out the sock pattern. For each wind sock, fold a piece of newspaper in half lengthwise, trace the sock onto the folded edge of the paper, and cut it out. Paint the sock, if desired. Roll the "leg" of the sock into a tube and tape with masking tape. Then glue or tape the "foot" end together. Tape string onto the edge of the open end and lightly stuff the "foot" end with crumpled newspaper.
Now find a breezy day and fly your wind sock!

A Week of Wind Watching

SCIENCE, REFLECTIVE THINKING

Materials

(for each child)

reproducible pages 34 and 35

scissors

stapler

In 1805, a British naval admiral named Sir Francis Beaufort invented a wind-measuring scale based on observations of waves and ship sails. Wind strengths were divided into 13 categories called forces. This Beaufort scale was later adapted for land use and is still used today to estimate winds. In this activity students use their powers of observation to estimate wind speed, comparing what they see to the Beaufort scale.

Directions

1 Reproduce page 34 and distribute it to students.

2 Ask students to read through the descriptions of wind effects at different speeds. If possible, designate a place for observing wind, either outside the classroom or at a large window. (A place where trees or a flag are visible would be great!) Make a few trips to your observation point on one or more days and encourage students to rate the wind according to the scale. Students can compare their estimations of wind speeds determined with the Beaufort scale with more precise ones—such as reported weather, or those taken with the anemometer on page 29. How accurate are their estimations compared to other methods?

3 Once students are comfortable using the Beaufort scale, invite them make a mini-book titled *A Week of Wind*. Photocopy page 35 and distribute it to students.

4 Ask students to cut out the six pages, assemble them into a mini-book, and staple them together.

5 Invite students to fill in their books every day for a week. You may wish to allow students to go to your wind-observing place if you notice a wind blowing outside, set up a time for wind observing each day, or assign students to observe the winds at home. After the week has passed, have the class compare results. How different were their observations?

6 As students become expert windwatchers, they may be able to add their own observations to the Beaufort scale.

MEASURE THE WEATHER:

Make a Wind Gauge

SCIENCE

S tudents can measure wind speed by making and using this wind gauge, or *anemometer* (AN-uh-MOM-uh-ter).

Directions

Divide the class into small groups. Make a copy of the wind gauge on page 36 for each group and have students follow these instructions:

1 Cut out the wind gauge and glue it to cardboard. After it has dried, cut it out, including the rectangle that makes the handle.

2 Use an unbent paper clip to poke a hole where the black dot appears on the top of the scale.

3 Thread a 12-inch piece of thread through the hole and tape it securely to the back.

4 Tape the table tennis ball to the other end of the thread. It's done!

5 To use the wind gauge, face into the wind and hold the gauge so the top line is level. The thread's height indicates the speed. Record the winds twice a day on a chart and compare your readings with your Beaufort scale observations (page 28).

Book Break

What better way to see the wind in action than to fly a kite? As a class, read a book about kite flying, make a kite together, and fly one on a windy day. A terrific resource is *Catch the Wind! All About Kites* by Gail Gibbons (Little, Brown, 1995). This book is out of print but still easy to find in stores and libraries.

Materials

(for each group)

reproducible page 36

table tennis ball

one 12-inch length of brightly colored heavy thread or thin cord

tape

glue

scissors

paper clip

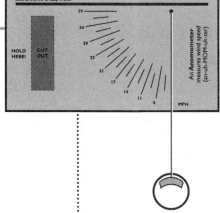

MEASURE THE WEATHER:

Make a Wind Vane

SCIENCE

Materials

(for each group)

reproducible page 37

heavy cardboard or plastic foam meat plate or egg carton lid

unsharpened pencil

pen cap that fits loosely over pencil end

scissors

masking tape

compass (optional)

glue

clean, empty soup can (or can of a similar size)

sand or fine gravel

modeling clay

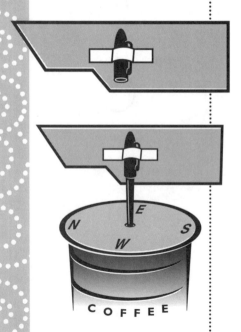

We know that high-pressure areas usually mean fair weather, and low-pressure areas usually mean precipitation. We also know that the wind blows away *from* high pressure areas and *toward* low pressure areas. For this reason, knowing the wind direction is an essential element in weather forecasting. People have been monitoring the direction of winds for thousands of years, and the wind vane or weather vane is probably the oldest of all meteorological instruments. This activity allows students to make a wind vane and track the direction of winds over time.

Directions

Divide the class into small groups and make one copy of page 37 for each group. Have students follow these instructions:

1 Cut out the two patterns on the page.

2 Use the wind pointer pattern to cut a pointer out of heavy cardboard or plastic foam. Glue the direction disk onto cardboard, paperboard, or plastic foam and cut it out. Poke a hole in the dot in the center of the disk. The hole needs to be big enough for a pencil to fit through.

3 Push the pencil eraser-side down through the hole in the direction disk, then stick the eraser end into a small ball of clay and set it in the bottom of an empty soup can. Fill the can with enough sand or gravel to make it stable.

4 Tape the pen cap onto one side of the wind pointer. Then set the wind pointer on top of the pencil by fitting the pen cap over the unsharpened pencil end. Make sure the pointer is level and if not, retape the pen cap. Also give the pointer a spin to make sure it moves freely. (If it doesn't, use a different kind of pen cap.)

5 When your wind pointers are ready, place them outside in an open area, away from high walls and tall trees. Use a compass—or the sun—to set the north point on the direction disk toward north. The wind pointer's narrow end will swing into the wind, indicating the way the wind is coming from. If the pointer is pointing to the west, the wind is blowing from the west and is called a westerly wind.

6 Check the wind direction using the wind vanes twice daily and record the direction on the Week of Weather chart (page 16).

A World of Winds

LANGUAGE ARTS, GEOGRAPHY

The world's people have named local winds for centuries. Below is a list of ten local winds from around the world, where they blow, and a description of the wind. The wind names make excellent starting points for stories and reports.

Materials

(for whole class)

empty coffee can

copy of wind names chart

Directions

Photocopy the list and cut into strips. Put the strips in an empty coffee can or box. Make a label for the can that says, "Pick a wind from around the world. Imagine that you are standing in the wind. What do you see around you? Write a paragraph describing what you see." Put the can in your weather learning center and encourage students to use encyclopedias, the Internet, and books to learn more about the place their wind is found.

haboob/Sudan/sandstorm or duststorm

kona/Hawaii/southwesterly, brings rain

chinook/western United States and Canada/dry, warm, westerly wind

dadur/Ganges Valley of India/down-valley wind

helm/Eden Valley of northern England/cold, northeasterly

junk/Vietnam/south or southeast monsoon wind

khamsin/Egypt/desert wind, southerly

Extension

A World of Wind (Geography) Divide the class into groups and give each group one wind name. Challenge the student groups to locate where their winds blow. Have them make a label with their wind name and use push-pins to hold it in place on the map.

Book Break

Read aloud *The Wind and the Sun* by Tomie de Paola (Silver Press, 1995). Invite students to write a fable with the same moral: Kindness is a better way than force to achieve what you want.

Wind Whirler

Color and cut out the wind whirler flower.

Great Weather Activities Scholastic Professional Books

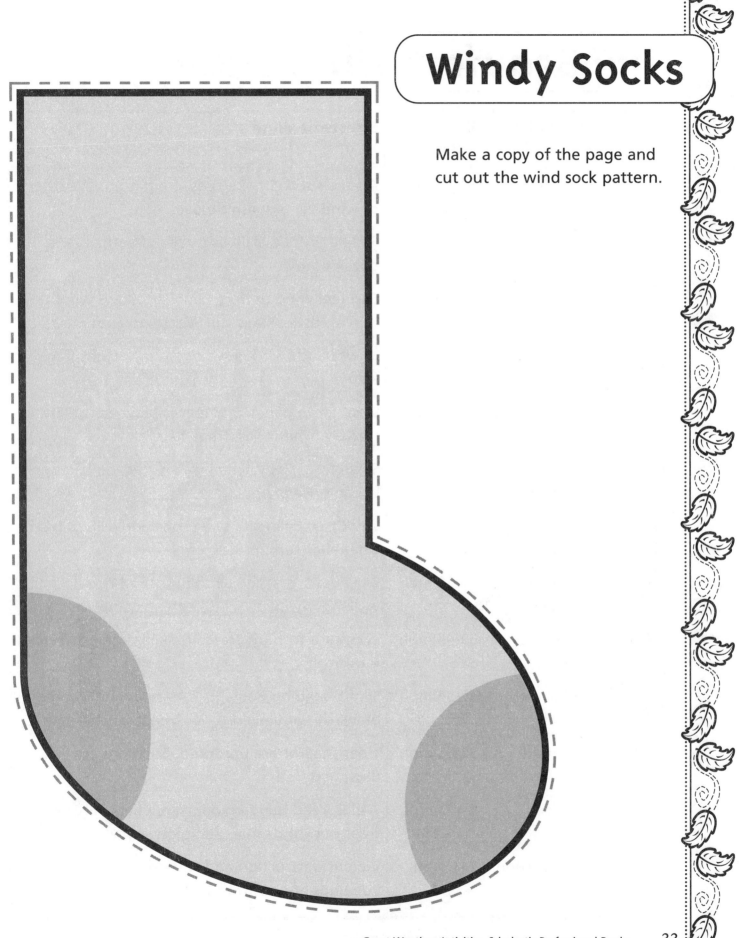

Windy Socks

Make a copy of the page and cut out the wind sock pattern.

The Beaufort Wind Scale

Beaufort Number	Kind of Wind	Wind Speed	Effects of Wind
0	Calm	less than 1 mph	Air feels still. Smoke rises straight up. Weather or wind vane doesn't move.
1	Light air	1-3 mph	Smoke drifts a little as it rises. Weather vane doesn't move.
2	Slight Breeze	4-7 mph	Can feel wind on face. Smoke follows wind. Leaves rustle. Flags stir. Weather vanes move.
3	Gentle Breeze	8-12 mph	Leaves and twigs move constantly. Light flags extend.
4	Moderate Breeze	13-18 mph	Dust, loose paper, and leaves blow about. Thin tree branches sway. Flags flap.
5	Fresh Breeze	19-24 mph	Small trees sway. Small waves crest on lakes and streams. Flags ripple.
6	Strong Breeze	25-31 mph	Thick tree branches sway constantly. Flags beat. Umbrellas turn inside out.
7	Moderate Gale	32-38 mph	Big trees sway. The wind pushes when walking against it. Flags extend completely.
8	Fresh Gale	39-46 mph	Twigs are torn off trees. Walking against wind is difficult.
9	Strong Gale	47-54 mph	Slight building damage–antennas and shingles blow off and awnings rip. Tree branches break.
10	Whole Gale	55-63 mph	Trees snap or are uprooted. Buildings are damaged.
11	Storm	64-73 mph	Widespread building damage. Cars overturn, trees uproot or snap and blow away.
12	Hurricane	74+ mph	Violent destruction and widespread damage. Buildings are destroyed.

A Week of Wind

Cut out the pages.

Staple them together to make a book.

Watch the wind for a week and write down your observations in your book.

A Week of Wind

by

_____
(your name)

Monday

What's the wind like today?

_____

_____

_____

Beaufort scale number _____

Tuesday

What's the wind like today?

_____

_____

_____

Beaufort scale number _____

Wednesday

What's the wind like today?

_____

_____

_____

Beaufort scale number _____

Thursday

What's the wind like today?

_____

_____

_____

Beaufort scale number _____

Friday

What's the wind like today?

_____

_____

_____

Beaufort scale number _____

Measure the Weather:

Make a Wind Gauge

Copy and cut out the scale to make a wind gauge for your class.

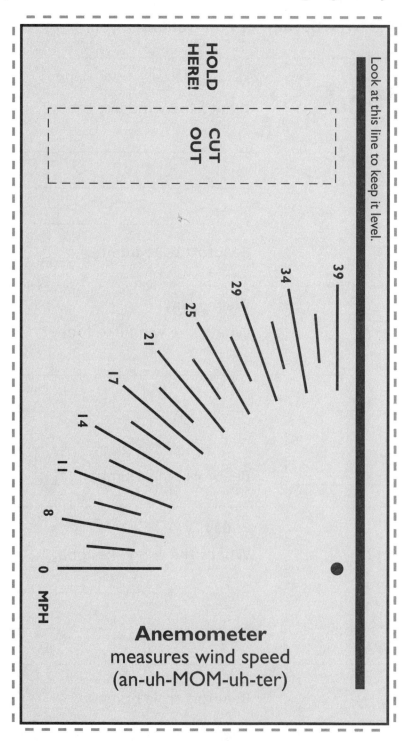

HOLD HERE!

CUT OUT

Look at this line to keep it level.

39

34

29

25

21

17

14

11

8

0

MPH

Anemometer
measures wind speed
(an-uh-MOM-uh-ter)

Make a Wind Vane

Copy and cut out the pieces to make a class wind vane.

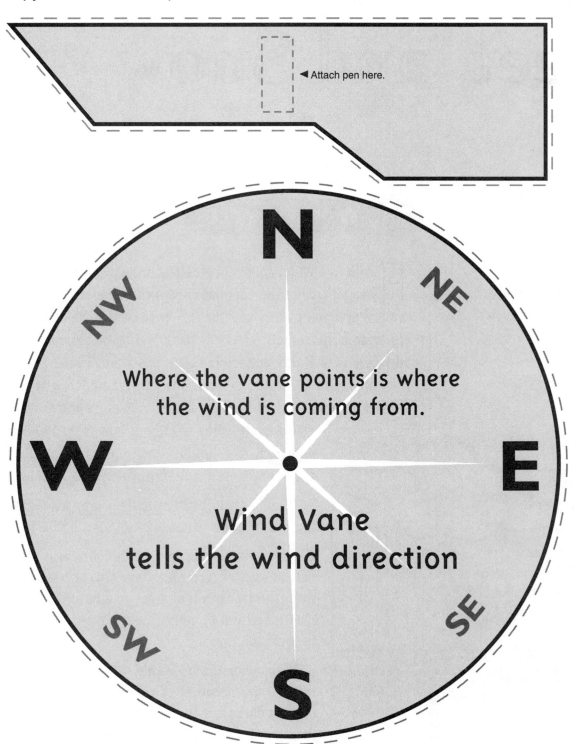

◄ Attach pen here.

N

NE

NW

Where the vane points is where
the wind is coming from.

W

E

**Wind Vane
tells the wind direction**

SW

SE

S

Clouds, Rain, Sleet, and Snow

THE WATER CYCLE

E arth is a watery planet. Ocean alone covers more than 70% of the surface of the earth and even the air around us contains an enormous amount of water in the form of water vapor, a gas. The continuous movement of water back and forth between the earth's surface and the atmosphere is called the water cycle. It means that the molecules of water in your morning coffee might have once bathed an ancient dinosaur! As water molecules move through the water cycle, they change phase from liquid to a gas and back to a liquid—and sometimes a solid (ice) in between. Here's how the water cycle works:

1. Heated liquid water changes into water vapor during evaporation (the transition of a liquid to a gas).

2. As the water vapor rises, it cools, and the molecules of water form droplets. This is called condensation (the transition of a gas to a liquid) or deposition (the transition of a gas to a solid) if it's cold enough to form ice crystals.

3. Water vapor condensing into tiny droplets around needed dust, smoke, or other condensation nuclei creates clouds. If the droplets grow too large and heavy to be held up by air currents, they fall to the ground as precipitation.

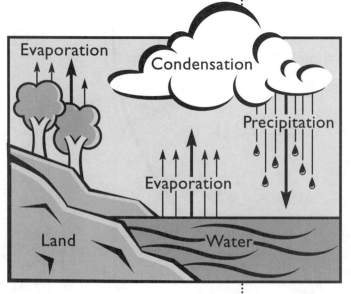

Whether that precipitation is rain, snow, sleet, or hail depends on its size, the temperature of the cloud, and the temperature of the air on the way down. Drizzle, for example, is made up of liquid drops smaller than .02 inches (.5 mm) in diameter. Rain is liquid precipitation larger than .02 inches (.5 mm). Freezing rain falls to the ground as water and freezes into ice on contact with any surface, whereas sleet is made of raindrops that have frozen in midair. Snow, on the other hand, is made up of ice crystals. Hailstones are balls of ice, but they don't usually have anything to do with winter weather. They form from clusters of raindrops repeatedly frozen in thunderstorm updrafts.

Humidity and Dew Point

Humidity is how much water vapor is in the air. All air holds some water vapor, even dry desert air. The amount of water vapor air can hold depends on the temperature. Cold air can hold less water vapor than warm air before that water vapor condenses and forms a liquid. The faster-moving molecules in warm air mean that more water can remain as vapor without being condensed into liquid. Air's capacity to hold water vapor roughly doubles with each temperature increase of 10°C. The temperature at which air loses its ability to hold water vapor (is saturated), and condensation occurs, is the dew point. It's the temperature of the air when dew—water vapor condensing to liquid—forms. If the dew point temperature is below freezing, frost forms.

Clouds

Clouds are made of tiny water droplets and/or ice crystals suspended by air and updrafts. This is possible because the water droplets in clouds are very small—it takes a million cloud drops to make a single raindrop. When cloud droplets or ice crystals grow large enough, they fall as precipitation. Clouds are classified into many different identifiable types. The names of clouds are made up of Latin words. Most cloud names are one of three cloud shapes—cirrus, stratus, and cumulus. Cirrus are curly, or stringy-looking clouds made of ice crystals. Stratus clouds are stratified, or layered, and flat. Cumulus are lumpy, fluffy, piled-up clouds. The shape name can be combined with a prefix such as *cirro, alto,* and *nimbo. Cirro-* means the cloud is high, a base above 20,000 feet or so. *Alto-* means the cloud is mid-level, or about 6,000 to 20,000 feet. There is no prefix for low. The prefix or suffix *nimbo* means the cloud is making precipitation. Therefore, a cirrocumulus is a high, fluffy cloud, whereas a cumulonimbus is a fluffy rain-making cloud.

Because clouds are made of "weather" they give insight into what the weather is like—and what's on the way. For example, altostratus clouds usually mean that rain or snow is on the way.

Words to Know

condensation: when water vapor turns into liquid water

dew: water drops formed by condensation of water vapor on grass, plants, or other objects

evaporation: when liquid water turns into water vapor

frost: water vapor that has turned to ice on the surface of something

precipitation: the falling of water from clouds in the form of rain, snow, sleet, hail, etc.

water vapor: what water is called when it becomes a gas

Wise Weather Fact

In the nineteenth century, scientists thought that clouds were composed of bubbles because bubbles float.

39

Water=Go=Round

SCIENCE

ater changes form as it moves between land and air. The water cycle is an important part of weather because it explains the formation of clouds and precipitation. In this activity students create a miniature water cycle where they can observe evaporation, condensation, and precipitation.

Materials

(for the whole class)

glass loaf pan with a clear lid or a clear plastic food container with clear lid

small bowl

warm water

ice cubes

plastic bag that closes

strong lamp

Directions

1 Set the bowl inside the pan at one end. Fill the bowl with warm tap water. This is your "lake." Close the lid.

2 Put the lamp a few inches over the box's lid directly over the bowl of water. The lamp is the "sun." Turn the "sun" on and let it shine over the "lake" for two hours. After two hours, ask: *What happened?* (Some of the water in the bowl has evaporated.) *Where is the water?* (It's in the air inside of the box, and some condensed into drops inside the lid.)

3 Put ice cubes into the plastic bag and close it. Set the bag of ice on top of the lid at the opposite end as the lamp. Leave the lamp on and wait another two hours. Ask: *What happens?* (It rained.) *Why?* (The cooling ice caused the temperature inside the box to drop, and water in the air condensed into rain.) *Did you observe clouds before it rained in the box? Why?* (The water vapor in the air first condensed into clouds before condensing into raindrops.)

Extensions

Follow a Raindrop Filmstrip (Language Arts) The story of a raindrop journeying through the water cycle lends itself to great storytelling possibilities while reinforcing many important concepts. Students can make and view a filmstrip version of this story using the reproducible on page 46 and an empty milk carton.

Hand out a copy of page 46 to each student and invite them to color it, if desired. Have students cut out the two filmstrip pieces along the dashed lines, then tape these together to make one long strip. Next help students make the projectors. Provide each student with an empty pint-sized milk carton and help them to cut off both ends of the carton to make a tube. About an inch or so from one end of the tube, cut slits on two opposite sides of the carton. The slits should run the length of the sides and allow for easy passage of the filmstrip. Students view their filmstrips by threading their strips through the viewer and holding it up to a light or window as they pull the strip through picture by picture. Invite student groups to write scripts for the filmstrip. Encourage them to be creative and include the fish, birds, and people the raindrop meets along its journey through the water cycle.

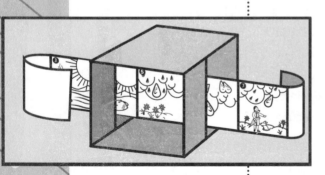

Sweaty Plants (Science) A great deal of water evaporates into the air through plants. Plants losing water through evaporation to the surrounding air is called *transpiration*. Students can observe *transpiration* by placing plastic bags around several leaves of a houseplant and observing the water droplets that form.

Poster: Meet the Clouds

The full-color poster bound in the back of this book features a fun and informative cloud poem describing major cloud types and the weather they bring. The clouds mentioned in the poem are depicted on the poster. Consider hanging the poster in the classroom at the beginning of your unit on clouds or as part of a weather learning center. It also makes a great added reference for the Cloud Finder activity (page 42).

Extensions

Name a Cloud (Language Arts) Invite students to rename the cloud types featured on the poster. Challenge them to come up with descriptive names that tell something about the clouds' shape, texture, color, height, or the weather they bring.

Classroom Clouds (Science) Help your students better understand how clouds form by doing this classroom demonstration. First collect some chalk dust from a chalk tray or by crushing a piece of chalk. Next fill a plastic bag with ice. Now fill a large clear jar with very hot water and put its lid on. After two or three minutes, dump out most of the water, re-cover it, and set the bag of ice on top. After about three minutes, quickly remove the lid and sprinkle a pinch of chalk dust into the jar and re-cover it. A cloud appears when water vapor forms tiny droplets of water in the jar, through condensation. The chalk dust gives the water droplets a place to form and helps pull the water vapor out of the air and create cloud droplets. The chalk dust acts as condensation nuclei.

Book Break

The Magic School Bus at the Waterworks, an award-winning book by Joanna Cole (Scholastic, 1986) is a fun, friendly way to introduce the water cycle to students. Use the information in the book to make a bulletin board display that shows how the cycle works.

Cloud Finder Wheel

SCIENCE

Materials

(for each child)

reproducible
pages 47-49

brass paper fastener

scissors

[ONLINE]
[LINK]

Is there a class in another part of the country or the world that you communicate with online? If so, set up a cloud-watch exchange with that class for one week. Each day, exchange descriptions of what the clouds look like in the sky above you. How are your skies different? If possible, draw or photograph the clouds you see each day, scan in the art, and exchange these pictures, too!

Identifying clouds is a fun way to introduce your students to weather watching. Learning about the kind of weather that clouds bring is a perfect opportunity to allow students to make predictions and observe outcomes. Students will assemble a wheel-shaped Cloud Finder identification key and use it to identify clouds and make predictions about the weather. (Note: Identifying clouds isn't always easy. Encourage students to make their best guesses based on the dominant kind of clouds they see, or to list more than one type. Also remember that identifying cloud types is only one part of weather forecasting; air pressure, winds, and other factors also play important roles.)

Directions

1 Make a copy of each reproducible page for each student. Show students how to make the Cloud Finder Wheel by cutting out both circles on pages 47 and 48, cutting out and discarding the two shaded areas on page 47, and fastening the wheels together. Page 47 goes on top.

2 To use the key, move the wheel until the cloud you want appears. Then read the name, weather description, and forecast information in the box.

3 Hand out a copy of page 49 to each student. Invite students to fill in the chart every morning for a week, comparing their predictions to the actual weather in the afternoon. Invite students to use the international cloud symbols pictured on the cloud wheel instead of the cloud names when filling in their charts, if they wish. (Note: Consider making the cloud poster bound in the back of this book available to students.)

4 After a week of collecting data, ask: *Is observing clouds a good way to predict weather? What kind of weather was easiest to predict?*

Extensions

Frame a Cloud (Art, Science) A fun way to become familiar with cloud shapes is to capture one in a "frame." Use masking tape to frame a cloud seen through a window. Have students draw the cloud a number of times over a few minutes as the cloud moves out of the frame. Ask students: *How does it change? Which way does it move? What kind is it?*

Cloudy Books (Language Arts, Art) Invite students to make a cloud book. Draw a fluffy cloud shape on a sheet of paper and photocopy it. Hand out a number of the sheets to each student. Ask students to cut out their book pages. Invite students to draw and label cloud shapes, write cloud poems, write facts about clouds, write a first-person story about what it would be like to be a cloud, etc. Once students have finished bind the books with a stapler.

Precipitation Map

SCIENCE, GEOGRAPHY

Precipitation is any form of moisture that falls out of clouds—snow, rain, hail, sleet, freezing rain, etc. Various symbols are used to represent the different kinds of precipitation on weather maps. In this activity, students will use a weather map to answer questions about precipitation falling across the country.

Directions

Photocopy and hand out a copy of page 50 to each student. Review the key with students, checking for understanding of the symbols. Ask students to follow the instructions to complete their worksheets.

Answers: 1. Washington and Oregon 2. Texas and Louisiana 3. Kansas, Nebraska, Iowa, and Missouri 4. Colorado, Wyoming, and Maine 5. Florida 6. Virginia, North Carolina, and South Carolina 7. probably winter because of the sleet and snow

Extensions

Precipitation Poems (Language Arts) The different kinds of precipitation—hail, snow, sleet, drizzle, etc.—make great poem themes. Have students choose a kind of precipitation and write a poem about its shape, feel, effects, etc. Invite students to illustrate their poems with rainy or snowy scenes. (If you wish, combine it with the Rainy-Day Pictures activity on page 44. Students can write poems to describe the pictures they've made.)

TV Weather Report (Language Arts) Challenge students to write a "current precipitation" paragraph summarizing the information on the weather map. Consider making a fun "TV" by cutting a window out of a large cardboard box and decorating it like a TV. Then students can take turns reporting the country's precipitation "on TV" as they hold the box over their heads.

Book Break

Read the stunningly illustrated book *Rain Player* by David Wisniewski (Clarion Books, 1991) to your class. It's the Mayan story of a brave boy who challenges Chac, the god of rain, to a game of pok-a-tok to win his people relief from drought. A number of Mayan words, such as pok-a-tok, are used in the story and are defined on the author's note page. Challenge students to define the words using context clues as you read the story and then see how close they were once the story is finished.

Materials

(for each student)

reproducible page 50

ONLINE LINK

www.weather.com

On the Weather Channel's website, it's easy to find out if it will be sunny or rainy in any part of the country. Next to the computer, keep a can or folder filled with weather challenges such as, "I'm going to Dallas on Friday. Do I need an umbrella?" written on slips of paper. Label the folder or can with the website's address. Students can go online, type in the city name, and answer the questions.

MEASURE THE WEATHER:
Make a Rain Gauge
SCIENCE

Materials

(for the whole class)

empty 1- or 2-liter plastic bottle

small weights (marbles, aquarium gravel, clean stones, or pennies work well)

scissors

clear packing tape

reproducible page 51

Rain Gauge measures precipitation

This rain gauge will give your students the opportunity to measure rainfall.

Directions

1 Carefully cut the plastic bottle where the sides start to slope up to the mouth. Put tape around both cut edges. The top will act as a funnel.

2 Place enough weights into the bottom of the large half of the bottle to stabilize it.

3 Set the funnel inside the bottle so the taped edges touch.

4 Cut out the scale on page 51 and tape it onto the outside of the bottle. Make sure the 0 line is above the weights and at a level where the bottle's shape is uniform. Use clear packing tape to completely cover the scale so it's waterproof.

5 Pour water into the gauge until it reaches the 0 line on the bottom of the scale. The gauge will need to be reset to this level each day that rainfall is to be measured.

6 Set the rain gauge outside in an open area, away from trees and building overhangs. Have students record the rainfall with units on a chart.

Extensions

Snowy Measurements (Science) If it's snowing in your area at this time of year, students can measure snowfall. Find a flat, level area on the ground and measure the snow that has accumulated there with a ruler. Then invite students to convert the inches of snow into inches of precipitation. Have students fill a container with snow to the height of snow they measured outside. Once the snow has melted, students measure the height of water in the container to get inches of precipitation. (Note: The average ratio is 10 inches of snow to 1 inch of rain.)

Rainy-Day Pictures (Art) Invite students to celebrate rain by creating rainy-day pictures. (Note: This can be messy! Have students work on newspaper and wear smocks or old shirts.) Students first draw a rainy-day scene on paper—without the rain. Then help students use an old flour sifter filled with blue tempera paint to sprinkle paint lightly over the pictures. Next spray the pictures with a spray bottle filled with water and watch the rain appear. Students can also come up with ways to use other classroom art materials to make snowy-day pictures.

Making Dew and Frost

SCIENCE

Your students have seen how glasses filled with cold drinks "sweat." But do they realize that this is also how dew forms on grass? The cold of the drink cools the air surrounding it, causing water vapor in the surrounding air to condense into water droplets on the outside the glass. The same thing happens at night when the temperature drops and water condenses out of the air, settling on grass as dew. If it's below freezing, frost forms instead of dew. Students can explore dew and frost formation in this activity.

Materials

(for each group)

two empty metal cans with labels and tops removed

ice

water

rock salt

two spoons

thermometer (optional)

Directions

1 Instruct students to fill one can about halfway with water and add a few ice cubes, then fill the other can with ice and rock salt. Students should make sure the outside of each can is dry.

2 Have students place a spoon in each and stir both cans.

3 Carefully watch the outside of the can with water in it for "sweat" droplets to form. This is dew, formed when water vapor in the air condenses into droplets on the cooling can. The can with ice and salt will form frost, as the room's water vapor freezes onto the can.

Extension

Frosty Crystals (Science) Frost is made up of crystals of frozen water. A frost-covered glass can have amazing and beautiful patterns. Invite students to observe those patterns with magnifying lenses. Quickly dip glass jars or glasses in water and put them in a freezer. Make sure students are ready with their magnifying lenses and science journals before passing out the glasses—they won't stay frosty for long! Encourage students to sketch the patterns they see in their science journals and then to compare shapes with classmates. (Note: This is a good at-home activity if freezers are unavailable at school.)

Follow a Raindrop

Color the pictures.

Cut out the two strips.

Tape them together to make one long filmstrip.

Cloud Finder Wheel

Cut out the wheel.

Cut out the two shaded areas inside the wheel.

This is the top wheel of your cloud finder.

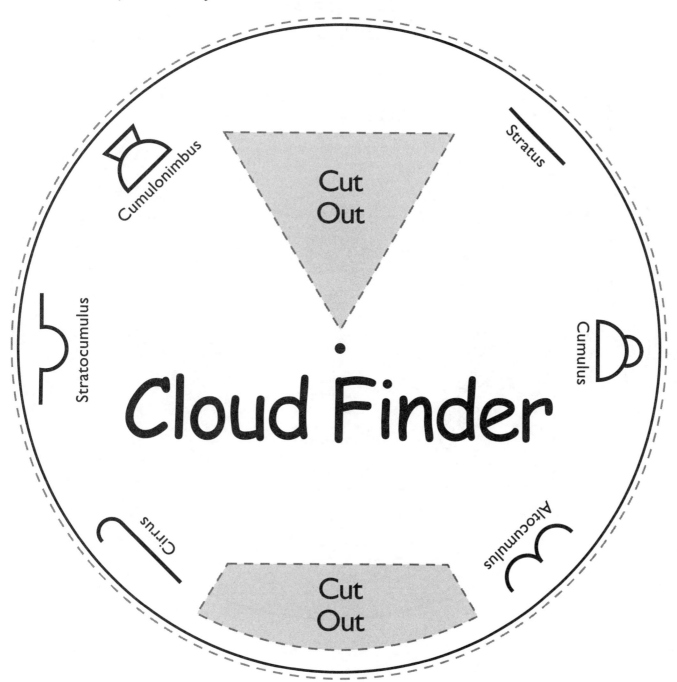

Cloud Finder Wheel

Cut out the wheel.

This is the bottom wheel of your cloud finder.

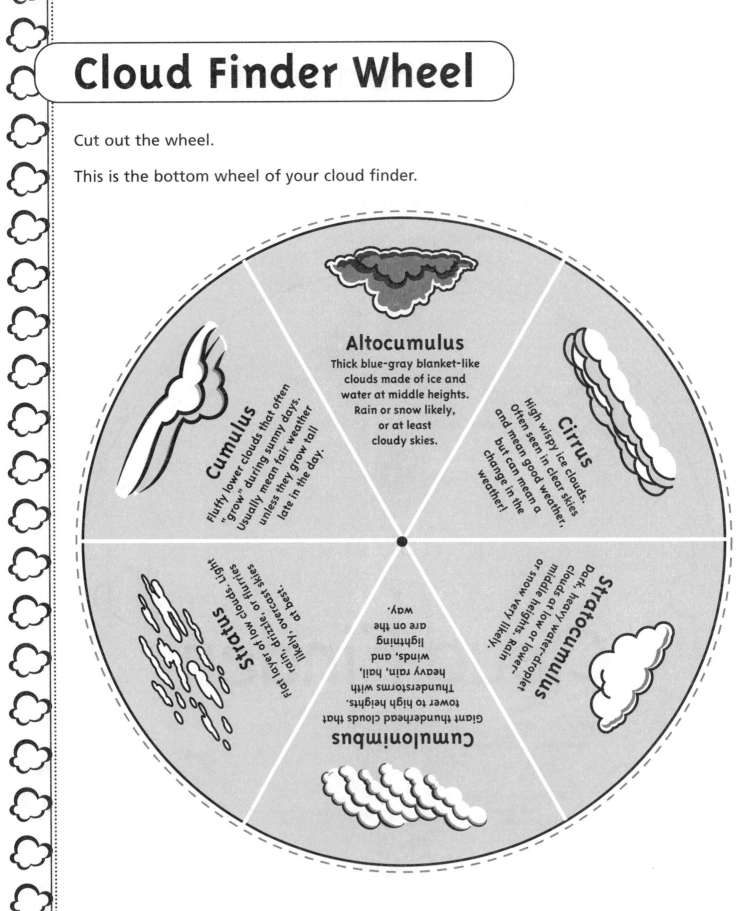

Altocumulus
Thick blue-gray blanket-like clouds made of ice and water at middle heights. Rain or snow likely, or at least cloudy skies.

Cirrus
High wispy ice clouds. Often seen in clear skies and mean good weather, but can mean a change in the weather!

Cumulus
Fluffy lower clouds that often "grow" during sunny days. Usually mean fair weather unless they grow tall late in the day.

Stratocumulus
Dark, heavy water-droplet clouds at low or lower middle heights. Rain or snow very likely. Lightning are on the way.

Cumulonimbus
Giant thunderhead clouds that tower to high heights. Thunderstorms with heavy rain, hail, winds, and lightning are on the way.

Stratus
Flat layer of low clouds. Light rain, drizzle, or flurries likely, overcast skies at best.

Name _____

Watch the Weather Chart

Watch the weather for a week.

Fill in the chart.

	Today is _____	Today is _____	Today is _____	Today is _____	Today is _____
What's the morning weather like?					
What kind of clouds are in the sky? Use your Cloud Finder Wheel!					
What do you think the weather will be like this afternoon? Use your Cloud Finder Wheel!					
What's the afternoon weather like?					
Was your weather prediction right?					

Precipitation Map

Precipitation can be rain, snow, sleet, flurries, freezing rain, or hail. Weather

maps use different symbols to tell you what's falling where. Look at the key below.

It shows you the symbols. Use them to read the map and answer the questions.

Questions:

1. In what states is it raining? _____

2. In what states is it drizzling? _____

3. What states are getting flurries? _____

4. What states are getting snow? _____

5. Where are there thunderstorms? _____

6. In what states is sleet coming down? _____

7. What season do you think the map shows? _____

8. Does the map show any precipitation where you live? _____

Measure the Weather:

Make a Rain Gauge

Cut out the scale.

Tape it to the bottle. Make sure you attach the scale to a part

of the bottle that is a uniform shape.

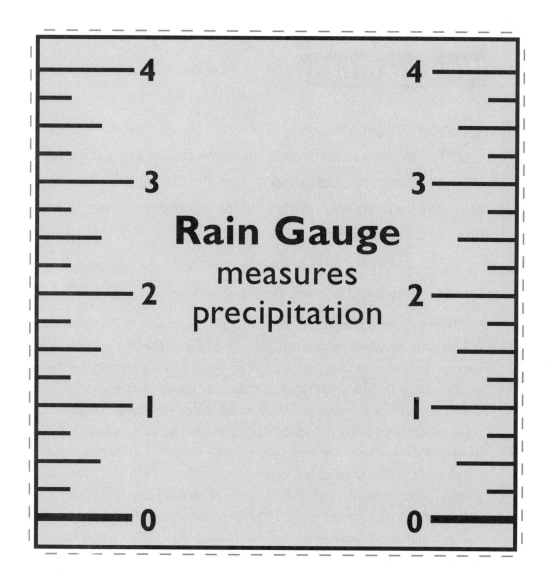

Rain Gauge
measures
precipitation

4   4

3   3

2   2

1   1

0   0

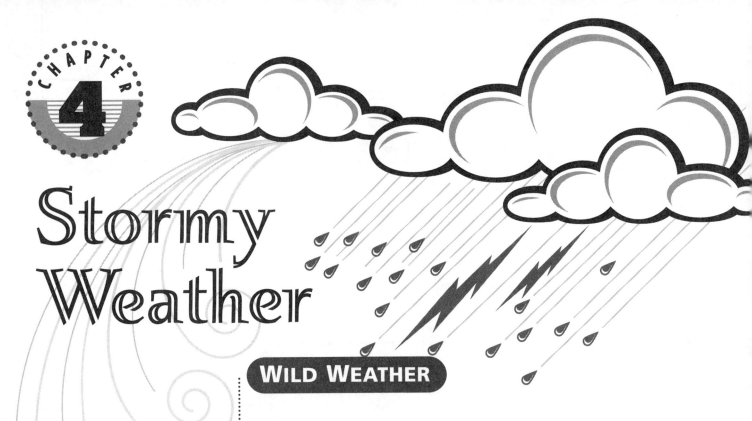

CHAPTER 4

Stormy Weather

WILD WEATHER

Storms are periods of violent weather caused by disturbances in the atmosphere that create strong winds and often bring rain, snow, or other precipitation that is sometimes accompanied by lightning. The main types of storms are thunderstorms, winter storms, tornadoes, and hurricanes.

Fronts, Updrafts, and Downdrafts

The change or disturbance in the atmosphere that results in a storm is often caused by a front. A front results when two different huge masses of air collide. An air mass is a chunk of atmosphere that has a uniform temperature and humidity. Air masses are huge, often the size of two states. Different air masses don't easily mix; their distinct temperatures give them differing densities, so they remain separate like oil and water. The boundary where the different air masses crash is a front—a battleground of weather, where one air mass advances while another retreats, often creating storms in the process. If it's the warm air that's advancing, it's called a warm front. If cold air is pushing on the boundary, it's a cold front. If it's a standoff, it's a stationary front.

Though not all storms are caused by fronts, all are fueled by heating and cooling. Heating of the earth's surface by the sun causes air above the surface to rise. Rising air cools, and the water vapor in that air condenses into clouds and precipitation. These regions of rising air are called updrafts. However, inside a storm, air can be cooled from ice falling from high clouds. The cooled air sinks (it's more dense), creating downdrafts. Downdrafts that crash into the earth's surface can turn into strong, potentially damaging horizontal winds.

Wise Weather Fact

The updrafts and downdrafts in thunderstorms zoom up and down the cloud as fast as 5,000 feet (1,500 meters) per minute.

Thunderstorms and Lightning

Every day as many as 45,000 thunderstorms boom and drop rain over parts of the planet. They are the world's most common kind of storm, bringing drenching rain, hail, lightning and thunder, and sometimes spawning tornadoes. In North America, most thunderstorms happen in the spring and summer, when air near the ground is at its warmest. This produces an unstable atmosphere in which giant clouds can form. These unstable air conditions spawn the giant anvil-shaped cumulonimbus clouds that produce thunderstorms. The warm, moist air rises off the ground, cools, and forms a cloud. The latent heat given off during cloud formation warms the surrounding air, allowing the air to rise even higher. This is how the tall, towering shape of the thunderhead evolves.

Inside the cloud, updrafts keep pumping warm humid air into the storm—further fueling it. Meanwhile, some ice and water droplets grow large enough to fall out, dragging air down with them and creating downdrafts. Ice caught in the updrafts can be recirculated, adding layer upon layer of ice until it falls out as hail.

Thunderstorms got their name from the dangerous lightning they produce. Lightning happens when electricity travels between negatively and positively charged parts of a cloud. Lightning is how a charged cloud "dumps" its charge. How a cloud becomes charged isn't completely understood. Scientists think the updrafts and downdrafts in a thunderhead may cause it. Updrafts carry some water upward where it becomes ice; other water in the cloud exists as liquid. This may cause different sections of the cloud to have a different charge.

When a cloud discharges and lightning flashes, it can heat up the air as much as 50,000°F (27,760°C) along its path. That air expands and immediately contracts because the lightning is moving so fast—60,000 miles (96,000 km) per second. The quick expansion and contraction of the air creates sound waves, called thunder. Sound travels much slower than light, so we see the flash and then hear the thunder.

Tornadoes

What are the most violent storms on the earth? Tornadoes. A rare product of thunderstorms, tornadoes are a swirling vortex of spinning air that forms a funnel shape. The largest tornadoes can have winds as fast as 300 mph (480 km), the fastest winds on the planet's surface. Winds of this intensity can smash houses and make projectile missiles out of cars. The average tornado lasts only a few minutes and forges a path much less than a mile long. A tornado's strength is determined by its wind speeds and measured on a scale called the Fujita scale.

Thunderstorms spawn tornadoes. The biggest twisters come from supercell storms—giant, towering cumulonimbus thunderstorms that soar toward the stratosphere and are often ten miles or more in diameter.

Fujita Tornado Scale

Fujita number	Wind speed mph	Observed Damage
F0	40-72	**Light:** Knocked-over chimneys and billboards, broken branches.
F1	73-112	**Moderate:** Roof and garage damage, mobile homes moved.
F2	113-157	**Significant:** Trees snapped, roofs torn off, boxcars overturned
F3	158-206	**Severe:** Trees uprooted, cars lifted and tossed, trains overturned.
F4	207-260	**Devastating:** Well-built homes leveled, cars become missiles.
F5	261-318	**Incredible:** Strong homes lifted off foundations and destroyed, steel-reinforced concrete structures badly damaged.

Wise Weather Fact

Although tornadoes are intense storms that do millions of dollars of damage and kill dozens of people a year in North America, most are short-lived and confined to small areas.

Wise Weather Fact

The energy output of a single hurricane is equivalent to the amount of electricity used in the United States during six months!

Words to Know

blizzard: a snowstorm with high winds

hurricane: a violent rainstorm that starts over warm oceans, with winds of 74 mph (119 kmph) or more. Can have heavy rains and cause flooding along coastlines.

lightning: a giant spark that occurs within thunderstorms. Lightning can occur inside a cloud, or jump from the cloud to the ground.

rainbow: an arc of different colors caused by the bending of sunlight through water vapor

sleet: rain that has frozen on the way down to the ground

snow: ice crystals

thunder: the loud, rumbling sound that lightning creates

tornado: a funnel-shaped storm with swirling winds that comes with thunderstorms

It's no coincidence that Tornado Alley runs from Iowa to Texas. Springtime supercell storms form in this part of the United States as warm, moist air from the Gulf of Mexico interacts with cold and warm fronts that have jet streams above them pulling air upward, like a chimney. Varying winds can cause some of the air in the cloud to begin rotating and drop out, creating a tornado.

Winter Storms

Blizzards, ice storms, and sleet storms are all winter storms that occur when the temperature is below freezing. During ice storms, rain falls and freezes as it hits the ground, trees, and power lines that are colder than the air. In an ice storm, water doesn't freeze until it makes contact with objects on the earth's surface; in contrast, sleet is rain that freezes as it falls down through the sky, hitting the ground as tiny pellets of ice.

A blizzard is a snowstorm with winds of 35 mph (56 km) or faster, and low temperatures. The winds blow snow into a blinding whirlwind, reducing visibility to one-quarter mile or less. The kind of precipitation that falls during winter storms is very difficult to predict. A rise or drop of just a few degrees in temperature in any number of places between cloud and ground can change snow to sleet or sleet to freezing rain.

The winds during winter storms can make relatively moderate temperatures feel well below freezing thanks to the windchill factor. The windchill factor is a temperature that represents how cold it feels (not just the air temperature). Wind blows away the normal layer of warmed air covering human skin. The body heat escapes, and it feels colder. The faster the wind, the faster the heat is carried away, the colder it feels, and the more likely the body is to become dangerously cold.

Hurricanes

Storms that form in the oceans are the planet's largest. Hurricanes and typhoons—their West Pacific Ocean cousins—are typically 300 miles (480 km) in diameter and have sustained winds of 100-150 mph (160-240 km per hour). They start in the band of warm ocean near the equator when the water is at its warmest. Warm water of 80°F (27°C) or more is the required fuel for these giant storms. The moisture from the warm water evaporates into the air hanging above it, creating warm, moist low-pressure air that's on the rise. As it rises, the air cools and the moisture condenses—releasing tremendous amounts of heat. This released heat warms up the surrounding air, causing its pressure to lower. Outlying higher pressure air rushes into the new low-pressure area as fast-moving updrafts and eventually a huge whirling mass of air called a tropical depression can form. If the depression continues to be fueled by the heat and low pressure of warm water, it's classified as a hurricane once its winds have reached 74 mph (119 km per hour).

Crackling Balloons

Storm clouds build up charges which they eventually release through bolts of lightning. Lightning is a form of static electricity, but it's much stronger than the kind that causes clinging clothes and zapping doorknobs. This activity invites students to experiment with static electricity.

Materials

(for each student)

balloon

large metal paper clips

1-by-4-inch aluminum foil strip

wool glove or scarf (optional)

Note: Do this activity on a day with low humidity.

Directions

1. Pass out a balloon and a paper clip to each student. Ask students to blow up the balloons and knot them (younger students may need help with this).

2. Have students rub one side of the balloon on their hair or on a wool glove or scarf.

3. Ask students to hold the paper clip in one hand and slowly move it toward where the balloon was rubbed until it touches. Ask: *What happens?* (They will hear a crackling sound.) *What is the sound?* (discharges of static electricity, like tiny claps of thunder) (Note: If students can do this activity in a very dark room, they can see the sparks.)

4. Have students repeat steps 2 and 3, slowly touching the opposite side of the balloon. Ask: *Were the results the same?*

5. Now have students unbend their paper clips into a dipper shape and fold the strip of foil over the end, as shown.

6. Ask students to recharge their balloons on their hair or wool.

7. Tell students to hold the paper clip by its long side and move the charged balloon toward it. Ask: *What happens?* (The strip of foil moves toward the balloon.) *Why?* (It's charged.)

8. Challenge students to find other objects in the classroom that make their foil strips move. Hint: Electronics like television screens work especially well, but avoid computers because it could cause damage.

Extensions

Thunder Math (Math) Thunder is the sound of air expanding and contracting when it's heated by the lightning flash. Because light travels much faster than sound, the bolt is seen before the thunder is heard. It takes sound about 5 seconds to travel one mile, so timing the seconds between lightning and thunder and dividing by 5 gives an estimate of how many miles away the lightning struck. Create word problems for students asking them to calculate how far away lightning struck if it took 10 seconds to hear the thunder, or 5 seconds, or 20 seconds, etc.

Homemade Rainbow

SCIENCE, ART

N othing's nicer after a storm than seeing a beautiful rainbow. Rainbows are often seen after storms because rain is falling in another part of the sky while the sun is to the viewer's back. A rainbow's colors come from white sunlight being split into a spectrum by raindrops acting like tiny prisms. A rainbow's arc is part of a circle made by the roundness of raindrops. In this activity students will discover how water can break up light into the colors of a rainbow.

Materials

(for each group)

small mirror

clear bowl or container

8-by-11-inch piece of white posterboard

water

sunny window

Directions

1 Divide the class into three or four groups, and instruct each group to fill the bowl or container with water and set it in direct sunlight. Have students place the mirror in the water facing the sunlight. Show them how to set the posterboard between the container and the window. (Note: If you only have one sunny window available, consider doing this as a whole-class activity.)

2 Instruct students to adjust the angle of the mirror until it casts a rainbow on the posterboard. Ask students to name the colors in order and draw them.

Extensions

Prism Art (Science, Art) Raindrops act as prisms, splitting white light into its individual colors to create a rainbow. Students can further explore the colors of the spectrum with handheld prisms. Provide students with prisms (or use old pieces from glass lamps or chandeliers, available at flea markets), white paper, and colored pencils or crayons. Help students set up their prisms in a stream of light so that the prisms cast a spectrum of color on their papers. Then have students trace and color the "rainbows" created. Ask: *Are the colors the same as were seen in the rainbows made with water?*

Fun Phenomena (Science) Rainbows are only one kind of optical weather phenomena. Challenge student groups to choose another meteorological phenomenon and report on it. They may choose from sundogs, coronas, halos, moonbows, and glories.

[ONLINE]
LINK

Go to http://www. brainpop.com/rainbow to watch a rainbow movie, take a rainbow quiz and do a printable rainbow activity.

Pop Bottle Tornado

SCIENCE

Tornadoes are vortexes of spinning air. In this activity, students can make a similar vortex of spinning water.

Directions

Divide the class into small groups.
Have students follow these instructions:

1 Fill one of the bottles about three-quarters full of water and then add a few drops of food coloring.

2 Set the other bottle on top of the first bottle and tape them together with the duct tape.

3 Carefully invert the bottles. Hold one hand firmly on the bottom bottle. Use your other hand to swirl the top bottle in a circle. A vortex is created.

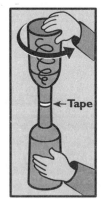

←Tape

Materials

(for each group)

two empty 1- or 2-liter clear plastic bottles

duct tape

water

food coloring

ACTIVITY

Tornado Tally

GEOGRAPHY, MATH

Tornadoes may be run-of-the-mill in Texas, but they are rare in Washington State. Challenge students to use their map-reading skills to answer the questions about tornadoes in the United States during 1997 in this activity.

Directions

Reproduce page 62 and distribute it to students. Make sure students understand what the numbers represent. Provide students with a reference map of the states, if needed.

Answers: 1. Texas 2. Florida 3. four states 4. Vermont, Rhode Island, Connecticut, and Delaware 5. sixteen states 6. four states 7. Texas, Florida, Kansas, and Oklahoma

Materials

(for each student)

reproducible page 62

[ONLINE] LINK

www.usatoday.com/ weather

Click on the word *tornadoes* to find maps of the United States that show where tornado watches and tornado warnings are in effect. Ask students to pick one tornado watch and keep track of its progress during the day: Does a tornado form?

Sleet vs. Snow

SCIENCE, MATH

S now and sleet are both frozen precipitation, but they fall very differently from the sky due to their weight and surface area. Snowflakes are large crystals of snow that float easily in the air. Sleet is bits of solid ice that speed toward the ground. In this activity students conduct an experiment to see which falls faster—snow or sleet.

Materials

(for each pair of students)

uncooked rice

cornflakes

chair

newspaper

Directions

1 Divide the class into pairs. Instruct students to spread newspaper on the floor and set a chair on it.

2 Have one student mix a half cup of rice and a half cup of cornflakes in the cupped hands of the partner.

3 Ask the students with the cereal and rice to stand on a chair. The other student should stand back five feet or so from the chair.

4 Instruct the student on the chair to hold her or his hands high and let the rice and cereal fall while the other student watches. Ask the observing students: *Which hits the ground first?* (rice) *Why?* (less air resistance) *Which is more like snow?* (cornflakes) *like sleet?* (rice) *Which falls faster, snow or sleet?* (sleet)

Extensions

Make Snow Globes (Art) Students can make "shake and snow" snow globes out of baby food jars or other small jars. Have students form snowpeople out of white plasticine clay and other waterproof accessories. (Make sure their figures can fit in the jar.) Glue snowpeople onto the inside jar lid for students. (You'll need to use a waterproof glue such as hot glue or Duco cement—do not allow children to come in contact with either of these.) Let the glue completely dry. Fill the jars about three-quarters full with water and add a pinch of silver and/or white glitter. Top the jar with the lid, carefully slipping the snowperson inside. Tightly screw the lid closed. (If it isn't watertight, seal with glue.) Students can gently shake and invert their jars to make a snowy scene.

Blizzard Books (Language Arts) Invite students to interview parents, grandparents, or other relatives about the worst blizzard they can remember. What happened? How did they cope? Challenge students to write paragraphs or mini-books about it, titled *The Blizzard of 1982,* etc.

Book Break

Before asking students to do the Blizzard Books extension activity, consider reading *Anna, Grandpa, and the Big Storm* by Carla Stevens (Clarion Books, 1982) to hear the story of what happens during a big snowstorm.

Chilly Wind

SCIENCE, MATH

Blizzards are snowstorms with high winds. Those winds can make for dangerous conditions because they make cold temperatures feel even colder. That's because the normal layer of warmed air covering human skin is blown away. This is called the windchill index or factor. Students can discover the chilling difference wind makes in this activity.

Directions

Make copies of page 63 and hand one out to each student. Review with students how to read the table. The actual air temperature runs across the top and the wind speed on the left. The windchill temperature is found by intersecting the two. Ask students to use the table to answer the questions. Answers: 1. 40°F 2. 9°F 3. 27°F 4. 20 mph

Extension

Winter Wisdom (Health) Challenge student groups to find out more about the warning signs of hypothermia and frostbite. Have students make Winter Weather Wisdom posters advising their classmates on how to read the signs of hypothermia and how to prevent it.

Book Break

In some parts of the world, keeping safe in freezing weather is an important concern. Read *Arctic Hunter* by Diane Hoyt-Goldsmith (Holiday House, 1992), the nonfiction account of an Inupiat family and their annual spring trip to their camp. Have students make a list of all of the things that the family needs to survive in the cold climate. How is the main character's life different from theirs? How is it the same?

Materials

(for each student)

reproducible page 63

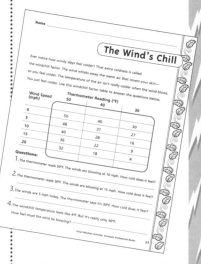

Wise Weather Fact

The lowest ever recorded temperature was -128.6°F (89.2°C) at Vostok Station in Antarctica during July, 1993.

Brrr!

Hurricane Swirl

SCIENCE

Materials

(for the whole class)

water

shallow cake pan

cornstarch

food coloring

spoon

paper and pencil (optional)

A hurricane is a huge storm over the ocean that has winds and clouds swirling around its calm center. In this activity students will model the shape and pattern of those winds and clouds using water instead of air.

Directions

1 Stir a few spoonfuls of cornstarch into the pan of water. The amount doesn't have to be exact, it just needs to look milky.

2 When the water is more or less still, add one or two drops of food coloring into the middle of the pan. Have students observe the color's movement and pattern for a few minutes. (Your results will vary, but likely some color will sink at the center while some color will form a slow-moving spiral with additional tiny spirals along its arms.) Consider asking students to draw what they see.

3 Pull the spoon very slowly through the water. Ask: *What follow in the wake of the spoon?* (spirals) Again, consider asking students to draw what they see.

4 Erase the color by completely mixing it in and let the water settle. Then add two or three more drops of food coloring in the center.

5 This time try to use the handle of the spoon to make a circle around the drops. Is what happens different? (A spiral is created inside the path of the spoon handle.) Invite students to draw their observations, if desired.

6 Help students connect what's happening in the pan to how conditions in the atmosphere could cause swirling winds. Ask: *Which would be more like a wider band of wind, the handle or round part of the spoon?* (round) *How did the speed of the moving spoon affect it?*

Book Break

Read *The Magic School Bus Inside a Hurricane* by Joanna Cole (Scholastic, 1995). Ask students to pick out any interesting facts they find about hurricanes and other storms. Write the facts in question form on index cards and use the questions to hold a Hurricane Quiz Show in the classroom.

Stormy Story Starters

LANGUAGE ARTS

Storms are exciting. That's probably why so many books and movies center around storms! Your students will find that writing about storms gets their imaginations swirling faster than the winds of a hurricane.

Directions

1 Decorate an empty box or can with stormy symbols, such as lightning bolts or snowflakes.

2 On small slips of paper or index cards, write story starters having to do with stormy weather, such as:

I'll never forget the blizzard we had last winter.

We were sailing a boat on the lake when the hurricane warning came through on the radio.

I looked out the window and saw the swirling tornado in the distance.

I knew the storm was bad when the wind picked up the garbage can and sent it flying down the street.

3 Put the story starters in your decorated box. Make an instruction sheet or label that reads, "Stormy Story Starters. Pick a story starter. Write a short story. Try to include at least three real facts about storms in your story."

4 If you wish, save the finished stories for a rainy day. Then sit in a circle and take turns reading stories aloud.

Book Break

In the book *Hurricane* by David Wiesner (Houghton Mifflin, 1992), two brothers weather a storm safely inside their home. The hurricane leaves a fallen tree in their backyard that sparks the boys' imagination in countless ways. Use this book as a springboard to discuss students' personal experiences during a storm. Encourage students to write or draw about a storm they remember. What did they see? hear? How did they feel?

Materials

(for the whole class)

empty box or can

index cards or slips of paper

Twister Totals

All states are not equal when it comes to tornadoes. Some states hardly ever have them. Other states have many. The map below shows how many tornadoes each state had during 1997 (except for Alaska and Hawaii). Use the map to answer the questions.

WA 14
9 MT
ND 31
MN 47
VT 0
ME 3
NH 2
MA 8
OR 14
6 ID
SD 30
WI 14
MI 18
NY 6
RI 0
CT 0
NJ 2
WY 26
IA 25
PA 14
DE 0
MD 4
NV 2
UT 1
CO 47
NE 31
IL 32
IN 15
OH 15
WV 1
VA 10
CA 17
KS 64
MO 12
KY 39
NC 10
TN 36
SC 17
AZ 5
NM 11
OK 57
AR 45
MS 34
AL 30
GA 22
TX 191
LA 19
FL 115

Questions:

1. What state had the most tornadoes? _____

2. What state had the second most tornadoes? _____

3. How many states had no tornadoes in 1997? _____

4. Name the states with no tornadoes. _____

5. How many states had fewer than 10 tornadoes? _____

6. How many states had more than 50 tornadoes? _____

7. Name the states with more than 50 tornadoes. _____

The Wind's Chill

Ever notice how windy days *feel colder*? That extra coldness is called

the windchill factor. The wind whisks away the warm air that covers your skin—

so you feel colder. The temperature of the air isn't really colder when the wind blows.

You just feel colder. Use this windchill factor table to answer the questions below.

Wind Speed (mph)	Thermometer Reading (°F)		
	50	**40**	**30**
0	50	40	30
5	48	37	27
10	40	28	16
15	36	22	9
20	32	18	4

Questions:

1. The thermometer reads 50°F. The winds are blowing at 10 mph. How cold does it feel?

_____

2. The thermometer reads 30°F. The winds are blowing at 15 mph. How cold does it feel?

_____

3. The winds are 5 mph today. The thermometer says it's 30°F. How cold does it feel?

_____

4. The windchill temperature feels like 4°F. But it's really only 30°F.

How fast must the wind be blowing? _____

Additional Resources

Books for Teachers

Discover the Seasons by Diane Iverson (Dawn Publications, 1996)

A Field Guide to the Atmosphere by Vincent J. Schaefer and John A. Day (Houghton, 1981)

How the Weather Works by Michael Allaby (Reader's Digest, 1995)

It's Raining Cats and Dogs: All Kinds of Weather and Why We Have It by Franklyn M. Branley (Houghton, 1987)

Looking at Weather by David Suzuki (Stoddart, 1991)

Nature All Year Long by Clare Walker Leslie (Greenwillow Books, 1991)

Science for Kids: 39 Easy Meteorology Experiments by Robert W. Wood (Tab, 1991)

Weather by Brian Cosgrove (Dorling Kindersley, 1991)

Weather by Janice VanCleave (Wiley, 1995)

The Weather Book by Jack Williams (Vintage Books, 1992)

The Weather Report by Mike Graf (Fearon Teacher Aids, 1989)

The Weather Sky by Bruce McMillan (HarperCollins, 1991)

Books for Students

Air Is All Around You by Franklyn M. Branley (Crowell, 1986)

Bringing the Rain to Kapiti Plain: A Nanda Tale by Verna Aardema (Dial Press, 1981)

The Cloud Book by Tomie de Paola (Holiday House, 1975)

Cloudy with a Chance of Meatballs by Judi Barrett (Atheneum, 1978)

A Drop of Water by Walter Wick (Scholastic, 1997)

Lightning by Seymour Simon (Morrow Junior Books, 1997)

Rain by Andres Llamas Ruiz (Sterling, 1996)

Rainy Day: Stories and Poems by Caroline Feller Bauer HarperCollins, 1987

The Reasons for Seasons by Gail Gibbons (Holiday House, 1995)

Snow Is Falling by Franklyn M. Branley (Crowell, 1986)

Storms by Seymour Simon (Morrow Junior Books, 1989)

Thunder Cake by Patricia Polacco (Philanel Book, 1990)

Weather by Seymour Simon (Morrow Junior Books, 1993)

Weather Words and What They Mean by Gail Gibbons (Holiday House, 1990)

Poetry Books

Sky Words by Marilyn Singer (Maxwell Macmillan International, 1994)

Weather Lee Bennett Hopkins (HarperCollins, 1994)

Websites

How the Weatherworks http://www.weatherworks.com

National Weather Service Homepage http://www.nws.noaa.gov

USA Today http://www.usatoday.com/weather

The Weather World 2010 Project http://www.2010.atmos.uiuc.edu

Weather Online http://www.weatheronline.com

The Weather Channel http://www.weather.com

Software

WeatherTracker V3.0.1 for Macintosh (Trexar Technologies Inc.)

Weather Tracker V3.5 for Windows 95/98/NT (Kidware)